EXPECTED UTILITY HYPOTHESES AND THE ALLAIS PARADOX

EXPECTED UTILITY HYPOTHESES AND THE ALLAIS PARADOX

Contemporary Discussions of Decisions under Uncertainty with Allais' Rejoinder

Edited by

MAURICE ALLAIS

Centre d'Analyse Economique,
Ecole Nationale Supérieure des Mines de Paris
Centre National de la Recherche Scientifique

and

OLE HAGEN

Oslo Institute of Business Administration,
Bedriftsoekonomisk Institutt

D. REIDEL PUBLISHING COMPANY

DORDRECHT : HOLLAND / BOSTON : U.S.A.
LONDON : ENGLAND

Library of Congress Cataloging in Publication Data

CIP

Main entry under title:

Expected utility hypotheses and the Allais Paradox.

(Theory and decision library; v. 21)
Bibliography: p.
Includes indexes.
1. Risk--Addresses, essays, lectures.
2. Decision-making--Addresses, essays, lectures.
3. Utility theory--Addresses, essays, lectures.
I. Allais, Maurice. II. Hagen, Ole, 1921–
HB615.E79   658.4'01   79-12137
ISBN 90-277-0960-2

Published by D. Reidel Publishing Company,
P.O. Box 17, Dordrecht, Holland

Sold and distributed in the U.S.A., Canada and Mexico
by D. Reidel Publishing Company, Inc.
Lincoln Building, 160 Old Derby Street, Hingham,
Mass. 02043, U.S.A.

Printed in The Netherlands

TABLE OF CONTENTS

v

EDITORIAL PREFACE

Utility theory or, value theory in general, is certainly the cornerstone of decision theory, game theory, microeconomics, and all social and political theories which deal with public decisions.

Recently the American School of utility, founded by von Neumann–Morgenstern, encountered a far-going criticism by the French School of utility represented by its founder Allais. The whole basis of the theory of decisions involving risk has been shaken and put into question. Consequently, basic research in the fundamentals of utility and value theory evolved into a crisis. Like any crisis in basic research, and this one was not an exception, it was very fruitful.

One may simply say: Allais versus von Neumann–Morgenstern, or the French School of utility versus the American School, became one of the battlefields of scientific development which proved to be a most creative source of new advances and new developments in all those sciences which are based on evaluation of utilities.

I have to thank here all participants who have contributed to the success of this volume which is dedicated to one of the most important scientific disputes of this century in the social sciences. The history of bringing together the different scholars was in fact as dramatic as the controversial issues presented in this volume and at one point the whole project seemed to come to a deadlock. I have to thank Professor Morgenstern and Professor Allais not only for their support to start this research but I am also indebted to Professor Allais' willingness to serve as the co-editor of the whole project. It is worthwhile to note that his impartiality in this controversy, which he himself originated, helped us to conceive and conclude the project and to bring the different opinions of all participating international scholars to a most fruitful and creative cooperation – guided only by a search for truth.

I want to thank Professor Ole Hagen for his active editorship; without his unusual combination of strength and understanding the book could not have been completed at all. Finally, I have to thank all contributors for their patience in this long exchange of ideas centering on the controversial dispute regarding the American versus the French School of utility.

WERNER LEINFELLNER
Series Editor

vii

PART I

EDITORIAL INTRODUCTION

FOREWORD

This volume can be published today through Professor Werner Lein-fellner's initiative, the understanding of the Reidel Publishing Company, and the perseverence of Ole Hagen. I wish to thank them especially.

Although in November, 1974, I agreed to be co-editor with Ole Hagen, I should stress that my many other activities and obligations reduced my participation almost to a purely nominal level, and that the considerable work of preparing this volume was carried out by Ole Hagen who assumed its responsibility. It was he who together with Professor Leinfellner secured the cooperation of Professors Morgenstern and Marschak in soliciting and organising the contributions made by the authors presented here, and the credit for this is his.

To be frank, I would have preferred – as I told Ole Hagen several times – to participate only as a contributor. The purpose of my new memoir was to reply as clearly as possible to the criticisms addressed to my 1952 work, and to set forth my position in the light of the subsequent developments in the literature. In this regard, my role as co-editor, albeit mostly a formal one, was an embarrassment, impairing somewhat my freedom to respond to the criticisms, often rather sharp, advanced by Morgenstern and Amihud in their contributions. I felt this even more strongly when I learnt of the death, first of Morgenstern at the beginning of August, then of Marschak in September, 1977. Neither could now comment on my own contribution, though on receiving the contributions of Morgenstern and Amihud, and in his letter of 16th August, 1974, Ole Hagen had indicated to Morgenstern that we all could comment on our respective contributions.

It was only the friendly, but firm, insistence of Ole Hagen and Werner Leinfellner that led me finally to agree that my name be kept as co-editor. Considering their arguments, I must recognize that effectively what should prevail, was not my own preferences, but the interest of diffusion of the book.

3

Maurice Allais and Ole Hagen (eds.), Expected Utility and the Allais Paradox, 3–11.
Copyright © 1979 by D. Reidel Publishing Company.

At all events, the book was, and is, essentially intended to give freely the clearest possible statement of the various conceptions of the theory of random choice (choice involving risk) that have been presented. Thus the criticisms of my 1952 study by Morgenstern and Amihud were particularly welcome, and I trust that my rejoinders will help contribute to make the elements of the debate clearer. Naturally, it is the ideas and the ideas alone which are important.

The mimeographed version of my contribution was sent, as soon as it was available for comment, to all those who had contributed to this volume. In Hagen's Introductory Survey it is explained how Amihud was invited to reply to my rejoinder. His note is included in the present volume.

Regarding my replies to Morgenstern's criticisms, I should have wished Karl Borch to reply in his place, for his thorough knowledge of Morgenstern's thought is allied to an outstanding authority and intelligence. To my deep regret, he declined the offer which was made to him.

I should also say that *I am alone responsible* for the delay of three years in publication. The main reason is that I wanted to be able to give the results of the 1952 survey. The processing and analysis could only be carried out over the period 1974–1976 and took a long time to complete: the amount of work went far beyond any possible forecast. I also realised that the scope of certain of the results obtained is so considerable that they should be established beyond any doubt. Unfortunately, I have only been able to present a short summary of them in Appendix C to the contribution I wrote in 1977. Be this as it may, I wish to apologize for the delay to all those who have contributed to this volume, since the first draft of my contribution was available only on 16th August, 1977.

I am especially grateful to the Reidel Publishing Company, Theory and Decision Library, and Professor Werner Leinfellner and Ole Hagen for the publication of the English version of my 1952 memoir on risk, in which is set forth a general theory which I believe explains why the so-called Allais Paradox, which has raised so many debates since 1952, is not a paradox at all.

*

The purpose of my new memoir at the end of this book is to complete my 1952 study and to add some further comments making allowance for the criticisms received and the results of the experiment that was carried out at that time. It is designed to show that in the same way as the *St. Petersburg Paradox* led Daniel Bernoulli to modify the initial principle of the mathematical expectation of monetary values, the consideration of the *Allais Paradox* leads to the modification of Daniel Bernoulli's formulation.

Actually, the first principle which was put forward for random choice was the principle of maximising the mathematical expectation of monetary values

$$(1) \qquad M = \sum_i p_i g_i$$

corresponding to a random prospect $(g_1, g_2, \ldots, g_n, p_1, p_2, \ldots, p_n)$ in which the p_i represent the probabilities of gains g_i. This principle has been subject to major objections in the case of the *St. Petersburg Paradox*, because, in this instance, no subject behaves according to the principle of the mathematical expectation of monetary gains. In order to explain this, Daniel Bernoulli considered not the monetary gains g_i, but the corresponding *moral values*

$$(2) \qquad u_i = \log (C + g_i)$$

defined up to a linear transformation, in which C denotes the estimate of the subject's capital; and he substituted the principle of maximising the mathematical expectation of 'moral values'

$$(3) \qquad \mathcal{M} = \sum_i p_i u_i$$

for the principle of maximising the mathematical expectation M of monetary gains. The monetary value V of a random outcome is then defined by Daniel Bernoulli by the relation

$$(4) \qquad u(C + V) = \mathcal{M}.$$

Cardinal utility in the post-Daniel Bernoulli literature corresponds to his concept of 'moral value'. This is the case of cardinal utility in Jevons' sense, but the logarithmic form is only a special case of it.

Von Neumann and Morgenstern's neo-Bernoullian theory substituted in place of the equations (2), (3) and (4), the expressions

$$(2^*) \qquad B_i = B(g_i),$$

$$(3^*) \qquad \mathcal{M} = \sum_i p_i B_i,$$

$$(4^*) \qquad B(V) = \mathcal{M}.$$

B being an index defined up to a linear transformation whose existence is deduced from a system of axioms. All the later neo-Bernoullian theories reduce to the relations (2^*), (3^*) and (4^*), but differ through the systems of axioms that they involve.

Just as the principle of maximising monetary values engendered objections as regards the St. Petersburg Paradox, the neo-Bernoullian formulation has given rise to new difficulties in the case of the *Allais Paradox*, corresponding to the random choices made by a large number of subjects in violation of the neo-Bernoullian formulation. In order to explain this new paradox, Allais in 1952 proposed that the expressions (2), (3) and (4) of Bernoulli's formulation be replaced by the expressions

$$(2^{**}) \qquad \gamma_i = \gamma_i(C + g_i),$$

$$(3^{**}) \qquad \omega = h[\gamma_1, \gamma_2, \ldots, \gamma_n, p_1, p_2, \ldots, p_n],$$

$$(4^{**}) \qquad \gamma(C + V) = \omega,$$

in which the γ_i, defined up to a linear transformation, denote the psychological values of the $C + g_i$ and h is a certain function that is assumed only to comply with the principle of absolute preference. In Allais' mind, one must not only substitute the psychological values $\gamma(C + g_i)$ for the monetary values $C + g_i$, but also, in place of the mathematical expectation of psychological values, consider the full probability distribution of the psychological values $\gamma(C + g_i)$.

By taking a new axiom into account, the axiom of iso-variation, Allais was led in 1976 to consider that

$$(3^{***}) \qquad \begin{aligned} \omega &= \mathcal{M} + f, \\ \mathcal{M} &= \sum_i p_i \gamma_i, \end{aligned}$$

the function f being a function of the second order and higher moments of the probability distribution of psychological values γ_i. The function f represents the psychological value of the distribution of psychological values about their mean. This, for him, is the specific element of psychology vis-à-vis risk.

Empirical research carried out by Allais in 1974–1975 led him to consider that Daniel Bernoulli's log–linear expression is indeed valid over a wide domain. However, for extremely large values of $C + g$, the psychological value $\gamma(C + g)$ does not increase as $\log(C + g)$ but tends towards a maximum corresponding to a state of satiety.

In the light of the above, it appears that the consideration of the *St. Petersburg Paradox* and then the *Allais Paradox* has led to the replacement of the mathematical expectation M of monetary gains g_i by the mathematical expectation $\mathcal{M}$ of psychological values, and to the replacement of this in turn by the sum of $\mathcal{M}$ and the psychological value f of risk.

*

The reader will find many different points of view expressed in this volume; but all cast fresh light on the heavily debated issue of the conditions for rationality in making random choice decisions. What are the proper definition and interpretation of the fundamental concepts of probability and utility? Should the neo-Bernoullian formulation, which maximises an index of 'utility', be taken as a general rule, or considered as a precept of very limited scope, valid only under very specific conditions? How can this index be determined and used? Do the examples presented to invalidate the neo-Bernoullian approach reflect the ignorance or lack of information of the subjects, or do they correspond to a specific reality, namely, greater or lesser preference for security or risk? These are the questions dealt with in this volume, and it is the hope of all who have contributed to it that the reader will find useful grounds for thought. The subject is so difficult, so vast, that the book's only ambition is to shed a little more light on it to foster future exchanges of views.

Without prejudging the content of the various contributions to this volume, it is worth stressing that in all the literature, and even in this volume, the same words may refer to entirely different realities.

To von Neumann and Morgenstern, 'utility' is cardinal utility in Jevons' sense: it represents the intensity of preferences. However, for them, it can only be determined by referring to random choices. In fact, they identify the neo-Bernoullian index whose existence they demonstrate with cardinal utility in Jevons' sense.

In de Finetti's mind, cardinal utility in Jevons' sense exists, but the neo-Bernoullian index takes into account both the curvature of cardinal utility and psychology vis-à-vis risk.

To Savage, cardinal utility in Jevons' sense is an "undefined, now almost obsolete, completely discredited, and mystical" concept, which does not exist (Savage, 1954, §5.6). What he claims corresponds to reality is the neo-Bernoullian index whose existence he demonstrates.

To Allais, the concept of psychological value (or cardinal utility) is an undisputable reality. However, this index cannot be determined from the consideration of certain choices or of random choices without making arbitrary and questionable assumptions, such as those of Irving Fisher and Frisch for certainly available goods, or those of von Neumann and Morgenstern for random choices. For Allais, the index of cardinal utility can only be determined directly from appropriate questions following processes similar to those used by psycho-physiologists such as Fechner and Weber.

If it is taken that cardinal utility $\gamma(C + g)$ in Jevons' sense exists for a given subject, and if his psychology being neo-Bernoullian, the neo-Bernoullian index $B(g)$ exists also, the question is what relation links both these indexes. To Allais, this relation is an identity up to a linear transformation.

The concept of probability also takes on entirely different meanings, depending on the authors. Von Neumann and Morgenstern consider "the perfectly well founded interpretation of probability as frequency in long runs". Marschak also holds this position. However, de Finetti and Savage think that there is only subjective probability, and that it can only be determined by considering random choices. To Allais, the concept of probability can only be defined in relation to drawings from reference urns which secure conditions of symmetry and it is proper to found it on the basis of the *axiom of equal possibility* implicit in Laplace's classical theory. To him, in the case of the reference urn process, probability must be defined as the ratio of the number of favourable cases to the number of possible cases, since for this process all cases can be regarded as equally possible (Axiom of equal possibility). This is a *subjective* definition of an *objective* probability.

For Ramsey, de Finetti and Savage, 'utility' and 'probability' can only be determined by considering random choices, and they are determined simultaneously by interpreting them from a certain system of axioms.

Similarly, great differences appear as far as the field of application of probabilities is concerned. Following D'Alembert, Buffon and Cournot, certain authors consider that small probabilities should be neglected. Others, such as Morgenstern, dispute that probabilities below 1% can be estimated correctly. Still, others, including myself, consider these positions to be unacceptable.

In the light of these various conceptions, there is a deplorable liability to error unless different names are given to the different concepts of 'utility' and 'probability'.

All theories of random choices assume the same group of axioms: the existence of ordered fields of choice, axiom of absolute preference, the application of the principle of total and compound probabilities, etc. However, the neo-Bernoullian theories all introduce, in one shape or another, an additional restrictive condition, and they all lead to the same principle of maximising the mathematical expectation of a 'utility' index $B(g)$.

In fact, each neo-Bernoullian author bases his theory of random choice on a system of axioms which appears unquestionable to him, and much effort has been devoted to finding axioms which would force conviction of anyone; but in each of these systems of axioms there is always one (von Neumann and Morgenstern's axiom 3Ba and 3Bb, Samuelson's independence axiom, Savage's sure-thing principle, etc.), whose presence implies the validity of the neo-Bernoullian formulation.

For critics of the neo-Bernoullian theories, this restriction cannot be justified; but their theories are considered by the neo-Bernoullians as 'void'.

It should be stressed that, according to von Neumann and Morgenstern, the neo-Bernoullian formulation does not take into consideration "the positive or negative utility of the mere act of *taking a chance*". However, most of the neo-Bernoullian authors, such as de Finetti and Savage, think that the neo-Bernoullian formulation effectively takes the utility or disutility of risk into account.

There is another fundamental divergence within the neo-Bernoullian school. Some authors, such as Savage, think that the neo-Bernoullian principle is necessary even in the case of a one-time choice, or an event which will never recur. For others, such as Marschak, the justification of the principle relies on the success of its application "on average in the long run". To Allais, the neo-Bernoullian formulation appears as asymptotically valid in the case of a very large number of games for which the corresponding probability of ruin is negligible.

Like the concept of 'utility' and 'probability', the idea of 'rationality' is a concept of which the reader should be wary. For certain authors, the rationality of the neo-Bernoullian formulation results from the obviousness of the axioms on which it is based. For others like myself, not only these axioms do not appear self-evident, but, in some cases, it would be irrational to follow the neo-Bernoullian formulation. However, there seems to be an agreement on one point. It would not be rational to admit a system of axioms and not accept its implications (principle of consistency), but it is still an open question whether rationality should be defined on the basis of *criteria* relating only to random choice, or following *criteria* which are independent of all consideration of random choice.

In the light of the radical divergences of the approaches to the construction of a satisfactory theory of random choice, the main purpose of this volume is not to present *one* theory of random choice, but to set forth various viewpoints. The editors of this book have therefore accepted the various contributions as they were submitted, even where they cannot share the same opinions and even where they may see errors in the reasoning. This should have gone without saying, but because of certain reactions, it seems necessary to underline that in a field in which there has been so much controversy, the role of an editor cannot be to censor opinions or reasoning which he considers as open to criticism or simply wrong. This is the principle I defended in 1952, in requesting the editor of *Econometrica* to publish my paper on the behaviour of the rational man in the face of risk, and this is the principle which underpins the conception of the present volume.

*

Lastly, I wish to pay tribute to the memory of my late friends and colleagues Jacob Marschak and Oskar Morgenstern, whose premature disappearance deprives economic science of two of its most brilliant representatives. In various ways, both made exceptional contributions to economics in general and risk theory in particular. Both were extensively and decisively helpful to Ole Hagen in preparing the present book, in particular in regard to the choice of participants.

I learnt of Morgenstern's death just as I was preparing to forward my contribution to this volume to him for comment. The parcel and my letter to Marschak were returned with only a mention of his death. I very much regret that neither could bring to the book, as we had hoped, the benefit of their views on my contribution. They would have been especially valuable and instructive.

As regards my new memoir, and in particular the Appendix C on the analysis of the 1952 survey, I would like to say that Jacob Marschak compiled the 1952 Questionnaire in full detail, and added many comments, and that he always expressed his friendly understanding of my work on risk. It was Marschak who took the initiative of having my 1954 paper on mining prospection in the Sahara translated for publication in the review *Management Science.*

From the standpoint of the central debate treated in this book, may I recall that it was von Neumann and Morgenstern who first underlined that the neo-Bernoullian formulation does not take account of the positive or negative specific utility of risk. This is another example of their breadth of vision and their insight into this hotly debated issue.

MAURICE ALLAIS
Saint-Cloud, this 6th December 1977

INTRODUCTORY SURVEY

This is a volume of discussion centering around the controversies frequently associated with the issues mentioned in the title. The idea of this project originated with Professor Werner Leinfellner, who also invited us to act as guest editors.

We accepted this invitation with pleasure and recognition of the trust shown us by the Theory and Decision Library in giving us this assignment.

In the preparation of this book. Professor Leinfellner and Dr Eckehart Köhler, then his assistant, played a major role at an early stage. At a crucial point, decisive assistance was given by Professor Oskar Morgenstern and Professor Jacob Marschak by agreeing to contribute and by suggesting other contributors, and thereby helping towards a balanced selection. The editorial responsibility on this point is mine.

To avoid misunderstanding, let it be mentioned that this volume has in some cases in the past been referred to as 'Rational Decisions under Risk. Contemporary Discussions'.

In my own paper, I have presented my views as a participant in the debate. Here, I shall try my best to give an objective orientation on what it is all about. I will not, however, try to present a fair distribution of attention to authors according to their merits. It is to be hoped that the book as a whole will do that. I shall give the mere outline of the history of thought and the problems presently facing us in the field concerned.

The types of problems we are dealing with concern several of the traditional academic subjects such as philosophy, psychology, statistics, management and economics. I think it must be tolerated that my outlook is limited by my background, as a managerial economist.

THE CONCEPT OF CARDINAL UTILITY

In the choice between actions, of which each leads to one certain result coming all at the same time and all measured in money, we can

13

Maurice Allais and Ole Hagen (eds.), Expected Utility and the Allais Paradox, 13–24.

use a static and deterministic model, and the objective is simple, as much money as possible. If the outcome of each action is not known for sure, each action represents a game. If the probabilities are known, it can be presented as a probability distribution.

Now the objective is not always easily defined. One rather obvious case is when the cumulative probability for any level is either the same or more favourable for the game A than for the game B and more favourable at one point at least. Then A is preferred (it has 'preference absolue' or 'stochastic dominance of the first order'). When there is no dominance of the first order then we have 'preference relative'.

The first thought that then comes to the mind is to prefer the game with the highest expected value. The classical counterexample to this is the St. Petersburg game. The prize in this game is won the first time a tossed coin comes up heads, and the size of the prize is doubled for each time it shows tails. The expected value of the game is infinite so it is higher than any price that could be charged for it. Still people would pay at most a few times the prize that would be won if the first toss showed heads. Bernoulli's solution to this "paradox" was a theory that people maximize the expectation of the logarithm of the sum of capital and prize.

Later objections to the credibility of the promise made in the game can be met by modifications, but even modified versions still show that the theory of maximizing the expected gain is untenable.

The original Bernoulli theory is rather special. Why exactly the logarithm? The development of the theory, including the discussions of controversies, has been furthered by a drive towards higher levels of generality, and has been stimulated by presentation of new paradoxes.

Early attempts to explain value in exchange from value in use, or as we would say utility, foundered on the paradox of the low price for some essential goods versus the high price of luxuries. This problem was solved by the introduction of marginal utility and the interplay between that concept and that of marginal cost.

The Austrians introduced a concept of utility that was quantitative in nature, and the increase in utility won per additional unit consumed was decreasing with increasing quantity consumed. Dividing this marginal utility of a good with its price gives the marginal utility of money, the same for all goods if utility is maximized under the budget constraint. Now producers maximizing profit and consumers maximizing utility under perfect competition implied: marginal cost = marginal utility/marginal utility of money, for all producers, all consumers and all goods.

Originally the total utility of the consumer was supposed to be the sum of independent utilities of the goods. This concept of additivity was dropped with the consideration of complementarity or more generally the dependence of the marginal utility of one good on the consumption of other goods.

But this did not strip the utility of its quantitative nature. Marginal utilities could still be ranked, which also implied that the ratios between utility differences were meaningful. One could transform a utility function but only by a positive linear transformation, i.e., one could change zero and unit, just as between scales of temperature. The utility scale was an interval scale, the concept of utility was cardinal. It will henceforth be referred to as cardinal utility in the classical sense. The assumption of declining marginal utility of wealth was a consequence of the declining marginal utilities of goods, which explained the falling demand curves (price at the vertical and quantity demanded on the negative axis).

Thus the economic theory developed for explaining consumers' behaviour was in full harmony with Bernoulli's theory of behaviour under risk. The derivative of a logarithmic function of wealth varies in inverse proportion with wealth. Call the function utility of wealth, and we have declining marginal utility of wealth. If economists had been more aware of this analogy at an early stage, perhaps both fields of theory would have developed quicker.

Bernoulli's theory has been developed by such eminent spirits as Laplace, but the trend went away from cardinal utility.

It was namely discovered by Pareto that in order to describe a consumer's preferences between goods (for one-period consumption and without risk) the assumption of cardinal utility was needless. Preferences described by one utility function could also be described by any other function that was a positive monotonous (not necessarily linear) transformation of it. It was sufficient to rank utilities and unnecessary to rank utility differences.

This discovery was given much more attention than the fact that cardinal utility could be used to explain e.g. borrowing and saving for consumption purpose. Now positive utility theory turned *ordinalist*.

Cardinal utility survived mainly in welfare economics where one even
assumed interpersonal comparability of utility differences, which was
not implied in the cardinalism of positive theory.

THE THEORY OF GAMES–ALLAIS VERSUS
VON NEUMANN–MORGENSTERN

An axiomatically developed and more general model of decisions
under risk, was presented by John von Neumann and Oskar Morgenstern in 1947. The conclusion they drew from their axioms, and there
is no controversy over the logic of their deduction, was that preferences between games was determined through the expected value
of numbers attached to situation's, originally by definition, then by
indifferences between certain situations and games with numbers
already attached as "prizes".

An example will show the implications. Attach a number to a
person's actual situation and another and higher number to his situation after receiving $100. For simplicity, we choose 0 and 1, respec-
tively. Assume that the person is indifferent as to whether he receives
X or a lottery ticket that gives a probability of π for winning $100
and $(1 - \pi)$ for remaining in his present situation. If we now attach
the number π to receive X for certain we find that the expected
value of the equivalent alternatives are: $0 \cdot (1 - \pi) + 1 \cdot \pi = \pi$ and
$\pi \cdot 1 = \pi$. If now the same person is found to be indifferent between
receiving Y $(0 < Y < X)$ or a game with probability p of winning $
and $(1 - p)$ if remaining in status quo, then by one of von Neumann
and Morgenstern's axioms the number $p\pi$ is attached to receiving Y.
Then Y is equivalent to a game with the probability $p\pi$ for getting
$100 and $(1 - p\pi)$ for nothing.

The determination of probabilities as described is easily interpreted
as a kind of evaluation of situations, and one that not only ranks
them, but also determines ratios between differences. On top of that
von Neumann and Morgenstern used the term "utility", and even
"numerical utility". Economists at that time were mostly convinced
ordinalists. Utility had no content but ranking according to preference. Comparing strength of preferences was considered as impossible, unnecessary and, most likely, meaningless. But here was
presented a formal logical language which implied that a utility index

was operational that was cardinal in the sense that differences could be compared.

The first ordinalist reaction to von Neumann and Morgenstern's utility theory was to raise doubt about the validity of the theory. The second was to give it an interpretation which did not conflict with ordinalism in general. The von Neumann–Morgenstern or neo-Bernoullian utility index served only to describe a person's preferences under risk, and its difference ratios had no significance in any other contexts.

This was the situation when Maurice Allais criticized what he termed 'The American School' at a Conference in Paris in 1952, followed up by publications mainly in the volume of the Conference.

The position taken by Allais is characterized by: (1) the assumption of a cardinal utility (psychological value) in the classical sense, (2) that games are valued under the influence of this utility and of a possible subjective deformation of probabilities, (3) that the valuation of games depend not only of the expected values of the utility, but on the whole shape of the probability distribution over utility, (4) that rationality implies consideration of objective probabilities when they exist and observance of the axiom of absolute preference, (5) that *if* the psychology of a person is at the same time rational and conforms with the neo-Bernoullian formulation, the index of which the expectation is maximised is necessarily identical with the cardinal utility in the classical sense.

It follows from (3), (4) and (5), that, in general, the existence of a von Neumann–Morgenstern utility index is denied. To support this conclusion, he presented examples of pairs of hypothetical choice situations in which introspection and interrogation suggest that conflicting conclusions concerning the utility index could be derived from two decisions by the same person.

All these examples have been chosen in order to show the complementarity effect caused by the strong propensity towards certainty, demonstrated by the majority of the subjects, in the neighbourhood of certainty when important amounts are concerned.

These examples have been named by others 'Allais Paradoxes'. These differ from the problem posed by the same person avoiding risk through insurance and buying risk in a lottery ticket, by the impossibility of solving them through any reshaping of the utility function.

In the discussion following Allais' criticism, the defenders of the expected utility principle all appeared to be ordinalists, which does not at all follow from the original von Neumann–Morgenstern presentation. Also the reservation made by them about the possibility of a specific utility of risk seemed to be forgotten. It has not been repeated in later axiomatic systems by other authors leading up to an expected utility theorem.

In the following, I will only try to survey some positions and views that are *apparently logically possible.*

- One could accept the existence both of a cardinal utility in the classical sense (operating in riskless contexts) and the von Neumann–Morgenstern utility index as describing actual behavior. This would imply either that they were identical or that they were independent or that the effects operating besides utility in the classical sense transformed this into a new function having the von Neumann–Morgenstern characteristics.

- One could deny the existence of classical cardinal utility and accept the existence and descriptive power of a von Neumann–Morgenstern utility index.

- One could accept the existence of classical cardinal utility and deny the existence of a von Neumann–Morgenstern index. The possibility of measuring cardinal utility through choices under risk could be accepted or rejected.

- One could deny both.

- One could neither axiomatically assume nor deny either, and adopt the working hypothesis that one function of wealth and another function of specific utility of risk, will emerge through choices under risk.

- One could adopt the expected utility principle as a normative principle only. This could be combined with any view on the descriptive power of expected utility hypotheses or any other hypotheses of actual behaviour.

There are of course possibilities of further subdivision and there is also the possibility that some possible position may have been overlooked. On the other hand some of these 'hatboxes' may be empty.

But roughly this is the field in which the contributors to this book place themselves.

In fact, Oskar Morgenstern has not publicly commented on Allais' criticism, nor has Maurice Allais commented on the counter-criticism. Not till now. Here they are both represented, along with other contributors to a debate which will no doubt go on, but hardly on the basis of repeating postulates from the nineteen forties and fifties.

SURVEY OF THIS BOOK

In Part II appears, for the first time in English, Allais' theory of decisions under risk, as presented in French in his 1952 memoir. An outline of this, I have tried to give above. Without this extensive exposition the debate would have been very difficult to follow from that majority of readers who do not read French well.

In Part III, the outright defenders of the neo-Bernoullian position have the floor, in alphabetical order.

Yakov Amihud very vividly rejects Allais' (and Hagen's) criticism of the vN–M expected utility theory partly as based on misconception and partly as based on ill-constructed and inconclusive experiments. The alternative to the expected utility theory is just a framework of *ad hoc* explanations of debatable observations. His exposition is eminently clear.

Bruno de Finetti in a concise declaration confirms adherence to the neo-Bernoullian utility theory.

Jacob Marschak very instructively sets out likeness and difference between the two theories. Neither reflects actual behaviour of un-trained decision makers. Psychologists should train rational decision makers.

Oskar Morgenstern in this, his last article, explains the background for the von Neumann–Morgenstern theory of utility, the need for a numerical concept of utility in (other parts of) the theory of games. The admittance from 1947 of the lack of including a specific utility of risk is maintained. But the criticism made by Allais and Hagen do not solve this problem.

The Allais experiments as set out in Part I and the Hagen tests of before 1973 are criticised for too large values and/or too small probabilities. He excludes games with probabilities smaller or more complicated that one quarter from the proper domain of this theory.

This dissociates him from e.g. attempts to explain simultaneous buying of insurance and lottery tickets as expected utility maximizing.

In Part IV, the contributions reflect more diverse positions and angles of approach.

Karl Borch maintains that stochastic dominance of the first order is the main axiom in Allais' theory from 1952. Admitting the neo-Bernoullian formulation, the logical implications of portfolio elimination through stochastic dominance of higher orders for the characteristics of a neo-Bernoullian utility index are shown. This is a valuable contribution to eliminating confusion in this field.

A. Camacho introduces a new risk-less definition of utility of single events, based on repetitive games. Under restricted circumstances the answer to the question: how many times must your preference for x_2 to x_3 be satisfied to compensate for one time that your preference for x_1 to x_2 is not satisfied? will give the ratio between the respective utility differences. If the pursuit of long-run success in terms of this utility is rational, then vN–M consistent behavior can only be rational if the vN–M utility index is consistent with that defined in Camacho's paper. From this new angle, the vN–M–Allais controversy is discussed.

Richard M. Cyert and Morris DeGroot describe the individual's discovery of its real utility function as a change in the anticipated utility function through actual experience, this being a Bayesian process. The assumption of a fixed utility function gives rise to inconsistency, as exemplified in the 'Allais Paradox'.

Peter C. Fishburn presents an expected utility theory with weaker axioms, which retains important von Neumann–Morgenstern aspects while overcoming some of the criticism. But even this weaker theory cannot explain some phenomena uncovered by Allais, Tversky, and others.

Samuel Gorovitz deals with modifications of the original St. Petersburg game which make it immune to the original objections, but still exposed to reasonable refusal contrary to Bayesian analysis. Refusal can be rationally explained if possibilities of very low likelihood are excluded by some standard incorporated in the theory.

Ole Hagen argues that the utility of a game is the expectation of utility plus a function of the moments of the distribution, in a simplified approximation: standard deviation and third moment/variance. Utility as a function of probabilities of given outcomes is non-linear. Tests of persons including faculty of science show that preference tends to shift from high-prize-low-probability to low-prize-high-probability when both probabilities are increased in common ratio. An alternative presentation expressed in ordinalistic language is given.

Werner Leinfellner and Edward Booth discuss the fundamental differences between the naturalistic, or behavioristic and the intuitive school of values. The first reflects the idea of cognitive presentation of past preferences. The second holds that value orders, in mente, may influence future preferences. Another difference is compatibility versus incompatibility of value. It is proposed to formalize the leeway of dispersion for incompatible values to complete the demonstration that the difference between the two schools can be defined by exhibiting differences in their structural frames.

Kenneth MacCrimmon and Stig Larsson present a systematic analysis of the interrelations between the axioms of the systems which have in common that they conclude in a neo-Bernoullian utility index, and an empirical investigation in the violation of these axioms when people are asked for preferences. The inconsistencies of accepted rules and decisions depend on probabilities and pay-off parameters. This dependency is mapped out in detail over a wide field. Part of their investigation concerns the 'common ratio' problem covering a wider field than Hagen (see above) and giving very conclusive results. The general conclusion of their empirical studies is that people often violate the rules they accept in their actual preferences.

Günter Menges discusses six decision models of which one with transformed consequences and *a posteriori* probabilities turns out to be epistomologically justifiable and practically the most important. It has its weak points. It is improved through a restatement of the von Neumann–Morgenstern utility's independence property, new techniques and flexible decision criteria for exploiting available information.

In Part V, Allais surveys the development of his own theory which is essentially the same today as in 1952. The emphasis is somewhat shifted, and two new axioms are added. Critical analysis is applied to the neo-Bernoullian theories developed after 1952. In replying to the criticism against his theory, which over the years since 1952 has been extensive but fragmented, he concentrates on contributions to this volume and a correspondence, which together can be assumed to be representative. The most striking points in his counter-criticism seem to be misrepresentation of his theory, and arguments where the conclusion is built into the premises. Modestly placed, as Appendix C, comes part of what the world has been waiting for, selected findings from the 1952 experiment. Among other results it shows discrepancies between Bernoullian indexes over the same values obtained in different ways, and a remarkable consistency in index of cardinal utility based on introspection and without reference to risk. Since the preparation of this has held up the publication, I must be allowed to say here, without violating the impartiality of 'the chair', that this may be the most important part of this volume. It may be that the Allais Paradox will turn out to be a turning point in the theoretical development comparable to the St. Petersburg Paradox. The crucial point seems to be that utility and risk attitude are considered explicitly as two distinct elements forming preferences under risk.

CONCEPTION OF THIS BOOK

Nothing is perfect, and viewed in retrospect much could have been done better in preparing this volume. In view of the fact that both editors have very similar views on the basic questions in the field under discussion one might raise the question of partiality.

As for selection of contributors, we consulted two of the more prominent representatives of the "other side". All their suggestions were followed. Even others who might be expected to take a strong position in that direction were invited. Among those invited were Paul Samuelson, Kenneth Arrow, Milton Friedman, R. Luce and Howard Raiffa, as well as Daniel Ellsberg, Shackle, Littlechild. Those who did not accept, mostly gave very good reasons, one of which I must confess was an inability to meet the deadline set in the invitation.

Much of this volume is taken up by contributions from Allais himself. Should this be criticised, let me refer to Mark Twain who once said he had heard so much about and against the devil, but never his own story, which he found unfair. Now, since 1953, criticism of what was alleged to be Allais' position has been a part of the curriculum even down to undergraduate level, and a recurrent theme in articles and dissertations where reference could only be made to the original presentation in French. Much discussion has taken place in collective volumes and at conferences to which Allais was never invited.

It has been expressed in private that Allais, as an editor, should not include a rejoinder to criticism from other contributors. I think I can easily reply to that. Over the years when Allais was silent on this topic this was interpreted as an admission of being wrong. Now after the sharp criticism from Amihud and Morgenstern, what would have been said in the same quarters if there was no reply from Allais in this volume?

In the correspondence between Morgenstern and myself there was never any misunderstanding on this: we were preparing a forum for sharp discussion. Also, at the time when I received his contribution, I suggested to him an exchange of comments in the book between those with the most marked opposing views.

When, in the summer of 1977, Allais' second contribution had reached a stage where it could be sent to the other contributors, this was done with an invitation to comment. When I visited him in August, he told me that Morgenstern had recently died. Later, we learned that Marschak was dead. This left us in a state of conflicting feelings, and I might as well admit this and the fact that Allais first of all wanted to give an opportunity of a reply to his comments to Amihud's and Morgenstern's paper, while I was reluctant to agree to anything that might cause further delay. I gave in when events took a turn that strengthened the reasons for it. Since no rule states which side should have the last word, I always saw this as a practical question. Professor Allais has preferred to give Amihud the last word. (See Amihud's comment on Allais' rejoinder of Part V to be found in 'A Reply to Allais', p.185.)

Concerning the criticism against Allais as an editor, I think he took it too much to heart, particularly when he suggested that he would step down as editor and leave the fort to me. Further: the contributors had not been asked to, and therefore not accepted to, participate in a volume edited by me alone, also the prospects for sales would suffer. With the help of Professor Leinfellner, he was in the end convinced that it was his duty to stay on.

I feel it is in order if I use this opportunity to stress the role of Jacob Marschak and Oskar Morgenstern in preparing this volume. As a person, I had special reasons to appreciate their true scientific spirit, their willingness to cooperate for progress through clarifying disagreement, and their warm humanity. In one of his last letters, Morgenstern impressed on me how this volume was awaited by "a considerable number of some very gifted and eager colleagues".

Well, here it is.

OLE HAGEN
Oslo Institute of Business Administration,
Bedriftsøkonomisk Institutt
January 1978

PART II

THE 1952 ALLAIS THEORY
OF CHOICE INVOLVING RISK

MAURICE ALLAIS

THE FOUNDATIONS OF A POSITIVE THEORY OF CHOICE INVOLVING RISK AND A CRITICISM OF THE POSTULATES AND AXIOMS OF THE AMERICAN SCHOOL (1952)*

This is the direct English translation, which appears for the first time, of 'Fondements d'une Théorie Positive des Choix Comportant un Risque et Critique des Postulats et Axiomes de L'Ecole Americaine' which was published in French as Memoir III annexed to *Econometrie*, Colloques Internationaux du Centre National de la Recherche Scientifique, Vol. XL, Paris, 1953, pp.257–332 (see p.447 below).

This memoir has also appeared as a special issue of the *Annales des Mines*, Vol. 144, 1955; and as a separate volume under the same title by the Imprimerie Nationale, 1955.

27

Maurice Allais and Ole Hagen (eds.), Expected Utility and the Allais Paradox, 27–145
Copyright © 1979 by D. Reidel Publishing Company.

TABLE OF CONTENTS

CHAPTER III / MATHEMATICAL APPENDICES

SUMMARY

The most important points in the following study may be summarised as follows.

(1) Contrary to the view of the majority of authors, the concept of psychological value (cardinal utility) $\gamma = \bar{s}(x)$ can be defined operationally by considering either psychologically equivalent variations Δx of x, or minimum perceptible thresholds (Weber–Fechner).

Thus to each monetary value x there can accordingly be made correspond a psychological value $\bar{s}(x)$.[1]

(2) Any theory of risk must *necessarily* take account of four factors, *even in a first approximation*, if it is to be realistic and is to bring out what is absolutely essential to any choice involving uncertainty.

   I. The distinction between monetary and psychological values.

   II. The distortion of objective probabilities and the consideration of subjective probabilities.

   III. The consideration of the mathematical expectation of psychological values (the first-order moment of the probability distribution of psychological values).

   IV. The consideration of the dispersion (i.e. the second-order moment) *and*, generally, of *the overall shape of the probability distribution of psychological values.*

The last of these four factors seems to be *the specific element* of any theory of risk. In many cases, its influence may be far greater than that of the three others.[2]

(3) Other factors affect choices involving risk, such as the costs of gaming, the pleasure of gaming as such, the magnitude of the minimum perceptible threshold, etc. *They may however be considered as secondary, and can be neglected in a first approximation.*[3]

(4) It is unanimously accepted that *real behaviour* does not follow the neo-Bernoullian formulation. However, there are fundamental differences of view in regard to what *rational behaviour* should be.

33

The American School holds that it should follow the neo-Bernoullian formulation. The author's view is that this is a mistake, *which in fact amounts to omitting the fourth fundamental factor above, which is specific to the psychology of risk.*[4]

(5) If rationality is defined as obedience to one of the systems of axioms which lead to the neo-Bernoullian formulation, discussion is obviously impossible. *Such a definition is therefore devoid of any scientific interest.*

In other words, to be of interest from a scientific standpoint, the author believes that rationality should be defined *either*:
- abstractly, in terms of the criterion generally used in the social sciences of non-self-contradiction, implying the consistency of the ends sought and the use of means appropriate to achieve them, or
- experimentally, by observing the conduct of persons who, one has reason in other respects* to believe, act rationally.

(6) The principle of non-self-contradiction implies only:
- *the use of objective probabilities*, when they exist.
- *the axiom of absolute preference*, according to which, of two situations, that which procures higher gains in all cases is to be regarded as certainly preferable.

These two conditions in conjunction are *less restrictive than the neo-Bernoullian formulation*. It follows that behaviour patterns exist which are rational (in the sense defined above), but do not obey the neo-Bernoullian formulation. It is therefore impossible to say that a rational man ought to act according to that formulation.[5]

(7) Actual observation of the behaviour of persons who are generally considered as rational invalidates the neo-Bernoullian formulation.

There are five classes of particularly significant facts:
- simultaneous purchase of lottery tickets and insurance policies.
- the behaviour of very prudent people in choosing between random prospects involving small sums.
- random choices in the neighbourhood of certainty which refute Savage's principle of independence.
- random choices in the neighbourhood of certainty which refute Samuelson's principle of substitutability.
- the behaviour of entrepreneurs when great losses are possible.[6]

(8) However more or less attractive in appearance they might be, none of the fundamental postulates of the American School leading to the neo-Bernoullian formulation stands up to analysis. All are based on pseudo-evidence.[7]

(9) For the rational man there does not exist, in general, a neo-Bernoullian index $B(x)$ such that the optimum situation could be defined by maximising the expected value $\Sigma\, p_i B(x_i)$ of $B(x_i)$ (*the neo-Bernoullian formulation*).[8]

(10) In the special case in which the psychology of the rational man is such that such an index exists, it necessarily follows that $B(x) \equiv \bar{s}(x)$ up to a linear transformation, $\bar{s}(x)$ denoting psychological value (or cardinal utility).[9]

(11) The justification of the neo-Bernoullian formulation by the law of large numbers, *even as a first approximation*, is pure illusion.[10]

(12) In the most general case, the link between psychological and monetary values and the influence of the shape of the distribution of psychological values are *inextricably interwoven, and no experiment concerning choice among uncertain prospects can be relied on to determine psychological value* (*cardinal utility*) $\bar{s}(x)$.[11]

In the most general case, the psychological value (cardinal utility) can be determined *only* by introspective observation of either psychologically equivalent increments or minimum perceptible thresholds.

It is *only* in the *very special* case in which the neo-Bernoullian index $B(x)^{**}$ would be identical to the psychological value $\bar{s}(x)$ that the psychological value $\bar{s}(x)$ could be determined by observation of random choices.[12]

Notes added in 1977
* That is on *criteria* that are free of all reference to any consideration of random choice.
** §10 above.
Note 1: §11, pp.45–46; §72, p.103; §74, pp.107–110. Note 2: §§14–23, pp.47–55; §§45–46, pp.67–69. Note 3: §§25–36, pp.57–60. Note 4: §47, pp.69–70; §§49–50, pp.74–77; §73, pp.104–106. Note 5: §47, pp.69–70; §§51–59, pp.77–86; §§82–85, pp.112–124; §§86–88, pp.124–128. Note 6: §§60–66, pp.86–95. Note 7: §§67–71, pp.95–103. Note 8: §§66–70, pp.95–99; §73, pp.104–106. Note 9: §50, pp.75–77; §69, pp.97–98. Note 10: §48, pp.70–73; §§80–81, pp.110–111. Note 11: §21, pp.53–54; §72, p.103; §§74–79, pp.107–110. Note 12: §69, pp.97–98; §§72–73, pp.103–106; §§89–90, pp.128–130.

The history of science largely confirms how difficult it is to absorb a new scientific conception. Our thinking inevitably follows the beaten path, even if it does not lead to the goal, and even if the new superior approach does not involve any special difficulties.

The essence and the function of fixed habits of thought in saving time and trouble is the outcome of their having become subconscious. Automatically deduced results are sheltered from criticism and eventually from the contradiction of individual facts. But when its time has come, this function becomes a brake on further progress.

JOSEPH SCHUMPETER, 1912[1]

The fine mind will commonly bring principles to bear before the eyes of all...all that is involved is good vision, but that vision must be good...for omission of a single principle leads to error...

Thus all geometricians would be fine geometricians were but their vision good, for they do not reason faultily on the principles they know.

What blunts their thought is that they do not perceive what is before them. Accustomed to the clear but rough principles of geometry, and to abstain from reasoning until their principles have been thoroughly perceived and deployed, they are lost when subtle questions arise to which their principles do not lend themselves. These questions can hardly be perceived; they are sensed rather than perceived and it is infinitely difficult to render them palpable by those who do not sense them. They are such delicate things that a highly attuned sense is needed to become aware of them, and then to judge directly and accurately in consequence.... The question must be seen at a single glance. It cannot be discovered, at least up to a certain point, by a process of reasoning.

BLAISE PASCAL, 1657[2]

But of all these paths, which will lead us most promptly to the goal? Who will tell us which to choose? We need a faculty which will help us perceive the goal from afar. This faculty is intuition....

Logic and intuition both have a necessary part to play. Both are indispensable. Logic alone can convey certainty: it is the instrument of proof. Intuition is the instrument of invention.

HENRI POINCARÉ, 1906[3]

The purpose and scope of this study

1. The bulk of this study[4,5] is devoted to a critical exposition of the postulates and axioms of the Theory of Risk put forward in recent American literature.

To facilitate the critical analysis, the discussion is divided into two parts. The first is devoted to a statement of the author's own approach and concepts. This is used as the basis of a critical analysis of the neo-Bernoullian formulation in the second part, with particular reference to the different axioms of the American School.

Generally speaking, *intuition is appealed to as far as possible, and unduly abstract mathematical formulations are avoided. Only too often, too high a degree of mathematical abstraction diverts attention from the real difficulties and obscures the essential aspects of a problem.*[6]

Mathematics are merely a tool for transforming statements. Real importance attaches only to the discussion of the premisses adopted and the results obtained.[7]

CHAPTER I

THE FOUNDATIONS OF A POSITIVE THEORY
OF CHOICE INVOLVING RISK

1. *FIELDS OF CHOICE INVOLVING RISK*

A. INDIFFERENCE SURFACES

Ordinal Preference Index

2. Let (P) be a random prospect[7] of positive or negative gains whose discounted present values are $g_1, g_2, \ldots, g_n$,[8] each with a corresponding probability of occurrence $p_1, p_2, \ldots, p_n$ such that

(1) $\qquad p_1 + p_2 + \cdots + p_n = 1.$

Assume that a person (X), whose initial capital is C[9] can choose between various random prospects (P), and can rank them in order of preference. He can then attach an ordinal index of preference to each prospect (P):

(2) $\qquad S = S(C + g_1, C + g_2, \ldots, C + g_n, p_1, p_2, \ldots, p_n),$

such that for any prospect (P_2) which is preferred to prospect (P_1)

(3) $\qquad S_1 < S_2.$

To simplify the notation, C can be taken as origin of the monetary values and we can write

(4) $\qquad S = S(g_1, g_2, \ldots, g_n, p_1, p_2, \ldots, p_n),$

subject of course throughout to replacement of each value g_i by the value $g_i + C$ in all the relations derived whenever C is to be taken into account explicitly.

In the most general case, all that can be said of the function S is that:

38

(a) it is an increasing function of the g_i;

(b) it is a symmetrical function of the g_i and of the p_i;

(c) the function $(g, g, \ldots, g, p_1, p_2, \ldots, p_n)$ is a well determined function of g independent of the p_i;

(d) the function s is independent of g_i when $p_i = 0$.

If the quantities studied are assumed continuous, then using the corresponding notation, the preference index S is a functional[9]

(5) $$S = S[\varphi(g)]$$

of the probability density $\varphi(g)$.

Consistent Choices. The Axiom of Absolute Preference[10]

3. Consider an urn containing n identical balls. Each is associated with a gain g_i whose probability is $1/n$. This random prospect can be shown geometrically as a stair-step diagram in which each step is represented by successive segments of the horizontal axis of length $1/n$. Gains g_i are measured on the vertical axis, successive gains being ranked in growing order of size from left to right.[11] (Figure 1)

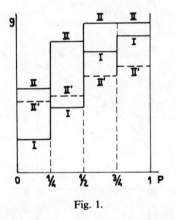

Fig. 1.

It is clear that if we consider a second set of random prospects (II) in which the gain provided by each ball is larger, (II) is necessarily preferable to (I) if the individual is consistent with himself. This assumption will be referred to as the *axiom of absolute preference*.

If, by contrast, we consider a random prospect (II') whose curve

intersects that of (I), nothing more can be said a priori. (II') may or
may not be preferred to (I); whether it is depends of course on the
psychology of the individual concerned.

In order to distinguish between the two cases, the first will be
referred to as *absolute preference* and the second as *relative preference*, and they will be denoted symbolically as

(1) $(I) \ll (II)$, $(I) < (II')$.

A random prospect that is mathematically continuous can similarly be
represented by an increasing function (Figure 2)

(2) $g = \psi(P)$,

and it is clear that P is nothing other than the probability that the gain
obtained will be less than a given value of g. The inverse

(3) $P = F(g)$

of the function $\psi(P)$ therefore defines the total probability function
corresponding to the random prospect considered, and we have
(Figure 3)

(4) $P = F(g) = \int_{-\infty}^{g} \varphi(g) \, dg.$

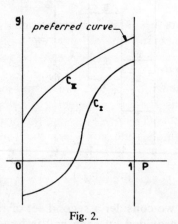

Fig. 2.

It can be seen immediately that the transition from the conventional
total probability curve C' to the curve C is obtained by a symmetrical
shift with respect to the axis OP followed by a 90° clockwise rotation.

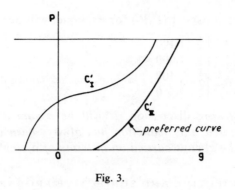

Fig. 3.

A random prospect (II) will be absolutely preferred to a random prospect (I), if, in Figure (2), the curve C_{II} representing prospect (II) is wholly located above the curve C_I representing prospect (I), or in Figure (3), if the curve C'_{II} representing (II) is wholly located *below* the curve C'_I representing (I).

Equivalence of a Series of Random Prospects and a Single Random Prospect[11']

4. Now assume that the person (X) is to make a certain number of successive choices among random prospects. For example, we may consider the successive choices between the random prospects (P_0) and (P'_0), (P_1) and (P'_1), . . . , (P_n) and (P'_n), etc.

Clearly this sequence of choices can be reduced to a single choice between the various random prospects. All that is necessary is to combine the prospects (P) and (P') using the principles of probability theory. If, for example, one considers the four independent prospects[12]

$$(P_0)\begin{cases}\frac{1}{2} & \$100 \\ \frac{1}{2} & 0\end{cases} \qquad (P'_0)\begin{cases}1 & \$100 \\ & \end{cases} \qquad (P_1)\begin{cases}\frac{1}{2} & \$1000 \\ \frac{1}{2} & 0\end{cases} \qquad (P'_1)\begin{cases}1 & \$300, \\ & \end{cases}$$

the successive choices between (P_0) and (P'_0) and between (P_1) and (P'_1) can be reduced to a single choice between the four prospects (P_0P_1), ($P_0P'_1$), (P'_0P_1) and ($P'_0P'_1$) found by applying the principle of compound probabilities to combine the basic probabilities. The distribution of prospect (P_0P_1) for example, will be

$$(P_0P_1)\begin{cases} \frac{1}{4} & 1.100 \\ \frac{1}{4} & 1.000 \\ \frac{1}{4} & 100 \\ \frac{1}{4} & 0 \end{cases}.$$

In the following discussion, *it will be assumed that, unless the contrary is stated, this reduction has always been done, so that the analysis can be always carried on in terms of a single choice.*[13]

B. OBJECTIVE AND SUBJECTIVE PROBABILITIES

Objective and Subjective Probabilities

5. *The objective probability of an event should be understood as a magnitude whose experimental measurement is given by its observed frequency.*

A distinction should be made between the frequency as actually measured – the *experimental* frequency – which indicates the objective probability, and the *psychologically* appraised frequency, which represents the subjective probability.

There are certainly people who, when tossing a coin, believe that the observed frequency of heads will differ from the value expected by non-participant scientific observers. Similar in nature would be the case of a person who, unaware of the findings of calorimetry, thought that water boils at 80°C, and acted accordingly.

Clearly, *an individual will only allow for the probabilities he believes to obtain, and not those that actually obtain.* There is therefore no reason for the subjective and objective probabilities of an event to be identical. Only a professional statistician, for example, can have an accurate idea of the meaning of a probability of one per cent.

In what follows the symbols p_i and $\overline{p_i}$ will be used respectively to denote objective and subjective probabilities.

Measuring Subjective Probabilities

6. *Objective probability can only be defined for an event that repeats itself.* It is a meaningless concept as regards an event which can only occur once and never again thereafter. However, there is nothing to prevent a person from behaving as if he attributes a probability to such an event. This is necessarily a subjective probability, and Borel has developed a method for measuring it,[14] the "method of gains".

Borel considers the choice made by an individual who will receive the same amount, say $1000, if he throws a one-spot on a die or if a given unique event (E) occurs – for example, if it rains tomorrow. Since the probability of the first of these two events is known, the choice made by (X) indicates whether he assesses the chance of (E) occurring is above or below $\frac{1}{6}$. By successive approximations, taking as benchmarks other events whose objective probabilities are known (casting dice, or drawing balls from a bag), it is possible to determine the value $\bar{p}$ of the subjective probability assigned by (X) to the event (E).[15]

The example shows that subjective probabilities exist, but that they can only be measured by reference to objective probabilities. It may reasonably be claimed that it would have been impossible to develop the concept of subjective probability if experience had not first taught us that objective probabilities exist.

C. CARDINAL UTILITY AND PSYCHOLOGICAL VALUE

The Cardinal Utility[15'] *Attaching to a Random Prospect*

7. For a given field of choice defined by an ordinal preference function

(1) $S = S(A, B, \ldots, C)$

in which $A, B, \ldots, C$ represent quantities consumed, it is possible to specify a cardinal preference function

(2) $\bar{S} = \bar{S}(A, B, \ldots, C),$

determined up to a linear transformation, such that for two increments of utility that are deemed equivalent, the variation $\Delta\bar{S}$ will have the same value.[16,17] Similarly, it is possible, in the case of random prospects, to specify for any field of choice defined by the function

(3) $S = S(g_1, g_2, \ldots, g_n, p_1, p_2, \ldots, p_n),$

a function of cardinal preference

(4) $\bar{S} = \bar{S}(g_1, g_2, \ldots, g_n, p_1, p_2, \ldots, p_n)$

which, in the field of the economic psychology of risk, is the equivalent of the Fechner–Weber functions expressing psycho-physiological sensation as a function of excitation.

Monetary and Psychological Values

8. Let $\bar{s}$ be the cardinal utility associated with a certain sum X. This cardinal utility represents the psychological value attaching to a certain capital $(C + X)$.

To the extent that the Fechner–Weber results in the psycho-physiology can be extrapolated to economic behaviour, we have

(1) $\bar{s}(X) = K \log (X + X_0)$

in which K and X_0 are two constants (Figure 4). The function $\bar{s}(X)$ will be referred to hereafter as the "psychological value". Naturally, it should be true that

(2) $\bar{s}(X) = \bar{s}(X, X, \ldots, X, p_1, p_2, \ldots, p_n)$.

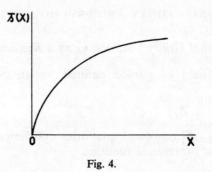

Fig. 4.

The Impossibility in General of Determining the Cardinal Utility by Considering Choices among Random Prospects

9. Obviously in the most general case in which the ordinal field of choice

(1) $S = S(g_1, g_2, \ldots, g_n, p_1, p_2, \ldots, p_n)$

is known, it cannot be used to determine the scale of cardinal utility $\bar{s}$

in the plane defined by the relations

(2) $p_1 + p_2 + \cdots + p_n = 1,$

(3) $g_1 = g_2 = \cdots = g_n,$

i.e. the scale of the psychological values $\bar{s}(X)$.[18]

The Monetary Value of a Random Prospect

10. Let V be the certain monetary value which an individual (X) deems equivalent to a random prospect (P). It follows from the foregoing that

(1) $\bar{s}(V) = \bar{S}(g_1, g_2, \ldots, g_n, p_1, p_2, \ldots, p_n)$

with

(2) $p_1 + p_2 + \cdots + p_n = 1.$

In continuous notation,

(3) $\bar{s}(V) = f[\varphi(g)],$

the function f being a functional of the probability density $\varphi(g)$.

A given random prospect (P) of value V can be thought of as a lottery ticket whose value is estimated as V.

If instead of considering monetary values g, valuation is in psychological units,

(4) $\gamma = \bar{s}(g),$

and if $\psi(\gamma)$ is used to designate the density of the distribution of the probabilities of the γ, we have

(5) $\bar{s}(V) = h[\psi(\gamma)],$

where h is a functional of the density $\psi(\gamma)$.

For the individual to be consistent with himself, all that is required is that the functions S, f and h comply with the axiom of absolute preference.[19]

The Concept of Psychological Value (Cardinal Utility)

11. The writer's view is that the concept of cardinal utility and psychological value is *fundamental* to the theory of random choice.

As this concept has come under sharp fire from a number of authors, a few further words on it are not out of place.

Firstly, *this concept, which in any event responds to intuition, can be given an operational definition by introducing either the notion of equivalent psychological increments or the notion of minimum perceptible thresholds.*[20]

Hardly anybody would fail to reply "yes" *without any hesitation* if asked "would you prefer to inherit $100 million rather than $10,000 more strongly than you would prefer to inherit $10,000 rather than $1000?". The absence of hesitation demonstrates without any doubt that the notion of equivalent psychological increments indeed corresponds to a psychological reality.[21]

Further, *as a practical matter*, a concept of this kind is applied effectively by the legislator in imposing progressive income tax. It may reasonably be suggested that (in a democracy, at least), the legislator assigns the same weight to the minimal threshold values perceived by different persons. In the most general case of any political organisation, it may be argued that the same magnitudes are taken into account, the difference lying in the weighting coefficients used.

It is curious to observe that so important a concept, lending itself so easily to the discussion of numerous issues,[22] seems gradually to have dropped out of the literature after Pareto's time.[23,24]

2. PSYCHOLOGICAL FACTORS OF CHOICES INVOLVING RISK

FUNDAMENTAL AND SECONDARY FACTORS

12. A careful distinction must be made between those components[24'] of a choice involving risk which are fundamental and those which are of secondary importance only.

The distinction is well illustrated by a simple example. It is possible to build up the theory of price determination by using demand and supply curves, abstracting the cost of purchasing and selling proper from the analysis as a first approximation: on examination, these factors are found to play generally a minor role. To include them at this stage would mask the fundamental issues to which price theory adresses itself.

The same distinction can be made for risk. Many psychological influences affect choice. *Some of them are basic, and to ignore them, even as a first approximation, would seriously falsify the phenomena studied.* Others, by contrast, are relatively secondary and can be allowed for at a later stage by making appropriate adjustments.[25,26]

A. FUNDAMENTAL FACTORS

13. There are four fundamental factors which must *necessarily* form part of any theory of risk that is meant to be realistic, and to bring to light the basic considerations that are relevant to choice among uncertain prospects.

I. THE PSYCHOLOGICAL DISTORTION OF MONETARY VALUES
AND THE CURVATURE OF CARDINAL UTILITY (FACTOR AI)

14. What a person takes into account in choosing among random prospects is not the monetary value g of the possible gain, but the psychological value $\bar{s}(g)$ of that gain.

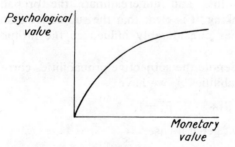

Fig. 5.

It follows that if marginal cardinal utility $d\bar{s}/dg$ is declining and shows a sufficiently marked rate of decline (i.e. strong curvature), a gain whose monetary value may be ten times that of another may be only worth twice as much, or even less, in psychological terms.[27]

II. THE SUBJECTIVE DISTORTION OF OBJECTIVE

PROBABILITIES (FACTOR AII)

15. People who believe in their lucky star underestimate the probability of an unfavourable outcome and overestimate the likelihood of success. Those who believe that misfortune dogs their steps err in the opposite direction.

The subjective distortion of objective probabilities generally seems to depend on whether gain or loss is at issue, as well as the amounts involved. In the most general case, all outcomes are possible. An individual may well overestimate small probabilities of gain and underestimate small probabilities of loss. He may underestimate high probabilities of small loss, but overestimate high probabilities of large gains. Again, he may overestimate small probabilities of large gains or losses alike.

The same person is perfectly capable of cautiously buying insurance protection against fire, and losing all his fortune at the races.

The gambler may differ from the prudent man in the way he distorts objective probabilities. Generally speaking, the gambler overestimates the probability of gain and underestimates the likelihood of loss. Prudent people by contrast, tend to overestimate the probability of loss and underestimate the probability of gain.[28] Generally speaking, it is clear that the subjective distortion of objective probabilities considerably influences the attitude of economic agents to risk.

Using $\overline{p_i}$ to denote the subjective probabilities corresponding to the objective probabilities p_i, we have

(1) $\overline{p_i} + \overline{p_2} + \cdots + \overline{p_n} = 1,$

and, in the most general case,

(2) $\overline{p_i} = \overline{p_i}(g_1, g_2, \ldots, g_n, p_1, p_2, \ldots, p_n).$

In continuous notation, $\bar{\varphi}(g)$ and $\bar{\psi}(\gamma)$ will be used to denote the subjective probability densities of the monetary (g) and psychological (γ) values.

As has already been noted, cases exist in which the concept of objective probability completely disappears, although a subjective probability continues to be assigned. This corresponds to the case of isolated events. Here, it is impossible to define a frequency, yet a subjective probability can be defined by comparison with a phenomenon for which an objective probability exists.[29]

III. THE PROBABILITY WEIGHTING OF PSYCHOLOGICAL
    VALUES AND THE CONSIDERATION OF MATHEMATICAL
    EXPECTATION (FIRST-ORDER MOMENTS OF THE
    DISTRIBUTION OF THE PROBABILITIES OF MONETARY
    VALUES) (FACTOR AIII)

16. As a first approximation, it is possible to consider mathematical expectation instead of considering the distribution of the probabilities of psychological values. This is fully analogous to representing a set of figures by a single figure, namely their average. The advantages and disadvantages are the same.

If the first three elements are considered together, the valuation of a random prospect is assessed, not as the mathematical expectation of monetary values, but as the monetary value whose psychological value is equal to the mathematical expectation of the psychological values attaching to different possible gains, using psychological probabilities $\overline{p_i}$ as weights. This leads to consideration of the relationship

(1) $\bar{s}(V) = \overline{p_1}\bar{s}(g_1) + \overline{p_2}\bar{s}(g_2) + \cdots + \overline{p_n}\bar{s}(g_n),$

which will be referred to as the neo-Bernoullian formulation in honour of its originator. Thus what are combined, using the standard rules for combining probable values, are not the monetary values but the psychological values.

The Combined Effect of Factors AI and AIII

17. By combining Factors AI and AIII, it can be seen *that two prospects with the same mathematical expectation of monetary gain may not be at all equivalent from a psychological point of view.*

If my total capital amounts to 1 million units, I may well be loath to stake it against a bet of 10 million in a heads-or-tails game. This will be particularly true if my cardinal utility $\bar{s}(g)$ is such that the possible reduction $[\bar{s}(0) - \bar{s}(-1)]$ is much greater than the possible increase $[\bar{s}(10) - \bar{s}(0)]$, where the unit of measurement of monetary gain is equal to one million.[30] Although the two prospects have the same objective probability, I may well deem that the possible increase $[s(10) - s(0)]$ of my cardinal utility, associated with a probability of $\frac{1}{2}$, is not sufficient to outweigh the risk of psychological loss $[\bar{s}(0) - \bar{s}(-1)]$ associated with the same probability of $\frac{1}{2}$.

In other words, it would be wrong to consider a game as psychologically attractive if the mathematical expectation of the monetary values involved is positive. It may not be so if cardinal utility $\bar{s}(g)$ does not rise linearly with g and if $d\bar{s}/dg$ declines with g.

The Case of Small Gains

18. Where all the g_i are small enough, relation (1) of §16 yields

$$(1) \qquad V = \sum \bar{p}_i g_i.$$

This case reproduces the calculation based on the mathematical expectation attaching to monetary values. Since the curvature of the cardinal utility function does not operate in this particular case, it is normal for the individual to pattern his behaviour on the principle of mathematical expectation.

The Combined Effect of Factors AI, AII and AIII

19. To illustrate the combined operation of the factors AI–AIII consider the special case in which there are only two outcomes, respectively a gain of G or a loss of P, and in which the distortion of the probabilities is independent of G and P. We then have

$$(1) \qquad \bar{s}(V) = \bar{p}(p)\bar{s}(G) + [1 - \bar{p}(p)]\bar{s}(-P).$$

If the subject considered overestimates his chances of a win, we will have

$$(2) \qquad \bar{p} > p,$$

and vice-versa $(p > \bar{p})$ if he is overly cautious.

Using $p'(p)$ to denote the function representing the distortion of probabilities in case of loss, we have

$$(3) \qquad \bar{p}'(1 - p) = 1 - \bar{p}(p).$$

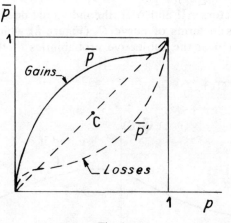

Fig. 6.

This relationship states that the curve of the function $\bar{p}'(p)$ is symmetrical with the curve of the function $\bar{p}(p)$ with respect to the point C whose coordinates are $(\frac{1}{2}, \frac{1}{2})$.

IV. CONSIDERATION OF THE SHAPE OF THE PROBABILITY DISTRIBUTION OF PSYCHOLOGICAL VALUES, AND IN PARTICULAR, OF THEIR DISPERSION (SECOND-MOMENTS) (FACTOR AIV)

20. A random prospect is, in fact, described by the curve C_1, the distribution of the probability of different gains. This curve plots the values $\varphi(g)$ of the objective probability density (Figure 7). However, in

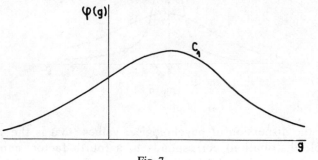

Fig. 7.

the light of Factors AII and AIII, the individual does not refer to this curve. He acts in terms of curve C_2 (Figure 8) which translates the distribution $\bar{\psi}(\gamma)$ of the subjective probabilities of the psychological values

(1) $\gamma = \bar{s}(g)$.

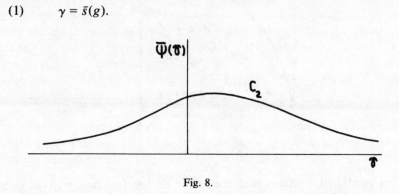

Fig. 8.

A cautious individual choosing between two random prospects which have Laplace–Gauss distributions of the psychological values γ and the same average value, will select the distribution with the least dispersion. In Figure 9, this is distribution (I). By contrast, if he likes risk, he will choose distribution (II) with the greatest dispersion.

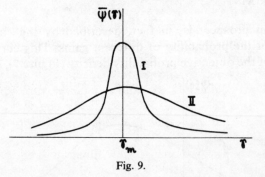

Fig. 9.

Thus, the dispersion of psychological values (that is the shape of the whole distribution) corresponds to a fourth factor, namely the pleasure – or aversion – inherent in the fact of taking a risk[31] i.e. in taking part in games in which different shapes of the distribution of the psychological values are possible.

This explains why roulette may be viewed as an attractive pastime, even though (as is likely for small sums) there is no psychological distortion of the monetary values, or indeed, even if the probabilities concerned are appraised at their objective values as revealed by experience. Similarly, it may be considered as well worthwhile pitting oneself against a stronger poker player if the pleasure drawn from participating in a game in which there is a great dispersion of outcomes, is great enough to offset the probable loss.

The pleasure or aversion attaching to risk-taking constitutes an additional element which modifies the results derived from the pure calculation based on a simple probability weighting (objective or subjective) of the psychological values to be drawn from the different outcomes possible. It should be carefully distinguished from the first factor (AI) listed above (the psychological distortion of monetary values), although the two are commonly *found in close association and may give rise to completely similar effects.*

The Dispersion of Monetary and Psychological Values

21. As a matter of fact it should be noted that the responsiveness of an individual to the dispersion of monetary gains about their average reflects the *simultaneous* influence of Factors AI, AIII and AIV.

Even if an individual were not sensitive to the dispersion of psychological values (Factor AIV), he would be affected by the dispersion of monetary values through the curvature of cardinal utility. Two changes Δg_1 and Δg_2 of g, equal in absolute value, but of opposite sign, are associated with changes $\Delta \gamma_1$ and $\Delta \gamma_2$ in psychological values of unequal absolute size (see Figure 10).

It is the symmetry of effect of Factors AI and AIV, in terms of monetary value, that has cast a cloud of obscurity over current discussion of the topic.

This symmetry is particularly well illustrated by the following concrete example. A traveller ends up at Marseille low in funds, but must get back to Paris at all costs. If he has $10 left, whatever game offers him the greatest chance of winning the price of his ticket is the most advantageous for him. The rule of maximising the mathematical expectation of this monetary gain is irrelevant to his case, *even as a*

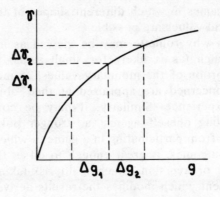

Fig. 10.

first approximation. Our traveller's behaviour in this example can be explained equally well either by the psychological distortion of monetary values (Factor AI), with a high value attributed to any psychological value $\bar{s}(g)$ exceeding his fare; or, alternatively, by the advantages stemming from taking part in a game offering a chance of winning a greater sum than the fare (Factor AIV).[32-34]

In point of fact, the sensitivity to the dispersion of the monetary values by reason of the curvature of cardinal utility is of a completely different nature compared with the sensitivity to the dispersion of psychological values. In fact it does not take into account *the fundamental feature characterising the psychology of risk, that is the dispersion of psychological values.*

The Psychological Value of Dispersion Considered in Itself

22. Most individuals are, in practice, sensitive to the existence of the possibility of great losses or great gains. Admittedly, they evaluate these losses or gains using another scale, namely their scale of psychological values, but once this is done, the mere existence of these losses or gains is an intrinsically important fact in itself.

For someone who desires a large sum of money above all else, gaming may be the only rational answer. Further, this has nothing to do with any of the first three factors AI–AIII.

In reality, Factor AIV, the impact of the spread of gains and losses when evaluated in psychological units, is, as far as this author can see, an absolutely basic component of choices involving risk.

In many cases, it may exert much more influence than the consideration of mathematical expectation, the subjective distortion of monetary values, or the subjective distortion of objective probabilities. It may be a greater error to neglect the dispersion of psychological values than it is to treat them on the same footing as monetary values.

In the most general case, it can be taken that as regards the simplified rule under which monetary values are weighted by objective probabilities, Factors AI, AII and AIV (respectively, psychological distortion of monetary values and objective probabilities, and the dispersion of psychological values) are correction factors of *substantially equal importance.*

It would be wrong, therefore, to neglect the dispersion of psychological values even in the frame of a first approximation; indeed, I contend that this factor is the specific characteristic of the psychology of risk.

It is very unfortunate that its effect is so often masked by the operation of the first factor, namely, the psychological distortion of monetary values.

In reality, Factor AIV operates in all cases, and *it is absolutely impossible to carry out any experiment in which it could be presumed absent.* The result is, as already noted, that the cardinal utility function $\bar{s}(g)$ cannot be determined by observing random choices.

Analytical Formulation

(a) General Formulation

23. The most general formulation specifying the relationship of the value V of a random prospect to its components γ is:

$$\bar{s}(V) = h[\bar{\psi}(\gamma)],$$

where h is a certain functional of the density of the psychological probabilities $\bar{\psi}$ of the psychological values γ.

(b) Special Formulations

24. From certain points of view, it may be of interest to consider other formulations.

(1) If Factor AIV were non-operative, the monetary value V' of a random prospect would be given, as has been noted (§16), by

$$(1) \qquad \bar{s}(V') = \sum_i \overline{p_i}(g_1, g_2, \ldots, g_n, p_1, p_2, \ldots, p_n)\bar{s}(g_i).$$

If Factor AIV is allowed for, this monetary value becomes V. Thus the difference $(V - V')$ in a sense is the monetary premium, which may be positive or negative, attaching to the *shape* of the random distribution describing the prospect considered.

It is always possible to write

$$(2) \qquad \bar{s}(V) = \sum_i \overline{p_i}(g_1, g_2, \ldots, g_n, p_1, p_2, \ldots, p_n)\bar{s}(g_i + v),$$

where v has the same sign as $(V - V')$, since all the subjective probabilities $\overline{p_i}$ are positive. The value v represents the additional gain to be attached to each outcome if the value is to be given by the formula for the mathematical expectation of the psychological values. It will be positive if the subject likes risk, negative if he is averse to it.

(2) If the axiom of absolute preference is assumed to be satisfied, the monetary value V will certainly lie between the two extreme values of g, and there will exist *positive* functions $\alpha_i(g_1, g_2, \ldots, g_n, p_1, p_2, \ldots, p_n)$ such that

$$(3) \qquad \bar{s}(V) = \sum \alpha_i(g_1, g_2, \ldots, g_n, p_1, p_2, \ldots, p_n)\bar{s}(g_i),$$

with

$$(4) \qquad \sum \alpha_i(g_1, g_2, \ldots, g_n, p_1, p_2, \ldots, p_n) = 1.$$

This formulation is wholly analogous to the neo-Bernoullian formulation and we see that behaviour with respect to risk is as it would be if the individual used positive weighting coefficients α_i, summing to unity, to combine the psychological values which correspond to the monetary values of the random outcome considered. *There is, of course, no reason for these α_i coefficients necessarily to be equal to the corresponding subjective probabilities*, even though they are positive and sum to unity.

This formulation is in fact *purely formal*, and is only of interest to the extent that it contrasts with the neo-Bernoullian formulation.

B. SECONDARY FACTORS

25. When subjected to analysis, the gaming phenomenon turns out to be very complex. Many other elements affecting choices subject to risk can be identified. Basically, however, they play a secondary role, and can be neglected in a first approximation. The main ones only are examined below.

1. *The Expense of Playing (Factor B1)*

26. The mere act of playing means giving up time. A stock exchange speculator is doomed to follow the market. A race course or casino gambler, in addition to the time spent, must pay an entrance fee. Gaming involves a cost which must be allowed for by the player.

Let us assume that a cost F is associated with the game

$$(g_1, g_2, \ldots, g_n, p_1, p_2, \ldots, p_n).$$

In all cases, this cost must be deducted from wins and losses, and relation (2) of §24 becomes

$$(1) \qquad \bar{s}(V) = \bar{p}_1 \bar{s}(g_1 + v - F) + \cdots + \bar{p}_n \bar{s}(g_n + v - F).$$

As before, it is easy to see that positive coefficients β_i can be defined so that relation (3) of §24 will be verified. However, as the axiom of absolute preference is no longer necessarily verified for gross winnings g_i, we will have in general

$$(2) \qquad \sum \beta_i(g_1, g_2, \ldots, g_n, p_1, p_2, \ldots, p_n) \neq 1.$$

2. *The Intrinsic Pleasure of the Act of Playing (Factor B2)*

27. For some people, participating in the unfolding of a game is a source of pleasure. Others get bored: gaming is a loss of satisfaction for them.

Although, at first sight, the distinction between factors AIV and B2 seems very subtle, it is nonetheless clear. If a person enjoys playing cards, this may because he can participate in this way in an activity with different possible outcomes (Factor AIV), or because gaming is in itself a pleasant pastime (B2). Several writers in English use the terms "pleasure of gambling" and "pleasure of gaming (or, of the game)" to refer to these two elements.

The process is the same as for Factor B1, except that the parameter F (relation 1 of §26) is negative when gaming conveys pleasure.

3. *The Pleasure of Winning Considered in Itself* (*Factor B3*)

28. It is obvious that a player who wins a cup of coffee in a friendly dice game can derive more pleasure from the fact of having won than he attaches to the mere increase in his income. The same is true of the disappointment produced by the fact of losing.[35]

Similar circumstances are to be encountered in the business world. An entrepreneur may consider that his prestige will rise if his project succeeds, and decline if it fails. This factor should evidently not be confused with Factor AIV (the intrinsic pleasure of risk-taking) or with Factor B2 (the pleasure of gaming). It can be allowed for analytically by a weighted formulation using β_i coefficients whose sum differs from unity.

4. *The Minimum Perceptible Threshold* (*Factor B4*)

29. If a lottery ticket costs an amount below my minimum perceptible threshold whereas the daydream of a big win produces a tangible degree of pleasure, it is perfectly rational for me to buy it.

Similarly, consider a person who has 5000 units of currency to spend on a holiday, who cannot think of anything he would like to do costing that price, but believes he would have a splendid time if he had 50,000 units. He would be acting perfectly rationally in plunging his 5000 units in a visit to a casino or a racecourse, or by buying lottery tickets – even if he has a markedly curved function of cardinal utility, overestimates the risk of loss, dislikes both gambling and gaming, and is perfectly aware that his mathematical expectation is lower than the value of his stake.

When the loss $-g$ is less than the minimum perceptible threshold, $\bar{s}(g)$ should be replaced by $\bar{s}(0)$. As can be seen, the weighted formulation can be maintained by choosing an appropriate set of β_i weighting coefficients whose sum will differ from unity.

5. *The Interval between the Bet and the Draw* (*Factor B5*)

30. The attraction of a random prospect is, in general, dependent on the time elapsing between the decision to stake and the drawing. The further in the future the drawing lies, the longer the pleasure attaching to the hope of winning will last. Impatience, of course, has exactly the opposite effect.

6. *Self Justification (Factor B6)*[36]

31. Some people are consciously aware of the pleasure of risk and admit it. Others are subconsciously attracted by risk, but their conscious mind condemns it. They must have some outside justification (e.g., indirect contributions to charity by purchase of raffle tickets, amusement of children, etc.).

7. *Relations with Others (Factor B7)*[36]

32. The attitude of third parties to the subject's decision to play or not to play may have an important role. There are two extreme attitudes here, with all the possible intermediate gradations. Mr. X may wish to be different, and will take a risk as long as he is alone in doing so. Mr. Y may prefer to remain in conformity with the psychology of his social milieu, and will accept risk if everybody else does too.

8. *The Existence of Some Indeterminacy (Factor B8)*[37]

33. In reality, it cannot generally be affirmed that a random prospect P_1 is preferred to another P_2. All that can be said is that there is a certain probability π that P_1 will be preferred to P_2.

9. *The Nature of the Game (Factor B9)*

34. All the accessory factors in set (B) may depend on the nature of the game considered. All other things being equal, their influence will not be the same in a friendly game of poker as in the case in which a fortune is staked on a stock exchange speculation or invested in an industrial project.

10. *Other Factors (Factor B10)*

35. Many other factors affecting gaming behaviour could be distinguished, for reality is very complex. However, it seems that the

items enumerated above suffice for present purposes: the factors
labelled as (A) must be allowed for in any first approximation, and
those listed under (B) should be taken into account when further
refinement is called for.

As has already been noted, the (A) factors are the essential elements of any approach in which it is desired to focus on the
fundamental aspects of the psychology of risk. It is the same for the
theory of risk as for the theory of price determination. As a first
approximation, the theory can be built up without paying regard to
associated expenditure, the pleasure of "shopping around", or minimum perceptible thresholds.

11. *The Complexity of Reality*

36. Finally, it must be stressed that in many cases it is extremely
difficult to distinguish between the various operative factors. *They
may be so closely interwoven that they seem indissociable in practice.*
Pascal's statement about the gambler is apt: "Some people live a
perfectly pleasant existence in which they continually gamble small
amounts. Give one of them every morning the amount he could have
won during the day, providing he does not gamble, and you will make
him miserable. You may think that this is because he is looking for
the pleasure of the game, rather than the winnings involved. If so, just
try letting him play without stakes. He will betray no enthusiasm,
only boredom".[38]

C. GENERAL FORMULATION

General Analytical Formulation

37. In the light of the foregoing, it can be seen that in the most
general case it is possible to consider that the value V of a random
prospect may be considered as given by an expression of the form

$$(1) \qquad \bar{s}(V) = \sum \beta_i \bar{s}(g_i),$$

in which the β_i coefficients are positive, in general do not sum to
unity,

(2) $\sum \beta_i \neq 1,$

and are functions of all the influences affecting the process of choice.

Thus, in the most general case, the quantities by which the levels of cardinal utility corresponding to the various gains g_i should be multiplied are neither objective probabilities nor subjective probabilities. They are mere weighting coefficients that do not sum to unity. Of course they are functions, in particular, of the possible gains $g_1, g_2, \ldots, g_n$ and the objective $(p_1, p_2, \ldots, p_n)$ or subjective $(\overline{p}_1, \overline{p}_2, \ldots, \overline{p}_n)$ probabilities associated with these g_i, but the shape of these functions depends on the influence of all the secondary factors (B).

At any event, as has been noted earlier in connection with the fundamental factors, this formulation is purely formal, and is of interest only insofar as it stands in contrast to the neo-Bernoullian formulation.

Comments on the General Formulation

(a) *The General Nature of the Formulation*

38. As has been noted,[39] in the most general case the monetary value V of a random prospect may be considered as given by a relationship of the form

(1) $\bar{s}(V) = \bar{S}(g_1, g_2, \ldots, g_n, p_1, p_2, \ldots, p_n).$

Whatever this function $\bar{S}$, it can always be written in the form[40]

(2) $\bar{s}(V) = \sum_i \beta_i(g_1, g_2, \ldots, g_n, p_1, p_2, \ldots, p_n)\bar{s}(g_i),$

in which the function $s(g)$ represents cardinal utility and the β_i are positive functions whose sum differs from unity.

Thus the use of relation (2) involves no loss of generality vis-à-vis relation (1). This purely mathematical property confirms the generality of the analysis presented above.

(b) *The Sum of the Weighting Coefficients*

39. It should be stressed that in general, the β_i weights introduced in the transition from form (1) to form (2) of the general formulation *will not normally add to unity*.

In other words, *in general*, there are no functions

$$\beta_i(g_1, g_2, \ldots, g_n, p_1, p_2, \ldots, p_n),$$

such that

(1) $$\bar{S}(g_1, g_2, \ldots, g_n, p_1, p_2, \ldots, p_n)$$

$$= \sum \beta_i(g_1, g_2, \ldots, g_n, p_1, p_2, \ldots, p_n)\bar{s}(g_i),$$

with

(2) $$\sum \beta_i(g_1, g_2, \ldots, g_n, p_1, p_2, \ldots, p_n) = 1.$$

To confirm this, it is only necessary to consider two special cases:

(a) Assume that all the g_i are equal to the same amount g. If the β_i summed to unity, we would have

(3) $$\bar{s}(V) = \bar{s}(g).$$

However, this equality may be not verified, due to the possible influence of the pleasure of gaming (Factor B.2); it follows that

(4) $$V > g.$$

It might be objected that if the g_i are all equal, there is no game. This is a wrong view.[41] Consider the case of a person who is equally happy with either of two gifts (A) and (B) suggested by the donor, and tosses a coin to determine which he will receive. The game in this example is not neutral, although the two outcomes are equivalent.

(b) A second example refuting the unit-sum hypothesis with particular clarity is as follows:

Assume that there are only two outcomes, a gain G_1 or a loss G_2 and that the (B) elements are such that

(5) $$V > G_1.$$

Since, according to relation (2) of §38, we have

(6) $$\bar{s}(V) = \beta_1 \bar{s}(G_1) + \beta_2 \bar{s}(G_2),$$

it is clearly impossible to have

(7) $$\beta_1 + \beta_2 = 1.$$

Possible Generalisation of the neo-Bernoullian Formulation

40. It follows from what has been said above that providing regard is paid not to gross gains g_i, but to net gains G_i, the sum of the gross gains g_i and the monetary equivalent values v_i of the various factors affecting risk-bearing choices other than the first three listed in group (A), *the two fundamental relations below will always hold*:

(1) $$\bar{s}(V) = \sum_i \beta_i[G_1, \ldots, G_n, p_1, \ldots, p_n]\bar{s}(G_i),$$

(2) $$\sum_i \beta_i(G_1, \ldots, G_n, p_1, \ldots, p_n) = 1,$$

in which the p_i are the *objective probabilities* of the prospects $G_1, G_2, \ldots, G_n$, and in which the β_i functions are positive.

The Different Formulations of the Psychology of Risk

41. From the above analysis, it can be seen that alongside the most general case

(I)
$$\bar{s}(V) = \sum_i \beta_i(g_1, g_2, \ldots, g_n, p_1, p_2, \ldots, p_n)\bar{s}(g_i),$$
$$\sum_i \beta_i(g_1, g_2, \ldots, g_n, p_1, p_2, \ldots, p_n) \neq 1,$$

in which the g_i represent the gross gains and in which the weighting coefficients are not necessarily subjective probabilities, four especially interesting special cases can be distinguished. They are listed below, in increasing order of restrictiveness under the Roman numerals II, III, IV and V:

(II)
$$\bar{s}(V) = \sum_i \alpha_i(g_1, g_2, \ldots, g_n, p_1, p_2, \ldots, p_n)\bar{s}(g_i),$$
$$\sum_i \alpha_i(g_1, g_2, \ldots, g_n, p_1, p_2, \ldots, p_n) = 1;$$

(III)
$$\bar{s}(V) = \sum_i \overline{p_i}(g_1, g_2, \ldots, g_n, p_1, p_2, \ldots, p_n)\bar{s}(g_i),$$
$$\sum_i \overline{p_i}(g_1, g_2, \ldots, g_n, p_1, p_2, \ldots, p_n) = 1;$$

(IV)
$$\bar{s}(V) = \sum_i \overline{p_i}(p_i, p_2, \ldots, p_n)\bar{s}(g_i),$$

$$\sum_i \overline{p_i}(p_1, p_2, \ldots, p_n) = 1;$$

(V)
$$\bar{s}(V) = \sum_i p_i\bar{s}(g_i),$$

$$\sum_i p_i = 1.$$

In each of these cases except (II), the weighting coefficients correspond to probabilities. In (III) and (IV), subjective probabilities are involved, while those in case (V) are objective probabilities. In case (IV), the distortion of the objective probabilities is a function of the objective probabilities themselves, whereas in case (II), the values of the gains g_i are also a determining factor.

As will be seen later, the von Neumann–Morgenstern and Marschak theories only apply to case (V), so that they must be considered as being of very limited generality. Savage has reasoned in terms of case (III), so that his approach is much more general.

It should of course be borne in mind, as was noted in §3 above, that for self-consistency of the individual concerned, the axiom of absolute preference should be verified, *the probabilities relevant for this purpose being naturally the subjective probabilities* $\overline{p_i}$.

In case (IV), and in case (V) which is only a sub-case of (IV) in which $\overline{p_i} = p_i$, it can be seen immediately that the axiom of absolute preference is indeed verified.

In cases (II) and (III), the axiom is verified only if the functions in the respective formulations are subjected to restrictive conditions, but, as can easily be seen, these conditions do not suffice on their own to determine the form of the functions.[42,42']

Finally, in case (I), the axiom of absolute preference cannot be satisfied in general. The axiom implies that (V) will lie within the two extreme values of the distribution of the g_i, and, as has been pointed out earlier, the (B) factors may operate in such a way that this does not happen.

Explanation of the Facts

42. Clearly, in the most general case, the formulation

$$\bar{s}(V) = \sum \beta_i(g_1, g_2, \ldots, g_n, p_1, p_2, \ldots, p_n)\bar{s}(g_i),$$

$$\sum \beta_i(g_1, g_2, \ldots, g_n, p_1, p_2, \ldots, p_n) \neq 1,$$

or the equivalent formulation

$$\bar{s}(V) = \sum \alpha_i(g_1, g_2, \ldots, g_n, p_1, p_2, \ldots, p_n)\bar{s}(G_i),$$

$$\sum \alpha_i(g_1, g_2, \ldots, g_n, p_1, p_2, \ldots, p_n) = 1,$$

provides an explanation of all actually observed behaviour.

But it should be stressed that *the problem is not just that of explaining observed behaviour by a formula containing undetermined coefficients. That is always feasible. The real problem is to attempt to determine the form of the coefficients and that of the cardinal utility function*, using the data given by experience.

Scope of the Theory

43. The theory presented has a number of advantages:

(1) It accurately specifies the various relevant psychological factors.

(2) It can explain *all* the phenomena observed.

(3) It provides a link between different phenomena (cardinal utility in the Fechner–Weber sense and fields of choice involving risk).

(4) It is *very simple*.

The theory therefore has all the characteristics of a theory that is "scientifically true" in Poincaré's understanding of that term.

The Scientific Character of a Theory

44. It has been contended[43] that this theory is not scientific, being so general as to explain any kind of observed behaviour. A scientific theory, it has been suggested, is not necessarily true or false, nor does it necessarily attempt to explain the facts; for a theory to be scientific, it should be such that it is open to contradiction by confrontation with observed fact.

From this standpoint, the neo-Bernoullian theory should be preferable to that advanced here. The neo-Bernoullian approach, leads to the formulation

(1) $B(V) = \sum p_i B(g_i)$

with, of course

(2) $\sum p_i = 1,$

in which the function $B(g)$ is a certain function of g which is not necessarily identical to $\bar{s}(g)$,[44] whereas the present theory leads to the formulation

(3) $\bar{s}(V) = \sum \beta_i(g_1, g_2, \ldots, g_n, p_1, p_2, \ldots, p_n)\bar{s}(g_i)$

with, in the general case

(4) $\sum \beta_i(g_1, g_2, \ldots, g_n, p_1, p_2, \ldots, p_n) \neq 1.$

Relations (3) and (4) do indeed cover every conceivable case, whereas (1) and (2) are very restrictive.

At first sight, this reasoning may seem very attractive, but it is in fact quite specious. This can readily be illustrated by a few examples.

(a) Consider the case of a physicist who has determined the law governing the displacement of a magnetised needle under the influence of a magnet, and who has further observed that the needle is influenced by the action of an electric current in a neighbouring circuit, but has not as yet been able to discover exactly how this action is exerted.

Would it be scientific for him to continue to maintain the formula which excludes the effect of the nearby current? Would not the true scientific approach be for him to include an unknown function in his calculations which would allow for this as yet inadequately specified factor, and to attempt to determine it accurately by experiment?

The effect of the current in this example is wholly analogous to the role played by Factors (AII), (AIV) and the factors in group (B) in the theory above. There are strong reasons for believing that they have bearing, but in the present state of our knowledge, this can be proved scientifically only by introspection. But would it be scientific to ignore them in building up a theory of risk?

(b) A similar situation is met in mechanics when indeterminate frictional terms are introduced into equations. Initially, they are brought into the calculations in a very general form. Attempts are then made to refine and clarify them by experiment.

(c) *It can even be held that this successive approach is the general process of any science.* In every case, the starting point is to allow in an indeterminate way for the effect of those factors whose influence cannot at this stage be specified accurately. It would never enter a scientist's mind to neglect them on the pretext that he does not yet know how to calculate their effect.

(d) The classical theory of choice itself bases all its calculations on preference functions $S = S(A, B, \ldots, C)$ which are not specified. Nevertheless, it has turned out to be extremely useful.

A similar situation obtains in the theory of choice involving risk. Even though the shape of indifference surfaces cannot be stated exactly, the mere fact that the equations for them can be written in their most general form makes it possible to generalise both the theory of general economic equilibrium and the theory of maximum efficiency.[44']

(e) It is certainly incorrect to contend that a theory A [45] which patently omits certain relevant factors, and is therefore necessarily invalid, can be superior to a theory B [46] of broader generality, merely because experience provides a touchstone to prove that A is false, whereas it is impossible to prove that theory B is false. As has already been said, the scientific problem raised by B is not that of explaining observed behaviour, since B covers all possible cases. The true problem is to bring experience to bear to specify the indeterminate functions to which it leads.

3. THE PURE PSYCHOLOGY OF RISK AND RATIONALITY

The Pure Psychology of Risk

45. Risk will be referred to as *pure* when the four fundamental factors (A) operate alone, without any effect arising from the action of the secondary factors in group (B).

Current discussion is entirely in terms of "pure" risk as thus defined, and there is therefore no drawback, at least as a first approximation, in ignoring the (B) factors.

The Historical Development of the Theoretical Concept
of the Pure Psychology of Risk

46. The theoretical view of the pure psychology of risk has passed through four successive stages.[47]

(a) In a *first stage*, it was thought that the value V of a random prospect is equal to its mathematical expectation

$$\text{(I)} \qquad V = p_1 g_1 + p_2 g_2 + \cdots + p_n g_n,$$

i.e. the average value of the possible gains weighted by their objective probabilities.

(b) In a *second stage*, psychological values were introduced to replace the monetary values in the initial formulation. This led to

$$\text{(II)} \qquad \bar{s}(V) = p_1 \bar{s}(g_1) + p_2 \bar{s}(g_2) + \cdots + p_n \bar{s}(g_n),$$

in which the p_i are objective probabilities.

In this formulation, the rule of probable values is used to combine the utility attaching to different possible gains rather than the gains themselves. This is the hypothesis that Bernoulli naturally came to develop to explain the St. Petersburg paradox, and it was later adopted by Laplace in his theory of *moral expectancy*.[47'] More recently, Von Neumann and Morgenstern were led to develop a formula corresponding to this approach in their *Theory of Games*.[48]

(c) In a *third stage*, the idea took root that the individual does not take account of objective probabilities as such, but acts in terms of his psychological perception of these probabilities, i.e., in terms of subjective probabilities. This leads to the formulation

$$\text{(III)} \qquad \bar{s}(V) = \overline{p_1}\,\bar{s}(g_1) + \overline{p_2}\,\bar{s}(g_2) + \cdots + \overline{p_n}\,\bar{s}(g_n),$$

in which the $\bar{p}$ are subjective probabilities. This is still the neo-Bernoullian formulation, but allowing for the replacement of objective by subjective probabilities.[49]

(d) The *fourth stage* consists of the realisation that it is not enough to consider the probability-weighted average psychological value $\gamma = \bar{s}(g)$; the distribution of the probabilities must also be allowed for. This produces the formula

$$\text{(IV)} \qquad \bar{s}(V) = h[\psi(\gamma)],$$

in which h is a functional of the probability density $\psi(\gamma)$ of the psychological values.

The present author's thinking is in terms of this fourth stage, whose implication is that the *dispersion* of the psychological values about their mean is at least as important a factor as the psychological distortion of monetary values and objective probabilities, so that *even in a first approximation*, it is necessary to take account of the shape of the distribution of psychological values, and in particular of the second-order moments of this distribution.

Actual Behaviour of Man and the Psychology of the Rational Man

47. There seems to be general agreement that the neo-Bernoullian formulation does not successfully represent actual behaviour, and that the various factors (A) and (B) are relevant and should be introduced. However, difficulties arise in specifying how a rational person would be expected to behave under conditions of risk.

To simplify the discussion, the secondary factors in group (B) can be neglected in a first approximation; examination will be limited to appraising the characteristics which the pure psychology of risk should possess in order to be rational.

In the first instance an accurate definition must be given of what is meant by the adjective "rational".

The author considers that a person's conduct can be considered rational if it satisfies the general principle of not being self-contradictory. This, in turn, implies two conditions. The first is that the ends pursued should be logically consistent; the second, that the means employed should be appropriate to these ends.

As regards the pure psychology of risk, the first condition implies, on the one hand, that the various random prospects can be classified to constitute an ordered set, and on the other hand, that the axiom of absolute preference[50] is verified. Both are necessary for logical consistency.

The second condition implies that the individual takes account of objective probabilities; from a scientific point of view, this is necessary for action to be efficient.

The author further considers that these two conditions are both necessary and sufficient for the psychology considered to be viewed as rational.

Using the notation presented above, rational psychology can be
described in the most general case by

(1) $\bar{s}(V) = f[\psi(\gamma)]$,

in which f is a functional of the objective frequency function $\psi(\gamma)$ of
the psychological values $\gamma = \bar{s}(g)$ under the single constraint that this
function must satisfy the axiom of absolute preference.

In particular, there is no reason to consider that where an individual's conduct fails to satisfy the relation

(2) $\bar{s}(V) = \sum p_i \bar{s}(g_i)$,

it must necessarily be irrational, since an attitude which takes account
of the *dispersion* of psychological values, could not be considered as
irrational.

In point of fact, it would be improper to brand a cautious man
irrational because he is willing to accept a lower psycho-mathematical
expectation as the price of lower dispersion. Nor can a person who
enjoys risk as such be labelled as irrational, merely because he
accepts a lower psycho-mathematical expectation as the counterpart
of the availability of some chance of extremely high psychological
gain. He may be felt to be imprudent – this is as may be[51] – but it
seems impossible to say that he is irrational.

It cannot be too strongly emphasized *that there are no criteria for
the rationality of ends as such other than the condition of consistency.*
Ends are completely arbitrary. To prefer highly dispersed random
outcomes may seem irrational to the prudent, but for somebody with
this penchant, there is nothing irrational about it. This area is like that
of tastes: they are what they are, and differ from one person to the
next.[52]

The neo-Bernoullian Formulation and the Law of Large Numbers

48. Basically, the intuitive justification of formulations founded on
the mathematical expectation of psychological values[53] is the law of
large numbers.

Consideration of monetary values

(A) *To simplify the discussion, first assume that psychological gain is equal to monetary gain.* This assumption is approximately true over any region of the cardinal utility curve in which the curve and its tangent are practically indistinguishable.

The law of large numbers tells us that in the long run, the average gain will tend, in the sense of the statistical theory, to its mathematical expectation. In other words, there is always a number of trials or events, n, which is large enough for the probability of a deviation between the average gain and the mathematical expectation to become smaller than any pre-selected number ε. The conclusion drawn is that the rule of mathematical expectation holds.

This rule has already generated much heated debate, and in all likelihood, there is still more to come.[54] The following points are worth making:

(1) *If I am able to participate in a long series of games, but could be ruined early on, possibly even in the first round, it is obvious that the justification of the rule of mathematical expectation by the law of large numbers is invalid.* There would be little consolation for me in the knowledge that, had I been able to hold on, my winnings would probably have tended to the value of their mathematical expectation.

(2) *At all events, there is a limit to the number of rounds in which I can participate,* if only because my life span is limited. Thus there is always some dispersion of the average gain to be allowed for. In practice, the concept of a very long series of trials is not realistic, and the dispersion of the average gain is never negligible in practice.[55]

(3) *Even if I were genuinely able to participate in an extremely large number of trials, it is by no means evident that my optimum strategy would be to rely on the rule of mathematical expectation.* What matters to the player is not the average gain but the cumulative gain and its distribution.

Let us assume for example, that the gain in a unit round of a game is distributed according to the Laplace–Gauss law, with an average value of m_1 and a standard deviation of σ_1. In a series of n rounds, the mathematical expectation will be

(1) $M = nm_1,$

and the standard deviation

(2) $\Sigma_1 = \sqrt{n}\,\sigma_1.$

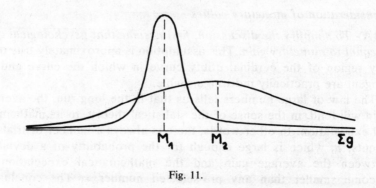

Fig. 11.

If I have a choice between the strategy (m_1, σ_1) and the strategy (m_2, σ_2) (see Figure 11) with $m_1 < m_2, \sigma_1 < \sigma_2$, there is no reason for me necessarily to prefer the second. It is true that for n rounds, my mathematical expectancy would be

$$M_2 - M_1 = n(m_2 - m_1),$$

but at the same time,

$$\Sigma_2 - \Sigma_1 = \sqrt{n}(\sigma_2 - \sigma_1)$$

would hold, and there is no difficulty in finding examples in which a prudent, rational man should clearly prefer the first strategy, even though it is associated with a lower mathematical expectancy and the number of rounds is high.[56-58]

(4) Finally, it is clear that *in the case of an isolated event or trial which is not to be repeated, the justification based on the law of large numbers does not apply at all.*

At the same time, *the specific characteristic of most of the cases in which random decisions are taken is that they in fact relate to isolated events.* In the author's view, the law of large numbers is utterly without relevance here. Everything depends on the special circumstances involved.

The governing factor here is personal psychology. Some will prefer to rely on mathematical expectation, others will attach greater importance to the form of the distribution. No one rule of conduct can be considered as more rational than another.

(5) *The only value of the rule of mathematical expectation is that it*

provides an overall indication. In this context, as has already been noted,[58'] its service is exactly that yielded by the use of a mean value to summarise a set of numbers. No less, and no more.

Consideration of psychological values

(B) If allowance is now made for the psychological values $\bar{s}(g)$ rather than for the monetary values g, *all the foregoing statements can be transposed without difficulty,* providing the probability distribution of g is replaced by that of $\bar{s}(g)$. Here again, the justification of the rule of mathematical expectation provided by the law of large numbers is a sheer *illusion.*

It is precisely to avoid all these difficulties, which *needlessly and uselessly* complicate the study of the psychology of risk, that we have based all our reasoning on the case of an isolated choice.[59]

Moreover, it is essential to stress here that *it would be wrong to consider that a strategy of maximising the mathematical expectation*

$$\sum p_i \bar{s}(g_i)$$

would be a good first approximation rule in all circumstances, when we have to take a decision concerning a random choice.[60]

CHAPTER II

CRITICISM OF THE NEO-BERNOULLIAN
FORMULATION AS A BEHAVIOURAL RULE
FOR RATIONAL MAN

•

1. *THE STATE OF THE DISCUSSION*

THE VIEWS OF THE SUPPORTERS OF THE NEO-BERNOULLIAN FORMULATION

49. As far as can be judged, the neo-Bernoullian formulation, as originally presented by von Neumann and Morgenstern,[60'] has three characteristics:

(1) It applies to *anybody* whose field of choice is ordered.

(2) It results in *an index $B(g)$ which is identified with cardinal utility $\bar{s}(g)$*.[61] By observing actual random choices it should be possible to determine cardinal utility. This thesis naturally implies that the neo-Bernoullian formulation is capable of providing a suitable portrayal of the behaviour of real man, and therefore of forecasting it.[62]

(3) It uses *objective probabilities* as weighting coefficients.

Marschak's formulation[62'] has the three following characteristics:

(1) It relates not to the actual behaviour of real man, but to what a *rational* man's behaviour ought to be.[63]

(2) It yields *an index $B(g)$ which*, according to the statements of the proponents of this formulation (Marschak, Samuelson, Friedman), is claimed to be *distinct from cardinal utility $\bar{s}(g)$*.[64]

(3) Like the preceding formulation, it uses *objective probabilities* for weighting.

The third formulation is that given by Savage, and it also has three distinguishing features:

(1) Like the second, it applies only to *rational* behaviour.

(2) It yields an index $B(g)$ which, like the second formulation, is claimed to be *distinct from cardinal utility* $\bar{s}(g)$.

(3) It uses *subjective probabilities*.

As can be seen, *these three positions are very different*. In particular, the American School has in fact put forward two claims:

(1) Actual behaviour can be represented by the neo-Bernoullian formulation, and in conjunction with the observation of choices involving risk, this formulation provides a means of determining cardinal utility.

(2) The neo-Bernoullian formulation is capable of portraying only the behaviour of rational man.

THE QUESTIONS PRESENTLY UNDER DISCUSSION

50. *At present*, the following points seem to be accepted by all proponents[64'] of the neo-Bernoullian formulation:

(1) The formulation does not apply to actual behaviour. It is used only to describe the behaviour of a "rational" man.

(2) The index $B(g)$ is distinct from the indicator of cardinal utility $\bar{s}(g)$.

The view that the two indexes $B(g)$ and $\bar{s}(g)$ would be one and the same has gradually had to be abandoned,[65] and there is currently no support[65'] for the thesis that cardinal utility can be measured by examining empirical data on choices involving risk, a thesis which would imply that real behaviour can be suitably portrayed by the neo-Bernoullian formulation.

It is easy to see why this view had to be abandoned. *If the identity*

$$B(g) \equiv \bar{s}(g)$$

were accepted, the neo-Bernoullian formulation would clearly ignore the dispersion of psychological values (Factor AIV of the analysis above), *and this would lead to considering as irrational the attitude of a careful person who attaches weight to this dispersion. Such a position is manifestly untenable.*[66]

Thus the original contention of the Bernoullian school has been laid aside, and at present the only difference in viewpoint relates to the definition of the concept of probability. Savage and de Finetti claim that only subjective probabilities exist, whereas Marschak uses objective probabilities. However, as regards the behaviour of a rational man, Savage would no doubt agree that it is proper to consider objective probabilities defined with reference to experimentally observed frequencies.

If this can be taken as so, the central argument of the proponents of the neo-Bernoullian formulation[66'] is that an index $B(g)$ necessarily exists for any rational individual such that the value V of any random prospect is given by the relation

(1) $B(V) = \sum_i p_i B(g_i)$

with

(2) $\sum p_i = 1,$

the p_i being objective probabilities.

From this standpoint, the index $B(g)$ is considered to include allowance both for the psychological distortion of monetary values and the utility (or disutility) associated with the shape of the probability distribution of the psychological values (i.e., elements AI and AIV of the analysis above).

It may be noted in passing that these two elements are not considered to be 'irrational'. It is accepted that a rational individual's scale of psychological values may differ from the monetary scale, and that he may have a greater or lesser propensity for safety or for risk. There seems to be agreement that this is an issue of psychology and not of 'rationality'.

The argument developed below *casts doubt on the validity of relation* (1) *for a rational man*. It will be argued that the neo-Bernoullian formulation is not only incapable of representing the behaviour of real man properly, or of determining cardinal utility, but more, that *even for a rational man*, the linkage between the value V and gains g_i is in general of much more complex form:

(3) $\bar{s}(V) = f(g_1, g_2, \ldots, g_n, p_1, p_2, \ldots, p_n),$

a relation which, in the case of the pure psychology of risk can be written in the form

(4) $\bar{s}(V) = \sum_i \alpha_i(g_1, g_2, \ldots, g_n, p_1, p_2, \ldots, p_n)\bar{s}(g_i),$

in which

(5) $\sum_i \alpha_i(g_1, g_2, \ldots, g_n, p_1, p_2, \ldots, p_n) = 1,$

but the α_i are in general distinct from the probabilities p_i [66''] so that in general *no index B(g) exists which satisfies the neo-Bernoullian formulation.*

The author accepts that a rational man may well act according to the Bernoulli formulation, but in this case, his index B(g) will necessarily be identical to his cardinal utility, and we will have[67] $B(g) \equiv \bar{s}(g)$ so that if he does follow the Bernoulli formulation, this is because of his specific psychology vis-à-vis risk, which renders him indifferent to the dispersion of psychological values. But in general, there is no reason for this to be so; rather the opposite.

In the light of the remarks made earlier on the dispersion of psychological values (Factor AIV), our point of view is that *the American School's psychological theory of risk neglects the specific feature of this psychology, namely the dispersion of psychological values, which is omitted in its initial axioms.*

The sophisticated mathematical deductions with which the American School has conducted its analysis should not mislead us. Only the initial premisses and the interpretation of the results are of real significance. However complex the mathematical development of the deductions, it has no intrinsic value beyond its purely mathematical interest, which is irrelevant from the standpoint of economic analysis that concerns us here. *The complexity or scientific value of the deductive process can never confer scientific value on the premisses.*

DEFINITION OF RATIONALITY

51. To derive the neo-Bernoullian formulation, the American School starts from various systems of axioms or postulates. But in fact it is clear – and this is an important point – that it is not relevant to define rationality in terms of obedience to any of these systems, for, in this case, *there could not possibly be any discussion.*

The neo-Bernoullian formulation is in fact rigorously equivalent to any one whatsoever of these systems of axioms, and there is clearly *no interest at all* in discussing the view that a rational man should behave according to the neo-Bernoullian formulation when rationality is itself defined in terms of obedience to one of the systems of axioms from which that principle is deduced. *This is a tautological proposition, and therefore useless scientifically.*

To discuss the proposition "should a rational man act according to the neo-Bernoullian formulation" is meaningful *only if rationality is defined other than by direct or indirect reference to that formulation.*

It is therefore necessary to define what is meant by "rationality". In practice, two definitions are possible, depending whether the standpoint taken is that of abstract reasoning or that of experience.

(a) *Abstract Definition of Rationality*

52. Other than the pseudo-definition of rationality in terms of respect of their systems of axioms, the proponents of the neo-Bernoullian formulation offer nothing by way of a precise statement. Given this gap, and as we have already indicated,[68] we must have recourse to the definition which is suggested by scientific logic: a man will be deemed to act rationally

(a) if he pursues ends that are mutually consistent (i.e. not contradictory),

(b) if he employs means that are appropriate to these ends.

As has been noted, the only consequences which these two conditions entail are:

(1) that the field of choice is ordered;
(2) that the axiom of absolute preference is satisfied;
(3) that objective probabilities are considered.

Points (1) and (2) are contested by nobody. As regards point (3) it seems hard to dispute that it would be of advantage to replace the objective probabilities by subjective probabilities which would be distinct from them.

It is important to underline that the three points listed are the *only* consequences of the consistency condition. In particular, it cannot be accepted that either Savage's fifth axiom of independence[68'] or Samuelson's substitution axiom[68"] constitute conditions of consistency.

So far as Savage's fifth axiom is concerned, if in the diagram in §3 two equivalent prospects share a common component, there is no necessary reason for this equivalence to subsist if the common component undergoes a shift. To the contrary: it is clear that this shift will alter the form of the probability distribution of the psychological values.[69]

Similarly, it is impossible to take Samuelson's substitution axiom as absolutely indispensable from the standpoint of rationality. Let (P_1) and (P_2) be two equivalent prospects, whose equivalence is expressed by the symbolic relation $(P_1) = (P_2)$.

The substitution axiom signifies that if (P_3) is any random prospect whatever, then, for any α, we should have

$$\alpha(P_1) + (1 - \alpha)(P_3) = \alpha(P_2) + (1 - \alpha)(P_3),$$

where the symbol $[\alpha(P_1) + (1 - \alpha)(P_3)]$ stands for a lottery ticket which offers the probability α of prospect (P_1) and the probability $(1 - \alpha)$ of prospect (P_3). This axiom is justified, it is claimed, because whether or not the event whose probability is α occurs, the individual concerned will ultimately be in possession of two equivalent prospects. In reality, this claim is unacceptable, for it assumes that the first drawing, corresponding to the probabilities $[\alpha, (1 - \alpha)]$ is *neutral*. In fact *it is not*. This is an *ex post* conclusion, whereas the problem must be viewed *ex ante*.[70]

If the above definition of rationality is not accepted, another must be put forward. So far, none has, and it seems idle to discuss what might be proposed in its place. Actually, it is hard at this stage to see what could be.[71]

(b) *Experimental Definition of Rationality*

53. If it is not felt possible or desirable to use an abstract definition of rationality, the only option is to rely on experience, *and to observe the behaviour of men whom one has reason in other respects to believe act rationally.*

In the author's view, *the adherents of the neo-Bernoullian school should be asked to reply clearly to the three following questions*:

(1) Do you directly or indirectly define rationality as meaning obedience to your axioms?

(2) If not, do you accept an abstract definition, and if so, which one?

(3) In the absence of an abstract definition other than one couched in terms of obedience to your axioms, do you accept that rationality

can be defined by having regard to the behaviour of persons who are commonly considered as rational?[72]

2. *REFUTATION OF THE NEO-BERNOULLIAN FORMULATION*

CONDITIONS FOR REFUTATION OF THE NEO-BERNOULLIAN FORMULATION

54. As the neo-Bernoullian formulation is claimed to be general, it may be refuted by providing as little as *one example* of rational behaviour which does not correspond either to the final formulation or any of the systems of postulates to which it is equivalent.

This having been stated clearly, the refutation presented below comprises two parts. In the first, using the abstract definition of rationality, we show that the rational man will not necessarily follow the neo-Bernoullian formulation. The second part is an analysis of the behaviour of persons who are generally considered as rational, and which is absolutely incompatible with the neo-Bernoullian formulation.

For reasons set forth earlier,[73] the discussion will deal with in the case of a single choice involving risk.[74]

A. REFUTATION OF THE NEO-BERNOULLIAN FORMULATION BASED ON THE ABSTRACT DEFINITION OF RATIONALITY

1. THE NEO-BERNOULLIAN FORMULATION IS MORE RESTRICTIVE THAN THE AXIOM OF ABSOLUTE PREFERENCE

55. It will first be shown that the axiom of absolute preference does not suffice in itself to entail the existence of an index $B(x)$ which satisfies the neo-Bernoullian relation.[75]

This can be seen as follows. Let (P_1), (P_2) and (P_3) be random prospects which can take material shape as three lottery tickets, and assume that (P_3) is preferred to (P_1) and (P_2). Using $>$ to denote preference, we have

(1) $(P_1) < (P_3),$ $(P_2) < (P_3).$

It can be shown[76] that if the inequalities (1) necessarily entail the inequality

(2) $[\alpha(P_1) + (1 - \alpha)(P_2)] < (P_3),$

(using the symbol $[\alpha(P_1) + (1 - \alpha)P_2]$ to denote a lottery ticket with a probability α of winning the ticket (P_1) as prize and $(1 - \alpha)$ of winning the ticket (P_2), α having any value whatever,[77] then there necessarily exists an index $B(x)$ which satisfies the neo-Bernoullian formulation. Conversely, if the neo-Bernoullian formulation is verified, the conditions (1) imply condition (2).

However, if it is assumed only that the axiom of absolute preference is verified it cannot in general be affirmed that conditions (1) *imply condition* (2). All that can be said is that the conditions

(3) $(P_1) \lll (P_3),$ $(P_2) \lll (P_3),$

necessarily entail

(4) $[\alpha(P_1) + (1 - \alpha)(P_2)] \lll (P_3),$

using the sign $\lll$ to denote absolute preference,[78] and this in turn implies

(5) $[\alpha(P_1) + (1 - \alpha)P_2] < (P_3).$

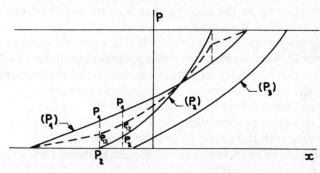

Fig. 12.

Let P be the total probability that the outcome will be some figure between $-\infty$ and x. Then, from the principle of compound probabilities

(6) $P_{12} = \alpha P_1 + (1 - \alpha)P_2,$

where P_{12} is the probability P that the compound lottery ticket

$$[\alpha(P_1) + (1 - \alpha)(P_2)]$$

will yield a gain exceeding g. Thus we have in Figure 12 the geometric equality

(7) $P_1P_{12} = (1 - \alpha)P_1P_2.$

In this figure, the curve representing the random prospect P_{12} lies between the curves of the prospects P_1 and P_2, so that geometrically, and in the light of the earlier analysis, it can be verified immediately that the conditions (3) do indeed imply condition (4) and therefore condition (5).

At the same time, it can be verified that the axiom of absolute preference is less restrictive than the neo-Bernoullian formulation or any of the equivalent systems of axioms.

2. RATIONALITY IN NO WAY IMPLIES THE NEO-BERNOULLIAN FORMULATION

56. The foregoing yields an immediate refutation of the neo-Bernoullian formulation as the rational man's guide to behaviour, using an abstract definition of rationality.

Such a definition was given earlier.[78'] If it is accepted – and no other has been put forward apart from some pseudo-definitions which can only lead to tautological propositions in the areas that concern us here – then the *only implications* of rational conduct are:
(a) use of an ordered field of choice;
(b) use of objective probabilities;
(c) conformity with the axiom of absolute preference.[79]

Now, these three properties are insufficient to deduce the existence of an index $B(g)$ such that[80]

$$B(V) = \sum_i p_iB(g_i),$$

where V is the value of the random prospect

$$(g_1, g_2, \ldots, g_n, p_1, p_2, \ldots, p_n).$$

It follows that:

(1) To be rational, an individual's behaviour need not necessarily be what the neo-Bernoullian formulation would have it be.

(2) In reality, given that the consequences of the abstract definition of rationality are less restrictive than the axioms of the neo-Bernoullian school, the latter contain one or more additional constraints which *may* actually be *irrational*.

3. EXAMPLES OF RATIONAL BEHAVIOUR SATISFYING THE AXIOM OF ABSOLUTE PREFERENCE WITHOUT SATISFYING THE NEO-BERNOULLIAN FORMULATION

It is easy to find a number of particularly simple examples of a psychology that meets the criterion of absolute preference without satisfying the neo-Bernoullian formulation.

(1) *The Choice between Different Gains g of Probability p*

57. Consider an individual having to choose between random prospects each consisting of a gain g_i whose probability is p_i, and assume that his ordinal preference function is given by

(1) $S = f(g, p)$.

This function satisfies the criterion of absolute preference if we have

(2) $\partial f / \partial g > 0, \qquad \partial f / \partial p > 0$.

But in general it does not satisfy the neo-Bernoullian formulation, which would require

(3) $S = f[pB(g)]$,

where f and B are increasing functions. In other words, according to the neo-Bernoullian formulation, the preference index should be an increasing function of the product $pB(g)$.

This verifies the markedly greater restrictiveness of the neo-Bernoullian formulation.[81]

(2) *The Choice between Prospects Distributed According to the Normal Law*

58. Consider an individual having to choose between a number of random prospects (P) that can be described by *normal distributions* of mean M and standard deviation Σ, and assume that in order to make this particular choice,[82] his preference index is of the form

(1) $S = f(M, \Sigma)$.

For the axiom of absolute preference to be satisfied, it is necessary and sufficient that *for given* Σ, the index S should be an increasing function of M, i.e. that[83,84]

(2) $\partial f / \partial M > 0$.

It is easy to see that in general no index $B(x)$ exists such that we could have

(3) $$f(M, \Sigma) = \int_{-\infty}^{+\infty} B(x) \frac{\exp\left[-(x - M)^2 / 2\Sigma^2\right]}{\sqrt{2\pi}\Sigma} \, dx,$$

with[85]

(4) $B'_x > 0$.

This further example again shows that the neo-Bernoullian formulation is much more restrictive that it need be in terms of rationality alone.[86]

(3) *The Choice between Alternative Prospects with an Average Gain of M and a Probability P of a Loss Exceeding X*

59. Now consider an individual who has to choose between various prospects each of which is characterized by an average gain M and a probability P of experiencing a loss in excess of a given value X.[86']

Any field of choice

(1) $S = f(M, P)$

satisfies the axiom of absolute preference providing that it is true simultaneously that

(2) $\partial S / \partial M > 0, \qquad \partial S / \partial P < 0.$

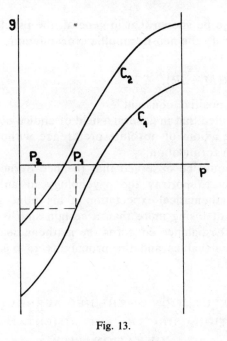

Fig. 13.

Consider the two curves C_1 and C_2 of Figure 13. If the curve C_2 lies above the curve C_1, the two conditions

(3) $M_1 < M_2$, $P_1 > P_2$,

hold (Figure 13). Figure 14 shows that these conditions indeed imply the conditions (2), and vice-versa.[87]

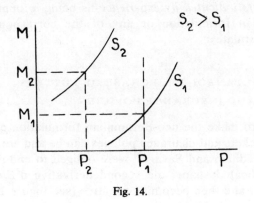

Fig. 14.

But it can also be shown that in general, the psychological pattern (1) does not satisfy the neo-Bernoullian formulation, which requires a function of the type

(4) $S = f(M - aP)$,

in which a is a positive constant.[88]

Thus it is verified that in general a field of choice of the type (1) and (2) satisfies the axiom of absolute preference without verifying the neo-Bernoullian formulation.

Finally, it should be observed that the neo-Bernoullian formula's general inability to portray the psychology of an individual who balances the mathematical expectation of his monetary gains against his probability of losing more than a certain sum is repeated in the case in which the balance concerns the mathematical expectation of the psychological values and the probability of a loss exceeding a certain threshold.[89]

B. REFUTATION OF THE NEO-BERNOULLIAN
FORMULATION USING THE EXPERIMENTAL DEFINITION
OF RATIONALITY

60. In the absence of an abstract definition of rationality that leads to anything but tautological propositions, recourse must be had to the experimental definition yielded by *observation of the behaviour of men who may be considered as rational and who are fully familiar with the calculus of probabilities.* It is then possible to cite the following *facts indicated by experience* as being in opposition to the neo-Bernoullian formulation or any of the corresponding sets of axioms of postulates:

1. THE SIMULTANEOUS PURCHASE OF LOTTERY
TICKETS AND INSURANCE POLICIES

61. In order to make the neo-Bernoullian formulation cover the fact that lottery tickets and insurance policies can be and are brought concurrently, Friedman and Savage[90] were obliged to endow their index with a complicated shape, the second derivative d^2B/dg^2 being initially positive and then becoming negative (see Figure 15).

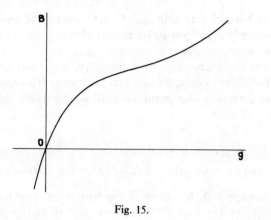

Fig. 15.

To the extent that one accepts, *as they did in 1948*, that

(1) $\bar{s}(g) \equiv B(g)$,

the conclusion must be that in some cases the marginal utility of money could be an increasing function of the gain, which I consider to be in flagrant contradiction to introspective data. Any tests that could be invented in this area would lead to the same conclusion.

The objection evidently vanishes if it is claimed, *as Friedman and Savage now do*, that the index $B(g)$ is distinct from the utility function;[91] but as will be seen below,[91'] this claim is difficult to maintain.

2. THE BEHAVIOUR OF THE VERY PRUDENT IN CHOICES
WITH RISK INVOLVING SMALL SUMS

62. In the local domain, for *small values* of gains g, changes in the index $B(g)$ may be considered as practically linear, and in this case the component producing its curvature is eliminated. Thus if a neo-Bernoullian index exists, it implies in this case that $V = \Sigma\, p_i g_i$, i.e. the value of a random prospect is equal to its mathematical expectation.

Nevertheless, experience shows that very cautious people who are commonly considered as rational may prefer \$4 to one chance in two of winning \$10; or a gain of \$400 to one chance in two of winning

$1000, etc. In formulating this question, it should be made clear that this is a *once-only offer*, not to be repeated, i.e. a single choice.[92]

This is an incontestable experimental observation, and it is hard to see how, from the standpoint of rationality, a person with a marked preference for safety could be open to criticism. *However this type of behaviour undermines the fundamental position of the American-School.*[93]

3. CHOICES IN THE NEIGHBOURHOOD OF CERTAINTY
UNDERMINING SAVAGE'S PRINCIPLE OF INDEPENDENCE

63. Under Savage's fifth axiom,[93'] the order of preference of two random prospects (1) and (2) having a part in common is left unchanged by any displacement of this part. This can be called the independence principle, for it brings out an essential aspect of the neo-Bernoullian formulation (see Figure 16).

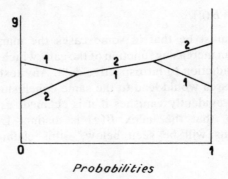

Probabilities

Fig. 16.

It is easy to build up many examples in which the answer given by reputedly rational people would run counter to Savage's fundamental axiom.[94] One need only, as a general rule, choose extreme cases in which the advantages (or drawbacks) of complementarity may be particularly strong. This is particularly true of the choice between certain and uncertain gains whose value is high by comparison with the player's fortune. It is easy here to show the considerable psychological importance attaching to the advantage of certainty as such.

Figures 17(a) and (b) present the geometrical portrayal of two follow-ing questions:[94']

(1) *Do you prefer Situation A to Situation B?*
Situation A:
– *certainty* of receiving 100 million.
Situation B:
– *a* 10% *chance* of winning 500 million,
– *an* 89% *chance* of winning 100 million,
– *a* 1% *chance* of winning nothing.

(2) *Do you prefer Situation C to Situation D?*
Situation C:
– *a* 11% *chance* of winning 100 million,
– *an* 89% *chance* of winning nothing.
Situation D:
– *a* 10% *chance* of winning 500 million,
– *a* 90% *chance* of winning nothing.

If Savage's postulate were justified, the preference $A > B$ should entail $C > D$.

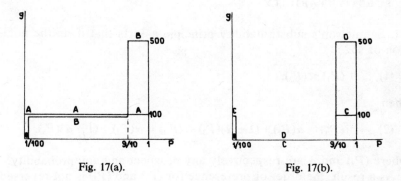

Fig. 17(a).   Fig. 17(b).

What one finds, however, is that the pattern for most highly prudent persons, the curvature of whose satisfaction curves is not very marked, and who are considered generally as rational, is the pairing $A > B$ and $C < D$. This contradicts Savage's fifth axiom.

It should be noted that the mathematical expectations attaching to the four situations are (in millions of units)

$$a = 100, \qquad b = 139, \qquad c = 11, \qquad d = 50.$$

Given the curvature of their cardinal utility function and the advantages of safety, most prudent persons prefer A, even though its mathematical expectancy is some 40% below that of B. However, this curvature is not generally marked enough for them to prefer D to C, although the ratio of mathematical expectations is 1 to 5. It will be remarked that for questions C and D, the complementarity effect corresponding to the 1% chance of a zero win is small.

This example is a good illustration of the *pseudo-evident* character of Savage's axiom V. *That it is accepted by so many is due to the fact that not all its implications are perceived although far from being rational, some of them are in certain psychological situations wholly irrational* (as for example, in the case described above of the highly prudent individual whose personal assessment of value continues to increase perceptibly in the neighbourhood of 100 million).

4. CHOICES IN THE NEIGHBOURHOOD OF CERTAINTY

UNDERMINING SAMUELSON'S PRINCIPLE OF

SUBSTITUTABILITY

64. Samuelson's substitutability principle asserts that if, in the notation of §52

(1) $(P_1) < (P_2),$

then

(2) $(P'_1) \equiv \alpha(P_1) + (1 - \alpha)(P_3) < (P'_2) \equiv \alpha(P_2) + (1 - \alpha)(P_3),$

where (P_3) and α are respectively any prospect and any probability.

As a result, the order of preference for (P_1) and (P_2) is not reversed by compounding them with any other outcome whatsoever (P_3). *This clearly implies that there is no complementarity effect capable of upsetting this order.*[95]

This being so, examples of rational persons' behaviour invalidating this axiom are easy to find. *All that is needed is to find cases in which the complementarity relations of (P_3) with (P_1) and (P_2) (or the absence of such relations) may change the order of preference.*

To illustrate this, let (P_2) be a certain gain, and (P_1) an uncertain one. Any compound prospect (P'_1) removes the certainty (i.e. the advantage of complementarity) attaching to the right-hand member of the inequality (1), whereas the left hand member is not affected in this way. Thus, using the notation of §4, consider the following case:

$$P_1 \begin{cases} 98\%: 500 \text{ million} \\ 2\%: 0 \end{cases} \qquad P_2 \begin{cases} 100 \text{ million} \\ \text{certain} \end{cases} \qquad P_3 \begin{cases} 1 \text{ certain} \end{cases}.$$

Experience shows that the acknowledgedly rational but prudent will prefer the *certainty* of 100 million to be received to a 98% chance of winning 500 million, associated with a 2% chance of not winning anything. For them we will have:

(1) $(P_1) < (P_2)$.

But *at the same time*, they may prefer a 0.98% chance of winning 500 million (mathematical expectation: 4.9 million) to a 1% chance of winning 100 million (mathematical expectation: 1 million) because, *once far away from certainty, they weight psychological values by probabilities*, i.e. according to the rule $\bar{s}(V) = \Sigma \, p_i \bar{s}(g_i)$ and their $\bar{s}(g)$ functions may attach a markedly higher psychological value to 500 million than to 100 million.

For such persons, this second preference pattern yields:

$$(P_1') = \frac{1}{100}(P_1) + \frac{99}{100}(P_3) > (P_2') \equiv \frac{1}{100}(P_2) + \frac{99}{100}(P_3).$$

We have the following:

$$(P_1') = \frac{1}{100}(P_1) + \frac{99}{100}(P_3) \equiv \begin{cases} 0.98\%: 500 \text{ million} \\ 99\%: \quad 1 \\ 0.02\%: \quad 0 \end{cases}$$

or approximately

$$\begin{cases} 0.98\%: 500 \text{ million} \\ 99.02\%: \quad 0 \end{cases}$$

and

$$(P_2') = \frac{1}{100}(P_2) + \frac{99}{100}(P_3) \equiv \begin{cases} 1\%: 100 \text{ million} \\ 99\%: \quad 1 \end{cases}$$

or practically

$$\begin{cases} 1\%: 100 \text{ million} \\ 99\%: \quad 0 \end{cases}$$

This is *an observation from experience* which invalidates Samuelson's substitution principle.

In the author's opinion, *nobody could say that persons acting in this way are behaving irrationally* because they attach a high value to certainty, but, where the outcome is far from certain, weight psychological values by their probabilities. If somebody does wish to argue the contrary, it would be quite fascinating to hear his grounds!

5. ENTREPRENEURIAL BEHAVIOUR WHEN LARGE LOSSES
MAY BE INCURRED

65. Observation shows that prudent businessmen act as though they were balancing the probable gain g against the probability P of a loss exceeding X.[95'] In other words, their ordinal preference index is of the form

(1) $S = f(M, P)$,

with[96]

(2) $\partial S / \partial M > 0$, $\partial S / \partial P < 0$.

Once the probability P attaching to an activity becomes at all significant its potential yield must be substantial, or it will not be undertaken. The ultra-cautious will purely and simply eliminate all random prospects for which the probability of ruin exceeds a certain threshold value.

As we have seen earlier, a preference of type (1) and (2) satisfies the axiom of absolute preference, but can only satisfy the neo-Bernoullian formulation if it is of the form[97]

(3) $S = f(M - aP)$.

If it is accepted (*as seems psychologically very natural and at all events highly rational*) that M increases more quickly than P for a given level of the preference index, this linear structure of preference curves is absolutely excluded.

Is it really possible to consider as irrational a person who, for each choice among random prospects, takes his decision by weighing the probable gain M against the probability P of losing more than a certain sum X which he wishes not to exceed in any circumstances, acting according to the neo-Bernoullian formulation *for small values* of M and P (parallel lines), but abstaining completely from any project which he judges has a 90% or greater probability of losing X? His indifference function would be of the form shown in Figure 18, and this is, in general, absolutely incompatible with the neo-Bernoullian formulation.

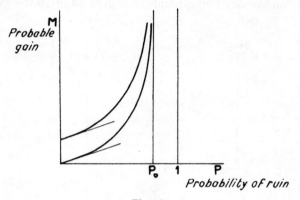

Fig. 18.

If, as seems psychologically admissible, the psychology of uncertainty is continuous, a linear form of the type (3) is absolutely impossible.

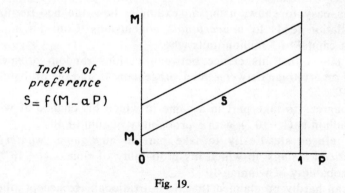

Fig. 19.

Consider a sum M_0 whose psychological value is great, for instance $M_0 = \$1$ million. On the same indifference line we would have

$$1 = M - aP,$$

which relation intimates that any random prospect providing a probable gain of M million with a probability P of ruin is worth 1 million.
Now, if $P = 1$, ruin is certain, and the value of the certainty of the
ruin cannot be valued at \$1 million. This is inadmissible and in fact no
indifference curve can cut the vertical axis $P = 1$. Figure 19 is really
impossible and reality corresponds to Figure 18 or 20.[98]

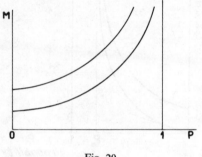

Fig. 20.

At all events, any form of behaviour corresponding to $S = f(M, P)$
functions, which satisfy the general conditions (2), seems to be perfectly possible psychologically, and there seems no reason for branding it as irrational.[99,100]

It is easy to show, using an example, how the neo-Bernoullian
formulation leads to *unacceptable* conclusions. Consider a person
with a capital of 5 million units who:

(a) states that his choice between various random prospects is
based on arbitrage between the average gain M and the probability of
ruin P;

(b) agrees to take part in a game in which his chance of winning
100 million is $(1 - 10^{-6})$, with a probability of ruin of 10^{-6};

(c) refuses steadfastly to take part in any game, *whatever the
potential winnings*, in which his probability of ruin is $(1 - 10^{-6})$, and
the probability of winning 10^{-9}.

It can hardly be claimed that he is irrational. He accepts the first
alternative because it offers *the virtual certainty of winning* 100
million,[101] and refuses the second because he is *virtually certain to be
ruined*. Yet it can easily be seen that this behavioural pattern stands in
total contradiction with the neo-Bernoullian formulation.[102]

It may, of course, be objected that this is an extreme case. But if the absurdity of the conclusions stemming from a theory is to be demonstrated, the only way is to pick cases whose absurdity is painfully evident – in other words, extreme cases. As was noted earlier, the critic can select his own ground here, for it is enough to find *one* example in which the neo-Bernoullian formulation is manifestly erroneous to rebut it in general.

In the case of individual choices among random prospects similar behaviour is often observed when the persons concerned are both rational and prudent. People of this ilk start by laying down the *maximum* loss they are willing to suffer in any circumstances, and then choose by balancing the mathematical expectation against their probability of ruin. Here, the arbitrage relates not to the mathematical expectation M of the monetary values g, but to the mathematical expectation μ of the psychological values γ, so that $S = S(\mu, P)$.

As was shown above, this behaviour pattern is incompatible with the neo-Bernoullian formulation, apart from the exceptional case in which the psychological value is linearly dependent on the monetary gain and in which S is of the form[103]

$$S = S(M - aP).$$

THE BEHAVIOUR OF RATIONAL MAN AND THE EXISTENCE OF A NEO-BERNOULLIAN INDEX

66. To summarise, whether one proceeds from the abstract definition of rationality or from actual observation of the behaviour of persons whom it is reasonable to consider as rational, the conclusion reached is that for a rational man, in general no index $B(x)$ exists such that the optimum situation can be defined by maximising the expectation $\Sigma \, p_i B(x_i)$.

3. *CRITICAL ANALYSIS OF SOME ASPECTS OF THE THEORIES OF THE AMERICAN SCHOOL*

67. The foregoing discussion has shown the theoretical and observed opposition between rational behaviour and the formulation of it developed by the American School.

The reader who is strongly attached to the neo-Bernoullian formulation may still not be entirely convinced, and it is therefore useful to add to what has already been said a few critical remarks concerning some of the central features of the theories of the American School.

1. THE NEO-BERNOULLIAN INDEX AND THE DISPERSION OF PSYCHOLOGICAL VALUES

68. In the view of the American School, the dispersion of psychological values $\bar{s}(g)$ enters the neo-Bernoullian formulation via the index $B(g)$, which would *imply that the index allows simultaneously for the psychological distortion of monetary values and the probability distribution of psychological values.*[103'] *This view does not appear to be correct.*

(a) As has been seen,[104] we have

(1) $\bar{s}(V) = h[\psi(\gamma)],$

where h is a functional of the probability density of the psychological values $\gamma = \bar{s}(g)$, subject only to the constraint that it must satisfy the axiom of absolute preference.

If an index $B(g)$ existed that allowed simultaneously for the distortion of monetary values and the dispersion of psychological values, there would exist a transformation

(2) $\gamma = \gamma(B),$

such that relation (1) could be written

(3) $B(V) = \sum p_i B(g_i).$

In general, this transformation cannot exist. If it did, this would imply that, in general, the axiom of absolute preference would suffice on its own to imply the neo-Bernoullian formulation. This is not so.[105]

(b) At all events, with the psychological weight allotted in the formulation

(4) $B(V) = \sum_i p_i B(g_i)$

to any income g_i depending only on that income and the probability associated with it, it is impossible to see how the function $B(g)$ can allow for the dispersion of the psychological values $\bar{s}(g_i)$. Indeed, it cannot take the shape of the distribution of the $\bar{s}(g_i)$ into account, *inasmuch as the calculation of the psychological value of a random prospect attributes to each possibility of a weight that is absolutely independent of that shape.*[106]

2. DISTINCTION BETWEEN THE NEO-BERNOULLIAN INDEX
AND PSYCHOLOGICAL VALUE (CARDINAL UTILITY)

69. The following argument is not identical to the preceding one, although closely related to it. As has already been stated,[107] if the neo-Bernoullian index and psychological value were the same thing, the neo-Bernoullian formulation would be unable to allow for the dispersion of psychological values. *This fact forced the proponents of the neo-Bernoullian formulation, during the 1952 Paris Colloquium, to beat a retreat to a fallback position in which they claim that their index must be distinguished from psychological value.*

In our opinion, there are strong reasons for believing that *when a neo-Bernoullian index does exist*, the two quantities are one and the same thing.[108]

(a) It may first be noted that in all the experimental cases which can be analysed without ambiguity, and in which *the person's behaviour pattern is such that he takes account of the dispersion of psychological values*, the neo-Bernoullian formulation is refuted. Since it goes without saying that where the subject is insensitive to the dispersion of psychological values, a neo-Bernoullian index exists *ex hypothese* and is identical to psychological value, we are led to conclude that *when* a neo-Bernoullian index exists, it and psychological value are one and the same.

(b) Assume that a neo-Bernoullian index actually exists. We consider the formulation

$$(1) \qquad B(V) = \sum p_i B(g_i),$$

in which the p_i are subjective probabilities, and are equal to objective probabilities in the case of a rational man.

Let $E_1, E_2, \ldots, E_n$ be the events, to which there attach probabilities $p_1, p_2, \ldots, p_n$. If they occur, they yield gains of $g_1, g_2, \ldots, g_n$. We make the further *essential* assumption that the individual concerned makes his choice by conducting an *a posteriori* examination of each *independently* of the other values. *This is the fundamental hypothesis of the American School.*

Now assume that all the gains g_i increase by an amount Δg_i, but that the Δg_i are all below the minimum perceptible thresholds Δg_i^m corresponding to the g_i. Since this is so for *each outcome considered* separately, it may be deduced that the value V of the random prospect considered increases, but that the increase ΔV is less than the minimum perceptible threshold ΔV^m corresponding to the level of gain V.

It could similarly be shown that if the increases Δg_i exceed the minimum perceptible thresholds Δg_i^m corresponding to the g_i, the increase ΔV itself exceeds the minimum perceptible threshold ΔV^m corresponding to V. It follows that if

(2) $\Delta g_i = \Delta g_i^m,$

for all i, then also:[109]

(3) $\Delta V = \Delta V^m.$

It is easily shown that if this is so, the scale of the index $B(V)$ is necessarily identical to that of the psychological values, subject only to application of a linear transformation.[110]

Thus if a neo-Bernoullian index exists, the conclusion must be that it is identical to psychological value.[111] If so, it is obvious that the neo-Bernoullian formulation implicitly neglects the dispersion of psychological values (Factor AIV of the analysis in Part I), which we regard precisely as the factor which is specific to risk.

3. THE CONSEQUENCES OF THE PRINCIPLE OF INDEPENDENCE

70. The principle of independence expressed by the neo-Bernoullian formulation calls for the following comments:

(a) If the neo-Bernoullian formulation were justified, there would exist an index $B(x)$ such that

(1) $B(V) = \sum p_i B(g_i).$

In this case, the indifference surfaces would be portrayed by an ordinal index S whose most general form would be

$$(2) \qquad S = F\left[\sum p_i B(g_i)\right],$$

and cardinal utility would be of the form:

$$(3) \qquad \bar{S} = G\left[\sum p_i B(g_i)\right],$$

in which F is any increasing function and G an increasing function that is determined up to a linear transformation. This situation could *only* occur if the goods represented by the accruals $g_1, g_2, \ldots, g_n$ whose probabilities are $p_1, p_2, \ldots, p_n$ could be considered as psychologically independent,[112,113] but *there is no reason for this to be so in general.*

The fact that the event whose probability p_1, by its occurrence, excludes all the others, is not enough on its own to generate such a situation, for the desirability $d\bar{S}/dg_1$ of a gain g_1 whose probability is p_1 obviously depends in general on the amount g_2 attaching to the occurrence whose probability is p_2.[114]

In fact, as has just been noted, there may be *a very strong complementarity effect* in the neighbourhood of certainty, and in the most general case, a $B(x)$ function satisfying relation (1) cannot exist.

(b) In the neo-Bernoullian formulation, the expression $pB(g)$ represents the psychological value attributed in random choices to a gain g whose probability is p. It is hardly feasible to assume that this value in general remains the same *whether it is or is not associated* with the value $(1-p)B(g)$, since the association of the probabilities p and $1-p$ attaching to the gain g yields the *certainty* attaching to g_i. *There is clearly a complementarity effect here which is not allowed for by the neo-Bernoullian formulation.*

4. THE DECEPTIVE APPARENTLY RATIONAL NATURE OF SAMUELSON'S PRINCIPLE OF SUBSTITUTABILITY

71. Returning to the notation used in §52, Samuelson's substitutability principle can be expressed as follows.[115] If we have

$$(1) \qquad (P_1) = (P_2),$$

it should be true that

$$(2) \qquad \alpha(P_1) + (1 - \alpha)P_3 = \alpha(P_2) + (1 - \alpha)P_3,$$

whatever α and (P_3), and conversely.

As before, (P_1') and (P_2') will be used to designate the compound prospects respectively on the left-hand side and the right-hand side of relation (2).

It was indicated above[116] that this axiom is invalidated by the behaviour of persons who are generally acknowledged to be rational. It remains to show why this is so.

Samuelson's reasoning is the following: "Consider two compound lottery tickets corresponding to the prospects (P_1') and (P_2'), and examine the choice between them. If the event whose probability is $(1 - \alpha)$ occurs, the two tickets lead to the same outcome, (P_3), and they are equivalent. However, if the event whose probability is α occurs, the first ticket yields prospects (P_1) and the second prospect (P_2). Since the prospects (P_1) and (P_2) are considered as equivalent by hypothesis, the second ticket is no more and no less advantageous than the first".[117]

There is no denying that at first sight, this is a very appealing argument, and that its obviousness seems perfectly natural.[118] *Nevertheless, it is specious*, like all those which are put forward to justify the character of rational obviousness of the initial axioms of the American theories. It is easy to show where the flaw is.

When an individual has to choose, he is not aware of the result of the drawing. He must choose *ex ante* whereas Samuelson's reasoning is from an *ex post* standpoint. There is a substantial difference between *ex ante* and *ex post* reasoning. The latter eliminates an essential component of the operation of combining random prospects. To see this, consider the special case in which

$$(3) \qquad (P_3) \equiv (P_1).$$

According to the Samuelson's axiom of substitutability, the equality

$$(4) \qquad (P_1) = (P_2)$$

should entail

$$(5) \qquad (P_1) = \alpha(P_1) + (1 - \alpha)(P_2) \equiv (P).$$

This is Marschak's fourth postulate.[118']

Revert to Savage's diagrammatic presentation[118"] (see Figure 21). Let (P_1) and (P_2) be portrayed by two rectilinear segments, AB horizontal, and CD sloped, intersecting at their central points at point Q the abscissa of which is $\frac{1}{2}$. Under the rules of graphical combination obtained earlier,[119] the prospect (P) defined by relation (5) is represented by the broken line CEFD, the points E and F being the barycentres of the points A and Q and the points B and Q respectively, weighted by the coefficients α and $(1 - \alpha)$.

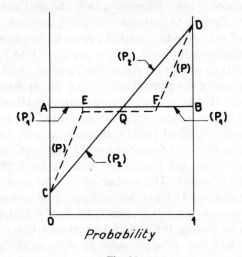

Probability

Fig. 21.

Granted that *ex post*, the conclusion is that (P) should be judged equivalent to (P_1) or (P_2), *ex ante there is no reason for this to be so. The special shape of (P) as a broken line CEFD may perfectly well be considered as an advantage by the individual making a choice, if such is his psychology,[120] and behaviour of this kind is in no way irrational in itself.[121]*

In reality, the *"ex ante"* standpoint is the only one that may properly be taken in considering choices involving uncertainty. *In taking an ex post stance the element specific to risk, to wit, the importance of the shape of the distribution of uncertainty, is eliminated unawares.[122,123] That this is happening is absolutely obvious only in extreme cases such as that discussed in §64, but in fact it is happening throughout.*

Returning to the example used earlier,[123'] one might share Samuelson's contention that, should the event whose probability is 1% occur, one of the persons considered prefers a certain 100 million to a 98% chance of winning 500 million, whereas should the event whose probability is 99% occur, he will obtain 1 unit in any case, and he *ought* to prefer 1 chance in 100 of winning 100 million to 0.98 chances in 100 of winning 500 million. But it is clear from this example that by reasoning *a posteriori*, and restricting consideration to the two possible outcomes *under the assumption that the first drawing has been completed, the effect is to introduce a new condition surreptitiously.*

The author of this memoir, *who is perfectly familiar with Samuelson's arguments,* unhesitatingly prefers prospect (P_2) to prospect (P_1) and prospect (P_1') to prospect (P_2') of §64, and he thinks that most of his readers will share his preference[124]; yet, to the best of his knowledge, he believes that he is not irrational. He is perfectly aware that 2 chances in 100,000 is a non-negligible quantity, but his view is that this quantity does not offset for him the reduction in the possible gain from 500 to 100 million, whereas for him by contrast, the achievement of *certainty* by raising the chance of winning from 98% to 100% is well worth this reduction. The author of this memoir, *very carefully pondered over and worked out* his attitude, and nobody could convince him to change his mind should he *really* find himself in the happy position of facing the random prospects described. *His psychology makes him prefer safety more strongly in the neighbourhood of certainty than he does in the neighbourhood of high risk.* He is absolutely convinced there is nothing about this view that could justify it as being regarded in any way as irrational.

Finally, it can be seen that the axiom of substitutability can be taken as a condition of consistency of choice *only if random prospects are independent, and in general, they are not.*

Just as it may be conceived that a very great effort is justified to perfect a whole, where only a detail remains to be remedied, albeit that detail on its own is of negligible importance, it may similarly be considered that it is *in no way irrational to accept a heavy reduction of possible gain as the price of achieving certainty, although this same reduction would not be felt acceptable for the same increase in the probability of gain if that increase is far removed from certainty.*

The decomposition of a drawing into two stages, as done by Samuelson, necessarily induces erroneous conclusions, for *it leads to the comparison of random prospects which are not comparable and to the formulation of unsubstantiated value judgements.*

This is particularly clear in the example given above. If I must choose between 0.98% chance of winning 500 million and a 1% chance of winning 100 million, I am in an altogether different probability region from that which offers me a 98% chance of winning 500 million and a 100% chance of winning 100 million. From the standpoint of rationality, there is no obligation to establish a link between the choices made in one region and those made in another.

In reality, these choices relate to entirely different situations. The contention that behaviour in such different situations must be the same to be rational, is a postulate that is neither evident nor attractive in contrast to the substitutability postulate.

Samuelson's two-stage reasoning is a perfect example of the fallacious arguments which the American School has continually brought to bear to justify the fundamental axioms used as its starting point. All that counts in the area of choice under uncertainty is the probability distribution of the gains that ultimately emerge. Decomposition into two or more stages can only lead to blunders.

On reflection, it seems quite amazing that Savage should have been able to persuade Samuelson to abandon his original correct position, crushing him into a logic which, in actual fact, is a pseudo-logic.

5. THE DETERMINATION OF CARDINAL UTILITY

72. From the foregoing,[125] it can be seen that there is *an indissoluble link* between the psychological distortion of monetary values and the importance attached to the shape of the probability distribution of psychological values, and consequently that any attempt to determine cardinal utility through observation of choices among random prospects is illusory. One of the fundamental errors of the von Neumann–Morgenstern *Theory of Games* lies here.

It should also be stressed that the other members of the American School seem generally content, as was pointed out above,[126] to hold that the concept of cardinal utility is non-operational, i.e. incapable of undergoing experimental measurement. Some even go so far as to deny its mere existence. *Nevertheless, by a singular paradox, it follows from the analysis in this study that the one case in which a neo-Bernoullian index exists is the case in which this index merges with cardinal utility or psychological value.*[127]

4. CONCLUSION: THE FUNDAMENTAL ERROR
OF THE AMERICAN SCHOOL

73. The analysis has shown that the *fundamental error of the entire American School*[128] *is its indirect and unconscious neglect of the dispersion of psychological values.* Whatever the system of axioms taken as starting point, there is always somewhere one axiom that is based on pseudo evidence, and whose psychological signification has not been sufficiently thought through.

In general, no index $B(x)$ exists such that the value V of a random prospect to a rational man is given by the relation

$$B(V) = \sum p_i B(g_i).$$

Where it does exist, it can be affirmed that it is indistinguishable from cardinal utility or psychological value,[129] and in addition, that the individual considered is insensitive to the dispersion of psychological values, which, when all is said and done, is a simple matter of taste.

At all events, the aesthetical beauty of the very general mathematical constructs based on the axioms retained has diverted the American School from examination of the real problem.[130]

From the standpoint of the economic psychology of risk, the neo-Bernoullian formulation is of no greater, and no lesser, interest than any formulation purporting to represent a set of numbers by a single figure. The median or the geometric mean of psychological values could equally well have been taken. They would have been just as interesting.

The implicit neglect in the neo-Bernoullian formulation of the dispersion of psychological values vitiates its use, despite the successive claims of its American supporters, as an instrument for portraying the actual behaviour of man in the process of choice, for determining cardinal utility, or even for providing a "reasonable rule of conduct for a reasonable man".

By contrast, what is very interesting in the American theories is that the neo-Bernoullian formulation could be derived from certain axioms which at first sight appear to be a far cry from it. But on thinking it over, we easily realize that these axioms, in their essence, imply an assumption of linearity.

Further, the mathematical constructions based on these axioms are very complex only because it was desired to make them very general. They could be simplified enormously by restricting consideration to essentials. Concern for excessive formal generality has, in the upshot, obscured the question of the psychology of risk and diverted attention from what was truly important. In this context, it is symptomatic that in all the American papers relative to the neo-Bernoullian formulation, almost the full contents of each are devoted to working out the mathematical consequences of the axioms, whereas the discussion of these axioms is itself dismissed in a few lines.

Of course it is quite disappointing to have to exert so much effort to prove the illusory character of a formulation whose oversimplification is evident to anyone with a little psychological intuition. But it is clearly somewhat difficult to show the error inherent in the claim that a rational individual should follow a certain rule because he would be irrational if he did not.

To paraphrase what Paul Levy, in his excellent analysis of the theory of probable gain[131] had to say of Joseph Bertrand's formulation based on the mathematical expectation of monetary values we may finally say that: "The error of the American School, basically, is to express itself as if the theory of the probable value of the moral gain were an ideal which reality has the defect of failing to approach. It brings to mind the astronomer who, on discovering that Mercury does not exactly follow the trajectory forecast by Newton's law, thought that Mercury must be wrong and in describing his calculations took to saying 'we have calculated what Mercury's trajectory would be if it was rational, that is, if it had better understood the harmony of the universe and Newton's work. But we should bear in mind that Mercury is wrong, and allow for its error'. Just as Newton's law is no more than an approximate formulation that holds only in certain conditions, the law of large numbers is only an approximation that in general is more satisfactory the larger the set of numbers considered. *But it must not be applied where it is not applicable*".

The fundamental reason for this error is that in treating the psychology of risk, the American School has been more occupied with pretty logical constructs than with factual observation. This is not without spice for a country whose concern, we are told, is with facts first and foremost.

In defence of the American School, we can say that this is not the first time – nor, unfortunately, the last – that very brilliant minds have caged themselves in a logically coherent and beautiful system, but one which has no real link with reality. The history of physics swarms with such examples.

As was noted by that eminent and courageous physicist Bouasse writing about his science, "we have seen hundreds of times that there is no gross absurdity that we cannot be convinced to accept if it is drawn rigorously from premises adopted without due consideration. The solidity of the chain of reasoning blinds us to the exactness of the principle at its far end".[132]

CHAPTER III

MATHEMATICAL APPENDICES

APPENDIX I: SYMMETRY OF EFFECTS OF THE PSYCHOLOGICAL DISTORTION OF MONETARY VALUES AND OF THE DISPERSION OF PSYCHOLOGICAL VALUES (§§20–21)[133]

74. The symmetry of the effects of the psychological distortion of monetary values (Factor AI) and of the dispersion of psychological values (Factor AIV) may be easily illustrated by the analysis of a specific model.

THE MODEL

Probability Density of Gains

75. We assume that the probability density of gains g (see Figure A1) is

$$\text{(1)} \quad \begin{aligned} \varphi(g) &= r \quad \text{for} \quad -A < g < A, \quad (2Ar = 1) \\ \varphi(g) &= 0 \quad \text{for} \quad |g| > A. \end{aligned}$$

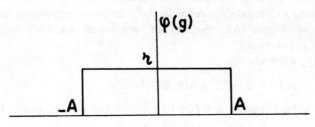

Fig. A1.

107

Cardinal Utility Function

76. We assume that the cardinal utility function is written

(2) $\gamma = \bar{s}(g) = a + bg - cg^2$ with $b > 0, c > 0$.

This is an increasing function for

(3) $g < b/2c$,

and *it will be assumed therefore that*

(4) $A < b/2c$.

Mathematical Expectation of Monetary and Psychological Values

77. Using M and Σ to denote the mean and standard deviation of the monetary gain g, and $\mathcal{M}$ and σ to denote the mean and standard deviation of the psychological value $\gamma = \bar{s}(g)$ we find easily

(5) $M = 0,$ $\Sigma = A/\sqrt{3},$

(6) $\mathcal{M} = a - c\Sigma^2,$ $\sigma^2 = b^2\Sigma^2 + \frac{4}{5}c^2\Sigma^4.$

Psychological Value of a Random Prospect

78. If it is now *assumed* that in order to select between different random prospects of the type considered, we have

(7) $\bar{s}(V) = \displaystyle\int_{-\infty}^{+\infty} \bar{s}(g)\varphi(g)\,\mathrm{d}g - \lambda \int_{-\infty}^{+\infty} [\bar{s}(g) - \bar{s}_m(g)]^2\varphi(g)\,\mathrm{d}g,$

or

(8) $\bar{s}(V) = \mathcal{M} - \lambda\sigma^2.$

This function is psychologically acceptable since *it satisfies the axiom of absolute preference* as regards the outcomes envisaged (as can be seen from Figure A2, the set of outcomes includes no case of absolute preference).

Finally, we find

(9) $\bar{s}(V) = a - c\Sigma^2 - \lambda(b^2\Sigma^2 + \frac{4}{5}c^2\Sigma^4),$

or, for example taking $a = b = 1$ (without any loss of generality)

(10) $\bar{s}(V) = 1 - (c + \lambda)\Sigma^2 - \frac{4}{5}\lambda c^2\Sigma^4.$

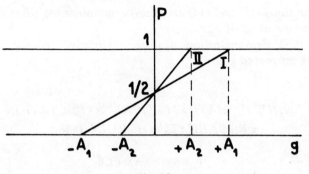

Fig. A2.

If, in relation (10), we consider that c represents the curvature of cardinal utility (Factor AI), Σ represents the dispersion of monetary values, and λ represents aversion to risk (Factor AIV), it can be seen that the curvature of cardinal utility and the aversion to risk operate in an exactly analogous way for given values of Σ. Since each of the factors considered produces analogous effects, it is not surprising that they should be so hard to dissociate.

NON-EXISTENCE OF A NEO-BERNOULLIAN INDEX $B(g)$ FOR THE MODEL CONSIDERED

79. Lastly, it should be noted that there exists no index

$$(11) \qquad B = B(g) = B'[\gamma = \bar{s}(g)] = f(\gamma),$$

such that

$$(12) \qquad B(V) = \int_{-\infty}^{+\infty} B(g)\varphi(g)\,dg,$$

f being a well determined function of γ.

If it did, we would have, according to (2), (11) and (12)

$$(13) \qquad B(V) = \frac{1}{2A}\int_{-A}^{+A} f(a + bg - cg^2)\,dg = F(a, b, c),$$

where F is a certain function of a, b and c. Then according to (9), (11) and (13) we would have

$$(14) \qquad F(a, b, c) = f[a - c\Sigma^2 - \lambda(b^2\Sigma^2 + \tfrac{4}{5}\lambda c^2\Sigma^4)].$$

Thus equations (13) and (14) are clearly incompatible since expression (13) is independent of λ.

[The 1952 demonstration has been slightly changed and some misprints corrected.]

APPENDIX II: MATHEMATICAL EXPECTATION AND PROBABILITY OF RUIN (§48)[134]

FIRST EXAMPLE

80. Consider an individual whose fortune is F, using a martingale system with a probability p that an individual bet will win, and $(1 - p)$ that it will lose. If for each unit bet the mathematical expectancy is e, we have

$$pg - (1 - p)m = em,$$

in which m is the amount staked and g the amount to be won on that bet.

Whatever the amount staked on an individual round, the average winnings per unit staked over a large number of rounds will tend, in probability, to e, and from this point of view the various systems of playing are all equivalent.

But, psychologically, this is far from true. If a player makes a high bet m each round, he has some hope of getting rich quickly, but he also increases his likelihood of ruin. Conversely, if he regularly wagers low amounts, he can diminish the probability of ruin to any desired level, but he will get rich much less quickly.

SECOND EXAMPLE

81. Another good example is given by a player with a capital of x who makes n successive bets, for each of which the outcome is distributed according to the Gaussian law with average value m and standard deviation σ. For n bets, the mathematical expectation is

$$M = nm,$$

and it can be shown that if x is fairly large by comparison with m, and n is a large number, our player's probability of ruin P is approximately

$$P = \exp(-2mx/\sigma^2).$$

(Bachelier, 1912, *Calcul des Probabilités*, No. 349.)

Now consider two games J_1 and J_2 for which the data are (in dollars)

$$J_1 \begin{cases} m_1 = 10^{-4} \\ \sigma_1 = 1 \end{cases} \qquad J_2 \begin{cases} m_2 = 10^{-3} \\ \sigma_2 = 10^3 \end{cases},$$

$x = 1$ million
$n = 100$ billion bets: 10^{11}

$$J_1 \begin{cases} M_1 = nm_1 = 10 \text{ million} \\ \Sigma_1 = \sqrt{n}\,\sigma_1 = 3.16 \times 10^5 \\ \Sigma_1/M_1 = 3.16 \times 10^{-2} \end{cases} \quad J_2 \begin{cases} M_2 = nm_2 = 100 \text{ million} \\ \Sigma_2 = \sqrt{n}\,\sigma_2 = 3.16 \times 10^8 \\ \Sigma_2/M_2 = 3.16 \end{cases}.$$

For J_1 and J_2, we have respectively

$$J_1: 2m_1x/\sigma_1^2 = 200, \qquad J_2: 2m_2x/\sigma_2^2 = 0.002$$

and

$$J_1: P_1 \simeq \frac{1.38}{10^{87}}, \qquad J_2: P_2 \simeq \frac{998}{1000}.$$

Thus the mathematical expectation attaching to J_2 is \$100 million, against \$10 million only for J_1. But with J_2, the player has a 99.8% chance of ruin, whereas for J_1, this probability is only 1.4×10^{-87}. It is hard to see who, with a capital of \$1 million, would prefer J_2 to J_1. Yet this is a situation in which the law of large numbers is fully applicable, since a series of 100 billion bets is involved (notice that for the winnings associated with J_1, the standard deviation about the mathematical expectation is below $\frac{1}{30}$ of the average winnings after $n = 10^{11}$ bets).

This is, of course, an extreme example, but its demonstrational value is complete, for so clear a situation in a limiting case will not fail equally to occur to some degree in intermediate cases.

APPENDIX III: SOME PROPERTIES OF THE PREFERENCE
INDEX $S = f(M, \Sigma)$ (§58)[135]

THE TRADE-OFF $S = f(M, \Sigma)$ BETWEEN MATHEMATICAL
EXPECTATION AND STANDARD DEVIATION OF MONETARY
GAINS AND THE AXIOM OF ABSOLUTE PREFERENCE

82. Consider the preference index

(1) $S = f(M, \Sigma)$,

in which M represents the mathematical expectation and Σ the standard deviation of monetary gains.

It can be verified from Figure 2 in §3 that all Gaussian distributions *with the same standard deviation* can be derived from any one of them by a simple vertical transformation. Correspondingly, if one of two normally distributed prospects is to be absolutely preferred to the other, the necessary and sufficient condition is that its mathematical expectation should have a higher value. So we should have

(1') $\partial f / \partial M > 0$.

INCOMPATIBILITY IN GENERAL OF THE TRADE-OFF
$S = f(M, \Sigma)$ WITH THE PRINCIPLE OF ABSOLUTE PREFERENCE

83. *Whereas for a normal distribution the preference index* (1) *under the condition* (1') *satisfies the absolute preference principle, this property does not hold for the most general random prospects.* This can be seen from the following.

Assume that

(1'') $\partial f / \partial \Sigma < 0$.

Returning to the geometrical presentation in §3 above, consider a curve C_1, and the curve C_2 derived from it by raising the ordinates of a over a segment PQ of length q located to the far right of the abscissae (see Figure A3), and assume that

(2) $aq = \varepsilon$, $a > 0$,

where ε is a very small number.

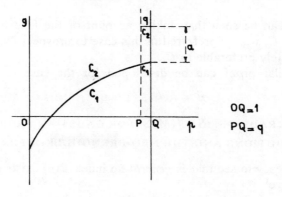

Fig. A3.

We have

$$a = 0 \quad \text{for} \quad 0 < p < 1 - q,$$
$$a \neq 0 \quad \text{for} \quad 1 - q < p < 1.$$

According to the axiom of absolute preference, C_2 should be preferred to C_1. Now, we have

(3) $$dS = f'_M \, dM + f'_\Sigma \, d\Sigma.$$

Since

(4) $$M = \int_0^1 g \, dp, \qquad \Sigma^2 = \int_0^1 (g - M)^2 \, dp = \int_0^1 g^2 \, dp - M^2,$$

there follows

(5) $$dM = aq, \qquad 2\Sigma \, d\Sigma = \int_{1-q}^1 [(g + a)^2 - g^2] \, dp - 2M \, dM$$
$$= a^2 q + 2a g_m q - 2Maq,$$

using g_m to denote the average value of g *over the interval q.* Hence according to (2), (3) and (5)

(6) $$dS = \left[f'_M + \frac{f'_\Sigma}{2\Sigma} [a + 2(g_m - M)] \right] \varepsilon.$$

Hence, since according to (1″) f'_Σ is negative, it is always possible to find a number a sufficiently large to make

(7) $$dS < 0.$$

Thus it can be seen that, taking account of the field of choice (1), prospect C_1 will be preferred in this case to prospect C_2, although C_2 is absolutely preferable to C_1.

A similar proof can be developed for the case in which f'_Σ is positive.

THE TRADE-OFF $S = f(M, \Sigma)$ FOR GAUSSIAN PROBABILITY DISTRIBUTIONS AND THE NEO-BERNOULLIAN FORMULATION

84. It is easy to see that *in general* no index $B(g)$ exists such that we could have

$$(8) \qquad S = f(M, \Sigma) = \int_{-\infty}^{+\infty} B(g) \frac{\exp\left[-(g-M)^2/2\Sigma^2\right]}{\sqrt{2\pi}\Sigma} \, dg,$$

up to a linear transformation, with

$$(9) \qquad dB/dg > 0.$$

Consider the function

$$(10) \qquad F(M, \Sigma) = \Sigma f(M, \Sigma).$$

An easily performed differentiation of the integral (8) shows that condition (8) would imply

$$(11) \qquad \frac{\partial^2 F}{\partial M^2} = \frac{1}{\Sigma} \frac{\partial F}{\partial \Sigma} - \frac{F}{\Sigma^2},$$

and according to (10)[136]

$$(12) \qquad \Sigma \frac{\partial^2 f}{\partial M^2} = \frac{\partial f}{\partial \Sigma}.$$

This condition is, in general, not verified by the most general function $S = f(M, \Sigma)$. Thus the function

$$(13) \qquad f(M, \Sigma) = M + \lambda\Sigma,$$

used by this author in the model of economic equilibrium in his 1953 *Econometrica* paper, 'L'extension des théories de l'équilibre économique et du rendement social au cas du risque' ('Extension of the Theories of General Economic Equilibrium and Economic Efficiency to the Case of Risk') *does not* satisfy condition (12), but it satisfies the axiom of absolute preference.

Condition (12), moreover, is necessary but *not sufficient*, for it neglects the fact that if an index $B(g)$ does exist, the inequality

(14) $dB/dg \geq 0$

should be true at all points.

THE FULL IMPLICATIONS OF THE NEO-BERNOULLIAN FORMULATION FOR THE TRADE-OFF $S = f(M, \Sigma)$ AND GAUSSIAN PROBABILITY DISTRIBUTIONS

85. It is easy to see the implication of condition (14) using an illustrative example. We have

(15)
$$\frac{1}{\sqrt{2\pi}\Sigma} \int_{-\infty}^{+\infty} \exp\left[-(g - M)^2/2\Sigma^2\right] dg = 1,$$

$$\frac{1}{\sqrt{2\pi}\Sigma} \int_{-\infty}^{+\infty} (g - M)^2 \exp\left[-(g - M)^2/2\Sigma^2\right] dg = \Sigma^2,$$

$$\frac{1}{\sqrt{2\pi}\Sigma} \int_{-\infty}^{+\infty} g \exp\left[-(g - M)^2/2\Sigma^2\right] dg = M,$$

$$\frac{1}{\sqrt{2\pi}\Sigma} \int_{-\infty}^{+\infty} g^2 \exp\left[-(g - M)^2/2\Sigma^2\right] dg = \Sigma^2 + M^2.$$

Thus we have

(16)
$$\int_{-\infty}^{+\infty} \left[B_0 + B_1 g + \frac{B_2}{2} g^2\right] \frac{\exp\left[-(g - M)^2/2\Sigma^2\right]}{\sqrt{2\pi}\Sigma} dg$$
$$= B_0 + B_1 M + \frac{B_2}{2}(M^2 + \Sigma^2);$$

B_0, B_1 and B_2 being constants.

Thus we verify that there corresponds to the family of functions

(17) $$f(M, \Sigma) = B_0 + B_1 M + \frac{B_2}{2}(M^2 + \Sigma^2)$$

a family of indexes

(18) $$B(g) = B_0 + B_1 g + \frac{B_2}{2} g^2,$$

(B_0, B_1 and B_2 being constants) satisfying condition (8) since according to (8) and (18) we have

(19) $S = f(M, \Sigma) = B_0 + B_1 M + \dfrac{B_2}{2}(\Sigma^2 + M^2).$

This function satisfies condition (12), but since

(20) $dB/dg = B_1 + B_2 g,$

condition (14) is not satisfied at all points.

Any preference function for Gaussian prospects having the form of relation (17) is thus *incompatible with the neo-Bernoullian formulation.* Condition (14) thus turns out to be *much more restrictive than it seems at first sight.*

Of course there is the trivial solution

(21) $f(M, \Sigma) = B_0 + B_1 M,$

but the standard deviation Σ has disappeared from it.

ANNEX

Integration of the Equation $\Sigma \, \partial^2 f/\partial M^2 = \partial f/\partial \Sigma.$ (Note added in 1977)

Partial Differential Equation $\Sigma f''_{M^2} = f'_\Sigma$

85.1. Setting

(22) $U = \Sigma^2/2,$

the relation (12)

(23) $\Sigma \, \partial^2 f/\partial M^2 = \partial f/\partial \Sigma$

is written

(24) $\partial^2 f/\partial M^2 = \partial f/\partial U.$

This equation is no other than the classical equation of heat.

Relying on the general theory of this equation, one can prove that the most general solution of equation (12) satisfying the limit condition

(25) $f(M, \Sigma = 0) = B(M),$

in which $B(M)$ is an arbitrary function, is that given by relation (8) [See Bronstein–Semendjajew, *Taschenbuch der Mathematik*, Teubner, Leipzig, 1958, pp.417–419]. Condition (25) corresponds to the fact that when $\Sigma = 0$ the random prospect considered reduces the assured gain M.

Two cases are of particular interest:

(a) The function $B(M)$ can be expanded as a Taylor series.

(b) The function $B(M)$ can be expanded as a Fourier series.

(a) *The function $B(M)$ can be expanded as a Taylor series*

85.2. Assume that, considering the argument g, we have

$$(26) \qquad B(g) = B_0 + B_1 g + \frac{B_2}{2!} g^2 + \cdots + \frac{B_n}{n!} g^n + \cdots,$$

with

$$(27) \qquad B_n = \frac{d^n B}{dg^n} (g = 0).$$

One can always assume

$$(28) \qquad B_0 = 0, \qquad B_1 = 1,$$

without loss of generality, as $B(g)$ is defined up to a linear transformation.

Setting

$$(29) \qquad u = (g - M)/\Sigma,$$

we have from (8)

$$(30) \qquad S = f(M, \Sigma) = \int_{-\infty}^{+\infty} B[M + u\Sigma] \frac{\exp(-u^2/2)}{\sqrt{2\pi}} \, du,$$

whence, from (26)

$$(31) \qquad S = f(M, \Sigma) = B_0 + B_1 M + \int_{-\infty}^{+\infty} \frac{B_2}{2} (M + u\Sigma)^2 \frac{\exp(-u^2/2)}{\sqrt{2\pi}} \, du +$$

$$+ \cdots + \int_{-\infty}^{+\infty} \frac{B_n}{n!} (M + u\Sigma)^n \frac{\exp(-u^2/2)}{\sqrt{2\pi}} \, du +$$

$$+ \cdots.$$

As

$$(32) \quad \int_{-\infty}^{+\infty} u^{2p-1} \frac{\exp(-u^2/2)}{\sqrt{2\pi}} du = 0,$$

$$\int_{-\infty}^{+\infty} u^{2p} \frac{\exp(-u^2/2)}{\sqrt{2\pi}} du = 1.3.\ldots(2p-1),$$

it can be seen that relation (31) yields the expression for the expansion of function f as a Taylor series.

Thus we have

$$(33) \quad S = f(M, \Sigma) = B_0 + B_1 M + \frac{B_2}{2!}(M^2 + \Sigma^2) +$$

$$+ \frac{B_3}{3!}(M^3 + 3M\Sigma^2) + \cdots.$$

The nth order term is a polynomial of degree n, which is homogeneous in M and Σ and it may easily be verified that each of them is a solution to equation (23). For $\Sigma = 0$, we find expansion (26).

Naturally, similar results are obtain if it is assumed that the function f can be expanded as a Taylor series. We could then write

$$(34) \quad f(M, \Sigma) = f_0 + f_1 M + f_2 \Sigma + \frac{1}{2!}(f_{11}M^2 + 2f_{12}M\Sigma + f_{22}\Sigma^2) + \cdots,$$

by setting

$$(35) \quad f_0 = f(0, 0), \qquad f_1 = \frac{\partial f}{\partial M}(0, 0), \qquad f_2 = \frac{\partial f}{\partial \Sigma}(0, 0),$$

$$(36) \quad f_{1,1} = \frac{\partial^2 f}{\partial M^2}(0, 0), \qquad f_{1,2} = \frac{\partial^2 f}{\partial M \partial \Sigma}(0, 0), \qquad f_{2,2} = \frac{\partial^2 f}{\partial \Sigma^2}(0, 0).$$

By carrying the expansion of the function $f(M, \Sigma)$ into relation (23), we would find the conditions

$$(37) \quad f_2 = 0, \qquad f_{1,2} = 0, \qquad f_{1,1} = f_{2,2}, \ldots,$$

whence

$$(38) \quad f(M, \Sigma) = f_0 + f_1 M + \frac{f_{1,1}}{2!}(M^2 + \Sigma^2) + \cdots.$$

This again yields the expansion (33).

(b) *The function B(M) can be expanded as a Fourier series*
    in the interval $(0, l)$

85.3. Consider the interval

(39) $0 \leq M \leq l,$

and assume that in this interval $B(M)$ can be defined by the series

(40) $B(M) = \sum_n A_n \sin n\pi M/l.$

It can be proved that the most general solution to equation (24) satisfying the limit condition (25) is given by relation

(41) $f(M, \Sigma) = \sum_n A_n \exp\left(-\frac{n^2\pi^2}{l^2}\frac{\Sigma^2}{2}\right) \sin n\pi M/l$

(Ch. Fabry, *Propagation of Heat*, Armand Colin, Paris, 1949, pp.82–87). It can be immediately verified that the nth order term is a solution to equation (23).

Solutions to the partial differential equation in f

85.4. Overall, it can be seen that there are an infinite number of functions $B(g)$ which satisfy condition (8), but all imply that the function $f(M, \Sigma)$ has a special structure defined by condition (12).

Case in which the preference index considered is a function of the average $\mathcal{M}$ and the standard deviation σ of cardinal utility $\gamma = \bar{s}(g)$, the neo-Bernoullian formulation being assumed satisfied

85.5. Assume that for normal distributions of cardinal utility

(42) $\gamma = \bar{s}(g)$

we have the field of choice

(43) $S = f^*(\mathcal{M}, \sigma),$

and assume further that the neo-Bernoullian formulation is also satisfied.

In this case, an index

(44) $B = \beta(\gamma)$

should exist, such that

$$(45) \qquad S = f^*(\mathcal{M}, \sigma) = \int_{-\infty}^{+\infty} \beta(\gamma) \frac{\exp\left[-(\gamma - \mathcal{M})^2/2\sigma^2\right]}{\sqrt{2\pi}\sigma} \, d\gamma.$$

All the deductions above may immediately be transposed by simply replacing M and Σ by $\mathcal{M}$ and σ. In particular we should have

$$(46) \qquad \sigma \frac{\partial^2 f^*}{\partial \mathcal{M}^2} = \frac{\partial f^*}{\partial \sigma},$$

which corresponds to relation (23).

Here again, the most general solution to this partial differential equation satisfying the limit condition

$$(47) \qquad f^*(\mathcal{M}, \sigma = 0) = \beta(\mathcal{M})$$

is that given by relation (45). The limit condition (47) corresponds to the fact that for $\sigma = 0$, the random prospect considered reduces to the assured gain M whose psychological value is $\mathcal{M}$.

If the function $\beta(\gamma)$ can be expanded as a Taylor series, we can write as previously

$$(48) \qquad \beta(\gamma) = \beta_0 + \beta_1 \gamma + \frac{\beta_2}{2!} \gamma^2 + \cdots + \frac{\beta_n}{n!} \gamma^n + \cdots,$$

with

$$(49) \qquad \beta_n = \frac{d^n \beta}{d\gamma^n} \quad (\gamma = 0).$$

This yields

$$(50) \qquad S = f^*(\mathcal{M}, \sigma) = \beta_0 + \beta_1 \mathcal{M} + \frac{\beta_2}{2}(\mathcal{M}^2 + \sigma^2)$$

$$+ \frac{\beta_3}{6}(\mathcal{M}^3 + 3\mathcal{M}\sigma^2) + \cdots.$$

Suppose that, e.g.

$$(51) \qquad \beta_4 = \beta_5 = \cdots = \beta_n = \cdots = 0.$$

For the axiom of absolute preference to be verified, we should have from (1')

$$(52) \qquad \partial f^*/\partial \mathcal{M} = \beta_1 + \beta_2 \mathcal{M} + \frac{\beta_3}{2}(\mathcal{M}^2 + \sigma^2) > 0,$$

for all values of $\mathcal{M}$ and σ characterizing the normally distributed random prospects considered.

If $\mathcal{M}$ can take any value, condition (52) entails

(53) $\beta_1 > 0, \qquad \beta_3 > 0.$

As

(54) $\partial^2 f^* / \partial \mathcal{M}^2 = \beta_2 + \beta_3 \mathcal{M},$

we see that when $\mathcal{M}$ varies the minimum value of $\partial f^* / \partial \mathcal{M}$

(55) $\beta_1 - \dfrac{\beta_2^2}{2\beta_3} + \dfrac{\beta_3}{2}\sigma^2,$

will certainly be positive for $\sigma = 0$ if

(56) $\beta_3 > \dfrac{\beta_2^2}{2\beta_1}.$

As

(57) $\partial f^* / \partial \sigma = \sigma(\beta_2 + \beta_3 \mathcal{M}),$

and

(58) $\sigma > 0,$

we have correspondingly

(59) $\partial f^* / \partial \sigma > 0,$ for $\mathcal{M} > -\beta_2/\beta_3,$

(60) $\partial f^* / \partial \sigma < 0,$ for $\mathcal{M} < -\beta_2/\beta_3.$

There would therefore be a preference for risk for values of $\mathcal{M}$ *greater than* $-\beta_2/\beta_3$ and a preference for security for *lower* values of $\mathcal{M}$.

It also follows from this that a general preference for security or risk would imply the condition

(61) $\beta_3 = 0,$

and from (56)

(62) $\beta_2 = 0,$

so that

(63) $\beta = \beta(\gamma) = \beta_0 + \beta_1 \gamma,$

which would imply the identity of the neo-Bernoullian index B and cardinal utility γ.

This is a general result. Assume that the function f^* reduces to a polynomial of degree n and that there is a general preference for security, which implies

(64) $\partial f^*/\partial\sigma < 0.$

From (46), we will then have

(65) $\partial^2 f^*/\partial\mathcal{M}^2 < 0.$

It follows that the function $\partial f^*/\partial M$ would be ever-decreasing. As it is a polynomial in $\mathcal{M}$, conditions (64) and

(66) $\partial f^*/\partial\mathcal{M} > 0$

implied by the axiom of absolute preference for a normal distribution of $\gamma(g)$ could not be satisfied for all values of $\mathcal{M}$, except naturally if all β_n would be equal to zero for $n \geqslant 2$.

This would likewise be true if there was a general preference for risk.

Thus, however far one expands the function f^*, a general preference for security or risk is translated by the conditions

(67) $\beta_2 = \beta_3 = \cdots = \beta_n = \cdots = 0,$

i.e., by the identity of the two indexes $B(g)$ and $\gamma(g)$ up to a linear transformation.

Thus we verify that in the case considered the neo-Bernoullian formulation is *extremely restrictive.*

The analysis of the psychology towards risk for the neo-Bernoullians who admit the existence of an index of psychological value (cardinal utility)

85.6. It should be stressed that, for the study of psychology vis-à-vis risk, the only series expansion of the neo-Bernoullian index that is of interest, is the expansion of this index as a function $B = \beta(\gamma)$ of cardinal utility γ (relation 48), and that the expansion of the index $B = B(g)$ as a function of the monetary gain (relation 26) can only lead to regrettable confusion between the effect of transformation of monetary values into psychological values and the effect of the propensity for risk (or security).

Assume that the function $\gamma = \gamma(g)$ can be expanded as a Taylor series. We have

(68) $\qquad \gamma(g) = \gamma_0 + \gamma_1 g + \dfrac{\gamma_2}{2} g^2 + \dfrac{\gamma_3}{3!} g^3 + \cdots.$

We can write without loss of generality

(69) $\qquad \begin{aligned} & B_0 = 0, \qquad \beta_0 = 0, \qquad \gamma_0 = 0, \\ & B_1 = 1, \qquad \beta_1 = 1, \qquad \gamma_1 = 1, \end{aligned}$

since the indices B, β and γ are defined up to a linear transformation. From (48), (68) and (69), we then deduce

(70) $\qquad \begin{aligned} B(g) = \beta[\gamma(g)] &= \left[g + \dfrac{\gamma_2}{2} g^2 + \dfrac{\gamma_3}{3!} g^3 + \cdots \right] + \\ &+ \dfrac{\beta_2}{2!} \left[g + \dfrac{\gamma_2}{2} g^2 + \cdots \right]^2 + \dfrac{\beta_3}{3!} [g + \cdots]^3 + \cdots \\ &= g + \dfrac{\gamma_2 + \beta_2}{2!} g^2 + \dfrac{1}{3!} [\gamma_3 + 3\gamma_2\beta_2 + \beta_3] g^3 + \cdots. \end{aligned}$

Hence, according to (26), we finally deduce that

(71) $\qquad \begin{aligned} & B_2 = \gamma_2 + \beta_2, \\ & B_3 = \gamma_3 + 3\gamma_2\beta_2 + \beta_3, \\ & B_4 = \cdots. \end{aligned}$

The coefficients B_n represent the conjugated effect of the psychological estimate of monetary values and the effect of psychology vis-à-vis risk *in the case where we assume the existence of an index of cardinal utility $\gamma = \gamma(g)$ and of a neo-Bernoullian index $B = B(g)$ which can be developed in Taylor's expansions according to relations (68) and (48).*

May I recall that in the case considered and according to my theory, relation (48) should reduce to

(72) $\qquad \beta(\gamma) = \beta_0 + \beta_1 \gamma,$

which expresses the identity of the two indices B and γ, but *for the neo-Bernoullians who, like de Finetti, admit the existence of an index of cardinal utility, and who maintain that the neo-Bernoullian index does not reduce to cardinal utility, it is the function $\beta(\gamma)$ and its expansion (48) which indeed represent the effect of the psychology* towards risk. For these neo-Bernoullians, relations (71) represent the conjugated effect of psychological values (cardinal utilities) and propensity to risk (or security) in the case considered.

APPENDIX IV: THE TRADE-OFF BETWEEN MATHEMATICAL EXPECTATION AND PROBABILITY OF RUIN, AND THE NEO-BERNOULLIAN FORMULATION (§59)[137]

THE TRADE-OFF BETWEEN MATHEMATICAL EXPECTATION OF MONETARY VALUES AND PROBABILITY OF RUIN, AND THE NEO-BERNOULLIAN FORMULATION

86. Consider the ordinal index of preference

(1) $S = f(M, P)$,

where M represents the mathematical expectation of monetary values and P the probability of experiencing a loss in excess of a given value X representing the fortune of the subject.

For the function (1) *to satisfy the neo-Bernoullian formulation*, it must satisfy any equivalent axiom, and in particular, therefore, Marschak's fourth postulate. Thus in the notation of §52, the condition

(2) $(P_1) = (P_2)$

would have to entail the condition

(3) $(P_1) = \alpha(P_1) + (1 - \alpha)(P_2)$,

whatever the value of α $(0 \leqslant \alpha \leqslant 1)$.

Then if (P) is used to denote the prospect on the right-hand side, the properties of compound probabilities yield

(4) $M = \alpha M_1 + (1 - \alpha)M_2$,

(5) $P = \alpha P_1 + (1 - \alpha)P_2$.

Thus in the space (P, M) any point (P) located on the segment joining two equivalent points (P_1) and (P_2) should also lie on the indifference curve joining these two points. It follows that these indifference curves are necessarily straight lines.

Further, these straight lines are necessarily parallel. Let (P_3) be any prospect whatever, and (P'_1) and (P'_2) be the prospects

(6) $(P'_1) = \beta(P_1) + (1 - \beta)(P_3),$ $(0 \leqslant \beta \leqslant 1)$

(7) $(P'_2) = \beta(P_2) + (1 - \beta)(P_3).$

By Samuelson's axiom, the prospects (P'_1) and (P'_2) are equivalent, so that the points P'_1 and P'_2 are on the same linear indifference curve. $P'_1 P'_2$ being parallel to $P_1 P_2$, it immediately follows that the indifference curves are parallel (see Figure A4).

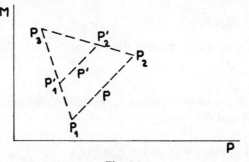

Fig. A4.

Since for a given level of the index of preference, the average gain M must rise together with the probability P, it can be seen finally that the index S must indeed be an increasing function of the binomial expression $(M - aP)$, in which a is a positive constant. Thus we should have

(8) $S = f(M - aP).$

EXPRESSION OF THE NEO-BERNOULLIAN INDEX
FOR $S = f(M, P)$

87. By similar reasoning we may deduce that

(9) $B = B(M - aP),$

B representing the neo-Bernoullian index.

In fact the neo-Bernoullian formulation is even more restrictive than relation (9).

The random prospect considered may be defined by the gains g_i associated with probabilities p_i:

gains: $g_1, g_2, \ldots, g_i, \ldots, g_n$,

probabilities: $p_1, p_2, \ldots, p_i, \ldots, p_n$,

with

$$(10) \qquad \sum p_i = 1.$$

Let g_j and g_k be the gains such that

$$(11) \qquad g_j + X > 0,$$

$$(12) \qquad g_k + X \leqslant 0.$$

The probability of a loss greater than X, or equal to X, is

$$(13) \qquad P = \sum_k p_k.$$

According to the neo-Bernoullian formulation, we must have according to (9), (10) and (13)

$$(14) \qquad B\left(\sum_i p_i g_i - a \sum_k p_k\right) = \sum_i p_i B(g_i),$$

and then

$$(15) \qquad F[p_j, p_k] = B\left[\sum_j p_j g_j + \sum_k p_k(g_k - a)\right]$$
$$- \sum_j p_j B(g_j) - \sum_k p_k B(g_k) = 0,$$

for all p_j and p_k satisfying the conditions

$$(16) \qquad \begin{aligned} \sum_j p_j &= 1 - P, \\ \sum_k p_k &= P. \end{aligned}$$

If we put

$$(17) \qquad H(p_j, p_k) = F(p_j, p_k) + G(p_j, p_k)$$

with

$$(18) \qquad G(p_j, p_k) = \lambda\left[1 - P - \sum_j p_j\right] + \mu\left[P - \sum_k p_k\right],$$

we must have identically

(19) $\partial H/\partial p_j = 0,$ $\partial H/\partial p_k = 0,$

λ and μ being regarded as constants.

Let

(20) $K = \sum_j p_j g_j + \sum_k p_k (g_k - a).$

We must have according to (19)

(21)
$$\frac{\partial H}{\partial p_j} = g_j \frac{\partial B}{\partial K}(K) - B(g_j) - \lambda = 0, \qquad \text{for } g_j > -X,$$

$$\frac{\partial H}{\partial p_k} = (g_k - a)\frac{\partial B}{\partial K}(K) - B(g_k) - \mu = 0, \qquad \text{for } g_k \leqslant -X.$$

These relations must remain valid for $K = 0$. Thus from (21) we deduce

(22)
$$B(g_j) = \alpha g_j + \beta, \qquad \text{for } g_j > -X,$$
$$B(g_k) = \alpha(g_k - a) + \gamma, \qquad \text{for } g_k \leqslant -X.$$

α, β, γ being constants.

Finally we see that the expression for the neo-Bernoullian index, *up to a linear transformation*, is[138]

(23)
$$B(g) = g, \qquad \text{for } g > -X,$$
$$B(g) = g - a, \qquad \text{for } g \leqslant -X.$$

THE TRADE-OFF BETWEEN MATHEMATICAL EXPECTATION OF PSYCHOLOGICAL VALUES AND PROBABILITY OF RUIN, AND THE NEO-BERNOULLIAN FORMULATION

88. In a similar way it is easy to see that *in general* the trade-off between *the mathematical expectation of psychological values* and the probability of ruin, is incompatible with the neo-Bernoullian formulation.

Consider for example the random prospects $(g_1, g_2, \ldots, g_n, p_1, p_2, \ldots, p_n)$ such that a loss in excess of the threshold figure X corresponds to gain g_n only. Then by hypothesis,

(24) $S = f\left[\sum p_i \gamma(g_i), p_n\right],$

where the $\gamma(g_i)$ represent psychological values.

To portray this psychological pattern by the neo-Bernoullian for-mulation would require the existence of a function $B(g)$ such that

$$(25) \qquad \sum p_i B(g_i) = F\left[\sum p_i \gamma(g_i), p_n\right],$$

whatever the values of the $g_1, g_2, \ldots, g_n, p_1, p_2, \ldots, p_n,$ *linked by the relation*

$$(26) \qquad p_1 + p_2 + \cdots + p_n = 1.$$

It can easily be seen that no function F depending on the prob-ability p_n can satisfy this condition. Differentiating with respect to $p_1, p_2, \ldots, p_n,$ equating $p_1, p_2, \ldots, p_{n-1}$ to zero and particularising some gains, we easily see[139] that we should have

$$(27) \qquad B(g_i) = \lambda \gamma(g_i) + \mu,$$

in which λ and μ are two constants. Thus putting

$$(28) \qquad h = \sum p_i \gamma(g_i),$$

we should have according to (25), (27) and (28)

$$(29) \qquad \lambda h + \mu = F(h, p_n),$$

from which it follows that F *cannot depend on* p_n.
Thus according to (24) we should have

$$(30) \qquad S = f\left[\sum p_i \gamma(g_i)\right].$$

It may be noted that this conclusion is not in contradiction with that arrived at in the preceding §87. According to relation (30) the index S depends only on $\sum p_i \gamma(g_i)$. But according to relation (8) the index S depends only on $M - aP$ so that it does indeed depend on P when *monetary and not psychological values* are considered.[140]

APPENDIX V: INDEX OF CARDINAL UTILITY AND THE NEO-BERNOULLIAN INDEX (§69)[141]

89. In §69 we applied the following theorem:
If there exist an index $\bar{s}(g)$ *of psychological value and a neo-Bernoullian index* $B(g)$ *and if the condition*

(1) $\Delta g_i = \Delta g_i^m$,

for every gain g_i, involves the condition

(2) $\Delta V = \Delta V^m$,

the index m corresponding to threshold values, then

(3) $B(g) \equiv \bar{s}(g)$,

up to a linear transformation.

Proof
90. Since equivalent psychological increments are equal to the same multiple of minimum perceptible thresholds, the property indicated signifies that if all the increases Δg_i of the g_i correspond to equivalent increments, the corresponding increase ΔV in V will also correspond to the common value of these increments.

In other words, if, e being an arbitrary constant, we have

(4) $\bar{s}(g_i + \Delta g_i) - \bar{s}(g_i) = e$

for all i, then

(5) $\bar{s}(V + \Delta V) - \bar{s}(V) = e.$

Now, we have according to the neo-Bernoullian formulation

(6) $B(V) = \sum_i p_i B(g_i)$,

(7) $B(V + \Delta V) = \sum_i p_i B(g_i + \Delta g_i).$

Writing

(8) $\gamma = \bar{s}(g),\qquad \omega = \bar{s}(V),$

then

(9) $B(g) = \beta(\gamma),\qquad B(V) = \beta(\omega),$

where β is an increasing function. It follows from the above that the function β should be such that the two relations

(10) $\beta(\omega) = \sum p_i \beta(\gamma_i)$,

(11) $\sum p_i = 1,$

entail the relation

(12) $\beta(\omega + e) = \sum p_i\beta(\gamma_i + e),$

for any e.

91. It is easy to see that the three equations (10), (11) and (12) require either that

(13) $\beta = \lambda\gamma + \mu,$ i.e. $B(g) = \lambda\bar{s}(g) + \mu,$

or

(14) $\beta = \lambda a^\gamma + \mu,$ i.e. $B(g) = \lambda a^{\bar{s}(g)} + \mu,$

λ and μ being constant.

Condition (14) is psychologically unacceptable, as incapable of portraying the obviously possible situations in which

(15) $\bar{s}(V) = \sum p_i\bar{s}(g_i).$

Thus only condition (13) remains and the neo-Bernoullian index is indeed identical to cardinal utility up to a linear transformation.

It should be stressed that even were relation (14) retained, such a restrictive linkage of the indicator $B(x)$ to cardinal utility $\bar{s}(x)$ could not possibly allow in the most general case for the probability distribution of the psychological values, which depends on an infinite number of parameters.[142]

NOTES

* This memoir is the direct English translation of the 1952 French text, except for a few changes of presentation and notation *which are indicated in brackets.*

In addition the proof of relations (23) of Appendix IV, not given in the original French version is given here in §87.

[1] Joseph A. Schumpeter, *Theorie der Wirtschaftlichen Entwicklung*, Chapter II, Section III; French translation, *Théorie du développement économique*, Dalloz, 1935, p.346.

[2] *Pensées*, Garnier, 1925, pp.65–66.
French text: "Dans l'esprit de finesse, les principes sont dans l'usage commun et devant les yeux de tout le monde . . . , il n'est question que d'avoir bonne vue, mais il faut l'avoir bonne . . . , car l'omission d'un seul principe mène à l'erreur . . .

Tous les géomètres seraient donc fins s'ils avaient la vue bonne, car ils ne raisonnent pas faux sur les principes qu'ils connaissent.

Ce qui fait que des géomètres ne sont pas fins, c'est qu'ils ne voient pas ce qui est devant eux, et qu'étant accoutumés aux principes nets et grossiers de la géométrie, et à ne raisonner qu'après avoir bien vu et manié leurs principes, ils se perdent dans les choses de finesse, où les principes ne se laissent pas ainsi manier. On les voit à peine, on les sent plutôt qu'on ne les voit; on a des peines infinies à les faire toucher à ceux qui ne les sentent pas d'eux-mêmes: ce sont choses tellement délicates qu'il faut un sens bien net pour les sentir, et juger droit et juste selon ce sentiment . . . Il faut d'un coup voir la chose d'un seul regard, et non pas par progrès de raisonnement, du moins jusqu'à un certain degré".

[3] *La Valeur de la Science* (*The Value of Science*). Flammarion, 1927, pp.27–29.

[4] The present study is an extract from a more general analysis *Foundations of the Economic Theory of Risk*, to be published shortly. An early draft was submitted to the European Econometric Congress at Louvain in September 1951 under the title: *Theoretical Notes on Risk and Future Uncertainty.*

The following pages contain a further extension of the approach originally presented and defended by the author in the International Colloquium on Risk sponsored and organised by the French National Center for Scientific Research in Paris in May 1952. Eminent proponents of the Bernoulli formulation, including de Finetti, Friedman, Marschak, Samuelson and Savage participated in this Colloquium. *The impassioned and fascinating debate that extended into several sessions demonstrates the need for total clarity in an area involving extreme difficulties.* Hence the length of the examination that follows: we felt indispensable to consider all the relevant aspects of the questions studied. In a sense, furthermore, there was no choice, given the many lines along which counter-arguments were put forward by the participants.

The author first learnt of the conclusions reached in the recent American literature a few years ago, in 1947. His view has remained very firm since: *it is that these conclusions are wrong.* But he has encountered such tenacious resistance in attempting to convince others of this (such is the authority of received ideas in this mortal world!)

131

that it seemed to him essential to develop the argument on the terrain chosen by his adversaries if there was to be any chance of success. In retrospect, this has been to some extent a waste of time for him: little or nothing emerged which he had not already perceived at the outset.

This is the first time in the author's scientific career that he has entered into a controversy with such total engagement, and the only reason for doing so is his great esteem for the intellectual qualities of his opponents, and his firm conviction that they can be led to revise their position. When all is said and done, the field is that of the psychology of games, and this particular game is worth at least as much as the others.

[The volume of the 1952 Paris Colloquium published in 1952 by the National Center of Scientific Research presents the records of the very enlightening discussions which took place. Unfortunately it was published under the very unattractive title *Econometrie*. Even more unfortunately it is not available in English.]

[5] Special thanks are due to MM. Capoulade, de Finetti, Mathieu, Lavaill, Lesourne, Massé, Mercier and Morlat for their many excellent comments and suggestions.

[6] Some theories of the psychology of risk are so swathed in a garment of mathematics that they escape critical appraisal by many otherwise qualified persons.

Even those in a position to understand them fully may have to devote so much attention at a purely mathematical level to unravelling their deduction that their attention may be diverted from an efficient discussion of the basic axioms, which is much more important. However, this latter effort is the only one that is worthwhile from the point of view that concerns us here. The deployment of mathematical techniques is and should remain completely *secondary*.

[7] See Allais, 1952, *Traité d'Economie Pure* (*Treatise on Pure Economics*), Introduction to the second edition, Nos. 31 to 40.

NOTES TO CHAPTER I: THE FOUNDATIONS OF A POSITIVE THEORY OF CHOICE INVOLVING RISK (Notes 7'-60)

1. *Fields of Choice Involving Risk* (Notes 7'-24)

[7'] [In French: 'perspective aléatoire'].

[8'] The present value of a sum x to be received n years hence is $x/(1 + I)^n$ where I is the annual rate of interest.

[9] C may be considered as the present value of his current and future income.

[9'] [In French: '*fonctionnelle*'. A *functional* is a function which depends on a given function.]

[10] The concept of absolute preference is due to MM. Massé and Morlat (see their paper on risk, read at the Paris International Colloquium in 1952).

[11] This presentation is the presentation used by M. Savage.

[11'] [In French: "équivalence d'une suite de choix aléatoires avec un choix aléatoire unique".] Some writers use the terms 'random outcome' as well as 'uncertain prospect', but this is a matter of variety of expression.

[12] The notation

$$\begin{array}{cc} 1/2 & \$100 \\ 1/2 & 0 \end{array}$$

indicates an even chance of winning $100 or nothing.

[13] As will be seen, this procedure avoids certain difficulties arising from the *repetition* of a given choice among random prospects. See, in particular, §48 below (pp.70–73).

[14] *Valeur Pratique et Philosophique des Probabilités* (*The Philosophy and Practical Value of Probabilities*), §39, p.73, and §48, pp.84–86.

[15] It may be noted in passing that the equality and addition of subjective probabilities can be defined directly. If a person is willing to wager the same sum on two mutually exclusive events, he clearly assigns the same probability to each, and the sum of the two probabilities can be defined as the probability that one or the other event will actually occur.

[15'] [French text: 'satisfaction absolue'.]

[16] See Allais, 1943, *A la Recherche d'une Discipline Economique* (indicated as A.R.D.E. below), pp.156–177 and Introduction to the second edition, 1952, No. 12. See also Lange, 1934, *The Determinateness of the Utility Function*, pp.218–225, and, Armstrong, 1939, *The Determinateness of the Utility Function*, pp.453–457.

[17] It is worth recalling that the problem of determining cardinal utility is identical to the problem of determining the marginal utility of money.

[18] A similar conclusion may be reached for the case of perfect foresight. Notwithstanding the view expressed by many authors, in the case of risk-free choice there is no way in which the choices actually made by an individual can be used to develop an indicator of his scale of cardinal utility (see Allais, 1943, *A la Recherche d'une Discipline Economique*, p.158, Note 51).

[19] This question is returned to below. See especially §41.

[20] It is fruitless to pursue a line of reasoning unless one is absolutely clear what one is talking about.

[21] [This paragraph was Note 21 of the French text of 1952.]

[22] Such as the theory of choice (see Allais, 1943, A.R.D.E., especially pp.373–375), or the theory of risk.

[23] It should be underscored at this point that the only purpose of using the concept of cardinal utility in the discussion below is to ensure that the author's standpoint is clearly understood. As the reader will see in Part II, the theses of the American School can be completely refuted without introducing this concept at all (pp.74–106).

[24] A lapse of which the author himself was guilty during the first six years of his teaching career (1943–1949).

2. *Psychological Factors of Choices Involving Risk* (Notes 24'–46)

[24'] [In French: '*éléments.*]

[25] In the analysis which follows, fundamental factors will be designated using Roman numerals, secondary ones by Arab numerals.

[26] This distinction was suggested to the author by de Finetti.

[27] It is worth noting that the criterion of absolute preference is independent of the

distortion of monetary values. In Figure 2 of §3, two curves which do not intersect are necessarily associated with two distorted curves which likewise do not intersect.

[28] Massé expresses a very similar point of view in : *Reserves and the Management of the Future*, Vol. II, p.16.

[29] See §6.

[30] Taking the owned capital (1 million) as origin (see §2).

[31] This is referred to in the English literature as the *pleasure of gambling*. It should be carefully distinguished from the *pleasure of playing*, which should be considered as a secondary factor only (see §27 below).

[32] [This paragraph was Note 32 of the French text of 1952.]

[33] See also the suggestive example discussed in Appendix I [which was originally Note 33 of the 1952 original French text, but was too long to be positioned here].

[34] This also explains why observed values of random prospects *cannot* be used to determine cardinal utility. Factors AI and AIV are actually *indissociable* (see the discussion in §9 above).

[35] Massé has drawn the writer's attention in correspondence to "the gap between expectation and achievement, which procures a feeling of disappointment or windfall pleasure unknown in a world of perfect foresight".

[36] These observations are by de Finetti who has drawn the author's attention to this point.

[37] Marschak has drawn attention to this factor.

[38] Edn. Garnier, Paris 1925, pp.107–108.

[39] See §10.

[40] Moreover, this is possible in an infinite number of ways.

[41] In fact all that may be said is that Factor AIV corresponding to dispersion (i.e. pleasure of or aversion to risk) has no influence.

[42] As Massé has pertinently observed, absolute preference in the field of random choice is absolutely parallel to the preference, for certainly available goods, of point M to point M_0 (Figure N1) when

(1) $A > A_0, \qquad B > B_0.$

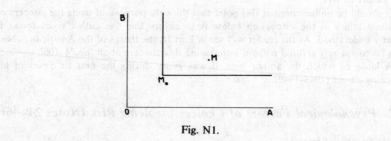

Fig. N1.

This preference is utterly insufficient to determine the shape of the indifference curves

(2) $S = S(A, B).$

[42'] Consider the relations IV, for example. *If we have* $g_i < g_j$ the axiom of absolute preference implies that $\bar{s}$ rises if a decrease in p_i is accompanied by an equal increase in p_j. It should therefore be true that

$$\frac{\partial \bar{s}}{\partial p_j} - \frac{\partial \bar{s}}{\partial p_i} > 0, \qquad \text{for } g_i < g_j.$$

These conditions are analogous to the conditions

$$S'_A > 0, \qquad S'_B > 0,$$

in the case of certainly available goods, where the index of preference is

$$S = S(A, B).$$

[43] By Milton Friedman, at a seminar held by the author, Paris, December 15th, 1950.
[44] See §50 below (pp.75–77).
[44'] See Allais, 1953, L'Extension des Théories de l'Equilibre Economique Général et du Rendement Social au Cas du Risque (Extension of the Theories of General Economic Equilibrium and Efficiency to the Case of Risk).
[45] Relations (1) and (2) of §44.
[46] Relations (3) and (4) of §44.

3. The Pure Psychology of Risk and Rationality (Notes 47–60)

[47] In point of fact, some authors do not seem to have got beyond the third. There are even a few who refuse to go beyond the third.
[47'] [In French: 'espérances morales'.]
[48] In our opinion the same can no doubt be said of Marschak (Rational Behaviour, Uncertain Prospects and Measurable Utility, 1950) despite his claim that his indicator $B(g)$ also takes account of the dispersion of psychological values.
[49] Savage seems to find his place in this stage, although he, like Marschak, claims that his indicator allows for the dispersion of psychological values.
[50] §3 above.
[51] Although again, there are cases in which a cautious, rational subject could well prefer dispersion to mathematical expectation.
[52] This is a real truism, but in an epoch in which totalitarian tendencies are rife, no language is too strong to denounce the propensity of many of our contemporaries for branding as irrational any behaviour that is not to their taste. In Calvin's day, it was considered irrational to play cards, and this activity was therefore forbidden in Geneva.
[53] Formulations III to V of §41 (pp.63–64).
[54] The best analysis, to the author's knowledge, is that of Paul Lévy, 1925, Calcul des probabilités, pp.111–133.
[55] If it were to become negligible, there would no longer be any problem.
[56] It would be enough to consider cases in which σ_1 is very small and σ_2 very large (see Appendix II) (pp.110–111).
[57] See Appendix II (this note of the French text is too long to be placed here) (p.110).
[58] It must nevertheless be noted that the mathematical expectation formulation is, in general, justified in the sense that it is generally advantageous to participate for an infinite period in a game whose mathematical expectation is positive, and disadvantageous if it is not.

This does not contradict the hypothesis discussed above, namely, that if two games have positive mathematical expectations, the more advantageous of the two may still be that with the lower expectation (see Appendix II below) (pp.110–111).

[58'] §16 above.

[59] §4 above (pp.41–42).

[60] This error is especially well demonstrated by the behaviour of a businessman or a gambler who balances the mathematical expectation of the outcome against the probability of ruin (see §65 and Appendix II below). *In this case, the rule of mathematical expectation is, in general, a poor guide, even as a first approximation* (pp.92–95).

NOTES TO CHAPTER II: CRITICISM OF THE NEO-BERNOULLIAN FORMULATION AS A BEHAVIOURAL RULE FOR RATIONAL MAN
(Notes 60'–132)

1. *The State of the Discussion* (Notes 60'–72)

[60'] Von Neumann and Morgenstern, 1947, *Theory of Games and Economic Behavior*, pp.8–31 and 617–632.

[61] Subject, of course, to a linear transformation, a point which must be underlined once for all.

[62] This is the position taken by Friedman and Savage in their 1948 paper 'The Utility Analysis of Choices Involving Risk', and by Frederick Mosteller and Philip Nogee in their 1951 paper 'Experimental Measurement of Utility'.

[62'] Marschak, 1950 and 1951.

[63] It should be noted that the von Neumann–Morgenstern analysis *nowhere* makes any mention of a rationality condition, at least explicitly.

[64] Milton Friedman initially argued that the two indexes B and $\bar{s}$ were identical subject only to a linear transformation, a point of view similar to that of von Neumann–Morgenstern. He subsequently felt constrained to adopt this fallback position.

[64'] Who participated in the 1952 Colloquium in Paris, i.e. de Finetti, Friedman, Marschak, Samuelson and Savage.

[65] In their 1948 article, 'The Utility Analysis of Choices Involving Risk', Friedman and Savage interpreted the Bernoulli formula as relating to cardinal utility. They no longer argue this, and speak only of a choice-generating index. However, in a number of papers, Friedman still seems to be identifying the two concepts.

[65'] Among the participants in the 1952 Colloquium (see Note 64' above).

[66] [This paragraph was Note 66 of the original French text.]

[66'] In particular Baumol, de Finetti, Friedman, Marschak, von Neumann–Morgenstern, Samuelson and Savage. It should be noted that Samuelson, whose point of view was similar to the present author's as recently as two years ago (i.e., 1950) has now gone over to the other camp.

[66"] See §24(2) above (p.56).

[67] Possibly subject to a linear transformation it is recalled once again (See §69(b) and Note 110 below).

[68] §47 above (pp.69–70).
[68'] Savage, 1952.
[68"] Samuelson, 1952.
[69] See §63 below for a detailed criticism of Savage's fifth axiom (pp.88–90).
[70] See §§64 and 71 below (pp.90–92, 99–103).
[71] It may be noted in passing that no objection to the proposed definition was raised in the discussion of the present paper during the 1952 Paris Colloquium.
[72] The end of §53 was Note 72 of the original French text.

2. Refutation of the neo-Bernoullian Formulation (Notes 73–103)

[73] §§4 and 48 above (pp.41–42, 70–73).
[74] This same frame is admitted by the American School.
[75] This demonstration is due to MM. Massé and Morlat.
[76] See the works of the American School, especially the investigations of Marschak (1950 and 1951), Samuelson (1952) and Savage (1953 and 1954).
[77] This property, taken as an axiom by the American School, is merely a variant of the substitutability axiom which considers two equivalent prospects (P_1) and (P_2) as substitutable in a compound prospect, implying

$$\alpha(P_1) + (1 - \alpha)(P_3) = \alpha(P_2) + (1 - \alpha)(P_3),$$

where (P_3) is any prospect whatsoever.
[78] See §3 above (pp.39–41).
[78'] §52 above (pp.78–79).
[79] A very important point in the context of the present discussion is that we have not defined rationality by referring to the axiom of absolute preference. To have done so would have been to fall into the same trap as the American School.

The axiom of absolute preference (so-called in order to align our terminology on that of Massé and Morlat) is merely a *consequence* of the mutual consistency that ought to characterise the ends pursued by a rational individual.
[80] To see this, it is enough to verify, as was done above (§55), that the axiom of absolute preference is much less restrictive than any of the systems of axioms that imply the neo-Bernoullian formulation.
[81] It should be stressed at this point that there seem no particularly good grounds for considering an individual's psychology as irrational if his preference index is given by relation (1) subject to the conditions (2) of §57.
[82] For this purpose, it is enough to assume that the functional (§10 above) $S = h[\varphi(g)]$ of the subject reduces to expressions (1) of §58 when the density $\varphi(g)$ is distributed according to the normal law.
[83] See Appendix III, §82. §82 of Appendix III was Note 83 of the original 1952 French text (p.112).
[84] See Appendix III, §83 (§83 was Note 84 of the original 1952 French text).
[85] See Appendix III, §84 (same observation as for Note 84) (pp.114–115).
[86] It is again hard to see how an individual whose behaviour when choosing among various Gaussian i.e. normal distributions is represented by relation (1) of §58, the distribution being normal, could be considered as irrational.

138   MAURICE ALLAIS

[86'] If X is the player's fortune, P represents the probability of his ruin.

[87] [The last paragraph is Note 87 of the original French text of 1952.]

[88] See Appendix IV, §86 below (Appendix IV, §§86 and 87 correspond to Note 88 of the original French text of 1952) (pp.124–127).

[89] See Appendix IV, §88 below (Appendix IV, §88 corresponds to the Note 89 of the 1952 French text) (pp.127–128).

[90] *The Utility Analysis of Choices involving Risk*, 1948.

[91] Although even here, the shape of the index $B(g)$ should be assumed to be complicated enough.

[91'] §69 below (pp.97–98).

[92] See what we have already said on this point in §4 and §48 above (pp.41–42, 70–73).

[93] Savage has objected that marked curvature of the index could serve to explain such behaviour. A priori, this explanation is not very convincing (although it is of course theoretically possible). *In practice, it is invalidated by the fact that the index determined by the analysis of other random prospects is necessarily only slightly curved for small sums.* This is a decisive proof that, in general, no index exists which is capable of explaining choices involving risk by the neo-Bernoullian formulation.

The sample taken subsequently in 1952 provided *decisive confirmation of the views expressed above* (see Note 94 below).

[93'] Savage, 1952, *An Axiomatisation of Reasonable Behavior in the Face of Uncertainty*.

[94] After the May 1952 symposium, a sample was run using many similar examples (See Allais, 1953, 'La psychologie de l'homme rationnel devant le risque').

The results will be published as soon as possible. The subjects were all people who are generally considered as eminently rational, and all in all, the results provided very strong support of the author's views. All the tests used were based on the fundamental idea that the psychological value of a gain with which a given probability is associated is not independent of the gains attaching to the other probabilities, although according to the neo-Bernoullian formulation, it should be.

[94'] [All the examples which follow were given in French francs at 1952 prices. 100 French francs in 1952 were worth about the same as 10 dollars in 1975.]

[95] A parallel with certainly available goods shows this particularly well. Suppose I am appraising three pieces of furniture (M_1), (M_2) and (M_3), and prefer (M_2) to (M_1), then

(1) $(M_1) < (M_2)$.

It does not follow that

(2) $(M_1) + (M_3) < (M_2) + (M_3)$,

for (M_3) may be *complementary* to (M_1), but not to (M_2), which can upset the preference ordering. Condition (1) can entail (2) *only if the items considered are independent*.

The consequence of the independence hypothesis for certainly available goods is the relation

(3) $\bar{S}(A, B, \ldots, C) = \varphi_A(A) + \varphi_B(B) + \cdots + \varphi_C(C)$

in which $\bar{S}$ is cardinal utility, or the relation

(4) $S(A, B, \ldots, C) = F[\varphi_A(A) + \varphi_B(B) + \cdots + \varphi_C(C)]$

in which S is ordinal utility and F any increasing function, which shows how utterly close is the connection between this independence hypothesis and the neo-Bernoullian formulation.

[95'] See Note 86' above.

[96] As for the player considered in Appendix II below, who must balance his probable winnings after n plays against the corresponding probability of ruin.

[97] §59 above (pp.84–86).

[98] [These two paragraphs are Notes 98 and 99 of the original French text of 1952.]

[99] In this regard, see also the very interesting remarks by Massé and Morlat on the behaviour of the insurers described in Dubourdieu's mathematical theory of insurance (Massé et Morlat, 1952, 'Sur le Classement Economique des Perspectives Aléatoires').

[100] It is of interest to note that if the behavioural rule was such that any random prospect is eliminated if its probability P of a loss more than X exceeds a threshold of ε, while the principle of selection among the remaining random prospects is to maximise the probable value of the psychological gain, this would be compatible with the neo-Bernoullian formulation, by taking $\bar{s}(g)$ as equal to $-\infty$ for all gains below $-X$.

However, observed behaviour indicates that there is some dependence between this probable value and the probability of ruin P. Where this is so, the neo-Bernoullian formulation is of course not verified.

[101] Borel considers that a probability of 10^{-6} is considered as negligible by human agents (*Le jeu, la chance, et les théories scientifiques modernes*, 1941, p.108).

[102] From condition (a), if the neo-Bernoullian formulation is valid, then, for the individual considered, we have

$$(1) \qquad S = f(M - aP),$$

S being the ordinal index of preference.

To say that he will play if the game offers a probability $(1 - p_0)$ of winning n_0 million and a probability p_0 of being ruined, i.e. of losing his fortune F, is to say that

$$(2) \qquad 0 < (1 - p_0)n_0 - p_0 F - ap_0,$$

with the notation of §§3 and 55 above and taking (1) into account.

To say that he will abstain from participating in another game, whatever the potential winnings n_1, if his probability of ruin is $(1 - q_1)$ is to say that according to (1)

$$(3) \qquad 0 > q_1 n_1 - (1 - q_1)F - a(1 - q_1),$$

for any value of n_1.

From (2) and (3) we deduce

$$(4) \qquad \frac{q_1}{1 - q_1} n_1 - F < a < \frac{1 - p_0}{p_0} n_0 - F,$$

whence

$$(5) \qquad n_1 < \frac{1 - p_0}{p_0} \frac{1 - q_1}{q_1} n_0.$$

This condition is independent of F and cannot be satisfied whatever the value of n_1.

In the example given in the text ($p_0 = q_1 = 10^{-6}$, $n_0 = 10^8$), the inequality (5), implied by the neo-Bernoullian formulation for the considered subject, is equivalent for practical purposes to the inequality.

$$n_1 < 10^{20}.$$

To upset it, the value of n_1, must of course be taken fabulously high, *but there is no reason for not doing so*, since the subject considered is assumed to maintain his choice (*c*) *whatever the value of* n_1.

Clearly there is a close connection between this example and the statement above regarding the impossibility of conceiving of indifference curves which intersect the vertical $q = 1$ other than at infinity.

[The 1952 analysis of the example was partially erroneous. It has been corrected in 1977.]

[103] §59 above *in fine*.

3. *Critical Analysis of Some Aspects of the Theories of the American School* (Notes 103′–132)

[103′] See especially de Finetti, Colloquium volume, C.N.R.S., 1953, pp.159–162 and 196–197.

[104] §10 above (p.45).

[105] §55 above (pp.80–82).

[106] Since it remains the same when the form changes. This is therefore *a sheer mathematical impossibility*.

[107] §50 above (pp.75–77).

[108] Subject of course to a possible linear transformation.

[109] It is essential to note that this equality results fundamentally from the assumption that the psychological value of the gain g_i having probability p_i is *independent* of the gains attaching to other probabilities.

It is evident that, the psychological value of a set of complementary uncertain gains exceeds the sum of their psychological values when they are considered separately. Thus in the case of complementarity the increase ΔV of V is greater than ΔV^m when all the Δg_i are equal to the minimum perceptible threshold Δg_i^m.

[110] See Appendix V below. [This Appendix was Note 110 of the original French text.]

[111] From the standpoint (not the author's) of those who justify the rule of mathematical expectation by the law of large numbers and admitting the existence of cardinal utility, the rule to be adopted should be clearly

$$(1) \qquad \bar{s}(V) = \sum p_i \bar{s}(g_i).$$

It would necessarily follow that, subject to a possible linear transformation, psychological value $\bar{s}(g_i)$ would be identical to the neo-Bernoullian index. *This would be a third argument in favour of the identity*

$$(2) \qquad B(g) \equiv \bar{s}(g).$$

[112] See Allais, 1943, A.R.D.E., pp.143–144, especially Note 17.

[113] It will be recalled that for an individual whose psychology is portrayed by the indifference surfaces

(1) $S = S(A, B, \ldots, C)$,

the two goods (A) and (B) are referred to as independent if there exists a transformation $\varphi(S)$ such that

(2) $\partial^2 \varphi / \partial A \, \partial B = 0$.   (See Note 95, p.138 above.)

[114] Von Neumann and Morgenstern do not seem to have perceived this clearly, at least if one is to judge by the following passages, whose meaning, it must be admitted, is somewhat obscure, no definition of complementarity being given anywhere in their text:

> By a combination of two events we mean this: let the two events be denoted by B and C and use, for the sake of simplicity, the probability 50% – 50%. Then the 'combination' is the prospect of seeing B occur with a probability of 50%, and (if B does not occur) C with the (remaining) probability of 50%. We stress that the two alternatives are mutually exclusive, so that no possibility of complementarity and the like exists (pp.17 and 18).

> Simply additive formulae, like $(3 : 1 : b)$ (the third axiom) would seem to indicate that we are assuming absence of any form of complementarity between the things the utilities of which we are combining. It is important to realise that we are doing this solely in a situation where there can indeed be no complementarity. As pointed out in the first part of 3.3.2., our u, v are the utilities not of definite – and possibly coexistent – goods or services, but of imagined events. The u, v, of $(3 : 1 : b)$ in particular refer to alternatively conceived events u, v of which only one can and will become real. I.e. $(3 : 1 : b)$ deals with either having u (with the probability α) or v (with the remaining probability $(1 - \alpha)$), but since the two are in no case conceived as taking place together, they can never complement each other in the ordinary sense (p.628. This passage was added in the second edition).

[115] *Basically, this axiom is only a variant of von Neumann–Morgenstern's axioms 3Ba and 3Bb and Marschak's fourth postulate.* Marschak's fourth postulate can be deduced from Samuelson's postulate by writing $(P_3) \equiv (P_1)$.
[Although in my 1951 Louvain study I presented axioms 3Ba and 3Bb as the key axioms, the reference to the axioms 3Ba and 3Bb was unfortunately replaced by inadvertance by a reference to axiom 3Cb in Note 115 of the original 1952 French text. The present text has been corrected. Note added in 1977.]
[116] §64 above (pp.90–92).
[117] Samuelson, 1952, *Utility, Preference and Probability*.
[118] Of all the axioms of the American School, it is by far the most attractive.
[118'] Marschak, 1952.
[118"] §63 above (pp.88–90).

[119] §65 above (pp.92–95).

[120] In other words, when two equivalent random prospects are combined, a new shape of distribution is introduced, and the advantage (or drawback) thus created destroys the equivalence of the new prospect to the two original prospects.

[121] It should further be stressed that in some cases, successive combinations may yield very substantial changes in shape of the probability distributions, whose psychological impact could become very strong.

[122] At any event, it should be noted that Samuelson's reasoning surreptitiously reintroduces the case of *successive* drawings, whereas it is clear that the only way to approach the problem is to consider a *single* choice among random prospects (See what we have already said in §4 and §48) (pp.41–42, 70–73).

Samuelson's treatment of a single drawing on the same footing as two successive drawings seems furthermore potentially to contain the law of large numbers, whose consequence is the neo-Bernoullian formulation (which applies in this case alone, for the ratio $\sqrt{n}\sigma/nm = \sigma/m\sqrt{n}$ of the standard deviation to the average gain tends to zero with the number n of successive gains and the influence of dispersion disappears). The consequence of this treatment is that a single drawing is assimilated to an infinite number of successive drawings.

[123] It is not useless to examine the parallel with certainly available goods. Writing the indifference surfaces as

(1) $S = S(A, B, \ldots, C)$,

Samuelson's axiom is equivalent to saying that, having consumed a quantity A_0 of A, two combinations (A_1, B_1) and (A_2, B_2) which were equivalent *before* A_0 was consumed remain equivalent *afterwards*. It might be objected that in the case of risk, no consumption of a material good occurs during the first drawing $[\alpha, (1 - \alpha)]$, but this would be a misunderstanding of the nature of the problem. Material consumption is not at issue here; what is being considered is "consumption of risk", and in the case under examination, the first drawing cannot be considered as a neutral operation. *This would only be possible if the substitutability axiom held, but the whole point is precisely that the axiom itself has to be justified, so that the argument is in a vicious circle and begs the question.*

[123'] See §64 above (pp.90–92).

[124] Those, at least, for whom there is a marked psychological difference between 500 million and 100 million. For those who consider that there is no clear distinction between 100 and 500 million, the rational attitude would of course be to prefer (P'_1) to (P'_2). For this latter group, it is always possible to repeat the test using 50 million and 10 million, and if that is still not enough, 5 million and 1 million. There is always a region such that in general, Samuelson's substitutability axiom is defective when applied to highly prudent individuals.

It should be underlined in passing that if our test is to invalidate the neo-Bernoullian formulation, the lowest figure A (here $A = 100$ million) must be high enough for the subject to give great weight to certainty, and the highest figure B (here $B = 500$ million) must be sufficiently in excess of A for the subject to make a clear psychological distinction between the two figures. (The same remark applies to the example in §63.)

This is an important observation, for it shows that there is a clear possibility that many of those undergoing our tests would reply consistently with the neo-Bernoullian formulation. It follows that although replies incompatible with the neo-Bernoullian principle invalidate the views of the neo-Bernoullian school, replies that are in line with it do not invalidate at all the theory presented here.

[125] Especially §21 above (pp.53–54).

[126] §11 above (pp.45–46).

[127] It may be noted in passing that the index derived from the Mosteller–Nogee experiments may perfectly well be something other than cardinal utility for *if the psychological experimentation is limited to a certain region*, a single index may portray the combined effect of the curvature of cardinal utility and the dispersion of psychological values. If so this index will be unusable for purposes of describing choices in tests involving a marked complementarity effect.

[128] For instance Friedman, Marschak, von Neumann–Morgenstern, Samuelson and Savage.

[129] French 1952 text: '*satisfaction absolue*'.

[130] On the dangers of abusive use of mathematical techniques, see Allais, 1952, *Introduction of the second edition of the Treatise on Pure Economics*, §§31 to 40.

[131] Paul Levy, 1925, *Calcul des Probabilités*, p.118.

[132] Bouasse, Preface to *Résistance des Matériaux*, p.XIX.

NOTES TO APPENDICES (Notes 133–142)

[133] Appendix I was originally Note 33 of the 1952 French text (§21 above) (pp.53–54).

[134] Appendix II was originally Note 57 of the 1952 French text (§48 above) (pp.70–73).

[135] Appendix III was originally Notes 83–85 of the 1952 French text (p.84).

[136] See the Annex to this Appendix (§§85.1–85.5). This Annex was added in 1977 (pp.116–123).

[137] Appendix IV was originally Notes 88 and 89 of the 1952 French text (§59 above) (p.86).

[138] [It seemed useful to give here the proof of relations (23). The original French 1952 version only stated these relations without giving the demonstration of them.]

[139] The demonstration is similar to that given in §87 (pp.125–127).

[140] The circumstance may be made clear by the consideration of relations (23), p.127.

[141] Appendix V was originally Note 110 of the 1952 French text (§69 above) (p.98).

[142] [Relation (14) would give according to (8), (9) and (11) $B(g) = \lambda \exp[\bar{s}(g)] + \mu$. If we had $\bar{s}(g) = \log(U_0 + g)$, U_0 being a constant, we would have $B(g) = \lambda g + \lambda U_0 + \mu$.] (Note added in 1977).

BIBLIOGRAPHY

Allais, M.: (1943). *A la Recherche d'une Discipline Economique.* – Première Partie: L'Economie Pure, Ateliers Industria, Paris, 1943, 2 Vol. 852 p. and Annexes 68 pp. Republished as:
Traité d'Economie Pure (*Treatise on Pure Economics*), Imprimerie Nationale and Centre National de la Recherche Scientifique, 5 Vol., Paris, 1952 (This second edition is identical to the first with the addition only of a new Introduction).

Allais, M.: (1951). 'Notes Theoriques sur l'Incertitude de l'Avenir et le Risque' ('Theoretical Notes on the Uncertainty of the Future and Risk'), Paper submitted to the *European Congress of the Econometric Society* at Louvain, Sept. 1951. Mimeo, 39 pages with three Appendices of 17, 6 and 20 pages. (the first version of this paper was drafted in April 1951).

Allais, M.: (1953a). 'L'Extension des Théories de l'Equilibre Economique' ('Extension of the Theories of General Economic Equilibrium and Social Output to the Case of Risk'), *Econometrica*, Vol. 21, No. 2, April 1953, pp.269–290.
A more complete text has been published in *Econométrie XL, Colloques Internationaux du Centre National de la Recherche Scientifique*, Colloque de Mai 1952, Fondements et Applications de la Théorie du Risque en Econométrie, Collective Volume, Centre National de la Recherche Scientifique, Paris, 1953, pp.81–120.

Allais, M.: (1953b). Le Comportement de l'Homme Rationnel devant le Risque (The Behaviour of Rational Man under Conditions of Risk), *Econometrica*, Vol. 21, No. 4, Oct. 1953, pp.503–546.
A more complete text has been published in the collective volume of the 1952 Colloquium (see Reference 1953a above), pp.257–332. This memoir has been republished in 1955 with very few additions and with an Index by the Imprimerie Nationale.

Allais, M.: (1953c). 'Interventions lors du Colloque International sur le Risque de 1952' ('Statements during the Discussion: International Symposium on Risk, 1952'). Colloques Internationaux du Centre National de la Recherche Scientifique, *Econométrie*, Vol. XL, Paris, 1953, pp.150–163, 194–197 and 245–247.

Allais, M.: (1953d). 'La Psychologie de l'Homme Rationnel devant le Risque: la Théorie et l'Expérience' ('The Psychology of the Rational Man under Conditions of Risk: Theory and Experience'), *Journal de la Société de Statistique de Paris*, Jan. 1953, pp.47–52 and later article. This study reviews the principles and the results of the sample survey on the psychology of risk carried out by the author between June and September 1952.

Bachelier: (1912). *Calcul des Probabilités* (*Probability Calculus*), Gauthier–Villars, 1912.

Baumol, William J.: (1951). The Neumann–Morgenstern Utility Index, An Ordinalist View. *The Journal of Political Economy*, Vol. LIX, Feb. 1951, No. 1, pp.61–66.

Borel: (1939). *Valeur Pratique et Philosophique des Probabilités* (*Probability: Its Philosophy and Practical Value*), Gauthier–Villars, 1939, Paris. See especially the discussion of the St. Petersburg Paradox, pp.60–66 and of the concepts of subjective and objective probabilities, pp.70–77, 84–107 and 134–146.

Centre National de la Recherche Scientifique: (1953). *Fondements et Applications de la Théorie du Risque en Econométrie*, International Colloquium on Risk, Paris, May 1952; Collection des Colloques Internationaux, Vol. XL, Paris, 1953.

Friedman, M., and Savage, J. L.: (1948). 'The Utility Analysis of Choices Involving Risk', *Journal of Political Economy*, August 1948, pp.279–304.

Levy, Paul: (1925). *Calcul des Probabilités (Probability Calculus)*, Gauthier–Villars, Paris 1925. Chapter VI (pp.113–133) of this work 'Criticism of the Theory of Probable Gain' contains an excellent analysis of the theory of moral expectations.

Marschak, J.: (1950). 'Rational Behavior, Uncertain Prospects and Measurable Utility', *Econometrica*, Vol. 18, No. 2, April 1950, pp.111–141.

Marschak, J.: (1951). 'Why "Should" Statisticians and Business Men Maximise Moral Expectation?' *Proceedings of the second Berkeley Symposium on Mathematical Statistics and Probability*, University of California Press, 1951.

Massé, P.: (1946). *Les Réserves et la Régulation de l'Avenir dans la Vie Economique (Reserves and the Regulation of the Future in Economic Life)*, Paris, Herman, 1946. See in particular Vol. II, Chapters V, VI and XII.

Massé, P., and Morlat: (1952). 'Sur le Classement Economique des Perspectives Aléatoires' ('On the Economic Classification of Uncertain Prospects'), Paper submitted to the International Symposium on Risk, May 1952, *Colloques Internationaux*, Vol. XL, Symposia, Centre National de la Recherche Scientifique, Paris 1953, pp.165–199.

Mosteller, Frederick, and Nogee, Philip: (1951). 'An Experimental Measurement of Utility', *The Journal of Political Economy*, October 1951, pp.371–404.

Von Neumann, J., and Morgenstern, O.: (1947). *Theory of Games and Economic Behavior*, 2nd Edition, Princeton University Press, 1947, pp.8–31 and 617–632.

Pascal, Blaise: (1957). *Pensées*, Editions Garnier, Paris, 1925, pp.107–108.

Samuelson, P. A.: (1952), 'Utility, Preference and Probability', Paper submitted to the International Symposium on Risk, Paris, May 1952, Symposia, Centre National de la Recherche Scientifique, *Colloques Internationaux XL, Econométrie*, Paris, 1953, pp.141–150.

Savage, L. J.: (1952). 'An Axiomatization of Reasonable Behavior in the Face of Uncertainty', Paper submitted to the International Symposium on Risk, Paris, May 1952. Symposia, Centre National de la Recherche Scientifique, *Colloques Internationaux XL, Econométrie*, Paris, 1953, pp.29–33.

PART III

THE NEO-BERNOULLIAN POSITION
VERSUS THE 1952 ALLAIS THEORY

YAKOV AMIHUD*

CRITICAL EXAMINATION OF THE
NEW FOUNDATION OF UTILITY

ABSTRACT. The paper examines some of the postulates of the new foundation of utility theory which was developed by Allais and Hagen, and criticizes it on two counts: First, Allais' criticism on the vN–M expected utility theory results from misinterpreting their definition of rationality as descriptive, rather than normative, given acceptance of the underlying axioms; those of the axioms criticized are not necessary to derive the expected utility theorem; and the experiments on which the criticism relies is ill-constructed and inconclusive. Second, the attempted theory does not prove to be an adequate alternative mainly because it lacks predictive power. The moment preference method it suggests does not define strictly which moments should be considered in various statistical distributions, nor how they should be applied as a general decision rule; this sometimes leads to contradictions between decision rules. The attempted theory is not derived systematically from an axiomatic system but rather relies on observations, which are debatable, and develops a framework which explains them *ad hoc*. As such, it does not outperform the prevailing expected utility theory of the American school.

To the list of quotes which open Allais' book, implying that the American school is resisting the progress in science, I would add one more:

The act of judgement that leads scientists to reject a previously accepted theory is always based upon more than a comparison of that theory with the world. The decision to reject one paradigm is always simultaneously the decision to accept another, and the judgement leading to that decision involves the comparison of both paradigms with nature *and* with each other. (Kuhn (1970), p.77.)

I shall try to show that Allais' criticism is not sufficiently convincing to reject the expected utility theory, and that the alternative theory suggested by Allais is far from being able to replace that of von Neumann and Morgenstern.

Much of the criticism of Allais against the von Neumann–Morgenstern expected utility theory is based on examples of choices which may be generally considered as rational but (according to Allais) are labelled as irrational by the expected utility theory which, he believes, proposes that "un homme rationnel doit se conformer a la formulation de Bernoulli" (Allais, 1953, p.518). This is an erroneous interpretation. The theory merely claims that if in a certain situation, given a choice between certain lotteries, an individual agrees that his

149

Maurice Allais and Ole Hagen (eds.), Expected Utility and the Allais Paradox, 149–160.

behavior is in accordance with the von Neumann–Morgenstern axioms – then an inconsistency in choices may be pointed out as irrational. Or, as Morgenstern put it:

Consider an individual who *professes to possess* a utility function as described by the von Neumann–Morgenstern axioms of expected utility. If it is shown to him that in his actual behavior he deviates from that function, the theory being absolutely convincing, will tell him how he should modify his behavior in order to conform to his own chosen preference system. (Morgenstern (1972), p.712, my italics.)

Clearly, any observation of any pattern of choice whatsoever is insufficient by itself to determine rationality (or irrationality). Irrationality is rather a *result* of an action taken by an individual who has agreed to accept this particular definition of rationality.

On the other hand, Allais defines rationality as *either* the criterion of "internal consistency," implying the coherence of desired ends and the use of appropriate means for attaining them; *or*, the observed behavior of "people who can be regarded as acting in a rational way" (p.504). This definition is subjective and may be wrong. Is rationality synonymous with 'normality?' Is it defined statistically? In an experiment cited below, a group of business executives presented with Allais' paradox was split almost evenly in their answers; who, then, is rational and who is not?[2] Moreover, it can be shown that there are rational types of behavior (in Allais' sense) which do not obey his basic axiom of absolute preference.[3] Consider a man who gambles against his good friend and wants to let him win. He is perfectly rational by Allais' definition, yet he intentionally does not choose the lottery which yields the greatest gain for all possible outcomes, thus violating the axiom of absolute preference. Is he rational or is he not?

It follows that the subject of criticism should not be the expected utility proposition – which is a well proven theorem – but its underlying axioms. Yet it is hard to find out which one of those suggested by von Neumann and Morgenstern is considered incorrect by Allais. The much criticized axioms of independence and substitution are not necessary to establish the existence of a measurable utility (in the von Neumann–Morgenstern sense). Even when the substitution axiom is introduced by Herstein and Milnor (1953) – which enables them to drop the much criticized continuity axiom[4] – it is introduced in a very weak form: If $u \sim v$ then for any w, $\frac{1}{2}u + \frac{1}{2}w \sim \frac{1}{2}v + \frac{1}{2}w$.[5] This axiom is not subject to the criticism mounted against he independence axiom, nor is it sensitive to the threshold criticism.[6]

It seems that the deviation of an individual's choices from the pattern suggested by the von Neumann–Morgenstern expected utility theory is contingent upon the form in which a lottery is presented to him. This seems to be in direct violation of the von Neumann–Morgenstern 'algebra of combining' (3:C:b) axiom which states that: $p(ru + (1 - r)v) + (1 - p)v = tu + (1 - t)v$; where $0 < r < 1$, $0 < p < 1$, u and v are entities and $t = pr$. This axiom may look rather like an algebraic identity, but as a behavioral axiom it implies the exclusion of the 'utility of gambling', i.e., it is irrelevant whether a lottery is presented in two stages or in one, provided the (compounded) probabilities of the final outcomes remain the same. A violation may occur when the individual draws a certain pleasure from the particular structure of the lottery. (For example, it may be useless to tell a gambler at Las Vegas that dice offer him better odds than roulette or vice versa.)

But, if no preference for any particular form is admitted – as is the case in Allais' experiment – what accounts for the violation? The reason may be a mistake arising from difficulty in calculations or laziness. If it was not so, the individuals who chose in an inconsistent manner would not have reversed their initial choices after being presented with a detailed breakdown of the lottery, as happened in Markowitz's, Savage's and MacCrimmon's cases.

I would also venture that the so called 'threshold phenomenon' may be caused by careless violation of the above axiom (3:C:b). It is always possible to present one-stage lotteries with almost identical odds as multi-stage lotteries which enable the decision maker to distinguish clearly between them. A businessman whose success may depend on such a lottery should do just that, rather than making a casual choice (as in an experiment).

Now it may be that the set of axioms proposed by von Neumann and Morgenstern is not as general as Allais would like it to be. Yet, a more general formulation of the axioms takes its toll in a poorer predictive power, as is the case with Allais' theory. The determination of the trade-off between the generality of the theory and its precision is made so that it adequately explains those phenomena and problems which are of the greatest importance to the behavioral science practitioners.

I do not think that Allais' paradox can be considered to offer such a problem. It deals with a most unrealistic situation which has a very little relevance to the economics of uncertainty,[7] for which the von Neumann–Morgenstern theory provides so well.

The problem of ill-constructed and poorly controlled psychological experiments which claim to test for one effect but actually test for another is well known. It may be suspected that Allais' experiment which led to the paradox is just of that kind: What does it test for, finess of perception, or consistency (in the von Neumann and Morgenstern sense)? Or, it may be claimed that its first part presents the individual with entirely different situations than the second one, or at least make him perceive so. Then, the individual uses different preferences in each part, and inconsistencies arise.[8] It may be wrong to infer from the individual's choice in one situation to his choice in another, if he himself does not consider the situations as equivalent and if he does not claim to employ the same set of rules in each of them. To make this sharper, I do not think that Allais' penniless traveler who is stuck in Marseille and bets on the lottery with the highest variance will be considered irrational by anyone in the American School. It is expected, however, that if this traveler states some preference (in particular, $U(\alpha P_1 + (1 - \alpha)P_2) < \alpha U(P_1) + (1 - \alpha)U(P_2)$ where $0 < \alpha < 1$ and $P_1 \neq P_2$ are the lottery outcomes) he will choose the lottery that yields the highest expected utility. When he finally arrives in Paris and visits his insurance agent, he may state different preferences (e.g., the inequality above reversed). Then, again, he is expected to choose the insurance policy in a manner which is consistent with his preferences, i.e., yields the highest expected utility.

Formally, this has been known in the American School as the "state preference approach."[9] This theory states that the individual may not possess a unique von Neumann–Morgenstern utility function for money, but his utility is contingent upon the different "states of the world." Moreover, in each state of the world, the von Neumann–Morgenstern utility function (being homogeneous up to a linear transformation) can be expressed such that $U_k(L_k) = 0$, $U_k(M_k) = 1$, where L_k is the maximum loss in state k, and M_k is the maximum gain in that state.[10]

This approach then, 'exempts' the individual from consistency of preferences between states, but requires such a consistency within each state. This may explain the inconsistencies cited by Allais, and it may also account for his famous paradox.

Consider the solution to the paradox suggested by Morrison (1967), which is in accordance with the von Neumann–Morgenstern expected utility theory. His analysis hinges on the distinction between the 'asset position' perceived by the individual in each part of the experiment. In each part he defines the individual's utility function on the interval (L_k, M_k) as above, which is $(-1, 4)$ in the first part and $(0, 5)$ in the second. Then, the individual's choices, as reported by Allais, may be viewed as consistent.

A different formulation of Allais' experiment suggested by Markowitz,[11] proved to give perfectly consistent results. He suggested arranging the lotteries as in Figure 1. It is required that the choice should be made before the draw of the lottery has begun. Then, since the two parts of the experiment are compatible with each other – no inconsistencies arise!

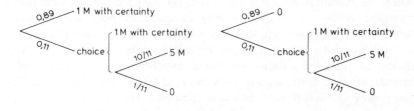

(M = 100 million French francs)

Fig. 1.

The same holds for the reformulation of Allais' experiment by Savage, who ultimately corrected his choice, having recognized his mistake. It is regrettable that Allais does not discuss these reformulations of his famous experiment, nor that he confronts their arguments with his. This has been done by McCrimmon (1968). He presented a group of subjects (business executives) with Savage's version of Allais' question. Over 60% of them chose in conformity with the von Neumann–Morgenstern expected utility theory.[12] Then they were presented with both Allais' and Savage's reasoning why a choice should be made in a certain way. After having reconsidered their choices – some have revised them to be in conformity with the von Neumann–Morgenstern axioms. Some of those whose choices were still conflicting the axioms indicated that they would have generally agreed to them, but that their answers differed in this particular case because of the special nature of the situation.[13] It was also suggested that the reason for answers to be in disagreement with the von Neumann–Morgenstern axioms is laziness or difficulties in computing, which result in mistakes. However, "the results of the experiment is that although the descriptive value may not be as high as one would like it to be, the (von Neumann–Morgenstern expected utility) theory is a very good one as a norm".[14] It is exactly here where the difference between the Allais and von Neumann–Morgenstern theories emerges.

*

When we consider Allais' Foundation on its own merits, one thing emerges: While Allais' theory may describe *ex post* why choices between risky lotteries are made in a certain way, it fails to suggest a method to predict these choices *ex ante*; while it can explain any choice as 'rational', based on some psychological (or any other) consideration, it is exempted from the acid test of proving its predictive power as correct, and thus it is sheltered from any paradox.

The poor construction of Allais' theory is particularly apparent in that its scope is not defined at all. I shall relate to what he calls "l'element specifique de la psychologie du risque" (p.512), namely the variance of the subjectively distorted probability distribution of the psychologically distorted monetary outcomes of a lottery. It is not clear what this proposition is based on. It does not have any theoretical ground, and its empirical support is very weak at best. Researchers in psychology have not been able yet to determine this one way or the other. In a recent carefully constructed study, Slovic and Lichtenstein (1968) wrote:

> The variance of outcomes in a gamble is presumed by many to be an important determinant of the gamble's attractiveness. However, because the variance is confounded with the gamble's probabilities and pay-offs, behaviors that have been interpreted in past studies as indicative of variance preferences are subject to alternative interpretations. The present study reports three experiments in which variance was manipulated without changing the particular probabilities and pay-offs that were explicitly displayed to S (subjects). This manipulation was made possible by the use of a specially constructed 'duplex gamble'. Results indicated that variance is at best a minor determinant of gambling decisions. Variance preferences observed in previous studies appear to be artifacts generated by other decision strategies.

This is definitely not the last word on the subject, and many researchers obtain different results. In a review article, Edwards (1961) states that "variance preferences are necessarily confounded with utility, and skewness preferences with probability, for two alternative bets. So all research on variance preferences so far is ambiguous." (p.481). Luce (1967) expresses the same opinion, and a more recent survey (Lee, 1971) confirms that "at the present time it is difficult to foresee whether the concepts 'variance and skewness preferences' have a useful future within decision theory", since the research results in this field may be adequately explained by using the expected utility (or subjective expected utility) theory (Lee, p.114).[15]

Therefore it may be suspected that what Allais suggested will result in double-counting the effect of the variance of the monetary outcomes of a lottery: once through the distortion of the monetary values, and once through accounting directly for their variance.

Next to be asked is why Allais focuses only on the second moment of the subjectively distorted probability distribution of the psychologically distorted monetary outcomes of a lottery?[16] Hagen (this book, p.272ff.) considers the third moment (again: why?).[17] Then, one may ask whether determining the 'relative preference' in terms of the first two (or three) moments is a convenient approximation of some 'true' preference function, or whether higher moments are just added at will when needed to explain a choice which cannot be explained with lower moments. If the answer is that the second alternative is the correct one, then I do not think that this is much of a theory. At most, it is an experimental hypothesis to which one may add the hypotheses that preference is a function of any other statistic of the distribution of the distorted monetary outcomes, e.g., the mode, the median, other quantile or interquantile range, or any other conceivable statistic.

If the Allais–Hagen models of choice in terms of the first two or three moments are a matter of convenient *approximation* to a complete preference model in terms of *all* the central moments,[18] then it may be shown that Hagen's explanation of his paradox can be also explained by the von Neumann–Morgenstern expected utility theory, where instead of using an exact utility function we use an *approximation*. Hagen suggests a model where a cardinal utility U is defined on the first three moments of a preference function u of monetary gain or loss, where U is an increasing function of the first and third moments of u and a decreasing function of the second. Hagen carries on the analysis of four lotteries whose moments of monetary outcomes are as given in Table 1. Then, in an empirical study, he found that there were more persons who preferred A to B than those who preferred X to Y.*

TABLE 1

Moments	Lotteries			
	A	B	X	Y
1st	$M_{1A} = M_{1B}$		$M_{1X} = M_{1Y}$	
2nd	$M_{2A} < M_{2B}$		$M_{2X} < M_{2Y}$	
3rd	$M_{3A} = M_{3B}$		$M_{3X} < M_{3Y}$	

The utility function of some lottery Z can be expanded by a Taylor series around the first central moment of Z, M_{1Z}.[19] We then obtain a polynomial in all central moments:

$$EU(Z) = U(M_{1Z}) + \frac{1}{2!} U''(M_{1Z})M_{2Z} +$$
$$+ \frac{1}{3!} U'''(M_{1Z})M_{3Z} + \cdots + R_n,$$

where R_n is the remainder, as small as desired. Let us assume for the moment that the convergence of the series is fast enough, so we may arbitrarily ignore the terms beyond the third one.

The weight of the various moments depends on the attitude of the decision maker towards risk. An assumption about risk aversion implies $U(\cdot)$ concave, hence $U''(\cdot) < 0$. The prevalent assumption about the type of risk aversion is of decreasing absolute risk aversion, which means that "... the willingness to engage in small bets of fixed size increases with wealth, in the sense that the odds demanded diminish." (Arrow (1965), p.35). Then it can be shown[20] that $U'''(M_{1Z}) > 0$.

Returning to Hagen's lottery, we have in its first part

$$EU(Z_A) - EU(Z_B) = \tfrac{1}{2}U''(M_{1A})(M_{2A} - M_{2B}) > 0,$$

and hence clearly A is preferred to B for risk-averse individuals. But when comparing the approximated expected utility of lotteries X and Y, we have

---

* [*Editorial Note*: See pp.288–293. The author's comments are based on a shorter, unpublished presentation – O.H.]

$$EU(Z_X) - EU(Z_Y) = \frac{1}{2} U''(M_{1X})(M_{2X} - M_{2Y}) +$$

$$+ \frac{1}{3!} U'''(M_{1X})(M_{3X} - M_{3Y}).$$

The first term on the right-hand side is positive and the second is negative. Hence, preference between X and Y is not so clearly defined as between A and B. This explains the empirical results. One should observe that, indeed, Hagen's example does not amount to much more than that.

It is also possible to construct experiments involving lotteries whose outcomes are equivalent in the first three moments but differ in the fourth moment. I suppose that Allais and Hagen would add it then to the determinants of the preference of the individual, as they do with lower moments. Yet, while the meaning of the first three moments is clear and one can easily hypothesize about their preference – not much can be hypothesized about preference of kurtosis off-hand. On the other hand, if the functional form of the von Neumann–Morgenstern utility is known, it is possible to predict the preference of the individual regarding the fourth (and any higher) moment of the lottery, without the necessity to directly observe (or assume anything about) preferences for these moments.

It is also possible to show that some of the decision rules suggested by Allais are leading to conflicting choices. In one case, Allais suggests choosing between lotteries by the mean and variance of their outcomes, where preference is positively related to the first moment and negatively related to the second. In another case, he suggests choosing by the mean and the probability of loss (the loss being greater than the gain), with positive and negative preference, respectively. Let us assume, then, two preference functions

$$S_1 = f(M - a\Sigma), \qquad S_2 = g(M - bQ),$$

where S is Allais' 'satisfaction' index, M is the mean, Σ is the variance, Q is the probability of loss. Now consider the following two lotteries:

(1) $\quad P(X) = \begin{cases} 0.2 \text{ for } X = \$0 \\ 0.8 \text{ for } X = \$2.5 \end{cases},$

(2) $\quad P(X) = \begin{cases} 0.5 \text{ for } X = \$0 \\ 0.5 \text{ for } X = -\$4 \end{cases}.$

Then we have $M_1 = -2.0$, $\Sigma_1 = 1.0$, $M_2 = -2.0$, $\Sigma_2 = 4.0$.

It can be easily seen that by S_1, lottery (1) is preferred because it has a smaller variance, while by S_2, lottery (2) is preferred, having a smaller probability of loss. It may be argued, in this example, that S_1 is applied only to the normal[21] distribution while S_2 is applied only to a binomial one. Then it should be expected that Allais' theory provides a complete set of decision rules for all infinitely many conceivable probability distributions – something which is inconceivable by itself. On the other hand, the von Neumann–Morgenstern expected utility theory has a completely general application, regardless of the probability distribution of the outcomes of a lottery. Compared to it, what Allais suggests looks rather an *ad hoc* theory.

Tel Aviv University and New York University   1974

NOTES

* I wish to thank Professor Oskar Morgenstern for a very helpful discussion and suggestions. Support by the Office of Naval Research through grant N0014–67–A–0467–0020 to New York University is gratefully acknowledged.
[1] Some of these 'irrationalities' can be explained as being different choices in different situations, as will be discussed below.
[2] The same holds for the results of some of Hagen's experiments reported in this book.
[3] This axiom states that out of two situations, one is certainly preferable, if, for all possible outcomes, it yields a great gain.
[4] The continuity axiom states that for every $u > v > w$ where is $0 < p < 1$ such that $pu + (1 - p)w \sim v$, where $\sim$ is a binary relation of indifference. They prove this as a theorem.
[5] A somewhat more restrictive form of this axiom is $pu + (1 - p)w \sim pv + (1 - p)w$, and is proved as a theorem.
[6] See Axiom B5 in Fishburn (this book, p.248) and his discussion.
[7] See comments by Edwards (1954) and Borch (1968).
[8] It is to be assumed that the individual's preferences are in accordance with the von Neumann–Morgenstern axioms.
[9] See Hirshleifer (1965), Meyer (1968), Robichek (1969).
[10] See Hirshleifer (1965), pp.531–36.
[11] Markowitz (1959), pp.220–23.
[12] A higher percentage – 68% to 71% – of responses which were consistent with the expected utility theory was achieved in a recent experiment by Moskowitz (1974), who used Allais' type of problem. The percentage of consistent answers increased after clarification and discussion with the subjects in the experiments.
[13] Incidentally, most of the persistent violations in MacCrimmon's experiments occurred among lower level executives. The final result was that 75% of the subjects chose in a consistent manner.

[14] Stael von Holstein, in discussion following MacCrimmon (1968), p.24.

[15] Also, Luce and Raifa (1957, p.32) discard any consideration of the distribution of utilities as a fallacy.

[16] Allais (1953) suggests "the need to consider the dispersion (i.e. the second-order moment) and, generally speaking, the overall shape of the probability distribution of psychological values" (p.504). However, his analysis is focused on the second moment only, and does not give any clue as to how higher-order moments should be treated.

[17] Hagen bases his assertion to positive skewness preference on the observation that "negative skewness, as lack of insurance, creates anxiety and sleepless nights". Yet, most ("rational") people are not insured for everything! [The passage quoted from Hagen (see Bibliography) is not included in the shortened version appearing in this volume, pp.271–302 – O.H.]

[18] It is not clear which is the highest central moment which should be included in the preference function. It seems that Allais and Hagen stop adding moments at the first one which solves their particular problem.

[19] See Samuelson (1970), Tsiang (1972). Borch, in an unpublished paper, "Uncertainty and Indifference Curves" (1972) investigated the conditions under which the von Neumann–Morgenstern utility can be expressed as a linear function of the moments.

[20] The Arrow–Pratt measure of absolute risk aversion is defined as:

$$R = - \frac{U''(W)}{U'(W)} \quad (W = \text{wealth})$$

and decreasing absolute risk aversion implies

$$\frac{d}{dW}\left(-\frac{U''(W)}{U'(W)}\right) = -\frac{U'''(W)U'(W)-(U''(W))^2}{(U'(W))^2} < 0,$$

hence $U'''(W) > 0$. The last inequality also holds for the constant absolute risk aversion (exponential) utility function, but is undetermined for increasing absolute risk aversion. See Arditti (1967), Levy (1969).

[21] Tobin (1958) showed that for the normal distribution, the mean-variance decision rule is compatible with the von Neumann–Mogenstern utility theory. For other distributions it holds only for a quadratic utility. But the mean-variance analysis is also abandoned by Allais for non-normal distribution.

BIBLIOGRAPHY

Allais, M.: (1953). 'Le Comportement de l'Homme Rationnel devant le Risque: Critique de Postulates et Axioms de l'Ecole Americaine', *Econometrica*, pp.503–46.

Arditti, F. D.: (1967). 'Risk and Required Return on Equity', *Journal of Finance*, pp.19–36.

Arrow, K. J.: (1965). *Aspects of the Theory of Risk Bearing*, Yrjo Jahnssonian Saatio, Helsinki.

Borch, K. H.: (1968). *The Economics of Uncertainty*, Princeton University Press, Princeton, New Jersey.

Edwards, W.: (1954). 'The Theory of Decision Making', *Psychological Bulletin*, pp.380–417.

Edwards, W.: (1961). 'Behavioral Decision Theory', *Annual Review of Psychology*, pp.473–98.

Fishburn, P. C.: (1979). 'On the Nature of Expected Utility', this volume, pp.243–257.

Hagen, O.: 'New Foundations of Utility. Allais versus Morgenstern', unpublished seminar paper.

Herstein, I. N., and Milnor, J.: (1953). 'An Axiomatic Approach to Measurable Utility', *Econometrica*, pp.291–97.

Hirshleifer, J.: (1965). 'Investment Decisions Under Uncertainty – Choice Theoretic Approach', *Quarterly Journal of Economics*, pp.509–36.

Kuhn, T. S.: (1970). *The Structure of Scientific Revolution*, The University of Chicago Press, Chicago, Illinois.

Lee, W.: (1971). *Decision Theory and Human Behavior*, John Wiley and Sons, Inc., New York.

Levy, H.: (1969). 'A Utility Function Dependent on the First Three Moments', *Journal of Finance*.

Luce, R. D.: (1967). 'Psychological Studies of Risky Decision Making'. In W. Edwards and A. Tversky (Eds.), *Decision Making*, Penguin Books, Baltimore, Maryland, pp.334–52.

Luce, R. D., and Raiffa, H.: (1957). *Games and Decisions*, John Wiley and Sons, Inc., New York.

MacCrimmon, K. R.: (1968). 'Descriptive and Normative Implication of the Decision-Theory Postulates'. In K. Borch and J. Mossin (Eds.), *Risk and Uncertainty*, St. Martin's Press, New York, pp.3–32.

Markowitz, H. M.: (1959). *Portfolio Selection*, John Wiley and Sons, Inc., New York.

Meyer, S. C.: (1968). 'A Time-State-Preference Model of Security Valuation', *Journal of Finance and Quantitative Analysis*, pp.1–31.

Morgenstern, O.: (1972). 'Descriptive, Predictive and Normative Theory', *Kyklos*, Fasc. 4, pp.699–714.

Morrison, D. G.: (1967). 'On the Consistency of Preference in Allais' Paradox', *Behavioral Science*, pp.373–83.

Moskowitz, H.: (1974). 'Effects of Problem Representation and Feedback on Rational Behavior in Allais and Morlat-type Problems', *Decision Science*, pp.725–42.

Pratt, J. W.: (1964). 'Risk Aversion in the Small and in the Large'. *Econometrica* 32, 122–35.

Robichek, A. A.: (1969). 'Risk and the Value of Securities', *Journal of Finance and Quantitative Analysis*.

Samuelson, P. A.: (1970). 'The Fundamental Approximation Theorem of Portfolio Analysis in Terms of Means, Variances and Higher Moments', *Review of Economic Studies*, pp.537–42.

Slovic, P., and Lichtenstein, S.: (1968). 'Importance of Variance Preferences in Gambling Decision', *Journal of Experimental Psychology*, pp.646–54.

Tobin, J.: (1958). 'Liquidity Preference as a Behavior Towards Risk', *Review of Economic Studies*, pp.65–86.

Tsiang, S. C.: (1972). 'The Rational of the Mean-Standard Deviation Analysis, Skewness Preference, and the Demand for Money', *American Economic Review*, pp.354–71.

BRUNO DE FINETTI

A SHORT CONFIRMATION OF MY STANDPOINT

Because of the delay in receiving the invitation, I feel obliged to confine in a few lines my answer to the question without examining new literature. Moreover, I think I have nothing to add to the remarks already made on this old issue.

No doubt seems to me possible about the validity of the von Neumann–Morgenstern rule of preference under uncertainty, consisting in maximizing the expected utility. Utility is, in fact, precisely so defined as to suit such requirement: that is, to be linear in mixtures where the weights are probabilities. It is, usually, a convex function of the monetary value, since aversion to risk usually exists (and is admitted as the "normal" assumption in economic theory), so that a sure amount is preferred to an uncertain one with the same expectation.

The thesis is even better clarified starting from Wald's notion of *admissibility* and Savage's reference to such idea for a general foundation of a theory including the necessary axioms both for subjective probability and utility. Essentially, it is the same view as that roughly suggested by Daniel Bernoulli and Blaise Pascal in the 18th century.

The objection by Allais, if it is the same of 20 years ago, consists in asserting that the same correction should be repeated about the utility. This seems tantamount to asserting that, when the deflection of a bridge owing to a given load is computed, the deflection from the deflected position should be computed again because the load acts also on the deflected line (missing to note that, by definition, the deflected line is just that one for which elasticity exactly reacts so that the weight of the load is balanced).

University of Rome

Maurice Allais and Ole Hagen (eds.), Expected Utility and the Allais Paradox, 161.
Copyright © 1979 by D. Reidel Publishing Company.

J. MARSCHAK

UTILITIES, PSYCHOLOGICAL VALUES, AND THE TRAINING OF DECISION MAKERS[1]

ABSTRACT. M. Allais and the 'American School' have formulated two alternative hypotheses for the decision-making under uncertainty. Although Allais concentrates on the case when the consequences are money-amounts, his hypothesis can be applied to more general sets of consequences, as used in the 'American' discussion. In both hypotheses, subjective probabilities can be revealed by similar observational methods, but Allais' 'psychological values' and the 'Bernoullian utilities' are, in general, not identical concepts. In particular, Allais' maximand depends, not only on the mean but also on the dispersion of 'psychological values' – an assumption that Allais considers necessary to explain attitudes towards the variance of money amounts.

Neither hypothesis can claim to describe the 'actual' behavior of untrained, un-experienced, non-reflecting members of our or other cultures. Rather, these, or some other, weaker hypotheses claim to be models of 'rational' behavior. A challenge to psychologists: develop methods to train rational decision-makers!

I. DESCRIBING OR PRESCRIBING?

On a May day in 1952, between sessions of the International Colloquium on Risk, Professor Allais drove his luncheon guests to the Racing Club de France on the outskirts of Paris. The guests – Ragnar Frisch, L. J. Savage and myself – alighted from his car. Maurice Allais manoeuvred to park it, got out, and began to cross the road hurriedly, causing the driver of an oncoming car to brake sharply. Allais just avoided being hit. Instantly, Savage snapped his fingers and exclaimed, "Bob Thrall should be here!" For our host's actions contradicted the lexicographical preference ordering that Professor Thrall had defended in the morning session and that would, of course, rank "surviving but letting one's guests wait one more minute" ahead of the smallest chance of being run over.

Savage was thus arguing from observed behavior. Yet his *Foundations of Statistics* published two years later profess to be mainly normative, prescriptive, – not descriptive.[2] Yet the boundary is not easy to trace. Before reporting (*Foundations*, 5.6) on his own reactions to Allais' brilliant, deeply searching experiment (see now Allais: §63) Savage reminds us that D. Bernoulli was indeed led by observed behavioral facts (the St. Petersburg paradox) to replace mathematical

163

Maurice Allais and Ole Hagen (eds.), Expected Utility and the Allais Paradox, 163–174.

by moral expectation. When subjected to Allais' experiment, Savage "immediately expressed preference" in a way contradicting his own 'sure-thing principle'. But, by tabulating two pay-off matrices, with drawn numbered lottery tickets as events, and two pairs of alternative prospects as acts, the problem became transparent. He must revise the choice he made either between the members of the first, or of the second pair of acts.* He has thus

... corrected an error. There is, of course, an important sense in which preferences, being entirely subjective, cannot be in error; but in a different, more subtle sense they can be. Let me illustrate by a simple example containing no reference to uncertainty. A man buying a car for $2,134.56 is tempted to order it with a radio installed, which will bring the total price to $2,228.41, feeling that the difference is trifling. But, when he reflects that, if he already had the car, he certainly would not spend $93.85 for a radio for it, he realizes that he has made an error.

I would add: "and he regrets the loss caused by his inconsistency". For this may be the crucial test. It is instructive to read how it solved some of B. de Finetti's hesitations (1972, p.150ff) about the nature of subjectivistic probability theory.

Another example of 'reflection and regret': in essence, Pratt, Raiffa and Schlaifer (1965, Section 2.3.4) convince you that you would regret your 'intransitive' ('cyclical') behavior, as follows: "You own A and prefer A to B, B to C, and (cyclically!) C to A. Therefore, give us A and pay us a premium, to obtain C. Now pay a premium to exchange C for B. Finally, pay a premium to get A in exchange for B. You end up with your original possession of A, minus three premiums .... *Don't you now regret having acted as you did?*"

We are reminded of Socrates' dialogues, teaching wisdom by facing you with the consequences of your folly. And again: the distinction between prescriptive logic (and mathematics, and formal ethics if it exists) and descriptive psychology is a subtle one. We first proceed to contrasting two psychological hypotheses.

II. TWO HYPOTHESES AND SOME COMMENTS

II.1. It seems to me that, as a matter of descriptive psychology, the two hypotheses contrasted by M. Allais – his own and that of the 'American School' – can be stated on Figure 1.

* [*Editorial Note*: Compare MacCrimmon and Larson, this volume, pp.333–409 – O.H.]

TWO HYPOTHESES

Allais	Ramsey (1926), De Finetti (1974,
(§§13–24: 'Fundamental Factors')	Sec. 3.2), the 'American School'

The subject's choices reveal the existence of: (1) a 'subjective probability measure', $\bar{p}$, on the set $(1, \ldots, n)$ of events, and (2) a real-valued function of the 'consequences' q_i $(i = 1, \ldots, n)$, denoted by:

$\bar{s}(g_i)$ for 'satisfaction' $B(g_i)$ for 'Bernoullian utility'

with the following property: when offered to choose from a set whose generic element is a 'prospect' of receiving g_i $(i = 1, \ldots, n)$ when i happens, the subject will choose a prospect which maximizes

a function of M and Σ^2 increasing in M, where $\qquad\qquad$ M_B where

$$M \equiv \sum \bar{p}_i \bar{s}(g_i) \qquad\qquad\qquad M_B \equiv \sum \bar{p}_i B(g_i)$$

$$\Sigma^2 \equiv \sum p_i(\bar{s}(q_i) - M)^2$$

[$\equiv$ 'expectation and dispersion of psychological values'; notations in Allais, Note 33] $\qquad\qquad\qquad\qquad$ ($\equiv$ 'expected utility')

Fig. 1.

II.2. *Discreteness of Events.* As in much of Allais' article the case when the set of events is continuous has been omitted on Figure 1, for simplicity's sake.

II.3. *Symbol $\bar{p}$.* For subjective probability, we have used the *same* symbol $\bar{p}$ in stating both hypotheses. For the present author and, I believe, others of the 'American School' do agree with the suggestion (Allais, §6) to elicit $\bar{p}_i$ by Emil Borel's method: that is, to observe the subject's choices between a bet on the event i and a succession of bets on drawing a red ball from a bag with an appropriately varying proportion of red balls, known each time to the subject. In must be added, in the 'subjectivist' spirit, that preliminary tests should assure the experimenter beforehand that the subject is indifferent between bets on any of the individual balls, thus revealing that he is indeed assigning to each the same subjective probability of being drawn (= 1/100 if there are 100 balls).[3]

II.4. *Symbols $\bar{s}$ and B.* By contrast, the symbols $\bar{s}(g_i)$ and $B(g_i)$ denote, in general, different quantities, to be revealed, in principle, by different experiments. The function $\bar{s}$ is to be "determined by intro-spective observation of equivalent increments or minimum perceptual thresholds" [Allais: Summary, item (12); also text, §11; and Note 21]. The function B, on the other hand, is to be determined by observing the subject's choices between bets: see, e.g., Mosteller and Nogee, cited by Allais; Swalm (1966) applied the method to study the choice behavior of business executives.

II.5. *Real-valued and Other Consequences.* In the bulk of Allais' discussion the consequences g_i are identified with monetary gains and thus can be represented by (possibly negative) real numbers. He does, however, refer occasionally (Allais, §7) to a preference function on the set of vectors whose components are real numbers, viz., the quantities consumed. One might, then, consider as a 'prospect' a probability distribution of such vectors: points in a multi-dimensional real space. Under the name of 'multi-attribute choices under un-certainty' (see, e.g., Raiffa, 1968, Chapter 9) the problem has recently acquired great practical importance in applications to public policy.

Still more generally, the consequences need not be numerical, of any dimensionality. The set of consequences $(g_1, g_2, \ldots)$ may be, for example: 'victory, defeat, stalemate'; 'good health, pneumonia, tuberculosis'; and so on. This extension of the choice problem to non-numerical consequences – thus bringing political, military, medi-cal decisions to join economic ones – is one of the greatest merits of von Neumann and Morgenstern. It has been widely applied by the 'American School'; and nothing stands in the way of thus generalizing also Allais' hypothesis.

II.6. *Effect of the Shape of the Satisfaction Function $\bar{s}$ on the Desirability of the Variance of Money Gains.* If the consequences g_i are real-valued (money gains or, for that matter, the number of patients cured or prisoners taken), expand $\bar{s}(g_i)$ in the neighborhood of some arbitrary origin:

$$\bar{s}(g_i) = \bar{s}(0) + q_i \cdot \bar{s}'(0) + g_i^2 \cdot \bar{s}''(0)/2 + g_i^3 \cdot \bar{s}'''(0)/6 + \cdots;$$

then the "expectation of psychological values" is

$$M \equiv \sum \bar{p}_i \bar{s}(q_i) = \bar{s}(0) + \mu_1 \cdot \bar{s}'(0) + \mu_2 \cdot \bar{s}''(0)/2 +$$

$$+ \mu_3 \cdot \bar{s}'''(0)/6 + \cdots,$$

where the μ_k $(k = 1, 2, \ldots)$ are the moments of the distribution $\bar{p}$ about the origin. If the second derivative $\bar{s}''$ is negative (positive) over the considered range of money gains, the function $\bar{s}$ is strictly concave (strictly convex) over that range, and we have the case of diminishing (increasing) 'marginal satisfaction': Allais, §14. Accordingly, when all moments but μ_2 are fixed, M, the expectation of psychological values, will decrease (increase) when the variance $(\mu_2 - \mu_1^2)$ of the distribution p increases. To explain why a subject, over a given range of monetary gains, prefers their lower (higher) variance it is thus sufficient to assume that he maximizes M and has a concave (convex) satisfaction function $\bar{s}$ that, along with $\bar{p}$, describes his 'psychology'. It is not necessary to assume that, in addition, it must be characterized by his preferring, for M given, a low or a high 'dispersion of psychological values', Σ^2. This is clearly stated by Allais in the first two paragraphs of his section 21. But the clarity is removed in his subsequent paragraphs.

II.7. *Analogous Effect of the Shape of the Utility Function B.* In the above expansions, replace $\bar{s}$ by B and, correspondingly, 'marginal satisfaction' by 'marginal utility'. This reconstitutes, in part, Alfred Marshall's (1890, Mathematical Appendix 9) reasoning: if the Bernoullian decision-maker has decreasing marginal utility of money he will prefer lower to higher variance of money gains. More particularly, Marshall seems to have regarded a strictly concave money utility function B as a psychological fact – or perhaps as a moral prescription against gambling, in a Victorian spirit, an heir to Calvin (Allais, Note 52)? ... More generally, M. Friedman and L. J. Savage, in a paper cited by Allais, explained the gambling of people who are insured, by the Bernoullian function being convex in some neighborhoods and concave in others ... The same reasoning might apply to Allais' satisfaction function $\bar{s}$.

Note the advantage of restricting a hypothesis as little as possible. Maximizing moral expectation is less restrictive than maximizing expected gain. Concave utility is less restrictive than Bernoulli's logarithmic one. And the inflexions of the money utility curve, introduced by Friedman and Savage are less restrictive and more realistic still. (On the other hand some considerations may impose restrictions: as pointed out by Arrow the utility function must be bounded, to meet the Petersburg paradox!)

II.8. *Predicting Choices from Words or from Observed Choices?* In Borel's method recommended by Allais and by ourselves, the subject's choices are observed. This is also the case when students of Bernoullian utility try to elicit it, – sometimes by actually paying the subject's lottery gains. On the other hand, the "introspective" comparison of "satisfaction increments" by the subject provides the experimenter with words not with observed choices; so would the subject's naming probability numbers, or their increments. I suppose we are more interested in predicting actions than words; and such predictions are probably better based on recorded actions than on recorded words.

II.9. If one could assume that, by good luck, the functions $\bar{s}$ and B do coincide, it would be possible to *test the 'American' hypothesis against Allais'* in the special form of his Note 33, Equation (8): the decision-maker maximizes $M - \lambda \Sigma^2$ [but see also Allais, Note 85]. Consider a triple of probability distributions ψ_1, ψ_2, ψ_3 below; M and Σ^2 are evaluated in the last two columns:

$s(g) = 0$	1	4	M	Σ^2
ψ_1	0	0.5	0.5	2.5	2.25
ψ_2	0.25	0.5	0.25	1.5	2.25
ψ_3	0.5	0.5	0	0.5	0.25

If the functions s and B are identical, so are the quantities M and M_B; and the 'American' hypothesis would predict the ordering $\psi_1 > \psi_2 > \psi_3$ of prospects. But Allais' hypothesis would predict this ordering only if $\lambda > \frac{1}{2}$. It would predict $\psi_3 > \psi_1 > \psi_2$ if $\lambda > \frac{5}{4}$, and $\psi_1 \geqslant \psi_3 \geqslant \psi_2$ in the intermediate case. For a consistent subject a series of such experiments would decide the issue.

III. ACTUAL BEHAVIOR

Common to both hypotheses of our Figure 1 are certain underlying assumptions about human behavior. Unfortunately, they are often contradicted by facts.

Are we sure that – as assumed by Allais, §4 – people do derive the subjective probabilities of compound prospects by properly combining those of the constituent prospects? This is made very doubtful by the experiments of Tversky and Kahneman (1974), and the studies of Slovic, Kunreuther and White (1974). It would be worthwhile to follow them up, using subjective probabilities established by Borel's method.

Further: the assumption that a person ranks the prospects in order of preference – Allais, §2; Savage's Postulate 1 – was violated in many experiments: by 27% of students tested by May (1954), by 10% of students tested by Davidson and Marschak (1959); although, interestingly, by only 4% of business executives tested by MacCrimmon (1965). Experimental psychologists (unlike the economists and some logicians) are not astonished. It is not even sure that a person consistently chooses the same object from an offered set, even within the same hour or day. As in the experiments of Fechner (1860) on the perceived comparative heaviness or loudness, to the sentence "the person chooses this particular object" the words "with such and such probability" are added. Accordingly, preference ordering is replaced by various competing "stochastic models of choice". The transitivity requirement appears in modified, weakened forms. One of these implies the existence of a numerical function f on the set of objects with the following property: the probability of choosing A rather than B is the larger, the larger the difference $f(A) - f(B)$. Thus $f(A)$ is analogous to Fechner's measure of subjective sensation of the stimulus A. It may be called 'stochastic utility' or, for that matter, 'stochastic satisfaction'.[4] Other models, both weaker and stronger have been proposed and some of them were submitted to tests.[5]

In our Section I, we described how a subject may be led to reflect; and to regret his failure to rank objects consistently. Similarly with what Allais, §3, calls the 'axiom of absolute preferences' (also known as the 'admissibility requirement of A. Wald (1940), and identical with Savage's 'Theorem 3'). Here is a test (see Marschak (1968), Section III). Let the subject pick up one of many sealed envelopes, with the experimenter not present. The subject opens it, it contains v dollars. He tells a third person his asking price, a dollars, for the contents of the envelope, after being told that there is a written bid, x dollars; and that if the bid exceeds his asking price he will receive x dollars, and will otherwise keep the v dollars.

If the subject would tabulate the pay-off matrix showing the results of the bid x when he has asked a dollars, he would see that he should ask the amount $a = v$. A lower or higher price asked will not give him, for any level of x, any higher results and will, for some ranges of x, give him less. In my experience with students and in K. MacCrimmon's with business executives, not using pencil and paper, they usually ask more than v, thus violating the principle of absolute preferences. After being invited to tabulate and to reflect they 'regretted'.

Most psychological studies of children, but also of adults, the bulk of the anthropology of primitive people, much of sociology and, of course, all of psychiatry deal with actual behavior. But it is also supposed that psychiatrists, and psychologically trained teachers, will help the patient or the pupil to approach in their behavior some norms of logic, of arithmetic. It is similar with the decision behavior: it is important to describe, but also to improve it.

IV. TRAINING FOR RATIONALITY

IV.1. Young children are taught arithmetic (and, nowadays, also set-theoretical logic) using the abacus, colored blocks etc. and avoiding technical words as long as possible (except for bad teachers and bad writers of textbooks of new maths). Also, to train people not to confuse 'if' and 'only if', simple exercises must be used.

I believe that, similarly, procedures can be developed to train people for decision-making. To educate future decision-makers, possibly future persons with great responsibilities, is a task similar to, and socially at least as important as, the education of future accountants and lawyers in arithmetic and logic.

Psychologists practiced in cognitive experimentation (studies of problem-solving) know how the manner of presenting a problem, – even the trivial, detailed features of its presentation, – affect the subject's ability to get the necessary insight. At the same time as MacCrimmon presented problems to executives, I used the same problems with the students in my class. But by the time I presented the 'substitution' problem my students had become used to drawing pay-off matrices, thus translating the verbal, syntactically complicated statement of the problem into a visually clear form – unlike Mac-Crimmon's subjects. (You may have noticed, when discussing a car purchase with a dealer, that he uses the paper for doodling, placing figures, percentage calculations and additions in odd corners of the sheet and foregoes the advantages of clear visual sequences or tables.) A large majority of my students obeyed the substitution axiom, in contrast to MacCrimmon's executives, and this may be due to their having drawn up and contemplated pay-off matrices.

As quoted in Section I above, Savage did change his decision, and complied with his axiom, after having drawn pay-off matrices. In the case of a less sophisticated person, training for rationality would also succeed, I believe, if Allais' experiment on the substitution postulate were not phrased in terms of numerical probabilities, or numbers of lottery tickets, but in terms of events: to-morrow's sunshine, clouds, rain, gale. This would avoid the influence of any school-bench memories of urns and chances, yet capture the essence of the experiment, and of its possible application in real life. (Remember also, that Savage's subjective probabilities do not exist for a person disobeying his axioms!)

While Savage, on reflection, changed his decision, "nobody could convince the author (viz., Allais, §71) to change his mind should he *as a practical matter* find himself in the happy position of facing the uncertain prospects described" (i.e. with a small chance of an immense gain, yet, in Savage's 'contradicting' Allais' previous choice). This difference in attitudes suggests that it may be worthwhile considering methods of training for alternative types of 'rationality'. It should be possible to face a person with decisions that would gradually reveal to him *his* true satisfaction function s and the other function also characteristic of his tastes, which, according to Allais, depends on the expectation and the dispersion of 'psychological values'.

This raises the question of possible modification of norms. Recently, thoughtful authors (P. Fishburn, (1970), and A. Sen, (1969)), while retaining the transitivity of preference, have proposed to discard the transitivity of indifference, essentially on the grounds of non-discriminability of small increments: while I prefer 110 to 100 cents, I am indifferent between 100 and 105 cents, and between 105 and 110; and so is the automatic computer, condemned to rounding-offs. And A. Tversky (1972) has deepened both the logic and the psychology of discrimination as a concomitant of choices. One might say it is indeed non-rational, non-economical to avoid rounding-offs. Both engineers and accountants do round off. Even replacing deterministic by stochastic decision models may be 'economical': it requires too much effort to be perfectly consistent!

I suggest then, that (1) the most obvious modifications (mostly weakenings) of 'rational' axioms should be formulated and their logical implications studied. That is, the personal utilities and probabilities would exist only as 'approximations' – this term to be defined as precisely as possible and applied operationally to well-trained decision-makers. (2) Effective, partly non-verbal *training devices* should be developed which would make a given modified norm to a habit – similar to the mathematician's or a good lawyer habit of distinguishing between necessary and sufficient conditions.

The task of developing methods of training is a psychological one. It must be distinguished from another, also psychological, or anthropological, task, more in the tradition of these disciplines: to describe the actual behavior of people of a given culture, social group, age, physical condition. A decision-maker dealing with people will need this information – as an engineering decision-maker may need information on the properties of metals. At the same time, both must be trained to apply norms of logic, mathematics, and of decision-making, albeit modified ('rounded-off') to avoid uneconomical efforts.

University of California at Los Angeles

NOTES

[1] The present comments deal with M. Allais' paper 'The Foundations of a Positive Theory of Choice Involving Risk and a Criticism of the Postulates and Axioms of the American School' which appears as Part II of the present volume [See also Part V – O.H.] I shall cite by number the sections and notes (not the pages) of that paper. As far as possible, the notations of M. Allais will be used. My list of references (provided with the publication year in the text) will include only those not already contained in the bibliography attached to M. Allais' paper.

[2] "Two very different sorts of interpretations can be made of ... the ... postulates ... First, ... as a prediction about the behavior of people, or animals, in decision situations. Second, ... as a logic-like interpretation of consistency in decision situations. For us, the second interpretation is the only one of direct relevance, but it may be fruitful to discuss both, calling the first *empirical* and the second *normative*". I strongly recommend pondering Savage's subsequent discussion of the two interpretations. (*Foundations*, 2.6).

[3] I take this opportunity to correct M. Allais' impression (§6, Case V) that I have persisted in the 'objectivist' stance of my early articles of 1950–51. On the contrary: see Marschak (1954), (1954a), (1968), (1970). Borel's procedure is described in the latest

two of these essays. This and other methods of eliciting subjective probabilities were surveyed by Savage in his posthumous paper (1971).
[4] Fechner tells us that when assuming the 'sensation' to be logarithmic in the amount of the physical stimulus, he was inspired by Daniel Bernoulli's logarithmic function (our *B*) of the gambler's achieved amount of money. It is only fair that students of gambling now, in return, imitate Fechner's stochastic hypothesis!
[5] Luce's pioneering work (1959) was followed by various authors including my collaborators and myself: (1959, 1960, 1960a, 1963, 1963a, 1963b, 1964). For a survey see Luce and Suppes (1965).

REFERENCES

de Finetti, B.: (1972). *Probability, Induction and Statistics: The Art of Guessing*, Wiley, New York.

de Finetti, B.: (1974). *Theory of Probability*, Vol. I, Wiley, New York, (translated from the Italian edition, 1970).

Fechner, G. T.: (1860). *Elemente der Psychophysik*, 2 Vols., Leipzig, (English translation of Vol. I, Holt, New York, 1966).

Fishburn, P. C.: (1970). 'Intransitive Indifference in Preference Theory', *Operations Research* **18**, 207–228.

Luce, R. D.: (1959). *Individual Choice Behavior: A Theoretical Analysis*, Wiley, New York.

Luce, R. D., and Suppes, P.: (1965). 'Preference, Utility, and Subjective Probability'. In R. D. Luce, R. R. Bush and E. Galanter (Eds.), *Handbook of Mathematical Psychology*, Vol. 3, Wiley, New York.

MacCrimmon, K. R.: (1965). 'An Experimental Study of the Decision-Making Behavior of Business Executives', Ph.D. Dissertation, University of California, Los Angeles.

Marschak, J.: For convenience, the references are to *Selected Essays* (S.E.) published in *Economic Information, Decision and Prediction*, Vol. I, D. Reidel, Dordrecht, Holland, 1974: 'Scaling of Utilities and Probabilities', S.E. 3 (1954); 'Probability in the Social Sciences', S.E. 4 (1954a); (With D. Davidson) 'Experimental Tests of a Stochastic Decision Theory', S.E. 6 (1959); (With H. D. Block) 'Random Orderings and Stochastic Theories of Responses', S.E. 7 (1960); 'Binary-Choice Constraints and Random Utility Indicators', S.E. 8 (1960a); (With G. M. Becker and M. H. DeGroot) 'Stochastic Models of Choice Behavior', S.E. 10 (1963); (With G. M. Becker and M. H. DeGroot) 'An Experimental Study of Some Stochastic Models for Wagers', S.E. 12 (1963a); (With G. M. Becker and M. H. DeGroot) 'Probabilities of Choices Among Very Similar Objects: An Experiment', S.E. 14 (1963b); 'Actual Versus Consistent Decision Behavior', S.E. 9 (1964); 'Decision-Making: Economic Aspects', S.E. 16 (1968); 'The Economic Man's Logic', S.E. 17 (1970).

Marshall, A.: (1890). *Principles of Economics*, 9th edn., Macmillan, New York, 1961.

May, K. O.: (1954). 'Intransitivity, Utility and the Aggregation of Preference Patterns', *Econometrica* **22**, 1–13.

Pratt, J. W., Raiffa, H., and Schlaifer, R.: (1965). *Introduction to Statistical Decision Theory*, McGraw-Hill, New York.

Raiffa, H.: (1968). *Decision Analysis: Introductory Lectures on Choices under Uncertainty*, Addison-Wesley, Reading, Massachusetts.

Ramsey, F. P.: (1926). 'Truth and Probability'. In R. B. Braithwaite (Ed.), *The Foundation of Mathematics and Other Logical Essays*, The Humanities Press, New York, 1950.

Savage, L. J.: (1971). 'Elicitation of Personal Probabilities and Expectations', *Journal of the American Statistical Association* **66**, 783–801.

Sen, A. K.: (1969). 'Quasi-Transitivity, Rational Choice and Collective Decisions', *Review of Economic Studies*.

Slovic, P., Kunreuther, H., and White, G. F.: (1974). 'Decision Processes, Rationality, and Adjustment to Natural Hazards'. In G. F. White (Ed.), *Natural Hazards: Local, National, and Global*, Oxford Press, New York.

Swalm, R. O.: (1966). 'Utility Theory – Insights with Risk-Taking', *Harvard Business Review* 123–136.

Tversky, A.: (1972). 'Elimination by Aspects: A Theory of Choice', *Psychological Review* **79**, 181–199.

Tversky, A., and Kahneman, D.: (1974). 'Judgement under Uncertainty: Heuristics and Biases', *Science* **185**, 1124–1131.

Wald, A.: (1950). *Statistical Decision Functions*, Wiley, New York.

OSKAR MORGENSTERN

SOME REFLECTIONS ON UTILITY*

ABSTRACT.** The von Neumann–Morgenstern 'expected utility hypothesis' as presented in Chapter I of *The Theory of Games and Economic Behavior* (1944) was the first attempt at a rigorous axiomatization of a fundamental concept of economics, namely, a general theory of utility. There is no *a priori* notion of 'rationality' in the theory; rather, that is a concept to be derived and given meaning to from the theory. The theory is 'absolutely convincing' in the sense that if behavior deviates from that predicated by the theory, after explanation of the theory, behavior would be adjusted. The von Neumann–Morgenstern 'expected utility theory' was the first approximation to an undoubtedly much richer and far more complicated reality. Critics of the theory, such as Allais and others, have centered their criticism of the theory not on the internal consistency of the axioms of which the theory is composed but rather on the validity of the axioms themselves. In that sense, the attacks on the theory are misplaced. It is common knowledge throughout scientific circles that axiomatic systems are often modified as axioms are more precisely specified, qualified, or, at times, replaced, as our understanding of physical laws is expanded. Not unexpectedly, the evolution of the von Neumann–Morgenstern 'expected utility theory' over the past thirty years is in complete concordance with scientific progress.

It is natural that the 'expected utility hypothesis' as presented in Chapter I of *Theory of Games and Economic Behavior* (von Neumann, Morgenstern, 1944) would have been challenged. After all, the theory goes a significant step beyond the thus far accepted version of a theory of utility which deals only with sure prospects and yields a number for utility only up to *monotone* transformations. What von Neumann and I have done is: (a) we recognize the undeniable fact that in our world some prospects are uncertain and that probabilities must be attached to them. This is clearly an empirical observation or assertion. (b) We have established a set of axioms expressing precisely the assertions. For these axioms, we have carefully shown that they are free of contradictions and have all the properties a true axiomatic system has to exhibit. It is clearly not enough to call any assertion an 'axiom'. If a new one is to be introduced, either being

* Support by the Office of Naval Research through Grant N0014–67–A–0467–0020 to New York University is gratefully acknowledged.
** Abstract compiled by Ira Sohn.

175

Maurice Allais and Ole Hagen (eds.), Expected Utility and the Allais Paradox, 175–183.
Copyright © 1979 by D. Reidel Publishing Company.

added to, or replacing, an existing one, it has to be shown that the new set has all required properties and to prove what the implications of the new system are.

Incidentally, our axiomatic system appears to have been one of the first in economics for which an actual, rigorous proof was given; in this case, the proof is that the axioms imply precisely what we postulated, namely, that an expected utility could be demonstrated to exist which is numerical up to a positive *linear* transformation, leaving the zero and the unit scale open.

Now, to my knowledge, that proof has never been challenged anywhere in the extensive subsequent literature as, indeed, it cannot be. The proof is valid. But in the usual manner, later authors have attempted to weaken our axioms or have given simpler proofs or done both, but all have arrived at the same result. This is a typical development in science and mathematics and must be welcomed. There is no reason to discuss these matters here; one is essentially confronted with questions of aesthetics, convenience and taste. Perhaps not surprisingly, I still prefer our original axioms because they appear to me quite natural and transparent. But, as I said, this is a matter of taste.

The next question is whether there are phenomena relating to our intuition which neither the original von Neumann–Morgenstern axioms nor later ones capture. There are so far two possibilities to be considered (perhaps later on additional ones may appear).

The *first* is the question whether the probabilities used are always already numerical – as we have assumed *expressis verbis* – or whether they might, perhaps more typically, be subjective, i.e., non-numerical. That is a good question. Von Neumann and I have anticipated this matter and we have stated specifically that in the latter case axioms could be found from which one could derive the desired numerical utility *together with* a number for the probabilities (cf. p.19 of von Neumann and Morgenstern, 1944). We did not carry this out; it was demonstrated by Pfanzagl (1967, 1968) with all the necessary rigor.

The *second* is the question whether the scheme of choosing between risky alternatives allows for a possible preference for, or aversion against, gambling, which, if it exists, could perhaps distort the resulting numerical utility. The possibility that this argument might be raised was also anticipated by von Neumann–Morgenstern as discussed in 3.7.1 (1944) as follows (and I quote): "May there not exist in an individual a (positive or negative) utility of the mere act of 'taking a chance', of gambling, which the use of the mathematical expectation obliterates?... Since [our axioms] (3:A)–(3:C) secure that the necessary construction can be carried out, concepts like a 'specific utility of gambling' cannot be formulated free of contradiction on this level." (*loc. cit.*, p.28). We have furthermore added a footnote: "This may seem to be a paradoxical assertion. But anybody who has seriously tried to axiomatize that elusive concept, will probably concur with it." On the same page we state that the notion of a 'utility of gambling' would require "a much more refined system of psychology ... than the one now available for the purposes of economics." Finally, on page 29 (*loc. cit.*) we say "that the analysis of the methods which make use of mathematical expectation ... is far from concluded at present". That was written in 1944. Has this more refined system of psychology been developed since then, and is it implied and used by Allais and the others who have taken up his argument? In my view the answer is negative.

What has been done instead by Allais and others can be characterized as an attempt to show *counterexamples* which would conclusively demonstrate that individuals have a 'utility of gambling' such that these examples would destroy the universal claim of the theory.

Regarding counterexamples: it is easy to falsify the statement 'all swans are white' by showing one black swan. But it is not as easy to contradict an axiomatic theory which fulfills all the requirements of such a theory, as ours does. Instead of generalities one would expect that a new axiom be established and be fitted into the existing system, however modified. Then a proof should be given for the type and kind of utility that the modified system defines. Or, perhaps, one would show that there cannot be any 'utility' of any kind. Nothing of this seems to have been done.

It is necessary to realize that a modification and extension of a theory can only be made in the proper *domain* of the theory.

To give some illustrations: Newton's mechanics cannot explain how light gets into the system. There simply is no provision for it. Nor is Newtonian mechanics applicable when the velocity of bodies exceeds certain magnitudes: If bodies travel with speeds near that of light, the classical theory is no longer useful. It has to be replaced – or complemented – by relativity theory. Maxwell's theory accounts for electricity but has no place for atoms. Quantum mechanics in its turn also has its domain and is in character quite different from classical mechanics. There are more such examples. This shows that there is no absolute truth; all theories are only approximations. But together these theories make up physics and they are not in conflict with each other.

Now the von Neumann–Morgenstern utility theory, as any theory, is also only an approximation to an undoubtedly much richer and far more complicated reality than that which the theory describes in a simple manner.

In the light of these observations, one should now point out that the domain of our axioms on utility theory is also restricted. Perhaps we should have pointed that out, instead of assuming that this would be understood *ab ovo*. For example, the probabilities used must be within certain plausible ranges and not go to 0.01 or even less to 0.001, then to be compared to other equally tiny numbers such as 0.02, etc. Rather, one imagines that a normal individual would have some intuition of what 50 : 50 or 25 : 75 means, etc. Naturally, one may *postulate* that he might be able to calculate correctly. But then this need and ability must be introduced explicitly into the experiments; yet this has not been done by the critics.

Besides this difficulty of exposing individuals to almost unrecognizably small probabilities, there is added another one. And it is difficult to say which is more formidable: that is, the matter of the objects which are being offered: Millions, even tens of millions of Norwegian crowns, French francs, or even dollars. The chances are offered to school teachers, for example, (as Hagen does) or to otherwise not specified persons, but presumably ordinary individuals (economically speaking) who do not normally, if ever, contemplate coming into possession of millions! This then corresponds to letting bodies move with speeds approaching that of light, thereby going far beyond the limits of classical mechanics, as mentioned above.

What, for example, would one say to the 'decision' – whatever it be – of a man who is supposedly confronted with either the sure prospect of being hung, or the possibility either of escape or else being slowly tortured to death with the respective probabilities of, say, 0.01 vs. 0.99. Do the very notions of 'preference', 'rational', 'gambling' apply to such situations? Clearly not. This is beyond the bounds of a possible theory as known today and therefore the answers, whatever they be, are worthless. Observe that the above question is asked of a man who is not, and never expects to be in his lifetime, in situations remotely resembling the awful dilemma described in the above example. Therefore, it is doubtful that *any* answer he gives can be used. In this manner, a 'test' can never be made. The frequent remarks about this or that decision as being 'rational' or not are also open to doubt. For example, in game theory one does not start out with an idea of 'rationality'; rather, that is a concept to be *derived* and given meaning to from the theory. One merely assumes that the players prefer a greater pay-off to a lesser one. But the behavior necessary to achieve this is deduced from the theory. Similarly here: there is no *a priori* notion of 'rational' that could be used in describing the action of an individual of whom one does not know in advance whether he is risk-averse or not. If he is, one kind of action is indicated; if he is not, another one. Only then could one say – if one had a theory! – whether the individual was acting rationally: after all, even a risk-averter can make mistakes!

The point that for testing individuals – for anything! – in regard to a possible preference for gambling, one has to consider situations within their normal experience and not outlandish situations, was already made by W. Edwards (1944). This eminent psychologist spoke from the basis of an experience with experiments which it is indispensable to have but which, as far as I know, may not be possessed by either Allais or Hagen. It is, of course, much to be welcomed that one even wishes to experiment in economics, where this is a much neglected field (Morgenstern, 1954). It is interesting, however, that there are even supporters of the von Neumann–Morgenstern theory who discuss such hypothetical situations (in order to reject Allais' strictures). One of them is Markowitz in his otherwise valuable book on portfolio selection (1959).

The matter of design of experiments is a very complicated one. As Einstein said more than once to me: "Most scientists naively think that they know what they should observe and how they should measure it." He had in mind the physical sciences. How much more difficult is the observation of humans and especially when they are put into hypothetical situations far removed from their ordinary life circumstances. Incidentally this is a further comment on the naiveté of the so-called 'revealed preference' theory (Morgenstern, 1972).

If one goes outside the range of normal experience of the individuals questioned, it becomes also clear that statements about their alleged consideration of variance, skewness, first, higher moments, etc., are subject to the same doubts as their gross 'decision' noted above. This matter is treated competently by Y. Amihud in this Volume (p.149) and I fully agree with his observations.

This also takes care of the matter whether those questioned would 'correct' their behavior if it were pointed out to them that they 'act' in violation of the expected utility hypothesis. That theory, as formulated by the von Neumann–Morgenstern axioms, is normative in the sense that the theory is 'absolutely convincing' which implies that men will act accordingly. If they deviate from the theory, an explanation of the theory and of their deviation will cause them to readjust their behavior. This is similar to the man who tries to build a *perpetuum mobile* and then is shown that this will never be possible. Hence, on understanding the underlying physical theory, he will give up the vain effort. Or, an individual making a mistake in, say, long division, will clearly correct himself when shown the mistake. Naturally, it is assumed that the individuals are accessible intellectually whether it be physics or arithmetics or utility that is being explained to them. In that sense there is a limitation since there are certainly persons for whom this is impossible. Whether they then should be called 'irrational' is a matter of taste.

In a Colloquium regularly held by me at New York University, students who, however, were well versed in the von Neumann–Morgenstern theory, were exposed to several of the same experiments made by Allais and Hagen. The result was that they conformed immediately and exactly to the expected utility hypothesis, quite differently from Hagen's school teachers. It was interesting that the conformity to the theory was significantly greater when the amounts offered were modest, i.e., ranged from a few cents to a few dollars. When millions of dollars were introduced in the experiments and very small probabilities were used, deviations in the sense of inconsistencies became significant. When they were in agreement with the theory, was this due to their familiarity with the theory? Or did they not enjoy the uncertainty? Did they discount the fact that my 'experiment' was phony – as all the others carried out by Allais, Hagen, etc., – in the specific sense that there were no millions of dollars in my possession which I would cheerfully offer just to discover how to determine and measure the possible existence of the pleasure of gambling? Were the persons used in the experiments made by Allais and others equally capable of calculating as properly as the students and were they also aware that the millions of francs and crowns were not forthcoming? Did they *know* what problems the experiments wanted to settle?

I want to make it absolutely clear that I believe – as von Neumann did – that there may be a pleasure of gambling, of taking chances, a love of assuming risks, etc. But what we did say and what I do feel I have to repeat even today after so many efforts have been made by so many learned men, is that the matter is still very elusive. I know of no axiomatic system worth its name that specifically incorporates a specific pleasure or utility of gambling together with a general theory of utility. Perhaps it will be offered tomorrow. I am not saying that it is impossible to achieve it in a scientifically rigorous manner. I am only saying (as we did in 1944) that this is a very deep matter. I would be delighted if one could go beyond the instinctive feeling – which I share – that there is such an inclination towards, or aversion against, gambling and nevertheless establish a rigorous theory of utility.

Finally, let me repeat that in my view the matter of finding a comprehensive theory of utility is far from settled. What von Neumann and I have done was simply to straighten out some issues and to point out others that were not resolved at the time of our writing. We needed a good number for the pay-off matrices in game theory. We were, of course, aware of the debate regarding ordinal and cardinal utilities. We realized the importance of uncertainty which dominates all our life. But instead of merely postulating the existence of such a number for the purposes of game theory, as we easily could have done, we decided that we could obtain a number by looking at the basic fact of uncertainty. We were greatly stimulated by the splendid paper on the St. Petersburg Paradox by Karl Menger (1967). It took very little time to formulate our axioms and to give the necessary motivation. The proof that the axioms yield a number having the desired properties was published, with some additional comments, only in the second edition of our work in 1947, although we naturally had the proof already in 1944 and even earlier. This theory is not a fundamental building stone for game theory, but it is, of course, most welcome.

Neither von Neumann nor I thought in the least that what we said would be the last word on preferences and utility. We did think, however, that it was nice to offer one of the first rigorous axiomatizations of a fundamental concept of economics. It is one of the great pleasures of my life that those few passages we wrote on utility theory have provided so much stimulus for others to concern themselves deeply and in a fresh manner with the notion of utility which is forever basic for any economic theory.

What the ultimate theory of utility will look like is hard to imagine even after so many works have been published on the basis of the von Neumann–Morgenstern theory. I believe one will have to take time into consideration as I have tried to outline in an early paper elsewhere (1934). It is also possible that preferences form an only partially-ordered set with subsets, some of which are completely ordered and possess the Archimedean property and others which fail to have it. It is amusing to contemplate what 'optimal allocation of resources' would mean and possibly have to look like, should reality be as contemplated.

It would be difficult enough, for example, to have a single completely-ordered set without the Archimedean property, which means that there is no continuity or, putting it differently, that differences in utility are infinite. Would that not mean that one should go on indefinitely allocating resources to the most important want, since every other is inferior? There is no evidence that this happens in reality, which apparently means that no such non-Archimedean ordering exists. But that is not true: an astronomical observatory in space, outside the atmosphere, is clearly better than one on earth. No amount of additional earthly observatories is ever the equal of one outside. And if our preferences are only partially ordered – which means, grossly speaking, that they are in considerable disarray – then there is no presently known guiding principle for optimal allocation. Yet we do hope to have one in our personal affairs and we struggle to arrive at one in social situations. This is achieved by a variety of acts and decisions which *impose* a greater order and it is that system we are looking at when as economists we discuss preferences, orderings, etc. A complete order can be achieved by compromise, by democratic processes of voting or by dictatorial, authoritarian *fiat*. It is therefore clear that, should the utility field be only partially ordered, such 'political' processes will have to be studied, to be synthesized with the simultaneously given uncertainty.

It is in this light in which matters have to be looked at which, though they appear to have been thoroughly investigated by Arrow and others, certainly need further exploration. We are thus at least several steps removed from the underlying reality. These facts seem to me to be more important than the question whether a possible utility of gambling has to be axiomatized, welcome though that would be.

New York University

REFERENCES

Allais, M: 'The Foundations of a Positive Theory of Choice Involving Risk and a Criticisim of the Postulates and Axioms of the American School'. (Part II of this Volume.)

Amihud, Y.: 'Critical Examination of the New Foundation of Utility'. (p.149, this Volume.)

Borch, K.: (1968). *The Economics of Uncertainty*, Princeton.

Edwards, W.: (1944). 'The Theory of Decision Making', *Psychological Bulletin* 51, No. 4, 380–417.

Hagen, O.: 'Towards a Positive Theory of Preferences under Risk'. (p.271, this Volume.) [Includes material that was not available when this article was written, notably the Oslo test, pp.293–296. The author reserved possible comments for a later occasion – O.H.]

Markowitz, H. M.: (1959). *Portfolio Selection*, New York.

Menger, Karl: (1967). 'The Role of Uncertainty in Economics'. In M. Shubik (Ed.), *Essays in Mathematical Economics in Honor of Oskar Morgenstern*, Princeton, pp.211–231, (originally published in German in 1934).

Morgenstern, O.: (1954). Experiment and Large Scale Computation in Economics. In O. Morgenstern (Ed.), *Economic Activity Analysis*, New York, pp.483–549.

Morgenstern, O.: (1934). 'Das Zeitmoment in der Wertlehre', *Zeitschrift für Nationalökonomie* 5, No. 4, 433–458. Published in English in A. Schotter (Ed.), *Selected Economic Writings*, New York, 1975.

Morgenstern, O.: (1972). 'Thirteen Critical Points in Contemporary Economic Theory: An Interpretation', *Journal of Economic Literature*, 10, 1163–1189.

von Neumann, J., and Morgenstern, O.: (1944). *Theory of Games and Economic Behavior*, Princeton, Third edn., 1953.

Pfanzagl, J.: (1967). 'Subjective Probability, derived from the Morgenstern–von Neumann Utility Concept'. In M. Shubik (Ed.), *Essays in Mathematical Economics in Honor of Oskar Morgenstern*, Princeton, pp.237–251.

Pfanzagl, J.: (1968). *Theory of Measurement*, Würzburg, pp.213–218.

YAKOV AMIHUD

A REPLY TO ALLAIS

In my reply, I shall have to be somewhat repetitious, due to a certain imprecision in the representation of my arguments by Allais. I shall relate to his 1953 article and his recurrent rejoinder, and not to any of his memoires or other publications.

I think that refutation of an existing theory is a necessary, but not a sufficient condition to accept a competing theory. For example, in spite of the anomalies in the relation of the Ptolemaic theory with nature, it was rejected only when the new Copernican theory proved to produce predictions which were better than those derived by its predecessor.

In our case, Allais did not supply the necessary nor the sufficient conditions to reject the expected utility (EU) theory: The results of his experiments leave many unclear points as to the applicability and the analysis of the results. But above all, even if Allais was right in his criticism of the EU theory, he is yet to come up with a better theory of a risk choice. In my opinion, what he suggests can hardly be so qualified. He does not give a clear and definite criterion to rank lotteries; his theory is so loosely defined that any choice is admissible as 'rational' and there is no way in which the theory can ever be refuted. To use Allais' example (§35.3), he does not ask us to choose whether the earth is a sphere or a spheroid; he rather suggests that we choose between the earth being a sphere or being *any possible shape*. The exact sciences would not admit of such a 'theory'; there is no reason why it should be admitted into the social sciences.

1. I was disturbed by the poor predictive power of Allais' theory because I was taught that "the aim of a good theory is prediction, and in prediction lies the ultimate test of its validity".* Hence, I expected that after pointing out the failure of the EU (expected utility) theory to make accurate prediction of risk choice, Allais would have demonstrated that his theory can better predict such choice.

What we get instead is a list of factors which affect risk choice to a

---

* Morgenstern (1972), p.704.

Maurice Allais and Ole Hagen (eds.), Expected Utility and the Allais Paradox, 185–190.

first and second (etc.?) approximation (1953, p.504), and a collection of examples of how these factors could be used to justify the choice of 'rational' individuals as being 'rational': *After* having observed a choice (*any* choice), Allais conveniently fits it to one of the preference functions from his arsenal, defined over a subset of the factors in the above list. Sometimes, a combination of some moments can explain choice. Sometimes, the probability of loss is in order. And, when difficulty arises, there is a magic variable $\bar{S}$ which enters the preference function and explains everything not fully explained by the pay-offs and their probabilities (see §38). Thus, the harmony of the theory with reality is guaranteed under any circumstances; the theory cannot be put to test against reality, and can never be refuted.

Allais does not suggest any general rule for ranking lotteries (except for the obvious case of 'complete dominance', i.e. $S(A_1, \ldots, A_n) > S(B_1, \ldots, B_n)$ if $A_i > B_i$ for all $i = 1, \ldots, n$). The acceptance of his set of axioms does not imply anything as to how to use his list of factors in a risk choice. It does not even support his assertion that under some circumstances the maximization of the expected value of the psychological values (as the EU theory suggests) is appropriate. When a rule for ranking lotteries is lacking, the use of the theory for prediction is impossible.

I hope that this clarifies what I meant when I claimed that Allais' theory lacks a predictive power. I certainly did not have in mind (as Allais strangely puts it) that a theory should enable to "forecast *a priori* whether a subject taken at random will prefer frankfurters or hot dogs" nor whether he would like his meat "rare or well done" (Allais, §35.2).

To illustrate the poor predictive power of Allais' theory, consider a variant on his experiment: if an individual agrees with the vN–M axioms and prefers certainty [A: \$100; $P = 1.0$] over a lottery [B: \$500, \$100, \$0; $P = 0.10, 0.89, 0.01$, respectively], then the EU theory *predicts* that he will prefer the lottery [D: \$100, \$0; $P = 0.11, 0.89$] over [C: \$500, \$0; $P = 0.10, 0.90$]. If he prefers B and A, he is expected to prefer C over D. (From my experience, this prediction is successful in the great majority of cases.)* Now, does Allais' theory enable us to make such a prediction? I doubt it.

---

* Moreover, even when millions of dollars are involved, most respondents choose as the EU theory predicts. This is also the result in similar experiments reported in the literature, which are in contrast with Allais' result that *all* choose in contradiction with the EU theory.

2. Allais does not settle my wonder at Factor AIV in his theory, i.e. the effect of the distribution of psychological values. He admits that it is 'indissociable' (1953, p.511) from Factor AI (the psychological distortion of monetary values), as was confirmed by later researchers. In light of this difficulty, we would expect Allais to suggest how these two elements can be distinguishedly measured and used in his theory. His examples of the use of Factor AIV are unsatisfactory. Instead of using the whole available information from the distribution of psychological values, he focuses on the *variance* (as was also perceived by others, see his f.n. 193). Hagen (this Volume, p.271) used the third moment to explain his results. Is the use of lower-order moments the theory itself or its convenient approximation? Why is it that higher-order moments are so often ignored? What is the rule by which moments are introduced into the preference function and what is their effect? It seems that the answers are as many as the examples one can conceive.

The same applies to Allais' examples which use the probability of loss as a decision rule. What is the rule by which this element supercedes the moments of the distribution in the individual's preference function?

3. Allais misrepresented (or just missed) my arguments regarding 'rationality', hence his reply is misplaced (I think the same applies to his comments on the arguments laid out by Professor Morgenstern). I neither claimed that 'rationality' is defined as "conformity with the axioms of the Theory of Games" (Allais' §38) nor that a person can be branded irrational "on the sole ground that his behavior violates the axioms of the Neo-Bernoullian formulation". I merely suggested that the rationality of a risk choice should be assessed in the light of the set of rules, or axioms, which guide the individual's behavior. *It is not the choice of the particular set of axioms which shows rationality, but a consistency with it.* Hence, an inconsistency of a choice with the EU theory may be pointed out as erroneous, or irrational, only *if* the individual has agreed with the vN–M axioms. To illustrate, the results of the non-Euclidean geometry cannot be considered erroneous because they differ from those of the Euclidean geometry, since they are derived from a different set of axioms. It is therefore useless to test whether an individual who disagrees with the vN–M axioms acts in consistency with the EU theory; it is also insufficient to infer that an individual is 'rational' from the mere fact that his choice is consistent with the EU theory. *It is only against the adopted postulates that a choice can be assessed as 'rational'.*

Now, since the vN–M EU theory hinges on the applicability of their axioms to human behavior, I would have expected to see a study on people's agreement with those axioms. (MacCrimmon did it to some extent.) Unless the applicability of the vN–M axioms is explicitly investigated, it is hard to say, based on the failure of the EU theory to make accurate prediction, as to which axiom is the one responsible for this failure. Hence, Allais' claim that I erred in suggesting that the inconsistent choice might be due to a disagreement with Axiom 3Cb, and his suggestion that the crucial axioms are 3Ba and 3Bb, is a mere hypothesis.

4. Allais' own definition of 'rationality' (1953, p.504) hovers between inclarity and tautology. One definition is "coherence of desired ends and ιne use of appropriate means to attain them", where nowhere does he suggest how to sort out those human actions which do not serve his desires, nor does he define exactly the scope of "appropriate means". However, more confusing is the suggestion that *"Rationality* can be defined experimentally by observing the actions of people who can be regarded as acting in a *rational* way". Throughout his paper, Allais supports his claims by examples from the behavior of "des gens jugés comme parfaitement rationnels" (p.529). Who are those 'rational' men whose actions are 'rational' since they are 'rational', etc.? How are they judged 'rational'? Indeed, when things are not precisely defined, everything, any choice, is admissible, and the theory can never be put to test.

5. Unfortunately, Professor Allais did not privilege me (or Professor Morgenstern) with an analysis of his 1952 experiment at the time that we wrote our papers, nor since then (excluding the few days preceding the writing of these lines). It is therefore weird that he requires us to refer to details of an experiment which he kept unpublished. My comments referred to what was published in 1953. I was unaware that an analysis of Allais' experiment had appeared in the *Journal de Societe de Statistique de Paris*.

The applicability of Allais' experiments may be questioned on the grounds that they lie outside of the domain of the EU theory and deal with magnitudes which are beyond the grasp of the subjects in the experiment.

In two separate experiments we presented subjects (students who had not been exposed to the expected utility theory) with two question-naires, similar to Allais' (1953, p.527): In the first, prizes were in millions of dollars, and in the second, in hundreds. As can be expected (also by Allais), most of those who chose in inconsistency with the EU theory in the first questionnaire switched into a "consistent" pattern in the second. (Each questionnaire consisted of a single game, and the subject was not told after the first one whether his/her choice was 'right' or 'wrong'.) Appropriate statistical tests showed that (i) the fact that most subjects choose as the EU theory predicts is not due to a mere chance; (ii) that the switch from an "inconsistent" into a "consistent" pattern of choice, when amounts are reduced, is overwhelmingly significant.

6. There is still the issue of why subjects who choose inconsistently with the EU theory generally reverse their choices to be consistent. The fact is (and anyone can easily perform this experiment) that when subjects are presented with the Markowitz's (1959) version of Allais' experiment, the great majority of them choose, in consistency with the EU theory. They do so even when they know nothing about the vN–M axioms, nor about the EU theory (So a 'brain-wash' of the subjects cannot be implied). Markowitz presented Allais' lotteries in two successive stages so that the subject does not know the result of the first stage before making a decision in the second stage. Thus, it withstands Allais' comments in §36.3. Also, by Allais' own "axiom of composition", Markowitz's lottery should be regarded equivalent to his own. Now, why are the results of the two tests so different? Why those subjects who have chosen inconsistently with the EU theory switch (in the great majority of cases) to a consistent choice when presented with the Markowitz version of the Allais' experiment? One is led to think that maybe the inconsistent choice in the Allais-type experiment is a result of an error, confusion or misperception. Un-fortunately Allais did not tackle this problem of 'switching' nor did he offer an alternative explanation.

As to Allais' contention that the reversal of choice (to be consistent with the EU theory) is because the subjects "realized that these [the inconsistent – Y.A.] choices violated the axioms of the neo-Ber-noullian formulation, whereas they had postulated that these axioms defined Rationality" (§36.3): The results of Moskowitz's (1974) experiment refute this. In that experiment, subjects were presented with an Allais' type lottery and exposed to the reasoning of *both* Allais and the EU theory regarding risky choices. Most chose inconsistency with the EU theory. Those who switched from an inconsistent to a consistent choice outnumbered the switchers in the opposite direction. Although there was a considerable degree of accidental choice in both groups (consistent and inconsistent), the author concluded that when subjects were presented with both arguments, "Conforming (EU) reasoning was also found to be more persuasive than the Allais and Morlat reasoning" (p.239).

Tel Aviv and New York University   1977

BIBLIOGRAPHY

See the Bibliography of Amihud, Y.: 'Critical Examination of the New Foundation of Utility', this volume, pp.149–160.

PART IV

CONTEMPORARY VIEWS ON THE NEO-BERNOULLIAN THEORY AND THE ALLAIS PARADOX

KARL BORCH

UTILITY AND STOCHASTIC DOMINANCE

ABSTRACT. In portfolio theory, the principle of stochastic dominance can be used to eliminate certain portfolios as inefficient, provided the underlying utility function has certain properties. The paper gives a brief survey of the relationships between the utility functions and stochastic dominance of different orders. It is pointed out that the principle of stochastic dominance of the first order is the main axiom in the theory which Allais outlined in 1952.

1. The problem of making a decision under uncertainty can – possibly with some over-simplification – be reduced to the problem of selecting the best, or most preferred element in a set of probability distributions. This leads to the problem of establishing a preference ordering over a set of probability distributions, which we shall study in this paper. For the sake of simplicity we shall take the set to consist of all distributions over the non-negative half-line. A member of this set, F can then be interpreted as a lottery in which $F(x)$ is the probability that the gain shall be an amount of money at most equal to x.

The natural approach to our problem is the *Bernoulli Principle*, which states that the distribution F is preferred to the distribution G $(F > G)$ if and only if

$$\int_0^\infty u(x)\, dF(x) > \int_0^\infty u(x)\, dG(x). \tag{1}$$

Here $u(x)$ is Bernoulli's 'emolumentum', which today usually is referred to as the 'utility function'.

2. It is clear that (1) gives an ordering over the set considered. In the simplest possible case, when $u(x) = x$ the distributions will be ordered by their expected values. This ordering was rejected by Daniel Bernoulli, because it does not take the risk into account. Bernoulli himself argued that the utility function should be $u(x) = \log(x + c)$, but he was ready to accept Cramer's suggestion that the function $u(x) = \sqrt{x + c}$ might also give a reasonable preference ordering. Marshall's discussion of the question about 150 years later, seems to

Maurice Allais and Ole Hagen (eds.), Expected Utility and the Allais Paradox, 193–201.
Copyright © 1979 by D. Reidel Publishing Company.

indicate that the prevailing view was that any concave function could serve as utility function and generate a reasonable preference ordering. Marshall apparently considered the different possible shapes of the utility function as "interesting guesses", and did not commit himself to any statement about whether rational people did, or should make their decisions in accordance with the Bernoulli Principle.

3. Von Neumann and Morgenstern [1] gave the Bernoulli Principle a mathematical foundation. Their result can be derived from the two assumptions:

(i) There exists an ordering over a convex set of probability distributions.

(ii) This ordering has the property that if the relation $F > G$ holds for two arbitrary members set, and $H = \alpha F + (1 - \alpha)G$, then $F > H > G$ for $0 < \alpha < 1$.

From these assumptions one can prove that there exists a function $u(x)$ so that the ordering can be represented in the form (1).

This is a mathematical result of some importance. There is no controversy about the possibility of deriving the representation (1) from the two assumptions, which must be given in a more precise form in order to prove the theorem with full mathematical rigor. The assumptions have however been the subject of considerable controversy, and they have been presented in many different, although equivalent forms, in order to meet objections of various kind.

4. The theorem of von Neumann and Morgenstern gives the conditions that a utility function exists so that a preference ordering can be represented in the form (1). The theorem has nothing to say about the shape of the function $u(x)$. In our special case, when the distributions are one-dimensional, and interpreted as lotteries with amounts of money as prizes, it is natural to assume that $u(x)$ is an increasing function of x. This assumption, which just says that a larger amount of money is preferred to a smaller one, cannot be derived from the two original assumptions. It must be introduced as an additional, and independent assumption.

5. In an outline of an alternative set of axioms, Allais takes this last assumption as his starting point, and refers to it as "Axiome de Préférence Absolue" ([2] p.267). This axiom states that F is preferred

to G if the inequality

$$F(x) \leq G(x) \qquad (2)$$

holds for all x, with strict inequality for at least one value of x. The axiom has an immediate appeal. For any x, F offers a higher probability that the prize shall exceed x.

It is clear that this axiom will give only a partial ordering over the set of all probability distributions.

6. The axiom of Allais is too simple to be entirely new.* As a reasonable decision rule, it has been suggested by many authors, and at least one of these ([3] p.38) claims that the rule was first formulated by James Bernoulli in *Ars Conjectandi* from 1713. The rule has been rediscovered several times in the theory of finance, and is currently referred to as "Stochastic Dominance". If F is preferred to G when (2) holds, one says that F is preferred to G by the principle of stochastic dominance of first order.

The concept can obviously be generalized. To simplify the exposition, assume that $F(0) = 0$. We shall write

$$F_n(Z) = \int_0^Z F_{n-1}(x)\,dx, \qquad (3)$$

where $n = 2, 3, 4, \ldots$, and $F_1(x) = F(x)$.

If F is preferred to G when the following relation holds for all Z, with strict inequality for some Z

$$F_n(Z) \leq G_n(Z), \qquad (4)$$

we shall say that F is preferred to G by the principle of stochastic dominance of the nth order.

It is easy to verify that the stochastic dominance of the nth order implies dominance of higher order.

7. The principle of stochastic dominance of higher order may not have the same immediate appeal as the axiom of Allais, but we shall give it an interpretation which makes some sense. Before we do this, we shall derive some useful relations.

---

* [*Editorial Note*: Compare Allais' reference to Massé and Morlat as originators, Part II, Note 10, which is identical with the original – O.H.]

We first note that for $n > 1$ we have

$$F_n'(Z) = F_{n-1}(Z).$$

Partial integration of (3) gives

$$F_n(Z) = [xF_{n-1}(x)]_0^Z - \int_0^Z xF_{n-2}(x)\,dx$$

$$= \int_0^Z (Z - x)F_{n-2}(x)\,dx,$$

or in general

$$F_n(Z) = \frac{1}{(n-2)!}\int_0^Z (Z - x)^{n-2}F(x)\,dx. \qquad (5)$$

If a density $f(x) = F'(x)$ exists, we have

$$F_n(Z) = \frac{1}{(n-1)!}\int_0^Z (Z - x)^{n-1}f(x)\,dx. \qquad (5')$$

8. First-order stochastic dominance will, as we noted in §5, give only a partial ordering. It is natural to ask if we can obtain a complete preference ordering by considering stochastic dominance of higher orders.

Let us assume that $F(x) < G(x)$ for $0 \leqslant x \leqslant C$, and let $M_1 > 0$ be the smallest value of the difference $G(x) - F(x)$ in this interval. Let further M_2 be the smallest value of the same difference for $C < x$. Clearly $M_2 < 0$, unless there is first-order stochastic dominance. We then have

$$G_n(Z) - F_n(Z) = \frac{1}{(n-2)!}\int_0^Z (Z - x)^{n-2}\{G(x) - F(x)\}\,dx >$$

$$> \frac{M_1}{(n-2)!}\int_0^C (Z - x)^{n-2}\,dx + \frac{M_2}{(n-2)!} \times$$

$$\times \int_C^Z (Z - x)^{n-2}\,dx,$$

or

$$G_n(Z) - F_n(Z) > \frac{1}{(n-1)!}\{M_1 Z^{n-1} - (M_1 - M_2)(Z - C)^{n-1}\}.$$

By choosing n sufficiently large, we can make certain that this inequality holds for all Z. We have thus proved that the decision rule:

F is preferred to G if for some n the inequality
$F_n(Z) < G_n(Z)$ holds for all Z,

gives a complete ordering of the set of all probability distributions. Moreover the ordering is strict, i.e. no two distributions can be equivalent – except of course if they differ only in a set with measure zero.

This result is more than we asked for, and may be more than we wanted. A preference ordering of this form is inconsistent with the Bernoulli Principle, and cannot be represented in form (1).

9. From (5) we see that increasing n implies that greater relative weight is assigned to the small values of x. This means that with increasing n more "risk aversion" is brought into the decision rule. In the limit we obtain a mini-max rule, which represents the extreme risk aversion, or the extreme pessimism. When comparing two distributions, the decision maker will consider only the worst possible outcome, and prefer the distribution which gives the lower probability to this outcome. This is in a sense well known.

There is a considerable literature on stochastic dominance, and a fairly complete survey has been given in a recent paper by Bawa [4]. He sums up the basic results in the following manner:

(i) Preferences based on first-order stochastic dominance are consistent with the Bernoulli Principle with a non-decreasing utility function, i.e. $u'(x) \geq 0$.

This amounts to consistency, combined with the assumption that more money is preferred to less, and expresses the same as the "Axiome de Préférence Absolue" of Allais.

(ii) Preferences based on second-order stochastic dominance are equivalent to the Bernoulli Principle with positive aversion, i.e. with a utility function such that $u'(x) \geq 0$, $u''(x) \leq 0$.

(iii) Preferences based on third-order stochastic dominance are equivalent to the Bernoulli Principle with a utility function such that $u'(x) \geq 0$, $u''(x) \leq 0$ and $u'''(x) \geq 0$.

To give an intuitive meaning to the condition $u'''(x) \geq 0$, it is convenient to introduce the "risk aversion"

$$R(x) = -\frac{u''(x)}{u'(x)},$$

and its inverse, the "risk tolerance"

$$T(x) = -\frac{u'(x)}{u''(x)}.$$

From the latter definition we find:

$$u'''(x) = \frac{u''(x)^2}{u'(x)}\{1 + T'(x)\}.$$

Hence, we have $u'''(x) \geqslant 0$ if the risk tolerance is not decreasing at a rate exceeding unity.

10. Stochastic dominance of the third order was first studied by Whitmore [5]. So far there seems to be no studies of dominance of higher order, and apparently no attempts have been made to place the basic results above in a general framework. The explanation of this apparent neglect of an important question may be that most advocates of stochastic dominance have been concerned with practical applications, and have shown little interest in formulating axioms or proving theorems.

The situation which these authors have in mind can be described as follows: A decision maker has to choose an element from a large set of probability distributions, representing, for instance, the returns on different investment projects. If this decision maker is rational he can use the principle of stochastic dominance of the first order (i.e. Allais' axiom) to eliminate some projects as inferior, or 'inefficient'. If the decision maker is a risk averter, he can eliminate another set of projects by using stochastic dominance of the second order. Finally, if the decision maker feels that his attitude to risk is such that it must be represented by an increasing, or a moderately decreasing risk tolerance function, he can eliminate more projects by considering third order dominance. By this three-stage process, the initial set of distributions may be considerably reduced, and this will make the decision problem simpler, although not necessarily easier. The decision maker will still have to devise a rule for selecting an element from the reduced set. He can of course go on using stochastic dominance of ever higher order, until the set is reduced to just one element. This procedure is as we have seen equivalent to a mini-max rule, which the decision maker probably will find unacceptable. He may however ask if there is anything magic about the number three, and apply the principle of stochastic dominance of say fourth and fifth order, before seeking a different principle for choosing an element from the remaining set.

11. To simplify our discussion of this question we shall consider the set of all probability distributions confined to the domain $(0, C)$. For any distribution in this set we have $F(x) = 1$ for $x > C$.

Let us now consider two such distributions, F and G, and assume that F is preferred to G when the condition

$$F_n(Z) \leqslant G_n(Z) \tag{4}$$

holds for all Z, and for any $n \geqslant N$. From (5) it follows that for $Z > C$ we have

$$\int_0^Z (Z - x)^{N-2}\{G(x) - F(x)\}\, dx$$
$$= \int_0^C (Z - x)^{N-2}\{G(x) - F(x)\}\, dx > 0,$$

and that

$$\int_0^C (Z - x)^{N-1}\{g(x) - f(x)\}\, dx > 0.$$

This means that F is preferred to G by the Bernoulli Principle when the underlying utility function is

$$u(x) = -(Z - x)^{N-1}.$$

12. For the utility function found above, we derive the following expression for the risk aversion:

$$R(x) = -\frac{u''(x)}{u'(x)} = \frac{N-2}{Z-x}.$$

The risk tolerance is:

$$T(x) = \frac{1}{R(x)} = \frac{Z}{N-2} - \frac{x}{N-2} \quad \text{for } N > 2.$$

As Z is an arbitrary number, greater than C, we can write:

$$T(x) = K - \frac{x}{N-2} \quad \text{with} \quad x < (N-2)K.$$

We see that the risk tolerance is a decreasing linear function, and the rate of decrease is $1/(N-2)$. This observation enables us to continue the argument from §10 above.

If the decision maker, after searching his soul, concludes that he is a risk averter, with increasing risk aversion – i.e. with decreasing risk tolerance, – he can simplify his problem by using the principle of stochastic dominance of third order to eliminate some distributions as inferior. If after a further search of the same soul, the decision maker can determine how fast his risk tolerance decreases, he can also decide how far he can simplify his problem by using stochastic dominance of higher order to eliminate more distributions from considerations.

13. The conclusions above are formulated in a rather loose manner. They could – at a certain cost – be stated in a more precise mathematical form. I doubt, at the present stage, if this is the most pressing problem.

A decision maker must search his soul to determine what his objective actually is. His real problem is to find a good search technique. He can find a sequence of principles, which will give a sequence of partial orderings converging to a complete ordering. He can also follow Bernoulli, and assume that the ordering exists, and set out to determine the underlying utility functions.

Stochastic dominance is related to both these approaches, and may be a useful search technique. It may turn out to be more valuable as such, than as an efficient method for handling the computations involved in the decision problem.

Bergen, February 1975

REFERENCES

[1] Neumann, J. von, and Morgenstern, O.: (1947). *Theory of Games and Economic Behavior*, Second Edition, Princeton University Press.
[2] Allais, M.: (1953). 'Fondements d'une théorie positive des choix comportant un risque', *Colloques Internationaux du CNRS XL*, pp.257–332, Paris.
[3] Schneeweiss, H.: (1967). *Entscheidungskriterien bei Risiko*, Springer-Verlag.

[4] Bawa, V. S.: (1975). 'Optimal Rules for Ordering Uncertain Prospects', *Journal of Financial Economics* **2**, 95–121.
[5] Whitmore, G. A.: (1970). 'Third-order Stochastic Dominance', *The American Economic Review*, pp.457–459.

A. CAMACHO

MAXIMIZING EXPECTED UTILITY AND THE RULE OF LONG RUN SUCCESS

ABSTRACT. Axioms on the preference ordering of infinite sequences of a finite number of prizes are used to derive utility indices for these prizes which are constant up to positive linear transformations and satisfy certain conditions. These utility indices and "the rule of long run success" which is formally stated in the paper are then used to determine how an individual should rank lotteries assigning the different prizes with given probabilities. The implications of our results are finally discussed in relation to the von Neumann–Morgenstern axioms and a contention made by M. Allais in his 1953 *Econometrica* paper.

1. INTRODUCTION

In the utility theory developed by von Neumann and Morgenstern [1] (see also Marschak [2]), the preference ordering of probability distributions by an individual is used to derive his utility indices of a finite set of prizes $x_1, \ldots, x_n$ to which the probabilities are assigned. It is shown there that if the ordering of probability distributions satisfies certain, so called, rationality conditions or rules (rules that any rational man, according to Marschak [2] *should* follow in ordering the probability distributions), then utility indices, u_i^v, constant up to positive linear transformations, can be assigned to the prizes x_i in such a way that the individual orders the probability distributions as if he were maximizing the expected value of the utilities u_i^v.

Professor Marschak in [3], pp.504–5, proposes the alternative approach of starting by defining what he calls the rule or aim of *long run success* and then trying to study whether this aim can be satisfied by applying the rule of maximizing expected utility. In other words, what Professor Marschak proposes is to start out with the intuitively very appealing common sense definition that "the best policy or rule is the one that succeeds in the long run" and then try to determine whether the rule of maximizing expected utility is a best rule according to this common sense definition. A related problem was also studied later by J. Marschak and R. Radner in the context of 'long run subjective probabilities'. See in particular [4], Chapter 2, Sections 9, 10, 11.

In this paper, we plan to follow a similar approach to that initiated by Marschak in [3]. To this end, we will proceed as follows: First, I

203

Maurice Allais and Ole Hagen (eds.), Expected Utility and the Allais Paradox, 203–222.

will define how the individual orders sequences of prizes $x_{h_1}, \ldots, x_{h_i}, \ldots, x_{h_k}$, for $k = 1, 2, \ldots$. Then, from the ordering of these sequences of prizes, utility indices $u_i^c = u^c(x_i)$ $(i = 1, \ldots, n)$ will be obtained, which are constant up to positive linear transformations, and possess the property that the sequence $x_{h_1}, x_{h_2}, \ldots, x_{h_k}$ is at least as good as the sequence $x'_{h_1}, x'_{h_2}, \ldots, x'_{h_k}$ if and only if

$$\sum_{i=1}^{k} u^c(x_{h_i}) \geq \sum_{i=1}^{k} u^c(x'_{h_i}).$$

By using these utility indices u_i^c, utility functions for finite sequences of prizes $U_k^c(x_{h_1}, \ldots, x_{h_k})$ are then defined in the obvious way. The rule of long run success is then formally stated. Finally, we will show that given two lotteries L and L' assigning the prizes x_i $(i = 1, \ldots, n)$ with probabilities P_i and P'_i respectively

$$\left(0 \leq P_i \leq 1, 0 \leq P'_i \leq 1, \sum_{i=1}^{n} P_i = \sum_{i=1}^{n} P'_i = 1\right),$$

the rule that prescribes choosing L over L' whenever $\sum_{i=1}^{n} u_i^c P_i$ is greater than $\sum_{i=1}^{n} u_i^c P'_i$ implies that the rule of long run success, as stated by us, will be satisfied. We will also discuss the von Neumann and Morgenstern rationality axioms and the utility indices u_i^v derived from them in relation to the utility indices u_i^c derived from our model and the rule of long run success.

I would like to point out here that we, like Marschak, do not assume the successive random variables $U_1^c, U_2^c, \ldots, U_k^c$, to be statistically independent. Neither do we assume, unlike Marschak, that their corresponding variances $\sigma_1^2, \sigma_2^2, \ldots, \sigma_k^2$ converge to zero as $k \to \infty$.

Given the extremely subtle character of the problem of rationalizing decision making under uncertainty, we will rely for the developing of our model mainly on a very simple example. We will do this, even at the expense of sacrificing generality, with the hope of reducing the probability of misunderstandings to acceptable levels.

2. THE ORDERING OF SEQUENCES OF PRIZES

The theory of utility to be presented here is a simplified version of the one developed by this author in [5] (see also [3]).

Consider the following simple situation. An individual, say Mr. A, will be offered every day after lunch either x_1, a cup of coffee, or x_2, a cup of tea, or x_3, a cup of camomile. Let us assume that Mr. A prefers to have, after lunch, a cup of coffee to a cup of tea, and a cup of tea to a cup of camomile. Thus he prefers x_1 over x_2 and x_2 over x_3. Suppose that our hostess for some reason, can serve each day only coffee or only tea or only camomile, but that she can decide every day which of the three different drinks will be served. Suppose further that besides Mr. A, there are other guests with tastes different from his. And that our hostess, who is a fair minded person, wants to know more about the preferences of Mr. A (and the other guests, of course) in order to find out what could be a fair proportion of days serving coffee, days serving tea, and days serving camomile. Thus, she asks Mr. A the following question: Suppose that one day I serve tea which, I know, is not your favorite, instead of coffee that like the best. But other days, I can serve tea instead of camomile, that you like the least, and thus compensate you for the loss of pleasure suffered the day that I give you tea instead of coffee. How many days do I have to serve tea instead of camomile in order for you to feel compensated? We will assume that Mr. A can answer this question precisely. We will also assume that if during a period of a *finite* number of days, say k, coffee is served during k_1 days, tea during k_2 days and camomile during k_3 days (of course $k_1 + k_2 + k_3 = k$), Mr. A would not care regarding the order in which the different drinks are served whenever the number of times that he has coffee, tea and camomile remain k_1, k_2 and k_3.

These and other less crucial conditions will be presented below in a formal way in the form of axioms characterizing the preferences of an individual. And from these axioms utility indices $u_i^c = u^c(x_i)$ will be derived which are constant up to positive linear transformations, and such that, for any finite k, the sequence $x_{h_1}, x_{h_2}, \ldots, x_{h_i}, \ldots, x_{h_k}$ is at least as good as the sequence $x'_{h_1}, x'_{h_2}, \ldots, x'_{h_i}, \ldots, x'_{h_k}$ if and only if

$$\sum_{i=1}^{k} u^c(x_{h_i}) \geqslant \sum_{i=1}^{k} u^c(x'_{h_i}).$$

We will proceed now to this formalization.

Let $X = \{x_1, \ldots, x_i, \ldots, x_n\}$ represent the set of the n alternative prizes or consumption incomes. Thus in our previous example, n was set equal to 3 and x_1 represented a cup of coffee, x_2 a cup of tea and x_3 a cup of camomile. Let $N = \{1, \ldots, i, \ldots, n\}$ be the set of the n natural numbers $1, 2, \ldots, i, \ldots, n$.

Write $X^\infty = X \times X \times \cdots$: the countable infinite Cartesian product of X times itself; and let x^∞ be a generic element of X^∞. Thus in a more explicit way x^∞ represents an infinite sequence $x_{h_1}, \ldots, x_{h_i}, \ldots$, with $h_i \in N$ for all i.

Our first axiom now states:

Total Ordering Axiom. It is assumed that the individual possesses a preference ordering Q (also written $\geq$)[1] of the elements of X^∞, i.e. Q is a transitive, reflexive, connected relation defined on X^∞. In economic terms, Q is the relation "is at least as good as".

In terms of our example what the total ordering axiom means is that Mr. A imagines himself having an after lunch drink day after day, after day . . . forever (he has not learned yet that he is going to die some day), and that he is able to rank, according to his tastes, all the possible alternative infinite sequences.

Remark. It should be emphasized that the preference ordering among infinite sequences of prizes postulated in the previous axiom is to be considered here in a timeless context. It is true that it is difficult to think of a person receiving a sequence of prizes without time being involved. We used a time reference in our example regarding Mr. A's after lunch drinks and we will use a time reference again when presenting further examples in order to facilitate their description and understanding. But we will assume that our individual makes abstraction of the time intervals elapsing between successive consumptions (because, say, these time intervals were previously fixed by custom or otherwise and cannot be changed) and cares only about the sequences of consumptions that he can receive.

Let us turn at this point to the *permutation axiom.* This *axiom* roughly states that the preferences of the individual with regard to the infinite sequences $x^\infty = x_{h_1}, \ldots, x_{h_i}, \ldots, h_i \in N$ for $i = 1, 2, \ldots$, do not depend on the way in which the prizes of any *finite* part of the sequence are arranged. In other words, the individual does not care if the order of any finite number of prizes of a sequence is altered. This is certainly a very strong restriction on the preferences of the individual. To begin with, habit forming consumptions have to be excluded from our set of prizes. Also, even if we exclude habit forming consumptions as prizes, we might still have the case where the order in which the prizes are received and consumed really matters. Consider for instance, the situation where a consumer is offered dinners for two years, half of them fish food and the other half meat food. There is no reason, of course, to assume that our consumer should be indifferent between, say, dining on fish during the whole first year and meat during the whole second year, or dining on meat one night and fish the following night, etc., throughout the two years. This last difficulty can be overcome to a certain extent by assuming that each prize represents not a concrete consumption as a cup of coffee or a steak, but a kind of 'opportunity set', as it is the case when each prize represents a certain amount of money. Thus, using a gastronomic example again, we can consider prize x_1 as a menu of fish and meat dishes of high quality from which the consumer can choose, x_2, as a similar menu but with lower quality, etc. – In this case the order in which the individual receives the prizes seems to us less important and the axiom can be accepted as a good approximation of reality. In any event, the case where the individual can alter his future preferences by means of his present consumptions or through moral persuasion or through advertising, etc., although extremely interesting, is beyond the scope of this paper.

We now present in a formal way the

Permutation Axiom. Let k be any natural number greater than 0. Let π_k and π'_k be arbitrary one to one functions from the set of natural numbers $\{1, 2, \ldots\}$ onto itself such that $\pi_k(m) = \pi'_k(m) = m$ for all $m > k$. Then we have: for any finite natural number $k > 0$ and any π_k and π'_k,

$$(x_{h_1}, \ldots, x_{h_i}, \ldots)Q(x_{h_1^*}, \ldots, x_{h_i^*}, \ldots) \Leftrightarrow$$
$$\Leftrightarrow (x_{h_{\pi_k(1)}}, \ldots, x_{h_{\pi_k(i)}}, \ldots)Q(x_{h_{\pi'_k(1)}^*}, \ldots, x_{h_{\pi'_k(i)}^*}, \ldots),$$

where h_i and h_i^* both belong to N for $i = 1, 2, \ldots$.

The Independence Axiom. Using the example of Mr. A's after lunch drinks, this axiom simply states that if two sequences of drinks $x_{h_1}, \ldots, x_{h_i}, \ldots$ and $x_{h_1^*}, \ldots, x_{h_i^*}, \ldots$ coincide from the $(\nu + 1)$th term on, and Mr. A prefers the sequence $x_{h_1}, \ldots, x_{h_i}, \ldots$ to the sequence $x_{h_1^*}, \ldots, x_{h_i^*}, \ldots$, he will also prefer drinking $x_{h_1}, \ldots, x_{h_\nu}$ to drinking $x_{h_1^*}, \ldots, x_{h_\nu^*}$ the first ν days no matter what he is offered to drink the rest of the days whenever these drinks are the same in both cases.

Before we present in a formal way the independence axiom, it might be convenient to develop some notation. Consider an infinite sequence

(1) $x_{h_1}, \ldots, x_{h_\nu}, \ldots = (x^\infty).$

We will also represent the sequence (1) by $(x^\nu; x^{\infty-\nu})$, where x^ν represents the first ν terms of the sequence and $x^{\infty-\nu}$ the remaining terms. Suppose we obtain a new sequence from the sequence (1) by changing some, all or none of the first ν terms. The resulting sequence will be represented by $(x^{*\nu}; x^{\infty-\nu})$. Similar changes on the remaining part of sequence (1) will be represented accordingly.

We can now formally present the *Independence Axiom*. For any natural number $\nu > 0$,

$$(x^\nu; x^{\infty-\nu}) \gtreqless (x^{*\nu}; x^{\infty-\nu}) \Leftrightarrow (x^\nu; x^{*\infty-\nu}) \gtreqless (x^{*\nu}; x^{*\infty-\nu}).$$

Remark. A preference ordering Q defined on x^∞, satisfying the Permutation and Independence axioms, induces a preference ordering Q_ν, which also satisfies the corresponding Permutation and Independence axioms, on the Cartesian product $X^\nu = X \times \cdots \times X$ (ν times; ν being any finite natural number greater than 0) as follows: write

$$x^\nu = (x_{h_1}, \ldots, x_{h_\nu}); \qquad x^{*\nu} = (x^*_{h_1}, \ldots, x^*_{h_\nu}).$$

Then

$$(x_{h_1}, \ldots, x_{h_\nu}) Q_\nu (x^*_{h_1}, \ldots, x^*_{h_\nu})$$

if and only if there is a $(x^{\infty-\nu})$ such that $(x^\nu; x^{\infty-\nu}) Q(x^{*\nu}; x^{\infty-\nu})$. In particular, we have the preference ordering Q_1 defined on the set of prizes X. We may write $\geq$ instead of Q_ν when it is clear from the context on which Cartesian product X^ν the preference ordering is defined.

The *rate of substitution axiom* tries to formalize the intuitive notion that if an individual is disappointed because in one instance he is given prize x_q instead of prize x_p that he likes better, he can be compensated by giving him in a sufficiently large number of instances a prize x_{p^*} instead of a prize x_{q^*} that he likes less. Formally, we have

Rate of Substitution Axiom. If $x_{h_p} \geq x_{h_q}$ and $x_{h_{p^*}} > x_{h_{q^*}}$ then there exists a real and non-negative number (that depends on $h_p, h_q, h_{p^*}, h_{q^*}$), $R(h_p, h_q, h_{p^*}, h_{q^*})$ such that the following is true:

(a) If in a sequence $x_{h_1}, \ldots, x_{h_i}, \ldots$, we substitute x_{h_q} for x_{h_p} r times $(r > 0)$ and $x_{h_{p^*}}$ for $x_{h_{q^*}}$ s times $(s \geq 0)$, then the resulting sequence is $>$,

$<$, or $\sim$ with regard to the original one if and only if

$$s/r > R(h_p, h_q, h_{p*}, h_{q*}), \qquad s/r < R(h_p, h_q, h_{p*}, h_{q*}),$$

or

$$s/r = R(h_p, h_q, h_{p*}, h_{q*}),$$

respectively.

(b) If in a sequence $x_{h_1}, \ldots, x_{h_i}, \ldots$, we substitute x_{h_p} for x_{h_q} r times $(r > 0)$ and $x_{h_{q*}}$ for $x_{h_{p*}}$ s times $(s \geq 0)$, then the resulting sequence is $>$, $<$, or $\sim$ with regard to the original one if and only if

$$s/r < R(h_p, h_q, h_{p*}, h_{q*}), \qquad s/r > R(h_p, h_q, h_{p*}, h_{q*}),$$

or

$$s/r = R(h_p, h_q, h_{p*}, h_{q*}),$$

respectively.

We will sometimes represent a finite sequence containing c_1 times the term $x_{h_1}, \ldots, c_k$ times the term x_{h_k}, where the c_i's $(i = 1, \ldots, k)$ are integer and positive numbers, by $c_1 \times x_{h_1}, \ldots, c_k \times x_{h_k}$. This representation is legitimate in view of the Permutation axiom.

We now turn to our last axiom, the

Repetition Axiom. For any integer and positive numbers k and c,

$$x_{h_1}, \ldots, x_{h_k} \gtrless x_{h_1^*}, \ldots, x_{h_k^*} \Leftrightarrow$$
$$\Leftrightarrow c \times x_{h_1}, \ldots, c \times x_{h_k} \gtrless c \times x_{h_1^*}, \ldots, c \times x_{h_k^*}.$$

The following theorem, whose proof we will postpone until the appendix, enunciates some of the properties of the function $R(h_p, h_q, h_{p*}, h_{q*})$.

THEOREM 1. *The function* $R(h_p, h_q, h_{p*}, h_{q*})$, *that clearly is unique, satisfies the following properties:*

(i) $\qquad$ *If* $R(h_p, h_q, h_{p*}, h_{q*}) > 0$, *then*

$$R(h_{p*}, h_{q*}, h_p, h_q) = \frac{1}{R(h_p, h_q, h_{p*}, h_{q*})},$$

(ii) $\qquad$ $$R(h_p, h_q, h_{p*}, h_{q*}) = \frac{R(h_p, h_q, h_g, h_k)}{R(h_{p*}, h_{q*}, h_g, h_k)}.$$

(iii)   If $x_{h_1} > x_{h_2} > \cdots > x_{h_p}$ $(2 \leq p \leq n)$, and $x_g > x_k$, then

$$R(h_1, h_p, g, k) = R(h_1, h_2, g, k) + R(h_2, h_3, g, k) + \cdots$$
$$+ R(h_{p-1}, h_p, g, k).$$

Utility indices. We try to determine now if they exist, utility indices for the different prizes x_i, $u^c(x_i) = u_i^c$, $i = 1, \ldots, n$, that satisfy the following condition:

$$[\alpha] \qquad x_{h_1}, \ldots, x_{h_k} \gtreqless x_{h_1^*}, \ldots, x_{h_k^*} \Leftrightarrow \sum_{i=1}^{k} u_{h_i}^c \gtreqless \sum_{i=1}^{k} u_{h_i^*}^c,$$

where k is any finite natural number greater than 0.

THEOREM 2. (Proof in the Appendix.) *There exist utility indices u_i^c satisfying condition $[\alpha]$ if and only if:*

(i) $u_r^c > u_s^c \Leftrightarrow x_r > x_s$; *and*

(ii)   *if $x_r > x_s$ and $x_{r^*} > x_{s^*}$, then*

$$\frac{u_r^c - u_s^c}{u_{r^*}^c - u_{s^*}^c} = R(r, s, r^*, s^*).$$

Write $u^c = (u_1^c, \ldots, u_n^c)$. We will call the vectors u^c, utility vectors.

THEOREM 3. (Proof is in the Appendix.)

(i) *There exists a class $\mathcal{U}^c$ of utility vectors u^c that satisfy conditions (i) and (ii) of Theorem 2 and therefore condition $[\alpha]$. Two vectors $\bar{u}^c = (\bar{u}_1^c, \ldots, \bar{u}_n^c)$ and $\bar{\bar{u}}^c = (\bar{\bar{u}}_1^c, \ldots, \bar{\bar{u}}_n^c)$ belong to the class $\mathcal{U}^c$ if and only if $\bar{u}^c \in \mathcal{U}^c$ and $\bar{\bar{u}}_i^c = a u_i^c + b$ for $i = 1, \ldots, n$, where a and b are constants, $a > 0$.*

(ii) *If a utility vector u^c satisfies conditions (i) and (ii) of Theorem 2, then $u^c \in \mathcal{U}^c$.*

Now that we have developed a theory of utility for sequences of prizes, we can attack the problem suggested by Marschak in [3] of relating the rule of 'long run success' to the rule of maximizing expected utility. To this task we will turn in the following sections.

3. MAXIMIZATION OF EXPECTED UTILITY AND THE RULE
OF LONG RUN SUCCESS

Let us go back to our example regarding Mr. A and his after lunch drinks. Suppose that our hostess decides to determine each day by means of a random device, say a roulette, whether coffee, tea or camomile will be served. Thus, the set of all possible outcomes of playing once the roulette is partitioned into three events E_1, E_2 and E_3 and the commitment is made that those days in which the outcome of playing the roulette belongs to E_1 coffee will be served, those in which the outcome belongs to E_2 tea will be served, and those in which E_3 obtains camomile will be served.

Let P_i designate the probability of the event E_i ($i = 1, 2, 3$). The word probability here will be used in the objective or statistical sense. That is, P_i will be taken here as the limit to which the frequency of occurrence of the event E_i 'converges' when the random experiment is repeated infinite many times.

Let $\mathscr{E}$ be the random experiment that corresponds to a partition of all the possible outcomes of playing our roulette into three events E_1, E_2 and E_3 with probabilities P_1, P_2 and P_3, respectively. Let $\mathscr{E}'$ be the random experiment that corresponds to the partition into the events E'_1, E'_2, E'_3 with probabilities P'_1, P'_2, P'_3. Suppose now that our hostess presents Mr. A with the two random experiments and asks him which of the two he prefers that be used every day in order to determine whether coffee, tea, or camomile will be served. What random experiment should he choose $\mathscr{E}$ or $\mathscr{E}'$? Or equivalently, what probability distribution should he choose (P_1, P_2, P_3) or (P'_1, P'_2, P'_3)?

Remark. We want to stress here that for Mr. A to choose the random experiment, say $\mathscr{E}$, or equivalently its corresponding probability distribution (P_1, P_2, P_3), means that *each* and *every* day the roulette is played; and that coffee will be served when E_1 obtains, tea when E_2 and camomile when E_3. Also given the objective or statistical interpretation that we have adopted for the probabilities P_1, P_2 and P_3, this means that by choosing the probability distribution (P_1, P_2, P_3), Mr. A will obtain a sequence of drinks $x_{h_1}, x_{h_2}, \ldots, x_{h_k}$, such that the frequency with which coffee, tea and camomile will be served 'converges', respectively, to the probabilities P_1, P_2 and P_3 when $k \to \infty$.

The rule of long run success. Let $x_{h_1}, \ldots, x_{h_k}$ and $x'_{h_1}, \ldots, x'_{h_k}$ designate, respectively, the sequences of the first k prizes generated by the random devices $\mathscr{E}$ and $\mathscr{E}'$, or equivalently by their corresponding probability distributions (P_1, P_2, P_3) and (P'_1, P'_2, P'_3). Clearly, the sequences $x_{h_1}, \ldots, x_{h_k}$ and $x'_{h_1}, \ldots, x'_{h_k}$ are random and therefore we can calculate the probability that, say, the sequence $x_{h_1}, \ldots, x_{h_k}$ be preferred by Mr A to the sequence $x'_{h_1}, \ldots, x'_{h_k}$. In symbols $P_r[(x_{h_1}, \ldots, x_{h_k}) > (x'_{h_1}, \ldots, x'_{h_k})]$. Now, we say that Mr. A satisfies or follows the *rule of long run success* if he chooses the probability distribution (P_1, P_2, P_3) over the probability distribution (P'_1, P'_2, P'_3) whenever,

$$\lim_{k \to \infty} P_r[(x_{h_1}, \ldots, x_{h_k}) > (x'_{h_1}, \ldots, x'_{h_k})] = 1.$$

It will be easy to prove now the proposition that if Mr. A orders the possible sequences of prizes $x_{h_1}, \ldots, x_{h_k}, \ldots$ in a way that satisfies our permutation, independence, rate of substitution and repetition axioms, then the rule of maximizing the expected value of the utilities u_i^c *implies* that the rule of long run success, as stated above, is satisfied.

Proof. As it was shown in Section 2, if the preference ordering, by Mr. A, of the possible sequences $x_{h_1}, \ldots, x_{h_k}, \ldots$ satisfies our axioms, then utility indices $u^c(x_1)$, $u^c(x_2)$, $u^c(x_3)$, constant up to positive linear transformations, can be assigned to the prizes x_1, x_2, x_3 with the property that the sequence $x_{h_1}, \ldots, x_{h_k}$ is at least as good as the sequence $x'_{h_1}, \ldots, x'_{h_k}$ if and only if

$$\sum_{i=1}^{k} u^c(x_{h_i}) \geqslant \sum_{i=1}^{k} u^c(x'_{h_i}).$$

If the sequences $x_{h_1}, \ldots, x_{h_k}$ and $x'_{h_1}, \ldots, x'_{h_k}$ are generated, respectively, by the probability distributions (P_1, P_2, P_3) and (P'_1, P'_2, P'_3), then

$$Z_k = \frac{1}{k} \sum_{i=1}^{k} u^c(x_{h_i}) \quad \text{and} \quad Z'_k = \frac{1}{k} \sum_{i=1}^{k} u^c(x'_{h_i})$$

are random variables and by the *law of large numbers* we know that Z_k and Z'_k converge in probability respectively to $\sum_{i=1}^{3} P_i u^c(x_i)$ and $\sum_{i=1}^{3} P'_i u^c(x_i)$ as $k \to \infty$. Now, the rule of maximizing the expected value of the utilities $u^c(x_i)$ prescribes that the probability distribution (P_1, P_2, P_3) be preferred over the probability distribution (P'_1, P'_2, P'_3)

whenever $\Sigma_{i=1}^{3} P_i u^c(x_i)$ is greater than $\Sigma_{i=1}^{3} P_i' u^c(x_i)$, which implies that

$$\lim_{k \to \infty} P_r[Z_k > Z_k'] = 1.$$

But

$$P_r[Z_k > Z_k'] = P_r[kZ_k > kZ_k'] = P_r\left[\sum_{i=1}^{k} u^c(x_{h_i}) > \sum_{i=1}^{k} u^c(x_{h_i}')\right]$$

$$= P_r[(x_{h_1}, \ldots, x_{h_k}) > (x_{h_1}', \ldots, x_{h_k}')].$$

Thus

$$\sum_{i=1}^{3} P_i u^c(x_i) > \sum_{i=1}^{3} P_i' u^c(x_i)$$

implies that

$$\lim_{k \to \infty} P_r[(x_{h_1}, \ldots, x_{h_k}) > (x_{h_1}', \ldots, x_{h_k}')] = 1. \qquad \text{QED}$$

Remark. Observe that the rule of long run success, as stated by us, requires, to be satisfied, only that the probability distribution $P = (P_1, P_2, P_3)$ be ranked above the probability distribution $P' = (P_1', P_2', P_3')$ whenever $\Sigma_{i=1}^{3} P_i u^c(x_i) = E[u_i^c | P]$ is greater than $\Sigma_{i=1}^{3} P_i' u^c(x_i) = E[u_i^c | P']$. But it does not require that the probability distributions P and P' be ranked as indifferent to each other when $E[u_i^c | P] = E[u_i^c | P']$. Thus, if we designate by $\sigma[u_i^c | P]$ the standard deviation of the random utility given P, i.e., the standard deviation of the random variable taking the values u_i^c with probabilities P_i ($i = 1, 2, 3$), then the individual can order the probability distributions, without violating the rule of long run success, according to the following lexicographic ordering:

$$P > P' \begin{cases} \text{if } E[u_i^c | P] > E[u_i^c | P'], \\ \text{or if } E[u_i^c | P] = E[u_i^c | P'], \quad \sigma[u_i^c | P] > \sigma[u_i^c | P']. \end{cases}$$

4. SOME FINAL REMARKS

Remark 1. In this paper, we have presented a utility theory for sequences of prizes that allows us to discuss rational behavior in terms of the intuitively very appealing rule of long run success. Whether or not this utility theory is a 'good' one to deal with sequences of prizes remains to be seen. We are aware of the limitations of its applicability and we indicated this fact in Section 2 where we presented and discussed our axioms. But in cases similar to the example regarding Mr. A and his after lunch drinks we believe that both our axioms and the conclusions obtained from our model by defining rational behavior as that behavior that does not violate the rule of long run success are indeed reasonable. For those situations only we will claim that our model and its conclusions are valid.

Remark 2. It should be noted that the utility indices u_i^c that we have used in this paper are derived from axioms which do not involve the ordering of probability distributions or uncertain prospects. Thus, in the derivation of the u_i^c no uncertainty is involved. In the von Neumann and Morgenstern expected utility theory, on the contrary, the utility indices u_i^v are derived from axioms regarding the ordering of probability distributions or uncertain prospects.

Remark 3. An interesting question then arises: What is the relationship between the u_i^v and the u_i^c? More concretely, suppose that Mr. A satisfies our axioms and, consequently, by asking him the different rates of substitution postulated by the Rate of Substitution Axiom, we can calculate his utility indices u_1^c, u_2^c, u_3^c. Suppose also that Mr. A satisfies the von Neumann and Morgenstern, so called, rationality axioms and, consequently, by observing how he orders the different probability distributions (P_1, P_2, P_3) we can obtain his utility indices u_1^v, u_2^v, u_3^v. What is the relationship between these two sets of indices? Are the u_i^v equal to the u_i^c, up to a positive linear transformation? Or, are the u_i^v increasing concave or convex transformations[2] of the u_i^c?

Remark 4. In situations where our model applies, it appears *reasonable* to adopt as the only rationality criterion the rule of long run success. But then, the von Neumann and Morgenstern rationality axioms imply rationality in the sense of the rule of long run success only if the utility indices u_i^v derived from these axioms are equal to the utility indices u_i^c up to a positive linear transformation. Thus, suppose that after learning from Mr. A what are his rate of substitution values, we make the necessary calculations and obtain a set of utility indices u_i^c, say, $u_1^c = 2$ for the utility of coffee, $u_2^c = 1$ for the utility of tea and $u_3^c = 0$ for the utility of camomile. To calculate the utility indices u_i^v, assuming that Mr. A satisfies the von Neumann and

Morgenstern rationality axioms, we can put $u_1^v = 2$, $u_3^v = 0$ and then calculate u_2^v by asking Mr. A to reveal the probability distribution $(P_1, 0, 1 - P_1)$ that is indifferent from his point of view to having tea with certainty. In order for Mr. A to satisfy the rule of long run success, as stated by us, he must choose $P_1 = \frac{1}{2}$, that will give $u_2^v = 1$. But he can choose, without violating the rationality axioms, say, $P_1 = \frac{3}{4}$, that will give $u_2^v = \frac{3}{2}$; or $P_1 = \frac{1}{4}$, in which case $u_2^v = \frac{1}{2}$, etc. And in all these cases he will be violating the rule of long run success although he behaves in accordance with the von Neumann and Morgenstern rationality axioms.

Remark 5. If we define *rational behavior*, as we have proposed before for those situations where our model applies, as any behavior that does not violate the rule of long run success then it follows that the rationality axioms are neither necessary nor sufficient for rational behavior. They are not necessary because the lexicographic ordering of probability distributions

$$P > P', \quad \begin{array}{l} \text{if and} \\ \text{only if} \end{array} \begin{cases} E[u_i^c \mid P] > E[u_i^c \mid P'], \\ \text{or if } E[u_i^c \mid P] = E[u_i^c \mid P'], \sigma[u_i^c \mid P'] > \sigma[u_i^c \mid P] \end{cases}$$

does satisfy the rule of long run success but not the rationality axioms. They are not sufficient because the utility indices u_i^v derived from them are not necessarily equal to the utility indices u_i^c, up to a positive linear transformation, and when this is the case the rule of maximizing the expected value of the utilities u_i^v does violate the rule of long run success.

Remark 6. The conclusion of Remark 5 is similar to the contention made by M. Allais [See [7] p.505, (9) and (10)]. He asserts there that for the rational man there does not exist in general utility indices u_i^v (he calls them utility indicators $B(x_i)$) such that the decision maker orders the probability distributions as if he were maximizing the expected value of u_i^v. This would be the case if we define 'rational man' as one that does not violate the rule of long run success and he happens to order the probability distributions according to the lexicographic order described in Remark 4. He also asserts that when such utility indicator $B(x_i)$ exists, it must coincide, up to a positive linear transformation, with what he calls the psychological value $\bar{s}(x_i)$. If $\bar{s}(x_i)$ is equal to $u^c(x_i)$, up to a positive linear transformation, then the same conclusion is reached in this paper. M. Allais, however, does not justify his assertions by using the rule of long run success and the law of large numbers as we do.

Remark 7. Since no uncertainty is involved in obtaining the utility indices u_i^c, and, on the other hand, the u_i^v's are derived from the ordering of probability distributions, it appears attractive to try to characterize the behavior toward risk of Mr. A by the relationship between his utility indices u_i^c and u_i^v: $u_i^v = F(u_i^c)$. Thus, we propose on a tentative basis the following definitions:

(i) Mr. A is risk neutral if F is a positive linear transformation.

(ii) Mr. A is risk averse if F is a monotonic increasing and strictly concave transformation.

(iii) Mr. A is risk loving if F is a monotonic increasing and strictly convex transformation.

It is worth noting here that both risk averse and risk loving behaviors are not rational in the sense that they do not satisfy the rule of long run success. We do not plan to study here the advantages or disadvantages of these definitions. We want to point out however that they allow us to make comparisons of risk averseness with many commodities without restricting those comparisons, as Kihlstrom and Mirman do [8], to cases where the ordinal preferences are the same.

APPENDIX

Proof of Theorem 1

Part (i). Assume that $R(h_p, h_q, h_{p^*}, h_{q^*}) > 0$ and

$$R(h_{p^*}, h_{q^*}, h_p, h_q) \neq \frac{1}{R(h_p, h_q, h_{p^*}, h_{q^*})}.$$

Then, either

(α) $R(h_{p^*}, h_{q^*}, h_p, h_q) \cdot R(h_p, h_q, h_{p^*}, h_{q^*}) > 1,$

or

(β) $R(h_{p^*}, h_{q^*}, h_p, h_q) \cdot R(h_p, h_q, h_{p^*}, h_{q^*}) < 1.$

Assume that (α) holds. Since $R(h_p, h_q, h_{p^*}, h_{q^*}) > 0$ and

$$R(h_{p^*}, h_{q^*}, h_p, h_q) \cdot R(h_p, h_q, h_{p^*}, h_{q^*}) > 1,$$

there exist two numbers a and b integer and positive such that,

$$R(h_p, h_q, h_{p^*}, h_{q^*}) > a/b, \quad \text{and} \quad R(h_{p^*}, h_{q^*}, h_p, h_q) > b/a.$$

Consider now a finite sequence containing b times the term x_{h_p}, and a times the term x_{h_q}. We can write this finite sequence as follows: $b \times x_{h_p}, a \times x_{h_q}$. By applying the Rate of Substitution Axiom, we have:

(α_1) Since $R(h_p, h_q, h_{p^*}, h_{q^*}) > a/b$,

$$b \times x_{h_p}, a \times x_{h_{q^*}} > b \times x_{h_q}, a \times x_{h_{p^*}}.$$

(α_2) Since $R(h_{p^*}, h_{q^*}, h_p, h_q) > b/a$,

$$b \times x_{h_q}, a \times x_{h_{p^*}} > b \times x_{h_p}, a \times x_{h_{q^*}}.$$

(α_1) and (α_2) imply that $b \times x_{h_p}, a \times x_{h_{q^*}} > b \times x_{h_p}, a \times x_{h_{q^*}}$, which is impossible. Therefore (α) cannot hold. In a similar way we can show that (β) cannot hold, which completes the proof of Part (i).

Part (ii). Assume that $R(h_p, h_q, h_{p^*}, h_{q^*}) > 0$ and that

$$R(h_p, h_q, h_{p^*}, h_{q^*}) \neq \frac{R(h_p, h_q, h_g, h_k)}{R(h_{p^*}, h_{q^*}, h_g, h_k)}$$

$$= R(h_p, h_q, h_g, h_k) \cdot R(h_g, h_k, h_{p^*}, h_{q^*}).$$

Then either

(α) $R(h_p, h_q, h_{p^*}, h_{q^*}) > R(h_p, h_q, h_g, h_k) \cdot R(h_g, h_k, h_{p^*}, h_{q^*}),$

or

(β) $R(h_p, h_q, h_{p^*}, h_{q^*}) < R(h_p, h_q, h_g, h_k) \cdot R(h_g, h_k, h_{p^*}, h_{q^*}).$

Suppose that (α) holds. Then, there exist numbers b, c and d integer and positive such that:

$$R(h_p, h_q, h_{p^*}, h_{q^*}) > b/c; \quad R(h_p, h_q, h_g, h_k) < d/c;$$
$$R(h_g, h_k, h_{p^*}, h_{q^*}) < b/d.$$

Consider the finite sequence

$$c \times x_{h_p}, b \times x_{h_{q^*}}, d \times x_{h_k}.$$

By applying the Rate of Substitution Axiom we have:

(i) $c \times x_{h_p}, b \times x_{h_{q^*}}, d \times x_{h_k} > c \times x_{h_q}, b \times x_{h_{p^*}}, d \times x_{h_k},$

since $R(h_p, h_q, h_{p^*}, h_{q^*}) > b/c,$

(ii) $\quad c \times x_{h_p}, b \times x_{h_{q^*}}, d \times x_{h_k} < c \times x_{h_q}, b \times x_{h_{q^*}}, d \times x_{h_g},$

since $R(h_p, h_q, h_g, h_k) > d/c$,

(iii) $\quad c \times x_{h_q}, b \times x_{h_{q^*}}, d \times x_{h_g} < c \times x_{h_q}, b \times x_{h_{p^*}}, d \times x_{h_k},$

since $R(h_g, h_k, h_{p^*}, h_{q^*}) < b/d$.

(i), (ii) and (iii) cannot be satisfied simultaneously, therefore (α) cannot hold.

In the same way, we can see that (β) cannot hold, which completes the proof of Part (ii) of Theorem 1.

Part (iii). It suffices to prove that if $x_{h_1} > x_{h_2} > x_{h_3}$ and $x_g > x_k$, then

$$R(h_1, h_3, g, k) = R(h_1, h_2, g, k) + R(h_2, h_3, g, k).$$

Suppose not. Then, either

(α) $\quad R(h_1, h_3, g, k) > R(h_1, h_2, g, k) + R(h_2, h_3, g, k),$

or

(β) $\quad R(h_1, h_3, g, k) < R(h_1, h_2, g, k) + R(h_2, h_3, g, k).$

Assume that (α) holds. Then, there exist three numbers b_1, b_2, and c integers and positive such that $b_1/c > R(h_1, h_2, g, k)$, $b_2/c > R(h_2, h_3, g, k)$ and $(b_1 + b_2)/c < R(h_1, h_3, g, k)$. The rest of the proof consists in constructing an appropriate finite sequence as in Part (ii), and showing by using the Rate of Substitution Axiom that the assumption that (α) holds leads to an impossible result. Case (β) can be dealt with in a similar way.

Proof of Theorem 2. We will first prove that if there exist utility indices u_i^c satisfying condition [α], then they must satisfy conditions (i) and (ii) of Theorem 2. That they must satisfy condition (i) is obvious. We will then show that they must satisfy condition (ii). Suppose they do not. Suppose, for instance, that

$$x_r > x_s, x_{r^*} > x_{s^*} \quad \text{and} \quad \frac{u_r^c - u_s^c}{u_{r^*}^c - u_{s^*}^c} > R(r, s, r^*, s^*).$$

Then, there exist numbers b and c, integer and positive, such that

$$\frac{u_r^c - u_s^c}{u_{r^*}^c - u_{s^*}^c} > \frac{b}{c} > R(r, s, r^*, s^*).$$

Now compare the finite sequences $c \times x_r$, $b \times x_{s*}$ and $c \times x_s$, $b \times x_{r*}$. Since $c \times u_r^c + b \times u_{s*}^c > c \times u_s^c + b \times u_{r*}^c$, we should have $c \times x_r$, $b \times x_{s*} > c \times x_s$, $b \times x_{r*}$. But, since $b/c > R(r, s, r^*, s^*)$, we should also have $c \times x_s$, $b \times x_{r*} > c \times x_r$, $b \times x_{s*}$, which is not possible. Thus our assumption that

$$\frac{u_r^c - u_s^c}{u_{r*}^c - u_{s*}^c} > R(r, s, r^*, s^*)$$

cannot hold. We can dispose of the case

$$\frac{u_r^c - u_s^c}{u_{r*}^c - u_{s*}^c} < R(r, s, r^*, s^*)$$

in a similar way.

Let us now conclude the proof of Theorem 2. Suppose that we have utility indices u_i^c that satisfy conditions (i) and (ii) of Theorem 2, but not condition [α]. Suppose, for instance, that

$$x_{h_1}, \ldots, x_{h_k} > x_{h_1^*}, \ldots, x_{h_k^*} \quad \text{and} \quad \sum_{i=1}^{k} u_{h_i}^c < \sum_{i=1}^{k} u_{h_i^*}^c.$$

Without loss of generality, we can assume that

$$u_{h_i}^c < u_{h_i^*}^c, \quad \text{for } i = 1, \ldots, j \quad (1 \leq j \leq k);$$

and

$$u_{h_i}^c \geq u_{h_i^*}^c, \quad \text{for } i = j+1, \ldots, k.$$

By condition (i) of Theorem 2, we have:

$$x_{h_i^*} > x_{h_i}, \quad \text{for } i = 1, \ldots, j;$$

$$x_{h_i^*} \leq x_{h_i}, \quad \text{for } i = j+1, \ldots, k.$$

Since $\sum_{i=1}^{k} u_{h_i}^c < \sum_{i=1}^{k} u_{h_i^*}^c$, we have that

$$\sum_{i=1}^{j} [u_{h_i^*}^c - u_{h_i}^c] > \sum_{i=j+1}^{k} [u_{h_i}^c - u_{h_i^*}^c].$$

By now dividing both members of the previous inequality by $u_{h_1^*}^c - u_{h_1}^c > 0$ we obtain, taking into account condition (ii) of Theorem 2,

$$\sum_{i=1}^{j} R(h_i^*, h_i, h_1^*, h_1) > \sum_{i=j+1}^{k} R(h_i, h_i^*, h_1^*, h_1).$$

We can find integer and positive numbers $c, b_1, \ldots, b_k$ such that:

$$\sum_{i=j+1}^{k} R(h_i, h_i^*, h_1^*, h_1) < \sum_{i=j+1}^{k} b_i/c < \sum_{i=1}^{j} b_i/c <$$
$$< \sum_{i=1}^{j} R(h_i^*, h_i, h_1^*, h_1);$$

$$b_i/c < R(h_i^*, h_i, h_1^*, h_1), \qquad \text{for } i = 1, \ldots, j;$$

$$b_i/c > R(h_i, h_i^*, h_1^*, h_1), \qquad \text{for } i = j+1, \ldots, k.$$

Consider now the sequence,

$$c \times x_{h_1}, \ldots, c \times x_{h_j}, c \times x_{h_{j+1}}, \ldots, c \times x_{h_k}, \left(\sum_{i=1}^{j} b_i\right) \times x_{h_1^*}, \left(\sum_{i=j+1}^{k} b_i\right) \times x_{h_1}.$$

Since $b_i/c < R(h_i^*, h_i, h_1^*, h_1)$ for $i = 1, \ldots, j$, we have by using the Rate of Substitution Axiom that,

(i)

$$c \times x_{h_1}, \ldots, c \times x_{h_j}, c \times x_{h_{j+1}}, \ldots, c \times x_{h_k}, \left(\sum_{i=1}^{j} b_i\right) \times x_{h_1^*}, \left(\sum_{i=j+1}^{k} b_i\right) \times x_{h_1} <$$
$$< c \times x_{h_1^*}, \ldots, c \times x_{h_j^*}, c \times x_{h_{j+1}}, \ldots, c \times x_{h_k}, \left(\sum_{i=1}^{j} b_i\right) \times x_{h_1}, \left(\sum_{i=j+1}^{k} b_i\right) \times x_{h_1}.$$

Since $b_i/c > R(h_i, h_i^*, h_1^*, h_1)$ for $i = j+1, \ldots, k$, we can obtain by applying the Rate of Substitution Axiom,

(ii)

$$c \times x_{h_i^*}, \ldots, c \times x_{h_j^*}, c \times x_{h_{j+1}}, \ldots, c \times x_{h_k}, \left(\sum_{i=1}^{j} b_i\right) \times x_{h_1}, \left(\sum_{i=j+1}^{k} b_i\right) \times x_{h_1} <$$
$$< c + x_{h_1^*}, \ldots, c \times x_{h_j^*}, c \times x_{h_{j+1}^*}, \ldots, c \times x_{h_k^*}, \left(\sum_{i=1}^{j} b_i\right) \times x_{h_1}, \left(\sum_{i=j+1}^{k} b_i\right) \times x_{h_1^*}.$$

Since $\Sigma_{i=1}^{j} b_i > \Sigma_{i=j+1}^{k} b_i$, by using again the Rate of Substitution Axiom, we obtain,

(iii)

$$c \times x_{h_1^*}, \ldots, c \times x_{h_j^*}, c \times x_{h_{j+1}^*}, \ldots, c \times x_{h_k^*}, \left(\sum_{i=1}^{j} b_i\right) \times x_{h_1}, \left(\sum_{i=j+1}^{k} b_i\right) \times x_{h_1^*} <$$
$$< c \times x_{h_1^*}, \ldots, c \times x_{h_j^*}, c \times x_{h_{j+1}^*}, \ldots, c \times x_{h_k^*}, \left(\sum_{j=1}^{j} b_i\right) \times x_{h_1^*}, \left(\sum_{i+j+1}^{k} b_i\right) \times x_{h_1}.$$

(i), (ii) and (iii) imply that,

$$c \times x_{h_1}, \ldots, c \times x_{h_j}, c \times x_{h_{j+1}}, \ldots, c \times x_{h_k}, \left(\sum_{i=1}^{j} b_i \right) \times x_{h_1^*}, \left(\sum_{i=j+1}^{k} b_i \right) \times x_{h_1} <$$

$$< c \times x_{h_1^*}, \ldots, c \times x_{h_j^*}, c \times x_{h_{j+1}^*}, \ldots, c \times x_{h_k^*}, \left(\sum_{i=1}^{j} b_i \right) \times x_{h_1^*}, \left(\sum_{i=1}^{j} b_i \right) \times x_{h_1},$$

which in view of the Independence Axiom implies that $c \times x_{h_1}, \ldots,$ $c \times x_{h_k} < c \times x_{h_1^*}, \ldots, c \times x_{h_k^*}$. And by using now the Repetition Axiom, we finally obtain, $x_{h_1}, \ldots, x_{h_k} < x_{h_1^*}, \ldots, x_{h_k^*}$, which contradicts the assumption that $x_{h_1}, \ldots, x_{h_k} > x_{h_1^*}, \ldots, x_{h_k^*}$. We can dispose of the other cases in a similar way.

Proof of Theorem 3. Without loss of generality, we can assume $x_1 > x_2 > \cdots > x_{n-1} > x_n$. Consider now the following vector $\bar{u}^c = (\bar{u}_1^c, \bar{u}_2^c, \ldots, \bar{u}_i^c, \ldots, \bar{u}_{n-1}^c, \bar{u}_n^c)$:

$$\bar{u}_n^c = 0; \quad \bar{u}_{n-1}^c = 1; \quad \bar{u}_i^c = \bar{u}_{i+1}^c + R(i, i+1, n-1, n),$$
$$\text{for } i = 1, \ldots, n-2.$$

Since $R(i, i+1, n-1, n) > 0$ for $i = 1, \ldots, n-2$, it follows that the $\bar{u}_i^c$'s satisfy condition (i) of Theorem 2. They also satisfy the following condition:

(ii)′ $\quad \dfrac{\bar{u}_i^c - \bar{u}_{i+1}^c}{\bar{u}_{n-1}^c - \bar{u}_n^c} = R(i, i+1, n-1, n), \quad \text{for } i = 1, \ldots, n-1.$

By taking into account now conditions (i), (ii) and (iii) of Theorem 1, it can be seen easily that the $\bar{u}_i^c$'s also satisfy condition (ii) of Theorem 2.

If $\bar{\bar{u}}^c = (\bar{\bar{u}}_1^c, \ldots, \bar{\bar{u}}_i^c, \ldots, \bar{\bar{u}}_n^c)$ is any vector such that $\bar{\bar{u}}_i^c = a\bar{u}_i^c + b$, where a and b are real numbers, $a > 0$, it follows immediately that $\bar{\bar{u}}^c$ satisfies conditions (i) and (ii) of Theorem 2. This completes the proof of Part (i) of Theorem 3.

Part (ii) of Theorem 3 is easily proved by observing that if a vector u^c satisfies conditions (i) and (ii) of Theorem 2, then it also satisfies condition (ii)′ stated above and therefore

$$\frac{u_i^c - u_{i+1}^c}{u_{n-1}^c - u_n^c} = \frac{\bar{u}_i^c - \bar{u}_{i+1}^c}{\bar{u}_{n-1}^c - \bar{u}_n^c},$$

which implies that $u_i^c = a\bar{u}_i^c + b$, $a > 0$, for $i = 1, \ldots, n$.

University of Illinois at Chicago Circle

NOTES

[1] We will write $x^\infty > x^{*\infty}$ to mean $x^\infty \geq x^{*\infty}$ but not $x^{*\infty} \geq x^\infty$. $x^\infty \sim x^{*\infty}$ means $x^\infty \geq x^{*\infty}$ and $x^{*\infty} \geq x^\infty$. We will use also '$\geq$' ('$>$') to express that the real number written to the left of $\geq$ is greater or equal (greater) than the real number written to the right.

[2] A transformation F from the u_i^c's to the u_i^p's is said to be:

   (i) positive linear if $F(u_i^c) = au_i^c + b$, with $a > 0$;
   (ii) monotonic increasing if $u_j^c > u_i^c$ implies that $F(u_j^c) > F(u_i^c)$;
   (iii) strictly concave (convex) if $u_j^c > u_i^c$ and $u_h^c = \alpha u_j^c + (1 - \alpha)u_i^c$, $0 < \alpha < 1$, implies that $\alpha F(u_j^c) + (1 - \alpha)F(u_i^c) < (>)F[\alpha u_j^c + (1 - \alpha)u_i^c]$.

REFERENCES

[1] von Neumann, J., and Morgenstern, O.: (1947). *Theory of Games and Economic Behavior*, Second Edition, Princeton: Princeton University Press.

[2] Marschak, J.: (1950). 'Rational Behavior, Uncertain Prospects, and Measurable Utility', *Econometrica* 18, 111–41.

[3] Marschak, J.: (1951). 'Why 'should' Statisticians and Businessmen Maximize 'Moral Expectation'?', *Proceedings of the Second Berkeley Symposium on Mathematical Statistics and Probability*, University of California Press, Berkeley.

[4] Marschak, J., and Radner, R.: (1972). *Economic Theory of Teams*, Yale University Press, New Haven, Conn.

[5] Camacho, A.: (1974). 'Societies and Social Decision Functions'. In W. Leinfellner and E. Köhler (Eds.), *Theory and Decision Library Book: Developments in the Methodology of Social Science*, D. Reidel, Dordrecht.

[6] Camacho, A.: (1975). 'Social Choice in a Sequential Environment', *Theory and Decision* 6, 419–37.

[7] Allais, M.: (1953). 'Le Compartement de L'homme Rationnel devant le Risque: Critique des Postulats et Axiomes de L'ecole Americaine', *Econometrica* 21, 503–46.

[8] Kihlstrom, R. E., and Mirman, L. J.: (1974). 'Risk Aversion with Many Commodities', *Journal of Economic Theory* 8, 361–88.

RICHARD M. CYERT AND MORRIS H. DEGROOT

ADAPTIVE UTILITY*

ABSTRACT. This paper is concerned with applying the concept of learning through a Bayesian process to individuals discovering their utility functions. In the usual formulation of decision theory the utility function is assumed to be known and fixed. The assumption of a fixed utility function gives rise to inconsistencies of the type illustrated by the 'Allais paradox'. We have explored a series of examples in which the individual compares the expected utility from the consequences of a particular event before it occurs with the utility actually realized after the event occurs. Any discrepancy between the two is assumed to result in a change in the expected (anticipated) utility function. In other words, expected utilities can be changed as a result of actual experience. The process of discovering the parameters of the expected utility function through experience is assumed to be Bayesian.

INTRODUCTION

The two central components of a decision problem under uncertainty are the decision maker's subjective probabilities, which characterize his knowledge and beliefs, and his subjective utilities, which characterize his preferences and tastes. In the usual development of decision theory and descriptions of decision making, provision is made for the decision maker to change his probabilities in the light of new information, but no provision is made for him to change his utilities in the light of such information. As a result, examples such as the 'Allais paradox' have been constructed which show that a decision maker may make a sequence of choices which are inconsistent with any fixed utility function.[1] Attempts to allow for such inconsistencies in the choices of a decision maker have led to the development of stochastic models of choice behavior and the notion of a stochastic utility function.[2]

It is our belief that the concept of learning can be applied to utilities as well as to probabilities. For example, when utility is a weighted average of several variables, we will argue that the particular weights

---

* Reprinted by kind permission of the Editors from: R. H. Day and T. Groves (Eds.), Adaptive Economic Models, Academic Press, 1975. (Presented at the Symposium on Adaptive Economics, Oct. 1974, Sponsored by the Mathematical Research Center, Madison, Wisc.)

223

Maurice Allais and Ole Hagen (eds.), Expected Utility and the Allais Paradox, 223–241.
Copyright © 1975 by Academic Press, Inc.

used in the utility function are subject to change as a result of learning through experiencing particular values of the variables. The common use of utility functions assumes that an individual can calculate accurately the utility he will receive from any specified values of the variables. We are proposing instead the concept of an adaptive or dynamic utility function in which the utility that will be received by the individual from specified values of the variables is to some extent uncertain, and the expected utility from these values will change as a result of learning through experience.

We postulate a process in which the individual envisions the consequences of an event and derives in his mind the expected utility that he will realize from those consequences. A decision may be made on the basis of this expected utility but actually experiencing the consequences may result in the realization of a significantly different level of utility.[3] As a result of this experience, the expected utility of similar consequences will be changed and another decision under the same circumstances may be quite different. Once it is recognized that utilities can be uncertain and that expected utilities can change by virtue of experience, it becomes important to incorporate these concepts in the theory of decision making.[4]

In this paper we shall attempt to present a full description of the impact of adaptive utility functions on the theory of decision making and to present some formal models for incorporating adaptive utility into the standard theory.

EXPECTED AND REALIZED UTILITY

In classical utility theory, a utility function is assumed to exist for any individual decision maker.[5] It is also assumed that this function is fully known to the individual so that it is even possible for him to make hypothetical choices. Thus, the demand curve for a product can be determined by having each consumer indicate the quantity he would purchase given different prices. After a decision is made, it is assumed that the utility realized by the decision maker is the amount indicated by the utility function. Thus, it is implicitly assumed that the utility that the individual expects from a particular decision is the utility realized when the decision is made. There are no surprises with respect to the amount of utility received. There is no gap between the expectation and the utility realized for each possible set of values of the variables in the utility function. There is only one utility function. It is known by the decision maker and it accurately reflects the utility that will be realized from the consequences of a particular event.

In the approach that we are taking, it is assumed that there are two types of utility functions. The first one is represented by the concept of expected utility. Here the individual may have a complete utility function for consequences that have not been experienced previously, but for which the individual estimates his expected utility. This utility function is somewhat analogous to the a priori probability distribution that is used in Bayesian analysis. We assume that the individual is capable of deriving expected utility for any consequences that may be relevant to him. One way that this expected utility might be derived for any particular consequence or specified values of the variables in the utility function would be for the individual to utilize mathematical expectation. He would construct a probability distribution for the different amounts of utility he might realize from the specified values of the variables and then calculate the mathematical expectation of this distribution. This value would become a point on the expected utility function which is composed of all such points. We do not believe that each individual actually goes through such calculations in determining his expected utility function. Rather we believe that the expected utility function is a heuristic used by the decision maker and is not typically derived by him from the kind of detailed calculation just described. However it is derived, the expected utility function becomes the basis for the individual's decision-making behavior.

Once a decision is made, and the individual experiences the consequences, the actual utility experienced is compared with the expected utility. There can be a gap between these utilities. For example, in trying out a new food or in buying a new product, the prior expectation may not be realized. In a different type of problem, an individual may have an expected utility for a particular price of a product that he is selling. However, when the price is actually offered in the market, he may experience utility that was different from the expected and he may reject a price that he had expected to accept. Similarly, when an individual buying a product has particular characteristics in mind, the actual utility of a product that does not meet the precise standards may exceed the expected utility, and the individual may purchase a product that did not meet his original specifications.

The result of the difference between the actual and expected utility is that the individual modifies the expected utility function when it is relevant for future decisions. In order to treat the problem formally, which we do in subsequent sections, we will assume that the expected utility function has been derived from the calculation of mathematical expectations as described earlier, and that this function is modified by the standard Bayesian analysis. This updating of the expected utility function could be based on a variety of assumptions, depending on the type of information extracted by the individual from the realized utility. For example, the individual might be able to perceive only that the actual utility was above or below the expected value and must apply Bayes theorem to these limited observations to determine a new expected utility function.

We do not explore the trivial case of modification in which the actual and expected functions can be brought into conformity on the basis of a few observations. This would be the case if the actual utility function depended on a small number of parameters which could be determined exactly from a small number of observations. Rather, we shall consider utility functions in which there is some element of randomness that prevents the parameters from ever being determined exactly.

The approach that we are postulating concentrates on the interactions between these two functions – the expected utility function and the actual function. It should be emphasized that we assume that the individual is capable of comparing the actual realized utility with the expected utility of the consequences of an event.

MAXIMIZING EXPECTED UTILITY

If the individual does not know his utility function and gains information through experience, what kind of process does he follow to gain the maximum utility? Our assumption is that he has the objective of maximizing expected utility. Suppose, as in the classical theory of decision making under uncertainty, that an individual must choose a decision δ from some available class Δ of possible decisions, and that each decision $\delta \in \Delta$ induces a probability distribution $P(\delta)$ on a given space R of possible consequences r. (More precisely, δ induces a probability distribution $P(\delta)$ on a given σ-field of subsets of R.) In the classical theory, it is assumed that there exists a real-valued utility function V defined on the space R such that one decision δ_1 is preferred to another decision δ_2 if and only if $E[V \mid P(\delta_1)] > E[V \mid P(\delta_2)]$, where $E[V \mid P(\delta_i)]$ denotes the expectation of V with respect to the distribution $P(\delta_i)$. If a decision δ must be chosen from a specified subset Δ_0 of the set Δ, then one will be chosen for which $E[V \mid P(\delta)]$ is a maximum, assuming that such a decision exists.

In accordance with this theory, if an individual could simply choose a consequence r from a given available subset of R, he would choose one for which $V(r)$ was a maximum. The theory indicates that this choice would be straightforward and could be made without difficulty because there are no elements of uncertainty in the decision. Uncertainty enters the classical theory only if the individual is uncertain about the consequence that will result from at least one of the available decisions that he might consider. Thus, this theory assumes that an individual's preferences among sure things are fixed, and then determines his preferences among probability distributions involving the same consequences.

In our approach, however, there are no sure things. A person who can choose a consequence, or reward, from among an available set of rewards may have difficulty making a choice because he is uncertain about the utility of each of the rewards. Thus, regardless of whether the reward is a meal at a new restaurant, a new household appliance, a stock certificate, or twenty dollars, the utility of the reward will be uncertain. Therefore, the utility that the person does assign to a reward should itself be regarded as an expected utility. Here, the expectation is taken, formally or heuristically, over the possible values that the utility of the reward might have, and is taken with respect to the person's subjective distribution for these possible values. Thus, from our point of view, an individual will typically be uncertain about the actual utility of any particular consequence, no matter how well specified that consequence might be.

Nevertheless, in a single period decision problem in which the individual must choose a decision δ from some specified subset Δ_0 of Δ, it is irrelevant whether $V(r)$ is the actual utility that will be realized from the consequence r or merely the expected utility that will be realized from r. In either case, $E[V \mid P(\delta)]$ will be the overall expected utility from choosing the decision δ, and the individual will try to choose a decision that maximizes $E[V \mid P(\delta)]$.

However, in a multiperiod decision problem in which the individual must choose decisions from Δ_0 repeatedly, the definition and underlying structure of the function V can be important. In a multiperiod problem of this type, the individual will try to maximize the expectation of some function, such as the sum, of the utilities that are realized in each period. This maximization must, in general, now be a sequential process. The individual will typically be able to increase the total utility realized over the entire process by explicitly taking into account the fact that the utility $V(r)$ he assigns to a particular consequence r at the beginning of the process is merely an expectation and may be higher or lower than the actual utility he would realize from r in any given period. By exploring the actual utilities of various consequences in the early stages of the process, the individual can learn about his utility function. This learning will result in the elimination of some or all of the uncertainty that is present in his utility function. He can thereby make decisions in later periods that will have a high probability of yielding conformance between actual utility and expected utility.

To formalize our description, consider a process with n periods and suppose that in each period, a decision maker must choose a decision $\delta \in \Delta$ after observing the consequences of the preceding periods. Let u_i denote the utility function for period i ($i = 1, \ldots, n$). The function u_i is defined on the space R of possible consequences. It is assumed that the decision maker is uncertain about the exact values of the function u_i and that this uncertainty is represented by the presence in the function u_i of a parameter θ whose value is unknown. Thus, if the consequence r occurs in period i, the realized utility will be $u_i(r \mid \theta)$. The parameter θ will, in general, be a vector taking values in some parameter space Θ.

For $i = 1, \ldots, n$, we shall let r_i denote the consequence that occurs in period i, and we shall assume that the total utility U over the entire process is simply the sum of the utilities realized in each of the n periods. Thus, we assume that $U = \sum_{i=1}^{n} u_i(r_i \mid \theta)$.

As is typical in statistical decision problems, we shall also assume that the probability distribution on the space R induced by each decision $\delta \in \Delta$ is not completely known and depends on a vector parameter φ. We shall let $P(r \mid \varphi, \delta)$ denote that distribution. The parameter φ will, in general, also be a vector taking values in a parameter space Φ. In some problems, some of the components of φ may be related to, or even identical with, some of the components of θ. In other problems, the parameters θ and φ may be completely unrelated.[6]

At the beginning of the process, the available information about the value of θ and φ can be represented by specifying a joint prior distribution $\xi(\theta, \varphi)$ for these parameters. If θ and φ were completely unrelated, this joint prior distribution would be a product distribution of the form $\xi_1(\theta)\xi_2(\varphi)$.

In the first period, there are two types of information that become available to the decision maker. First, after he has chosen a decision δ_1 in period 1, he observes which consequence r_1 actually occurs. Second, he gains some information about the utility $u_1(r_1 \mid \theta)$ that he actually receives from r_1 in period 1. In general, he will not be able to learn the exact numerical value of $u_1(r_1 \mid \theta)$, but will only be able to learn this value subject to error. For example, he might learn only whether this value is greater than or less than his prior expected value $\int_\Theta u_1(r_1 \mid \theta) \, d\xi_1(\theta)$, where $\xi_1(\theta)$ denotes the marginal prior distribution of θ.

Together, these two types of information lead to a posterior joint distribution of θ and φ that serves as the relevant prior distribution when a decision $\delta_2 \in \Delta$ is chosen in the second period. The decision maker must choose a sequence of decisions $\delta_1, \ldots, \delta_n$ that will maximize the expected total utility $E(U)$.

In general, the optimal decision δ_1 in the first period of this multiperiod problem will be different from the decision specified by the myopic rule which considers only the first period and ignores future periods. It will, in general, also be different from the decision specified by the rule which ignores possible changes in utility and assumes that the same expected utility function which pertains to the first period will also pertain to all future periods. Indeed, even in a two-period problem in which the parameters θ and φ are independent, and the information obtained about θ in the first period does not depend on which decision δ_1 is chosen or which consequence r_1 occurs, the decision maker must take possible changes in utility into account when choosing δ_1. This fact can be shown as follows:

Suppose that θ and φ are independent under their joint prior distribution, and that information about θ is obtained at the end of the first period by observing the value x of a random variable X whose distribution $F(x \mid \theta)$ depends on θ but does not depend on which decision δ_1 was chosen or on which consequence r_1 occurred.[7] Then the information obtained about θ is independent of the information obtained about φ, and it follows that θ and φ will again be independent under their joint posterior distribution. We shall let $\xi_1'(\theta)$ and $\xi_2'(\varphi)$ denote the posterior distributions of θ and φ, given δ_1, r_1, and x. If a particular decision δ_2 is then chosen on the second (and final) period, the expected utility resulting from this decision will be

$$(1) \qquad \int_\Phi \int_\Theta \int_R u_2(r \mid \theta) \, dP(r \mid \varphi, \delta_2) \, d\xi_1'(\theta) \, d\xi_2'(\varphi)$$

$$= \int_\Phi \int_R v_2(r \mid x) \, dP(r \mid \varphi, \delta_2) \, d\xi_2'(\varphi).$$

Here $v_2(r \mid x)$ is the expected utility function for the second period, as determined by the relation

$$v_2(r \mid x) = \int_\Theta u_2(r \mid \theta) \, d\xi_1'(\theta).$$

Since the posterior distribution $\xi_1'(\theta)$ depends on x, so also will the expected utility function $v_2(r \mid x)$, and we have explicitly exhibited this dependence in the notation we are using. Next, for any possible decision δ_2, we can use the conditional distribution $P(r \mid \varphi, \delta_2)$ of r_2 given φ, together with the marginal distribution $\xi_2'(\varphi)$ of φ, to determine the marginal (or predictive) distribution $\bar{P}(r \mid \delta_2)$ of r_2. Since the posterior distribution $\xi_2'(\varphi)$ depends on the decision δ_1 that was chosen in the first period and on the observed consequence r_1, this marginal distribution should more properly be written as $\bar{P}(r \mid \delta_2, \delta_1, r_1)$. The expected utility (1) can now be expressed as follows:

$$(2) \qquad \int_R v_2(r \mid x) \, d\bar{P}(r \mid \delta_2, \delta_1, r_1).$$

At the beginning of the second period, a decision δ_2 should be chosen for which the integral (2) is a maximum. We shall let

$$(3) \qquad U_2(\delta_1, r_1, x) = \sup_{\delta_2 \in \Delta} \int_R v_2(r \mid x) \, d\bar{P}(r \mid \delta_2, \delta_1, r_1).$$

Then it follows from backward induction that at the beginning of the process, a decision δ_1 should be chosen for which the following expression is maximized:

(4) $$\int_{\Phi}\int_{\Theta}\int_{R} u_1(r \mid \theta)\, \mathrm{d}P(r \mid \varphi, \delta_1)\, \mathrm{d}\xi_1(\theta)\, \mathrm{d}\xi_2(\varphi) +$$

$$+ \int_{\Phi}\int_{R}\int_{\Theta}\int_{X} U_2(\delta_1, r_1, x)\, \mathrm{d}F(x \mid \theta)\, \mathrm{d}\xi_1(\theta)\, \mathrm{d}P(r_1 \mid \varphi, \delta_1)\, \mathrm{d}\xi_2(\varphi).$$

The important feature of this result from our present point of view is that when the decision maker chooses δ_1, he must consider the full range of possible new expected utility functions $v_2(r \mid x)$ that might be obtained from the observation x. It should be noted that both δ_1 and δ_2 will be different from the decisions that would be optimal in traditional theory. The optimal decisions in traditional theory would be based solely on the available information about φ. It is clear that the optimal δ_2 in our approach will be different from the one in the traditional theory because of the new information about θ that becomes available from x. It should be emphasized, moreover, that even though the decision maker has no control over the information about θ that will be generated in the first period, the optimal δ_1 in our approach will also be different from the one in the traditional theory.

In a more general problem, the space R_i of possible consequences in period i, the space Δ_i of possible decisions in period i, and the distribution $P_i(r_i \mid \delta_i, \varphi)$ induced on R_i by each decision $\delta_i \in \Delta_i$ can depend on the decisions that were chosen in preceding periods and on the consequences that were observed in those periods. Also, the total utility over the n periods can be an arbitrary function $U(r_1, \ldots, r_n \mid \theta)$ of the entire observed sequence of consequences. An optimal sequence of decisions that takes into account the adaptive nature of the utility functions can again be determined by backward induction.

UTILITY EFFECTS IN DEMAND THEORY

Demand theory is an area for which our approach has important implications. Although the standard analysis of consumption in terms of indifference curves is general enough to admit changes in the utility function, these changes have typically been ignored. Since change in the utility function is an integral part of our approach, we shall demonstrate how the standard analysis can include such changes.

Consider the choices of two commodities made by a particular household or individual. Let M denote the income of the household in a given period, let p and q denote the prices of the two commodities in that period, and let x and y denote the amounts of the commodities that are consumed in that same period. The values of x and y will be chosen to maximize the household's utility function $U(x, y)$ subject to the budget constraint $px + qy = M$.

The standard economic analysis[8] proceeds as follows: The utility function U determines a family of nonintersecting indifference curves in the xy-plane. In Figure 1, two of these indifference curves are denoted I_1 and I_2. In that figure, the line AB represents the budget constraint $px + qy = M$. The amounts x and y to be consumed are specified by the point $F = (x_1, y_1)$ at which the line AB is tangent to the indifference curve I_1.

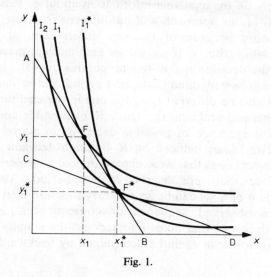

Fig. 1.

Now suppose that the household's utility function changes from U to a different function U^*. The new utility function U^* will determine a new family of indifference curves. In Figure 1, the curve I_1^* represents one of the new indifference curves. In particular, I_1^* is the new indifference curve that is tangent to the line AB. Thus, the consumption of the household will shift from the values x_1 and y_1 to the values x_1^* and y_1^* which are the coordinates of the point F^*.

It is also shown in Figure 1 that the *utility effect*, which results from changing the utility function from U to U^*, is equivalent to the effect of changing prices and income while retaining the original utility function. As indicated in the figure, among the original family of indifference curves, the curve I_2 passes through the point F* and the line CD is tangent to the curve I_2 at the point F*. Therefore, if the household retained its original indifference curves and its consumption had to satisfy the budget constraint represented by the line CD, then the household would consume the amounts x_1^* and y_1^* specified by the point F*. It follows that changing the utility function from U to U^* is equivalent to retaining the original utility function and changing the income and prices to new values M^*, p^*, and q^* such that $M^*/p^* = C$ and $M^*/q^* = D$. Clearly, there are an infinite number of different sets of values of M^*, p^*, and q^* which satisfy these two equations.

Another way to think of the utility effect is illustrated in Figure 2. The curves I_1 and I_1^*, and the points F and F*, are as before. The curve I_2^* is the indifference curve in the new family which contains the point F. Since both the points F and G lie on the curve I_2^*, the household is now indifferent between these points. The line ab is parallel to AB and tangent to the curve I_2^*. The point of tangency is denoted by G. Therefore, if the income of the household were reduced from M to the amount represented by the budget constraint ab, the household could still attain a consumption G equivalent to its

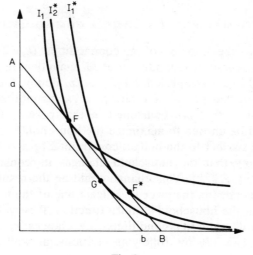

Fig. 2.

original consumption F. Thus, from the point of view of the household, this income difference $p(A - a)$, or equivalently $q(B - b)$, can be regarded as the *income effect* of the change in utility.

By analogy with the traditional economic analysis, we can say that we have represented the utility effect, which induces the change in consumption from F to F*, as the sum of the following two effects: (1) a substitution effect which induces the change from F to G along the curve I_2^*, and (2) the income effect which induces the change from G to F*.

It should be noted that since both the points F and F* satisfy the budget constraint, and income and prices are held fixed, the point F* must always yield a higher level of utility than F in the new family of indifference curves; and it must always yield a lower level of utility in the old family of indifference curves. Therefore, the income effect as defined here resulting from a change in utility must always be positive.

In our approach, we have distinguished between the actual utility and the expected utility functions. The curves drawn in Figures 1 and 2 would be based on the expected utility function. The change from F to F* would result from adapting the expected utility function in light of the experienced utility at the point (x_1, y_1).

FORMAL EXTENSION TO k COMMODITIES

Consider now the choices of k commodities $(k \geqslant 2)$ made by a particular household or individual. Let M again denote the income of the household in a given period, let $p_1, \ldots, p_k$ denote the prices of the commodities in that period, and let $x_1, \ldots, x_k$ denote the amounts of the commodities that are consumed in that period. The values of $x_1, \ldots, x_k$ will be chosen to maximize the household's utility function $U(x_1, \ldots, x_k)$ subject to the budget constraint $\Sigma_1^n p_i x_i = M$.

Suppose now that the household changes its consumption from $x_1, \ldots, x_k$ to $x_1^*, \ldots, x_k^*$. This change could be the result of a change in income, a change in the price of at least one of the n commodities, or a change in the household's utility function. It is well-known[9] that under standard regularity conditions, the choices $x_1, \ldots, x_k$ of the household will satisfy the following relations, as well as the budget constraint:

$$(5) \qquad \frac{U_1}{p_1} = \frac{U_2}{p_2} = \cdots = \frac{U_k}{p_k},$$

where $U_i = \delta U / \delta x_i$. Thus, there is typically a wide class of combinations of income, prices, and utility that will result in a particular set of values of $x_1, \ldots, x_k$.

For example, suppose that the values of $x_1, \ldots, x_k$ must be positive and that

$$(6) \qquad U(x_1, \ldots, x_k) = \sum_{i=1}^{k} \alpha_i \log x_i,$$

where $\alpha_i > 0$ for $i = 1, \ldots, k$ and $\Sigma_{i=1}^{k} \alpha_i = 1$. It is easily found that the optimal choices of $x_1, \ldots, x_k$, subject to the constraint $\Sigma_{i=1}^{k} p_i x_i = M$ are

$$(7) \qquad x_i = M \alpha_i / p_i \quad \text{for } i = 1, \ldots, k.$$

A change in the value of x_i means that there must have been a change in the value of M, p_i, or α_i. From the point of view of the consumer, a change from $\alpha_1, \ldots, \alpha_k$ to $\alpha_1^*, \ldots, \alpha_k^*$ in the utility function is equivalent to a change in prices from $p_1, \ldots, p_k$ to $p_1^*, \ldots, p_k^*$, where $p_i^* = p_i \alpha_i / \alpha_i^*$ for $i = 1, \ldots, k$, and income M is held fixed. More generally, the change from $\alpha_1, \ldots, \alpha_k$ to $\alpha_1^*, \ldots, \alpha_k^*$ is equivalent to any change in prices from $p_1, \ldots, p_k$ to $p_1^*, \ldots, p_k^*$ *and* in income from M to M^* that satisfies the following relations:

$$\frac{p_i^*}{M^*} = \frac{p_i}{M} \frac{\alpha_i}{\alpha_i^*}, \quad \text{for } i = 1, \ldots, k.$$

On the other hand, a change in prices from $p_1, \ldots, p_k$ to a new set $p_1^*, \ldots, p_k^*$ is equivalent uniquely to a change in income from M to $M^* = M \Sigma_{i=1}^{k} \alpha_i p_i / p_i^*$ accompanied by a change in weights from $\alpha_1, \ldots, \alpha_k$ to

$$\alpha_i^* = \frac{M}{M^*} \frac{p_i}{p_i^*} \alpha_i, \quad \text{for } i = 1, \ldots, k.$$

LEARNING ABOUT UTILITIES BY A BAYESIAN PROCESS

In this section, we shall demonstrate in a demand theory context how utility functions are learned through Bayesian analysis. Assume two commodities with prices p and q and consumption x and y. Let the utility function be

(8) $U(x, y \mid \alpha) = \alpha \log x + (1 - \alpha) \log y$,

where $0 < \alpha < 1$. Suppose that the consumer is uncertain about the exact value of α and assigns a prior p.d.f. $\xi(\alpha)$ to this value. Thus, although it is unrealistic, we are assuming that the learning process we have described has resulted in the consumer's knowledge of the general form of his utility function but not the exact weights.

If the consumer is going to choose x and y in only a single period, then he should choose the values for which the expected utility $E[U(x, y \mid \alpha)]$ is a maximum. Since

(9) $E[U(x, y \mid \alpha)] = E(\alpha) \log x + [1 - E(\alpha)] \log y$,

the consumer can simply replace the uncertain value of α in his utility function by its expectation $E(\alpha)$. The optimal choices of x and y would, therefore, be

(10) $x = \dfrac{E(\alpha)}{p} M$ and $y = \dfrac{1 - E(\alpha)}{q} M$.

We shall now consider a process with more than one period. After the consumer chooses the values of x and y in a given period and consumes those amounts of the two commodities, his experience will lead him to formulate a new posterior p.d.f. of α. The consumer should realize that the more quickly he can learn the precise value of α, the greater will be the utility that he can attain from his choices of x and y in each period. Because of this learning process, it will not be optimal in general to choose x and y in each period in accordance with (10), but rather to choose x and y to increase the rate of learning in order to maximize the total utility to be attained from the entire multiperiod process. We shall now present two examples based on plausible models for the learning process. In the first example, the optimal choices of x and y in each period can be made in accordance with (10), and in the second example they cannot.

Example 1. At the beginning of each period, the consumer has an expectation $E(\alpha)$ for α. Therefore, after he has chosen the values of x and y to be used in a given period, his expectation $E[U(x, y \mid \alpha)]$ for the utility that he will realize in that period is given by Equation (9).

We shall assume that after he has consumed the amounts x and y, he can determine whether the actual utility he has realized is larger than, smaller than, or equal to the expected utility given by (9).

The actual utility $U(x, y \mid \alpha)$ is given by Equation (8). Therefore, we are assuming that at the end of the given period, the consumer can determine which one of the following three relations is correct:

(i) $U(x, y \mid \alpha) > E[U(x, y \mid \alpha)]$,
(ii) $U(x, y \mid \alpha) < E[U(x, y \mid \alpha)]$,
(iii) $U(x, y \mid \alpha) = E[U(x, y \mid \alpha)]$.

It follows from Equations (8) and (9) that these three relations are equivalent, respectively, to the following three relations:

(i) $[\alpha - E(\alpha)](\log x - \log y) > 0$,
(ii) $[\alpha - E(\alpha)](\log x - \log y) < 0$,
(iii) $[\alpha - E(\alpha)](\log x - \log y) = 0$.

If $x \neq y$, then determining which one of these three relations is correct is equivalent to determining whether $\alpha > E(\alpha)$, $\alpha < E(\alpha)$, or $\alpha = E(\alpha)$. Therefore, if the amounts x and y consumed in a given period are not equal, the consumer will be able to determine whether the actual value of α is greater than, less than, or equal to the expectation $E(\alpha)$ that he held at the beginning of the period.

Suppose now that $x = y$ in a given period. In this case, it follows from Equations (8) and (9) that

(11) $U(x, y \mid \alpha) = E[U(x, y \mid \alpha)] = \log x$.

Therefore, the consumer will not gain any information about the value of α from the realized utility. He knows in advance that the realized utility will be equal to the expected utility.

The essential feature of this example is that the information that the consumer learns about α in any period does not depend on the values of x and y that he chooses in that period, provided that $x \neq y$. Therefore, it will be optimal for him to proceed by choosing x and y in each period to maximize his expected utility in that period, in accordance with Equation (10), provided that Equation (10) does not yield $x = y$. If Equation (10) does specify that $x = y$ in a given period, then strictly speaking there will be no optimal values of x and y in that period. The values $x = y$ will yield the maximum expected utility for that period but will yield no information whatsoever about the value of α. A procedure that will be almost optimal in this situation will be to choose x and y only very slightly different from each other.

With such values for x and y, the expected utility in the given period will be very close to the maximum expected utility that could be obtained by choosing $x = y$ and, in addition, the consumer will learn whether the actual value of α is greater than, less than, or equal to $E(\alpha)$.

Example 2. We shall continue to assume that the utility function has the form given in Equation (8). However, suppose now that instead of the special form for the learning process that we have just considered, we assume that this process has the following alternative form: After he has consumed any particular amounts x and y in a given period, the consumer can determine whether he would have preferred a slightly larger value of x and a slightly smaller value of y, or a slightly smaller value of x and a slightly larger value of y. In more precise terms, we shall assume that the consumer can determine whether the derivative $\partial U(x, y \mid \alpha)/\partial x$ of his utility function, evaluated at the particular values of x and y consumed in the given period, is positive, negative, or zero. We shall now derive some implications of this assumption.

The amounts x and y consumed in any period satisfy the relation

$$(12) \qquad y = \frac{1}{q}(M - px).$$

Therefore, it follows from Equation (8) that

$$(13) \qquad \frac{\partial U(x, y \mid \alpha)}{\partial x} = \frac{\alpha}{x} + \frac{1-\alpha}{y}\frac{\partial y}{\partial x}$$

$$= \frac{\alpha}{x} - \frac{1-\alpha}{y}\frac{p}{q}$$

$$= p\left(\frac{\alpha}{px} - \frac{1-\alpha}{qy}\right).$$

It can be seen from Equations (12) and (13) that the three relations
(i) $\partial U(x, y \mid \alpha)/\partial x > 0$,
(ii) $\partial U(x, y \mid \alpha)/\partial x < 0$,
(iii) $\partial U(x, y \mid \alpha)/\partial x = 0$,
are equivalent, respectively, to the following three relations:
(i) $\alpha > px/M$,
(ii) $\alpha < px/M$,
(iii) $\alpha = px/M$.

Hence, in this process, the consumer can determine which one of these relations is correct.

In a problem with n periods, a sequence of optimal decisions for the consumer can be found by backward induction. Since the information about α which the consumer gains in each period depends on his choice of x (and y) in that period, the optimal values of x and y in a given period will not typically be the values given by Equation (10).

CONCLUSIONS

It should be clear that this paper represents only the beginning exploration into an important topic. The concept of a well-defined utility function is central to most theories of decision making. At the same time, the empirical work on decision making indicates that human decision makers do not have well-defined utility functions.[10] Our approach has been an attempt to use the utility concept in a manner that is closer to actual behavior. We have removed the constraints that require the decision maker to have immediate knowledge of his utility function.

In our approach, the individual is assumed to be capable of determining an expected utility for the consequences of some event and to be capable of comparing the expected value with the actual value when the consequences are experienced. One criticism that can be made of the approach we have taken is that it represents the activity that preceded the standard theory. In other words, even if we are correct, our approach only justifies the traditional approach by showing how utility functions are learned.

We would not accept this criticism for several reasons. First, some of the population being analyzed at any time will be in the process of learning their utility functions, and this fact must be incorporated in any theory. Second, it is not clear that a utility function ever becomes completely known since there will be consequences never experienced by the individual. Finally, we do not believe that the utility function ever becomes completely stable. Individuals are always seeking new experiences as part of their nature. Knight[11] has referred to this aspect as "explorative activity". We try to deal with it in a formal way by utilizing a random variable in the utility function. One implication of this idea is that the standard concept of a stable equilibrium needs to be modified. The only equilibrium possible would be some kind of stochastic equilibrium.

The notion of explorative activity and utility being known only through experience is consistent with casual empiricism. We have reference to the fads in style, food, automobiles, soaps, and other products in the economy. Only a small number of the new products can lay claim to legitimate technical improvements over older products. In the marketing literature such shifts have been institutionalized in the concept of a product life cycle.[12] In other words, it is expected that products will have a limited life, partly because of preference changes.

One of the obvious concerns of an approach that challenges the existence of utility functions is whether it is possible to have an analytic science of decision making. In this paper, we have made a start toward a positive answer.

Carnegie-Mellon University

NOTES AND REFERENCES

[1] Allais, M.: (1953). 'Le comportement de l'homme rationnel devant le risque: Critique des postulats et axioms de l'école Americaine,' *Econometrica* 21, 503–546.
Savage, L. J.: (1954). *The Foundations of Statistics*, Wiley, New York, pp.101–103.
DeGroot, M. H.: (1970). *Optimal Statistical Decisions*, McGraw-Hill, New York, pp.93–94.
[2] Quandt, R.: (1956). 'Probabilistic Theory of Consumer Behavior', *Quarterly Journal of Economics* 70, 507–536.
Becker, G. M., DeGroot, M. H., and Marschak, J.: (1963). 'Stochastic Models of Choice Behavior', *Behavioral Science* 8, 41–55.
Luce, R. D., and Suppes, P.: (1965). 'Preference, Utility, and Subjective Probability'. In Luce, Bush, and Galanter (Eds.), *Handbook of Mathematical Psychology*, Vol. 3, Wiley, New York, pp.249–410.
[3] Cf. Simon, H. A.: (1955). 'A Behavioral Model of Rational Choice', *Quarterly Journal of Economics* 69, 99–118.
Simon has put this well: "The consequences that the organism experiences may change the pay-off function – it doesn't know how well it likes cheese until it has eaten cheese."
[4] Cf. Witsenhausen, H. S.: (1974). 'On the Uncertainty of Future Preferences', *Annals of Economic and Social Measurement* 3, 91–94.
In this paper, Witsenhausen emphasizes the need to incorporate these concepts in problems of long range planning.
[5] Von Neumann, J., and Morgenstern, O.: (1947). *Theory of Games and Economic Behavior, Second Edition*, Princeton University Press, Princeton, New Jersey;

DeGroot, M. H., *op. cit.*

[6] For example, the parameter θ which determines how much utility or enjoyment an individual will derive from ordering a steak dinner at a particular restaurant will be closely related to the parameter φ which determines whether or not the restaurant prepares good steak dinners. As another example, the parameter θ which determines how much utility an individual will realize from owning a stock that yields a particular gain is only slightly related to the parameter φ representing external conditions which determine whether or not the stock will yield that gain.

[7] The random variable X will in general be a function of the actual utility received from the realized consequence. For example, as mentioned earlier, X may be an indicator of whether the actual utility is greater or smaller than the expected utility for that consequence. The assumption made in the text that $F(x \mid \theta)$ does not depend on which consequence occurs is special and need not be retained in the general theory.

[8] Cf. Cohen, K. J., and Cyert, R. M.: (1965). *Theory of the Firm: Resource Allocation in a Market Economy*, Prentice-Hall, Inc., Englewood Cliffs, New Jersey.

[9] Slutsky, E. E.: (1915). 'On the Theory of the Budget of the Consumer', *Giornale degli Economisti*, Vol. LI, pp.1–26. Reprinted in *Readings in Price Theory*, Stigler and Boulding (Eds.), Richard D. Irwin, Inc., Chicago, 1952, pp.27–56.

[10] Simon, H. A.: *op. cit.*

[11] Knight, F. H.: (1935). *The Ethics of Competition*, Harper, New York, pp.22–23. Quoted in G. J. Stigler (1946), *The Theory of Price*, The Macmillan Co., New York, p.65.

[12] Cf. Nord, O. C.: (1963). *Growth of a New Product: Effects of Capacity-Acquisition Policies*, The M.I.T. Press, Cambridge, Massachusetts, Chapter 1.

Kotler, P.: (1967). *Marketing Management*, Prentice-Hall, Englewood Cliffs, New Jersey, Chapter 13.

PETER C. FISHBURN

ON THE NATURE OF EXPECTED UTILITY

ABSTRACT. The axioms of von Neumann and Morgenstern for a preference relation $>$ on a set P of probability distributions consist of an ordering axiom, an independence axiom, and an Archimedean condition. It is argued that the core of their idea is captured by parts of their first two axioms, namely that $>$ on P is asymmetric, and that $\lambda p + (1 - \lambda)r > \lambda q + (1 - \lambda)s$ whenever $0 < \lambda < 1$, $p > q$ and $r > s$. These less demanding axioms overcome criticisms of the original axioms which pertain to threshold phenomena and vagueness in human judgment, and they lead to a lexicographic expected-utility representation that retains important aspects of the representation used by von Neumann and Morgenstern. However, even this drastic weakening of the original expected-utility theory cannot fully account for failures of independence uncovered by Allais, nor can it handle the phenomenon of cyclic preferences which has been observed by Tversky and others.

1. INTRODUCTION

This paper discusses aspects and modifications of the axioms of von Neumann and Morgenstern (1944) for an individual's preferences on a set of risky alternatives. The modified axioms are designed in part to accommodate realities of psychological thresholds and vagueness in human judgment. We shall see that many properties of their expected utility model are implied by axioms which are considerably weaker than the original axioms. Proofs will be omitted since they are available elsewhere.

For simplicity of exposition, the set X of consequences $x, y, \ldots$ will be assumed to be finite. Examples will use monetary consequences, viewed as increments to present wealth, although the elements in X could be completely non-monetary. The set P with elements $p, q, r, s, \ldots$ denotes the set of all probability distributions or 'gambles' on X. Each $p \in P$ is a non-negative real function on X whose values sum to unity: $p(x)$ is the probability that x will be the resultant consequence if p is implemented. Given $p, q \in P$ and $0 \leqslant \lambda \leqslant 1$, $\lambda p + (1 - \lambda)q$ is the gamble in P whose probability for $x \in X$ is $\lambda p(x) + (1 - \lambda)q(x)$. Although $\lambda p + (1 - \lambda)q$ is written as a convex combination or 'mixture' of p and q, it should properly be viewed as a single entity or a simple function in P, which is precisely what it is.

243

Maurice Allais and Ole Hagen (eds.), Expected Utility and the Allais Paradox, 243–257.
Copyright © 1979 by D. Reidel Publishing Company.

The individual's binary preference relation $>$ is defined on P, with $p > q$ interpreted to mean that the individual (strictly) prefers p to q. The associated indifference relation $\sim$ signifies the absence of a definite preference, with $p \sim q$ if and only if neither $p > q$ nor $q > p$. By definition, $\sim$ is symmetric: $p \sim q$ if and only if $q \sim p$. Several of our modified axioms are designed to avoid the questionable assertion of transitive indifference.

The preference axioms of von Neumann and Morgenstern can be viewed as consisting of three conditions for $>$ on P. The first pertains to ordering and says that $>$ is *asymmetric* ($p > q$ and $q > p$ cannot both be true) and *negatively transitive* (if $p > q$ then either $p > r$ or $r > q$). This implies that both $>$ and $\sim$ are transitive. The second condition is an independence axiom which says that if $p > q$ and $0 < \lambda < 1$ then $\lambda p + (1 - \lambda)r > \lambda q + (1 - \lambda)r$ for any $r \in P$. The third axiom is an Archimedean or continuity condition which says that if $p > q$ and $q > r$ then $\lambda p + (1 - \lambda)r > q$ and $q > \mu p + (1 - \mu)r$ for some real λ and μ strictly between zero and unity. The three axioms noted here are shown by Jensen (1967) and Fishburn (1970) to be necessary and sufficient for the proposition that there is a real function u on X such that, for all $p, q \in P$,

(1) $p > q$ if and only if $E(u, p) > E(u, q)$,

where $E(u, p) =_{df} \Sigma_x p(x)u(x)$, the 'expected utility' of gamble p.

Ordering properties for $>$ on P will be discussed in the next section, and independence axioms will be analyzed in the third section. Implications of combinations of ordering and independence axioms are presented in the fourth section. We shall see there that the essence of the von Neumann–Morgenstern proposal, modified to take account of certain psychological limitations in human judgment, can be captured by two basic axioms, namely asymmetry of $>$ and the weak version of independence which says that if $p > q$, $r > s$, and $0 < \lambda < 1$, then $\lambda p + (1 - \lambda)r > \lambda q + (1 - \lambda)s$.

Archimedean axioms are briefly considered in the penultimate section. From a representational or computational standpoint, these axioms provide the convenience of single-valued utilities, as in (1), instead of vector-valued utilities as discussed in Section 4. The final section of the paper presents a brief summary.

2. ORDERING AXIOMS

A binary relation R on P is *acyclic* if it is never true that there is a positive integer n and $p_1, p_2, \ldots, p_n \in P$ such that $p_1 R p_2$, $p_2 R p_3, \ldots, p_{n-1} R p_n$ and $p_n R p_1$. And R is *transitive* if pRr whenever pRq and qRr for some $q \in P$. In the following list of ordering axioms, (A1) and (A4) constitute the ordering axiom used above for (1).

(A1) $>$ *is asymmetric.*

(A2) $>$ *is acyclic.*

(A3) $>$ *is transitive.*

(A4) $>$ *is negatively transitive.*

(A5) $\sim$ *is transitive.*

The assumption that strict preference $>$ is asymmetric is vital to our usual conception of preference and will be used throughout the paper. Evidence for a violation of (A1) might arise in an experiment in which the pair $\{p, q\}$ is presented to the subject in two separated trials and he indicates the choice of p on one trial and the choice of q on the other. However, apart from the problems posed by modes of presentation and changes of values over time, it could be argued that such behavior is likely to reflect the individual's indecision about which of p and q he prefers or that they are 'close enough' that it is not worth his effort to be careful about which he chooses, and in such a case it seems reasonable in an operational sense to say that he is indifferent between p and q.

Like the first axiom, the second is essential for any numerical model which seeks to represent $>$ by expected utilities, whether these be single-valued or vector-valued. However, there seem to be situations in which the acyclicity of $>$ may fail. The potential for such a failure of (A2) in a monetary context is suggested by experiments conducted by Tversky (1969), which take advantage of perceptual thresholds and the fact that monetary gambles are essentially two-dimensional, these two dimensions being pay-offs and risks. Call $p \in P$ a *T-gamble* when it has $p(\$x) = \lambda$ and $p(\$0) = 1 - \lambda$ for some x and λ. Such a gamble gives 'you' $\$x$ with probability λ or nothing ($\$0$) with probability $1 - \lambda$. We consider the following series of T-gambles:

	λ	$x(\$)$
p_0	0.400	10,000
p_1	0.401	9,950
p_2	0.402	9,900
	$\vdots$	
p_n	$0.4 + n/1{,}000$	$10{,}000 - 50n$
	$\vdots$	
p_{99}	0.499	5,050
p_{100}	0.500	5,000

(2)

Each successive T-gamble in the series increases the 'win' probability by 1 chance in 1,000 and decreases the pay-off by \$50. In either case the increment of change is small compared to the base figure. Consider p_0 versus p_1. Some people will welcome the additional chance of one in a thousand to win a prize that is almost as large as the original \$10,000 and so will have $p_1 > p_0$. Others will consider the probability differential quite insufficient to outweigh the potential 'loss' of \$50 and will firmly declare $p_0 > p_1$. And others would likely be indecisive or indifferent between p_0 and p_1. (Where do you fall?)

Consider a person who has $p_1 > p_0$. For much the same reason that he has $p_1 > p_0$, he may also have $p_2 > p_1, p_3 > p_2, \ldots$, and $p_{100} > p_{99}$. If he also has $p_0 > p_{100}$, preferring a 40 percent chance of getting \$10,000 to a 50 percent chance of getting \$5,000, which does not seem at all unreasonable, then $>$ is cyclic and (A2) does not hold.

There are of course several standard arguments which purport to show the unreasonableness of cyclic preferences. One of these is the so-called money pump, which suggests that if you prefer p to q then you would be willing to pay something to exchange ownership of q for ownership of p. By proceeding step by step around a cycle, you will eventually end up with the gamble you started with, minus the cash payments you made for the successive exchanges. It should be noted however that this procedure introduces several new aspects into a dynamic game situation that were not involved in the original pairwise preference judgments, and hence it seems to offer no more than tangential evidence for the unreasonableness of acyclicity. In fact, the willingness of an individual to behave like a money pump may speak more to the point of his naïvete or foolishness in getting involved in a game that is obviously unfair to him than to the fact that a series of pairwise comparisons reveals a cycle. The only serious attempt I am aware of to analyze the money pump has been made by Burros (1974).

A second argument for the unreasonableness of cyclic preferences involves the use of an independence or 'sure-thing' axiom and will therefore be postponed until the next section.

The third axiom, (A3), although it is slightly different than (A2), has much the same status as (A2) with regard to its reasonableness. It is judged by many writers to characterize at least part of their notion of 'rationality', but may of course fail to hold for some individuals in certain situations.

The final two axioms, for the negative transitivity of $>$ and the transitivity of $\sim$, can be criticized on somewhat different grounds than used above for acyclicity. To repeat an example I have used elsewhere, let p, q and r be three T-gambles with $p(\$36) = q(\$35) = 1$ and $r(\$100) = \frac{1}{2}$. That is, p and q are sure-thing options for \$36 and \$35 respectively, and r is a 50–50 gamble for \$100 or \$0. Most people would have $p > q$. On the other hand, because of the involvement of intermediate probability in r and difficulties in judging between such a gamble and a sure-thing option, it would not seem surprising to find $p \sim r$ and $r \sim q$, and in such a case both (A4) and (A5) fail. In the particular case used here, my own judgments agree with $p > q$, $p \sim r$ and $r \sim q$: for example, if I were offered the choice of p or r, I'd be happy to let you make the choice for me (or to flip a coin to decide between them), and similarly for q versus r. If you feel differently in this case, perhaps you can find figures other than \$35 and \$36 (e.g., \$28 and \$29, or \$44.17 and \$44.63) that would give a similar failure of (A4) and (A5).

In concluding this section, we note a few implications involving (A1) through (A5) as follows: (A1) and (A4) imply each of (A2), (A3) and (A5); (A1) and (A3) imply (A2); and (A1), (A3) and (A5) imply (A4).

3. INDEPENDENCE AXIOMS

In this section we shall consider six independence axioms which are implied by (1). They are to apply to all $p, q, r, s \in P$ and all $\lambda \in (0, 1)$.
(B1) If $p > q$ and $r > s$ then $\lambda p + (1 - \lambda)r > \lambda q + (1 - \lambda)s$.

(B2) If $p > q$ then $\lambda p + (1 - \lambda)r > \lambda q + (1 - \lambda)r$.

(B3) If $\lambda p + (1 - \lambda)r > \lambda q + (1 - \lambda)r$ then $p > q$.

(B4) If $p \sim q$ and $r \sim s$ then $\lambda p + (1 - \lambda)r \sim \lambda q + (1 - \lambda)s$.

(B5) If $p \sim q$ then $\lambda p + (1 - \lambda)r \sim \lambda q + (1 - \lambda)r$.

(B6) If $\lambda p + (1 - \lambda)r \sim \lambda q + (1 - \lambda)r$ then $p \sim q$.

The last three of these are obtained respectively from the first three by replacing $>$ by $\sim$ throughout. Using the definition of $\sim$, it is readily seen that (B2) implies (B6), and that (B3) implies (B5). I shall focus mainly on the independence axioms which use strict preference.

As is well known, the attractiveness of axioms like (B1), (B2) and (B3) is usually illustrated by a two-stage process with regard to the convex combinations. We shall note this using (B1). Illustrations with (B2) and (B3) are similar. Thus, consider the accompanying matrix

		Chance device	
		λ	$1 - \lambda$
Your	$\lambda p + (1 - \lambda)r$	p	r
Choice	$\lambda q + (1 - \lambda)s$	q	s

where you choose a row and a chance device independently selects a column according to the probabilities λ and $1 - \lambda$. If you choose the first row and chance selects the first column, then you receive x with probability $p(x)$. Thus, if you choose the first row, then your probability of getting x will be $\lambda p(x) + (1 - \lambda)r(x)$. Viewed in this way, the two rows do indeed amount to the gambles $\lambda p + (1 - \lambda)r$ and $\lambda q + (1 - \lambda)s$.

Now based on this construction it is argued that if you prefer p to q and also prefer r to s then, regardless of which column is selected by the chance device, you will be better off with the first row than with the second and hence 'should' choose the first row. To use a familiar term, the first row dominates the second, and it is this notion which lies behind both the von Neumann–Morgenstern independence axiom and Savage's sure-thing principle (1954). Thus, based on this way of viewing the situation, Axiom (B1) seems like an unassailable candidate for a 'rationality' axiom in risky decision situations.

But is it? Based in large part on the above reasoning and the examples in Allais' paper (1953), answers to this question range from a resounding 'yes' through the spectrum of hedged answers to a resounding 'no'. My understanding of the Allais criticism lies in the assertion that even though the above way of viewing (B1) seems appealing, an individual's preference judgment between $\lambda p + (1 - \lambda)r$ and $\lambda q + (1 - \lambda)s$ is properly based on a comparison of these two gambles in their full perspectives and not on a comparison of separate parts such as p versus q and r versus s. If we adopt this holistic comparison point of view, which seems to me to be what is intended by the formulation discussed in the introduction of this paper, then the status of (B1) and its companions is not as simple as the foregoing analysis would suggest.

To illustrate further along this line we consider two examples. The first involves the individual with cyclic preferences for (2) who has $p_0 > p_{100} > p_{99} > \cdots > p_2 > p_1 > p_0$. Granting (A1), this individual cannot satisfy (B1), for it is easily checked that (A1) and (B1) imply (A2) (acyclicity). The second argument for the unreasonableness of cyclic preferences alluded to in the preceding section is precisely this: if (A1) and (B1) are presumed to be reasonable, then (A2) must also be reasonable since it is implied by (A1) and (B1). Those who favor (B1) but not the sensibility of cyclic preferences might reason with the cyclic individual as follows, with the individual's reply recorded subsequently.

Decision Theorist to Cyclic Individual: "Consider the following array with two rows, p and q, and 101 columns. You can select the row and then one of the columns will be chosen randomly, each with

	1	2	3	...	99	100	101
p	p_1	p_2	p_3		p_{99}	p_{100}	p_0
q	p_0	p_1	p_2		p_{98}	p_{99}	p_{100}

the same probability of 1/101. Now according to your preferences, you prefer the entry in the first row to that in the second row for every column. Hence you should find p (first row) definitely more attractive than q (second row) and should be willing to pay something for the opportunity to select p rather than q. But that would be foolish since close examination of $p = (1/101)p_1 + (1/101)p_2 + \cdots + (1/101)p_0$ and $q = (1/101)p_0 + (1/101)p_1 + \cdots + (1/101)p_{100}$ reveals that $p = q$."

Cyclic Individual to Decision Theorist: "I agree with your judgment of my pairwise preferences in the columns of your matrix and, if offered any such pair I would unhesitatingly select the gamble in the first row. But I too can compute and am aware that p and q are identical. Thus, as between the two rows viewed holistically, I am quite indifferent and wouldn't pay you a farthing for the 'opportunity' to select p rather than q. As a prudent and reasonable man, these are my judgments and if they disturb you in some way then I am sorry for your sake."

So much for cyclic preferences. For our second example, which involves (B3), we turn to Allais' most famous example, based on the following four gambles:

p: \$500,000 with probability 1.

q: \$2,500,000 with probability 0.1,
$500,000 with probability 0.89,
$0 with probability 0.01.

r: \$500,000 with probability 0.11,
$0 with probability 0.89.

s: \$2,500,000 with probability 0.1,
$0 with probability 0.9.

My readings and conversations with others suggest that, up to the present time, hundreds of individuals in classrooms and elsewhere have made the comparisons between p and q and between r and s (or between similar types of pairs). A significant proportion of these individuals have $p > q$ and $s > r$ and therefore violate the combination of (A1) and (B3) since, with $t(\$2,500,000) = \frac{10}{11}$, $t(\$0) = \frac{1}{11}$, and $v(\$0) = 1$,

$$p = 0.11p + 0.89p$$
$$q = 0.11t + 0.89p,$$

and

$$r = 0.11p + 0.89v$$
$$s = 0.11t + 0.89v.$$

Hence (B3) would require $p > t$ from $p > q$, and $t > p$ from $s > r$ thus contradicting asymmetry. It is reported that many individuals who have $p > q$ and $s > r$ show no intention of changing their minds when faced with the fact that they violate the cited axioms or (1). Should these knowing violators of (A1) and (B3) be labeled as 'irrational' and be left without a satisfactory model for their preferences, or should we attempt, as has Allais (1953, 1972), to look for a model that will account for such preferences?

In the remainder of this section, I should like to consider a different criticism of some of the independence axioms that is similar in spirit to the criticism of transitive indifference in the penultimate paragraph of the preceding section. The nature of this can be seen with reference to (B2), which says that $p > q$ and $0 < \lambda < 1$ imply $\lambda p + (1 - \lambda)r > \lambda q + (1 - \lambda)r$. One difficulty with this seems to be that if λ is sufficiently near to zero then, despite the fact that p is preferred to q, the presence of $(1 - \lambda)r$ in both $\lambda p + (1 - \lambda)r$ and $\lambda q + (1 - \lambda)r$ may so overwhelm or mask the differences between p and q that the individual will be indifferent between $\lambda p + (1 - \lambda)r$ and $\lambda q + (1 - \lambda)r$. In substance, this criticism simply speaks against the preservation of strict preference under arbitrarily fine dilutions. An example in Fishburn (1972a, p.296) illustrates this in more detail.

Because (B1) has strict preference in both antecedents, with $p > q$ and $r > s$, it is not subject to the same criticism. Axiom (B3), which can be thought of as an antidilution independence axiom, also avoids the problem. For, reasoning from the above-challenged matrix (two-stage) paradigm, if $\lambda p + (1 - \lambda)r > \lambda q + (1 - \lambda)r$ then the basis of preference must arise from distinctions between p and q, and such distinctions will be more evident when r is removed, thus giving $p > q$.

Of the three independence axioms which use indifference, (B4) and (B6) are subject to criticisms based on dilutions and thresholds while (B5) is not. For example, if $p \sim q$ as in the hypothesis of (B5), then dilutions with r would appear only to strengthen the similarity between $\lambda p + (1 - \lambda)r$ and $\lambda q + (1 - \lambda)r$, and so one might expect indifference between $\lambda p + (1 - \lambda)r$ and $\lambda q + (1 - \lambda)r$ as in the conclusion of (B5). To illustrate a difficulty with (B4) we consider the earlier example in which $p(\$36) = q(\$35) = 1$ and $r(\$100) = r(\$0) = \frac{1}{2}$. If $p \sim r$ and $q \sim r$ then (B4) would require indifference between

$\frac{1}{2}p + \frac{1}{2}r$: $36 with probability 0.5,

$100 with probability 0.25,

$0 with probability 0.25,

and

$$\tfrac{1}{2}q + \tfrac{1}{2}r: \text{ \$35 with probability 0.5,}$$
$$\text{\$100 with probability 0.25,}$$
$$\text{\$0 with probability 0.25,}$$

which would violate the expected $\tfrac{1}{2}p + \tfrac{1}{2}r > \tfrac{1}{2}q + \tfrac{1}{2}r$. Axiom (B6), which is implied by (B2), is subject to the same form of criticism given above for (B2).

In summary, apart from the problems posed by the earlier examples in this section, Axiom (B2) is sensitive to dilution or threshold criticisms while (B1) and (B3) are not, at least within the two-stage paradigm that is often used. When $>$ is replaced by $\sim$ in these axioms, the situation is reversed with (B4) and (B6) but not (B5) liable to similar criticisms.

4. IMPLICATIONS

Several implications of the foregoing order and independence axioms which are also implications of the von Neumann–Morgenstern expected utility model (1) can be established without reference to utility functions. We have already noted that (A1) and (B1) imply (A2), and it can be shown that transitivity of $>$, or (A3), is implied by (A1), (B1) and (B3). Moreover, letting

$$P_1 = \{p \in P: q > p \text{ for no } q \in P\}$$
$$P_0 = \{p \in P: q > p \text{ for some } q \in P\},$$

so that P_1 is the subset of maximally preferred gambles in P with $P_1 \cup P_0 = P$ and $P_1 \cap P_0 = \phi$, Fishburn (1972a) shows that

(3)   (A1) and (B1) imply that P_1 is not empty and it contains a p which assigns probability 1 to some $x \in X$;

(4)   (A1), (A3) and (B3) imply that P_1 is not empty and for each $q \in P_0$ there is some $p \in P_1$ such that $p > q$.

The latter result shows that, under the appropriate axioms, every gamble which is nonmaximal in $(P, >)$ is less preferred than some maximal gamble in P_1. This is not generally true under Axioms (A1) and (B1) used in (3). That is, when (A1) and (B1) hold, it is possible that all gambles p for which $p > q$ when $q \in P_0$ will be in P_0.

Preference-preserving utility functions are implied by certain combinations of order and independence axioms, but, since no Archimedean condition is involved in these representations, the utilities of the consequence in X must usually be vector-valued with the order of $>$ preserved by means of the lexicographic order on expected utility vectors. Letting Re^n denote n-dimensional Euclidean space, the strict lexicographic order $>_L$ on Re^n is defined by $(a_1, \ldots, a_n) >_L (b_1, \ldots, b_n)$ if and only if $a_i \neq b_i$ for some $i \in \{1, \ldots, n\}$ and $a_i > b_i$ for the smallest i for which $a_i \neq b_i$.

A vector-valued utility function U on X is a function which maps each $x \in X$ into a real vector $U(x) = (u_1(x), \ldots, u_n(x))$ in a given Re^n with n a positive integer. Given $U: X \to \text{Re}^n$, the expected utility for $p \in P$ is the vector $E(U, p) = (E(u_1, p), \ldots, E(u_n, p))$ where $E(u_i, p) = \Sigma_x p(x) u_i(x)$ for each i. The following theorem results from an observation in Fishburn (1971a, p.575).

(5)   Suppose (A1) and (B1) hold and X contains $m > 1$ consequences. Then there exists a positive integer $n < m$ and a function $U: X \to \text{Re}^n$ such that, for all $p, q \in P$, $E(U, p) >_L E(U, q)$ whenever $p > q$.

The conclusion of (5), which establishes (3) in a straightforward way, says that strict preference is preserved by expected utility vectors under the natural lexicographic order in the sense that $p > q$ implies $E(U, p) >_L E(U, q)$, for all p and q in P. The converse need not hold, so that when $E(U, p) >_L E(U, q)$ we may have either $p > q$ or $p \sim q$. If P' is a subset of P and if $E(U, p)$ has a lexicographic maximum within P' at $p' \in P'$, meaning that $E(U, p') >_L E(U, q')$ or $E(U, p') = E(U, q')$ for each $q' \in P'$, then p' is a maximally preferred gamble within P'. It can also be shown that (A1), (A2), (B2) and (B3) imply the conclusion of (5), but I find these hypotheses less satisfactory than (A1) and (B1) since they involve the dilution axiom, (B2).

The observations in the preceding paragraph lead us to conclude that the crux of the von Neumann–Morgenstern utility theory, when modified to account for certain limitations in human judgment, can be captured by the two basic axioms of asymmetry (A1) and weak independence (B1).

As has been noted by several authors, including Hausner (1954), Chipman (1960, 1971) and Fishburn (1971b), when indifference as well as preference is assumed to be transitive and strong independence axioms are used, the lexicographic representation goes both ways:

(6)   Suppose (A1), (A4), (B2) and (B5) hold and X contains
        $m > 1$ consequences. Then there exists a positive integer
        $n < m$ and a function $U: X \to \mathrm{Re}^n$ such that, for all
        $p, q \in P$, $p > q$ if and only if $E(U, p) >_L E(U, q)$.

5. ARCHIMEDEAN AXIOMS

When certain Archimedean axioms are used in conjunction with order
and independence axioms, the vector-valued utilities in (5) and (6) can
be replaced with single-valued utilities as in (1). Besides allowing a
conceptually simpler expected utility model, this change has important implications in certain applications, as has been illustrated by
Fishburn (1972c) in the area of two-person zero-sum games.

We shall consider the following three Archimedean axioms to apply
to all p, q, r and s in P.

(C1) If $p > q$ and $q > r$ then there exist $\lambda, \mu \in (0, 1)$ such that
$\lambda p + (1 - \lambda)r > q$ and $q > \mu p + (1 - \mu)r$.

(C2) If $p > q$ and $r > s$ then there exists $\lambda \in (0, 1)$ such that $\lambda p +
(1 - \lambda)s > \lambda q + (1 - \lambda)r$.

(C3) If $\lambda p + (1 - \lambda)r > \lambda q + (1 - \lambda)s$ for all $\lambda \in (0, 1]$ then either
$r > s$ or $r \sim s$.

Axiom (C1) is the von Neumann–Morgenstern (1944) Archimedean
axiom, usually defended by the contention that if $p > q > r$ then there
should be some $\lambda \in (0, 1)$, perhaps very near to 1, such that $\lambda p +
(1 - \lambda)r > q$. A similar remark applies to $q > \mu p + (1 - \mu)r$ with μ
close to zero. Although in an objective sense $\mu p + (1 - \mu)r$ is virtually
the same as r when μ is near to 0, such as $\mu = 10^{-100}$, some people
seem to exhibit rather different attitudes towards something that is
'assured' with absolute certainty and something that is extremely
likely to occur but has a chance, however small, of not occurring. For
example, some individuals may prefer any T-gamble which gives a
positive probability of winning a million dollars to the certainty of
getting one nickel, and (C1) must fail for such individuals if they
prefer $1,000,000 to five cents and prefer five cents to nothing.

The second Archimedean axiom, (C2), is stronger than (C1) since it
implies (C1), but not conversely. In so far as (C1) is liable to criticism,
(C2) can be subjected to similar criticism. Intuitively, (C2) seems
appealing when λ is taken very close to unity.

Axiom (C3), which is similar to an axiom used by Aumann (1962), is designed for use with certain order and independence conditions, as are the others, and is more or less the weakest of the three axioms. Any single-valued utility function $u: X \to \mathrm{Re}$ which has $E(u, p) > E(u, q)$ whenever $p > q$ requires the satisfaction of (C3) but not of (C1) or (C2). With $p(\$1,000,000) = r(\$0) = q(\$.05) = s(\$.05) = 1$, (C3) will fail for the individual who has $p > q > r$ but prefers any chance at the \$1,000,000 to a nickel for sure.

The effect of (C2) in the context of (5) is as follows.

(7)   Suppose (A1), (B1) and (C2) hold. Then there exists $u: X \to \mathrm{Re}$ such that, for all $p, q \in P$, $E(u, p) > E(u, q)$ whenever $p > q$.

This is proved in Fishburn (1972b). As shown by Aumann (1962) and Fishburn (1970, 1971a), the conclusion of (7) also follows from (A3), (B2), (B3) and (C3). The absence of (A1) from the latter set of axioms is explained by the fact that (C3) and (A3) imply (A1).

The effect of (C1) on (6) has already been noted in the introduction: (A1), (A4), (B2) and (C1) imply the existence of $u: X \to \mathrm{Re}$ which satisfies (1). Although (B5) was used for (6) it can be omitted when (C1) is added since, as shown by Jensen (1967), it is implied by (A1), (A4), (B2) and (C1).

6. SUMMARY

In this paper, we have explored certain aspects of the three types of axioms for an individual's preference relation > on the set of probability distributions or 'gambles' defined on a finite set of consequences that were used by von Neumann and Morgenstern in their pioneering axiomatization of preferences on risky alternatives.

For ordering type axioms, examples were given which purport to show the general untenability of transitive indifference and to suggest that reasonable people may have cyclic preferences in some situations.

Following Allais (1953), we noted a basic argument against a variety of independence axioms and then argued that several of these axioms were also subject to criticism based on threshold phenomena and vagueness in judgment.

It was then suggested that the heart of the von Neumann–Morgenstern proposal, taking account of vagueness in human judgment, consists of the asymmetry of $>$ and the weak independence axiom which says that $\lambda p + (1 - \lambda)r > \lambda q + (1 - \lambda)s$ whenever $p > q$, $r > s$ and $0 < \lambda < 1$. The satisfaction of these two axioms implies the existence of a vector-valued utility function $U: X \to \text{Re}^n$ which gives $E(U, p) >_L E(U, q)$ whenever $p > q$. The addition of an Archimedean axiom allows the vector-valued utilities to be replaced by single-valued utilities.

Despite the fact that a number of criticisms of the von Neumann–Morgenstern axioms can be accommodated within the framework of the model in the preceding paragraph, certain other criticisms such as Allais' attack on independence axioms and cyclic preferences cannot be handled by that model. Possibilities of dealing with these other criticisms have been set forth by Allais (1953, 1972) and Tversky (1969), respectively.

College of Business Administration,
The Pennsylvania State University

BIBLIOGRAPHY

Allais, M.: (1953). 'Le Comportement de l'Homme Rationnel devant le Risque', *Econometrica* 21, 503–546.

Allais, M.: (1972). 'The Foundations of a Positive Theory of Choice Involving Risk and a Criticism of the Postulates and Axioms of the American School', Centre D'Analyse Economique, No. 2824, September, 1972. [Part II of this Volume; developed further in Part V – O.H.]

Aumann, R. J.: (1962, 1964). 'Utility Theory without the Completeness Axiom', *Econometrica* 30, 445–462; 32, 210–212.

Burros, R. H.: (1974). 'Axiomatic Analysis of Non-transitivity of Preference and of Indifference', *Theory and Decision* 5, 185–204.

Chipman, J. S.: (1960). 'The Foundations of Utility', *Econometrica* 28, 193–224.

Chipman, J. S.: (1971). 'Non-Archimedean Behavior Under Risk: An Elementary Analysis'. In J. S. Chipman, L. Hurwicz, M. K. Richter and H. F. Sonnenschein (Eds.), *Preferences, Utility, and Demand*, Harcourt Brace Jovanovich, New York, p.289.

Fishburn, P. C.: (1970). *Utility Theory for Decision Making*, Wiley, New York.

Fishburn, P. C.: (1971a). 'One-Way Expected Utility with Finite Consequence Spaces', *Annals of Mathematical Statistics* 42, 572–577.

Fishburn, P. C.: (1971b). 'A Study of Lexicographic Expected Utility', *Management Science* 17, 672–678.

Fishburn, P. C.: (1972a). 'Minimal Preferences on Lotteries', *Journal of Mathematical Psychology* **9**, 294–305.

Fishburn, P. C.: (1972b). 'Alternative Axiomatizations of One-Way Expected Utility', *Annals of Mathematical Statistics* **43**, 1648–1651.

Fishburn, P. C.: (1972c). 'On the Foundations of Game Theory: The Case of Non-Archimedean Utilities', *International Journal of Game Theory* **1**, 65–71.

Hausner, M.: (1954). 'Multidimensional Utilities'. In R. M. Thrall, C. H. Coombs and R. L. Davis (Eds.), *Decision Processes*, Wiley, New York, p.167.

Jensen, N. E.: (1967). 'An Introduction to Bernoullian Utility Theory: I. Utility Functions', *Swedish Journal of Economics* **69**, 163–183.

Savage, L. J.: (1954). *The Foundations of Statistics*, Wiley, New York.

Tversky, A.: (1969). 'Intransitivity of Preferences', *Psychological Review* **76**, 31–48.

von Neumann, J., and Morgenstern, O.: (1944). *Theory of Games and Economic Behavior*, Princeton University Press, Princeton.

SAMUEL GOROVITZ

THE ST. PETERSBURG PUZZLE[1]

ABSTRACT. The standard Bayesian account of rational decision-making leads to the St. Petersburg paradox. Jeffrey's response to the paradox suggests a modification of the St. Petersburg game. The puzzle is that it seems reasonable to refuse to play the game, contrary to Bayesian analysis, yet the game is immune to Jeffrey's original objections. A partially systematic account of the rationality of refusal can be based on the observation that in making decisions there is an implicit level of likelihood below which possible events are discounted, and properly so. A thorough account of rational decision-making should incorporate some standard of how the refusal to consider extremely unlikely contributions to expected utility can be warranted.

The standard Bayesian account of rational decision-making leads to the well-known St. Petersburg paradox. R. C. Jeffrey's response to the paradox suggests what I call the St. Petersburg puzzle – a puzzle which, while not a paradox, should nonetheless prompt consideration by the defenders of present formulations of Bayesian decision theory. For the sake of completeness, I shall recount the St. Petersburg paradox and Jeffrey's reply before introducing the puzzle.

The ideally rational decision, according to the standard Bayesian view, is made by taking all available relevant evidence into account, in a way that can be rigorously characterized. The available alternative courses of action are identified, the possible outcomes of each alternative action assessed as to probability and desirability, and the choice made of that action which has the maximum expected utility. But the St. Petersburg paradox seems to defy this logic. It arises out of the St. Petersburg game, in which A offers B a chance to purchase, for a fee, an opportunity to toss a fair coin until a tail comes up, with the understanding that A will then pay B 2^n dollars – where n is the number of the toss on which that first tail appeared. The question then is: How much is it rational for B to pay A in order to play? Clearly, it cannot be less than two dollars, since even if the first toss yields the dreaded tail, B will receive a pay-off no less than that. One assumes that the reasonable fee, as B judges the opportunity, will be a function of his wealth, his taste for gambling, the intensity of his desire for greater riches, his psychological disposition in the face of victory and defeat, etc. But, surprisingly, none of these factors

Maurice Allais and Ole Hagen (eds.), Expected Utility and the Allais Paradox, 259–270.
Copyright © 1979 by D. Reidel Publishing Company.

matters. For, the expected gain of playing is infinite, and hence any rational man should be willing to pay all he has for a chance to play. Yet that is absurd, and therein lies the paradox. The calculation looks like this:

$$g = \sum_{n=1}^{\infty} 2^n = 1 + 1 + 1 + \cdots = \infty,$$

where n = toss of first tail and g = expected gain of playing. (The expected gain is the sum over all possible outcomes of the probability times the value of each outcome.)

The most promising way out of the paradox may seem to lie in the observation, made by Bernoulli (1738), that the expected gain is not equivalent to the expected utility – that the utility of each additional dollar tends to diminish as one's wealth increases, and thus the above computation yields too large a figure. We should restate the calculation thus:

$$u = \sum_{n=0}^{\infty} f(n) = t_0 + t_1 + t_2 + \ldots,$$

where u = expected utility of playing and where f is some function of n that increasingly discounts the desirability of increasingly large monetary pay-offs. Here, t_i is the contribution to expected utility of the possibility of an outcome of i consecutive heads. The paradox would disappear if there were some point beyond which additional gain were of no desirability at all – i.e., if there were some specific k such that $t_i = 0$ if $i > k$. That such an assumption is warranted is, at best, debatable. Indeed, its denial, according to Friedman and Savage ([1948], p.303) is "implicit in the orthodox theory of choice", which holds that the marginal utility of money income is "everywhere positive". The paradox would also disappear if f is such that even though each term t_i is positive, the summation approaches some limit. There is reason to believe that for a particular agent in a specified situation, if the agent's preferences are already clear and satisfy certain conditions such as transitivity and coherence, it is possible to write a bounded function of n such that the agent acts in accordance with his preferences if and only if he acts so as to maximize the value of that function. Such a function, tailored to the circumstances, in effect describes the agent's preferences at the point in time under consideration. Whatever normative force it has derives from the constraints that are placed on the original preferences. Those constraints require, for example, that a rational agent prefers winning to losing. But it is not clear that they provide a basis for computing a single, plausible game playing fee.

Yet the paradox must be dispelled, or the Bayesian account of the rational decision is threatened. Jeffrey ([1965], p.143) agrees, writing:

Our theory, like Ramsey's, is incompatible with the existence of a proposition of positive probability to which the agent assigns infinite positive or negative desirability. Therefore it is essential that we avoid the St. Petersburg paradox; it is essential that we block the argument that seems to lead from the existence of a sequence of propositions of finite but unbounded desirability to the existence of a proposition of positive probability and infinite desirability.

He goes on to reject the paradox, continuing:

In fact, we can do this very easily .... Put briefly and crudely, our rebuttal of the St. Petersburg paradox consists in the remark that anyone who offers to let the agent play the St. Petersburg game is a liar, for he is pretending to have an indefinitely large bank.

Thus, the paradox cannot arise, since the game itself is a deception, and cannot be played. This argument, incidentally, echoes that offered much earlier by Menger, who also argued that the St. Petersburg game is a sham ([1934]; see also Hagen [1972], pp.55–6).

Having dispensed with games of infinite expected desirability, Jeffrey observes that a nation could play the St. Petersburg game by printing a special note in the amount of any required pay-off. He is untroubled by the prospect, however, holding that "in that case there would clearly be a finite upper bound on the desirabilities of the possible pay-offs." And further, "Due to the resulting inflation, the marginal desirabilities of such high pay-offs would presumably be low enough to make the prospect of playing the game have finite expected desirability" ([1965], p.144).

Granting the presumption, we note that it is not enough simply that the expected utility of the game be reduced from the infinite to the finite. Rather, what is necessary is that the expected utility of playing the game be reduced to what on other grounds would be judged reasonable to pay for the privilege of playing. If the calculated expected utility, albeit finite, exceeds such an amount, then a challenge to the Bayesian account remains. Such a challenge may be dispelled only by elimination of the gap between the Bayesian calculation and the independent assessment – either by rejecting the independent assessment as not credible, or by revision of the Bayesian calculation.

The St. Petersburg puzzle is intended as precisely this sort of challenge. Suppose, after Jeffrey's suggestion, that a nation does undertake to play a version of the St. Petersburg game. Let us examine a possible scenario. The United States, to distract public opinion from foreign policy blunders, announces that a truncated version of the classical St. Petersburg game will be offered to the public. Citizens will be picked at random, seriatim, and offered a single chance to play for a fee of 33 dollars. The pay-off is to be 2^n dollars (where $n - 1$ is the number of consecutive heads) subject to a maximum run of 34 heads. With such a limit imposed, the maximum governmental risk at any one time is not quite 35 billion dollars, well within the range of dubious governmental expenditures. Assume I am picked; is it rational for me to accept the offer, pay the fee, and play?

If utility were equivalent to monetary pay-off, the Bayesian computation of expected utility would be simply:

$$u = \sum_{n=1}^{n=35} \frac{1}{2^n} 2^n = 35.$$

But I would refuse to play, even though the fee, less than the expected pay-off, would seem at least initially to be a Bayesian bargain.

There are ways of trying to close the gap between what I would pay and the Bayesian expected gain, short of calling my decision irrational. Most obvious is the acknowledgment, as above, that the actual utility to me of very large pay-offs is not proportional to the dollar yield – i.e., that utility and monetary gain are not equivalent. Further considerations might include the facts that I cannot afford the playing fee without great sacrifice to some other venture of high value, that I have a marked aversion to risk, or that I suffer disproportionate anxiety in the face of uncertain outcomes.

With respect to the truncated version of the game, infinite desirability is no longer an issue. It will suffice if f maps monetary gains into utilities in such a way as to lower the expected utility of playing the game to a level comparable to what one might reasonably pay in order to play the game.

Von Neumann and Morgenstern (1947) have shown that, given a set of preferences in a choice situation (assuming those preferences to satisfy certain plausible conditions, such as coherence and transitivity) it is possible to *describe* the preferences with a utility function such that one acts in accordance with one's preferences if and only if one maximizes expected utility as given by that function. Such descriptive possibilities, however, do not themselves constitute a normative account of rational betting behavior. Nor did von Neumann and Morgenstern claim normative force for them.* There is thus no shortage of functions that will do the job; the question is whether they make sense as part of a normative characterization of rational betting behavior.

Dorling suggests trying a logarithmic function, such as:

$$f(n) = k \sum_{n=1}^{35} \frac{1}{2^n} \log_2 \left(1 + \frac{2^n}{c}\right),$$

where c is the player's capital, and k is a normalizing constant, perhaps equal to c.

The idea of using a logarithmic function to measure utility goes back to Daniel Bernoulli [1738], who, according to Savage ([1945], p.92):

went further than the law of diminishing marginal utility and suggested that the slope of utility as a function of wealth might, at least as a rule of thumb, be supposed, not only to decrease with, but to be inversely proportional to, the cash value of wealth. This, he pointed out, is equivalent to postulating that utility is equal to the logarithm (to any base) of the cash value of wealth. To this day, no other function has been suggested as a better prototype for Everyman's utility function.

But Bayesians do not purport to characterize any single utility function for "Everyman." Rather, they claim to provide an account of how to determine a utility function that is normative for a particular person, in a specific situation, whose preferences are antecedently clear. Whatever general normative force the theory has seems to lie in the constraints on preferences.

Using such a logarithmic function, the expected utility of the game would be given by:

$$u = k \sum_{n=1}^{35} \frac{1}{2^n} \log_2 \left(1 + \frac{2^n}{c}\right).$$

This function characterizes a diminishing marginal utility, but it

---

* [*Editorial Note*: Compare now Morgenstern, p.180 – O.H.]

nonetheless yields unacceptable expected utility values for any situation in which I can readily imagine myself. For example, at $c = \$15,000$, u is about $22 -$ still too high a figure. For a man with half a billion dollars (and there are some), the expected utility is about $42 -$ also surely a counter-intuitive result, exceeding as it does the expected monetary gain.

Any such function reflects the view that the utility of additional funds diminishes – perhaps logarithmically, perhaps otherwise, but steadily – as one's capital increases. But in fact, the utility of additional income depends on one's aspirations as well as on one's capital, and one's aspirations often rise with rising income. Thus, the assumption of steady diminution is implausible. Indeed, were my capital or prospects sufficient to enable me realistically to aspire to underwrite programs of social welfare that I judge my government remiss in neglecting, I might well endow the possibility of additional income with a utility function that does not yield steady diminution of utility as gain increases, but rather, for some ranges of the value of n, goes the other way.[2] If this be the case, then functions like the one above cannot do after all, in spite of their relativization of utility to level of capital. What would be required in an adequate characterization of rational betting behavior along the suggested lines is a function that reflects individual aspirations as well as wherewithal. My worry is that the von Neumann–Morgenstern conditions do not constrain preferences in such a way as to yield, for each potential player, such a function, the expected utility of which corresponds to what he would reasonably pay to play.

What I am suggesting here is that my refusal to play the game as offered does not after all seem readily amenable to a plausible, systematic, normative account along Bayesian lines, even when that account takes into consideration the diminishing marginal utility of money. Further, I can afford the playing fee, I have a moderate taste for a gamble, and I do not have a particularly low tolerance for uncertainty. Still, I submit, my refusal to play is rational.[3]

My claim to rationality may be challenged, but it cannot be refuted by any argument based on calculations of expected outcomes in the long run. The game at issue provides what is strictly a short run situation, and rational betting behavior differs in the long and short runs. Thus, I would reject an opportunity to buy for $10 a single, non-repeatable ten percent chance at winning $200, on the grounds that the odds were 9 to 1 in favor of my losing the initial stake. Yet I would welcome most eagerly an opportunity to purchase such chances repeatedly, confident that in the long run I would profit well.

This observation provides the key to what I wish to suggest as a direction in which might be found an explanation of the reasonableness of my refusal to play the revised St. Petersburg game. In order to avoid losing money at the game, I must win at least the playing fee. That requires an initial run of six heads. The chances of my getting such a run are just one in sixty four. It isn't that I'm unduly pessimistic, or that I won't ever bet on a long shot. Rather, it is simply that in this situation the shot is just too long to represent a reasonable investment of a non-trivial sum. The possible large pay-offs are far too unlikely for their possibility to have real bearing on my decision.

In claiming this, I explicitly discount on strictly probabilistic grounds certain possible outcomes as irrelevant to my decision. This should not be viewed as unusual; we do it commonly. For example, consider a bet on a cross-country race between a train and an automobile. We would take many factors into account in assessing the wisdom of such a bet. But we would not likely consider as relevant the fact that a meteor might strike either road or rails, and that a car could more easily circumvent the resulting damage. We concede that such an event would be causally relevant to the outcome of the race, but we do not include its possibility as relevant to the assessment of odds, because it is simply too unlikely. This view is in contrast with the more traditional Bayesian view that we discount such an event because its probability is so low that, even multiplied by an enormous utility, it is too small to affect the direction of the inequalities among the expected utilities of the acts under consideration.

Let us assume that in every decision-making context there is an implicit level of probability below which possible events are discounted. We can now explain my gaming behavior. If in this case I set that minimum level of probability at one chance in sixty four, then the calculation of the expected utility of playing the truncated St. Petersburg game is itself truncated – the summation only includes those terms the probabilistic component of which equals or exceeds 1/64. The value of the summation thus shrinks to six dollars. I am far more likely to play for that.

Of course, it is not merely lowness of probability that matters here, but lowness of probability of some outcomes relative to others. Low probability alone does not discriminate against an outcome. Allais saw this point long ago. Speaking of the probability distributions of utility in situations involving risk ([1953], p.504), he held that:

The dispersion (variance) as well as general properties of the form of the probability distribution [must be taken into account] even in a first approximation, by every theory of risk if it is to be realistic and is to bring out what is absolutely essential in every choice involving risk.

In a lottery, for example, all the outcomes available for consideration may share very low probabilities. But in the St. Petersburg puzzle, the very low probabilities are contrasted with others as high as 0.5. I do not mean to suggest that such comparative lowness of probability is, in general, a decisive factor; rather, I seek merely to have it recognized as one relevant consideration. Indeed, in some cases it seems plainly not to be dominant. For example, a moderately hungry man faced with an opportunity to purchase for his remaining cash of five dollars a one in a thousand chance to save his three thousand dollar equity in securities from utter collapse might reasonably make the purchase, forgoing a chance to purchase for the same money a highly likely prospect of a decent dinner.[4] In this case the high utility of the unlikely outcome seems to be the dominant factor, whereas in the St. Petersburg puzzle no such dominance occurs. There must be some factor that differentiates these two circumstances, but I do not know what it is.

In the case at hand, my selection of 1/64 as the appropriate value is admittedly somewhat arbitrary. Although the consequences of its selection accord fairly well with my inclinations in the gaming situation at issue, I can provide no general procedure to justify its selection or to guide the selection of similar truncation point values for other situations. Still, there seems to me something appealing about a model that eliminates from the calculation of utilities such factors as we in fact seem reasonably to ignore.

Jeffrey, objecting quite properly to the Procrusteanism of an arbitrarily selected truncation level, raises (but rejects) the possibility of incorporating a function that discounts low probabilities more and more, the lower they get. Expected utilities would then be given by an expression of the form $g(p)f(n)$, where f is a function accounting for decreasing marginal utilities and g is a function that discounts terms on the basis of low probabilities. But with any such function, we still face this dilemma: either there is some point within the range of p values $(0 \leqslant p \leqslant 1)$ beyond which the value of the function is linear, or there is not. If there is, then that point seems arbitrary. If there is not, then we are discounting all terms in the summation, to varying degrees (assuming $g(p) < 1$ for $p < 1$) – in which case we are discounting not merely low probabilities, but all of them, as the price paid for avoiding arbitrariness. Such complications of the Bayesian model are distressing, and their consequences for probability theory and decision theory may be more so. They do not appear to provide a welcome way out of the puzzle.

The Bayesian logic of decision, as formulated by Jeffrey and others, is a normative account. It purports not to describe how decisions are made, but to reveal the structure of decisions made rationally. Even if the Bayesian calculation, by including in the summation of expected utilities the contributions from all terms regardless of probability, goes too far to describe the actual making of certain decisions, it is still open to the Bayesian to claim that all such terms must be included equally in the ideally rational decision. Such a response not only fails to account convincingly for the St. Petersburg puzzle, it fails to acknowledge or explain a deeply ingrained feature of conscientious decision-making. For, the case out of which the St. Petersburg puzzle arises, unlike the original St. Petersburg game, is not an anomalous curiosity. What it lacks in paradox, it makes up for by its correspondence with real decision-making situations, in which a conscientious incorporation into the deliberation of highly unlikely possibilities would be crippling or misleading.

I suggest that the failure or refusal to consider highly unlikely contributions to expected utility is not only common, but in some instances entirely reasonable. If that is so, then an account of rational decision-making should incorporate some standard of how such refusal should operate. It can be done well or badly, but I do not know how to characterize the difference in any systematic way.

I have posed the puzzle as an apparent exception to Bayesian theory taken as a normative account of rational behavior. I do not doubt that some sort of Bayesian resolution of the puzzle is possible. But, as Savage says ([1954], p.101):

Many apparent exceptions to the theory can be so reinterpreted as not to be exceptions at all . . . in general, the reinterpretation needed to reconcile various sorts of behavior with the utility theory is sometimes quite acceptable and sometimes so strained as to lay whoever proposes it open to the charge of trying to save the theory by rendering it tautological.

How serious a challenge to Bayesian theory the puzzle presents will depend on the strain that is required for resolution of the difficulty, as the process of adjustment of principles and cases to one another continues. Rawls ([1971], pp.20ff.) names this process well, calling it a search for "reflective equilibrium." But Savage ([1954, p.102) describes it succinctly:

A person who has tentatively accepted a normative theory must conscientiously study situations in which the theory seems to lead him astray; he must decide for each by reflection – deduction will typically be of little relevance – whether to retain his initial impression of the situation or to accept the implications of the theory for it.

The St. Petersburg puzzle is no counter-example to Bayesian theory. Rather, it is a case in which the theory seems to lead one astray. It is thus a criticism that may contribute either to the weakening or the strengthening of the theory. For, as Lindley ([1972], p.374) observes:

It is surely vital that statistics have a formal structure .... The only available structure at the moment is the Bayesian one. It is right that this should be criticized .... But Popper makes the point that there is no proof that any formal system is correct; all one can do is attempt to destroy the system, and every attempt at destruction that fails enhances the system.

Lindley makes his point in reference to a formal, axiomatic theory of statistics, but as a methodological observation it applies equally well to utility theory as a normative account of rational behavior.

The difficulty posed by the St. Petersburg puzzle underscores the fact that it is often simply not possible to attend to and reflect in deliberation outcomes that are highly unlikely in relation to the more probable outcomes confronting us. The limitations of rational capacity do not underlie the St. Petersburg puzzle, for we can well understand the choices and chances involved. But they do constrain the way we make choices in more complex situations. Whatever difficulties exist in accounting for the St. Petersburg puzzle are thus compounded in the development of a general theory of rational behavior. With Suppes ([1966], p.64), I want to emphasize:

...the difficulty of expressing in systematic form the mechanisms of attention a rationally operating organism should use. It is also worth noting that any interesting concept of rationality for the behavior of man must be keyed to a realistic appraisal of the powers and limitations of the perceptual and mental apparatus of humans.

The University of Maryland,
College Park

NOTES

[1] I am greatly indebted to Jon Dorling, Ray Nelson, Ilmar Waldner, and, especially, to Richard Jeffrey, for comments on earlier drafts of this discussion. None of its faults should be taken as theirs, however, nor should it be assumed that they are in essential agreement throughout.

[2] That such a 'wiggly utility curve' may be needed to characterize common choice behavior is well recognized by Friedman and Savage ([1948], pp.298ff.): "Increases in income that raise the relative position of the consumer unit in its own class but do not shift the unit out of its class yield diminishing marginal utility, while increases that shift it into a new class, that give it a new social and economic status, yield increasing marginal utility."

[3] I am supported in my perception of the refusal as rational by the fact that no person with whom I have discussed the game has disagreed, or held that he would do otherwise. The claim about amenability to Bayesian treatment is better read as an invitation than as any impossibility theorem.

[4] This example was suggested by Ilmar Waldner.

REFERENCES

Allais, M.: (1953). 'Le Comportement de l'Homme Rationnel devant le Risque: Critique des Postulats et Axiomes de l'Ecole Americaine', *Econometrica* 21, 503–546. [See also Part II of this Volume. Allais considers the St. Petersburg game in Part V of this Volume, p.498 – O.H.]

Bernoulli, D.: (1954). 'Exposition of a New Theory on the Measurement of Risk', English translation of 'Specimen Theoriae Novae de Mensura Sortis', *Commentarii Academiae Imperialist Petropolitanae*, (1730–1731) 5, (1738) 175–192, by Louise Sommer, *Econometrica* 22, 23–36.

Friedman, M., and Savage, L. J.: (1948). 'The Utility Analysis of Choices Involving Risk', *The Journal of Political Economy* LVI, 279–304.

Hagen, O.: (1972). 'A New Axiomatization of Utility under Risk', *Teorie A Metoda* IV 55–80.

Jeffrey, R.C.: (1965). *The Logic of Decision*, McGraw Hill, New York.

Lindley, D.V.: (1972). "Comments" on C. R. Blyth's 'Some Probability Paradoxes in Choice from Among Random Alternatives', *Journal of the American Statistical Association*, pp.373–4.

Menger, K.: (1934). 'Das Unsicherheitsmoment in der Wertlehre', *Zeitschrift für Nationalökonomie.*

Rawls, J.: (1971). *A Theory of Justice,* Harvard University Press, Cambridge.

Savage, L. J.: (1954). *The Foundations of Statistics,* Wiley, New York.

Suppes, P. C.: (1966). 'Probabilistic Inference and the Concept of Total Evidence'. In J. Hintikka and P. Suppes (Eds.), *Aspects of Inductive Logic,* North Holland Publishing Co., Amsterdam, pp.59–65.

von Neumann, J., and Morgenstern, O.: (1947). *Theory of Games and Economic Behavior,* second edition, Princeton University Press, Princeton, N.J.

OLE HAGEN

TOWARDS A POSITIVE THEORY OF PREFERENCES UNDER RISK

> A normally built truth lives – let me say – as a
> rule some 17–18, at the outside 20 years; rarely
> longer.
>
> 'Doctor Stockmann' in *An Enemy of the People*, by Henrik Ibsen.

ABSTRACT. A previously published model, based on introspective cardinalism, is summarized. A slightly revised version more clearly implies predictions of 'paradoxes' while excluding 'counter paradoxes', i.e. deviations from the Neumann–Morgenstern-consistent behaviour in the opposite direction.

Empirical tests on school teachers and a new test on science faculty confirm asymmetric deviation from N–M-consistent behaviour.

The result of the theoretical development and the empirical evidence is also expressed in ordinalistic language in a field of preferences.

In a space where coordinates are probabilities for prizes indifference sets are convex towards the origin and somewhat twisted as compared with the parallel and linear sets of equal expected utility.

I. EXTRACTS FROM AN AXIOMATIC MODEL (1969/1972)

A. INTRODUCTION

I have previously presented an axiomatic model for decisions under risk, Hagen 1969. This has been developed further in Hagen 1972. In this paper, I will give an outline of the general trend of the axioms and repeat those of the theorems which I consider to be of most interest to the general theme of this volume.

B. OUTLINE OF CHARACTERISTIC AXIOMS

The axioms are based on intuition. They concern probabilities and utilities. From these are derived theorems concerning preferences that can be compared to actual behaviour and to stated preferences concerning probabilities and money. Wealth is defined as the highest

271

Maurice Allais and Ole Hagen (eds.), Expected Utility and the Allais Paradox, 271–302.

loss that can be suffered without bankruptcy. All games are in cash.

The principles expressed in the axioms include the following:

(1) The existence of a cardinal utility of wealth in the classical sense, with decreasing marginal utility. Axioms (1)–(4).

(2) Absolute preference (A10).

(3) A uniform addition to all utilities in the probability distribution of a game adds the same amount to the utility of the game. Axiom (11).

(4) The utility of a game can be expressed as a function of the expectation ($\hat{u}$) and of all higher moments of around the expectation of the probability distribution of the utility of gains (u) resulting from the game.

(5) A better approximation to the utility of a game than the expectation alone is the sum of the expectation and a function approximating the utility of risk:

$$U = \hat{u} + f(s, z) + \varepsilon, \qquad \text{(Axiom (17))},$$

where U = utility of the game, $\hat{u}$ = expectation of utility of gains, f = approximative expression for utility of risk, s = standard deviation in terms of utility, $z = m_3/s^2$ = ratio between third order moment and variance in terms of utility (when $s = 0$, $z = 0$, by definition), and where ε = error element.

(6) In *unique* games (neither the identical nor a similar game can be repeated):

$$\delta f/\delta s < 0, \qquad \text{Axiom (16)},$$
$$\delta^2 f/\delta s^2 < 0, \qquad \text{Axiom (14)},$$
$$\delta f/\delta z > 0, \qquad \text{Axiom (15)}.$$

Axioms (14) and (15) are also valid for non-unique games.

C. COMMENTS TO AXIOMS AND CONCEPTS

The presentation is not complete, but limited to what seems essential and of relevance to the behaviouristic model and the empirical research presented later. The similarity with Allais' basic theory is obvious. Incidentally Allais has now added an axiom* corresponding to Axiom (11) and proved that it implies the additivity of expected utility of result and utility of risk. It has however its distinct characteristics as outlined in (5) and (6) in B above.

---

* [*Editorial Note*: Axiom of Cardinal Utility.]

To understand the psychological content of the axioms mentioned under B it is easiest if one considers two outcome games. In these, the sign of the third moment in the probabilities distribution over utilities is known because it must be the same as in the corresponding distribution over wealth.

Let us first consider a symmetric game. Axiom (16) states that the experience of risk has a negative effect in unique games (Axiom (16) is valid only for unique games). In any type of games, this negative effect increases with increasing the gap between the highest and the lowest outcome (which in symmetric two-outcome games is twice the standard deviation).

The symbol z stands for a special measure of skewness, and the use of that rather than the more conventional third moment, needs explaining. Consider the two possible outcomes with utilities 1, with probability p, and 0 with probability $(1 - p)$ and let us compare z with m_3 and m_{31}:

p	m_3	m_{31}	z
0.01	0.0097	0.0073	0.98
0.10	0.0720	0.0038	0.80
0.50	0.0000	0.0000	0.00
0.90	−0.0720	−0.0038	−0.80
0.99	−0.0097	−0.0073	−0.98

While m_3 shows a higher value for $p = 0.10$ than for $p = 0.01$, m_{30} shows a higher value for the smaller p in this case. This seems a more appropriate ranking of the psychological experience which is attached to skewness. But then, if $p = 0.001$, $m_{31} = 0.001 < 0.0074$. The measure z is, on the other hand, consistent in giving higher value with smaller p. As an expression for skewness it seems that z is superior to m_3 and for that matter m_{31}.

In dealing with two-outcome games which have three degrees of freedom it is obvious that a function of three statistics, like $\hat{u}$, s and z can give a complete and correct ranking of any number of games for any person. In games with n outcomes $(2n - 1)$ statistics would be necessary for this purpose. To rank all kinds of games one would need a function of an infinite number of statistics, e.g. moments, but to postulate the characteristics of such a function is impractical. Instead we postulate that for *all kinds of games* a function of $\hat{u}$, s and z with the postulated characteristics will give a *better approximation* than the expectation of utility or of any utility index alone.

The intuitive psychological assumptions underlying these axioms are:

Axioms (16) *and* (14): Uncertainty in terms of standard deviation in utility (e.g. half the distance between outcomes in 50–50 games given the expectation of utility) has a disutility growing worse with increasing speed when standard deviation increases.

Axiom (15): Given the expectation and the standard deviation. A small probability for a large increase in utility (lottery) creates hope and is attractive. A small probability for a large reduction in utility (non-insurance) creates anxiety and sleepless nights.

D. SELECTED THEOREMS

In the following, a few of the theorems presented and proved before (Hagen 1969, 1972) will be presented. Definitions are needed for $\hat{x}$, S and Z which are the opposite numbers in the probability distribution over gains in money, x, to $\hat{u}$, s and z in the probability distribution over utilities of gains, u.

$\hat{x}$ = expectation of x

S = standard deviation

$Z = M_3/S^2$ = 3rd moment/variance.

The Insurance/Lottery Paradox Solved

It is obvious that a person acting according to the model will buy insurance even if he must pay somewhat more than the mathematical expectation of compensation. This is expressed so:

THEOREM. T(AA)4. *A two outcome game with $Z < 0$ may be rejected even if $\hat{x}$ is positive* (*non-insurance*).

It is *not to insure* which is a game, normally with positive expectation. This can be rejected. At the same time lotteries may be accepted:

THEOREM. T(AA)5. *A two outcome game with $Z > 0$ may be accepted even if $\hat{x}$ is negative (lottery).*

Thus the insurance/lottery 'paradox' has a simple solution, the key is the effect of z, which has the same sign as Z.

Convexity Towards the Origin in Indifference Sets when Coordinates Represent Probabilities of Prizes

If a game has $(n + 1)$ outcomes we define the n preferred outcomes as prizes. When each possible outcome is defined, the utility of the game is a function of the probabilities of the prizes. Let p_0 be the probability of the inferior outcome and $p_1, \ldots, p_n$ the probabilities of the prizes. We then have the function $U(p_1, p_2, \ldots, p_n)$ given the utilities $u_1, u_2, \ldots, u_n$, and we define $u_0 = 0$, we know that the expectation of the final utility is a linear function:

$$\hat{u} = \sum u_i p_i.$$

If one accepts the expected utility principle, whatever the interpretation of utility, the utility of the game would be a linear function of the probabilities. Indifference sets will then be linear and parallel. My axioms imply that the utility of the game is a non-linear function of the probabilities of prizes. In Hagen, 1972, it is shown that in a set of equal expected utilities there may be a restricted maximum of the utility of the game, Theorem T(AAA)6b, which implies that there may be convexities towards the origin in indifference sets, Theorem T(AAA)6a.

It cannot be proved that concavity cannot occur on the basis of the axioms presented up to now.

II. IMPLICATIONS OF THE MODEL

A. THE CARDINAL UTILITY AND VON NEUMANN–MORGENSTERN INDICES

It may be of some interest to show the implications of the model for the relationship between the assumed cardinal utility of games and the equilibrating probabilities that could be expected for the same gains. For example: define the utility of receiving \$10,000 as unity and the utility of status quo as zero. What is the monetary certainty equivalent to the chance of winning \$10,000 with probability 0.5, or rather what is the cardinal utility of that certainty equivalent which is also the utility of the game?

$$(1) \qquad U = \hat{u} + f(s, z).$$

In this case

$$U = 0.5 + f(0.5, 0).$$

Assuming this to be a unique game, $f < 0$, then $U < 0.5$. That is, if we call the equilibrating probability π, then

$$u(x) < \pi(x) \text{ when } \pi(x) = 0.5.$$

If $\pi > 0.5$, $z < 0$:

$$u(x) < \pi(x) \text{ when } \pi > 0.5.$$

For lower values of π consider a more general expression:

$$(2) \qquad U = \pi + f(\sqrt{\pi(1 - \pi)}, 1 - 2\pi).$$

$$(3) \qquad \frac{df}{d\pi} = \frac{1 - 2\pi}{2s} \frac{\delta f}{\delta s} - 2\frac{\delta f}{\delta z}.$$

When $\pi < 0.5$, then $df/d\pi < 0$. This means that f increases as π decreases and there may be an interval where $f > 0$ and, accordingly, $U > \pi$. This is illustrated in Figure 1.

The equilibrating probability is one (not *the*) von Neumann–Morgenstern utility index for values in the $(0, \$10,000)$ interval. Corresponding comparisons of a neo-Bernoullian utility index and a cardinal utility, both being experimentally determined, is made in Charts X to XII in Appendix C of Allais, p.649. Another neo-Bernoullian index could be constructed through fifty–fifty games. The amount x which corresponds to the index value 0.5 would be the same, but the amount that corresponds to the value 0.25 would be the certainty equivalent to a fifty–fifty game between the 0.5 equivalent and status quo. There would be no skewness, and the effect of s would be partly cumulative. If we introduce $B_{1/2}$ for this type of index (Allais' symbol) and B_1 for the one defined as equilibrating probabilities over the same two outcomes, we can now deduce:

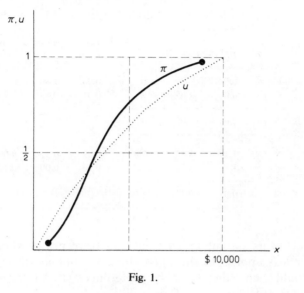

Fig. 1.

$B_1(x) < B_{1/2}(x)$ when $B_1 < 0.5$,
$B_1(x) = B_{1/2}(x)$ when $B_1 = 0.5$,
$B_{1/2}(x) > u(x)$ for all x $(0, \$10,000)$.

B. THE ALLAIS PARADOX IS SOLVABLE

In Table 1 is shown the values of the three arguments in the utility function for games in the four games of *the* Allais paradox, given utility values that gives the same expected value of utility in each pair.

It is obvious that the model implies the *possibility* of preferring E to F and Y to X. The difference in $\hat{u}$ is in both choices 0 in this case, it would have another value, but the same in both choices, with other utilities. The difference in s is in favour of the least risky alternative in both choices. The differences in z favours E and Y, respectively.

With the assumed utilities it would be impossible to get what might be called the '*counter paradox*': preference for F and X. But is the possibility of this implied in the model at all?

In the original as well as references to *the* Allais paradox the ratio between the two prizes is $5:1$. This exact ratio is, of course, im-

TABLE 1

| | $\hat{u}$ | s | z | Probabilities of Utilities | | |
				$u = 0$	10	11
E	10.0	0	0	0.00	1.00	0.00
F	10.0	1.05	-9	0.01	0.89	0.10
$E - F$	0.0	-1.05	9			
X	1.1	3.13	7.8	0.89	0.11	0.00
Y	1.1	3.30	8.8	0.90	0.00	0.10
$X - Y$	0.0	-0.17	-1.0			

material. Let us assume that we have a pair of prizes where the ratio 11:10 or less applies to the *utility* for all members of a population. They would then either have the preferences (E, X) or (E, Y), since all pulls towards preferring E over F.

To make some of them prefer F we must increase the utility of the higher prize. This could make some members change their preference from E to F. It could also change their preference from X to Y but not from Y to X. *So the model implies the impossibility of the 'counter paradox', but allows for the Allais paradox and for preferences not violating the expected utility hypothesis.* So it is not a vacuous theory.

C. THE BERGEN PARADOX

Let me present the Bergen game. You are offered the set of games:

$$(4) \qquad P(\$2^n) = (\tfrac{1}{2})^n, \qquad P(0) = 1 - (\tfrac{1}{2})^n,$$

where you choose n. The chosen n is called k. The choice implies that you prefer the game B where $n = k$ to the game A ($n = k - 1$), and this implies about the Bernoullian index B:

$$(5) \qquad B(\$2^{k-1}) < \tfrac{1}{2}B(\$2^k).$$

Now when given the choice

$$C: P(\$2^{k-1}) = 1, \quad \text{or} \quad D: P(\$2^k) = \tfrac{1}{2}, \qquad P(0) = \tfrac{1}{2}.$$

The preference might be for C, which implies:

(6) $B(\$2^{k-1}) > B(\$2^{k})$.

Now let us see what is implied by the model if for simplicity we assume:

$$u(\$2^{k-1}) = 1,$$
$$u(\$2^{k}) = 2.$$

The last assumption is really contrary to the axioms, it should be less than 2. We will consider the effect of that later.

TABLE 2

	u (prize)	P (prize)	$\hat{u}$	s	z
A	1	0.5^{k-1}	0.5^{k-1}	$\sqrt{0.5^{k-1}(1-0.5^{k-1})}$	$(1-0.5^{k-1})$
B	2	0.5^{k}	0.5^{k-1}	$\sqrt{0.5^{k}(1-0.5^{k})} \cdot 2$	$(1-0.5^{k}) \cdot 2$
A − B			0	<0	-1
C	1	1	1	0	0
D	2	0.5	1	1	0
C − D			0	-1	0

We compare the games assuming $k \geqslant 2$ in Table 2. We can see that it is possible to prefer B for A, but impossible to prefer D for C. If the utility of the prize in B and D is slightly reduced this still holds. *The Bergen paradox is implied in the model.*

To envisage the counter paradox in this case it would be if, when the preferred n was established, the certainty of receiving that prize was rejected in favour of a probability of 0.5 for winning the double amount. Let us now give the preferred n the name $k-1$ and the utility of that prize 1 and the above reasoning excludes the counter paradox.

What happens in Table 2 if we reduce the utility in B and D? Reducing $u(0.5^{k})$ below 2 favours A and C. It still holds open the possibility of the Bergen paradox, and still excludes the counter paradox.

D. ONE PRIZE VERSUS MULTIPRIZE LOTTERIES

Theorems T(AA)4 and T(AA)5 hold a key to solving the insurance/lottery paradox.

It is well known that buying both insurance and a lottery ticket can be explained as maximizing expectation of a function of wealth if it turns from convexity to concavity near the point of departure. What is not so well known is that the expected utility principle implies that lotteries should have one prize only if one wants to maximize the prospective buyer's expected utility under a given expenditure on prizes. It has been shown before (Hagen, 1972). Here it will be demonstrated that the applications of that information is easy. The only difficulty is that the prospective buyers have different utility functions even if they all have concavities.

Consider the following prospect:

> Number of tickets: 10,000,
> Prize per ticket: $10,
> 1 prize, $20,000 each,
> 10 prizes, $2,000 each.

Now instead of 10,000 tickets with 10,000 numbers one could have 10,000 tickets with 10 numbers each: either consecutive, or 4 digits identical (e.g. the last four). Now the prizes instead of being drawn on 11 numbers are distributed by drawing two times the four last digits and awarding each number having one of these characteristics $2,000. This means that if the gambler has Bernoullian preferences he can determine what expectation $\hat{B}$ of B is the highest:

(7) $\hat{B}_1 = 0.002B(\$2,000) + 0.998B(0),$

or

(8) $\hat{B}_2 = 0.0002B(\$20,000) + 0.9998B(0),$

one of which would necessarily be higher than

$$\hat{B}_3 = 0.001B(\$2,000) + 0.0001B(\$20,000) + 0.9989B(0)$$

(which would be the *only* option under the usual system) since:

(9) $\hat{B}_3 = 0.5(\hat{B}_1 + \hat{B}_2).$

Except for a borderline case:

(10) $\hat{B}_1 > \hat{B}_3,$

or

(11) $\hat{B}_2 > \hat{B}_3.$

If the theorists adhering to the expected utility principle as a descriptive theory are good citizens they should advise lottery managers to reform their lotteries to this effect. If this is not done, it means that they do not believe in their theory. No such advice can be deduced from my model, so it is not violated by the practice of lottery managers, which is probably based on experience. The possibility that multiprize lotteries are better than one prize lotteries, even with choices built in as above, follows from my Theorem T(AA)6, Hagen 1972.

III. A REVISED AXIOMATIC MODEL

A. A NEW AXIOM AND A NEW LEMMA

It is possible with a small change in the axiomatic base of the model to give answers to questions that are hitherto left open.

In the first published version (Hagen 1969) the *approximative* function was $U = f(\hat{u}, s, z)$, where U = utility of game, $\hat{u}$ = expectation of utility (u), s = standard deviation of distribution over u, m_3 = third moment of same distribution, and $z = m_3/s^2$, $z = 0$ when $s = 0$.

After an idea suggested by Leinfellner, I was led to assume additivity of expectation of utility and specific utility of risk:

Axiom (17): $U = \hat{u} + f(s, z) + \varepsilon,$

where f = specific utility of risk, and ε = error element $P(\varepsilon > 0) = P(\varepsilon < 0)$.

In 1973, I conducted experiments in Bergen over a theme where I expected the deviation from the results to be expected from the expected utility hypothesis to go in a particular direction. This expectation came through. Afterwards, I discovered that these outcomes could not always be rigorously deduced from my model. This is a weakness since the hypothesis, which will be presented as a theorem under B which follows, has strong intuitive appeal in itself.

The problem is solved by introducing this new axiom:

Axiom (18): $U = \hat{u} + g(s) + hz + \varepsilon,$

where g is a function, and h is a constant. It is not contradicting Axiom (17) and can formally be added to the system. It follows that f from Axiom (17) is now defined as

$$f(s, z) = g(s) + hz,$$

where g is a function, and h is a constant.

Previously I have used (AAA) to indicate Axioms (1) to (17). Now (AAAA) indicates Axioms (1) to (18). We further introduce a new Lemma.

LEMMA L(AAAA)7. *If $g(s)$ is transformed to a function of variance $G(s^2)$, then the second derivative of that function with respect to the variance cannot be zero or consistently negative.*

Proof. Assume the second-order derivative of the variance were constantly zero. Remember that $g(0) = G(0) = 0$ because the utility of a game with one certain outcome must be equal to the utility of that outcome and therefore to the expected utility. The disutility of the standard deviation $(-g)$ or that of the variance $(-G)$ would then be in strict and direct proportion to s^2. Therefore

(1) $(-g) = (-G) = \alpha s^2,$

α = constant.

(2) $\dfrac{d(-g)}{ds} = \dfrac{d(-G)}{d(s^2)}(2s),$

(3) $\dfrac{d^2(-g)}{ds^2} = \dfrac{d(-G)}{d(s^2)}(2) = \text{constant} > 0.$

If this were so, consider a game where the probabilities are $P(u_1) = \frac{1}{2}$, and $P(0) = \frac{1}{2}$. We would have $\hat{u} = \frac{1}{2}u_1$, $s = \frac{1}{2}u_1$, $s^2 = \frac{1}{4}u_1^2$, and:

(4) $U = \frac{1}{2}u_1 - \alpha\frac{1}{4}u_1^2,$

(5) $\dfrac{dU}{du_1} = \frac{1}{2} - \alpha\frac{1}{2}u_1.$

When $\alpha u_1 > 1$, which it will eventually be with increasing u_1, we would have a result which would violate Axiom (A10) ('Preference absolue').

So the Lemma is proved, clearly also with negative 2 derivative.

B. A NEW THEOREM OF PREFERENCES IN COMMON
RATIO GAMES

THEOREM T(AAAA)10. *Given a class of pairs of two outcome games where the lower outcome is zero, the higher a gain, or prize. The ratio between the probabilities for the two prizes is the same in all pairs. Probabilities are termed p and kp, $k < 1$. It is then possible that the preference will be for the low probability, high prize game when p is below a given value and for the high probability, low prize game when p is above this value. The reverse of this is impossible.*

Proof. Given two games No. (1) and No. (2) both with one prize, and with the same expected utility. Without loss of generality we can assume: In No. (1), the prize has $u = 1$, and the probability of winning is kp. In No. (2) the prize has $u = k$ and the probability of winning is p. So

$$(6) \qquad \hat{u}_1 = \hat{u}_2 = kp,$$

$$(7) \qquad s_1 = \sqrt{kp(1 - kp)} = \sqrt{kp - k^2 p^2},$$

$$(8) \qquad s_2 = \sqrt{p(1 - p)k} = \sqrt{k^2 p - k^2 p^2},$$

$$(9) \qquad z_1 = 1 - 2kp,$$

$$(10) \qquad z_2 = (1 - 2p)k = k - 2kp.$$

We will investigate what happens when p changes. We see at once that the difference in the expectation of utility is in any case zero and that the difference in z is in any case $(1 - k)$ which is in favour of game No. (1). It is also obvious that $s_1 > s_2$ which is in favour of game No. (2). What remains to be seen is then what happens to the size of the difference between the values of $g(s_1)$ and $g(s_2)$ when p changes from 0, where both s are 0, to 1, where $s_1 = \sqrt{k - k^2}$, and $s_2 = 0$.

$$(11) \qquad s_1' = \frac{k - 2k^2 p}{2s_1},$$

$$(12) \qquad s_2' = \frac{k^2 - 2k^2 p}{2s_2}.$$

The difference is

$$(13) \qquad s_1' - s_2' = \frac{k}{2s_1 s_2} [2kp(s_1 - s_2) - (ks_1 - s_2)].$$

It is a sufficient condition for this difference to be positive that $ks_1 < s_2$. It is easier to find out if

(14) $k^2 s_1^2 < s_2^2,$

(15) $k^2 s_1^2 = k^3 p - k^4 p^2,$ (compare (7)),

(16) $s_2^2 = k^2 p - k^2 p^2,$ (compare (8)),

(17) $k^2 s_1^2 - s_2^2 = k^2 p [p(1 - k^2) - (1 - k)],$

and, since $p \gtreqless 1$ and $k < 1$,

(18) $k^2 s_1^2 - s_2^2 < 0.$

This means that

(19) $s_1' - s_2' > 0,$

or

(20) $(s_1 - s_2)' > 0.$

With increasing p, and kp, the difference between standard deviations increase.

It follows from Axiom (14), compare Axiom (18), that

(21) $d^2 g / d s_2 < 0,$

so:

(22) $(g_1 - g_2)' > 0,$

as long as $s \geqq 0$, $(kp \gtreqless \frac{1}{2})$. *The difference in g in favour of Game No. (2) increases with increasing p when $kp \gtreqless \frac{1}{2}$.* Beyond this point both standard deviations and both variances are decreasing with increasing p.

(23) $s_1^2 - s_2^2 = pk(1 - k).$

The difference between the variances in favour of Game No. (2) increases with increasing p even when $kp > \frac{1}{2}$ and both variances decrease with increasing p. It then follows from the fact that the second-order derivative of G $(= g)$ with respect to the variance is negative that

(24) $(g_1 - g_2)' > 0$ even when $kp > \frac{1}{2}.$

The difference in g in favour of Game No. (2) *increases even when kp > 0 if the second order derivative of z* (= g) *with respect to the variance is positive.* Since it cannot be consistently negative or zero, movement in the opposite direction is impossible.

Remembering that the difference in g is constantly in favour of Game No. (1), the theorem is proved.

IV. EMPIRICAL TESTING OF COMMON RATIO GAMES

The following two investigations were carried out in 1973 in Bergen with students of the Norwegian School of Economics and Business Administration as interviewers and in 1975 in Oslo with the same aid of students in the Oslo Institute of Business Administration, a private counterpart to the Bergen school.

A. THE THEORETICAL BACKGROUND

The main purpose of the first investigation was to test the expected utility hypothesis. At the same time I wanted to test the extension of the expected utility hypothesis allowing for subjective aggrandizement of small probabilities. Further I wanted to test my 'Bergen Paradox'.

It so happens that the tests both come under the kind of problems for which MacCrimmon and Larsson in this book have coined the label "Common Ratio". This also goes for the test in the later Oslo investigation.

We have a class of pairs of games where the *two* prizes are the same in all *pairs*. All games have two outcomes, the inferior one is the same in all *games*. The *ratio* between the probabilities for winning the two prizes is the same in all *pairs*. In all pairs the game with the highest prize has the lowest probability for that prize.

It is now clear that in such a set of pairs of games, whatever is assumed about or meant by the utility of the outcomes there are three possibilities concerning the expectation of that utility.

(1) The least risky game has the highest expected utility in *all* pairs.

(2) The two games have the same expected utility in *all* pairs.

(3) The most risky games has the highest expected utility in *all* pairs.

Consistency with the expected utility principle therefore the demands that the ranking between the least risky and the most risky game is the same in all pairs.

What, then, is the alternative theory? At the time of the Bergen test, I had published the first version of my model (Hagen, 1969). I had not yet introduced the additivity of expected utility, and specific utility of risk in the second version, much less the additivity of expected utility, utility of standard deviation and utility of skewness in the form of a linear function of z (third moment/variance) introduced in this paper. Nevertheless, I could derive from my model the prediction that deviation from the expected utility maximization in this case could manifest itself through shifting the preference towards the least risky games in pairs where the probabilities for prizes were higher. The reasons given for the alternative hypotheses in the presentation submitted to Amihud and Morgenstern are not commented on by them.

However, I think that what valid conclusions can be drawn from an empirical investigation should not depend on what was in the investigators mind. In this paper, I have, with a small change, made it possible to prove from my axioms that, in common ratio games, preference can be for the least risky game when the probability for the prize is above some level and for the other game when it is below, and that the reverse is impossible. So the alternative theory is Theorem T(AAAA)10.

B. THE GENERAL SCHEME OF THE TESTS

A history of previous tests, not only concerning ratio of probabilities but also other tests relevant to the vNM–A controversy has been given in the contribution of McCrimmon and Larsson to this volume.

Without going into detail, let me point out how the following tests seem to differ from all or nearly all previous tests.

(1) In dealing with the common ratio problem.

(2) In putting the choices to be compared to different groups of persons.

Point (2) will provoke a predictable objection: When the questions are put to different people, a possible discrepancy between the allocation of answers between the two alternatives may be caused by differences in the utility functions between the two groups. The obvious answer is that when the individuals are sorted at random, the random element is taken account of in the test on significance of differences. However, I also took a practical measure. In addition to the questions relevant to the theme of the test, a question was added in identical form to both groups for the sole purpose of checking if a difference in utility function or risk attitude between the two groups were likely to exist.

To the members of the Alpha group was put choice situations with high probabilities for the prizes and to the Beta group choice situations with low probabilities in the same proportion. To both groups was put a question aimed at classifying them in respect to attitudes.

Given that it is admitted that my tests are fair, there remains the question why did I prefer this method to the one others have used? Let me first admit two advantages of putting the same question to all.

In the first case, it makes possible an exact measurement of the proportion of individuals in the sample who reveal vNM-inconsistent preferences, whereas with my method this can only be estimated. I do not attach great weight to this proportion at all. It does not measure how many people have vNM-inconsistent preferences only how many *reveal* them with *these* prizes and *these* probabilities. Take *the* Allais paradox. Multiply the prizes by a sufficiently large number, and everybody will prefer the least risky alternative in both cases. Divide both prizes by a sufficiently large number and everybody will prefer the most risky alternative, which has the highest monetary expectation. One can only estimate a lower limit to the number of persons in a sample who have vNM-inconsistent preferences by such questions. This limit can be increased by new questions if they are well chosen and varied. But even if all respondents have vNM-inconsistent preferences, it is possible to get no registration of this by choosing the questions well for that purpose.

The second advantage is as follows: What is of real interest in such investigations is the allocation of vNM-inconsistent answers between the two 'paradoxes', the one that is expected and the 'counter paradox'. For instance, using my symbols for 'the Allais Paradox' (E and X have the lower risk):

$$E \text{ Pf } F \quad \text{and} \quad Y \text{ Pf } X,$$

as opposed to the 'counter paradox':

$$F \text{ Pf } E \quad \text{and} \quad X \text{ Pf } Y,$$

where 'Pf' denotes 'preferred to'.

When I have chosen a method which cannot reveal this allocation, it is because it is now so well known that the 'counter paradox' practically does not occur, so this second advantage of putting both questions to all respondents is already exploited.

The main positive reasons for my decision to split the sample in an Alpha group to reply to one choice (between a pair of high probability lotteries) and a Beta group to reply a questions concerning two small probabilities, was this:

Such investigations are frequently commented on in a way that is very impolite to the respondents, and intellectuals tend to be sensitive about their intellects. I therefore wanted to be able to assure the respondents that no revelation of intellectual shortcomings was logically possible. Since no individual can give vNM-inconsistent answers when the questions are put to different groups, the truth of this statement is above discussion. A further advantage is of course that undue pro-vNM influence through knowledge of a theory of allegedly rational behaviour, is barred.

C. INVESTIGATION IN BERGEN, 1971

The technicalities of this investigation were given in minute and documented detail in Norwegian in the journal *Sosialøkonomen*, (Hagen 1973, No. 5), a journal, according to Frisch, that no Norwegian economist should be without. The strong Norwegian pro-vNM faction was explicitly and provocatively challenged to submit objections, but no one responded.

I will not go into detail here, but state the main points. The subjects were high school teachers in Bergen. These have, in most cases, 4–7 years university education. The selection of respondents as well as their division in two groups was made without systematic bias. The interviewers were students of the Norwegian School of Economics and Business Administration, participating in a seminar on decisions under risk, but at that stage (disregarding possible extra curricular knowledge) not informed about the significance of the investigation.

Question 1 was formed in order to test the expected utility hypothesis and, at the same time, had a specific purpose: It is often assumed that the Allais Paradox can be explained by specific utility of absolute certainty and/or subjective aggrandizement of small probabilities (such as 0.01). I therefore wanted a test that excluded these explanations. In the games of the Allais paradox, I kept the order of magnitude of the two prizes and the games where the probabilities for winning are 0.10 and 0.11, named X and Y in this paper. In the other choice situation, here referred to as between E and F, I arranged the game in such a manner that there would be no absolute certainty and that any effect of aggrandizement of the small probability (0.01) would be in favour of the most risky game.

The choice situations presented was then:

In the Alpha group:
$P(x)$ = probability of winning x N.kroner, (1 N.kr. a little less than 0.5 DM).

A:
$$P(5 \text{ Mill}) = 0.99,$$
$$P(0) \quad\;\; = 0.01,$$

or

B:
$$P(25 \text{ Mill}) = 0.90,$$
$$P(0) \quad\;\;\; = 0.10.$$

In the Beta group:

X:
$$P(5 \text{ Mill}) = 0.11,$$
$$P(0) \quad\;\; = 0.89.$$

Y:
$$P(25 \text{ Mill}) = 0.10,$$
$$P(0) \quad\;\;\; = 0.90.$$

Hypotheses, Question 1

The vNM theory clearly indicates the null-hypothesis. The expected proportion (Pr) preferring A in group Alpha is equal to the expected proportion preferring X in group Beta

H_0: $Pr(A) = Pr(X)$.

From my Theorem T(AAAA)10 follows the alternative hypothesis:

H_a: $Pr(A) > Pr(X)$.

Result Question 1

Out of a total number of 106 subjects, one was indifferent, and the remaining 105 were distributed as shown in Table 3.

TABLE 3

Alpha group		
A	37	70%
B	16	30%
Sub total	53	100%
Beta group		
X	15	29%
Y	37	71%
Sub total	52	100%
Whole sample		
A or X	52	49.5%
B or Y	53	50.5%
Total	105	100.0%

Difference in proportions: 0.41.

The normal distribution test is admissible since $0.495 \times 52 = 26$. This test gives

$$0.41/\sqrt{(1/53 + 1/52)(0.495)(0.555)} = 4.0.$$

Since this is greater than 1.645 (the 95% fractile) the null hypothesis is rejected in favour of the alternative hypothesis.

Question 2 is inspired by the Bergen paradox. It compares the choice between the certainty of one prize with the probability of one half of winning double that amount, with a choice where the prizes are the same, but both probabilities are divided by 50, to become 0.02 and 0.01.

The prizes were N.kr. 10,000 and N.kr. 20,000.

In the Alpha group:
$P(x)$ = probability of winning x N.kr.

A: $P(10000) = 1.00.$

B: $P(20000) = 0.50,$
       $P(0)\quad\ = 0.50.$

In the Beta group:

X: $P(10000) = 0.02,$
       $P(0)\quad\ = 0.98.$

Y: $P(20000) = 0.01,$
       $P(0)\quad\ = 0.99.$

Hypotheses, Question 2

By the same reasoning the vNM-based null hypothesis, expected proportions of preferences for A and for X are equal:

H_0: $Pr(A) = Pr(X),$

and deduced from Theorem T(AAAA)10:

H_a: $Pr(A) > Pr(X).$

Result, Question 2

Out of a total number of 106 subjects, one was indifferent in Question 2 also (the same person as in Question 1). The remaining 105 were distributed as shown in Table 4.

Difference in proportions: 0.33.
The normal distribution test is admissible since $0.28 \times 52 = 15$. This test gives

$$0.33/\sqrt{(1/53 + 1/52)(0.72)(0.28)} = 3.77.$$

Since this is greater than 1.645 (95% fractile) the vNM-based null hypothesis is rejected in favour of the alternative hypothesis based on Theorem T(AAAA)10.

TABLE 4

Alpha group		
A	47	89%
B	6	11%
Sub total	53	100%
Beta group		
X	29	56%
Y	23	44%
Sub total	52	100%
Whole sample		
A or X	76	72%
B or Y	29	28%
Total	105	100%

Question 3 has in itself no relevance to the test. It serves only to check if a difference in risk attitude has accidentally been introduced in the sorting of the respondents in the two groups.

The respondents in both groups were told that a real prize was to be issued to one among them, and, if they were to get the prize, would they prefer:

P: One whole ticket in the Norwegian Money Lottery,

or

Q: Two half tickets,

or

R: N.kr. 6.40 outright. (The expected monetary value of P and of Q.)

(Two half tickets give twice the chance of winning half of all prizes.)

Result, Question 3

The cross tabulation of answers to Question 3 with answers to the two first questions is given in Table 5.

The percentages of preferences for A and X, are indicated in Table 6 for those preferring P, Q and R, respectively. It can be seen that the slight correlation between high risk willingness and being placed in the Beta group cannot have influenced the result.

TABLE 5

	Question 1				Question 2			
Question 3	A	B	X	Y	A	B	X	Y
P	9	7	4	13	13	2	4	13
Q	25	9	8	24	30	4	23	9
R	4	0	2	0	4	0	2	0

TABLE 6

	Question 1		Question 2	
Question 3	A	X	A	X
P	53	24	87	24
Q	74	25	88	72
R	100	100	100	100

A Parallel Test

Two of my students later carried out a test using the same questions on a small sample of top level business executives, putting all questions to all respondents. The proportions of those giving NM-in-consistent answers, that deviated in the expected direction was significantly higher than $\frac{1}{2}$, nearly 1. (Holmer and Hvalvik, 1973).

D. TEST ON FACULTY OF SCIENCE, UNIVERSITY OF OSLO, 1975

In the spring of 1975, I had a class in decision theory at The Oslo Institute of Business Administration, and thus potential manpower for a new investigation.

In the meantime, a discussion paper by Oskar Morgenstern, a

preliminary version of his contribution to this volume (Morgenstern 1978), had contained critical comments on my Bergen test (above) on three points:

(1) Possible lack of experience in experimental psychology.

(2) Amounts of money exceeding respondent's experience and imagination, which presumably applies to question 1 only.

(3) Small probabilities in question 2, puts it outside the proper domain of the expected utility theory.

I thought that (1) is, of course, correct, and all I can do is to try and acquire it and also hope that experienced researchers will make similar tests. (See MacCrimmon and Larsson, 1979). Point (2) may well be justified, and (3) can be chalked up as an important theoretical statement leaving out the buying of insurance and lottery tickets from the domain of the von Neumann–Morgenstern theory.

I found that it would be more fruitful to profit from this criticism than to question its justification. This meant undertaking a new test, with amounts restricted within the horizon of the respondents, and with probabilities that can be expressed in quarts.

Further, from other quarters, objections can be raised based on the alleged inability of respondents to understand what probability is all about. In the search for a population large enough to provide statistically significant results, and with the best possible qualifications in this sense, I did not have to go far. The obvious selection was the academic staff and the academically educated laboratory staff of the Faculty of Mathematics and Natural Sciences at the University of Oslo. The first sample, which turned out to be sufficient, involved members found in their office on one out of two visits during a given day. This selection criterion should not be biassed in respect to conformity with Bernoullian preferences.

As before, the field work was carried out before students were acquainted with the theoretical issue involved.

The respondents were again asked alternatively the Alpha and the Beta version of Question 1, and then two common questions to check difference in risk attitude between groups. (The issuing of half tickets in the lottery was now discontinued.) The illustration of probabilities through references to a roulette was not used. Respondents were assured that there was no test of ability involved and asked not to discuss questions or answers with colleagues.

The alternatives in the first question were:

Alpha group:

A: P(N.kr. 10,000) = 1.00,

B: P(N.kr. 24,000) = 0.50, and P(0) = 0.50.

Beta group:

X: P(N.kr. 10,000) = 0.50, and P(0) = 0.50,

Y: P(N.kr. 24,000) = 0.25, and P(0) = 0.75.

Results, Question 1

The results are given in Table 7. Since $0.203 \times 30 = 18$ it is permissible to use the normal distribution. This gives

$$0.923 - 0.633 = 0.29$$
$$0.29/\sqrt{(1/39 + 1/30)(0.797)(0.203)} = 2.969.$$

Since this is greater than 1.645 (95% fractile) the null hypothesis is rejected in favour of the alternative hypothesis with the information so far taken into account.

TABLE 7

Alpha group			Beta group			Both groups		
A	36	92.3%	X	19	63.3%	A or X	55	79.7%
B	3	7.7%	Y	11	36.7%	B or Y	14	20.3%
Total	39	100.0%		30	100.0%		69	100.0%

Questions 2 and 3

To check whether there was an accidental difference between the risk attitudes among those drawn for the Alpha group and those drawn for the Beta group, the following questions were added:

Question 2: Have you during the last 12 months bought (for yourself) a ticket in the Norwegian Money Lottery?

Question 3: Have you during the last 12 months participated in private games or bets over money?

It was reported that some respondents were in doubt about the interpretation of Question 3. It was therefore disregarded in the analysis.

Results, Question 2

It turned out that frequency of the answer yes to Question 2 was highest in the Beta group. See Table 8. (The difference between 39 and 30 is caused by one interviewer who received his instructions second hand and put the Alpha question to all his subjects.)

TABLE 8

	Alpha group		Beta group		Both groups	
Yes	7	18%	9	43%	16	23%
No	32	82%	21	57%	53	77%
Total	39	100%	30	100%	69	100%

The difference between the distribution 18–82 and 43–57 is so big that it cannot be ignored. It is therefore necessary to look at the replies to Question 1 cross tabulated with the replies to Question 2. See Table 9. It turns out that those who had bought lottery tickets were less inclined to answer B or Y than the others. So the skewness in the yes/no distribution between the Alpha and the Beta group did not favour the alternative hypothesis after all. The conclusion above therefore stands.

TABLE 9

Question 1	Yes		No	
A or X	13	81%	42	79%
B or Y	3	19%	11	21%
Total	16	100%	53	100%

Morgenstern is probably right in assuming that such probabilities as were used in the Oslo-test are less likely to produce vNM-inconsistent replies than those used in Bergen. This could well be sufficient to explain why the estimate of the proportion revealed as vNM-inconsistent fell from 0.33 to 0.29. There is then very little room for correlation between mathematical training and vNM-consistency.

V. CONCLUSIONS

(1) Empirical evidence indicates the non existence of a unique utility index, the expectation of which can rank preferences expressed by persons a priori considered rational.

(2) Deviations from expected (neo-Bernoullian) utility index maximisation are *consistently* *asymmetric*, and *predictable* from a reasonably simple model.

Since the first of these conclusions has in fact for a long time been evident, but ignored as uninteresting because allegedly no better alternative was offered, it is the second conclusion to which I attach the greatest importance.

In this paper, I have presented theorems which explain classical and new deviations from the neo-Bernoullian preference pattern, so called paradoxes, and which exclude in most cases clearly what I have termed the 'counter paradoxes', i.e. deviations in the opposite direction. It is a misunderstanding that Allais' theory is neutral in this respect. One clear example: What he termed complementarity effect when probability is close to unity, explains *the* Allais Paradox, but not the counter paradox. It would therefore have been refuted by any evidence of the counter paradox being of comparable frequency.

VI. A REFORMULATION IN ORDINALISTIC LANGUAGE

What I have tried to show in this paper is the possibility of combining the classical theory of cardinal utility with a specific theory of utility of risk which conforms to reality. Here as elsewhere it may be possible, once this is done, to express the characteristics of the model for the field of decisions under risk without reference to the intuitive cardinal assumptions from which it was originally developed.

Let us define an n-dimensional system of coordinates as expressing probabilities for the n most preferred outcomes out of $n + 1$. Given equidistant points on the axis representing one outcome. On an axis representing an outcome that is preferred, the points representing games that are considered equivalent one by one to those already represented will be placed with increasing intervals when moving away from the origin. Given any point, the set of preferred points will be convex (seen from the origin) except for points representing the probability $= 1$ for outcomes slightly better than the certainty equivalent.

Most of what is expressed above is also expressed in Figure 2. Here the total number of outcomes is 3. The probabilities are in order of preference for the outcome: p_2, p_1 and $(1 - p_1 - p_2)$. The curved lines are indifference curves. Taking the intercept of the middle curve as a base, the corresponding mapping of 'Bernoullian' preferences would be the three parallel straight lines.

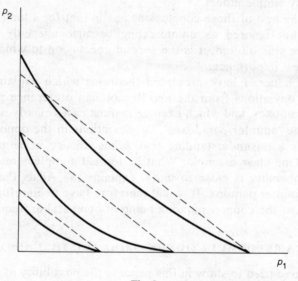

Fig. 2.

The same three lines also demonstrate the common ratio problem and the mixture of games problem. Comparing the two sets of lines illustrates Theorem T(AAAA)9, the 'common ratio paradox', and preference for mixture of equivalent games. Concerning games where the lowest outcome is always status quo and others are monetary prizes, 3 hypotheses emerge from this paper:

H1: Two equivalent two-outcome games are both inferior to a game whose probabilities of the 3 outcomes concerned are weighted averages of the two original probabilities.

H2: If the probabilities for the prizes in two equivalent two-outcome games are multiplied by k, the least risky game is preferred when $k > 1$, and the most risky if $k < 1$.

H3: If the prizes in two equivalent two-outcome games are multiplied by c, the least risky is preferred if $c > 1$, and the most risky if $c < 1$.

H1 and H2 contradict the expected utility principle. H3 is not implied by it.

ACKNOWLEDGEMENTS

This paper presents a selection of results from work in this field, carried out off and on since 1969, partly published before. Without provocative criticism, and encouragement, it would not have appeared. I wish to express deep acknowledgement for encouragement at crucial stages in chronological order from Peter Robson, Werner Leinfellner, Maurice Allais and Eckehart Köhler, as well as many others. Its contents is, of course, influenced first and foremost by Allais but also by the others mentioned. I also wish to thank Oskar Morgenstern for cultured and constructive criticism, which has had direct impact on my latest empirical test. My final conclusions rely to some extent on the work presented by MacCrimmon and Larsson in this volume. My empirical work could not have been carried out without the enthusiasm and effort of my students in Norges Handelshøyskole and Bedriftsøkonomisk Institutt.

T. Langeland has done some checking in the mathematics and statistics of Section IV. No remaining errors should, however, be blamed on him.

I thank Professors Gehard Stoltz and K. Berka for permission to use some material already published in Statsøkonomisk Tidsskrift and Teoria A Metoda.

To curb the tendency for this volume to exceed set limits to size I have split my contribution, the other half to be accommodated elsewhere. References by others have been adjusted.

Oslo Institute of Business Administration,
Bedriftsoekonomisk Institutt

BIBLIOGRAPHY

Allais, M.: (1953). *Fondements d'une Théorie Positive de Choix Comportant un Risque et Critique des Postulats et Axioms de l'Ecole Américaine*, Imprimerie Nationale. Also in Volume collectif *Econometrie*, Collection des Colloques Internationaux de C.N.R.S., Vol. XL, Paris, 1953b., pp.257–332.

English Translation of 1953a: 'The Foundations of a Positive Theory of Choice Involving Risk and a Criticism of the Postulates and Axioms of the American School', Part II of this volume, 1953/79.

'La Généralisation des Théories de l'Equilibre Economique Général et du Rendement Social au Cas du Risque', Volume collectif *Econometrie*, Collection des Colloques Internationaux du C.N.R.S., Vol. XV, Paris 1953c, pp.81–120.

'La Psychologie de l'Homme Rationnel devant le Risque – La Théorie et l'Expérience', *Journal de la Société de Statistique de Paris*, Janvier–Mars 1953d, pp.47–73.

'L'Extension des Théories de l'Equilibre Economique General et de Rendement Social au Cas du Risque', *Econometrica*, Vol. 21, No. 4, 1953e.

'Le Comportement de l'Homme Rationnel devant le Risque – Critique des Postulats et Axioms de l'Ecole Américaine', *Econometrica*, Vol. 21, No. 4, 1953f.

Allais, M.: (1957). 'Sur la Théorie des Choix Aléatoires', *Revue d'Economie Politique*, No. 3.

Allais, M.: (1979). 'The So-Called Allais Paradox and Rational Decisions Under Uncertainty, Part V of this Volume.

Arrow, Kenneth J.: (1965). *Aspects of the Theory of Risk-Bearing*, Helsinki.

Baumol, William J.: (1951). 'The von Neumann–Morgenstern Utility Index – An Ordinalist View', *Journal of Political Economy*, Vol. LIX, Feb., No. 1, pp.61–66.

Bernoulli, D.: (0000). 'Specimen Theoria Novae de Mensura Sortis', *Commentarii Academiae Scientiarium Imperialis Petropolitanae* 5, 138. Translation: 'Exposition of a New Theory on the Measurement of Risk', *Econometrica*, Vol. 22, No. 1, 1954, pp.21–36.

Booth, E.: See Leinfellner.

Borch, Karl H.: (1968). 'The Allais Paradox: A Comment', *Behavioral Science*, Vol. 13, No. 6.

Borch, Karl, and Mossin, Jan, (Eds.): (1968). 'Risk and Uncertainty', Proceedings of a Conference held by the International Economic Association, New York.

Buffon, G. L. L.: (1777). 'Essai d'Aritmetique morale', pp.72f in Volume IV of *Histoire naturelle, generale et particulière*.

Edwards, Ward: (1954). 'The Theory of Decision Making', *Psychological Bulletin*, Vol. 51, No. 4.

Ellsberg, Daniel: (1961). 'Risk, Ambiguity and the Savage Axiom', *Quarterly Journal of Economics*, pp.643–669.

Feldstein, M. S.: (1969). 'Mean-Variance Analysis in The Theory of Liquidity Preference and Portfolio Selection', *The Review of Economic Studies*, Vol. XXXI (1), Jan.

Fellner, William: (1965). *Probability and Profit: A Study of Economic Behavior along Bayesian Lines*, Homewood Ill, Richard D. Irwin Inc.

Freimer, Marshall and Gordon: (1968). 'Investment Behaviour with Utility a Concave Function of Wealth'. In K. Borch and J. Mossin (Eds.), *Risk and Uncertainty*, q.v.

Friedmann, Milton, and Savage, L. P. J.: (1948). 'The Utility Analysis of Choices Involving Risk', *The Journal of Political Economy*, Vol. LVI, pp.279–304.

Frisch, R.: (1926). 'Sur une probleme d'economie pure', *Norsk Matematisk Forenings skrifter*, Serie I, nr. 16.

Hagen, Ole: (1966). 'Risk Aversion and Incentive Contracting', *The Economic Record*, Sept., pp.416–4.

Hagen, Ole: (1967). 'Elements of Value', *Statsøkonomisk Tidsskrift*, No. 1.

Hagen, Ole: (1969). 'Separation of Cardinal Utility and Specific Utility of Risk in Theory of Choices under Uncertainty', *Statsøkonomisk Tidsskrift*, No. 3.

Hagen, Ole: (1972). 'A New Axiomatization of Utility under Risk', *Teorie A Metoda*, IV/2.

Hagen, Ole: (1973). 'Testing av nytteforventningshypotesen', *Sosialøkonomen*, No. 5.

Hicks, J. R.: (1959). *Revision of Demand Theory*, Oxford University Press, Oxford.

Holmer, Oddvar, and Hvalvik, Birger: (1973). *Beslutninger under usikkerhet og porteføljeteori*, The Norwegian School of Economics and Business Administration, Bergen.

Kroeber-Riel, W.: (1971). 'Constructs and Empirical Basis in Theories of Economic Behavior', *Theory and Decision*, 1, 337–349.

Krelle, Wilhelm: (1968). *Präferenz- und Entscheidungstheorie*, J. C. B. Nohr (Paul Siebek), Tübingen.

Lancaster, Kelvin J.: (1966). 'A New Approach to Consumer Theory', *Journal of Political Economy*, April.

Leinfellner, Werner: (1968). 'Generalization of Classical Decision Theory'. In K. Borch and J. Mossin (Eds.), *Risk and Uncertainty* q.v., pp.196–210, Discussion pp.210–218.

Leinfellner, W., and Booth, E.: (1979). 'The Naturalistic Versus and Intuitive Concept of Values', Part IV of this Volume.

MacCrimmon, Kenneth R.: (1968). 'Descriptive and Normative Implications of the Decision Theory Postulates'. In K. Borch and J. Mossin (Eds.), *Risk and Uncertainty* q.v., pp.3–22.

MacCrimmon, Kenneth R., and Larsson, Stig: (1979). 'Utility Theory: Axioms versus 'Paradoxes'', This Volume, p. 333.

Markowitz, Harry: (1952). 'The Utility of Wealth', *Journal of Political Economy*, Vol. LX, No. 1.

Menger, Karl: (1934). 'Das Unsicherheitsmoment in der Wertlehre', *Zeitschrift für Nationalökonomie*, p.459.

Menges, G.: (1968). 'On Some Open Questions in Statistical Decision Theory'. In K. Borch and J. Mossin (Eds.), *Risk and Uncertainty*, q.v., New York.

Morgenstern, Oscar, and von Neumann, John: (1953). *Theory of Games and Economic Behaviour*, Princeton University Press, Third Edition.

Morrison, D. G.: (1967). 'On the Consistency of Preferences in Allais Paradox', *Behavioural Science*, pp.373–383.

Mossin, Jan: (1973). *Theory of Financial Markets*, Prentice-Hall.

Raiffa, Howard: (1961). 'Risk Ambiguity and the Savage Axioms: Comment', *Quarterly Journal of Economics*, pp.690–694.

Ramsey, F. P.: (1931). 'Truth and Probability', *The Foundations of Mathematics and Other Logical Essays*, London, K. Paul, Trench, Trubner and Co.

Samuelson, Paul A.: (1947). *Foundations of Economic Analysis*, Harvard.

Samuelson, Paul A.: (1948). 'Consumption Theory in Terms of Revealed Preferences', *Economica*, N.S. 15, 243–253.

Samuelson, Paul A.: (1952). 'Probability, Utility, and the Independence Axioms', *Econometrica*, Vol. 20, pp.670–678.

302 OLE HAGEN

Savage, L. J.: (1954). *The Foundations of Statistics*, John Wiley and Sons, Inc., New York, Chapman & Hall Ltd., London.
Shackle, G. L. S.: (1955). *Uncertainty in Economics and Other Reflections*, Cambridge University Press.
Swalm, Ralph O.: (1966). 'Utility Theory – Insights into Risk Taking', *Harvard Business Review*, Dec.
Tobin, J.: (1958). 'Liquidity Preference as Behaviour Towards Risk', *The Review of Economic Studies*, No. 25.
Tobin, J.: (1965). 'The Theory of Portfolio Selection'. In F. H. Hahn and F. P. R. Brechling (Eds.), *The Theory of Interest Rates*, London, MacMillan.
Tobin, J.: (1969). 'Comment on Borch and Feldstein', *The Review of Economic Studies*, Vol. XXXI (1), Jan.
Wold, H.: (1952). *Demand Analysis: A Study in Econometrics*, Almquist and Wicksell, Stockholm, John Wiley and Sons, Inc. New York.

WERNER LEINFELLNER AND EDWARD BOOTH

THE NATURALISTIC VERSUS THE INTUITIONISTIC SCHOOL OF VALUES

ABSTRACT. The first part of this paper analyzes general foundational questions. It is maintained that naturalistic or behavioristic value theory is based on the idea of an order preserving representation of empirically given regular preferences of the past in a cognitive, passive sense. On the other hand, it is claimed that intuitive value theory holds that value orders, in mente, may actively influence and determine, in particular, future preferences. Behavioristic value theory was formalized and axiomatized very early. But the important question persists: what is the proper function of these axioms for making predictions concerning preference behavior? When an answer is sought for this question the difficulties inherent in behavioristic value theory are clearly revealed.

Proposals for eliminating these difficulties are discussed. One proposal is that a normative or rational argument can be used to insure that predictions concerning future preference behavior will be correct. It is demonstrated that, on the one hand, this normative or rational argument is borrowed from intuitive value theory, and, on the other hand, that intuitive value theory itself reduces to individual interaction with, or the manipulation of, values, especially where future preference behavior predictions are concerned.

In the second part of this paper, the formal extra-linguistic structural framework of value theories in general is analyzed and defined. The formal structure of classical behavioristic value theory is defined as a Brouwerian structure. The behavioristic value theory under uncertainty is defined as a modular structure. Thus the transition from classical to behavioristic structures under uncertainty and, finally, the transition to intuitive value theory is formally defined; these definitions will reveal the deep going changes in the structural frames of these theories. Both structures, the Brouwerian structure of classical value theory, and the behavioristic probabilistic structure of behavioristic value theory under uncertainty, possess a common characteristic formal feature: compatibility of values; in contrast, the structures of intuitive value theory are characterized by incompatible values. This incompatibility is based on the subjective manipulatability of values, in mente. In such a case values are no longer totally independent from each other. This incompatibility arises from a variety of reasons, e.g. psychological ones. Incompatibility, from a structural, formal, point of view, results in fundamental changes in the foundation of value theory. One of these changes is revealed in the notion of the dispersion of values and the effect of this dispersion upon predicting future preference behavior. Another change relates to the non-symmetrical properties of the modular structures of behavioristic probabilistic value theory.

Finally, a proposal is made to formalize the leeway of dispersion for incompatible values. This will complete the demonstration that the difference between behavioristic and intuitionistic value theories can be defined by exhibiting the fundamental differences in their structural frames.

Maurice Allais and Ole Hagen (eds.), Expected Utility and the Allais Paradox, 303–332.

In all value theories, beginning in early Greek value philosophy such as in Plato's 'Protagoras', and persisting in modern utility theory, values and utilities have been considered as abstractions which express, just as the ordinal numbers, degree, ranking or position within a series. This 'ranking' is accomplished with respect to an empirical field (D) of objects O, $(O \subseteq D)$, situations, etc. by an individual (i) employing his preference relations (P, I) upon these elements of the field (D). This ordinal aspect of utilities, or this order structure of values, is considered as a minimal representation of the structure of basic preferences (P, I) in naturalistic as well as in behavioristic utilitarian value philosophy.[1] Nevertheless, this order aspect belongs both to naturalistic and intuitive value theory.[2] It is considered as an a priori[3] independent and 'active' element in intuitive value philosophy, whereas the naturalistic-behavioristic order structure represents, in a passive cognitive sense, the ranking in D created by the individual's empirical preferences or wanting, desires, interests, pleasures.

Thus that values, as well as utilities, express a qualitative or quantitative order, or order structure, immediately gives rise to the question: What is more fundamental, values or preferences? Another question also arises: Are all values or utilities really only passive representations of preferential behavior (P, I) upon the objects O in the field (D)? Or, alternatively, is it the case that values are prior to, and in some sense, determine preferences and form preference behavior 'actively' either by manipulation or normative influence? Values as cognitive descriptive representations – (value = representation of preference behavior) – of preferential behavior will be considered as the typical behavioristic foundation of value theory. The notion that values form and prescribe preferences and preference behavior (value = norm) can be considered as the intuitive or conceptionalistic foundation of value theory. Therefore, value intuitionism or conceptualism may be roughly characterized as the view that values are prior to all empirical preferences and play an 'active' role in establishing these preferences. Further, the order which is expressed by these values is originated by the human mind. These values are primarily order products of a creative activity of the mind which are later imposed on preferences. Intuitive values are not platonistic, since according to value intuitionism values and their order can be considered as mental constructions which have no existence independent of the mind. The order aspect of values can be related to a pure hierarchical intuition of order which exists as some kind of inner sense of orientation which may be considered as having a psychological, cultural or introspective origin. Rationality as 'inner sense' has also been used together with ideological, moral, and religious principles, such as equality, freedom, to found decision theory, collective choice and democracy in recent literature.[4]

In any case, the order structure thus created in our consciousness or mind is based on the mind's awareness of its capacity to put objects of the world into a hierarchical serial preferential order. That is, humans first create a value order by mentally placing one object above another object (= mental manipulation). Thus, in a fashion which is similar to the intuitionistic reduction of the Peano axioms to a pure intuitively and mentally performed step by step counting procedure, the structure of a value or utility order-network, which is internally created, is cast upon the external preferential order of the objects of the world. This procedure serves to impose, so to speak, an internally created value order on the world and on our preference behavior. This order structure, once imposed, may be regarded, as was mentioned above, as the 'ethical, moral, or religious' principles and guidelines which regulate our social life.

Thus the following scheme, 'values determine preferences', is obtained:

Values → Preferences.

Contrary to this intuitive, non-naturalistic view of values, the strict empirical and behavioristic view assumes that preferences have to be given empirically by the empirical preference behavior, and that the empirical preference data are the only real basis for the abstract value order. This value order simply mirrors or represents the empirically established preference order.

Thus the following scheme, 'preferences determine values', holds:

Preferences → Values.

A third version of the nature of values, a neutral but cognitive oriented formalistic view,[5] assumes that values are nothing if taken in pure isolation; the same can be said for preferences if they are considered in total isolation. But the holders of the formalistic cognitive view would insist that both values and preferences exist simultaneously in such a fashion that, for example, a one-to-one (isomorphic) mapping of the preference order onto the value order and vice versa, is possible. As a result the following representational structure is assumed: (Here 'axiom' stands for the definition of the value order or structure by means of a set-theoretical axiomatization.)[6]

$$(1) \qquad \text{Axiom} \quad (V; >, \sim) = \{A\}$$
$$\updownarrow$$
$$(O; P, I)$$

In all formalistic reconstructions the mapping function, illustrated above by means of the double arrow, has to be established as a one-to-one or many-one utility function by means of a representation theorem. Whereas von Neumann–Morgenstern, Marschak, and others, proposed, and preferred, a certain value structure, known as an interval structure (the best one to use for the foundations of the differential calculus of classical economics, as well as for utility theory and game and decision theory, dealing, as they do, primarily with monetary values) the general scheme of a strict formalistic behavioristic evaluation theory is, nevertheless, amenable to any kind of axiomatization provided we have an adequate empirical interpretation '/' of $(V; >, \sim)/(O; P, I)$.

Therefore, for example, given an appropriate axiomatization for the quasi-order of $(V; >, \sim)$, all that is required of the formalist is that he finds an isomorphic preferential pattern $(O; P, I)$, or vice versa.

The problem of scaling, or the general question of the value measurement, comes down to the task of finding, for a specific empirically given domain $O \subseteq D$; $(O; P, I)$ of individual or collective preferential behavior, with the inclusion of random events (E) on which these preferences depend, a suitable axiom set $\{A\}$ which permits the finest scale possible, i.e. the best possible quantitative representation of the differences in the given preference behavior. This preferential behavior is revealed either by statements of the individuals making these choices – (linguistically in an empirical language (L_E)) – or effectively by the observation of compatible acts of preferences in a 'yes' or 'no' sense. Moreover, if it is assumed, as Bentham did, that man is always better off according to the fineness of his evaluation scale, what is sought is the finest possible representation of preference-differences by value differences of a value scale, given a specific empirical situation, i.e. an interval scale would be preferred to an ordinal scale, an equi-distant scale would be preferred to an hyper-ordinal scale, etc. The whole program of modern or 'formalistic' value theory is to derive, from the set of appropriate axioms, and given a theoretical framework of a specific value theory (Th), the representation theorem (RT) which guarantees an isomorphic or homomorphic mapping of $(O; P, I)$ onto: axiom $(V; >, \sim)$ so that the ranking structure in D is preserved in a specifically chosen scale.

For our simple case of an ordinal scale, the following holds:

(2) $P(o_1, o_2)$ or $P(o_2, o_1)$ or $I(o_1, o_2) \rightarrow v(o_1) > v(o_2)$

or $v(o_2) > v(o_1)$ or $v(o_1) = v(o_2)$.

It is interesting that the attempt to provide an empirical behavioristic foundation for formalistic value- and decision-theory, which from the beginning, was a descriptive, cognitive undertaking for compatible, i.e. simultaneously given preferences and values, ran into difficulties when used for predictions, i.e. when projected into the future. Suddenly a normative, prescriptive element had to be introduced into the descriptive value theory as some kind of 'deus ex machina' for this specific purpose. For consider that here the axioms have to be strengthened by regarding them, not as a mere representation acquired from the description of past regular preference:

(3) $\{A\} \rightarrow RT$,

but suddenly these axioms are supposed to dictate future behavior. Frequently this is done under the cover of maxims such as: everyone attempts to maximize his utility, or by means of principles such as those which characterize 'normative rational behavior'.

This is a decisive change for a descriptive theory. A change which was very often neglected when von Neumann–Morgenstern's or Marschak's axiomatization of utility was used for making predictions or future applications. Frequently, this step is taken by behavioristic value theorists by means of a normative device. For example, a businessman 'should', or is 'obliged', to behave in a manner prescribed by the axioms. Or perhaps the phrase is: If one wishes to be a rational evaluator then one should behave in a manner prescribed by the axioms. These few words are supposed to be sufficient to allow the transition from a mere descriptive to a prescriptive, normative view of evaluation, value, and decision theory. But this normative move entails enormous difficulties as Fleming, Goodman, Markowitz, and Harsanyi have shown.[7]

What is to be shown here is that any of these 'normative' attempts are borrowed from intuitive value theory. That is, whenever principles, norms, rules, etc., are imposed on an empirical or formalistic utility or decision theory this is done to guarantee that any individual (i) will, in the future, observe the following normatively enforced theoretical desideratum:

(4) $O[\{A\} \rightarrow RT]$.

This is indicated by using the deontic operator O"...". This means that the individual (i) should, or is obliged to, behave according to the axioms under consideration, in order to guarantee an isomorphic or homomorphic representation of his preferences onto his values.

Why is this change required? It may be assumed here, in a typical cognitive, descriptive sense, that the individual (i) always acted according to (4) in the past for (4) was obtained from the observations of the individual's past regular preference behavior which again can be taken as the specific representation theorem from a specific set of axioms of a specific value theory. Therefore, it may be assumed that, e.g., the regular behavioristic fulfillment of all the axioms required for a quasi-ordering actually may stem from an empirical past or present instinctive preference pattern of the type:

(5) $S \rightarrow R$,

i.e. given a certain well-defined experimental situation the preference reaction (R) takes place automatically.

Or, alternatively, in an empirical-behavioristic foundation of value theory, all past and present quasi-orderings of values or utilities may be regarded as following from and enforced by the empirically given sequence: $S \rightarrow R$.

(6) $(S \rightarrow R) \rightarrow (A \rightarrow RT)$.

It would be completely correct to assert (6), for it has been extracted from all past regular preferential behavior; this behavior having been exhibited under specified experimental conditions. Here, the consequent represents the theoretical reconstruction of an instinctively rooted or native pattern of preference behavior described in the antecedent ($S \rightarrow R$). (6) may be regarded as the explanatory principle of behaviorism. Whether it is a predictive principle is another question, for were it a predictive principle (6) would have to be reversed: $(A \rightarrow RT) \rightarrow (S \rightarrow R)$.

A foundation of utility on 'rationality' resulting from a rational attitude $(\mathcal{R})$ assumes even more than the above, namely, some kind of identification as follows:

(7) $\mathcal{R} = [(S \rightarrow R) \leftrightarrow (A \rightarrow RT)]$ or $\mathcal{R} = [(A \rightarrow RT) \leftrightarrow (S \rightarrow R)]$.

The individual's manipulation of values to create a quasi-ranking of objects, $O \subseteq D$, by adhering to the axioms $\{A\}$, may justify this ranking. But this justification presupposes that the individual (i) has accepted the axioms as norms via some kind of rational insight, or that he has accepted them through the influence of self-imposed principles, rules, etc. This foundation of utility theory on 'rationality' comes very near to the intuitive foundation of values, for it comes down to a purposeful 'manipulation' of future values by an individual with regards to axioms, principles, etc. 'Manipulation' means that the individual himself, not the axioms, principles, theories, etc., must act on his own order of values and then apply them.

Eventually the moment arrives when one can no longer only consider an individual's past preferential behavior but rather the individual's future behavior as a determinant of his value and preference behavior, as Churchman proposed. This temporal turning point may be called a Humean cut because here the individual's well-confirmed past preference behavior and experience must be projected into the relatively uncertain future. Hume's position with regards to the projection of laws into the future, especially causal laws, is very well known. It was Hume's contention that the projection of these laws could only be probabilistic. As Hume notes: it is merely custom which persuades us to believe that the sun will rise tomorrow. Today this situation can be more aptly characterized. For, since the possibility of a nova formation of our sun is very small, though it is not zero, it is only to be expected, with a very high probability, that the sun will rise tomorrow.

Hume proposed that our projection of even well-confirmed laws and past regularities into the future is based upon, and justified, only by an internal belief in their continuation. Hume's point of view will be adopted here along with the 'manipulation' assumption. The typical intuitive and non-natural view of evaluation consists simply in the awareness on the part of the individual that he may either believe in his present values and choose to be guided by a continuation of them, or he may change his future value orientation by manipulating his present values. The first case of maintenance will not be discussed here. However, these cases either constitute a conversion of the individual decision maker from a strict 'passive' empirical behaviorist of a cognitive type to an 'active' intuitive value theorist, or evaluator, of the normative-prescriptive type. Especially, the second case comes very close to the idea of a cybernetical learning process or a statistical automaton. The conversion occurs at the moment when the evaluator manipulates, i.e. changes, in mente, his past behavioristic experience before he projects it into the future. Thus the evaluator may become, according to Rickert, a 'value-creator' or, in a moderate sense, his own 'law-maker', by adding an intuitive weight or factor (F) to an already existing behavioristic prediction, as, for example, Bernoulli's theorem. The reasons for creating, or manipulating, a new value order in one's own mind, be they of a psychological, mental, rational or moral nature, will not be discussed here.

An individual's quasi-ranking of objects may be regarded as a learning experience confirmed by the individual's regular past (and regular present preference) behavior. With this assumption, value and decision theory acquires a partial empirical, behavioristic foundation, ex post, and a partial intuitive foundation, when an attempt is made to explain and predict an individual's future preferential behavior, ex ante. Thus behavioristic and intuitive value theory are in a kind of complementary relationship. A strict behavioristic value theory would doom any individual to continue his past preference pattern under all circumstances and thus the individual could be regarded as a deterministic automaton. But the situation changes completely if value and decision theory acquires an 'intuitive' prescriptive foundation.

Mere rational insight $(\mathscr{R})$, applied by an individual to his past and present preference behavior, even though that insight is abetted by an explicit utility theory, is not sufficient to guarantee that he will automatically behave as he did in the past. Here, it must be assumed that the individual's assent or active manipulation of his values, in an act of self identification with them, is of primary importance. This principle which the individual satisfies, or whatever rational insights will influence him, are of secondary importance.

From the above it can be seen why the behavioristic foundation of utility theory alone leads to an automatic maintenance or continuation of past behavior in accordance with a rationality norm or requirement. But perhaps utility-theorists borrow from the intuitive value theory the notion of 'manipulation' of hypothetical future values to serve as a formulation for their theory. This manipulation may result in a deviation from past preference behavior. To make the intuitive 'lemma' more clear this commitment to 'maintenance' may be construed as a moral one (Harsanyi), or as a rational commitment, or as a utilitarian commitment to the maximization of one's utility. This commitment relation (C) will be considered as a quite general deontic relation between our axioms, our value theory and their consequences (RT):

$$(8) \qquad C\{R[\{A\} \rightarrow RT]\},$$

and a set of rules (R). These rules may be moral obligations, juridical laws, in any case they are guidelines about how to change and manipulate future values. Of course, this amounts to an intuitive foundation for value theory as expressed by (8). Thus, the behavioristic prediction in value theory may be regarded as a dilemmatic one for it leads either to some kind of automaton-situation, namely, that any individual is considered to be an automaton without any degree of freedom, or, on the other hand, it leads to an intuitive complementary foundation for behavioristic value theory.

In summary, the modern empirical-behavioristic school of utility and value theory (the American School) presupposes that what is of primary concern is to maintain a past regular empirical preference behavior by borrowing intuitive elements, namely rules, principles, or, in general, 'manipulatability' of values. The intuitive-normative school (the French School) maintains just the reverse; they maintain that the active change produced by the internal subjective manipulation of past regular preference patterns is quite natural when the individual faces future hypothetical situations (in particular, the Allais questions). For the French School, it is of primary concern to learn how the individual will change or manipulate his values. But this can only be determined if the past regular and fixed preference behavior pattern exhibited by the individual is explicitly known. This information comes from, is borrowed from, the behavioristic value theories.

What happens if the behavioristic foundation of preference theory comes under fire, as has so often happened in the past? What behavioristic and formalistic response is there if, for example, transitivity of preferences is not fulfilled by certain individuals, given certain empirical situations, or if von Neumann–Morgenstern's third axioms are unfulfilled in ways such as those suggested by Mac-Crimmon?[8]

The rather facile solution offered to these problems by nearly all behaviorists is that the set of axioms can be changed in appropriate ways. For example, the requirement of transitivity of preference may be replaced by a weaker requirement of probabilistic transitivity, or, as has been suggested by Skala this transitivity requirement can be entirely eliminated.[9] Further, it has been suggested that utilities be considered as multi-dimensional or that 'fuzzy' utility orderings be used.[10] If any of these changes are effected, completely different axiom sets are obtained, any one of which might be used to explain preference behavior in special situations. Another way out of these difficulties would be to choose a coarser, weaker utility scale, i.e., instead of a cardinal scale use an ordinal scale. If all this tinkering mentioned above is to no avail perhaps both the fine-grained evaluation scale and the demanding axiom system {A} might have to be replaced. Generally, these kinds of radical changes are appropriate when the field of economics, with its monetary values and its sophisticated theories employing classical differential and integral calculus, is forsaken for the fields of aesthetics, culture and religion.

If all of the above-mentioned formalistic and behavioristic inventory of remedies is to no purpose, as has been vividly illustrated, for example, in the case of the Allais paradox, very often refuge is taken in an 'educational' rationality assumption $\mathcal{R}(7)$. This assumption is used to explain empirical anomalies with respect to certain axiom systems {A} as occurring because the agent, in these instances, was acting non-rationally owing to lack of proper 'education'; i.e., he deviated from the set {A} in a non-rational or non-common-sensical manner just as an untrained or uneducated person might. This fruitful approach has been taken by Borch, among others. In those cases in which the agent deviates from the von Neumann–Morgenstern axiomatic expectation, Borch views the deviation as resulting from: (1) an incorrect perception of the situation by the agent, and/or (2) lack of skill and training on the part of the agent. Borch proposed that the erratic behavior of the agent be eliminated by proper scientific and economic education. This proper education amounts to getting the agent to realize just how the von Neumann–Morgenstern axioms *really* do apply in a particular situation and thus disabusing the agent of his previous wrong-headedness.

Borch's learning procedure approach is certainly an interesting way out of the difficulty. But if this resolution is accepted doesn't the prescriptive normative transition from (7) to (8) occur, silently, but inevitably? Borch's solution is certainly an enlightened one: learn through rationalization. But, nonetheless, it offers a normative straight-jacket, which finally leads to the intuitive complementation of behavioristic value theories.

If irregularities in preference behavior still occur, in spite of all that Borch suggests, a final recourse is available. This is the well-known scientific method of forming hypotheses ad hoc, for the specific irregular cases. That is, provide specific additional unique axioms which will cover preference behavior in particular peculiar situations, such as that situation depicted in the Allais paradox.

In this paper, it will be shown that there are cases in which attempts to 'save the behavioristic theory' do not succeed in restoring the behavioristic foundation to utility or value theory, without, at least, an implicit resort to a partial intuitionistic foundation for value and decision theory. We simply have to abandon the notion that evaluation is a mere behavioristic passive formal category; a category which can be projected automatically into the future, if it has worked successfully in the past. 'Successfully' means that given an axiom system and a preferential order, this order can be mapped into future (formal) value-structures by, for example, a one-to-one utility function. This cognitive, descriptive conception that evaluation is exclusively a passive mirroring of past preference order is only the first step. It must be complemented, in all the situations already described with respect to future evaluations, by the intuitionistic 'active' conception of evaluation, and by a method to compute manipulation of values.

To conclude this section, it appears that any intuitive value structure may be superimposed upon the behavioristic structure. How this superimposition may internally change this descriptive pattern or structure and how a free manipulation may be understood and defined is described in the following.

1. THE STRUCTURE OF VALUE AND DECISION THEORY

1.1. THE BEHAVIORISTIC VALUE SPACE

It will be assumed that value and decision theories, as well as theories of society, may be based on, or refer to, an extra-linguistically given domain (D) of preference acts which belong to the effective or possible application of a theory (Th), i.e., the domain D is dependent ontologically and empirically on the structural properties of the configuration and combinations of the basic acts or preference behavior. These preferences are between objects, goods, situations, etc. $(o_1, o_2, \ldots, o_n \in O$, where $O \subseteq D)$. These preference acts are simple; i.e. an individual of normal-type, in a prescribed standard situation, exhibits preference, or indifference, towards the o_i's in O with respect to a specific theory of behavioristic type. Symbolically: $P(o_i, o_j)^B$ or $I(o_i, o_j)^B$ or $(O; P, I)^B$.

These fundamental acts constitute the behavioristic preferential data which are given, in the classic behavioristic case, completely independent of any observation, measurement or experiments, but, nevertheless, can be described by a behavioristic observational language (L_E^B). Here, it will be demonstrated that it is not necessary to express behavioristic preferential acts linguistically; that is, the structures discovered here are not obtained from the logic of the language of values. Behavioristic acts may be represented immediately (theoretically) in a given value space, i.e. a convex vector space. This representation may be called an extra-linguistic representation if set theory is not regarded as a language. Thus the order of these preferential acts may be represented in a linear vector space of convex character, symbolized by a language (L_T^B), or by a set-theoretical representational system (such as Suppes' and Adam's set-theoretical predicate[11]) or as behavioristic category, structural frame (more simply: structures):

$$
\begin{array}{ccccc}
(V; >, \sim) & & \mathrm{Str}^V & & \\
\updownarrow & \text{or} & \updownarrow & \text{or} & \mathrm{STR}^{B \to V}. \\
(O; P, I) & & \mathrm{Str}^B & &
\end{array}
$$

This representation of Str^B into Str^V is a mapping which must be either isomorphic or homomorphic. In contrast to the axiomatic approach of the previous section, in which the axioms and a representation theorem were the presuppositions for an isomorphic mapping of and within a specific value theory, the concern here is to find the widest structural frame, or the widest structural space for mapping $\text{STR}^{B \to V}$. This search resembles those efforts undertaken to find a suitable spatial framework for mechanics, or quantum physics, or thermodynamics, or a classification of structural types of value theories. The 'spatial framework' here is the value space, to be defined as a structure or a lattice which will impose its 'logic' on the underlying linguistic logic of value theory, not vice versa. In Section 1.2, the structure spanned up by the mapping of intuitively given preferential data $((O; P, I)^I$ or $\text{Str}^I)$ onto the value structure $((V; >, \sim)$ or $\text{Str}^V)$ will be precisely defined. This mapping may be abbreviated as: $\text{STR}^{I \to V}$ and may be regarded as a mathematical category, different from the category $\text{STR}^{B \to V}$.

Intuitive preferential data and values can be expressed by a language (L_E^I), or by a set-theoretical representational system, intuitive-type category, or structural frame (more simply structures):

$$
\begin{array}{ccccc}
(V; >, \sim) & & \text{Str}^V & & \\
\updownarrow & \text{or} & \updownarrow & \text{or} & \text{STR}^{I \to V}. \\
(O; P, I)^I & & \text{Str}^I & &
\end{array}
$$

Here, again, the attempt is to define precisely the widest and most general structural frame $(\text{STR}^{I \to V})$ which characterizes this 'intuitive' representation or mapping of Str^I onto Str^V. If this task can be accomplished it will be possible to compare both structural frames $(\text{STR}^{B \to V}$ and $\text{STR}^{I \to V})$ and determine if there exists a common embracing general structure (STR) from which both of these particular structures may be derived. If this is possible then the behavioristic, empirical value structure and the intuitive, mentalistic value structure may be classified formally as different structures or categories, or different types of theories.

The question of the relationship between the representational structures: $\text{STR}^{B \to V}$, $\text{STR}^{I \to V}$, STR, and the corresponding linguistic frameworks of predicate logical type will not be investigated here. It should be noted that the set-theoretical symbolization of scientific theories is to be regarded as independent of, or, at least, separable from, the normal predicate logic framework of scientific theories. Here set-theoretical representations will be considered as ontological reference models whereas the everyday language of normal predicate logic is seen as providing the communicative or informative language (meta- or epi-language) used in scientific research.

1.2. THE BROUWERIAN STRUCTURE: $\mathrm{STR}^{B \to V}$, THE STRUCTURE OF CLASSICAL BEHAVIORISTIC THEORIES

Here all preferential data will be considered as classical 'yes' or 'no' data. (In a semantic sense, all preference statements will be regarded as factually, or effectively, true or factually, or effectively, false. But a semantical definition of truth will not be used here.)

The structure of $(A; \subseteq, C)$ is called a classical behavioristic structure if and only if the following conditions are fulfilled:

(A0) The outcome of a normal-type individual's preferences or values with respect to objects, goods, situations, etc. in a standard situation should satisfy the following condition:

> if A is a 'yes' outcome of a preferential act or a 'yes' preferential datum then B is also a 'yes' outcome of a preferential act or a 'yes' preferential datum; semantically: A is true implies that B is true.

That is, if A is a correct outcome of a normal-type individual's preferences or values with respect to any two objects, goods, situations, etc. in a standard situation then B is a correct outcome of this same normal-type individual's preferences or values with respect to any other two objects, goods, situations, etc. in this standard situation; i.e., A and B are said to be value compatible or non-fuzzy.[10]

As was noted in the beginning, these preferential data are to be in reference to a single individual, of normal-type, in a precisely prescribed situation (standard situation) with respect to a freely chosen domain, $D \subseteq \mathrm{Th}$. If value statements (judgments) are dealt with, these statements (judgments) come from a single individual in a standard value state or situation in $D \subseteq \mathrm{Th}$.

The general relation described in (A0) denotes therefore '$\subseteq$' as $A \subseteq B$, i.e. strict consequence or implication or subjunction (in the sense of Churchman), as well as set-theoretical inclusion '$\subseteq$'. This axiom concerns only preferential data of the 'action–action' $(A \to A)$ type and '$\subseteq$' deals only with the 'situation $\to$ reaction' or the 'stimulus $\to$ response' $(S \to R)$, type of behavior. It concerns the 'event $\to$

action' $(E \to A)$ type only in those cases of 'yes $\to$ yes' outcomes, but not, for example, in probabilistic situations.

(AI) The relation '$\subseteq$' spans up a partially-ordered structure if and only if the following conditions are satisfied by the preferential data or value statements (judgments):

(1) $A \subseteq A$ for all $A \subseteq D$ or V (Reflexivity).

(2) $A \subseteq B$ and $B \subseteq A$ implies $A = B$ (Antisymmetry).

(3) $A \subseteq B$ and $B \subseteq C$ implies $A \subseteq C$ (Transitivity).

Axiom I(1) may be interpreted as the self-identity of correct value or preference outcomes. That is, a re-evaluation of an initial correct outcome of a normal-type individual's preferences or values with respect to the same two objects, goods, situations, etc. in this standard situation should also be correct.

Axiom I(2) may be interpreted as the commutativity of correct and equivalent value or preference outcomes. That is, if A is an initial correct outcome of a normal-type individual's preferences or values with respect to any two objects, goods, situations, etc. in a standard situation, with respect to $D \subseteq$ Th and B is a second correct outcome of this same individual's preferences or values with respect to any two other objects, goods, situations, etc., then, in this same standard situation, these outcomes will remain correct regardless of the order in which they are evaluated.

Axiom I(3) may be interpreted as requiring the transitivity of correct value or preference outcomes. If $A \subseteq B$ and $B \subseteq C$ are correct outcomes of a normal-type individual's preferences or values with respect to any two other objects, goods, situations, etc., in this same standard situation with respect to $D \subseteq$ Th, then a third outcome $A \subseteq C$ of this same individual's preferences or values with respect to any other objects, goods, situations, etc. (other than those evaluated in A and B) in this same standard situation should also be correct. Thus, if an initial correct outcome can be made all other outcomes of a normal-type individual's preferences or values, in this standard situation, will be correct regardless of the order or combination of the objects, goods, situations, etc., compared. One may, of course, replace 'correct' by 'effectively true' if one is dealing with the semantic concept of truth but this is not necessary for a language is not used here.

(AII) There exists a greatest minorant (lower bound) for every non-empty family of outcomes of a normal-type individual's preferential data or value statements (judgments) in the standard situation. This guarantees that there exists a substructure, denoted as: $\bigcap_U A_i$, such that (in symbols):

$$X \in A_i \text{ for all } i\text{'s } X \in \bigcap_U A_i.$$

It is assumed that the individual has, at least, a minimal preference ordering, that is, he has a threshold level for values. What is meant by 'minimal' is characterized by this axiom.

Since the concept of a greatest lower bound is co-ordinate to the concept of a least upper bound and since all the subsets of the preferential data have a greatest lower bound or meet (denoted by the intersection) and a lowest upper bound or join (denoted by the union) a complete Brouwerian value-structure is defined. With a lowest upper bound for the set of preferential data infinite values are excluded.

(AIII) This axiom defines the strict contrary preference act or complementary or contrary value, as well as the negation, in value theory.

(1) $(\text{non } A)' = A.$

(2) $A \cap A' = \emptyset$ or $\text{non } (A' \cap A) = 0.$

(3) $A \subseteq B \leftrightarrow B' \subseteq A'.$

Axiom III(1) defines the contrary preference act or contrary value and the strict negation or strict complementation for preference or value outcomes. This is required since, generally speaking, the negation – non (A_1) – could have been any of the following $A_2 \vee A_3 \vee , \ldots, \vee A_n$. Thus any many-valued negation is excluded in this type of value theory.

Axiom III(2) defines, together with III(1), the complete decidability of preference or value outcomes. Either an outcome, A, is correct or it is incorrect for an individual in the standard situation.

Axiom III(3) in formal logic is the de Morgan Law.

(AIV) (The Axiom of Atomicity or Foundation.) For every A there exists an 'atom', or a finite value or preferential datum, such that P, a point in the value space, or a value satisfies $P \subseteq A$.

An atom, or point, is an element P, belonging to a structure Str^V

(lattice), which is different from $\emptyset$ and such that:

$$\emptyset \subseteq X \subset P \to X = \emptyset \quad \text{or} \quad X = P.$$

Consequently, for any preferential or value datum, $A \neq \emptyset$, there exists a value P, such that $P \subseteq A$, or if Q is a value, then

$$A \subseteq X \subseteq A \cup Q \to X = A \quad \text{or} \quad X = A \cup Q.$$

This axiom insures the precision of preference and value measurement.

EPI-THEOREM 1: *Any representational value or decision theory which fulfills the axioms* (A0), (AI), (AII), (AIII), (AIV) *and, in addition, possesses the property of distributivity, is a classical 'behavioristic-effective' value or decision theory under certainty and no risk.*

This classical type of value theory has the epi-framework of a completely strict, or orthocomplemented structure. For example, the quasi-ordering of values, or an ordinal ranking or scale of values, would be included in this axiom system. This system is actually an epi-axiom scheme from which the underlying logic of classical value and decision theory can be derived. Note that this logic is not derived from the language but from the empirical structure of the basic preference acts. It is not quite identical with classical sentential or predicate calculus and is actually an intuitionistic type of logic.

1.3. A FURTHER GENERALIZATION OF CLASSICAL STRUCTURES: THE MODULAR STRUCTURES OF BEHAVIORISTIC VALUE THEORY UNDER UNCERTAINTY AND RISK[12]

For the von Neumann–Morgenstern's axiomatization of an interval utility-scale or space, the randomness of events E on which our preferences depend, introduces a completely new structure into the classical value space – a structure which is called a modular structure. The moment linear convex combinations are introduced into our finite 'Euclidean' value space the structure of this space is completely changed due to the empirical fact that those values are matched with probabilities α of the random events. A subset of any value space is said to be convex if and only if the line segment (set) joining any two points, V_1 and $V_2 \in V$, is defined by the following condition (which will be generalized for sets, V_i):

$$V_1, V_2 \in V \qquad \text{implies} \qquad \overline{V_1 V_2} \in V,$$

where $\overline{V_1 V_2}$ denotes the set connecting V_1 and V_2, or their linear combination. Convexity can be extended to the representation of value functions defined over the segments: $\overline{V_1 V_2}$, of the linear combinations of two values by probabilities. It is clear that the intersection of any number of convex sets is convex and therefore commutativity holds between convex sets.

But what happens when the union of convex sets is formed? Are these unions convex? The answer: not necessarily. For example, the union of set A and set B is not convex if a part of a line connecting set A and set B lies outside both sets.

To guarantee that the union of two sets is convex the conditions for the union of two sets has to be modified. Here $\bar{\cup}$ should be the smallest convex set that contains both A and B. This means that $A \bar{\cup} B$ is the least upper bound of A and B among the set of convex union sets.

Now while the set of all convex sets form a commutative and compatible structure (lattice) with respect to the operation $\subseteq$, they do not form a distributive lattice or structure. Take the three value sets: A, B, and C, where $B \bar{\cup} C$ and $A \cap (B \bar{\cup} C)$ is given, and the following holds:

$$A \cap B = \emptyset = A \cap C$$

and likewise:

$$(A \cap B) \bar{\cup} (A \cap C) = \emptyset \bar{\cup} \emptyset = \emptyset.$$

But the distributive law does not hold for the convex case:

$$(A \cap (B \bar{\cup} C)) \neq (A \cap B) \cup (A \cap C)$$

because:

$$(A \cap (B \bar{\cup} C)) > 0.$$

This means that the combined and iterated application of addition and multiplication, or the union and intersection operations, have to be generalized for convex structures. A structure for which the distributive law is no longer valid is called a modular structure.

Since the structure of $\text{STR}^{B \to V}$ under uncertainty and risk is not a

Brouwerian nor a Boolean structure the behavioristic or naturalistic value theories may be defined by the general structural criterion of modularity. Thus a definition for all types of non-classical behavioristic value theories is obtained if the modular axiom or law (M) is to be taken as such a structural criterion.

In any lattice-structure, i.e. a structure with two set-theoretical predicates, one always has distributivity:

$$X \cup (Y \cap Z) \subseteq (X \cup Y) \cap Z \quad \text{for} \quad X \subseteq Z.$$

But if the lattice-structure is such that for all $X \subseteq Z$ equality holds then the more general modularity is obtained:

$$X \cup (Y \cap Z) = (X \cup Y) \cap Z \quad \text{for} \quad X \subseteq Z.$$

Such a lattice-structure is called a modular structure. Modularity is the best known generalization of Brouwerian or Boolean structures. In such a sense, the introduction of the behavioristic matching assumption, or the linear convex combination assumption, into the value space, or, in other words, the shifting over to evaluation and decision making under uncertainty and risk, in von Neumann–Morgenstern type of axiomatizations, changes the general character of the structure $STR^{B \to V}$ from a classical Brouwerian or a Boolean one to a non-classical modular structure.

It is very striking that Birkhoff and von Neumann (1936) justified modularity by pointing out that on finite modular lattices one can always define a function, $f(a)$, with the ideal properties of a probability distribution matched, for our purposes, with a certain value. But this change, by way of introducing uncertainty and risk into the Boolean structure of certain or sure values, is not the only one of interest here. It will be demonstrated in the next chapter that the change from $STR^{B \to V}$ to $STR^{I \to V}$ induces a new and more fundamentally general structure on the modular structure $STR^{B \to V}$ under certainty and risk. It seems that the intuitive foundations of value and decision theory attacks a fundamental property underlying the Boolean and modular structures: the symmetry and a compatibility property.

The next problem is: Does there exist a common structure for both classical behavioristic value theory and behavioristic value theory under uncertainty? In both these theories the compatibility of values is maintained or preserved. The discriminating property for classical behavioristic value theory is distributivity whereas modularity is the discriminating property under uncertainty and risk.

The structure of a behavioristic value theory under uncertainty and risk is given if the Axioms (A0), (AI), (AII), (AIII), (AIV), plus 'modularity', are satisfied.

The general structure of both the classical and non-classical behavioristic value theory u.u.a.r. is given if the Axioms (A0), (AI), (AII), (AIII), (AIV), plus a weak modularity identical with compatibility (see Axiom (A0)) is satisfied.

One issue has not yet been discussed: the striking similarity of the structural frame of value theories and Quantum Theory as described by Birkhoff–von Neumann, Pyrron and Jauch.[12] In both cases, these structures are not obtained via extraction from the language of the corresponding theory, but from the empirical structural properties of experiments, in the case of Quantum Mechanics, and from the preferential outcomes, in the case of value theories. But in contrast to Quantum Theory, where only a single theory is analyzed, our investigation has covered a wide spectrum of different value theories and as a result is more a taxonomy of different types of value theories established by using formal structural criteria. This approach closely resembles the point of view of empirical logic[13] and the extra-linguistic approach for defining the structure of theories. This latter approach has been developed by the formalistic school of theory formation (Suppes, Adams).

An important question remains: How is one to account for the apparent structural similarities between physical theories and social theories? One simple answer may be: it is the introduction of probabilities which lead in both cases to ranges of uncertainty or fuzziness, which both structures have in common.

1.4. THE ATTACK AGAINST THE BEHAVIORISTIC COMBINING OF VALUES IN PROSPECTS

Most of the criticism of the intuitive school of values is directed against the axioms: 3:B and 3:C of von Neumann–Morgenstern's axiomatization of utility,[14] especially against "the algebra of combining".

It is very interesting that in this axiomatization, the basic situation of measurement of values, quite in the sense of 'empirical logic'

$$(9) \qquad x_2 \gtrless \alpha_1 x_1, \alpha_3 x_3,$$

is called an operation on a (value) system. The conditio sine qua non of the ordering and combining, as well as of the algebra of combining, has already been expressed in the Axiom (A0) as the compatibility of the values, v_1, v_2, v_3. But the situation may arise that, for example, the value statement v_2, which has to satisfy (9), may not always be compatible with both v_1 and v_3, i.e. these values may not always be determined or observed independently one from the other, so that the temporal order of the determination or observation would have an impact on the whole value state of the system. This again can be expressed quite generally as a violation of the Brouwerian, Boolean and Modular symmetry conditions, for example, of von-Neumann–Morgenstern's axiom: 3:C:a

$$\alpha_1 x_1 + (1 - \alpha)x_2 = (1 - \alpha)x_2 + \alpha_1 x_1.$$

Symmetry entailed by compatibility is important in determining the time period during which the values v_1, v_2, v_3 may be ascribed simultaneously to one and the same value state. Incompatibility means: (1) that at least two or more values, which are necessary for a complete description of the value state, cannot be determined, observed, or measured simultaneously and independent from each other for the determination of one would have an impact on the determination of the other, and (2) that in the case of an intuitive formation of a prospect for prognostic or predictive purposes at least two values interfere or interact in a manner which is difficult to control or describe. But this is exactly what may occur when values are manipulated as previously described.

In order to support his critique of the von Neumann–Morgenstern axiomatization Allais[15] created some hypothetical or possible choice situations and sent these, in the form of a questionnaire, to various people for their responses. Among those queried was L. J. Savage, a prominent adherent of the expected utility hypothesis.

Here are the Allais situations. The decision-maker is to select one alternative in each situation. The selection process for both situations is to occur 'at the same time'.

E: The certainty of getting 100 million French francs,

or

F: 10 chances in 100 of getting 500 million French francs,
          89 chances in 100 of getting 100 million French francs,
          1 chance in 100 of getting nothing.

X: 11 chances in 100 of getting 100 million French francs,
        89 chances in 100 of getting nothing.

or

Y: 10 chances in 100 of getting 500 million French francs,
        90 chances in 100 of getting nothing.

According to the von Neumann–Morgenstern axiomatization the prescribed solution should be:

(10) $F > E$ and $Y > X$ or $E > F$ and $X > Y$.

Many people, among them Savage,[16] do not make these choices, at least initially, but answered that they would prefer instead:

(11) $E > F$ and $Y > X$.

This combination of choices are, of course, contrary to what is prescribed by the von Neumann–Morgenstern axiomatization. For if the ratio, the utility of 500 million : the utility of 100 million, is more than 11 : 10, then the expected utility principle would indicate preference for F and for Y and in the opposite case, reverse preferences, i.e., one of the two in (10), but in no case the preference expressed in (11). If these choices were actually made then the von Neumann–Morgenstern axioms could be regarded as some kind of norm for future decision-making.[17]

But the intriguing question persists: Why do so many people deviate from the vNM-axioms? Is it because they actually change, or manipulate, values intuitively for future prospects according to their individual tastes?

This deviation unearthed by Allais actually has to be considered as a real paradox, if placed within the explanatory framework of the vNM ex post behavioristic axiomatization. But for Allais this problem is just a beginning. He wishes to impose his intuitive theory, which deals, according to our classification, with intuitive manipulatable values for future prospects, on the von Neumann–Morgenstern behavioristic foundations of utility under risk and uncertainty. The reason why people choose the unorthodox solution (11) – unorthodox with respect to the von Neumann–Morgenstern axiomatization – is, according to Allais, because they regard values as an intuitively created ranking where one has the possibility, in mente, to manipulate these comparisons intentionally according to psychological reasons.

The following kinds of manipulations are expressly mentioned by Allais:

(1) Psychological manipulations or distortions of the vNM comparisons.

(2) Subjective distortion or deviation of objective probabilities.

(3) Probability weighing of psychologically given factors of the specific choice which may influence the final outcome.

(4) Manipulations with respect to the shape of the probability distributions of intuitive values.

For example, Allais maintains that very small objective probabilities are manipulated, i.e., distorted, to somewhat higher subjective probabilities while, conversely, objective probabilities close to 1 are transformed to subjective probabilities somewhat smaller, or the individual cannot live without ignoring, at least in mente, very small probabilities (e.g. there is a very small probability of an outbreak of an atomic war, or of a nova formation of our sun, but this is something that humans must, for nearly all purposes, discount). We may regard the above-mentioned psychological distortion as raising or lowering the sensibility or the threshold of probability estimation for a particular individual in what is for that individual a very important situation.

Hagen (1969, 1972)[18] has gone a bit further than this general and formal description of the situation. He states postulates and axioms dealing with the situation (9) in an intuitive way and is concerned about just how the expected utility, predicted according to the vNM axioms, may be manipulated mentally by individuals. He expresses this formally by standard deviation and skewness, the skewness expressed by a special measure he has developed on the basis of his experimentations.

It has been proposed already that the common denominator of the 'intuitive deviation or dispersion', is, in fact, the possibility of a free manipulation, in mente, of possible or future value prospects. This manipulation factor will be investigated in the next section.

1.5. THE STRUCTURE OF INTUITIVE VALUE THEORY

The common denominator of the intuitive manipulation of the ex post behavioristic prospect behavior, for the purpose of future applications, can be seen as a general violation of the fundamental symmetry condition used, and required, by the von Neumann–Morgenstern axiomatization (in 3:B and 3:C). Therefore, intuitive manipulation is, formally, a symmetry violation and empirically it amounts to the incompatibility of values necessary for a complete value description. The basic idea is that prospects, intersections, or conjunctions may no longer be regarded as absolutely simultaneously commutative or symmetric if they are intuitively manipulatable. Intuitive manipulation means that the first member of the conjunction or intersection, which is necessary for the determination of a value state by an evaluator, influences the determination or observation of the second member, or vice versa.

In representing an actual choice situation within a behavioristic classical or modular structure it is always silently assumed that certain prospects, or value statements, or preferences are completely independent. That is, they are assumed to be completely independent from each other, which means completely independent from changes in the attitude of the evaluating individual, at least during the duration of the evaluation. A violation of this symmetry means that commutativity or symmetry of a conjunction, or intersection, necessary for the description of a value state, is given up. The outcome of the evaluation will depend, e.g. on the temporal or serial order by which the possible or future intersection or conjunction is expressed. That is:

$$v_1 \sim v_2 \neq v_2 \sim v_1 \quad \text{or} \quad \alpha_1 v_1, \alpha_2 v_2 \neq \alpha_2 v_2, \alpha_1 v_1.$$

But this clearly violates the von Neumann–Morgenstern 'algebra of prospects', as well as general Boolean and modular properties.

The notion of the compatibility of value statements or preferential acts can be best exhibited by again referring to the Allais case:[19]

Compatibility of value statements or preferential acts for all individuals, i, considered to be in the domain, D, of our theory, Th, is construed as implication as defined according to Section 1.1. For the Allais situation this would mean that if lottery (F) is preferred to lottery (E) then lottery (Y) should be preferred to lottery (X). In symbols:

$$L_F > L_E = A, \quad L_Y > L_X = B, \quad A \subseteq B \leftrightarrow A \, \text{comp} \, B.$$

But in the actual cases, since about 70% act in the sense of $-A \subseteq B$ and 30% act in the sense of $A \subseteq B$, not only does this constitute incompatibility, but, more radically, irreducibility, for the 70% : 30% ratio cannot be completely reduced to 'yes' and 'no' outcomes for a single individual. Even the single individuals change their preference from $-A \subseteq B$ to $A \subseteq B$ and vice versa, during the questioning period. The whole situation can be represented as follows (P = prefers):

70% $L_E P L_F \rightarrow L_Y P L_X = -A \subseteq B,$

30% $L_F P L_E \rightarrow L_Y P L_X = A \subseteq B.$

Accordingly, no strict deterministic behavioral one-to-one implication as defined by Axiom (A0) holds even between a single individual's value statements or preferential acts, with the result that smeared or fuzzy intervals are obtained. Irreducibility itself has been confirmed, interestingly by the Savage case, in which the single individual (Savage) changed his preferences. Needless to say the vNM system does not permit smeared or fuzzy intervals (outcomes) and thus the paradox arises within the von Neumann–Morgenstern axiomatization. From a systematic and structural point of view it must be noted that the intuitive manipulation or change of a behavioristic deterministic preference system, such as that noted in the Allais paradox[20] above, does not lead to a dissolution of behavioristic value theory, but has a certain well definable impact on the structure of this theory. Thus the situation that intuitive, or in Feigl's sense, mentalistic preferences may establish a completely chaotic situation which is beyond methodological control is avoided. Indeed, it is possible to define the limits of any intuitive or mentalistic 'generalization' of behavioristic value or preference theories by a certain leeway or range of deviation or dispersion.

The following definitions of incompatible values of a value state description refer exclusively to future possible and mentally manipulatable prospects and to non-classical incompatible state descriptions of irreducible character. Moreover, the introduction of irreducible values imposes an irreducible (intuitive) probabilistic character on our theory by restricting the classical multiplication theorem of probability.

Incompatible state descriptions of future or possible prospects may be defined, if the following empirical conditions are given, as follows:

(1) Prospects or preferences are possible – or future ones – and do not denote any actual preference patterns of the past; then and only then, they are intuitively manipulatable.

(2) There have to exist at least two possible preference statements or possible prospects, which form a sufficient and characteristic description of possible and future value states or outcomes – at least in mente.

(3) Since a complete independency between the agent and values and in between the values is no longer guaranteed, we obtain incompatible possible preferences or values-typical intuitive values. Hence, instead of compatible and sharp 'yes' or 'no' values, smeared intervals, Δv_i's, or fuzzy values, occur for the possible outcomes (predictions) influenced and determined by the intuitive factors (F). Consequently, we obtain:

$$F_1\alpha_1 x_1, F_2\alpha_2 x_2, \ldots, F_n\alpha_n x_n \quad \text{instead of} \quad \alpha_1 x_1, \alpha_2 x_2, \ldots, \alpha_n x_n.$$

The commas symbolize the 'and' or 'plus' connection. Future distributions are given by the condition c of uncertainty:

$$F_1 \times F_2 \times \cdots \times F_n = c,$$

where c is a constant, viz. the width of intuitive manipulatability, or change. This means that interdependency is symbolized by the product of all factors amounting to a certain constant, c, which is again dependent upon how the individual estimates his future situation. The width of c is therefore characteristic of the total leeway of manipulatability expressed by the product of the F_i's. This formulation expresses a generalized uncertainty condition[21] or relation with respect to the possible interdependency of the, in mente, mutually interdependent possible preferences or intuitive values. This strongest condition of intuitive manipulatability may be considerably weakened by the following considerations:

The experimentally determined degree to which possible values are manipulated around an average by individuals may be called the manipulation dispersion of intuitive values. The degree of dispersion expresses the average freedom (leeway) of manipulatability and is at the same time a measure of the deviation from the ex post deterministic naturalistic (behavioristic) vNM value behavior of the maximization of prospects. For example, the range may be given simply by quoting the smallest and the largest numbers. The mean deviation or average manipulation dispersion of possible x's: $x_1, x_2, \ldots, x_n$ may be defined by: $(x - \bar{x})$ where $\bar{x}$ is the arithmetic mean of the values and $(x_j - \bar{x})$ is the absolute measure of the deviation of x_j from $\bar{x}$.

The standard deviation of a set N of values: $x_1, x_2, \ldots, x_n$ is denoted by s and is defined by:

$$\sqrt{(x - \bar{x})^2} \quad \text{or} \quad \sqrt{\Sigma x^2 / N},$$

where x represents the deviations of each of the values: x_j from the mean $\bar{x}$. Thus s is the root-mean-square of the deviations from the mean or the root-mean-square deviations. Dispersion free states may be pure states or mixtures.

To conclude, a few remarks concerning the intuitive manipulation of values are offered. The 'maintenance' of previously established behavioristically given values for purposes of predictions has been discussed in the first part of this paper. But the most interesting case of the intuitive manipulation of values occurs when values, derived from one's past behavior, are 'rearranged'. This intuitive manipulation of values cannot occur without a behavioristic pre-ordering of values upon which this manipulation can take place. From this point of view, a wide variety of value-changes belong to the category of intuitive value manipulation, which are very well known in standard literature. It seems that most of them can be reduced to intuitive manipulations.

One group of intuitive manipulations of values may be that which has been very often believed to be the result of using subjective probabilities. But we agree with the 'antisubjectivists', e.g. Menges,[22] and others, that in these situations the subjective factor (element) is a consequence of the intuitive manipulation of values rather than the result of using subjective probabilities. In most cases, it is not the probabilities but the values that have been subjectively altered.

Another group of intuitive manipulations of values includes all those situations in which personalistic criteria are used in statistical decision making. Some of these criteria are: Savage's minimax regret criterion, Hurwicz's optimism parameters, as well as the intermediate decision criteria proposed by Hodges and Lehmann, Menges, Behara and Schneeweiss.[23]

The final group of intuitive manipulations of values includes a variety of attempts to specify the psychological factors influencing these situations. Among these attempts are Fishburn's[24] use of the degree of optimism and pessimism, or in microeconomics the role of the risk-loving or risk-averting businessman. But that is exactly what the intuitive group, or the Allais school, means, when they speak about psychological factors involved in the intuitive manipulation of values. Their contributions have been extensively discussed in this paper.

Finally, the main problem concerning the intuitive manipulation of values will become clear if one remembers that the intuitive manipulation of values is a 'subjective' superimposition upon the well-known behavioristic methods. What is required is that a reasonable limit of dispersion, for the range of dispersion, be established which would permit a reasonably good computation of value predictions within a given range of uncertainty c.

ACKNOWLEDGEMENTS

We would like to thank Professor O. Morgenstern for having read the paper and for helpful comments. We are also indebted to the Research Council of the University of Nebraska for financial support of the paper.

University of Nebraska

NOTES AND BIBLIOGRAPHY

[1] To this group belong amongst others: Epicurus, D. Hume, J. Bentham, J. S. Mill, K. Marx with his labor value theory, F. Brentano, the early Meinong, B. Russel, the Vienna Circle, A. J. Ayer, J. Dewey, Ch. J. Stevenson, M. Heidegger, the modern utility theorists, especially its founders: J. von Neumann, O. Morgenstern, J. Marshak, K. Menger, K. Borch, L. J. Savage, et al.

[2] To this group belong amongst others: Plato, Aquinas, J. G. Fichte, G. W. Hegel, the later Meinong, F. Nietzsche, the value theoretical Neo-Kantianism: W. Windelband, H. Rickert, H. Münsterberg, N. Hartmann, A. Weber, R. M. Toulmin, J. G. Urmson, R. W. Sellars, P. H. Nowell Smith, the intuitive school of value theory: M. Allais, O. Hagen, et al.

[3] F. Kant, H. Rickert; G. E. Moore (in *Principia Ethica*, 1903).

[4] F.e.: Braithewaite, R. B., *Theory of Games as a Tool for the Moral Philosopher*, Cambridge, 1955, Dobb, M. H., *Welfare Economics and the Economics of Socialism*, Cambridge, 1969, Harsanyi, J. C., 'Cardinal Welfare, Individualistic Ethics, and Interpersonal Comparison of Utility', *Journal of Political Economy*, Vol. 63, (1955) pp.309–321, Schick F., 'A Justification of Reason', *Journal of Philosophy*, Vol. 69, (1972), pp.835–840: Sen, A. K., *Collective Choice and Social Welfare*, Edinburgh, 1970, Leinfellner, W., 'A New Epitheoretical Analysis of Social Theories'. In W. Leinfellner and

E. Köhler (Eds.), *Developments in the Methodology of Social Science*, Dordrecht, 1974, pp.3–43, exp. pp.27–40.

[5] The formalistic point of view has its most famous representatives in: P. Suppes and J. L. Zinnes., 'Basic Measurement Theory'. In D. Luce, R. R. Bush and E. Galanter (Eds.), *Handbook of Mathematical Psychology*, New York, 1967, Vol. 1, pp.1–76.

[6] See von Neumann, J., and Morgenstern, O., *Theory of Games and Economic Behavior*, 3rd edn., Princeton, 1953, pp.26–29: Marschak, J., *Probability in the Social Sciences*, Dordrecht, 1974, pp.82–84: Leinfellner, W., 'A Generalization of Classical Decision Theory'. In K. Borch and J. Mossin (Eds.), *Risk and Uncertainty*, New York, 1968, pp.198–202.

[7] Fleming, M., 'A Cardinal Concept of Welfare', *Quarterly Journal of Economics*, LXVI (1952) pp.366–84: Goodman, L. and Markowitz, H., 'Social Welfare Functions Based on Individual Rankings', *Am. Journ. of Sociology*, Vol. LVIII, 1952, Harsanyi, see Note 4.

[8] MacCrimmon, K. R., 'Implications of Decision-theory Postulates'. In K. Borch and J. Mossin (Eds.), *Risk and Uncertainty*, New York, 1968, pp.3–32, especially pp.11–15, 20–22.

[9] Fishburn, P. C., 'Weak Qualitative Probability on Finite Sets', *Ann. Math. Stat.* 40, (1969) 2118–2126: Skala H. J., *Non Archimedian Utility Theory*, Chapter 5.

[10] Göttinger, H. W., 'Towards Fuzzy Reasoning in the Behavioral Sciences'. In W. Leinfellner and W. Köhler, *Developments in the Methodology of Social Science*, D. Reidel, Dordrecht, 1974, pp.287–307.

[11] Suppes, P., 'What is a Scientific Theory'. In *Philosophy of Science Today*, New Basic Books, 1967, pp.55–67. See the discussion of the formalistic view by Suppe, F., 'Theories and Phenomena'. In W. Leinfellner and E. Köhler (Eds.), *Developments in the Methodology of Social Science*, D. Reidel, Dordrecht, 1974, pp.45–55.

[12] This part of the article is taken from a research work, sponsored by the Research Council of the University of Nebraska, of W. Leinfellner, E. Leinfellner and E. Booth. The results will be published in the forthcoming book, Leinfellner W., *Philosophy of Social Science*, see also W. Leinfellner and E. Leinfellner, *Ontology, System Theory and Semantics*, Duncker and Humblot, Berlin, 1978 (in German): E. Booth, *Foundations of Value Theory* (diss). The ideas expressed in this chapter are partly generalizations of: Birkhoff, G., 'Lattice Theory', *Am. Math. Soc. Colloqu. Publ.* XXV 3rd edn. 1967; Piron C., 'Thèse de Piron', *Helvetica Physica Acta*, Vol. 37, Fasc. 4/5 pp.439–468, 1964: Jauch J. M., *Foundations of Quantum Mechanics*, Addison Wesley, Massachusetts, 1968: Randall C. H., and Foulis, D. J., 'An approach to Empirical Logic' *Amer. Math. Month.* 77, 1970, pp.363–374.

[13] See Note 12, Randall and Foulis.

[14] von Neumann, J., and Morgenstern, O., *Theory of Games and Economic Behavior*, 3rd edn., Princeton, 1953, pp.26–27: Marschak, J., 'Probability in the Social Sciences', *Selected Essays of J. Marschak*, Reidel, Dordrecht, 1974, Vol. 1, pp.82–84.

[15] Allais, M., 'The Foundations of a Positive Theory of Choice Involving Risk and a Criticism of the Postulates and Axioms of the American School', Centre d'Analyse Economique, No. 2824, pp.26–38. Also Part II of this volume.

Allais, M., 'Le Comportement de l'Homme Rationnel devant le Risque Critique des Postulates et Axiomes de l'Ecole Americaine', *Econometrica*, Vol. 21, No. 4, 1953, p.2.

[16] Savage, L. J., *The Foundations of Statistics*, New York, J. Wiley, pp.101–3.

[17] Booth, E., 'Attempted Resolution of the "Allais" Paradox', *Transactions of the Nebraska Academy of Sciences*, Vol. II, 1973, pp.94–104.

[18] Hagen, O., 'Separation of Cardinal Utility and Specific Utility of Risk in Theory of Choices under Uncertainty', *Statsokonomisk Tidsskrift*, No. 3, 1969. 'A New Axiomatization of Utility under Risk' *Theorie A Metoda* IV/2, 1972.

[19] Allais, M., 'La Psychologie de l'Homme Rationnel devant le Risk', *J. Societ. Statist.*, Paris, 1953, pp.47–72.

[20] Borch, K., 'The Allais Paradox: A Comment', *Behavioral Science* 13(6), pp. 488–489.

[21] Leinfellner, W., *Erkentnis and Wissenschaftstheorie*, B. I. Hochschultaschenbuch Nr. 41, 1967, 2nd edn. p.111n: Leinfellner W., and Leinfellner, E., *Ontologie, Systemtheorie und Semantik*, Duncker und Humblot, Berlin, 1978: Gottinger, H. W., and Leinfellner, W. (Eds.), *Decision Theory and Social Ethics*, Dordrecht-Boston, 1978.

[22] Menges, G., 'Objective Theory of Inductive Behavior'. In G. Menges (Ed.), *Information, Inference and Decision*, D. Reidel, Dordrecht, 1974, pp.3, 19, 21f, 45.

[23] See summary of criteria in Leinfellner, W., 'A New Epitheoretical Analysis of Social Theories'. In W. Leinfellner and E. Köhler (Eds.), *Developments in the Methodology of Social Science*, D. Reidel, Dordrecht, 1974, pp.3–45, esp. pp.37–40.

[24] Fishburn, P.C., *Decision and Value Theory*, J. Wiley, New York, 1964, pp.97, 195.

KENNETH R. MacCRIMMON AND STIG LARSSON

UTILITY THEORY: AXIOMS VERSUS 'PARADOXES'

ABSTRACT. Few attempts have yet been made to interrelate the major axiom systems of expected utility theory such as those presented by von Neumann–Morgenstern, Marschak, Savage, and Arrow. This paper attempts to consolidate the theoretical and empirical research on these axioms by showing the correspondences among the major axioms of each system and highlighting their similarities and differences in dealing with concepts such as probability and utility.

Allais, Ellsberg, and others have proposed decision problems which are designed to elicit choices which violate the utility axioms. To the extent that people accept the axioms, choices which violate the axioms can be considered 'paradoxical'. Whether people make such choices is an empirical matter, and we therefore investigate the rate of violation in previous and new experimental studies. Our results show that although there is considerable violation of the utility axioms, the rate can fall drastically as the probability and pay-off parameters are varied away from critical levels.

To provide a better understanding of the implications of the axioms and their relationship to some of the decision 'paradoxes', we have stated the implications as 'rules'. Since the subjects were asked to rate the appeal of each rule as a decision norm, we can determine the relative attractiveness of each rule and can show the relationship between subjects' actual choices and their agreement with the rules which guide choice. We found that people often prefer rules which contradict choices they have made.

1. INTRODUCTION

Since Bernoulli (1738), the standard criterion for rational decision-making in uncertain environments has been the maximization of expected utility. Presumably you should maximize expected utility because you will be sorry if you do not. If you are not convinced by this argument, you can turn to the axiomatic investigations initiated by Ramsey (1926) and von Neumann–Morgenstern (1947). They independently showed that expected utility can be justified on the basis of a set of relatively simple axioms. The virtue of this approach is that it allows you to obtain a better understanding of what underlies the acceptance of the rule of maximizing expected utility. If you accept all the axioms, then you are logically compelled to accept the maximization of expected utility as the choice criterion; but if you reject one or more of the axioms, then expected utility does not necessarily follow. How do you tell, though, whether to accept a

333

Maurice Allais and Ole Hagen (eds.), Expected Utility and the Allais Paradox, 333–409.
Copyright © 1979 by D. Reidel Publishing Company.

particular axiom? One way would be to study carefully the mathematical statement of the axiom and to think through its implications. An easier way might be to try to generate decision problems to see if the choices you would want to make, even upon careful reflection, would violate the axiom. To facilitate this latter approach, various problems have been constructed as challenges to the implications of the axioms. The more compelling of these problems have been called 'paradoxes'. By studying how you, and other 'reasonable' people, respond to these 'paradoxes', you may have a better basis for deciding whether to accept the axioms, and hence expected utility theory.

In considering axioms, though, you should realize that there is not a single set of axioms that will uniquely imply the maximization of expected utility. One can make different assumptions about the underlying sets of events or actions, about the existence of probabilities, etc., and hence end up with different sets of axioms. We would expect, however, that these sets of axioms would bear some close resemblances to each other. Even though a number of prominent sets of axioms have been proposed, little attention seems to have been directed toward comparing these sets with each other. As a preliminary to examining the utility theory axioms, then, it is necessary to look at some of the interrelationships among various sets of axioms. We shall focus on the axioms of von Neumann–Morgenstern, Marschak, Savage, and Arrow since, as we shall see, the four make different assumptions about which set their axioms are defined upon.

A number of the axioms deal with existence rather than preference and are of little interest. Within the preference class there are ordering axioms, continuity axioms and independence axioms.[1] Again, we shall devote little attention to the former groups, reserving our emphasis for axioms having the strongest practical relevance – those asserting *independence* between beliefs and values. For these axioms we shall pull together the most compelling 'paradoxes'. The relationship between particular 'paradoxes' and particular axioms has not always been made clear so we shall look at this in the process of describing the implications of various sets of choices in the 'paradoxes'. Choices violating axioms can be interpreted variously as implying that probabilities (satisfying the standard conditions) or utilities cannot exist, and we shall consider these, and other interpretations. Then we shall examine the existing empirical evidence on the extent to which the axiom or the 'paradox' is upheld. Finally, we shall report and discuss the results of a new empirical study designed to investigate the violation of the axioms at various levels of probability and payoff parameter values. In addition to results on the behavior of people for 'paradox' problems, we report information on the degree to which they find axiom versus 'counter-axiom' rules compelling and how these attitudes relate to their actual choices.

In Section 2, we give some basic notation, then we state and compare the main axiom systems of interest. Section 3 provides a transition by introducing rules which are implication of the axioms. In Sections 4–8, we present the strongest 'paradoxes' and examine the implications of particular sets of choices for the axioms. Existing and new empirical evidence is then considered. In Section 9, we examine some additional, important independence axioms in the light of the strongest challenges to them. Section 10 is the summary and conclusion.

2. UTILITY AXIOMS

2.1 BASIC NOTATION

The definitions and notation below will be used to state each of the axiom systems to be considered.

Probability space. Let (Ω, θ, μ) be a given probability space. Ω is the state space consisting of states ω. θ is a σ-algebra of subsets of Ω; an element of θ will be denoted as B and called an event. μ is a probability measure. For a given $B \in \theta$ we will denote the conditional probability of μ by μ_B.

Reward space. Let (R, Ψ) be a measurable space where R is an arbitrary set called the reward set, elements of R will be denoted by r. Ψ is a σ-algebra containing the set $\{r\}$ for all $r \in R$.

Function space. Let Γ be the set of all measurable functions from Ω to R.

Action space. Let A be an index set such that there exists a one-to-one mapping from A to Γ. For a given $a \in A$ we will denote the corresponding function in Γ by $f(\cdot, a)$. The set A is called the action set. For any subset A_0 of A we will denote the corresponding subset of Γ by Γ_{A_0}. For a given $B \in \theta$, the restriction of $f \in \Gamma$ to B will be denoted by f_B, i.e., $f(\omega, a) = f_B(\omega, a)$ for all $\omega \in B$.

Induced probability measure. For each function $f \in \Gamma$, a probability measure can be induced on (R, Ψ) by $P(C, a) = \mu\{\omega: f(\omega, a) \in C\}$ for all $C \in \Psi$, and let Π_{A_0} denote the set $\{P(\cdot, a): a \in A_0\}$. Similarly, we denote $P_B(C, a) = \mu_B\{\omega: f(\omega, a) \in C\}$ for all $C \in \Psi$.

Preference ordering. By a complete ordering on a set Z, we mean a binary relation, denoted by $\overset{Z}{\lesssim}$,[2] satisfying:

(1) for any $x, y \in Z$, either $x \overset{Z}{\lesssim} y$ or $y \overset{Z}{\lesssim} x$, and

(2) for $x, y, w \in Z$ and $x \overset{Z}{\lesssim} y$, $y \overset{Z}{\lesssim} w$, then $x \overset{Z}{\lesssim} w$.

Strict preference $x \overset{Z}{<} y$ is defined as $x \overset{Z}{\lesssim} y$ and not $y \overset{Z}{\lesssim} x$. Indifference, $x \overset{Z}{\sim} y$ is defined as $x \overset{Z}{\lesssim} y$ and $y \overset{Z}{\lesssim} x$. An ordering $\lesssim$ is called hereditary if for any subset Y of Z, $x \overset{Y}{\lesssim} y$ if and only if $x \overset{Z}{\lesssim} y$ for all $x, y \in Y$.

Utility functions. Given a complete ordering on A (or on Γ or on R or on Π), a utility function U is a real valued function defined such that

$$a_1 \overset{A}{\lesssim} a_2 \quad \text{if and only if} \quad E\{U(f(\cdot, a_1))\} \leqslant E\{U(f(\cdot, a_2))\},$$

where E is the expectation operator. For a particular reward $r \in R$, the number $U(r)$ is called the utility of r. If U is a utility function then $V = \alpha U + \beta$ is a utility function for any real numbers α, $\beta (\alpha > 0)$, since $E(V) = \alpha E(U) + \beta$. Any theorem stating the assumptions for the existence of U will be called an expected utility theorem.

Various sets of assumptions or axioms can be postulated from which the expected utility theorem can be derived. The differences in these approaches are due to particular assumptions made about the probability space and about the space on which preference is defined. We shall consider four of the most prominent approaches here. Each represents a different assumption about the space of preference orderings:

(1) von Neumann–Morgenstern (1947) defines preference orderings on the set, R,

(2) Marschak (1950) defines preference orderings on the set of probability measures Π,

(3) Savage (1954) defines preference orderings on the set of functions, Γ, and

(4) Arrow (1971) defines preference orderings on the set of actions, A.

The von Neumann–Morgenstern and the Marschak axioms are

similar, so we shall consider them together in the next subsection, first stating the axioms of each, then comparing them. Also, the Savage and the Arrow axioms are similar to each other, so they shall be stated and compared in the following subsection. Then we shall compare the von Neumann–Morgenstern/Marschak types of independence conditions with those of Savage/Arrow.[3]

2.2 VON NEUMANN-MORGENSTERN AND MARSCHAK AXIOMS

Von Neumann–Morgenstern Axioms

The von Neumann–Morgenstern (1947) approach does not directly make any assumptions on the underlying probability space (Ω, θ, μ) or on Γ. They, however, assume that Π, the set of all induced probability measures on R, is equal to the set of all discrete probability measures on R. They induce an ordering on Π from an ordering on R. To present their approach, we need some new definitions.

Let $\Pi'' = (0, 1) \times R \times R$, and let F be a function from Π'' to R. The set Π'' can be thought of as the set of those induced probability measures on R which are non-zero for exactly two elements of R. The value, $F(\alpha, r_1, r_2) = r_3$ can be thought of as the reward $r_3 \in R$ which would make us indifferent between the gambles,[4]

(1)   receiving r_1 with probability α
       receiving r_2 with probability $1 - \alpha$
(2)   receiving r_3 with probability 1.

In what follows, it is assumed that $r_1, r_2, r_3 \in R$ and that α, β, γ are real numbers on $(0, 1)$.

*Axiom NM*1: $\overset{R}{\lesssim}$ is a complete hereditary ordering.

*Axiom NM*2: $r_1 \overset{R}{\lesssim} r_2$ implies $r_1 \overset{R}{\lesssim} F(\alpha, r_1, r_2)$ and $F(\alpha, r_1, r_2) \overset{R}{\lesssim} r_2$ for all $\alpha \in (0, 1)$.

*Axiom NM*3: $r_1 \overset{R}{\lesssim} r_3 \overset{R}{\lesssim} r_2$ implies the existence of an $\alpha \in (0, 1)$ and a $\beta \in (0, 1)$ with $F(\alpha, r_1, r_2) \overset{R}{\lesssim} r_3$ and $r_3 \overset{R}{\lesssim} F(\beta, r_1, r_2)$.

*Axiom NM*4: $F(\alpha, r_1, r_2) \overset{R}{=} F(1 - \alpha, r_2, r_1)$,
$F(\alpha, F(\beta, r_1, r_2), r_2) \overset{R}{=} F(\alpha\beta, r_1, r_2)$.

These assumptions are sufficient to prove that a real valued function U exists such that

$$r_1 \overset{R}{\lesssim} r_2 \text{ implies } U(r_1) < U(r_2)$$

and

$$U(F(\alpha, r_1, r_2)) = \alpha U(r_1) + (1 - \alpha)U(r_2).$$

Marschak Axioms

Marschak (1950) was the first to adopt an approach of establishing an ordering on the probability measures. Samuelson (1952), Herstein and Milnor (1954) and other authors have also adopted this formulation. The axioms we shall give here are essentially the same as Jensen's (1964) axioms, and he has shown them to imply Marschak's axioms.

In this approach also, we ignore the underlying probability space since all assumptions are based on the induced probability measures. R is assumed to be a finite set.[5] Π is the set of all probability measures on R.

*Axiom M*1: $\overset{\Pi}{\lesssim}$ is a complete, hereditary ordering.

*Axiom M*2: If $P_1, P_2, P_3 \in \Pi$ and $P_1 \overset{\Pi}{\lesssim} P_2$, then for any real number $\alpha \in (0, 1)$,

$$\alpha P_1 + (1 - \alpha)P_3 \overset{\Pi}{\lesssim} \alpha P_2 + (1 - \alpha)P_3.$$

*Axiom M*3: If $P_1 \overset{\Pi}{\lesssim} P_2 \overset{\Pi}{\lesssim} P_3$ then there exist real numbers $\alpha, \beta \in (0, 1)$ such that

$$\alpha P_1 + (1 - \alpha)P_3 \overset{\Pi}{\lesssim} P_2 \quad \text{and} \quad P_2 \overset{\Pi}{\lesssim} \beta P_1 + (1 - \beta)P_3.$$

These three assumptions are sufficient to derive a utility function.

Von Neumann–Morgenstern/Marschak Comparison

It is easy to see that the von Neumann–Morgenstern and Marschak approaches are closely related since they both effectively consider orderings on probability distributions. Marschak's axioms do this directly while von Neumann–Morgenstern's axioms have the same effect by forcing the function F to satisfy similar conditions. Axiom M1 is stronger than Axiom vNM1 since R can be considered as a subset of P. In the Marschak approach, it is assumed that you can evaluate not only preferences on R but also complex probabilities on R. Hence Axiom vNM1 is less subject to criticisms of the possibility of complete orderings such as those of Aumann (1962).

Axiom M2 has been called the strong independence axiom by Samuelson (1952). Corresponding to the vNM approach, a function F

from $(0, 1) \times \Pi \times \Pi$ to Π could have been defined, such that $F(\alpha, P_1, P_2) = \alpha P_1 + (1 - \alpha)P_2$. In contrast to the vNM, the mathematical symbols are not confusing and have their usual meaning since we are dealing with combinations of probabilities rather than with combinations of rewards. The expression $\alpha P_1 + (1 - \alpha)P_2$ can also be interpreted in terms of gambles, similar to the vNM interpretation of the r combinations. It reflects a probability α of receiving the gamble P_1 and a probability $(1 - \alpha)$ of receiving the gamble P_2. By equating this meaning to the probability combination meaning, it implies that "it's no fun to gamble".

Axiom M3 is similar to Axiom vNM3 but note that the definition of it in terms of R in Axioms vNM3 and vNM2 requires that between every pair of rewards $r_1, r_2 \in R$ such that $r_1 \overset{R}{<} r_2$ there exists a reward r_3 such that $r_1 \overset{R}{<} r_3 \overset{R}{<} r_2$ and hence R cannot be finite.

2.3 SAVAGE AND ARROW AXIOMS

Savage Axioms

Savage (1954) starts with an underlying probability space (Ω, θ, μ). The theory does not hold, however, for an arbitrary probability space. There are restrictions on the cardinality of Ω (Axiom S6) and R must contain all subsets. The probability μ is not explicitly defined but is derived from preference relations on subsets of Ω.

Axiom S1: $\overset{r}{\leq}$ is a complete hereditary ordering.

Axiom S2: If $f_B(\cdot, a) = f_B(\cdot, b), \quad f_B(\cdot, c) = f_B(\cdot, d),$
$\qquad f_{\bar{B}}(\cdot, a) = f_{\bar{B}}(\cdot, c), \quad f_{\bar{B}}(\cdot, b) = f_{\bar{B}}(\cdot, d),$
$\qquad$ and $f(\cdot, a) \overset{r}{\leq} f(\cdot, b),$
$\qquad$ then $f(\cdot, c) \overset{r}{\leq} f(\cdot, d).$

Axiom S3: Let $f(\cdot, a) = r_1$ and $f(\cdot, b) = r_2$.
$\qquad$ If $f_B(\cdot, c) = f_B(\cdot, a), \quad f_B(\cdot, d) = f_B(\cdot, b),$
$\qquad$ and $f_{\bar{B}}(\cdot, c) = f_{\bar{B}}(\cdot, d),$
$\qquad$ then $f(\cdot, a) \overset{r}{\leq} f(\cdot, b)$ if and only if
$\qquad\qquad f(\cdot, c) \overset{r}{\leq} f(\cdot, d),$
for all $B \subset \Omega$ such that B is not null.[6]

Axiom S4: If $B, C \subset \Omega$ and $r_i \in R$, $i = 1, 2, 3, 4$, $r_1 > r_2$, $r_3 > r_4$, $a, b, c, d \in A$, and
$$f_B(\cdot, a) = r_1, \qquad f_{\bar{B}}(\cdot, a) = r_2,$$
$$f_C(\cdot, b) = r_1, \qquad f_{\bar{C}}(\cdot, b) = r_2,$$

$$f_B(\cdot, c) = r_3, \qquad f_{\bar B}(\cdot, c) = r_4,$$
$$f_C(\cdot, d) = r_3, \qquad f_{\bar C}(\cdot, d) = r_4,$$
$$\text{and } f(\cdot, a) \overset{\Gamma}{\leqslant} f(\cdot, b),$$
$$\text{then } f(\cdot, c) \leqslant f(\cdot, d).$$

Axiom S5: There is at least one pair of rewards $r_1, r_2 \in R$ such that

$$f(\cdot, a) = r_1 \overset{\Gamma}{<} f(\cdot, b) = r_2.$$

Axiom S6: If $f(\cdot, a) \overset{\Gamma}{<} f(\cdot, b)$ and r is any reward in R, then there exists a partition P of Ω, such that for any $B \in P$

$$f_B(\cdot, c) = r \quad \text{and} \quad f_{\bar B}(\cdot, c) = f_{\bar B}(\cdot, a)$$

implies $f(\cdot, c) \overset{\Gamma}{<} f(\cdot, b),$
and $f_B(\cdot, d) = r \quad \text{and} \quad f_{\bar B}(\cdot, d) = f_{\bar B}(\cdot, b)$
implies $f(\cdot, a) \overset{\Gamma}{<} f(\cdot, d).$

These six axioms are sufficient to guarantee a probability P and a function U such that the expected utility preserves the ordering when the consequences are finite. To extend the result to infinite consequences a seventh axiom is needed, but we will not use it here.

Arrow's Axioms

Arrow (1971) does not make the restrictions on the probability space, (Ω, θ, μ), that Savage does but his overall approach is similar to Savage's.

Axiom A1: $\overset{A}{<}$ is a complete, hereditary ordering.

Axiom A2: Given $a, b \in A$ where $b \overset{A}{<} a$, a consequence $r \in R$, and $\{E^i\}$ a sequence such that $E^{i+1} \subset E^i$ with $\bigcap_i E_i = \emptyset$. Define actions $a^i \in A$, $b^i \in A$ by

$$f_{\bar E^i}(\cdot, a^i) = f_{\bar E^i}(\cdot, a), \qquad f_{E^i}(\cdot, a^i) = c,$$
$$f_{\bar E^i}(\cdot, b^i) = f_{\bar E^i}(\cdot, b), \qquad f_{E^i}(\cdot, b^i) = c,$$

then for all i sufficiently large $b \overset{A}{<} a^i$ and $b^i \overset{A}{<} a$.

Axiom A3: For given E, $\overset{A}{<}$ satisfies Axiom A2 such that any two actions $a, b \in A$ where $f_E(\cdot, a) = f_E(\cdot, b)$ will be indifferent given E. This is denoted as $a \overset{A}{\doteq} b \,|\, E$. Weak preference is denoted as $a \overset{A}{\leqslant} b \,|\, E$ and strict preference as $a \overset{Ai}{<} b \,|\, E$.

Axiom A4: Let P be a partition. Given two actions $a, b \in A$, if, for every $E \in P$, $b \overset{A}{\leqslant} a \mid E$, then $b \overset{A}{\leqslant} a$. If in addition, there is a collection P' of events in P, whose union is non-null, such that $b \overset{A}{<} a \mid E$, $E \in P'$, then $b \overset{A}{<} a$.

Axiom A5: If $a, b, c, d \in A$ and

$$f(\omega_1, a) = f(\omega_2, b), \qquad f(\omega_1, c) = f(\omega_2, d),$$

$c \overset{A}{<} a \mid \omega_1$ implies $d \overset{A}{<} b \mid \omega_2$.

Axiom A6:[7] The probability distribution of states of the world is atomless. If the probability distribution of consequences is the same for two actions, they are indifferent.

Savage/Arrow Comparison

Since there is a one-to-one mapping between A and Γ, many of Savage's axioms can be directly translated to those of Arrow. For example, Axioms S1 and A1 are identical. Axiom S2 is called the sure-thing principle by Savage and is his most controversial assumption. Arrow's Axioms A3 and A4 are closely related to S2. Axiom A3 establishes the concept of conditional preference and Axiom A4 uses this concept to establish an unconditional preference based on dominance in conditional preference. Both these notions are found in Axiom S2. The relationship can be seen by writing S2 in the notation of actions as:

$$a \overset{A}{\doteqdot} b \mid B, \qquad c \overset{A}{\doteqdot} d \mid B,$$
$$a \overset{A}{\doteqdot} c \mid \bar{B}, \qquad b \overset{A}{\doteqdot} d \mid \bar{B}$$

and $a \overset{A}{\leqslant} b$. then $c \overset{A}{\leqslant} d$.

Note that by Arrow's Axioms A3 and A4, $a \overset{A}{\leqslant} b$ implies $a \overset{A}{\leqslant} b \mid \bar{B}$. Since $\{B, \bar{B}\}$ form a partition of Ω, by transitivity we have

$$a \overset{A}{\doteqdot} c \mid \bar{B} < b \overset{A}{\doteqdot} d \mid \bar{B}.$$

Arrow's Axiom A2 is called monotone continuity and has no direct equivalence in Savage's system but is related to Savage's S6. Axiom S5 which asserts that two rewards can be found such that one is strictly preferred to the other is completely innocuous and is taken for granted by Arrow. Axioms S3 and A5 are very similar and are needed to relate the choice on actions to the associated rewards.

The main difference between the Arrow and Savage approaches is embodied in Savage's S4 and Arrow's A6. Axiom S4 yields an ordering on subsets of Ω from the ordering on Γ and additionally it establishes the independence of this ordering from the particular rewards. It thus provides the crucial linkage needed to infer probabilities. Axiom A6, however, introduces probability directly and diverges sharply from Savage's approach. When this axiom is introduced, it is not clear what advantage Arrow gains by having the preference ordering on actions rather than on probability distributions directly. When Arrow replaces Axiom A6 by other axioms (see Note 7), his approach becomes similar to Savage's. For the correspondence to another important axiom system, that of Luce and Krantz (1971), see Larsson (1978).

2.4 COMPARISONS BETWEEN THE VON NEUMANN–MORGENSTERN/MARSCHAK AND THE SAVAGE AXIOMS

As we have seen, the correspondence between the von Neumann–Morgenstern axioms and the Marschak axioms is very close. The Savage axioms and Arrow axioms differ, however, in some key respects. Hence the comparisons we shall emphasize in this section are between vNM/M axioms and the S axioms.

Ordering Comparisons

Objections to the completeness of orderings of preference are more serious for S1/A1 than for vNM1/M1 since the cardinality of Γ and A is greater than the cardinality of R and Π. For the same reason, the transitivity of Γ and A is more open to challenge.

Probability Comparisons

Although we noted above some similarities between the Savage and Arrow approaches, the Savage axioms are unique in an important sense – no probabilities are initially assumed. Savage deals directly with events B and hence his approach can be applied to the following problem:

> Let Urn I contain 100 red and black balls but the exact composition is unknown. Urn II contains 50 red balls and 50 black balls. Would you prefer gamble 1 or 2?

(1) $1000 if a black ball is drawn from Urn I.
(2) $1000 if a black ball is drawn from Urn II.

With the other 3 approaches this would be an incompletely specified problem since we are not given the probabilities of drawing a black ball from Urn I, or from Urn II for that matter.

Since Savage's approach infers beliefs from preferences on actions (or more specifically, functions), it is important that these beliefs satisfy the standard probability axioms,[8] since the other approaches do by definition. The relation $\leqslant$ ('is not more probable than') on sets in R must satisfy the following axioms:

Axiom of ordering

(1)   if $A \in \theta, B \in \theta$, then either $A \overset{.}{\leqslant} B$ or $B \overset{.}{\leqslant} A$;

(2)   for any set $A \in \theta$, $A \overset{.}{\leqslant} A$;

(3)   if $A \overset{.}{\leqslant} B$ and $B \overset{.}{\leqslant} C$, then $A \overset{.}{\leqslant} C$;

(4) $\phi \overset{.}{<} \Omega$ and for any event A, $\phi \overset{.}{\leqslant} A \overset{.}{\leqslant} \Omega$.

We define $\overset{.}{<}$ ('is strictly less probable than') and $\overset{.}{=}$ ('is equiprobable with') in the usual way by:

$$A \overset{.}{<} B \text{ implies } A \overset{.}{\leqslant} B \text{ and not } B \overset{.}{\leqslant} A,$$
$$A \overset{.}{=} B \text{ implies } A \overset{.}{\leqslant} B \text{ and } B \overset{.}{\leqslant} A.$$

Axiom of monotony

(1)   if $B_1 \cap B_2 \equiv \emptyset$, $A_1 \overset{.}{\leqslant} B_1$ and $A_2 \overset{.}{\leqslant} B_2$,
        then $A_1 \cup A_2 \overset{.}{\leqslant} B_1 \cup B_2$,

(2)   if $B_1 \cap B_2 \equiv \emptyset$, $A_1 \overset{.}{\leqslant} B_1$ and $A_2 \overset{.}{<} B_2$,
        then $A_1 \cup A_2 \overset{.}{<} B_1 \cup B_2$.

The relation $\overset{.}{\leqslant}$ satisfying the above axioms is called a qualitative probability on the algebra θ. Savage's Axioms 1–5 imply these axioms. He assumes the algebra to be all subsets of Ω. However, these axioms are not sufficient to guarantee σ-additivity of the corresponding probability measure. For σ-additivity we need the following axiom:

Axiom of monotone sequence

For every monotone sequence of events $A_n \uparrow A$ and an event B such that $A_n \overset{.}{\leqslant} B$, for all n, then $A \overset{.}{\leqslant} B$.

As Kraft, Pratt and Seidenberg (1959) showed, these axioms are still not sufficient to guarantee a probability measure; we need additionally, an axiom such as this:

Axiom of partition of event

Every event can be partitioned into two equally probable events.

Villegas (1964) showed under certain assumptions that this is equivalent to an axiom that there are no atoms. Savage's Axiom 6 is of this form. With the four axioms above, there exists a unique probability measure such that $A \overset{.}{\leqslant} B$ if and only if $P(A) \leqslant P(B)$.

The one remaining problem with the Savage approach is that his definition of θ as the set of all subsets may preclude a σ-additive probability measure. We could, however, restrict Savage's theory to a class of sets, a σ-algebra, and add the monotone sequence axiom to obtain a σ-additive probability (although it would not necessarily be defined on all subsets).

On the other hand, the von Neumann–Morgenstern, Marschak and Arrow approaches deal with σ-additive measures, since they start with axioms on the probabilities. Intermediate between these and Savage is the approach of Anscombe and Aumann (1964) who start with a specified probability space called a roulette lottery (corresponding to the situations covered by vNM/M/A) in which the probabilities of the outcomes are given. They then focus on events, called horse lotteries, for which probabilities are not known. By assumptions similar to Savage's (except for Axiom S4) they extend the probabilities, and hence the basis for choice, to horse lotteries. Although this can be viewed as a link between the two different approaches, since there are no distinctively new axioms in Anscombe and Aumann, we shall not consider the details of their formulation, but just use their format to indicate the way in which Savage can be related to the other approaches. Hence we shall next consider the specifics of the independence axioms in the various theories.

Independence Axiom Comparisons

By adding the monotonic sequence axiom and restricting the number of sets in the σ-algebra, we can compare the axioms. The main independence axioms are Savage's sure-thing principle, S2, and the strong independence axiom, M2. These axioms are closely related in that if Axiom S2 is not accepted, then Axiom M2 would not be accepted. Similarly, if Axiom M2 would not be accepted, a probability space and set of random variables exist such that Axiom S2 cannot be accepted.

This can be seen by writing the sure-thing principle in terms of probability distributions. Assuming $\mu(B) = \alpha$, where $\alpha > 0$ and $1 - \alpha > 0$, the induced probability measure of $f_B(\cdot, a)$ can be written as $P_B(\cdot, a)$; similarly $f_{\bar{B}}(\cdot, b)$ induces measure of $P_{\bar{B}}(\cdot, b)$ and so forth. We can also write

$$P(\cdot, a) = \alpha P_B(\cdot, a) + (1 - \alpha)P_{\bar{B}}(\cdot, a).$$

Thus Axiom S2 can be written as:

$$\text{if } \alpha P_B(\cdot, a) + (1 - \alpha)P_{\bar{B}}(\cdot, a) \overset{\Gamma}{\lessgtr} \alpha P_B(\cdot, a) + (1 - \alpha)P_{\bar{B}}(\cdot, b),$$
$$\text{then } \alpha P_B(\cdot, c) + (1 - \alpha)P_{\bar{B}}(\cdot, a) \overset{\Gamma}{\lessgtr} \alpha P_B(\cdot, d) + (1 - \alpha)P_{\bar{B}}(\cdot, b).$$

This is clearly implied by Axiom M2. Hence we cannot accept the strong independence axiom and reject the sure-thing principle.

Unfortunately, it is not true that if the strong independence axiom, M2, is rejected we must reject the sure-thing principle, S2. The difficulty is that the probability space (Ω, θ, μ), and the set of random variables Γ, to induce the probability distribution on the rewards, are not uniquely defined. However, there will exist some probability space (Ω, θ, μ) such that Axiom S2 is not accepted. To see this consider the inequality

$$\alpha P(\cdot, i) + (1 - \alpha)P(\cdot, j) \overset{\Pi}{\lessgtr} P(\cdot, k) + (1 - \alpha)P(\cdot, j).$$

Let (Ω, θ, P) be a probability space such that $f(\cdot, i)$, $f(\cdot, j)$ and $f(\cdot, k)$ are random variables inducing the probability measures $P(\cdot, i)$, $P(\cdot, j)$, and $P(\cdot, k)$ respectively. Let $([0, 1], B, \lambda)$ be the probability space, with B the Borel sets and λ the Lebesque measure. Let $(\Omega \times [0, 1], \theta, \mu)$ be the product space.

Then $\mu(B \times [0, \alpha]) = \alpha P(B)$, $B \in \Omega$. Define a rv $f(\cdot, a): \Omega \times [0, 1] \to R$ by

$$f((\omega_1, \omega_2), a) = \begin{cases} f(\omega_1, i) & \omega_2 \in [0, \alpha) \\ f(\omega_1, j) & \omega_2 \in [\alpha, 1] \end{cases}.$$

Then the induced measure of $f(\cdot, a)$ is

$$\alpha P(\cdot, i) + (1 - \alpha)P(\cdot, j).$$

Similarly, define a rv $f(\cdot, b): \Omega \times [0, 1] \to R$

$$f((\omega_1, \omega_2), b) = \begin{cases} f(\omega_1, k) & \omega_2 \in [0, \alpha) \\ f(\omega_1, j) & \omega_2 \in [\alpha, 1] \end{cases}.$$

Then $f(\cdot, b)$ induces the measure

$$\alpha P(\cdot, k) + (1 - \alpha)P(\cdot, j),$$

and

$$f((\omega_1, \omega_2), a) = f((\omega_1, \omega_2), b),$$

for all $(\omega_1 \omega_2) \in \Omega \times [\alpha, 1]$.

Hence, to order $f(\cdot, a)$ and $f(\cdot, b)$, we need only to consider the consequences derived from $\Omega \times [0, \alpha)$ or equivalently consider the probability measure $P(\cdot, i)$ and $P(\cdot, k)$.

Savage's Axiom S6 is very closely related to Axiom 3 in Marschak's approach, i.e., if $r_1 \overset{R}{<} r_2 \overset{R}{<} r_3$ then there exists a $B \subset \Omega$ such that $P(B) > 0$ and $X_B(\cdot, a) = r_1$, $X_{\bar{B}}(\cdot, a) = r_3$ and $X(\cdot, b) = r_2$, then $X(\cdot, a) \overset{\Gamma}{<} X(\cdot, b)$.

3. AXIOMS AND EXPERIMENTS

We have described the major axiom systems of expected utility theory for two reasons: (1) to interrelate the axioms of particular systems, and (2) to clarify which axioms are being challenged by particular 'paradoxes'. In the preceding section, we indicated some similarities and differences among the axioms proposed by various researchers. In subsequent sections of this paper, we shall consider the relationship between specific axioms and the decision problems that have been designed to challenge the acceptability of the axioms.

Since the axioms we have studied seem to have been presented as normative theories,[9] we cannot, strictly speaking, talk about actual behavior as challenging the theory. Whether people behave in accordance with the axioms or not is not of relevance for normative theory. However, if the normative theory requires behavior that no one is capable of performing, or if very intelligent decision makers choose in violation of the axioms when making choices they think carefully about, then we must ask whether our normative theory is of much use. It is in this sense, then, that we examine the descriptive relevance of the expected utility theories.

The independence conditions of expected utility theory have been subjected to considerable scrutiny. One particularly pointed form has been the construction of small decision problems in which the choices made may be in conformity with particular independence axioms or may be in violation of such axioms. The problems, of course, have been constructed to elicit the maximum possible tendency to choose in violation of the axioms, and to the extent that a high degree of violation occurs, the problems are termed 'paradoxes'. By studying such situations, one can obtain a better understanding of some of the implications of the various axioms.

Which axioms apply to which problems has not been made clear. For example, a problem stated directly in terms of probabilities cannot be used to examine the validity of the Savage axioms because the probabilities have not been assigned by the decision maker who is to make the choices. In order to examine Savage's axioms, then, we would want to have any uncertainty stated in terms of events rather than probabilities. This point will be elaborated upon in the decision problem in Section 5.

In each of the next five sections, we first present a decision problem which you should respond to before reading further. We then present a list of rules which you may think are applicable to the problem at hand. Next we consider some of the implications of applying the rules to the problem. After this discussion, we examine the empirical evidence. After setting out some notation to characterize the type of problem, we look at previous experimental studies. Then, we analyze the overall experimental study we conducted. This study had as subjects 19 graduate degree students drawn from a course on decision making. The study was outside of class and prior to any discussion of relevant topics. A series of decision problems – the ones to be discussed herein and a few others – were presented to the subjects in a random order in a session of about 2 hours. The subjects were asked to indicate their choices in the problems and in some were asked to provide reasons for their choices. The choices of these subjects provide some evidence on the degree to which the axioms correspond with careful choices.

As an alternative check on the axioms, at the end of the session we presented the subjects with a list of 20 rules of decision. The rules were of four forms:

(a) Rules that stated direct implications of particular axioms.

(b) Rules that were direct contradictions to particular axioms.

(c) Rules that were associated with particular axioms but were incompletely specified (e.g., they only had partial conditions).

(d) Rules implying particular utility functions.

The subjects were asked to indicate their degree of agreement with each rule on an 11-point scale ranging from 'strongly disagree' (= 0) to 'strongly agree' (= 10).

Throughout the rest of this paper, we shall relate these rules to the decision problem we are considering. Some rules imply one set of choices in a particular problem while other rules imply other choices. It is also important to relate the rules to the axioms they are associated with. This is done in Figure 1. The column headings are the axioms we considered in the preceding section. The row labels are the rules. Those rules that are direct implications of an axiom are labelled '+'; those that are positively, but loosely related to an axiom are labelled P; those that are negatively related, but not in direct violation are labelled N; and those that are direct contradictions are labelled '−'. Only the rule number is given since it would be too cumbersome to list the rules themselves; however, the title given to each rule serves as a brief indication of what the rule is. The 20 rules are discussed throughout this paper. In the first column of Figure 1, we have indicated the section number in which the rule is considered.

In order to provide some further information we have renumbered the rules from the random order in which they were presented to the subjects. Instead, the rules are numbered according to their overall degree of acceptability. That is, we added the ratings given to a rule across all 19 subjects and then ordered the rules based on this overall rating. Throughout the paper, then, the rule number by itself gives you some information about how the rule compared to alternative ones. Rule 1 (Transitivity) was the rule that had the highest overall average rating (8.8) and Rule 20 (Common Consequence) had the lowest overall rating (5.0). Note that even the rule with the lowest rating was still on the acceptable side of the acceptable–unacceptable scale. Three rules that will be considered in various sections, but that were not presented in the experiment, are labelled U, V, and W at the bottom of Figure 1.

The rules will serve as linkages between the decision problems and the axioms. Since the rules express key implications of particular axioms, it is usually easiest to see the applicability of the axioms by

AXIOMS

Section number	Rule Name	Rule no.	vNM 1	vNM 2	vNM 3	vNM 4	M 1	M 2	M 3	S 1	S 2	S 3	S 4	S 5	S 6	A 1	A 2	A 3	A 4	A 5	A 6	Special utilities
10	Transitivity	1	+				+			+						+						
4, 7	Larger payoff	2			N				N		N								N			
9	Dominance	3		+							P	P										
9	Ethical neutrality	4				P						+	+						+			
7	Event complements	5	+			P	+			−	+			−					+			
4, 5	Win big	6			−		+	−		+									−			
10	Comparability	7	+		+		+	+	+	+	P	P				+		−	P		P	
4	Probability rates	8																				
6	Sure thing	9	+	P	N	P	+	P	N	+	+				N	+		P	+	N		
4, 6	Larger probability	10		+			+	+		+	N					+						
9	Irrelevant alternatives	11																				
7	Payoff over sureness	12			+		+			+			+			+		+	+		+	
4	Strong independence	13	+			P	+	+		+	P					+		P	P		P	
9	Sen's β	14		+			+	P		+			−			+		+	+		+	
*	Minimize variance	15																				×
5, 6, 7	Event-payoff irrelevance	16	+		+	P	+	P		+			+			+		+	+			
10	Substitutability	17				P	+	+		+						+		P	P	P	P	
*	Additivity of constant	18											−					+	N	+		×
6	Take a chance	19		P		P	+			+												
5	Common consequences	20		P												+		P	N	+		
4	Expected utility	U								+			+					P	P		P	
6, 7	Known chances	V		P				+		+	P							P	P		P	
5	Probability-payoff irrelevance	W		P				+		P			+					P	P		P	

* These rules, dealing with special utility functions, are not considered directly in this paper.

Fig. 1. Correspondence between axioms and rules.

considering the rule form. In each section, we shall use the rules to examine the relationship between subjects' actual choices and the rules they would accept in guiding their choices in general. If people choose inconsistently with a particular axiom but rate highly the rule expressing the relevant implication of the axiom (or vice versa), there is probably a communication problem. If, however, people choose inconsistently with the axiom *and* rate the corresponding rule low (and if they also rate the counter-rule high), then the validity of the axiom as a guide to actual behavior should be questioned.

4. COMMON RATIO OF PROBABILITIES

4.1 DECISION PROBLEM I

Decision Problem

Do you prefer A_1 or B_1?[10]

A_1: $1 million with probability 1.00,
B_1: $5 million with probability 0.80.

Do you prefer A_2 or B_2?[11]

A_2: $1 million with probability 0.05,
B_2: $5 million with probability 0.04.

Rules
In making your choice in each of these two sets of alternatives, you probably used some underlying rule to guide your choice – at least implicitly. Is the rationale for your choices contained in the rules below?

Rule 10: When two alternatives both have payoffs that are desirable, select the alternative having the larger probability.

Rule 2: When two alternatives have probabilities that are in the same range, select the alternative with the larger payoff.

Rule 6: When one alternative provides a sure (or almost sure) chance of obtaining a very desirable consequence, select it, even if it entails passing up a larger amount having a lower probability. When, however, the chances of winning are small and close together, take the option that provides the larger payoff.

Rule 8: If in one lottery, one alternative is preferred to another, and if a second lottery contains alternatives with the same payoffs and the same *relative* probabilities, select in the second lottery the same alternative that was preferred in the first lottery.

Rule 13: If when considering two alternatives A and B, A is preferred to B, then putting each into a lottery in which they are obtained with the same probability p (and some other alternative C is obtained with the probability $1 - p$) should not change the preference, i.e., the lottery based on A should be preferred to the lottery based on B.

Rule U: Maximize expected utility.

The type of decision problem given above was first posed by Maurice Allais (1952), who found that people generally prefer A_1 over B_1, and B_2 over A_2. The reasons that people commonly give for these choices are expressed in Rule 6, which can be viewed as a composite of Rules 10 and 2. Rule 10 applies to the first set because the probabilities are disparate and A_1 offers a sure $1 million; Rule 2 applies to the second set because the probabilities are in the same range and B_2 offers a chance at $5 million. The choice of A_1 and B_2 is, however, inconsistent with the applicable utility theory axioms, most specifically Marschak's Axiom M2. The verbal description is given by Rule 13; its formal statement was given and discussed in Section 2. To see how the rule applies take A_1 as A, B_1 as B, an alternative giving $0 for sure as C, and $p = 0.05$. Then, $A_1 > B_1$ means that the lottery 0.05 (1.00 of receiving $1 million) + 0.95 (1.00 of receiving $0) should be preferred to the lottery 0.05 (0.80 of receiving $1 million) + 0.95 (1.00 of receiving $0); but these terms simplify to 0.05 of receiving $1 million and 0.04 of receiving $5 million which are A_2 and B_2, respectively. Thus if A_1 is preferred to B_1 in the first set, Rule 13 would require that A_2 be preferred to B_2 in the second set.

Since Rule 13 is a necessary condition for maximizing expected utility (Rule U), a violation of Rule 13 does not allow utilities to be assigned. This relationship between Rule 13 and Rule U can be seen most directly by trying to express the A_1 and B_2 choices in terms of utilities[12] and noting the contradiction. The choices of A_1 over B_1 requires

$$1.00 \ U(\$1 \text{ million}) > 0.80 \ U(\$5 \text{ million}),$$

i.e., $$U(\$1 \text{ million}) > 4/5 \ U(\$5 \text{ million}).$$

The choice of B_2 over A_2 requires

$$0.04\,U(\$5\text{ million}) > 0.05\,U(\$1\text{ million}),$$

i.e., $U(\$1\text{ million}) < 4/5\,U(\$5\text{ million}).$

This contradiction shows that we must accept Rule 13 and reject Rule 6 if we want to maximize expected utility. The adoption of Rule 13 would require the choice of A_1 and A_2 or the choice of B_1 and B_2.

A particular form of Rule 13 relevant to this problem is given as Rule 8. The expressions above show that in both sets the probability of receiving $5 million was 4/5 of the probability of receiving $1 million. So Rule 8 requires us to pick the A alternative in each set, or the B alternative in each set, as long as the ratio of the probabilities is the same (in this case 4/5), regardless of the absolute level of the probabilities. Obviously, when the absolute values are large, the differences in probabilities between the A and B alternatives are relatively large and prominent, whereas when the absolute values are small, the differences are small and may seem insignificant. Note, then, that Rule 8 requires us to apply the same discrimination to ratios of probabilities no matter what part of the probability domain we consider.

The Savage axioms are not directly applicable to this problem since the problem is stated in terms of probabilities instead of events. It would be easy, however, to replace the probabilities by a standard urn situation.[13] When this change was made, then Axiom S2 would be directly applicable and what we have said above about violation of Axiom M2 would apply to Axiom S2.

If you thought both Rule 8 (or 13) and Rule 6 seemed to be worthwhile guides to choice, you obviously have a problem – you cannot follow them both here. If you thought you wanted to maximize expected utility, but chose A_1 and B_2, you should carefully reflect on those choices. If after careful reflection you prefer to accept Rule 13 and change your choices in one of the preceding sets, then you can continue to choose so as to maximize expected utility. If, however, you wish to retain your A_1 and B_2 choices, then you might search for ways of reconciling these choices with the rule of maximizing expected utility. One way would be to note when violations of Rule 13 occurred. For example, if violations occurred only when the probability p was small or only when the two money amounts were in the millions of dollars, as they are here, then you might maximize expected utility as long as such probability-consequence combinations did not occur in the choices you faced. We attempted to ascertain such boundary conditions in an empirical study to be discussed below.

4.2 EMPIRICAL STUDIES

Problem Representation

As noted above, different probability and payoff values can be expected to considerably affect whether one finds Rule 13 or Rule 6 the appropriate guide to choice. To highlight the effect of the parameter values and to efficiently characterize the empirical studies, we shall use the following notation:

> The basic alternative A will be denoted as (r, p) in which r is the amount of the payoff and p is the probability of this payoff. The higher payoff, less sure alternative B, will be denoted as $(\alpha r, \beta p)$.

The example at the beginning of this section, then, would have parameter values: $r = \$1$ million, $\alpha = 5$, $p_1 = 1.00$, $p_2 = 0.05$, and $\beta = 4/5$.

Previous Empirical Studies

The probability-domain problem we are considering appears to have been the subject of only a few previous studies. Allais, in his initial proposal of the problem (1953), referred to empirical studies. Hagen (1971) obtained some evidence from Norwegian teachers. Hagen used the problem with the following parameter values: $r = 5$ million Norwegian kroner, $\alpha = 5$, $p_1 = 0.99$, $p_2 = 0.11$, and $\beta = 10/11$. Because subjects were asked for choices in only one of the sets, Hagen could compare only the aggregate number of A versus B choices in the two sets; he could not compare each individual subject's choices across both sets. Hagen found that in the first set, 37 subjects out of 52 selected A_1 while in the second set 37 subjects out of 52 selected B_2. Hence there was a preference for the A alternative in the first set but the B alternative in the second set. Thus we can infer that if subjects had been presented with both sets, the majority would probably have violated Rule 13, and thus violated expected utility. In a second experiment, Hagen (1971) used the parameter values: $r = 10,000$ Norwegian kroner, $\alpha = 2$, $p_1 = 1.00$, $p_2 = 0.02$, and $\beta = \frac{1}{2}$. In the first set of choices, 47 of the 52 subjects selected A_1 while in the second set 23 of the 52 subjects selected B_2. Even though the A_2 alternative was the more favoured one in the second set, this pattern of choices again suggests some violation of Rule 13.

In view of the challenge to a basic independence axiom of utility theory, it seems desirable to make a more thorough study of the effect of different parameter values on the acceptance or rejection of Rule 13.

New Empirical Study

In this study we did not try to study the effect of varying all the parameter values but rather we concentrated on the effect of using different payoff and probability levels (i.e., values of r and p). We used two experiments. In the first we used positive payoffs; in the second we used negative payoffs (losses), to determine whether negative payoffs resulted in major differences in behaviour. The payoffs were all hypothetical but the subject was asked to act as if each would actually be realized and to treat each set independently of the others. The parameter values used were:

> On the positive expected value sets: $\alpha = 5$, $\beta = 4/5$, r took on the values $1,000,000$, $100,000$, $10,000$, $1,000$, 100, 10, and 1 while p took on the values 1.00, 0.75, 0.50, 0.25, 0.10, and 0.05.
> On the negative expected value sets: $\alpha = 5$, $\beta = 3/4$, r took on the values $-1,000$, -100, -10, and -1, while p took on the values 1.00, 0.80, 0.20, 0.04.

Twenty-one different positive expected value sets were presented, with four sets repeated to check for consistency. Eight different negative expected value sets were presented with two sets repeated to check for consistency. Not all combinations were presented since a pilot study had ascertained that some combinations (e.g., a low positive payoff and a low probability level) led to almost all subjects choosing the same alternative. (This is interesting in itself, but is not the best use of limited time for an experiment.) The 25 positive payoff sets and 10 negative payoff sets were presented in random order.

The particular combinations given can be seen from the graph of the results in Figure 2. The numbers show for each payoff-probability combination how many of the 19 subjects chose the higher probability (A) alternative.[14] So, for example, with the combination of payoffs and probabilities used in Decision Problem I above, 15 subjects chose A in set 1 while only 2 chose A in set 2 (as discussed in the footnote, this could equally well be treated as 14 and 1). Not surprisingly, the highest level of A choices, for positive amounts, occurs when there is a sure chance of getting a large amount of money. As the graph shows, when the probability levels decrease, or when the money payoff levels decrease, then there is a reduced tendency to pick the A alternative (i.e., the one giving the lower payoff with the higher probability). When the probability levels decrease the rationale is one of viewing the probability difference as insignificant and thus 'going for broke' on the larger payoff. When the payoff levels decrease, the

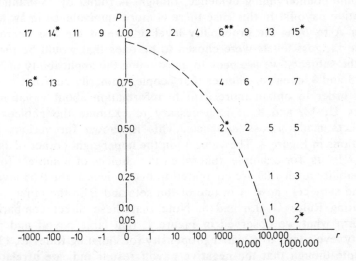

* One subject chose A on one presentation of this set, and B on the other presentation.
** Two subjects chose A on one presentation of this set and B on the other presentation.

Fig. 2. The number of subjects, out of 19, selecting the alternative (r, p) over the alternative $(5r, \frac{4}{5}p)$, in Decision Problem I: Common Ratio of Probabilities.

rationale is one of 'going for broke' since the amount you get for sure does not mean that much to you in terms of lifetime security, etc. The majority of the subjects would only select the A alternative when there was a certainty of getting a very large payoff (i.e., either $1,000,000 or $100,000). Even though each of our subjects made 25 (positive payoff) choices, they seemed to be quite alert to the changes in payoff and probability and hence chose differentially. It is clear, then, that the particular parameter values play a major role in whether one violates the utility independence conditions. Since almost all subjects can be expected to prefer the B alternative for payoff-probability combinations to the left and below the dashed line, then there would be no violation of Rule U (or Rules 13 and 8) if any of these combinations were compared to each other. Since in real choices the subjects would rarely have alternatives with payoffs such that they would be to the right of the line, we may question whether the possible violations in very unlikely cases has much relevance for utility theory.

Some countervailing evidence, though, is found by examining the negative payoffs. In this case there is more ambivalence in switching from A to B as the probability level or size of the loss decreases. Since the loss levels were chosen to be ones that would be realistic for the subjects, we are back to questioning the applicability of Rules U, 13 and 8, even for choices that people ordinarily confront.

In order to obtain more definite information about violations of Rules U, 13, and 8, it is necessary to examine the choices that subjects made across two sets. This is shown for various combinations in Figure 3. The value 12 in the upper-right corner of Figure 3(i), tells us, for example, that when the choices of a subject for the probability level 1.00 are compared to his choices at the 0.05 level, 12 of the subjects chose A in one of the sets and B in the other, hence violating Rules U, 13, and 8. Note that these direct comparisons confirm what we observed in Figure 1, that large payoff and probability levels lead to a higher propensity for violating Rules U, 13 and 8. Note though that the negative payoff results indicate a relatively low level of violation.

It is reasonable to ask whether an A choice in one set and a B choice in another set reflects a violation of Rules U, 13, and 8 or whether there is an alternative explanation. One possible explanation would be that the subject was bored, tired, disinterested or careless,

$\alpha = \$1,000,000$

p	1.00	0.75	0.50	0.25	0.10	0.05
1.00	1*	6	9	11	11	12
0.75			7	5	5	6
0.50				2	2	3
0.25					0	1
0.10						1
0.05						1*

(i)

$\alpha = \$1,000$

p	1.00	0.75	0.50
1.00	2*	6	4
0.75			4
0.50			1*

(ii)

$\alpha = -\$1,000$

p	0.80	0.20	0.04
1.00	1	1	3
0.80	1*	2	4
0.20			4

(iii)

* These subjects were inconsistent on the repeat of the same set, hence they were omitted from the tabulation of the remainder of the table. So the inconsistencies in Table (i) are out of 17 subjects, in Table (ii) out of 16 subjects, and in Table (iii) out of 18 subjects.

Fig. 3. Number of subjects inconsistent with utility axioms for various levels of α and p in Decision Problem I: Common Ratio of Probabilities.

and that the apparent inconsistencies reflect only this 'error variance'. To make an assessment of such error variance, we gave several repeats of exactly the same set. The number of instabilities on the same set can serve as a measure of the basic inconsistency. Overall on the 6 repeated sets (i.e., $6 \times 19 = 114$ subject-sets) there were 7 unstable choices, so an estimate of the underlying inconsistency is about 6% (i.e., 7/114).[15] Hence, looking at the 12 inconsistencies in the upper-right-hand corner of Figure 3(i), we can say that not all of this 70% inconsistency rate is due to an overt violation of the utility axioms; 6% is due to randomness in choice. Note, however, that this still leaves 64% attributable to the subjects' following Rule 6 instead of Rule 13.

If a subject's choices seem consistent with a particular rule, you would expect that he would agree with the rule when it was presented to him in the form given at the outset of this section. The subjects in this experiment were given the statement of the rules consistent with utility theory (Rules 8 and 13) and the statement of Rule 6, which is inconsistent with the utility independence condition. Twenty possible rules were presented to the subjects and they were asked to indicate their degree of agreement on an 11-point scale from 'completely agree' to 'completely disagree'. The results for Rules 13, 8, 6, 10, and 2 are shown in Figure 4.[16]

In order to compare the agreement and disagreement with the subject's own choices, we have divided the subjects into three categories: (1) the 3 subjects consistent with Rule 13 for both positive and negative payoffs, (2) the 4 subjects consistent with Rule 13 for negative payoffs but not for positive payoffs, and (3) the 12 subjects inconsistent with Rule 13 for both positive and negative payoffs.

Rules Actual choices	Utility independence conditions		Conditions inconsistent with utility		
	Rule 13	Rule 8	Rule 6	Rule 10	Rule 2
(1) Subjects consistent with Rules 13, 8, U on their own choices on both the positive and negative payoff series ($n = 3$).	5.2	5.0	5.0	5.3	8.5
(2) Subjects consistent with Rules 13, 8, U on the negative payoff set but not on the positive ($n = 4$).	7.0	7.3	7.5	8.5	8.5
(3) Subjects inconsistent with Rules 13, 8, U on both the positive and negative payoff series ($n = 12$).	6.0	7.2	7.4	6.5	8.5
Average Rating	6.1	6.9	7.1	6.7	8.5

Fig. 4. Correspondence between subjects' actual choices and their level of agreement with the relevant rules in Decision Problem I: Common Ratio of Probabilities.

The table shows that the level of agreement with all the rules is quite high (5.0 is the neutral point). Note that all subjects tend to agree more with Rules 10 and 2 than with the composite, Rule 6, which contains the direct counter proposal to the utility-based Rules 13 and 8.

There is a very slight tendency for the completely consistent subjects to agree more with Rule 13 than with Rule 6. Similarly, there is a tendency for inconsistent subjects, especially those inconsistent on both series, to prefer Rule 6 to Rule 13. The latter difference is interesting. Note that there is less difference between Rules 8 and 6 than between Rules 13 and 6. By looking down columns rather than along rows, we see that the inconsistent subjects tended to like all the rules more than did the consistent subjects, but the differential is most striking in their agreement with Rule 6, as we would expect.

4.3 SUMMARY

By no means did all the subjects in our new experiments act consistently with the utility independence conditions, specifically Axiom M2. For extreme values of payoffs (in millions of dollars) and for extreme values of probabilities (comparing the 1.00 level to the 0.05 level), the violation level reached about 65%, even after pulling out an estimate of random responses. However, for smaller values, those more likely to be actually encountered by the subjects, the choices were quite consistent. When the probability differences seem small or when the surer payoff does not guarantee a much better life-style, then there is a strong tendency for everyone to 'go for broke' with the alternative that is less sure but has a larger payoff. There is a tendency for subjects to agree more with the rule that reflects their choices rather than the rule in opposition to their choices.

The results suggest the need to look carefully at circumstances that are particularly favourable or unfavourable compared to normal, since inconsistent choices may be taken. Utility functions defined over large domains must also be used with caution.

5. COMMON CONSEQUENCE

5.1 DECISION PROBLEM II

Decision Problem

Do you prefer A_1 or B_1:[17]

A_1: $1 million with probability 1.00.

B_1: $5 million with probability 0.10,
           $1 million with probability 0.89.

Do you prefer A_2 or B_2?

A_2: $1 million with probability 0.11.

B_2: $5 million with probability 0.10.

Rules

In this problem as in the preceding one, you can probably identify some rules which guided your choice. Perhaps Rule 6 from the preceding section is relevant or perhaps Rules W, 16 or 20.

Rule 6: When one alternative provides a sure (or almost sure) chance of obtaining a very desirable consequence, select it, even if it entails passing up a larger amount having a lower probability. When, however, the chances of winning are small and close together, take the option that provides the larger payoff.

Rule W: If each of 2 alternatives has a common payoff having the same probability, that common payoff cannot help discriminate between the alternatives. If that payoff is changed, but still remains common to both alternatives and has the same probability in each alternative, then the choices between the alternatives should stay the same.

Rule 20: The choice between two alternatives should be independent of the particular consequences accruing from events for which both alternatives have common identical outcomes.

Rule 16: If each of two alternatives has a common payoff for some event *E*, that common payoff cannot help discriminate between the alternatives, and is therefore irrelevant in choosing between the alternatives. If that common payoff is changed, but still remains common to both alternatives, then the preferences between the alternatives should stay the same.

The problem given above is commonly referred to as the 'Allais Paradox'.[18] Presumably, it is a paradox because individuals choose A_1 and B_2. The reasons people give for their choices are similar to those reasons given in Rule 6 above and hence very similar to the choices in the problem in the preceding section. This combination of choices contradicts the independence conditions for utility theory. The violation of expected utility can be seen by noting that the choice of A_1 over B_1 implies that[19]

$$U(\$1 \text{ million}) > 0.10 \ U(\$5 \text{ million}) + 0.89 \ U(\$1 \text{ million}),$$

$$U(\$1 \text{ million}) > \frac{10}{11} U(\$5 \text{ million}).$$

The choice of B_2 over A_2 implies that

$$0.10 \ U(\$5 \text{ million}) > 0.11 \ U(\$1 \text{ million}),$$

$$\frac{10}{11} U(\$5 \text{ million}) > U(\$1 \text{ million}).$$

The most direct utility independence axiom, however, is not Rule 13 discussed in the preceding section, but rather Rule W stated above. This rule is not one of the ones considered at the beginning of the paper, but is a direct correspondence to Rule 16 or 20, which is Savage's sure-thing principle, Axiom S2. The sure-thing principle cannot be applied directly to the problem since it is stated in terms of probabilities instead of events. Savage, though, has related the problem to his theory by suggesting events by which such probabilities could be derived (1954, p.103). He proposes a lottery with 100 tickets numbered 1–100 with prizes given in the payoff matrix below:

	Ticket #1	Tickets #2–11	Tickets #12–100
A_1:	$1 million	$1 million	$1 million
B_1:	0	$5 million	$1 million
A_2:	$1 million	$1 million	0
B_2:	0	$5 million	0

When we apply Rule 16 or 20 to this payoff matrix, we see that if A_1 is preferred to B_1, then A_2 should be preferred to B_2 because tickets 12–100 can be ignored since they do not discriminate between the A and B alternatives – they yield common consequences. Without tickets 12–100, we see that A_2 is identical to A_1, and B_2 is identical to B_1; hence the A alternative should be chosen in both sets, or the B alternative should be chosen in both sets.

Hagen, however, has questioned Savage's translation of probabilities into events (1972). Consider the following alternative realization of the probabilities:

	Ticket #1	Tickets #2–11	Tickets #12–90	Tickets #91–100
A_1':	\$1 million	\$1 million	\$1 million	\$1 million
B_1':	0	\$5 million	\$1 million	\$1 million
A_2':	\$1 million	\$1 million	0	0
B_2':	0	0	0	\$5 million

In this format only tickets 12–90 can be ignored in both sets. When these common consequences are disregarded, we note that, unlike Savage's format, the two A alternatives are not identical, nor are the B alternatives; hence the sure-thing principle does not apply. Yet this realization is as legitimate as Savage's.

This formulation of the problem leads us to ask: if Axiom (S2) is not violated, which expected utility axiom *is* violated? Consider an alternative C_2:

	Ticket #1	Tickets #2–11	Tickets #12–90	Tickets #91–100
C_2	0	\$5 million	0	0

Axiom S2 does not allow us to assert a preference ordering between A_2' and B_2' but since $A_1' \geqslant B_1'$, we can assert by Axiom S2 that $A_2' \geqslant C_2$. What can be said about the relationship of B_2' and C_2? In setting up the events from the probabilities, we assumed that the events, tickets #2–11 and tickets #91–100, had the same probability. Since these events have the same probabilities, bets which only differ by being based on one rather than the other must be equivalent. If B_2' and C_2 are thus indifferent, then transitivity (Axiom S1) would imply

$A_2' \geqslant B_2'$. So if Axiom S2 is not violated, then Axiom S4 or Axiom S1 probably is violated.

The applicability of Rule W is more straightforward in this type of decision problem since it is not dependent on an event formulation; it is stated directly in terms of probabilities. Since A_1 and B_1 have a common consequence of $1 million with the probability 0.89, and A_2 and B_2 have a common consequence of $0 with the same probability 0.89, we can ignore this part of the sample space and find that in the remaining part A_1 and A_2 (also B_1 and B_2) are identical; that is, they have the same payoffs with the same probabilities.

The relationship between Rule W and the strong independence assumption, Axiom M2, can be seen by comparing the basic lotteries:

P_1:   1/11 of receiving $0,
         10/11 of receiving $5 million.

P_2:   certainty of receiving $1 million.

P_3:   certainty of receiving $0.

Then the 4 alternatives in Decision Problem II can be viewed as combinations of the following lotteries:

A_1: $11/100P_2 + 89/100P_2$,

B_1: $11/100P_1 + 89/100P_2$,

A_2: $11/100P_2 + 89/100P_3$,

B_2: $11/100P_1 + 89/100P_3$.

Hence, Axiom M2 would require that if $A_1 > B_1$, then $A_2 > B_2$, or vice versa.

In general, we would expect the A alternative to be chosen when its probability is high or when its payoff, relative to the payoff on B, is high. We shall now consider some empirical evidence about this expectation.

5.2 EMPIRICAL STUDIES

Problem Representation

The particular probabilities and payoffs in Decision Problem II have been carefully chosen to elicit violations of the utility axioms. As noted above, different levels of probabilities and payoffs can be expected to strongly influence the choice of the A or B alternatives. Hence it seems useful to set up a parametric representation.[20] Common consequence problems involve a binary choice of an A and a B alternative with three possible consequence parameters, r, s, t; and a probability parameter, p. The choice may be represented as:

A: $(s/p; t/1 - p)$,

B: $(r/0.10; s/p - 0.11; t/1.01 - p)$,

where the symbol before the slash is the consequence received with the probability given after the slash. It is assumed that $r > s > t$ and that $0.11 \leq p \leq 1.00$. The common consequence in these 'common consequence' problems is the outcome s with probability $p - 0.11$ and the outcome t with probability $1 - p$. Since a common consequence problem requires 2 pairs of choices, we have a p_1 and a p_2.

Using this notation, the problem at the beginning of this section can be written as $s = \$1,000,000$, $r = \$5,000,000$, $t = \$0$, $p_1 = 1.00$, and $p_2 = 0.11$. To reduce the number of parameters under consideration we shall assume, as does Allais, that $t = \$0$ and that $r = 5s$. In our empirical study, then, we can systematically vary the consequence and probability levels and do this in terms of only the parameters s and p.

Previous Empirical Studies

Previous studies of the common consequence have been made by MacCrimmon (1965), Moskowitz (1974), and Slovic and Tversky (1975). All these authors use problems having two pairs of choices and use the probability values $p_1 = 1.00$ and $p_2 = 0.11$.

MacCrimmon (1965) uses three common consequence problems. In order to relate directly to the Savage axioms, the consequences of all these are specified in terms of the occurrence of events rather than in terms of probabilities. In two of the problems, the events are based on standard urns, and from the events most people infer the same probabilities. In the other problem, the occurrence of events was described only verbally (e.g., 'very unlikely'); the subjects were senior business executives; the problems appeared in the context of investments for a hypothetical business; and the consequences were outcomes of the investment. The parameters of the problems may be summarized as:

Problem 1: $r = 500\%$, $s = 5\%$, $t =$ bankruptcy, $p_1 = 1.00$, $p_2 = 0.11$.

Problem 2: $r = 500\%$, $s = 5\%$, $t =$ bankruptcy, probabilities just verbal.

Problem 3: $r = 75\%$, $s = 35\%$, $t = 0\%$, $p_1 = 1.00$, $p_2 = 0.11$.

In all three problems a significant proportion of the 36 subjects chose an Allais-type answer (14, 15, and 13, respectively), and hence confirmed the claim made by Allais. Only 9 subjects conformed to the expected utility axioms in all 3 problems (15 had 1 deviation, 9 had 2, and 3 had 3). In addition to their own choices, the subjects were presented with responses supposedly from subjects in a previous session and were asked to critique them. Actually these responses were answers based on Rule 6 and Rule W. These results are even more compelling since 29 of the subjects (on problem 1) agreed with the Allais-type answer (i.e., Rule 6); only 7 agreed with the expected utility axioms-answer (Rule W). However, a hypothesis that, in critiquing these responses, subjects tended to pick the answer that most closely corresponded to their own answer, accounts for 32 of the cases. So we have to be careful in interpreting the general response as agreement with Rule 6 over Rule W.

Moskowitz (1974) presented each of 134 students with 3 problems involving course grades. For the first two problems, Moskowitz does not specify the numerical grades he used in the problems; in the third problem the grades were letter grades.[21] The parameters of his problem 3 were: $r = A$ grade, $s = B+$ grade, $t = F$ grade, $p_1 = 1.00$, and $p_2 = 0.11$. Moskowitz presented these problems in three different formats: word, tree, and matrix, as suggested in MacCrimmon (1967). He allowed some subjects to discuss the problems in a group while others had to proceed individually. In addition to presenting the problem, he presented pro and con arguments and afterward had the subjects choose again.

Overall, Moskowitz found a rate of violation of about 30%. The tree representation was the most difficult with a violation rate ranging from 29% to 50% (across the other conditions). In the word format, the violation rate was 17% to 40% and in the matrix format the violation rate was 21% to 42%.[22] There were only slight differences in problem types with Problem 1 having a violation range of 17% to 46%; Problem 2 having a violation range of 17% to 40%; and Problem 3 having a violation range of 17% to 45%. There was a significantly greater increase in consistency for discussion groups versus non-discussion groups, but both groups' answers were more consistent on the second presentation.

Slovic and Tversky (1975) used the standard Allais problem, that is, $s = \$1,000,000$, $p_1 = 1.00$, $p_2 = 0.11$. Of their 29 college student subjects, 17 chose the Allais response, and 12 chose consistently with the axioms. On a reconsideration, after reading arguments in favour of each position, 19 subjects chose the Allais response and 10 chose consistently with the axioms. Over the two presentations, 16 made the Allais-type choices, while 9 made the axiom-based choices. In a second experiment with 49 student subjects, the subjects first read and rated arguments for and against the axioms, then they made their own choices. With this format, consistency increased. In their actual choices, only 17 subjects made Allais-type choices, but 30 subjects made axiom-based choices. In rating their arguments for the axioms, 25 subjects rated the Allais argument higher while 21 subjects rated the axiom argument higher.

Across these previous studies, we see that the axioms are violated at a significant rate. The rate of violation ranges around 27% to 42% except for the high level in Slovic and Tversky's first experiment. However, there seems to be a considerable variation across the studies, and even within a single study. It seems useful to attempt to more systematically study the change in rate of violation with a change in parameter values.

New Empirical Study

In our new experiments, we were concerned with investigating the effect of changes in s and p. The parameter s took on the values \$1,000,000, \$100,000, \$10,000, and \$1,000, while the parameter p took on the values 1.00, 0.99, 0.50, and 0.11. Eleven different combinations of these parameters were presented plus 2 check points as a measure of the random component of the choices. From these we can form 12 different sets of two pairs of binary lotteries.

Figure 5 provides a summary of the results for the 19 subjects. The tables list the number of subjects making the A choice in the higher p

$s = \$1,000,000$

p_1 \ p_2	1.00	0.99	0.50	0.11
1.00	1	4	4	6
0.99			5	3
0.50				6
0.11				0

(i)

$s = \$100,000$

p_1 \ p_2	0.99	0.11
1.00	2	4
0.99		2

(ii)

$s = \$10,000$

p_1 \ p_2	0.99	0.11
1.00	4	4
0.99		6

(iii)

Fig. 5. Number of subjects inconsistent with utility axioms for various levels of s and p in Decision Problem II: Common Consequences.

set and the B choice in the lower p set. For example, in Figure 4(i), there were 6 subjects choosing A in the set $s = \$1,000,000$, $p = 1.00$, and B in the set $s = \$1,000,000$, $p = 0.11$ – that is, the standard Allais problem. Hence the rate of violation is 33% which is about the same as the preceding studies.[23] Note, though that we can now check the rate for other probability-payoff combinations. Not surprisingly, the highest rate of violation occurs for extreme probability-payoff values. There is not a higher rate of violation than the standard Allais problem, but two other combinations $s = \$1,000,000$. $p_1 = 0.50$, $p_2 = 0.11$, and $s = \$10,000$, $p_1 = 0.99$, $p_2 = 0.11$ also have six violations (out of 19 subjects though, not out of 18). It should be noted though that these violations are for significantly changed parameter values from the standard problem. We thus have found significant violations at the $\$10,000$ payoff level and (separately) at the 0.50 probability level.

As in the preceding section, it is interesting to look at the correspondence between the choices of the subjects and the extent to which they agreed with the statement of the applicable rule. We have classified the subjects into three categories: (1) subjects choosing consistently with the axioms (by always choosing *B*), (2) subjects with Allais-type choices throughout, and (3) subjects with mistakes or irregular choices. From Figure 6, it is obvious that each of the classes prefers the counter-axiom rule, Rule 6 (i.e. Allais's argument) better than either form of the independence Axiom S2 (i.e., Rules 16 or 20). In fact, one can see by the rule numbers that these rules were rated at or near the bottom of the list. It seems somewhat paradoxical that the 3 Allais-type subjects rated the axiom-based rules higher than did the other subjects, but this appears to be due to a higher rating they have in general. They certainly rate the Allais-type rule very highly. The reason for the difference in the ratings of Rules 16 and 20, which are slightly different statements of the same implication of Axiom S2, is not clear.

Rules Actual choices	Utility independence conditions		Condition inconsistent with utility
	Rule 20	Rule 16	Rule 6
(1) The subjects always choosing the *B* alternative and hence consistent with Rules 16 and 20. (*n* = 10)	5.5	4.9	6.2
(2) The subjects with Allais-type choices, that is, a choice of the *A* alternative for some set, the *B* alternative for others, with a regular pattern for switching. (*n* = 3)	5.8	6.8	8.5
(3) The subjects with obvious mistakes in choices or very irregular choice patterns. (*n* = 6)	3.8	6.8	8.0
Average Rating	5.1	5.8	7.1

Fig. 6. Correspondence between subjects' actual choices and their level of agreement with the relevant rules in Decision Problem II: Common Consequences.

5.3 SUMMARY

We can conclude that the violations in the Allais 'common consequence problem' are not due solely to the standard parameter values. Some degree of violation is found for quite different values. In comparing the rate of violation in this problem with that in the Allais 'probability ratio problem' (of Section 4), it is interesting to note a higher rate of violation in the preceding problem for roughly comparable parameter values. We might, then, tentatively conclude that the preceding problem is more of a challenge to the axioms than is this 'common consequence problem'. The preceding problem has the virtue of being less contrived. So even though the common consequence problem of this section is generally called the 'Allais Paradox', the preceding problem which is also due to Allais is more of a 'paradox' (if either is) in the sense that it elicits a higher rate of violation of the axioms.

6. KNOWN VERSUS UNKNOWN CHANCES

6.1 DECISION PROBLEM III

Decision Problem

Consider an urn containing 100 balls. You know there are 33 red balls but you do not know the composition of the remaining 67 black and yellow balls. One ball is to be drawn at random from the urn.

Which do you prefer: A_1 or B_1?

A_1 Receive \$1000 if a red ball is drawn.

B_1:   Receive \$1000 if a black ball is drawn.

Which do you prefer: A_2 or B_2?

A_2:   Receive \$1000 if a red or yellow ball is drawn.

B_2:   Receive \$1000 if a black or yellow ball is drawn.

If the urn contained 34 red balls and 66 black and yellow balls, what choices would you make, A_1 or B_1? A_2 or B_2?

Rules

In making a choice you were perhaps guided by particular rules. Do any of the rules below seem appropriate to you?

Rule V: When the payoffs are the same, take the alternative for which the chances are known over one in which the chances are uncertain.

Rule 9: If some alternative *A* is preferred to an alternative *B* knowing that some event *E* would occur, and if alternative *A* would be preferred to *B* knowing that event *E* would not occur, then alternative *A* should be preferred to alternative *B* overall.

Rule 10: When the alternatives both have payoffs that are desirable, select the alternative having the larger probability.

Rule 16: If each of two alternatives has a common payoff for some event, that common payoff cannot help discriminate between the alternatives and is therefore irrelevant in choosing between the alternatives. If that common payoff is changed, but still remains common to both alternatives, then the preferences between the alternatives should stay the same.

Rule 19: Select alternatives based on lotteries in which the chances of winning are known but small over ones in which the chances are unknown if the payoff is large enough. If the payoff is small, take a chance on the alternative with unknown chances.

Applying the Rules to the Decision Problem

This problem was first proposed by Daniel Ellsberg (1961) and is known as the 'Ellsberg Paradox'.[24] The term 'paradox' is applied because people presumably choose A_1 and B_2 and this combination violates one of the independence conditions of utility theory.[25] This violation can be seen most easily be setting up the problem in the form of a decision matrix.[26]

		67 balls	
	33 red balls	Black balls	Yellow balls
A_1:	1000	0	0
B_1:	0	1000	0
A_2:	1000	0	1000
B_2:	0	1000	1000

Using Rule 16, we note that the last event 'yellow ball' does not discriminate between the alternatives and hence can be ignored. Ignoring this event, we know that A_1 is then identical to A_2, and B_1 is identical to B_2; hence a choice of A_1 over B_1 would require a choice of A_2 over B_2.

Since unlike the preceding problems, this problem is stated directly in terms of events rather than probabilities, Savage's axioms are directly applicable. Rule 16 is one possible statement of Savage's sure-thing principle, i.e., Axiom S2.[27] Therefore the choice of A_1 and B_2 in this problem violates Savage's Axiom S2 and one could not maximize expected utility by these choices.

Since Axiom S2 is violated, it is natural to inquire as to the status of the strong independence axiom, M2.[28] In order to apply this axiom, though, we need to assign probabilities. Most people would agree to set $P(R) = 0.33$ and $P(B) + P(Y) = 0.67$. We then can try to infer the remaining probabilities from the expressed preferences. If $A_1 > B_1$, then

$$P(R) > P(B),$$

$$P(R) > 0.67 - P(Y).$$

If $B_2 > A_2$, then

$$P(B) + P(Y) > P(R) + P(Y),$$

$$0.67 > P(R) + P(Y) > 0.67 - P(Y) + P(Y) = 0.67.$$

Hence, probabilities (satisfying the usual probability axioms) cannot be assigned.[29] So the A_1, B_2 choices violate the underlying assumptions for the applicability of the von Neumann–Morgenstern/Marschak axioms, but we cannot attribute the difficulty specifically to Axiom M2.

We can, however, see the implications of Axiom M2 by forming the component lotteries,

$$C_1: \begin{cases} \dfrac{0.33}{0.33 + p} \text{ of } \$1000, \\[2mm] \dfrac{p}{0.33 + p} \text{ of } \$0, \end{cases} \qquad C_2: \begin{cases} \dfrac{0.33}{0.33 + p} \text{ of } \$0, \\[2mm] \dfrac{p}{0.33 + p} \text{ of } \$1000, \end{cases}$$

C_3: certainty of $0, C_4: certainty of $1000.

We can thus rewrite the original alternatives as:

A_1: $(0.33 + p)C_1 + (0.67 - p)C_3$.

B_1: $(0.33 + p)C_2 + (0.67 - p)C_3$.

A_2: $(0.33 + p)C_1 + (0.67 - p)C_4$.

B_2: $(0.33 + p)C_2 + (0.67 - p)C_4$.

Since Axiom M2 would directly assert $C_1 \geq C_2$ implies $A_1 \geq B_2$, $A_2 \geq B_2$, then choices of the Ellsberg-type can be seen to contradict Axiom M2.

In any case, the A_1, B_2 choices cause problems for any theory of expected utility because all of them require probabilities, and these choices reflect inconsistent beliefs for which probabilities cannot be assigned.

The rationale given by Ellsberg for the A_1, B_2 choices is reflected in Rule V. Rule V distinguishes between known and unknown chances, or, in Knight's (1921) terms, between 'risk' and 'uncertainty'. Presumably, there are some events for which probabilities can be assigned and hence one could maximize expected utility. Ellsberg contends, however, that there are other events, such as drawings from urns of unspecified composition, political and social changes, etc., for which probabilities cannot be assigned, since the attempt to assign probabilities will be thwarted by people's preference for selecting ventures based on known chances rather than on unknown chances. Such behavior would then obviate the additivity property of probability.[30]

Rule 19 suggests that the choice might be a function of the level of payoff. With large amounts at stake, you are likely to opt for the more known alternative – the one with the specified probabilities. However, if the stakes are small you may take a chance on the venture with incompletely specified probabilities.

6.2 EMPIRICAL STUDIES

In the preceding problems, the key parameters were both the probabilities and the payoffs. In this problem the interaction between them is not particularly interesting and so the main element is the probability. However, we should be careful to make the distinction that the problem is stated in terms of events rather than probabilities.

Indeed the question at issue is whether probabilities can be constructed.[31] Since we need to express these problems in terms of events rather than probabilities, we will characterize the problems by three events x_1, x_2, and x_3. These events consist of states and we know both the total number of states, n, and the proportion of states p in x_1. Hence there are $(1 - p)n$ states in the event 'x_2 or x_3'. The single payoff is denoted by r. The alternatives in decision problems of Type III can then be characterized as:

A_1: r if x_1 A_2: r if x_1 or x_3,

B_1: r if x_2 B_2: r if x_2 or x_3.

The problem at the beginning of this section can then be described as: $p = 0.33$, $x_1 = $ red ball, $x_2 = $ black ball, $x_3 = $ yellow ball, $n = 100$ balls, $r = \$1000$. The supplementary problem is the same except $p = 0.34$.

Previous Empirical Studies

Slovic and Tversky (1975) used the original Ellsberg problem ($p = \frac{1}{3}$, $x_1 = $ red ball, $x_2 = $ black ball, $x_3 = $ yellow ball, $n = 90$, $\alpha = \$100$). Of their 29 college students, 19 made Ellsberg-type violations when the problem was first presented to them. On a second presentation of the same problem, there were 21 Ellsberg-type violations. In a second group of 49 subjects who were presented with arguments before making their choices, 38 subjects agreed with an Ellsberg-type of argument and 39 made an Ellsberg-type violation in their choices.

New Empirical Study

As noted above, the most interesting parameter to vary in Type III decision problems is the proportion, p. This reflects the 'known' chances of winning with event x_1 and correspondingly, there is a $1 - p$ chance of winning with event 'x_2 or x_3'. We considered the following values of p: 0.20, 0.25, 0.30, 0.33, 0.34, 0.40, and 0.50. We would expect the highest tendency to make Ellsberg-type violations around $p = \frac{1}{3}$. To obtain some information on payoff level, we used $r = \$1000$ and $r = \$1,000,000$. For all variations we let $x_1 = $ red ball, $x_2 = $ black ball, and $x_3 = $ yellow ball. We set $n = 100$ balls in all cases except that we did give one presentation of the original Ellsberg problem with $n = 90$ balls (and $p = \frac{1}{3}$) for direct comparison purposes.

We wished to examine whether the axioms are, in fact, violated at a considerable rate, whether violations occur because the subject distinguishes between 'risk' and 'uncertainty', and if so, under what conditions the subject will maintain this distinction. For example, will a subject maintain such a distinction over wide changes in probability, and will he hold it if he gets a lower reward on the events with specified probabilities.

In the original Ellsberg problem, 11 of our 19 subjects made the Ellsberg-type violation (i.e., A_1, B_2). Only 5 individuals made choices conforming with the axioms (A_1, A_2 or B_1, B_2).[32] Hence there does seem to be a high rate of violation of Axiom S2 – or alternatively, a refutation of the notion that probabilities can be assigned to 'uncertain' events. In the form of the problem we used, (with $n = 100$ balls), the rate of violation tended to be even *higher*. For $p = 0.33$ or 0.34, 70% of the subjects made Ellsberg-type violations. So there was considerable violation for these particular parameters.

In an urn with 100 balls, proportion p of which are red, when p is close to 0 we would expect a choice of B_1, B_2, and when p is close to 1, we would expect a choice of A_1 and A_2. However, when p is around $\frac{1}{3}$, then individuals may be somewhat indifferent about the choices and may choose on the basis of how well known the chances are. Since the chances for alternatives A_1 and B_2 are specified, we would expect a much higher proportion of such violations around this value of p. As p deviates from $\frac{1}{3}$, then although the chances are still specified with alternatives A_1 and B_2, one is accepting a somewhat low chance of winning by taking A_1 when p is small or B_2 when p is large.

Regardless of whether this is the rationale for the choices, we definitely observe this kind of behavior. In Figure 7 we see that 70% of the choices for $p = 0.33$ or 0.34 are inconsistent with the axioms, but for $p = 0.20$, this percentage drops to 15% and for $p = 0.50$ it drops to 0%.[33]

On Type III problems, the correspondence between the subjects' choices and subjects' agreement with the associated rules is quite striking. In Figure 8, we see that the 5 subjects who are most consistent on this series of problems had a considerably higher level of agreement with the two axiom-based rules, 9 and 16, than did the 4 subjects with the highest level of violation. Correspondingly, the latter subjects had a significantly higher level of agreement with the two non-axiom-based rules, 10 and 19, than did the most consistent

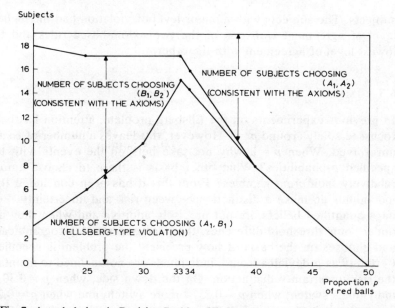

Fig. 7. Actual choices in Decision Problem III: Known versus Unknown Chances.

Actual choices	Rules	Utility independence conditions		Conditions inconsistent with utility	
		Rule 9	Rule 16	Rule 10	Rule 19
(1) Subjects consistent with axioms on all problems. ($n = 5$)		6.7	6.7	5.7	2.1
(2) Subjects inconsistent for values of Π near $\frac{1}{3}$. ($n = 4$)		4.4	5.6	8.4	7.0
(1) Subjects inconsistent even for $\Pi = 0.20$. ($n = 10$)		7.8	5.3	6.2	6.3
Average Rating		6.7	5.7	6.7	5.3

Fig. 8. Correspondence between subjects' actual choices and their level of agreement with the relevant rules in Decision Problem III: Known versus Unknown Events.

subjects. The subjects with a minor level of violation had the highest level of agreement with one of the two axiom-based rules and the lowest level of agreement with the other.

6.3 SUMMARY

In previous experiments on the Ellsberg problem, attention has been focussed solely around $p = \frac{1}{3}$. However, this leaves a number of issues unresolved. When $p = \frac{1}{3}$, why not take bets on the events with the specified probabilities? What other basis is there to choose among relatively indifferent gambles? From this it has been concluded that individuals do make a distinction between risk and uncertainty. Perhaps quantified beliefs are not precisely additive and when they are under some threshold difference, then one operates lexicographically and chooses on the basis of how precisely the problem is specified. Certainly as p deviates from $\frac{1}{3}$, individuals are not inclined to maintain the risk-uncertainty distinction. On the down side, when $p = 0.30$, 4 individuals switch; when $p = 0.25$, 4 more switch; and when $p = 0.20$, 3 more switch – leaving only three making such a distinction. On the up side, it is just as striking. At $p = 0.40$, 6 switch; at $p = 0.45$, 4 switch; and at $p = 0.50$ the remaining 4 switch. Individuals tend not to maintain a risk-uncertainty distinction (if they ever did) when they think it is costing them a significant chance of winning.

7. EVENT COMPLEMENTS

7.1 DECISION PROBLEM IV

Decision Problem

Consider the following two urns: Urn I contains 100 balls, each either red or black, but the precise composition of the urn is not known by you; Urn II contains 50 red balls and 50 black balls.

Do you prefer A_1 or B_1?

A_1:   Win $1000 if a red ball is drawn from Urn I.

B_1:   Win $1000 if a red ball is drawn from Urn II.

Do you prefer A_2 or B_2?

A_2:   Win \$1000 if a black ball is drawn from Urn I.

B_2:   Win \$1000 if a black ball is drawn from Urn II.

Then replace \$1000 by \$1010 in the A lotteries and choose again.

Rules

Is the rationale for your choice contained in any of the rules below?

Rule 2: When two alternatives have probabilities that are in the same range, then select the alternative with the higher payoff.

Rule 5: If you think the chances for an alternative based on an event in one lottery are higher than the chances on an event in another lottery, then the chances for an alternative based on the complement of the event in the first lottery should be lower than the chances on the complement of the event in the second lottery. With differing chances and the same stakes, take the alternatives offering the highest chances.

Rule 12: When your best estimate of the chances are the same for two alternatives, one of which seems more known than the other, take the one that offers the higher payoff.

Rule 16: If each of two alternatives has a common payoff for some event E, that common payoff cannot help to discriminate between the alternatives, and is, therefore, irrelevant in choosing between the alternatives. If that common payoff is changed, but still remains common to both alternatives, then the preferences between the alternatives should stay the same.

Rule V: When the payoffs are the same, take the alternative for which the chances are known over one in which the chances are uncertain.

Applying the Rules to the Decision Problem

This problem is also called the 'Ellsberg Paradox'. Ellsberg (1961) asserts that individuals choose B_1 and B_2 since they are bets on events with known, unambiguous probabilities. That these choices are a direct violation of Axiom S2 can be seen from the following matrix:

	red in Urn I red in Urn II	black in Urn I black in Urn II	red in Urn I black in Urn II	black in Urn I red in Urn II
A_1	1000	0	1000	0
B_1	1000	0	0	1000
A_2	0	1000	0	1000
B_2	0	1000	1000	0

The two alternatives A_1 and B_1 have common consequences for the event represented by the first two columns (event E in rule 16), and alternative A_2 and B_2 have common consequences for this same event. Hence this event can be ignored but then A_1 and B_2 are the same on event $\bar{E}$, and A_2 and B_1 are the same on $\bar{E}$; hence a choice of B_1 and B_2 violates this axiom.

The choices B_1, B_2, can also be seen to be a direct contradiction of the additivity condition for probabilities, assuming the maximization of expected utility.[34] Note, $B_1 > A_1$ implies

$$\tfrac{1}{2} > P(R_I)U_I(1000) + P(B_I)U_I(0),$$

and $B_2 > A_2$ implies

$$\tfrac{1}{2} > P(B_I)U_I(1000) + P(R_I)U_I(0).$$

If we can assume that winning or losing on Urn I gives the same utility as winning or losing the same amount on Urn II, then $U_I(1000) = 1$, $U_I(0) = 0$

$$\tfrac{1}{2} > P(R_I),$$

$$\tfrac{1}{2} > P(B_I).$$

Hence $P(R_I) + P(B_I) < 1$, and additivity does not hold. Rule 5 states the additivity condition directly in terms of events and their complements as we have here. Hence Axiom S2 is necessary for this probability axiom.

The applicability of the strong independence axiom, M2, can be seen by noting that the probability of winning on A_1 equals:

1/100P(exactly 1 red ball in Urn I) + 2/100P(exactly 2 red balls in Urn I) + $\cdots$ + 100/100P(exactly 100 red balls in Urn I).

If we now make a symmetry assumption that

P(exactly $50 - x$ red balls in Urn I) $= P$(exactly $50 + x$ red balls in Urn I) $= P(x)$, then by pairing up, we obtain

$$P(x) = \frac{50 - x}{100} P(x) + \frac{50 + x}{100} P(x) \quad \text{and} \quad \sum_{x=0}^{50} P(x) = \tfrac{1}{2}.$$

An alternative interpretation has been suggested by Smith (1969): Suppose additivity holds and the beliefs are consistent so that probabilities can be assigned: what do the choices of B_1 and B_2 imply about utility? This approach is interesting because it allows us to apply the von Neumann–Morgenstern/Marschak axioms, all of which require probabilities. In the expressions above, if instead of assuming $U_I(X) = U_{II}(X)$, we assume $P(R_I) + P(B_I) = 1$, we obtain

$$\tfrac{1}{2} > P(R_I)U_I(1000) + (1 - P(R_I))U_I(0),$$

and $\quad \tfrac{1}{2} > (1 - P(R_I))U_I(1000) + P(R_I)U_I(0),$

or $\quad \tfrac{1}{2} > P(R_I)(U_I(1000) - U_I(0)) + U_I(0),$

$$\tfrac{1}{2} > -P(R_I)(U_I(1000) - U_I(0)) + U_I(1000).$$

Adding these two expressions we obtain:

$$1 > U_I(0) + U_I(1000),$$

but since $U_{II}(0) + U_{II}(1000) = 1$, we see that the utility sum in Urn I must be less than the corresponding utility sum in Urn II.

This latter viewpoint suggests that perhaps instead of a risk-uncertainty distinction, we are observing the effect of a multi-level lottery. That is, Urn II may be considered a first level lottery, but Urn I may be thought of as a situation arising from drawing the urn or the balls in the urn as a sample from some population. For example, it may be thought of as having had 100 balls drawn from a large population of balls, 50% of which were red and 50% of which were black. Alternatively we may think of the urn itself as the sample unit, and assume that it was drawn from a population of urns. For example perhaps there were 101 urns, ranging from one having 0 red and 100 black up to one having 100 red and 0 black or perhaps there were only two urns in the population, the two described above. When someone is presented with an Urn I type of description perhaps he tries to build up a characterization of how it could have arisen. Different characterizations may lead to different choice patterns.

Raiffa (1961) proposed a compounding approach to remove the uncertainty in Urn I by first having a lottery on Urn II to select a color, and then if this color is drawn from Urn I, one wins. The probability of winning would be $\frac{1}{2}P(R_I) + \frac{1}{2}P(B_I)$ which equals $\frac{1}{2}\{P(R_I) + P(B_I)\}$. Since probabilities are additive, i.e., $P(R_I) + P(B_I) = 1$, (for non-additive assumption see, for example Fellner (1965)) and accepting the rule that if the payoffs are equal and the probabilities of obtaining those payoffs are equal, you should be indifferent between the alternatives.

Ellsberg (1961) and Becker and Brownson (1964) attempt to build a concept of ambiguity directly into the theory. For a critique of this work and for a new theoretical approach, see Larsson (1978).

7.2 EMPIRICAL STUDIES

Problem Representation

As with the preceding problem, the decision problem of this section is hard to represent succinctly since it is stated in terms of events rather than probabilities. We shall denote by X the situation which results in events x or $\bar{x}$ which have 'unknown' probabilities, if any. We shall denote by Y the situation which results in events y or $\bar{y}$ with 'known' probabilities, p and $1 - p$, respectively. The payoff on the Y events will be denoted as r, while the payoff on the X events will be denoted as αr. If $\alpha > 1$, then there is a premium for alternatives based on the 'unknown' events. The alternatives may be characterized as:

$$A_1: \alpha r \text{ if } x \qquad A_2: \alpha r \text{ if } \bar{x}$$
$$B_1: r \text{ if } y \qquad B_2: r \text{ if } \bar{y}.$$

An 'Ellsberg-type violation' is the choice B_1, B_2.

The problem at the beginning of this section can be described as X: urn with red balls (x) and black balls $(\bar{x})$ in unknown composition, Y: urn with 50 red balls (y) and 50 black balls $(\bar{y})$, $r = \$1000$, and $\alpha = 1$. In the supplementary question, below the problem statement, 'α' is changed to 1.01.

Previous Empirical Studies

In the study with 38 business executives, MacCrimmon (1965) used a series of Type IV problems. The main element varied in each was the type of event under consideration. We shall only discuss the two most relevant problems here. In the first problem the parameters were: X: a particular stock price, Pierce Industries, going up (x) or not going up ($\bar{x}$); Y: Deck with 26 red cards (y) and 26 black cards ($\bar{y}$), $r = \$1000$, and $\alpha = 1$. In the second problem, the parameters were: X: U.S. GNP being higher (x) or not higher ($\bar{x}$); Y: Coin landing heads (y) or tails ($\bar{y}$), $r = \$1000$, and $\alpha = 1$.

In the first problem 27 subjects were consistent with the axioms. That is, if they preferred event W over event Z in the first set, then they preferred the complement of Z over the complement of W in the second set. Seven subjects had violations of the event complement condition; five of these subjects had Ellsberg-type violations (i.e., they preferred the 'known' card bet both times), while the other two preferred the stock bet both times.[35] Hence the rate of violation was 21%. In the second problem there were 24 consistent subjects and 7 subjects who had Ellsberg-type violations. (The remaining 7 subjects had some degree of indifference.) Hence the rate of violation was 23%.

When the stakes were changed to yield $10 more on the 'unknown' event (i.e., $\alpha = 1.01$), then the proportion of Ellsberg-type violations dropped to 12% (4 out of 34) on the first problem and 17% (6 out of 35) on the second problem. Note here, though, that the choice of the 'unknown' stock bet in both sets cannot be called a violation with these payoffs since they pay more and would be the logical choice if the 'known' and 'unknown' events were deemed about equally likely.

On the first problem, the subjects were also presented with reasons supporting consistent (i.e., axiom-based) responses and with reasons supporting Ellsberg-type violations. Nineteen subjects judged the consistent argument the more reasonable, while 12 subjects preferred the violating argument. Thus overall, there was a rate of 39% accepting the Ellsberg-type violation. Among those subjects who had consistent answers themselves, the rate of acceptance of the Ellsberg-type answer was 22% (6 out of 27), while among those who had an inconsistent answer themselves, the acceptance rate was 57% (4 out of 7).

New Empirical Study

The 19 subjects in our study were presented with two sets of 11 alternative wagers and were asked to rank the wagers in each set in order of their preference.[36] The sets differed in terms of payoffs – in the first set $r = \$1000$, $\alpha = 1$; in the second set, $r = \$1000$, $\alpha = 1.01$. Let us first consider only the first set and only four of the 11 alternatives. We used the alternatives of the decision problem at the beginning of this section, i.e., X: urn with 100 balls either red (x) or black ($\bar{x}$); Y: urn with 50 red balls (y) and 50 black balls ($\bar{y}$).

Fifteen of our 19 subjects ranked both Y bets (i.e., bets on the 'known' urn) over either X bet. Another subject ranked three of the bets equally and one of the X bets lower. Two subjects ranked all four bets equally; while the remaining subject ranked one of the Y bets highest and the other lowest, with the X bets ranked between them. Hence only 3 of the 19 subjects behaved consistently with the utility axioms; there were 16 subjects with Ellsberg-type violations. This is a very high violation rate of 84%. Looking at it another way, 16 subjects prefer B_1 to A_1, and 3 subjects are indifferent. Of these 16 subjects, only one preferred A_2 to B_2 (i.e., the bets on the complements are in the right order).[37]

We can conclude from these results that bets on an urn with specified composition seem to be preferable to bets on an urn with unknown composition. Our general interest, though, is how people treat real situations of uncertainty. For example, do they act in making stock market investments in a manner that would force us to conclude that probabilities (satisfying the usual axioms) could not be assigned to stock price movements.[38] To obtain some information about this, we included the two stock price bets corresponding to the earlier MacCrimmon study, i.e., X': the price of Pierce Industries goes down (x') or does not go down ($\bar{x}'$).

Comparing the X' rankings to the Y rankings, we find that 10 subjects ranked both specified urn bets over either stock market bet. Two subjects ranked all four equally. The remaining 7 subjects gave rankings consistent with the utility axioms; 6 of them ranked one of the stock price bets first and the other last, while the other ranked the urn bet first and the other last.[39] Hence the rate of violation is lower with the stock price than with the 'unknown' urn. Still, the rate is 53% which is quite high.[40]

By obtaining rankings of all alternatives instead of just using pairs of bets on 'known' versus 'unknown' events, we can examine the degree to which the 'uncertain' events are perceived as uncertain. In discussing MacCrimmon's earlier study, Selten (1968, p.28) said, "Maybe the stock market events used here are not very good examples of uncertainty; many subjects may think that they can make a very good estimate of these probabilities." If this were so, we would expect, when we compare the stock price bets to the bets on the 'unknown' urn, that the stock price bets being more 'known' would both be ranked over either of the uncertain urn bets. A study of the data shows that this is true for only 6 of the 19 subjects. Another 6 subjects prefer both urn bets to either stock price bet. Hence it does not seem that the stock price bets are more certain.

It should not be forgotten that these comparisons provide still another test of the utility axioms, and obviously all 12 of the subjects identified above are inconsistent with the axioms. Another subject was indifferent among 3 of the 4 bets but ranked one of the urn bets

Rules / Actual choices	Utility independence conditions		Conditions inconsistent with utility	
	Rule 5	Rule 12	Rule 16	Rule 2
(1) Subjects consistent in one series, either Urn II versus Urn I, Urn II versus stock price, or Urn II versus Urn I with $\alpha = 1.01$. ($n = 10$)	6.4	6.5	5.3	8.3
(2) Subjects inconsistent ranking Urn II versus Urn I even with $\alpha = 1.01$, or Urn II versus stock price. ($n = 7$)	7.9	6.0	5.3	8.7
(3) Subjects indifferent throughout (or indifferent and inconsistent). ($n = 2$)	9.0	5.5	9.0	9.0
Average Rating	7.2	6.2	5.7	8.5

Fig. 9. Correspondence between subjects' actual choices and their level of agreement with the relevant rules in Decision Problem IV: Event Complements.

lower; hence he too was inconsistent. Two subjects were indifferent among all the four bets and the remaining 4 subjects ranked one of the stock bets first and the other stock bet last. Hence the rate of violation among two presumably uncertain situations was 68%.

The correspondence between the subjects' choices and the subjects' agreement with the relevant rules is given in Figure 9. The most applicable axiom-based rule is Rule 5 and it is puzzling why the 7 subjects who found it so acceptable managed to violate it each time they had the opportunity.

Summary

Ellsberg-type violations occur at a very high rate – much higher than in preceding studies. Perhaps the difference is due to our procedure of asking for rankings rather than for pair-wise choices. The high rate of violation occurring in the stock price choices causes doubt about whether people are sufficiently consistent in their beliefs to allow assessment of subjective probabilities. If the non-additivity of beliefs is such a prevalent behavior, then further theoretical and empirical study is warranted.

8. PAYOFF–PROBABILITY INTERACTIONS

8.1 DECISION PROBLEM V

Decision Problem

Consider an urn containing 100 balls, 20 of which are red; the other 80 are either black or yellow. The number of black balls is between 1 and 5 inclusive. One ball will be drawn from the urn and its color will determine the payoff you receive.

Do you prefer A_1 or B_1?

A_1:   \$100,000 if a red ball is drawn.
        \$1,000,000 if a yellow ball is drawn.
        \$0 if a black ball is drawn.

B_1:   \$0 if a red ball is drawn.
        \$1,000,000 if a yellow ball is drawn.
        \$1,000,000 if a black ball is drawn.

Do you prefer A_2 or B_2?

A_1: $100,000 if a red ball is drawn.
        $0 if a yellow ball is drawn.
        $0 if a black ball is drawn.

B_2: $0 if a red ball is drawn.
        $0 if a yellow ball is drawn.
        $1,000,000 if a black ball is drawn.

Rules

The rules applicable to this problem are those listed in the preceding sections; hence instead of listing the rules here, we shall provide an elaboration of the rules to this specific problem.[41]

(S) I would choose alternative A_1 over B_1 and alternative A_2 over alternative B_2.

In both situations, I note that if a yellow ball is drawn, it does not make any difference what I choose, since in the first situation alternatives A_1 and B_1 would both yield $1,000,000 while in the second situation alternatives A_2 and B_2 would both yield nothing. So I can focus only on what happens if a red ball or a black ball is drawn. But when I do this, the situations are the same. In both cases one alternative (A_1 or A_2) gives me $100,000 on a red ball and nothing on a black ball while the other alternative (B_1 or B_2) gives me nothing on a red ball and $1,000,000 on a black ball. Since I prefer the larger chance (20%) of getting $100,000 to the smaller chance (1%–5%) of getting $1,000,000, I choose alternatives A_1 and A_2.

(A) I would choose alternative A_1 over alternative B_1 and alternative B_2 over alternative A_2.

In the first situation, I have almost a sure chance of receiving at least $100,000 and a very good chance that it will be $1,000,000 by selecting alternative A_1. There is very little chance of getting nothing. Why should I take a 20% chance of getting nothing if a red ball turns up on alternative B_1?

In the second situation, the odds are against my receiving anything. Winning a million is so much better than winning $100,000 and the chances aren't that much worse, so I'll choose alternative B_2.

(E) I would choose alternative B_1 over alternative A_1 and alternative A_2 over alternative B_2.

In the first situation, alternative B_1 provides a guaranteed 80% chance of receiving $1,000,000. Alternative A_1, however, is more risky. This is a guaranteed chance of 20% of winning if a red ball comes up, but I would win only $100,000. Further, if a black ball comes up I don't win anything and there is up to a 5% chance that might happen. I know what the chances are with alternative B_1 but not with alternative A_1 – I'll take B_1.

In the second situation, alternative A_2 provides a guaranteed 20% chance of receiving $100,000. Alternative B_2 is riskier; there might be only one black ball and so the chances could be as low as 1% for winning $1,000,000. Since I don't know what the chances are with alternative B_2, but I do for alternative A_2 – I'll take A_2.

Applying the Rules to the Decision Problem

This problem was designed to attempt to capture the Allais and Ellsberg reasoning in the same problem. In the standard problems, two of the pairs of choices are consistent with the independence assumption and one violates it in a particular way, but that leaves one pair of choices violating the postulates in no particular way of interest. In addition to wanting a more efficient problem, the combination also allows a test of one type of violation versus the other (i.e., Ellsberg versus Allais) – something that cannot be done in separate problems.

The problems can be set up in a payoff matrix as follows:

	20 Red balls	Black	80 or Yellow balls
		1–5 Black balls	75–79 Yellow balls
A_1	$100,000	$0	$1,000,000
B_1	$0	$1,000,000	$1,000,000
A_2	$100,000	$0	$0
B_2	$0	$1,000,000	$0

From this matrix we can easily see that Axiom S2 would require the choices A_1 and A_2 or B_1 and B_2. The rationale is expressed above as Rule S and is a specific instance of Rules 16 and 20 discussed in Section 5. As was shown in Section 5, the A or B choices are implied by the strong independence assumption, Axiom M2. The earlier discussion also applies to this problem.

The A (for Allais) rationale is based on the reasoning discussed in Sections 4 and 5 and is represented in Rule 6.[42] That is, you choose A_1 over B_1 because you think conservatively when the environment is relatively good and you do not want to take the unnecessary chance of losing with B_1. When the environment is relatively bad, however, you become more of a gambler and select B_2 because although it does not have as good a chance of winning as A_2, it provides a chance to 'win big'. The E (for Ellsberg) rationale is based on the reasoning discussed in Sections 6 and 7 and represented by Rule V. That is, you note that any bet on the event 'red ball' or on the event 'black or yellow ball' gives a specified chance of winning. Bets on other events such as 'black ball' or 'red or black ball' give a range of chances rather than a specific number. When given an interval, you tend to assume that the low end of the interval will represent the chances and hence you end up taking B_1 and A_2. As before, these choices do not allow probabilities and utilities to be assigned.

8.2 EMPIRICAL STUDIES

Problem Representation

The given statement of this problem in terms of events again makes it difficult to develop a succinct representation. The problem requires three events, x_1, x_2, and x_3, which partition the state space. These events are composed of discrete states which are equally likely and whose total is n. The proportion of states in x_1 is p and the proportion of states in x_2 is an interval, q. There are three payoff values r, s and t with $r > s > t$. The alternatives in this problem can be characterized as:

A_1: s if x_1 $\qquad\qquad$ A_2: s if x_1
$\qquad$ r if x_2 $\qquad\qquad\qquad$ r if x_2 or x_3
B_1: t if x_1 $\qquad\qquad$ B_2: t if x_1 or x_2
$\qquad$ r if x_2 or x_3 $\qquad\qquad$ r if x_3.

Since there have been no previous empirical studies of this problem, the next part of the paper gives the results of our study. The problem used is exactly that given at the outset of this section and so has parameters: x_1: red ball, x_2: black ball, x_3: yellow ball, $n = 100$, $p = 0.20$, $q = [0.01, 0.05]$, $r = \$1,000,000$; $s = \$100,000$ and $t = \$0$. The choices A_1, A_2 or B_1, B_2 will be called 'consistent' (i.e., consistent with the utility axioms), the choices A_1, B_2 will be called 'Allais-type violations', and the choices B_1, A_2 will be called 'Ellsberg-type violations'.

New Empirical Study

In this combined problem, 15 subjects made consistent choices, 3 subjects had Ellsberg-type violations and 1 subject an Allais-type violation. Further evidence on propensity to favor Allais or Ellsberg comes in the ranking of reasons. The subjects were given reasons justifying each of the 4 pairs of answers and one would expect that those subjects making consistent choices would favor the postulate-based reasoning and those making a particular violation would favor the corresponding reason. Overall the most favored answer was one of the postulate answers, S, with $7\frac{1}{3}$ first-place votes and a rank order of 36. Next came the Allais reasoning with a first-place vote of $6\frac{1}{3}$ and a rank order of $30\frac{1}{3}$. Then came the other postulate-based reason ($3\frac{1}{3}$, 28) and finally the Ellsberg reason (2, $15\frac{1}{2}$). It should be noted, though, that the Allais reason got a majority in each of the pairwise comparisons.

In matching up the subject's own answer with the reason he favoured, we find only 1 true Ellsberg-type (i.e., someone who made an Ellsberg-type violation in his choices and who favoured the Ellsberg argument); 1 true Allais type (defined correspondingly); and 4 true utility axiom types. This latter condition requires subjects to favour both the postulate answers over the other two; if, however, we require just one of the axiom-based argument to be voted at the top, we can add another six subjects. The other subjects had mixed answers.

8.3 SUMMARY

An advantage of the combined problem is that it circumvents the problem of subjects agreeing with an answer simply because it had one of the choices similar to their own. With arguments for all 4 answers (unlike MacCrimmon 1965, and Slovic and Tversky 1975), we can observe the difference between closeness in choices and real agreement. Only 9 of the 19 subjects agreed with the reasons supporting the choices they had made themselves; 4 put the reason corresponding to their own choices in second place, 5 put it in third place, and 1 put it in last place.

We have omitted the rule-agreement part of the analysis of this experiment since this was essentially imbedded within the problem and has been discussed above. In the direct comparison we find a stronger tendency for subjects to make Ellsberg-type violations rather than Allais-type violations in their own choices, but there is a contrasting tendency to find the Allais rationale to be a more compelling one. At this stage we have no definite explanation for this behavior. Clearly the small sample size does not allow us to make any definite statements about the relative rates of violation, but the problem does seem to hold some promise of making such comparisons. The problem should be modified to make B_1 and B_2 relatively more attractive since 12 of the 18 subjects chose A_1 and A_2.

9. OTHER INDEPENDENCE CONDITIONS

9.1 INTRODUCTION

In the preceding five sections, we have discussed the main 'paradoxes' in utility theory, and we have shown that most of the challenges to the axioms have been directed toward the independence condition represented in axioms S2, M2, vNM2, or A4. Over the years, each of these has been the most controversial axiom in its system. In this section, we shall consider a few other interesting independence conditions.

One form of challenge to the general S2 axiom is in the form of decision problems that can be presented to anyone to find out whether his choice violates the axioms. A less convincing kind of challenge is presented in the form of an example of how some particular decision maker, faced with particular choices, violates the axioms. Since this format does not require you to make direct choices, you can try to decide only (1) whether it is reasonable for such a decision maker to choose in the manner asserted, (2) whether his choices really violate the axioms, and (3) whether the situation is serious enough to cause concern about the axioms. In this section most of the challenges to the axioms will be in 'example' form.

The independence conditions we shall focus on in this section are of three kinds:
(1) independence of events from alternatives,
(2) independence from irrelevant alternatives, and
(3) independence of beliefs from payoffs.

9.2 INDEPENDENCE OF EVENTS FROM ALTERNATIVES

Decision Problem

Consider the following situation:

Two closed Boxes A and B are on the table in front of you. Box A contains $1000. Box B contains either nothing or $1,000,000. You do not know which. You have a choice between two actions:
(i) Take what is in both boxes.
(ii) Take only what is in Box B.

At some time before this opportunity, a superior being made a prediction about what you will decide. The being is 'almost certainly' correct. If the being expects you to take action (i), he has left Box B empty. If he expects you to take action (ii), he has left $1,000,000 in Box B. If he expects you to randomize your choice, for example by flipping a coin, he has left Box B empty. In all cases, Box A contains $1000.

What action would you choose?

Discussion of the Decision Problem

As in the earlier problems, one can present fairly compelling arguments for the choice of either (i) or (ii). Consider the following arguments:

(i) Either the money is in Box B or it is not. If the money is in Box B and I take both boxes, I will have $1000 more than if I had only taken Box B. Alternatively, if the money is not in Box B, and I take both boxes, at least I will get $1000. Hence, taking alternative (i), i.e., selecting both boxes, is the better strategy.

(ii) If the being can guess with 'almost certainty' then I would only take Box B, since if I were to take both he would almost surely guess correctly and hence leave Box B empty.

This problem, and its associated arguments, was first published by Nozick (1969) and is called the 'Newcombe Paradox' after Newcombe who first formulated it. Because it was introduced some years after the other 'paradoxes', it has not yet received the attention of those problems. The Newcombe problem differs from the other ones in several ways. Perhaps most importantly, it presumes to set one of the axioms in opposition to the expected utility criterion, rather than to attack one of the axioms with a counter-axiom. Argument (i) is based on the dominance axiom, and argument (ii) is based on an expected utility formulation. Presumably you cannot have both.

It is useful to analyze more directly how the dominance and expected utility formulations apparently contradict each other. Let us look first at dominance, as expressed most directly in Arrow's Axiom A4. Dominance is almost universally accepted as a reasonable axiom to use when it applies and so it would be hard to choose in contradiction to it. Consider the following way of formulating the problem in a payoff matrix:

	$1,000,000 is in Box B	nothing is in Box B
(i) Take both boxes	$1,001,000	$1000
(ii) Take only Box B	$1,000,000	$0

If you accept this formulation of the problem, it would be difficult not to take alternative (i) because it dominates alternative (ii).

However, this formulation may be questionable because it fails to take into account the predictive ability of the superior being. Consider, instead, the following payoff matrix formulation:

	Being predicts correctly	Being does not predict correctly
(i) Take both boxes	$1000	$1,001,000
(ii) Take only Box B	$1,000,000	$0

Obviously in this formulation dominance does not apply and one would take alternative (ii) if $P(\text{being correct})U(\$1,000,000) + P(\text{being}$

incorrect)$U(\$0)$ is greater than P(being correct)$U(\$1000) + P$(being incorrect)$U(\$1,001,000)$. For any reasonable utility function, and assuming that P is close to one as implied in the problem, alternative (ii) would have the higher expected utility. Thus, if it were not for the different formulations, we would have the paradoxical situation in which dominance implies one action while the maximization of expected utility implies another action.

The major difference, then, between this challenge to the axioms and those considered earlier, is that the 'Newcombe paradox' is based on the way the problem is formulated, rather than in the choices offered in a specific formulation. Expected utility theory, as set forth in Section 2, requires an independence between the events and the alternatives. In the 'dominance formulation' of the problem, the probability of either event occurring is not independent of your choice of actions and is inappropriate. While this difficulty does not hold for the second formulation above, the second formulation does not take into account the amount in the boxes and hence may seem incomplete. In order to get both uncertain elements into the problem, we need to form the compound events:

	Being predicts correctly and put:		Being predicts incorrectly and put:	
	$1,000,000 in Box B	$0 in Box B	$1,000,000 in Box B	$0 in Box B
(i) Take both boxes		$1000	$1,001,000	
(ii) Take only Box B	$1,000,000			$0

The empty cells represent impossible combinations and an examination of the whole table shows that dominance cannot be applied. Hence one can choose only Box B and act in accordance with expected utility without violating dominance. If, there are very large, non-monetary satisfactions of exhibiting the 'free-will' of taking both boxes or of beating the being out of $1,001,000 and showing him up in the process, as asserted by Asimov (Gardner, 1974, p.123), then you might choose action (i). You would, however, be choosing it on an expected utility basis rather than on the basis of dominance.

Empirical Study

After a discussion of the Newcombe problem by Nozick (1974), 652 readers of *Scientific American* wrote in to express their choices and reasons. A large proportion, 483, selected only Box B; a great variety of reasons were given.

In our controlled, experimental study, using the subjects described earlier, the subjects also tended to select only Box B. Of the 19 subjects, only 2 stated that they would take both boxes, and these subjects, plus one other, were the only ones who thought that argument (i) – the dominance principle – was the more compelling basis for choice. As a check on the extent to which the large money amount in Box B might affect the choice, we also asked a question in which this amount was reduced to $1000. Ten of the 16 subjects who answered this question indicated a preference for both boxes. This increase in preference for both boxes does not necessarily vindicate the dominance formulation but rather it indicates that the expected utility of action (ii) is not sufficiently high. In the original problem, the subjects were asked at what point they would switch to action (i) if the money amount in Box B were decreased. The median and modal response of the 17 subjects selecting action (ii) was $500,000. They were also asked to state the probability of the being predicting correctly at which they would be indifferent between the two actions; the median response was 0.55 (and the mode was 0.75).

Although the expected utility criterion was not directly presented to the subjects, they were asked to rate their acceptance of a form of dominance, as expressed in the following rule:

Rule 3: If one alternative *A* has outcomes that are at least as good as the outcomes for another alternative *B*, for every possible state of the world, then alternative *A* is at least as good as alternative *B*.

As could be expected, there was a high level of agreement with the dominance criterion. It was ranked third in the set of 20 rules, and it received an average rating of 8.1.

Summary

While it may at first seem that dominance and expected utility collide in the Newcombe problem, both may be adhered to when the problem is correctly formulated to retain the necessary independence between events and alternatives. Many interesting issues are involved in formulating the problem and we have given only a cursory discussion. For a more detailed treatment, see Nozick (1969), and Bar-Hillel and Margalit (1972).

9.3 INDEPENDENCE FROM IRRELEVANT ALTERNATIVES

Decision Example

A gentleman wandering in a strange city at dinner time chances upon a modest restaurant which he enters uncertainly. The waiter informs him that there is no menu, but that this evening he may have either broiled salmon at $2.50 or steak at $4.00. In a first-rate restaurant his choice would have been steak, but considering his unknown surroundings and the different prices he elects the salmon. Soon after the waiter returns from the kitchen, apologizes profusely, blaming the uncommunicative chef for omitting to tell him that fried snails and frog's legs are also on the bill of fare at $4.50 each. It so happens that our hero detests them both and would always select salmon in preference to either, yet his response is "Splendid, I'll change my order to steak."

Luce and Raiffa (1957, p.288)

Discussion of the Decision Example

This is a particularly good example of a violation of the condition called the 'independence from irrelevant alternatives'. One would expect that a rational theory of decision would not allow the introduction of new alternatives, or the elimination of old alternatives, to reverse the preference between two alternatives available in both instances. This condition is incorporated in each of the axiom systems studied in Section 2. In each system it appears as the hereditary condition in the first axiom. The first axiom in each system requires a complete ordering and since it says nothing about what other alternatives are available, if action A is preferred to action B it must be preferred regardless of the other alternatives.

If the condition of the independence of irrelevant alternatives seems so acceptable, then how do we explain the example given above? Under the circumstances was it really unreasonable for the diner to change his order to steak? The information that the restaurant served snails and frog's legs indicated to him that it was probably a better restaurant than he had initially thought and that he could, therefore, probably get a good steak. This seems quite reasonable and so we must ask whether the axioms can account for his choices. Clearly they can if you consider the following alternatives:

A_1:   steak in a poor restaurant,

B_1:   salmon in a poor restaurant,

A_2:   steak in a first-class restaurant,

B_2:   salmon in a first-class restaurant.

By looking at the problem this way, we see that the diner was not really selecting between the same two alternatives in both instances. In situations when he thinks he is choosing in a poor restaurant, he takes B_1 over A_1; when he thinks he is choosing in a good restaurant, he takes A_2 over B_2. Since these are four distinct alternatives, there is no violation of the independence of irrelevant alternatives.

Empirical Study

There have been a few previous studies involving the independence of irrelevant alternatives, but these, along with one we conducted, tend to take up too much space to describe. We shall confine our attention here to the attitude part of our study. We presented the independence of irrelevant alternatives condition to our subjects in the form of two separate rules.

Rule 11: If some alternative *A* is preferred to another alternative *B*, then even when new alternatives are added or old alternatives are taken away, alternative *A* should still be preferred to alternative *B*.

Rule 14: If alternatives *A* and *B* are considered as equally good best alternatives when choosing from a restricted list of alternatives, when the list of alternatives is expanded, if alternative *A* is still one of the best alternatives, then alternative *B* also should be considered one of the best alternatives.

Rule 11 is the more standard form of the condition while Rule 14 asserts a particular implication that Sen (1970) has developed.[43] As the rule number suggests, the first form was found more acceptable than the second, although both were ranked in the lower half of the 20 rules considered. The average rating for Rule 11 was 6.5, while the average rating for Rule 14 was 6.0.

Summary

It seems, then, that whenever we face two alternatives that are described identically to ones encountered earlier, we must ask whether new information justifies a redefinition of the alternatives before we proceed to apply the independence of irrelevant alternatives condition. If however, we automatically redefine an alternative as different simply because it has occurred at another time, we may be sacrificing the guidance the decision axioms can provide.

There seem to have been no major empirical studies of the independence of irrelevant alternatives although the topic has been included as a part of several experiments. Because of the ambiguous interpretation of repeated alternatives, however, it is difficult to reach any conclusions about the rate of violation or even the applicability of the condition. It does seem to have some appeal to people, but in neither form we used was it ranked in the top half of the 20 rules considered.

9.4 INDEPENDENCE OF BELIEFS FROM PAYOFFS

Decision Example

Two friends on their way to a restaurant decide to order the chef's special of the day although neither knows what it is. On the way in, Tom makes Harry the following offer: Harry is to guess if it will be meat or fish – if he is right, Tom will treat them to the best bottle of white wine. Harry guesses fish. The wine steward overhears them talking about the wine and tells them that it is out of stock but the best red wine is in stock. Tom then changes the prize to the bottle of red wine. Harry changes his guess to meat.

Discussion of the Decision Example

Does Harry's behavior seem rational? If we use choices to infer the probability one assigns to events, then from Harry's first guess we may conclude that he thought that fish was more likely to be the special than was meat, since the payoff was the same in either case – a bottle of white wine. However, from his revised guess we would conclude that he thought meat was more likely to be the special.

Presumably if you think meat is more likely than fish, you should guess meat in each situation (and conversely). Such a dependence of beliefs on particular payoffs would seem to be a violation of rules of rational decision.[44] Specifically, it would be a violation of Axiom S4. This can be seen most easily by setting out the payoff matrix:

	special is fish	special is meat
Situation 1: guess fish	bottle of white wine	lose
guess meat	lose	bottle of white wine
Situation 2: guess fish	bottle of red wine	lose
guess meat	lose	bottle of red wine

The attempt to resolve the dilemma of why the choice might change can be made along somewhat different lines from the frogs-legs story. In this case we probably have an interaction between the event "the special is ..." and the type of wine available. The consequence is not just "a bottle of white wine" but rather it is "a bottle of white wine with fish" or "a bottle of white wine with meat"; similarly for the red wine. When we think of it this way, then the first guess implies:[45]

P(special is fish) U(fish and white wine) $> P$(special is meat) U(meat and white wine),

while the second guess implies:

P(special is fish) U(fish and red wine) $< P$(special is meat) U(meat and red wine).

Clearly there is nothing necessarily inconsistent about these beliefs and preferences.

In the terminology of Ramsey (1931), we would say that the events are not ethically neutral. We care which one occurs for particular payoffs. Hence in interpreting whether a rule such as Axiom (S4) is reasonable, we must correctly describe the consequences. Note though that if we were to always redefine the consequences whenever S4 was apparently violated, then S4 would be tautological. Thus there must be some balance struck between redefining consequences to avoid a violation and letting a violation stand. Among the situations that may yield an apparent violation of S4 are ones in which (a) the consequence valuation depends on the event outcome (as in the example above), (b) the consequence gives information on the event outcome, (c) the combination of events introduces new elements, (d) the event (e.g., death) obviates realization of the stated consequences, (e) the changed reward may make careful reflection worthwhile, and (f) the events themselves have an intrinsic attraction (e.g., gambling) or aversion (e.g., disaster).

Empirical Study

Only a few empirical studies of the independence of beliefs from payoffs have been made. In the earlier study by MacCrimmon (1965) there was a quite high degree of violation of the independence condition, but part of the reason was due to the difficulties in ranking a large number of alternatives. We did not include a test of this independence axiom in our empirical study but we did present a statement of the rule to ascertain the degree of agreement. It was stated as:

Rule 4: The probability assigned to a particular event should not be affected by the particular payoffs that are associated with the event occurring or not occurring.

As you can see from the rule number, it was ranked fourth out of the set of 20 rules, receiving an average agreement score of 7.4.

Summary

There is some difficulty in interpreting whether the condition of the independence of beliefs from payoffs is applicable because of the definition of payoffs. Since there are no standard decision problems designed to elicit violations, it would seem that it is a quite acceptable axiom once the payoffs are completely specified. This is supported by the level of agreement with a written statement of it in our study. See Marschak and Radner (1972) for a further discussion.

10. CONCLUDING REMARKS

10.1 OTHER AXIOMS

Focus of Attention

We have studied how the axioms of expected utility theory stand up to the attacks which have been made against them. As a basis for explaining which axioms are being challenged and on what grounds, it was first necessary to present some of the axiom systems and to derive some of the similarities and differences among them. The most interesting axioms are those which assert some kind of independence. Since the expected utility criterion involves the multiplication of probability by a utility of payoff term, it should not be surprising that the central type of independence is between probabilities and payoffs. As we have seen, this type of independence has a surprising number of implications, including the following: (a) the lack of meaning in distinguishing between known and unknown chances, (b) the use of probability ratios, (c) the invalidity of switching from a conservative style to one of trying to win big, and (d) the additivity of the relation between an event and its complement.

Even though we considered a number of such implications in the central sections of this paper (i.e., Sections 4–8), we were not able to consider all implications. For example, an important implication of axioms such as M2 and S2 is the notion of substitutability as expressed in the following rule:

Rule 17: If for some alternative A one of its outcomes is replaced by another outcome, possibly a lottery, for which it is deemed equivalent, then the modified alternative A will stand in the same preference relation to all other alternatives as the original A did.

This substitutability concept is a major focus in some axiom systems such as that of Pratt, Raiffa, and Schlaifer (1964). We used a substitutability experiment, but describing it would take too much space. The above rule was on the list of the 20 rules presented to the subjects, and, as you can see from its number, it was ranked relatively low in terms of acceptability. (It should be remembered, though, that the rules based on the 'common consequence' implication of S2 ranked just as low.) The substitutability implication has been related to the Allais 'common consequence' problem by Morrison (1967). A critique of this appears in MacCrimmon (1967).

In the main body of this paper, we have not focussed attention on ordering and continuity axioms since they seem relatively less interesting. However, it seems worthwhile to consider them briefly here, if only to raise some issues and to provide some references.

Ordering Axioms

Each of the four axiom systems we considered had an axiom that asserted the existence of a complete, hereditary ordering. We have, in fact, already considered one implication of these ordering axioms – the independence from irrelevant alternatives. The two main properties of a complete ordering, however, have not yet been examined. These properties are (a) completeness, and (b) transitivity, as we noted at the beginning of Section 2. Examples of presumed violation of both properties have been presented and experimental evidence has been gathered.

As a violation of completeness (alternatively, it is called comparability), consider the following demand: 'Choose which is better (i) a Mozart symphony or (ii) a Cezanne painting.' A natural answer would be that you cannot compare them and this response could be considered a violation of completeness. Note, though, that the completeness property of relevance to expected utility theory is completeness of *preference*. In the request above, you are not being asked to choose on the basis of preference but rather on some notion of 'betterness'. This is a different question. Hopefully if you were asked a preference-relevant question, such as 'Would you prefer to go to hear a Mozart symphony or see a Cezanne painting?', you could answer it. See Davidson, Suppes, and Siegel (1957), and Churchman (1961) for these aspects of completeness.

Another important issue on completeness is the reluctance to make a choice when the alternatives have distasteful or 'unthinkable' consequences. For example, you may refuse to choose which one of your two children be spared from execution. However, if your refusal will result in both dying, you may provide the necessary choice. See Rapoport (1967) for a further discussion of this example and its implications.

A particularly sticky issue involving the completeness property is the distinction between completeness and indifference. If you continue to refuse to make a choice, does that indicate incompleteness or solely indifference? Did Buridan's ass have incomplete preferences among the bundles of hay or were they equally attractive? For a good discussion of these aspects of completeness, see Sen (1973).

Some of the same issues arise when considering the property of transitivity. Examples of intransitivity are easiest to find in non-preference contexts. For example in sports: team A beats team B, team B in turn beats team C, but team C beats team A. See May (1954) for some interesting examples.

In a preference context, one can observe intransitivities most readily when the alternatives are characterized by multiple attributes. Hence, in considering A versus B, you may focus on one set of attributes, in considering B versus C you focus on other attributes, and in considering C versus A you consider other attributes, so that you end up with a circular choice. For further discussion of this topic, see Rose (1965), Weinstein (1968), and Tversky (1969). The money pump argument, that is, collecting money to keep cycling a person to (intransitive) choices he has indicated a preference for, is described nicely by Raiffa (1968).

One of the most interesting aspects of transitivity, as with completeness, involves the indifference relation. Most of the examples of intransitivity of simple (i.e., not multi-attributed) alternatives involve intransitivity of indifference. You may be indifferent between 10 grains of sugar in your coffee and 11 grains of sugar, and between 11 grains and 12 grains, and so forth, but there will come a point, say 1500 grains, which you will not find indifferent to 10 grains. See Armstrong (1951), Luce (1956), and Fishburn (1970) for a discussion of the intransitivity of indifference.

In the list of 20 rules presented to the subjects we included verbal statements of completeness and of transitivity. Transitivity was the highest rated overall rule with an average rating of 8.8. Completeness (stated in terms of being willing and able to compare any alternatives) was also relatively highly rated, having an average score of 6.9 which made it the seventh ranked, overall. For a further discussion of both these properties and some empirical summaries, see Marschak (1964, 1967) and MacCrimmon (1968).

Continuity

Various axioms assert the existence of particular payoffs or probabilities that will make two expected utility terms equal. If such values do not exist or cannot be found, then the axioms are, in a sense, violated. Consider the following example: alternative A yields you 1¢ for sure but alternative B is a lottery which yields you 2¢ with a particular probability $(1 - p)$ and which results in immediate death with probability p. For what value of p would you be just indifferent between the two alternatives? Your first tendency is probably to say that there is no p for which you would be indifferent, and hence you would violate axioms such as vNM7, M8, and A9. If you reflect more on the situation, though, you might be willing to say that if p were less than 10^{-100}, you would consider alternative B. In fact, when you think of the chance of a fatal heart attack due to bending over to pick up a penny you drop, you might be willing to consider alternative B even for probabilities considerably larger than 10^{-100}. For a further discussion of theoretical aspects of these axioms, see Thrall (1954) and Chipman (1960). Fishburn (1968, 1970) provides a comprehensive discussion of these and other axioms.

10.2 SUMMARY

In the theoretical part of this paper, we have considered four of the main axiom systems for expected utility theory. In the past, they have tended to be referred to interchangeably. Even when they have been presented jointly, little attempt has been made to demonstrate the similarities and differences among them. We have tried to do this by first developing some common notation, then by showing some of the most important correspondences. The interrelation is most difficult between Savage's axioms which attempt to derive a probability measure and the other systems which start with probabilities. Some of these distinctions have tended to be by-passed in previous work, but they are worthy of further exploration.

In the empirical part of this paper, we have presented the strongest challenges to the expected utility axioms. Where possible these challenges have been given in the form of decision problems and the linkage to the axioms has been by way of rules which present the relevant implications of the axioms. Our new experimental study was directed more at pointing out which parameters should be studied than toward obtaining definitive results. Even with a sample size of 19, however, we obtained some strong results. The various 'paradoxes' of Allais and Ellsberg do seem to elicit a high rate of violation of the relevant axioms. Directions for further study were pointed out.

Suppose individuals violate the axioms in the choices they make, and especially when these choices have been the result of careful thought. If they would like to rely on the assistance of a theory of decision making, they have three main options:

(1) they can maintain the choices they have made and conclude that the axioms are not relevant for them in this situation (or perhaps in any situation),

(2) they can change their choices to bring them in line with the axioms, or

(3) they can change the theory to make it consistent with their choices.

Of these options, (1) is not very satisfactory since you do not know which situation will be relevant, unless you can develop a theory which will tell you, but this puts it into category (3). Even if you can develop such guidelines, you still do not have a basis for assisting in your choice when the axioms do not apply. Alternative (2) is probably the easiest way out of the difficulty. You use the axioms to police your choices and if a violation occurs, you conclude that you have made a mistake which you would like to change. If upon careful reflection, or if in a variety of problems, you persist in such violations, you may begin, however, to be troubled about such a mechanistic way of resolving difficult choice situations. Alternative (3) is in many ways the most desirable solution to the quandry, but it is not at all clear what kind of revisions to make to the theory. The development of the axioms of expected utility theory has received a great deal of careful attention and it may be difficult to make a good modification. While the approaches taken along these lines by Allais, Ellsberg, and others troubled by their 'paradoxes' have some interesting aspects, they mainly strike one as quite ad hoc. Rarely are such approaches based on axioms which in turn can be carefully scrutinized. However, since many careful, intelligent decision makers do seem to violate some axioms of expected utility theory, even upon reflection of their choices, it does seem worthwhile exploring this third option of considering modifications to the standard theory. It would seem that, sooner or later, any convincing changes will have to be made at the level of the axioms.

ACKNOWLEDGEMENT

I gratefully acknowledge my great debt to Jacob Marschak. His support, guidance, suggestions, encouragement and criticisms made possible the study underlying an earlier paper, 'Descriptive and normative implications of the decision-theory postulates'. Subsequent contact as a colleague and as a friend has increased this debt.

The above acknowledgement was written in 1975 when this paper was completed. Sadly, I must add a postscript: The paper is dedicated to the memory of a true scholar and a wonderful person, Jacob Marschak – K.R.M.

University of British Columbia

NOTES

[1] See Fishburn (1968) for a discussion of these distinctions.
[2] $\overset{z}{\leq}$ is read 'is not preferred to'.
[3] We have changed the notation to facilitate comparisons.
[4] Sometimes $F(\alpha, r_1, r_2)$ is written as $\alpha r_1 + (1 - \alpha)r_2$ but this may be confusing since r_1 and r_2 are not necessarily numbers. Even if they are numbers, the mathematical definition of $\alpha r_1 + (1 - \alpha)r_2$ is not necessarily equal to r_3.
[5] R has been extended to infinite numbers of sure prospects by Herstein and Milnor. When R is extended to an uncountable set, other assumptions to guarantee measurability of U have to be added but we will not go into these here.
[6] A set $B \in \theta$ is null if $\mu(B) = 0$ but Savage does not yet define probability so a set B is null if $f_B(\cdot, a) \overset{\Gamma}{=} f_B(\cdot, b)$ for all $a, b \in A$.
[7] We have used the axioms Arrow presents in the first part of his Chapter 2 (1971). In the second part of the chapter Arrow replaces Axiom A6 with a set of axioms similar to those listed under our section on probability comparisons.
[8] Savage's derived probability does not necessarily satisfy the σ-additivity property of a probability measure.
[9] Whether the orientation of the authors is descriptive or normative is generally unclear, except that Savage is clearly normative.
[10] The residual probability (e.g., 0.20 in B_1) corresponds to $0, i.e., neither gaining nor losing.
[11] The residual probability (e.g., 0.95 in A_2) corresponds to $0, i.e., neither gaining nor losing.

[12] For simplicity, with no loss of generality, we set $U(\$0) = 0$.

[13] For example, B_1 would be reworded as: $5 million if one of the balls numbered 1–80 is drawn from the urn containing balls numbered 1–100.

[14] The number of asterisks in Figure 2 indicates the number of subjects choosing the A alternative in one presentation and the B alternative the other time the set was presented. We have arbitrarily recorded the choice as an A alternative choice but one could equally treat it as a B choice by subtracting the number of asterisks from each number.

[15] The number of inconsistencies was quite evenly distributed over the r, p conditions (see Figure 2) so it seems appropriate to use the average as a measure of underlying consistency applicable at all levels.

[16] Rules 10 and 2 are inconsistent only when taken together in the form of Rule 6, so we present the results here as supplementary information.

[17] In this problem as in the preceding one, the residual probability corresponds to getting nothing.

[18] Since Maurice Allais (1952) proposed both this problem and the preceding one, and the earlier one is as much of a 'paradox' as this, we shall call this problem the 'common consequence' problem. This problem has the same probability values as Allais's original problem, but we have increased the payoffs (another effect of inflation).

[19] For simplicity, with no loss of generality, we set $U(\$0) = 0$. We also assume that the choice allows us to infer strict preference.

[20] Borch (1968) discusses the problem based on a probability parameter.

[21] The second problem was formed from a Morlat type of format (1953) in which there are four possible events, with no alternative yielding a sure consequence.

[22] All the other experiments discussed in this section present the problems only in the word format.

[23] Because one subject chose the A alternative on one presentation of $s = \$1,000,000$, $p = 1.00$ and chose the B alternative the second time, as shown in the (1, 1) cell, we have omitted him from the rest of the first line of this table, so the results are out of 18 subjects.

[24] Ellsberg's original problem had 90 balls in the urn, of which 30 were known to be red; the remainder were either black or yellow.

[25] We shall call such a choice an 'Ellsberg-type violation'.

[26] For simplicity we discuss only the problem with 33 red balls since the 'paradox' holds only if we assume that a choice reflects strict preference, as Ellsberg did. Technically, though, a choice may reflect indifference and a second problem (e.g., the one with 34 balls) is needed to uncover a violation of the axioms.

[27] Rule 9 is another statement of the key part (i.e., conditional preference) of Axiom S2.

[28] It is clear from our comparison in Section 2.4 that M2 must also be violated.

[29] Clearly, the violation does not arise from the particular probabilities, 0.33 and 0.67, assigned. More generally, $A_1 > B_1$ implies $P(R) > P(B)$ and $B_2 > A_2$ implies $P(B) + P(Y) > P(R) + P(Y)$, thus $P(B) + P(Y) > P(B) + P(Y)$, and hence we obtain a contradiction. In this argument, note that we have used the Axiom S4 implication about action preference yielding ordinal probabilities.

[30] If additivity is not assumed, it has not been clear what it means to consider non-additive probability (Fellner, 1965). If some numerical counterpart of probability

can be reasonably developed, we could still apply Rule 10, and may even get a kind of expected utility, as a guide to choice. This will be considered in a subsequent paper.
[31] In order to relate such probabilities to behavior, we will need Savage's Axiom S2, the axiom of monotony or a similar assumption.
[32] For some reason, 3 subjects made the non-conforming B_1, A_2 choice.
[33] The results for $r = \$1,000,000$ differ only slightly; at one probability level, $p = 0.45$, there are 2 more violations; at another level, $p = 0.33$. there is one less.
[34] We assume that a choice of B_1 over A_1 indicates strict preference, $B_1 > A_1$, for ease of discussion. This can be specifically ascertained by allowing an indifference or by slightly increasing the payoff on A_1. Both these possibilities were incorporated in our empirical study. We denote the utility of outcomes in Urn i as U_i. Let $\text{Urn}_{II}(1000) = 1$, $U_{II}(0) = 0$. It seems reasonable to assume $P(R_{II}) = P(B_{II}) = \frac{1}{2}$.
[35] The other 4 subjects had some degree of indifference among choices making a definite categorization difficult.
[36] Subjects were allowed to indicate indifference.
[37] In both X and Y bets there were a majority of subject-choices (27 of 38) indifferent to color. The remaining 11 subject-choices, however, were for the red ball bet over the black ball bet.
[38] Assuming that they would choose the alternative with higher probability for a fixed payoff.
[39] The terms 'first' and 'last' here, as above, apply to the ranking within the particular quadruple under consideration.
[40] Within the stock price set, 10 subjects ranked x' higher; 4 subjects ranked $\bar{x}'$ higher; and 5 were indifferent.
[41] The discussion will be stated in the form of responses that might have been given to rationalize particular choices, since this format will be used in the subsequent presentation of empirical results. The three responses are labeled S, A, and E.
[42] This problem has the advantage of not defining one alternative as leading to a sure outcome, i.e., all four alternatives are lotteries.
[43] Rule 14 is usually called 'Sen's β' condition.
[44] Note that in this case, unlike the independence of irrelevant alternatives example, the new information does not give an additional clue about the available alternatives since we assume that the stock of an expensive wine is independent of a particular day's special.
[45] To simplify the expressions, we set $U(\text{lose}) = 0$.
[46] For particularly good discussions of this approach, see Savage (1954) and Marschak (1964, 1968).

BIBLIOGRAPHY

Allais, M.: (1952). 'Fondements d'une Theorie Positive des Choix comportant un Risque et Critique des Postulats et Axiomes de l'Ecole Americaine', Paris, CNRS.
Allais, M.: (1953). 'Le Comportement de L'Homme Rationnel Devant le Risque: Critique des Postulats et Axioms de l'ecole Americaine', *Econometrica* 21, 503–546.
Allais, M.: 'The Foundations of a Positive Theory of Choice Involving Risk and a

Criticism of the Postulates and the Axioms of the American School', (Translation of 1952, 1976), Part II of this volume.

Anscombe, F., and Aumann, R. J.: (1963). 'A Definition of Subjective Probability', *Annals of Mathematical Statistics* **34**, 199–205.

Armstrong, W.: (1951). 'Utility and the Theory of Welfare', *Oxford Economic Papers* **3**, 259–271.

Arrow, K.: (1971). *Essays in the Theory of Risk-bearing*, Markham Publishing Company, Chicago.

Aumann, R.: (1962). 'Utility Theory without the Completeness Axiom', *Econometrica* **30**, 445–462.

Bar-Hillel, M., and Margalit, A.: (1972). 'Newcombe's Paradox Revisited', *British Journal of Philosophical Science* **23**, 295–304.

Becker, S., and Brownson, F.: (1964). 'What Price Ambiguity? or the Role of Ambiguity in Decision-making', *Journal of Political Economy* **72**, 62–73.

Bernoulli, D.: (1738). 'Specimen Theoriae Novae de Mensura Sortis', *Comentarii Acadeiae Scientiarum Imperiales Petropolitanae* **5**, 175–192. (Trans. by L. Sommer in *Econometrica*, 1954, Vol. 22.)

Borch, K.: (1968). 'The Allais Paradox: A Comment', *Behavioral Science* **13**, 488–489.

Chipman, J.: (1960). 'The Foundations of Utility', *Econometrica* **28**, 193–224.

Churchman, C.: (1961). *Prediction and Optimal Decision*, Englewood Cliffs, N.J.: Prentice-Hall.

Davidson, D., Suppes, P., and Siegel, S.: (1957). *Decision Making: An Experimental Approach*, Stanford, Calif.: Stanford University Press.

Ellsberg, D.: (1961). 'Risk, Ambiguity and the Savage Axioms', *Quarterly Journal of Economics* **75**, 643–669.

Fellner, W.: (1961). 'Distortion of Subjective Probabilities as a Reaction to Uncertainty', *Quarterly Journal of Economics* **75**, 670–689.

Fellner, W.: (1965). *Probability and Profit*, Homewood, Richard D. Irwin, Inc., Illinois.

Fishburn, P.: (1968). 'Utility Theory', *Management Science* **14**, 335–378.

Fishburn, P.: (1970). *Utility Theory for Decision Making*, Wiley, New York.

Gardner, M.: (1974). 'Mathematical Games', *Scientific American* **230**, 116–121.

Hagen, O.: (1972). 'A New Axiomatization of Utility under Risk', *Teorie a Metoda* **IV-2**, 55–80.

Hagen, O.: (1971). 'New Foundations of Utility: Allais versus Morgenstern', seminar paper, University of Heidelberg, 15pp.

Hagen, O.: (1976). 'Toward a Positive Theory of Preferences under Risk', This volume.

Herstein, I., and Milnor, J.: (1953). 'An Axiomatic Approach to Measurable Utility', *Econometrica* **21**, 291–297.

Jensen, N.: (1967). 'An Introduction to Bernoullian Utility Theory', *Swedish Journal of Economics* **69**, 163–183.

Knight, F.: (1921). *Risk, Uncertainty and Profit*, Houghton Mifflin and Co., Boston.

Kraft, C., Pratt, J., and Seidenberg, A.: (1959). 'Intuitive Probability on Finite Sets', *Annals of Mathematical Statistics* **30**, 408–419.

Larsson, S.: (1978). 'Studies in Utility Theory', unpublished dissertation, University of British Columbia, Vancouver, Canada.

Luce, R.: (1956). 'Semi-order and a Theory of Utility Discrimination', *Econometrica* **24**, 178–191.

Luce, R., and Krantz, D.: (1971). 'Conditional Expected Utility', *Econometrica* **39**, 253–271.

Luce, R., and Raiffa, H.: (1957). *Games and Decisions*, Wiley, New York.

MacCrimmon, K.: (1965). *An Experimental Study of the Decision Making Behavior of Business Executives*, unpublished dissertation, University of California, Los Angeles.

MacCrimmon, K.: (1967). 'Consistent Choices and the Allais Problem: Theoretical Considerations and Empirical Results', Working Paper 130, Western Management Science Institute, UCLA, 20pp.

MacCrimmon, K.: (1968). 'Descriptive and Normative Implications of the Decision-theory Postulates'. In K. Borch and J. Mossin (Eds.), *Risk and Uncertainty*, Macmillan, New York, 3–23.

Marschak, J.: (1964). 'Actual versus Consistent Decision Behavior', *Behavioral Science* **9**, 103–110.

Marschak, J.: (1968). 'Decision Making: Economic Aspects'. In D. Sills (Ed.), *International Encyclopedia of the Social Sciences* **4**. Crowell Collier and Macmillan, New York, 42–55.

Marschak, J.: (1950). 'Rational Behavior, Uncertain Prospects, and Measurable Utility', *Econometrica* **18**, 111–141.

Marschak, J., and Radner, R.: (1972). *Economic Theory of Teams*, Yale University Press, New Haven, Chapter 1.

May, K.: (1954). 'Intransitivity, utility, and the aggregation of preference patterns', *Econometrica* **22**, 1–13.

Morlat, G.: (1953). 'Comment on an Axiom of Savage', *Econometrie*, CNRS, Paris, 156–7.

Morrison, D.: (1967). 'On the Consistency of Preferences in Allais Paradox', *Behavioral Science*, 373–383.

Moskowitz, H.: (1974). 'Effects of Problem Representation and Feedback on Rational Behavior in Allais and Morlat-type Problems', *Decision Sciences* **5**, 225–241.

Nozick, R.: (1969). 'Newcombe's Problem and Two Principles of Choice'. In N. Rescher (Ed.), *Essays in Honor of Carl S. Hempel*, D. Reidel Publishing Co., Dordrecht, Holland, 114–146.

Pratt, J., Raiffa, H., and Schlaifer, R.: (1964). 'The Foundations of Decision under Uncertainty: An Elementary Exposition', *American Statistical Association Journal*, **59**, 353–375.

Raiffa, H.: (1968). *Decision Analysis*, Addison-Wesley, Reading, Mass.

Raiffa, H.: (1961). 'Risk, Ambiguity and the Savage Axioms: Comment', *Quarterly Journal of Economics* **75**, 690–694.

Ramsey, F.: (1926). In R. Braithwaite (Ed.) 1931, *The Foundations of Mathematics and Other Logical Essays*, Routledge and Kegan Paul.

Rapoport, A.: (1960). *Fights, Games and Debates*, University of Michigan Press, Ann Arbor.

Roberts, H.: (1963). 'Risk, Ambiguity, and the Savage Axioms: Comment', *Quarterly Journal of Economics* **77**, 327–342.

Rose, A.: (1963). 'Conditions for Irrational Choice', *Social Research* **30**, 151–152.

Samuelson, P.: (1952). 'Probability, Utility and the Independent Axiom', *Econometrica* **20**, 670–678.

Savage, L.: (1954). *The Foundations of Statistics*, Wiley, New York.

Selten, R.: (1968). 'Comments on Paper by MacCrimmon'. In K. Borch and J. Mossin (Eds.), *Risk and Uncertainty*, Macmillan, New York, p.23.

Sen, A.: (1973). 'Behaviour and the Concept of Preference', *Economica* **40**, 241–259.

Sen, A.: (1970). *Collective Choice and Social Welfare*, Holden-Day, San Francisco.

Slovic, P., and Tversky, A.: (1974). 'Who Accepts Savage's Axiom?', *Behavioral Science* **19**, 368–373.

Smith, V.: (1969). 'Measuring Non-monetary Utilities in Uncertain Choices: The Ellsberg Urn', *Quarterly Journal of Economics* **83**, 324–329.

Thrall, R.: (1954). 'Applications of Multidimensional Utility Theory'. In R. Thrall, C. Coombs, and R. Davis (Eds.), *Decision Processes*, Wiley, New York, pp.181–186.

Tversky, A.: (1969). 'Intransitivities of Preferences', *Psychological Review* **76**, 31–48.

Villegas, C.: (1964). 'On Qualitative Probability σ-Algebras', *Annals of Mathematical Statistics* **35**, 1787–1796.

von Neumann, J., and Morgenstern, D.: (1947). *Theory of Games and Economic Behavior*, 2nd edn., Princeton University Press, Princeton, N.J.

Weinstein, A.: (1968). 'Individual Preference Intransitivity', *Southern Economic Journal* **34**, 335–343.

GÜNTER MENGES

COMPARISON OF DECISION MODELS
AND SOME SUGGESTIONS

ABSTRACT. Six decision models are distinguished by two criteria (consequences: original or transformed; probabilities: a priori or a posteriori or subjective). All six models are discussed, their axiomatic foundations characterized, and compared with each other. Model VI (transformed consequences, subjective probabilities) is shown to be epistemologically the most doubtful one. Model IV (transformed consequences, a posteriori probabilities) is epistemologically justifiable and turns out to be the most important one from a practical point of view. Some shortcomings of it are nevertheless to be stated. Three modifications of model IV which are suited to weaken the shortcomings are discussed: a restatement of the independence property of the von Neumann–Morgenstern utility, techniques which allow for an exploitation of all information available, and application of flexible decision criteria which can be adapted to the type and amount of information available.

1. INTRODUCTION: THE VARIOUS MODELS

The theory of decision is a theory of choice from among risky prospects. The latter, in their simplest form,[1] are characterized by two components:

(a) the outcomes are consequences which occur when a certain action or prospect[2] is adopted: $c_1, c_2, \ldots, c_n$;

(b) the probabilities of the consequences to occur: $p_1, p_2, \ldots, p_n$. Usually $p' = (p_1, p_2, \ldots, p_n)$ is considered a probability vector on the so-called state space. For a mathematically more rigorous formulation, see Menges [1964].

In some models one component or both are transformed, the consequences c_i are replaced by some function $u(c_i)$ called the utility of c_i (for the decision maker); the (a priori) probabilities p_i are replaced either by a posteriori probabilities $\pi(p_i)$ or by some function $\varphi(p_i)$, called subjective probabilities.

We compile the members of all 'constituents' to column vectors $(u_i = u(c_i), \pi_i = \pi(p_i), \varphi_i = \varphi(p_i))$

$$c = \begin{bmatrix} c_1 \\ \vdots \\ c_n \end{bmatrix} \quad p = \begin{bmatrix} p_1 \\ \vdots \\ p_n \end{bmatrix} \quad u = \begin{bmatrix} u_1 \\ \vdots \\ u_n \end{bmatrix} \quad \pi = \begin{bmatrix} \pi_1 \\ \vdots \\ \pi_n \end{bmatrix} \quad \varphi = \begin{bmatrix} \varphi_1 \\ \vdots \\ \varphi_n \end{bmatrix},$$

411

Maurice Allais and Ole Hagen (eds.), Expected Utility and the Allais Paradox, 411–433.
Copyright © 1979 by D. Reidel Publishing Company.

and observe $p'e = 1$, $\pi'e' = 1$, $\varphi'e = 1$, where ' indicates transposition and e is the column vector of respective length consisting of ones. Using c, p, u, π, and φ we can define six kinds of expectations evaluating the risky prospects:

$$C_p = c'p \quad (= E_p(c)),$$
$$C_\pi = c'\pi \quad (= E_\pi(c)),$$
$$C_\varphi = c'\varphi \quad (= E_\varphi(c)),$$
$$U_p = u'p \quad (= E_p(u)),$$
$$U_\pi = u'\pi \quad (= E_\pi(u)),$$
$$U_\varphi = u'\varphi \quad (= E_\varphi(u)),$$

and also four kinds of basic decision models (in brackets the corresponding expectations):

	original consequences c	transformed consequences u
original (a priori) probabilities p	(I) c, p (C_p)	(II) u, p (U_p)
a posteriori probabilities π	(III) c, π (C_π)	(IV) u, π (U_π)
subjective probabilities φ	(V) c, φ (C_φ)	(VI) u, φ (U_φ)

Model I is the classical gambling model, the c's are monetary values, the p's objective a priori probabilities. The expected value C_p is but the mathematical expectation of the random variable c. The decision rule, in general applied to this model, is sometimes called the μ-principle. It requires the choice of that C_p^* from among a set $\{C_p\}$ of competing expectations which is maximal (supremal). The competing alternatives C_p's can be considered as assigned to the competing actions. The idea goes back – if not further – to Jakob Bernoulli (*Ars conjectandi* [1713]). Model II is the equally old and well-known Daniel Bernoulli-version [D. Bernoulli 1731]. It allows, among other things, for a solution of the St. Petersburg game and explains the behaviour of people with regard to insurance companies (and vice versa), by taking the possibility into account that an individual has different attitudes towards risk.

The transformation $c \rightarrow u$ allows for concave (risk aversion) as well as convex forms (risk preference) as well as mixtures of both (see Mosteller–Nogee [1951]) expressing the fact that an individual may have different risk behaviours in different regions of c, e.g. with regard to lottery tickets and insurances. Whereas c itself may or may not be an objective measure, the measure $u(c)$ is to be considered a strictly personal one. I believe this is one of the very few things in decision theory which are generally accepted.

The decision rule usually applied to this model is the so-called *Bernoulli principle*: Choose that U_p^* from among a set of competing alternatives $\{U_p\}$ which is maximal (supremal).

Model III retains the original measures of consequences c but – without making use of the epistemologically weak subjective probabilities – takes account of the fact that in most practical situations, especially in the social and economic field, a priori probabilities are not available. Model III per se has found little attention in the literature. Only the transformation of a priori into a posteriori probabilities by means of Bayes' theorem is a standard procedure. The link between a posteriori probabilities and original outcomes is nevertheless as reasonable as, or even more reasonable than, the link between a priori probabilities and original outcomes. A decision rule in full analogy to the μ-principle can be applied in the framework of Model III: Choose that C_π^* from among the set of competing alternatives which is maximal (supremal). This decision rule may be called *empirical μ-principle*, 'empirical' for the reason that a posteriori probabilities, in one form or another, are always based upon empirical observations.

Model IV is the first to make use of transformations with respect to both the c's and the p's. c is transformed into u, p into π. This model has been discussed by Menges and Diehl [1973]. The corresponding decision rule, namely 'Choose that U_π^* from among the competing alternatives $\{U_\pi\}$ which is maximal (supremal)' may – for obvious reasons – be called the *empirical Bernoulli principle*.

Model V although of little practical importance, is nevertheless useful for the study of subjective probabilities. Contrary to Model VI which is not, Model V is suited for that purpose because – plainly speaking – in practical situations it is sometimes objectively possible to eliminate the part c in $C_\varphi = c'\varphi$ and thus to identify the subjective part φ.

The decision rule of Model V 'Choose that C_φ^* from among the set of competing alternatives $\{C_\varphi\}$ which is maximal (supremal)' is sometimes called *Bayes' principle*, cf. J. Marschak [1955].

Model VI like Model IV transforms c and p; c is transformed into u, p into φ. The corresponding decision rule is sometimes called the *Ramsey principle*. It has been celebrated by many writers (e.g. Savage [1954]) as a universal tool, particularly in its generalized form [Schneeweiss 1974, p.117]:

Utility can be attached to any kind of consequences, not necessarily describable by monetary values. Subjective probabilities, on the other hand, may be assigned to any event whose occurrence is unknown (to the decision maker), e.g. to events whose probabilities are unknown, or even to those events to which no frequentist would think of applying the probability concept.

The strong appeal of the Model VI rests upon this claimed universality, upon the deliverance to establish objective probabilities and also upon the integrated axiomatic system it allows for, an axiomatic system which is by some writers considered as the axiomatic foundation of decision theory altogether.

One main task of the present article is a critique of Model VI and its generalization.

*

In the sequel, we shall discuss and compare the six different models, and their axiomatic foundations. For the sake of brevity we name the models after the decision rule they employ.

2. THE μ-MODEL

The axiomatic foundation of Model I (original a priori probabilities, original consequences, μ-principle) is quite simple, since it is the same as that for probability. Although it is well known that Kolmogoroff's axioms are not sufficient as a basis for the whole body of probability calculus, the reference to Kolmogoroff [1933] and Hacking [1965] may suffice here.

Simplicity is the advantage of this model, its severe disadvantage on the probability side is the fact that a priori probabilities are often not available, and on the outcome side the fact that in "choices under uncertainty people try to maximize the expectation (not of wealth but) of a function of wealth, utility" (Hagen [1972], p.55), which is not only theoretically plausible (St. Petersburg problem!) but also empirically confirmed.

3. THE BERNOULLI MODEL

The Model II (utilities, a priori probabilities, Bernoulli principle) is the one which is extensively discussed by J. v. Neumann and O. Morgenstern in their famous book [1947]. The advantages of this model are well known (realistic outcome measures, theoretically unimpeachable probabilities), not so well known are the disadvantages. Critique against the Bernoulli model has mainly put forward by Allais [1953], Hagen [1972], and Blyth [1972a,b]; (see also the ordinalistic arguments by Baumol [1951] and Chipman [1960]). Allais and Hagen point at the incompatibility of the Bernoulli model with common behaviour of people like that of buying insurances and lottery tickets as well. They require – among other things – to consider all aspects of the probability distribution, mainly its dispersion and skewness, and not only the expectation.

From among the axioms[3] the order property is not open to severe criticism because it is confined to $\mathfrak{C}$, the outcome space, and is therefore weaker and much more plausible than the order property of Savage's system (see below, Section 7). The monotony and continuity[4] axioms have not found any severe criticism, but the independence property has (see the discussion by Samuelson [1952], Wold [1952] and others in *Econometrica*, Vol. 20, 1952). We shall return to it in Section 11.

4. THE EMPIRICAL μ-MODEL[5]

The c-part of Model III needs no special consideration, but the probability part does. It leads directly into the field of statistical inference and confirmation logic. First of all we have to specify what is meant by a posteriori probabilities. In their simplest form they are Bayesian probabilities as they result from Bayes' theorem. Their advantages then are their frequentist interpretability, their being σ-additive measures and also a high degree of plausibility and vividity which may be claimed for them. Their disadvantage is dependence of the knowledge of the a priori probabilities. Kolmogoroff's system of axioms in principle fits to them as probabilities but not to their role as degrees of confirmation (in Carnap's sense; c.f. Carnap and Stegmüller [1959]). However, this shortcoming can be removed.[6] As compared to the μ-model, the empirical μmodel is – from a practical point of view – much superior since it admits and takes into account the necessity to estimate the probability vector on the state space. (In Section 12, we shall consider other means of estimating the probability vector.)

5. THE EMPIRICAL BERNOULLI MODEL

An axiomatic foundation of the Model IV has not yet been established, but I see no difficulties as long as the u- and π-parts are axiomatized separately. It can be done by basing the u-part on the v. Neumann–Morgenstern system and the π-part on a system of confirmation axioms like those indicated in the previous section. The advantages and disadvantages hold correspondingly.

The combination (of u and π) as such seems in principle, and from a practical point of view, to be the most reasonable one as will become evident later on (see Sections 9 and 10) when we try to free both constituents from some of their 'classical' shortcomings. Plainly speaking, in principle the superiority of this combination stems from the fact that the π's are neither subjective quantities which are practically easy-to-get (but theoretically poor) nor (the theoretically finest but practically unattainable) a priori probabilities, and that the u's (in spite of the difficulties mentioned in Section 3) are better suited to real-life problems than the c's.

6. THE 'BAYES' MODEL[7]

Model V is only of subsidiary importance and not suited (and not intended) for the solution of decision problems proper. Its axiomatic foundation is the foundation of subjective probability and traces back to Stumpf [1893].

In our times, it has been discussed especially by Ramsey [1931], de Finetti [1937] and Koopman [1940], though from slightly different standpoints. Perhaps the most elegant and convincing foundation of the probability part of Model V has been given by de Groot [1970] in the sixth chapter of his book.[8] (However, instead of his notion of "relative likelihood" which is a standard terminus technicus for something quite different, I should prefer a notion like Meinong's [1915] "presumptive probability" or something of that kind.)

The leading idea is to start with ordinal probabilities, i.e. statements of the form 'A is more probable than B', 'B is more probable than C', etc., and to guarantee by appropriate axioms that for $AC = BC = \emptyset$ it holds that A is more probable than B if and only if $A \cup C$ is more probable than $B \cup C$. In this way necessary, but not sufficient, conditions for the existence of subjective probabilities are obtained.

The independence property of axiomatic systems of subjective probability is usually expressed by conditional probabilities analogous to objective probabilities (see de Groot's 6th axiom), however it might be worth mentioning that Savage's Sure-Thing-Principle is not, at least not necessarily, among the properties of subjective probability in the framework of Model V.

While in Section 8, I try to find arguments against subjective probabilities as sound tools of decision-making (i.e. as prescribing tools) they may (besides serving as substitutes for objective probabilities) well be sound tools for the analysis and explanation of actual decisions (i.e. describing tools). It is a reasonable question in psychology or sociology to ask if, to what extent, and why subjective probabilities depart from the corresponding objective probabilities. Strong deviations can, e.g., indicate certain mental diseases, like paranoia. In such 'describing contexts' the axiomatics of subjective probability, in particular in constructive forms (i.e. in forms which immediately allow for the numerical determination of subjective probabilities), like de Groot's system, seems to be reasonable and useful.

7. THE 'INTEGRATED' RAMSEY–SAVAGE MODEL

We now come to the most controversial model, Type VI, and its generalization.

A first system of this kind was established by Ramsey [1931]. Later on, Savage [1954], taking up ideas of de Finetti [1937] and turning around Ramsey's order (first utility, then probability), considerably improved the axiomatic foundation of Model VI. The axioms of this system recently found a clear and simplified interpretation by Schneeweiss [1974, p.131ff], on which I rely in the sequel.

The first axiom, an order axiom, states (somewhat loosely expressed) that the elements of the given action space can be completely ordered. Strictly speaking it says: Given a subset Z of the state space S, where Z is the relevant 'subworld', i.e., $S - Z$ contains all those elements s of S which are known to be impossible, then the order axiom states a complete $\gtrsim_z$-ordering on the space A of actions a. This property is much stronger than the corresponding order axiom of Model II (v. Neumann–Morgenstern utility), in fact, it is so strong that it suspends the concepts of probability and of decision-making altogether. As soon as the property of complete ordering of actions is fulfilled the decision maker knows all that is relevant for his decision: He will choose the most preferred action. One may argue that in addition he wants *consistency* in decision making and a *justification* (or rationalization) of his decision or his preference order, respectively. Regarding consistency: In fact, in model versions of Type V it would be reasonable to try and identify and retain consistency because there exist, in the form of objective probabilities, quantities which allow for an objective judgement of consistency. But if, as in model versions of Type VI, the decision maker is the one who produces both probabilities and utilities, he can likewise produce consistency. If, on the other hand, he were not able to bring about consistency by himself, the decision theory would hardly bring him help. (Perhaps instead of decision theory, concepts and methods of psychology may be competent to analyse ex post such a personal procedure.) In an actual decision problem who, besides him, could find out whether any inconsistency was caused by wrong evaluation of utility or by wrong evaluation of probability?

Similar arguments hold for the justification aspect. Since in Model VI there is no objective way of splitting up preferences into the utility and probability parts there is no objective way of intrinsic justification. Maybe, there is a non-intrinsic way, viz. by learning. Yet, for learning, i.e., observing consequences of actual decisions and modifying the behaviour, other models than decision models will likely be found more appropriate. Again[9], I want to express the opinion that the development of appropriate learning models could be a fruitful task. The further development of decision models, in my view, should not aim at more rigidity and (pseudo-) unification but at more receptivity for revision and modification. Another disadvantage (and source for inconsistencies) of the integrated axioms system is the fact that an action is often more than a combination of probabilities and utilities of the consequences of the respective events.

In order to demonstrate this disadvantage of the order axiom of Savage's integrated system consider the following example. If I ask you what you believe to be more probable, the event A that you will have a car accident next week or the event B that you will become heavyweight champion next week, you will answer: A is more probable than B. But if I offer you a certain fixed price (say 50 DM) you will receive if A happens or the same price (50 DM) you will receive if B happens, you will most likely prefer '50 DM if B happens'. This choice is apparently inconsistent. Such inconsistencies are likely to occur if the preferences refer to actions, i.e., to probabilities connected with consequences. The next axiom of the integrated axioms system, viz. the independence property, is also very problematic. It says virtually[10] for two actions $a, b \in A$: If $a \gtrsim_z b$ and $a \gtrsim_{\bar{z}} b$, then $a \gtrsim b$, where $\bar{Z} = S - Z$ and $\gtrsim_{\bar{z}}$ is the corresponding preference relation conditioned on $\bar{Z} \subset S$. Like the first axiom, it is not equivalent to, but stronger than, the corresponding axiom of the v. Neumann–Morgenstern utility concept (Model II); it has been discussed by Savage and others under the name Sure-Thing Principle. Blyth [1972a,b] recently showed that the Sure-Thing Principle can lead to paradoxical results. Indeed, by amalgamating both independence properties, that of utility and of probability, as the Sure-Thing Principle does, the so-called 'false correlation paradox' can occur [Blyth, 1972b, p.366], i.e., it can be shown that the following is possible: $a \gtrsim_z b$, $a \gtrsim_{\bar{z}} b$, and $b > a$.

It should also be mentioned that Allais' critique of Savage's independence axiom has not yet been refuted (cf. Allais [1953], Savage [1954], Morrison [1967], Borch [1968b], de Groot [1970], Hagen [1972], Schneeweiss [1974]).

The third axiom of the integrated system, the dominance principle, which seems to be very simple, leads to a certain difficulty. The axiom states for an action a_c ($a_{c'}$) which results in a consequence c (c') for all $s \in Z \subset S$:

$$a_c >_z a_{c'} \quad \text{if and only if} \quad c > c',$$

where $>_z$ again denotes preference under the condition $Z, Z \subset S$. Even Schneeweiss, a strong adherent of Savage's system admits the

problematical nature of this 'trivially and innocuously' seeming property, because: "In practice, it may be difficult to find or even to
perceive an action that has the same consequence . . . for all s of some
subworld . . ." Z (Schneeweiss [1974], p.133).

The last axiom of the integrated system, that of unique betting, says
for an action $a_{Xc\bar{c}}$ which results in c, if an $s \in X \subset S$ happens, and in
$\bar{c}$, if an $s \in \bar{X} = S - X$ happens: For $c > \bar{c}$ and $d > \bar{d}$ it follows for
any $X, Z \subset S$

$$a_{Xc\bar{c}} \succsim a_{Zc\bar{c}} \quad \text{if and only if} \quad a_{Xd\bar{d}} \succsim a_{Zd\bar{d}}.$$

The problem with this axiom is that although it is intended to aim at
cardinal (subjective) probabilities it leads only to ordinal ones. The
latter, it is true, can be transformed into cardinal probabilities by the
construction of artificial actions whose consequences depend on the
outcomes of multiple coin tossings. But the use of such a crutch
means the employment of objective probabilities in an axiomatic
system of subjective probability, which at least is a corporal defect
not to say an inconsistency.

*

Usually, in mathematics and mathematized theories, the axiomatic
system underlying the theory is considered good if the axioms are
useful and reasonable as well as plausible for an ordinary man.
Reasonableness and plausibility are the more required, if the axioms,
at least partially, are of deontic nature. The axioms of the integrated
system are bad because, as we have seen above, all four are problematical in themselves, unreasonable and implausible. They do have,
it is true, some use for a unification of the theories of probability and
of utility. But it is questionable that unification per se should have
such a high value that it is worth the sacrifice of reasonableness and
plausibility. Indeed, an 'integrated axiomatization' of utility and
probability is of no great use, it is inexpedient and improper as a basis
of a 'prescriptive' (Marschak) theory of decision making under uncertainty and/or risk. The same cannot be said of separate axiomatizations of objective probability a priori and a posteriori, of utility,
and of subjective probability.

Even the concept of subjective probability and a constructive
axiomatization of it is of great use, not to say, it is indispensable

because there are many phenomena, particularly in the social and economic field where neither objective a priori probabilities are known nor controlled observations can be found, which could serve as a basis for a posteriori probabilities. On the other hand, subjective probability is at best a substitute for objective probability, and its role as 'degree of belief' of a person is questionable. This will be made clear in the next section.

8. THE STORY OF SUBJECTIVE PROBABILITY

One can say that the temptation to use subjective probabilities is as old as the probability concept itself. Already Jakob Bernoulli [1713, 1899] had a peculiar ambivalent attitude towards probability subjectivism, as is best seen in his correspondence with Leibniz. In his book *Ars conjectandi* one finds passages which seem to indicate that he was a subjectivist. On the other hand, he warned of the use of only subjectively determined probabilities: fearing at the same time that the probability of phenomena which are governed by the free human will cannot be determined objectively. The ambivalence traces through the whole history of probability in the 18th century.[11] In the 19th century, it was revived by Laplace [1812], a genuine subjectivist, whose "alchemy of logic" was opposed by Cournot [1843] and later on by v. Kries [1886]. In our century, Keynes [1921] took up the controversy. He thought of probability theory as of a theory of "logical reasons which make us believe one thing more strongly than another", as v. Bortkiewicz [1923] put it in his critical review of Keynes' book. While in Keynes' view, probability rests equally on apriority and intuition, Ramsey [1931] substituted Keynes' notion of intuition by the concept of belief and weakened the aprioristic pillar in favour of stronger subjectivity. His views were mainly taken up by Savage, as is well known.

In the long history of the controversy mainly five arguments against probability subjectivism have been stated (c.f. Menges [1970], p.47): (1) Limited interpersonal communicability. (2) Degrees of belief and objective probabilities diverge, and the kind of deformation varies from person to person. (3) Emotional and intellectual circumstances exert uncontrollable influences on the determination of the degree of belief. (4) Human individuals are incapable of distinguishing between probabilities which lie closely together. (5) Human individuals are incapable of measuring their own degree of belief without technical help (e.g. by trained psychologists).

There are also numerous arguments put forward against objective probability. They have been collected by de Finetti [1974]. While it may be a matter of personal taste and standpoint which arguments seem more convincing there remains the problem of the epistemological foundation of probability which strongly speaks for the objective modality (cf. Hartwig [1956], Menges [1970], [1974]).

In earlier papers, I conceded that subjective probabilities, though epistemologically doubtful[12] and at best a substitute for objective measures, comparable to causal conjectures a natural scientist may use as long as a certain relationship is not fully analyzed and objectively known, may well serve as measures for the degree of belief a person has with regard to random phenomena. Two articles by Blyth [1972a,b] made me doubt if subjective probabilities can really play this role.

The problem arises when one admits that the degree of belief a person has with respect to a certain event is not simply a number but a random variable. It is the analogous statement Allais makes in his paper in this book with regard to what he calls the psychological variables. He claims that one needs not only to consider the mathematical expectation of psychological values (which would be a number analogous to the degree of belief) but also the overall shape of the probability distribution of the psychological variables. But while numbers can be ordered, random variables cannot and, even worse, the attempt to order random variables involves the risk of paradoxical results.[13] These paradoxes surely also cast some doubts on the reasonableness of the axioms of expected utility (v. Neumann–Morgenstern utility) and the Bernoulli principle altogether but they must be called crucial for the role of subjective probabilities as degrees of belief.

9. A RANKING OF THE MODELS

The considerations so far speak for a certain ranking of the six models, and a corresponding cognitive strategy. It runs as follows.

On the side of the outcomes:

(1) one should use the original (untransformed) quantities which measure the consequences of an action in all cases where it is

adequate to the problem on hand (Models I, II, III), if not

(2) one should use transformations into ordinal utilities (in all cases where they lead to a solution of the decision problem on hand) or into cardinal (expected) utilities (Models II, IV, VI).

On the side of probability:

(1) one should make use of objective a priori knowledge in all cases where it is at hand or obtainable through physical analyses (Models I, II); if one does not possess reliable objective a priori knowledge nor can obtain such knowledge,

(2) one should make statistical observations of the phenomena and infer the unknown probabilities (Models III, IV); if the phenomena are not observable for technical or pecuniary reasons, the matter becomes really subjective:

(3) some will turn to their beliefs or intuitions (Models V, VI), others will resign and consider the task as unattainable, others will use the minimax principle which leads in practically all situations to a solution. (The latter outlet, however, means the adoption of such a pessimistic behaviour that most modern decision theorists refrain from it, although Wald [1950] and many writers in the fifties seriously recommended such a behaviour. We shall return to this point in Section 13.)

As the reader will observe, the ranking is:

(1)   I > III > V,

(2)   II > IV > VI.

10. SUGGESTIONS FROM A PRACTICAL POINT OF VIEW

If it is true that in choices under uncertainty most people try to maximize not wealth but utility, and if it is true that the objective a priori assessment of probabilities is in most cases impossible and the subjective assessment is doubtful, then Model IV, the empirical Bernoulli model is the most important one from a practical point of view.

It would then be reasonable to enlarge the field of applicability of this model through weakening or overcoming of at least some of its shortcomings. Some suggestions along this line were made, mainly by Allais and Hagen, and though from quite a different standpoint, by Marschak [1973, 1974].

In my view the task can be fulfilled mainly by three modifications of Model IV,

(1) restatement of the independence property of the v. Neumann–Morgenstern utility,

(2) exploitation of all inference techniques offered by statistical theory (instead of confining to the Bayes method of determination of a posteriori probabilities), and

(3) application of flexible decision criteria which can be adapted to the type and amount of information available.

In earlier papers (Menges [1964, 1966, 1968, 1970, 1973, 1974], Menges–Diehl [1969, 1973], Leiner [1974]), we tried to tackle all three problems. In the sequel, I shall briefly repeat the main aspects and try to adjust them to the present discussion.

11. A MODIFICATION OF THE INDEPENDENCE AXIOM OF THE V. NEUMANN–MORGENSTERN UTILITY[14]

This axiom is the most crucial and most debated one of the v. Neumann–Morgenstern system. A shortcoming which was mainly put forward by Wold [1952] is its static nature. The independence axiom says that for any two probability mixtures of the outcomes (prospects) c', $c'' \in \mathfrak{C}$ with $c'' \sim c'$ for all $p \in (0, 1)$ it holds $c'pc \sim c''pc$ for all prospects $c \in \mathfrak{C}$.

Together with the monotony axiom and Axiom 7 (see Note 3) the relation $c' > c''$ even results in $c' = c'pc' > c''pc'$. That means that a person when preferring c' to c'' will prefer c' to any mixture of the form $c''pc'$. It is hardly credible that a person after some periods when c' was realized with probability 1 still prefers c'. Instead one would expect that the original relation $c' > c''$ becomes unstable or even reverts (Wold's paradox).

In order to overcome this difficulty it seems natural to consider, instead of a single outcome, *sequences of outcomes*

$$\gamma_j = (c_{j1}, c_{j2}, \ldots, c_{jr}),$$

(r is the number of periods; $j = 1, \ldots, m$; m is the number of states, for simplicity's sake assumed to be finite). Such sequences may be called *programs*. Accordingly, instead of single states s one considers *processes*

$$\sigma_j = (s_{j1}, s_{j2}, \ldots, s_{jr})$$

and instead of single actions *a plans*

$$\alpha_i = (a_{i1}, a_{i2}, \ldots, a_{ir}).$$

If one assigns a program to every combination of a process with a plan, we have

$$\gamma_{ij} = (c_{ij}^{(1)}, \ldots, c_{ij}^{(r)}), \quad i \in I, \quad j \in J,$$

where I and J are the corresponding index sets.

Let the set of processes be denoted by Σ, the set of plans by A, and the set of programs by $G = \{\gamma_{ij} \mid i \in I, j \in J\}$, then the *program function* is defined as:

$$g: A \times \Sigma \to G.$$

The programs are compiled to program prospects $\bar{g}, \bar{g}', \bar{g}'', \ldots$ with

$$\bar{g} = (g_{11}p_{11}, g_{12}p_{12}, \ldots),$$

$$\bar{g}' = (g_{11}p'_{11}, g_{12}p'_{12}, \ldots),$$

$$\bar{g}'' = (g_{11}p''_{11}, g_{12}p''_{12}, \ldots),$$

whose space is $\bar{G} = \{\bar{g}, \bar{g}', \bar{g}'', \ldots\}$. We can now establish four simple axioms:

(1) There exists a preordering on $\bar{G}$ (order axiom).[15]

(2) There exist at least two program prospects in $\bar{G}$ for which indifference is excluded (non-triviality axiom).

(3) For $\bar{g} > \bar{g}' > \bar{g}''$ there exists a $p \in (0, 1)$ such that $\bar{g}' \sim \bar{g}p\bar{g}''$ (continuity).

(4) From $\bar{g}' \sim \bar{g}''$ and $p \in (0, 1)$ follows $\bar{g}'p\bar{g} \sim \bar{g}''p\bar{g}$ (independence).

THEOREM. [Menges, Rommelfanger 1970]: *If $\bar{G}$ has the properties expressed by the four axioms then there exists a utility function of the v. Neumann–Morgenstern type on $\bar{G}$.*

The independence axiom of this system is no longer subject to the Wold paradox, since the number of periods r can be chosen in a way as to prevent the preference relations from reverting.

It would be an interesting question to check if and to what extent the Allais paradox holds. My conjecture is that it also disappears (perhaps provided the number of periods covers 'the buying of an insurance and of a lottery ticket').

12. FIDUCIAL AND LIKELIHOOD OPTIMALITY[16]

The Bayesian method of determination of the a posteriori probabilities is only one method statistical theory offers for the solution of the inference problem. The disadvantage of this method is the necessity to know the a priori distribution of the states (or – according to Section 11 – of the processes). Methods which come along without that knowledge are R. A. Fisher's well known fiducial method and D. A. S. Fraser's [1968] structural method. As long as a fiducial density or a structural density exists while no 'prior knowledge' is available, one of these techniques can successfully be applied.

If a fiducial or structural density is not attainable it may be defendable to use a likelihood function. Although there are some snares, it is pretty well-suited as a confirmation measure in Carnap's sense. (Cf. Carnap, Stegmüller [1958]).

The qualification of the likelihood function $L(\theta \mid x)$[17] as confirmation measure can be seen from the four following properties it possesses (cf. Menges [1974], p.28, Hacking [1965] and Stegmüller [1973]):

(1) (implication) From $\theta_1 \Vdash \theta_2$ $(\theta_1, \theta_2 \in \Omega)$ follows $L(\theta_1 \mid x) \leqslant L(\theta_2 \mid x)$.

(2) (conjunction) From $x \Vdash \theta_2$ follows $L(\theta_1 \mid x) \leqslant L((\theta_1 \wedge \theta_2) \mid x)$, $\theta_1, \theta_2 \in \Omega$.

(3) (transitivity) From $L(\theta_1 \mid x_1) \leqslant L(\theta_2 \mid x_2)$ and $L(\theta_2 \mid x_2) \leqslant L(\theta_3 \mid x_3)$ follows $L(\theta_1 \mid x_1) \leqslant L(\theta_3 \mid x_3)$; $\theta_1, \theta_2, \theta_3 \in \Omega$; $x_1, x_2, x_3 \in \mathfrak{X}$.

(4) (maximum) For all $\theta \in \Omega$ and all $x \in \mathfrak{X}$ and an arbitrarily chosen $\theta^* \in \Omega$, $L(\theta \mid x) \leqslant L(\theta^* \mid \theta^*)$.

Other advantages of the likelihood function, besides its analogy to Carnap's degree of confirmation, are its nearly universal applicability, its frequentist interpretability and its linkage to the so-called background knowledge (cf. Diehl, Sprott [1965] and Edwards [1972]).

On the other hand, as is well known, the likelihood function is in general not additive in a measure-theoretical sense. It can be given the properties of a probability function by standardization. But the standardization means Bayesian inference with the uniform distribution as 'prior'. A way off the snares may be the following: The likelihood function $L(\theta \mid x)$ – for the notation see above – is transformed into the relative likelihood function

$$R(\theta \mid x) = \frac{L(\theta \mid x)}{\sup_{\theta \in \Omega} L(\theta \mid x)},$$

which satisfies

$$R(\theta \mid x) \in [0, 1].$$

A real number $\varepsilon \in (0, 1)$ may indicate what is to be understood by plausible or likely values of θ, and the consideration can be confined to the set $\Omega^* \subset \Omega$ of these plausible values:

$$\Omega^* = \{\theta \mid \theta \in \Omega \wedge R(\theta \mid x) \geqslant \varepsilon \text{ and } R \text{ compact}\}.$$

After an a priori distribution $g(\theta)$, $\theta \in \Omega^*$ has been introduced the Bernoulli principle can be applied by choosing that action a^* out of the action space for which

$$\int_{\Omega^*} u(a^*, \theta)f(x; \theta)g(\theta) \, d\theta = \sup_{a \in A} \int_{\Omega^*} u(a, \theta)f(x; \theta)g(\theta) \, d\theta.$$

The problem of the determination of $g(\theta)$ remains, it is true, but even if $g(\theta)$ is determined subjectively the degree of subjectivity is smaller than if $g(\theta)$ were determined subjectively on the whole range of Ω.

If the determination of $g(\theta)$, $\theta \in \Omega^*$, is not possible or not defendable, instead of the sup-expectation-operator, the sup-inf-operator can be used which means the application of the maximin-principle though in a restricted form, restricted in the sense that the pessimism and other shortcomings of that principle are confined to the selection of the worst a priori distribution out of Ω^* and not out of Ω.

The application of the maximum likelihood principle would be an easy way out of the dilemma, but there would be a considerable loss of information to be suffered: This criterion discards any information about the shape of the likelihood function.

13. ADAPTIVE BEHAVIOUR[18]

Finally, I want to repeat my proposal to use, instead of the relatively rigid Bernoulli or minimax-principles, still non-restrictive but more versatile decision criteria, criteria that allow for different degrees of uncertainty, different amounts of information available, different orders of instability, modi of change and of action in time, and that

are adaptable to additional information. The general form of such an
adaptive criterion can be seen in the following: u and Ω are considered time-dependent; u_t, $\Omega(t)$, $\Omega(t)$ is decomposed into pairwise
disjoint subsets $\Omega_i(t)$ ($i = 1, \ldots, k$) allowing for distinctions between
domains of different uncertainty and instability. Furthermore, a time-
interval T is introduced during which the impact of the action upon
the world will happen; β_t is the density function of that impact. The
adaptive behaviour manifests itself in the specification of the constituents of the model[19] and in the choice of that action which
maximizes

$$\int_T \beta_t \inf_{\theta \in \Omega(t)} \sum_{i=1}^{k} \int_{\Omega_i(t)} u_t(a, \theta) f(x; \theta) \, d\theta \, dt.$$

Specializations of this criterion can be found in the literature quoted
in Note 17. The specializations rather than the generic criterion itself
can mediate application patterns and their rationality.

Note added in proof: In the meantime, a new theory of decision-making
under partial information has been developed by Kofler and Menges
(1976), which is in many aspects a generalization of the 'adaptive
behaviour'. Its main idea is to utilize fully all kinds of information,
incomplete or vague or partial as it may be, given a priori or a posteriori
and to close the ever remaining gap by decisions. The theory of
decision-making under partial information as developed by Kofler and
Menges has two main advantages: it is susceptible to any kind of
information and it allows to utilize every information according to its
vagueness, fuzziness, or incompleteness.

University of Heidelberg

NOTES

[1] In order to clarify the basic ideas, the notions of decision functions and strategies are
not considered in this article, c.f. Wald [1950].

[2] A prospect is a probability mixture of outcomes. An action is to be understood as the
adoption of a prospect.

[3] The axiomatic system of v. Neumann–Morgenstern [1947] reads as follows (with
Pfanzagl's [1959] supplements; c.f. Menges [1970], p.48f]): The set of outcomes c and
probability mixtures of outcomes be $\mathfrak{C}$.

(1) A complete preordering $>$ is given on $\mathfrak{C}$ (order).

(2) For any pair c_1, $c_2 \in \mathfrak{C}$ and any $p \in (0, 1)$ an element $c_1 p c_2 \in \mathfrak{C}$ is defined such that $c_1 < c_2$ implies $c_1 < c_1 p c_2$ for every $p \in (0, 1)$ (continuity).

(3) From $c_1 < c_2 < c_3$ follows the existence of p, $p' \in (0, 1)$ with $c_1 p c_3 < c_2 < c_1 p' c_3$ (monotony).

(4) From $c_2 \sim \bar{c}_2$ follows $c_1 p c_2 \sim c_1 p \bar{c}_2$ (independence).

(5) $c_1 p c_2 \sim c_2(1 - p)c_1$.

(6) $(c_1 p c_2)p' c_2 \sim c_1(p p')c_2$.

(7) $c_1 p c_1 \sim c_1$.

[4] For a deliverance of the continuity axiom by the use of non-standard models of the reals, see Skala [1973].

[5] The empirical μ- and Bernoulli models should not be confused with Robbins' empirical Bayes approach although there are some similarities; c.f. Robbins [1964] and Krutchkoff [1972] and the literature quoted there.

[6] C.f. Menges [1974]. For the sake of simplicity we describe the probability distribution over the state space by a parameter or parameter vector θ out of a specified parameter space Ω. Let $\mathfrak{X}$ be the sample space of a random variable X, whose realizations are $x \in \mathfrak{X}$. The confirmation axioms for Bayesian a posteriori probabilities then read as follows (Menges [1974], p.34):

(1) From $x_1 \sim_L x_2$ $(x_1, x_2 \in \mathfrak{X})$ follows $\pi(\theta \mid x_1) = \pi(\theta \mid x_2)$, (axiom of observational equivalence; $\sim_L$ means logical equivalence).

(2) From $\theta_1 \sim_L \theta_2$ $(\theta_1, \theta_2 \in \Omega)$ follows $\pi(\theta_1 \mid x) = \pi(\theta_2 \mid x)$ (axiom of equivalence of hypotheses).

(3) From $(x \wedge (\theta_1 \wedge \theta_2))$ logically false follows $\pi(\theta_1 \wedge \theta_2 \mid x) = \pi(\theta_2 \mid x)\pi(\theta_1 \mid x \wedge \theta_2)$ (axiom of incompatibility or of general multiplication).

(4) From $(x \wedge (\theta_1 \wedge \theta_2))$ logically false follows $\pi(\theta_1 \vee \theta_2 \mid x) = \pi(\theta_1 \mid x) + \pi(\theta_2 \mid x)$ (special addition axiom).

(5) From $x \Vdash \theta$ follows $\pi(\theta \mid x) = 1$ (standardization axiom).

(6) If

$$f(x \mid \theta) = \frac{\pi(\theta \mid x)}{g(\theta)} \int_\Omega f(x; \theta)g(\theta) \, d\theta$$

($g(\theta)$ being the a priori distribution and $f(x; \theta)$ the probability function on $\mathfrak{X}$) exists, then for given x, $f(x; \theta)$ is a likelihood function (frequency axiom).

(7) From $f(x_1 \wedge x_2; \theta) = f(x_1; \theta)$ $(x_1, x_2 \in \mathfrak{X})$ follows $\pi(\theta \mid x_1) = \pi(\theta \mid x_1 \wedge x_2)$ (irrelevancy axiom).

[7] I put the name of the disfigured classic in inverted commas here in order to avoid confusion with other misuses of the name of the late reverend.

[8] De Groot's axioms read as follows (de Groot [1970], pp.71ff):

(1) For any two events A, $B \in \mathfrak{A}$ ($\mathfrak{A} = \sigma$-field of events based on the event space S) it holds exactly either $A < B$ or $B < A$ or $A \sim B$, where $A < B$ indicates that B seems more likely to occur (to a certain person), and $A \sim B$ indicates that A and B are equally likely to occur.

(2) For A_1, A_2, B_1, $B_2 \in \mathfrak{A}$ with $A_1 A_2 = B_1 B_2 = \emptyset$ and $A_i \lesssim B_i$ $(i = 1, 2)$ it holds $A_1 \cup A_2 \lesssim B_1 \cup B_2$, and if either $A_1 < B_1$ or $A_2 < B_2$, then $A_1 \cup A_2 < B_1 \cup B_2$.

(3) If $A \in \mathfrak{A}$, then $\emptyset \subset A$ and $A > \emptyset$.

(4) If $A_1 \supset A_2 \supset \cdots$ is a decreasing sequence of events and $B \in \mathfrak{A}$ with $A_i \gtrsim B$

$(i = 1, 2, \ldots)$, then

$$\bigcap_{i=1}^{\infty} A_i \gtrsim B.$$

(5) There exists a random variable which has a uniform distribution on the interval $[0, 1]$.

(6) For any three events $A, B, C \in \mathfrak{A}$, $(A \mid C) \lesssim (B \mid C)$ if and only if $AC \lesssim BC$.

[9] Menges [1970], p.50.

[10] More precise: For two actions $a, b \in A$ and $Z \neq \emptyset$ it holds that if $a \gtrsim_z b$ and $a \gtrsim_{\bar{z}} b$, then $a \gtrsim b$, and if $a >_z b$ and $a \gtrsim_{\bar{z}} b$, then $a > b$. (c f. Schneeweiss [1974], p.132.

[11] See Menges [1970], p.43f.

[12] I do not want to enter in the philosophical discussion in the present article but instead refer to Hartwig's [1956] work on the etiality principle and my [Menges 1974] trial to formalize it in the context of confirmation logic.

[13] The three main paradoxes – according to Blyth – are the following; X, Y, Z being real-valued random variables:

(1) the clocking paradox: It is possible to have (a) $P(X > Y)$ arbitrarily close to 1 and (b) $P(X \leq a) < P(Y \leq a)$ for all a;

(2) the non-transitivity paradox: It is possible to have (a) $P(X < Y) > 0.5$, $P(Y < Z) > 0.5$, and (b) $P(Z < X) > 0.5$;

(3) the pairwise-worst-best paradox: It is possible to have (a) $P(X = \min(X, Y, Z)) < P(Y = \min(X, Y, Z))$, $P(Y = \min(X, Y, Z)) < P(Z = \min(X, Y, Z))$ and (b) $P(X < Y) > 0.5$, $P(X < Z) > 0.5$, $P(Y < Z) > 0.5$.

[14] Cf. Menges [1972].

[15] The axioms system, by departing from the prospects instead of from the outcomes, uses an idea of Marschak [1950].

[16] Cf. Menges–Diehl [1969, 1973].

[17] For the notation see Note 5.

[18] Cf. Menges [1964, 1966, 1968, 1973, 1974], Menges–Behara [1963], Kale [1963], Schneeweiss [1964, 1967], Kofler [1974].

[19] Cf. Menges [1965].

REFERENCES

Allais, M.: (1953). 'Le comportement de l'homme rationnel devant le risque – Critique des postulats et axiomes de l'école Américaine', *Econometrica* 21, 503–546.

Allais, M.: (1976). 'The Foundations of a Positive Theory of Choice involving Risk and a Criticism of the Postulates and Axioms of the American School', Part II of this Volume.

Baumol, W. J.: (1951). 'The v. Neumann–Morgenstern Utility Index – An Ordinalist View', *Journal of Political Economy* **LIX**, No. 1, pp.61–66.

Bernoulli, D.: (1731). 'Specimen theoriae novae de mensura sortis', *Comentarii Academ. Petrop.* 5, 1730/31, pp.175–192.

Bernoulli, D.: (1777). 'Dijudicatio maxime probabilis plurium observationum discripantium atque verisi millima inductio inde formanda', *Acta Academ. Petrop.*, pp.3–23.

Bernoulli, J.: (1713). 'Ars conjectandi. Opus post humum. Accedit tractatus de seriebus infinites et epistola gallice scripta de ludo pilae reticularis', *Basilea.*

Bernoulli, J.: (1899). *Wahrscheinlichkeitsrechnung*, Übers. von R. Haussner, Leipzig.

Blyth, C. R.: (1972a). 'On Simpson's Paradox and the Sure-Thing Principle', *Journal of the American Statistical Association* **67**, pp.364-365.

Blyth, C. R.: (1972b). 'Some Probability Paradoxes in Choice from Among Random Alternatives', *Journal of the American Statistical Association* **67**, pp.365-373.

Borch, K. H.: (1968a). *The Economics of Uncertainty*, Princeton University Press, Princeton.

Borch, K. H.: (1968b). 'The Allais Paradox: A Comment', *Behavioral Science* **13**, pp.488-489.

Bortkiewicz, L. v.: (1923). 'Wahrscheinlichkeit und statistische Forschung nach Keynes', *Nordisk Statistisk Tidskrift* **2**, pp.1-23.

Carnap, R., und Stegmüller, W.: (1958). *Induktive Logik und Wahrscheinlichkeit*, Springer, Wien.

Chipman, J. S.: (1960). 'The Foundation of Utility', *Econometrica* **28**, pp.193-224.

Cournot, A.: (1843). *Exposition de la théorie des chances et des probabilités*, Paris.

Diehl, H. und Sprott, D. A.: (1965). 'Die Likelihoodfunktion und ihre Verwendung beim statistischen Schluss', *Statistische Hefte* **6**, pp.112-134.

Edwards, A. W. F.: (1972). *Likelihood*, Cambridge University Press.

Finetti, B. de: (1937). 'Foresight: Its Logical Laws, Its Subjective Sources', *Anales de l'Institut Henri Poincaré*, **7**.

Finetti, B. de: (1974). 'Bayesianism: Its Unifying Role for Both the Foundations and Applications of Statistics', *International Statistical Review* **42**, No. 2, pp.117-130.

Fraser, D. A. S.: (1968). *The Structure of Inference*, Wiley, New York.

Groot, M. H. de: (1970). *Optimal Statistical Decisions*, McGraw Hill, New York.

Hacking, I.: (1965). *Logic of Statistical Inference*, Cambridge University Press, London.

Hagen, O.: (1972). 'A New Axiomatization of Utility under Risk', *Teorie a Metoda* **VI/2**, pp.54-80.

Hagen, O.: (1976). 'Towards a Positive Theory of Preferences under Risk', This Volume.

Hartwig, H.: (1956). 'Naturwissenschaftliche und sozialwissenschaftliche Statistik', *Zeitschrift für die gesamte Staatswissenschaft* **112**, pp.252-256.

Kale, B. K.: (1963). 'Decisions Opposite Markov Chains', *Statistische Hefte* **4**, pp.172-177.

Keynes, J. M.: (1921). *A Treatise on Probability*, London.

Kofler, E.: (1974). 'Entscheidungen bei teilweise bekannter Verteilung der Zustände', *Zeitschrift für Operations Research*, Serie A: Theorie, **18**, pp.141-157.

Kofler, E., and Menges, G.: (1976). *Entscheidungen bei unvollständiger Information*, Springer, Berlin.

Kolmogoroff, A. A.: (1933). *Grundbegriffe der Wahrscheinlichkeitsrechnung*, Springer, Berlin, 1933.

Koopman, B. O.: (1940). 'The Axioms and Algebra of Intuitive Probability', *Annals of Mathematics* **41**, pp.269-292.

Kries, J. v.: (1886). 'Die Principien der Wahrscheinlichkeitsrechnung', Freiburg i.B., 1886.

Krutchkoff, R. G.: (1972). 'Empirical Bayes Estimation', *The American Statistician* **26**, No. 5, pp.14-16.

Laplace, P. S. de: (1812). *Théorie Analytique des Probabilités*, Paris.

Leiner, B.: (1974). 'Notes on Etiality, the Adaptation Criterion, and the Inference–Decision Problem'. In G. Menges (Ed.), *Information, Inference and Decision*, Reidel, Dordrecht, pp.63–73.

Leinfellner, W.: (1965). *Struktur und Aufbau wissenschaftlicher Theorien*, Physica-Verlag, Wien und Würzburg.

Marschak, J.: (1950). 'Rational Behaviour, Uncertain Prospects, and Measurable Utility', *Econometrica* 18, pp.111–141.

Marschak, J.: (1955). 'Probability in the Social Sciences'. In P. F. Lazarsfeld (Ed.), *Mathematical Thinking in the Social Sciences*, The Free Press, Glencoe, Ill., 2nd edn., pp.166–215.

Marschak, J.: (1973). 'Information, Decision and the Scientist'. In L. Cherry (Ed.), *Pragmatic Aspects of Human Communication*, Reidel, Dordrecht, pp.145–178.

Marschak, J.: (1974). 'Prior and Posterior Probabilities and Semantic Information'. In G. Menges (Ed.), *Information, Inference and Decision*, Reidel, Dordrecht, pp.167–180.

Meinong, A. v.: (1915). 'Über Möglichkeit und Wahrscheinlichkeit', Leipzig.

Menger, K.: (1934). 'Das Unsicherheitsmoment in der Wertlehre', *Zeitschrift für Nationalökonomie* 5, pp.459–485.

Menges, G.: (1963). 'The Adaptation of Decision Criteria and Application Patterns'. Extrait des actes de la 3e Conference Internationale de Recherche Operationelle, Oslo, Dunod, Paris 1964, pp.585–594.

Menges, G.: (1965). 'Vorentscheidungen', Operations Research-Verfahren, Vol. II, Verlag Anton Hain, Meisenheim/Glan, pp.24–40.

Menges, G.: (1966). 'On the Bayesification of the Minimax Principle', *Unternehmensforschung*, 10, pp.81–91.

Menges, G.: (1968). 'On Some Open Questions in Statistical Decision Theory'. In K. Borch and J. Mossin (Eds.), *Risk and Uncertainty*, New York.

Menges, G.: (1970). 'On Subjective Probability and Related Problems', *Theory and Decision* 1, pp.40–60.

Menges, G.: (1972). 'Measuring Social Utility and the Substitution Axiom'. In W. Krelle (Ed.), *Operations Research-Verfahren*. (Methods of Operations Research), Vol. XIV, Anton Hain Verlag, Meisenheim/Glan, pp.109–117.

Menges, G.: (1973). 'Inference and Decision', *Selecta Statistica Canadiana* 1, pp.1–14.

Menges, G.: (1974). 'Elements of an Objective Theory of Inductive Behaviour'. In G. Menges (Ed.), *Information, Inference and Decision*, Reidel, Dordrecht, pp.3–49.

Menges, G. and Behara, M.: (1963). 'On Decision Criteria under Various Degrees of Stability', *Journal of the Indian Statistical Association* 1, pp.185–196.

Menges, G. and Diehl, H.: (1969). 'On the Application of Fiducial Probability to Statistical Decisions'. In *The Proceedings of the Fourth International Conference on Operational Research*. Wiley, New York, pp.82–91.

Menges, G. and Diehl, H.: (1973). 'Likelihood- and Fiducial-optimal Solutions of Decision problems under Uncertainty'. Transactions of the Sixth Prague Conference on Information Theory, Statistical Decision Functions, Random Processes, Academia Publishing House of the Czechoslovak Academy of Sciences, Prague, pp.639–647.

Menges, G. and Rommelfanger, W.: (1970). 'Die Messung des sozialen Nutzens', Unveröffentlichtes Manuskript, Heidelberg.

Morrison, D. G.: (1967). 'On the Consistency of Preferences in Allais' Paradox', *Behavioral Science* 12, pp.373–383.

Mosteller, F. R. and Nogee, P.: (1951). 'An Experimental Measurement of Utility', *Journal of Political Economy* **59**, pp.371–404.

Neumann, J. v. and Morgenstern, O.: (1947). *Theory of Games and Economic Behaviour.* Princeton University Press, Princeton, 2nd edn.

Pfanzagl, J.: (1959). *Die axiomatischen Grundlagen einer allgemeinen Theorie des Messens,* Physica-Verlag, Würzburg und Wien.

Ramsey, F. P.: (1931). *The Foundations of Mathematics and other Logical Essays,* London.

Robbins, H.: (1964). 'The Empirical Bayes Approach to Statistical Decision Problems', *Annals of Mathematical Statistics* **35**, pp.1–20.

Samuelson, P. A.: (1952). 'Probability, Utility and the Independence Axiom', *Econometrica,* **29**, pp.670–678.

Savage, L. J.: (1954). *The Foundations of Statistics,* New York, London.

Schneeweiss, H.: (1964). 'Eine Entscheidungsregel für den Fall partiell bekannter Wahrscheinlichkeiten', *Unternehmensforschung* **8**, pp.86–95.

Schneeweiss, H.: (1967). *Entscheidungskriterien bei Risiko,* Springer, Heidelberg, New York.

Schneeweiss, H.: (1974). 'Probability and Utility – Dual Concepts in Decision Theory'. In G. Menges (Ed.), *Information, Inference and Decision,* Reidel, Dordrecht, pp.113–144.

Skala, H.: (1973). 'Über einige Grundprobleme der Nutzentheorie – Nichtarchimedische Nutzentheorie', Habilitationsschrift, Universität Heidelberg.

Stegmüller, W.: (1973). *Probleme und Resultate der Wissenschaftstheorie und Analytischen Philosophie,* Vol. IV, Springer, Berlin und Heidelberg.

Stumpf, C.: (1893). 'Über den Begriff der mathematischen Wahrscheinlichkeit', Sitzungsberichte der philosophisch-philologischen und historischen Klasse der königlichen bayrischen Akademie der Wissenschaften zu München, Jg. 1892, München.

Wald, A.: (1950). *Statistical Decision Functions,* Wiley, New York.

Wold, H.: (1952). 'Ordinal Preferences or Cardinal Utility?', *Econometrica* **20**, pp. 661–663.

PART V

ALLAIS' REJOINDER: THEORY
AND EMPIRICAL EVIDENCE

MAURICE ALLAIS

THE SO-CALLED ALLAIS PARADOX
AND RATIONAL DECISIONS
UNDER UNCERTAINTY

Maurice Allais and Ole Hagen (eds.), Expected Utility and the Allais Paradox, 437–681.
Copyright © 1979 by D. Reidel Publishing Company.

TABLE OF CONTENTS

438

SUMMARY

The present memoir constitutes an extension of my 1952 study, *The Foundations of a Positive Theory of Choice Involving Risk and a Criticism of the Postulates and Axioms of the American School* (see Part II of this Volume), completing it and adding further comments in the light of the criticisms addressed to it and the analysis of the responses to the experiment carried out in 1952 by means of a Questionnaire. Its aim was to display the behaviour in situations of random choice of people who are generally considered by the common opinion as rational *on criteria* that are free of all reference to any consideration of random choice.

Out of the contents of this 1952 memoir one aspect only received wide attention: the so-called *Allais Paradox*. This paradox corresponds to the very numerous class of random choices violating the neo-Bernoullian formulation. Actually, this paradox is only apparent, and is the reflection of a fundamental aspect of reality: *the preference for security in the neighbourhood of certainty.*[1]

The theory presented differs utterly from the neo-Bernoullian theories which were developed with and after the publication in 1947 of the second edition of the *Theory of Games*. It is based on two groups of axioms, the first relating to the fundamental concepts of probability and psychological value, the second to fields of random choice.[2]

Whereas the latest neo-Bernoullian theories prove the existence of magnitudes which are labelled as *probability* and *utility* on the basis of a single system of axioms concerning random choice fields, the theory of random choice I propose takes as its starting point the existence of probabilities and psychological values, independently of any random choice, and, this existence being admitted, investigates the properties of fields of random choice.[3]

The probabilities considered are objective probabilities *defined on the basis of reference urns*, and the psychological values (cardinal utilities) representing the intensity of the preferences, can be determined *operationally* from the answers to the relevant questions. If C

represents the estimate of his worth made by himself by a subject and
g a certain gain, the results obtained show that, as a first approximation and up to a linear transformation, the Daniel Bernoulli
log–linear expression $\gamma = \log(C + g)$ of 'moral worth' (psychological
value or cardinal utility) may be considered as valid.[4]

The crucial difference between the theory presented and the neo-
Bernoullian theories lies in the substitution of the axiom of absolute
preference in place of the axiom of independence used in the neo-
Bernoullian theories (or to the equivalent axioms, as, for instance,
von Neumann and Morgenstern's axioms 3Ba and 3Bb).[5]

The theory presented makes it possible to refute the neo-Bernoullian theories by showing that they fundamentally neglect the
impact of the greater or lesser propensity for risk-taking or security,
the consequence of which is, in particular, a complementarity effect
in the neighbourhood of certainty. This theory also makes it possible
to show that the neo-Bernoullian theories are valid only asymptotically for a very great number of games when the probability of ruin in
an infinite number of games may be deemed negligible.[6]

The analysis of the replies to the 1952 experiment led to two
essential results: the direct determination of the cardinal preference
index (cardinal utility) of each subject from a set of appropriate
questions, independent of any consideration or random choice, and
the impossibility of determining for any given subject an index which
could depict his behaviour for different series of questions under the
assumption that the neo-Bernoullian formulation is valid.[7]

After a general introduction (Chapter I), this study presents general
comments on the 1952 study which seem the most important in the light
of the later debate (Chapter II), a critical analysis of the basic concepts
of the post-1952 theories of the American School (Chapter III), a
rejoinder to the criticisms made (Chapter IV), and finally, a general
interpretation of my analysis in relation to theory and experience
(Chapter V).[8]

The second Chapter sets out primarily to analyse the effective
structure of my theory and its implications, but by comparing *point by
point* the neo-Bernoullian theories and my own in the third and fourth
Chapters it will undoubtedly assist the reader to a better understanding
of certain complex and crucial aspects of the random choice theory.

Four appendices are presented, containing respectively a critical
analysis of the von Neumann–Morgenstern axioms (Appendix A),

mathematical complements (Appendix B), some of the results of the 1952 experiment (Appendix C), and a few considerations on the concept of probability (Appendix D).[9]

Among the very many analyses of this memoir, I would cite in particular: the nature and meaning of the concepts of objective and subjective probabilities, the axiom of cardinal isovariation and the neo-Bernoullian formulation, conditions for the asymptotic validity of the neo-Bernoullian formulation, the implications of the neo-Bernoullian formulation for the arbitrage between mathematical expectation and the probability of ruin, the analysis of the St. Petersburg Paradox and the theory of gambler's ruin, the respective meaning of Axioms 3Ba, 3Bb and 3Cb of von Neumann and Morgenstern, and the correspondence between the axioms of my theory and those of von Neumann and Morgenstern.[10]

Notes

[1] *Allais' Paradox*: Foreword, pp.4–7; §36, pp.533–541.

[2] *Axiomatic Foundation and Structure of Allais' Theory*: Foreword, pp.4–7; §10–13, pp.456–463; §21, pp.469–473; §23, pp.475–483; §39–40, pp.548–552.

[3] *Probability and Utility – Latest neo-Bernoullian Theories*: §28–29, pp.508–514. *Allais' Theory*: §10–13, pp.456–463; §21, pp.469–473; §23, pp.475–483.

[4] *Objective Probabilities*: §29, pp.510–514; §§D.1–D.3, pp.655–663. *Psychological Values*: §11, pp.460–462; §23, pp.475–483; §§C.5–C.9, pp.614–620; §C.18, pp.627–628; §C.21, pp.632–634.

[5] *Axiom of Absolute Preference and Axiom of Independence*: §10, p.457; §18, pp.466–467; §39–40, pp.548–552; §A.4, A.6, A.7, pp.594–599.

[6] *Non-Validity of the neo-Bernoullian Theories: Complementary Effect in the Neighbourhood of Certainty*: §14–19, pp.463–468; §22, pp.473–474; §27, pp.507–508. *Asymptotic Validity of the neo-Bernoullian Formulation*: §24, pp.483–490.

[7] *Analysis of the Replies to the 1952 Experiment*: §C.6, pp.451–454; §37, pp.541–543; Appendix C, pp.611–654.

[8] Chapter I, *Introduction*, pp.445–455; Chapter II, *The Allais 1952 Theory*, pp.456–506; Chapter III, *Critical Analysis of the neo-Bernoullian Basic Concepts*, pp.507–517; Chapter IV, *Criticisms of the Allais 1952 Theory: Rejoinder*, pp.518–546; Chapter V, *Theory and Experience*, pp.547–554.

[9] Appendices: A. pp.591–603; B. pp.604–610; C. pp.611–654; D. pp.655–663.

[10] *Objective and Subjective Probabilities*: §21, pp.469–473; §29, pp.510–514; Appendix D, pp.655–663; *Axiom of Cardinal Isovariation and the neo-Bernoullian Formulation*: Foreword, pp.4–7; §23, pp.481–483; §39–40, pp.548–552. *Asymptotic Validity of the neo-Bernoullian Formulation*: §24, pp.483–490. *Arbitrage between Mathematical Expectation and Probability of Ruin*: §1, pp.445–446; §25, pp.491–498. *Analysis of the St. Petersburg Paradox*: §26, pp.498–506. *Meaning of Axioms 3Ba, 3Bb and 3Cb of von Neumann–Morgenstern*: §A.6, pp.596–598; §A.8, pp.599–600. *Analysis of the Concept of Rationality*: §12, pp.462–463; §19, pp.467–468; §31, pp.514–517; §38, pp.543–546. *Nature of a Scientific Theory*: §35, pp.527–533; §41, pp.552–554.

The students nodded, emphatically agreeing with a statement which upwards of sixty-two thousand repetitions in the dark had made them accept, not merely as true, but as axiomatic self evidence, utterly indisputable . . . .

One believes things because one has been conditioned to believe them. Finding bad reasons for what one believes for other bad reasons – that's philosophy.

ALDOUS HUXLEY, 1932[1]

Most fallacies seem foolish when pinpointed, but they are not the prerogative of fools . . . . Great men make mistakes, and when they admit them remorsefully, they reveal a facet of their greatness . . . . Many fallacies . . . have their origin in wishful thinking, laziness, and business. These conditions lead to over-simplification, the desire to win an argument at all costs (even at the cost of over-complication), failure to listen to the opposition, too-ready acceptance of authority . . . , too great reliance on a formal system or formula . . . , and too-ready rejection of them . . . . These emotionally determined weaknesses are not themselves fallacies, but they provoke them. For example, they provoque special pleading . . . , the insistence that a method used successfully in one field of research is the only appropriate one in another, the distorsion of judgment, and the forgetting of the need for judgment.

IRVING JOHN GOOD, 1968[2]

Badly understood respect for personal authority would be superstition and a real obstacle to the progress of science; it would also be contrary to the examples set by great men of all times. The great men are those who have introduced new ideas and destroyed errors. They themselves did not respect their predecessors' authority, and see no reason why they should not be treated otherwise . . . .

Every epoch has its errors and truths. Some mistakes are in a sense an inherent part of their time, and will only be revealed by the future progress of science.

The scholastic mind always requires a fixed and unquestionable starting point . . . . Once this has been set, the scholastic or systematic usually deduces logically all the consequences, and may even invoke observation or factual experience as arguments when this suits it; the only condition is that the starting point remains immutable and will not be affected by experience and observation, and that to the contrary, the facts be interpreted to adapt them to the starting point . . . . The scholastic or systematic, the two mean the same thing, never doubts the starting point and refers everything to it, proudly and intolerantly refusing contradiction since he cannot admit that the starting point might change.

CLAUDE BERNARD, 1865[3]

CHAPTER I

INTRODUCTION

> There is ever a tendency of the most hurtful kind to allow opinions to crystallize into creeds. Especially does this tendency manifest itself when some eminent author, enjoying the power of clear and comprehensive exposition, becomes recognized as an authority.... But 'to err is human', and the best works should ever be open to criticism. If, instead of welcoming inquiry and criticism, the admirers of a great author accept his writings as authoritative,... the most serious injury is done to truth. In matters of philosophy and science authority has ever been the great opponent of truth. A despotic calm is usually the triumph of error.... In science and philosophy nothing must be held sacred.
>
> STANLEY JEVONS, 1871[4]

MY RESEARCHES IN 1936 INTO OPTIMAL STRATEGY IN THE FIELD OF UNCERTAINTY

1. About thirty years ago, just after the war, in 1947, I read the second edition of the von Neumann–Morgenstern *Theory of Games* (the first edition was published in 1944). My immediate reaction was that two of their fundamental conclusions were totally unacceptable: the conclusion that the psychological value (cardinal utility) of money can be measured by observation of choices between uncertain prospects, and their presentation of the principle of maximising the mathematical expectation of psychological value (cardinal utility) as the principle of optimum behaviour.

At the suggestion of a friend, I had already had the opportunity before the war, in 1936, of thinking about a method for successful racecourse betting, based on the use of newspaper forecasts. Initial statistical analysis indicated that the method could yield a slightly positive mathematical expectation, but with a high dispersion of gains and losses. The law of large numbers made very large winnings certain in the long term, but with one condition: not to have to discontinue during the process through excessive interim losses. The question thus boiled down to ascertaining how much to commit in each wager to reduce the probability of ruin to an acceptable level, taking into account my available capital. This is, of course, the classical problem of the probability of ruin of a player engaged in a long sequence of games, each with a positive mathematical expectation m. The optimal strategy was manifestly not based on the maximisation of the mathematical expectation E_n after n games, but on a compromise between this mathematical expectation and the probability of ruin P_n in n games. This compromise could be represented by the maximisation of an index of preference $S(E_n, P_n)$ for a large number of games, and I was led, as a first approximation, to consider a preference index

$$S = S(m, P),$$

a function of the mathematical expectation m for each game and the probability of ruin P for an infinite number of games.[5]

In reading the *Theory of Games*, I realised immediately that the principle of reasonable behaviour to which my pre-war thinking had led me was totally incompatible with the principle of maximising the mathematical expectation of an index of psychological value as suggested by the book. This induced me to seek out which postulates of the *Theory of Games* were responsible for such an unacceptable proposition, and in turn to make a critical analysis of the different theories in the American literature which favoured the neo-Bernoullian formulation. This analysis also led me to the conclusion that the observation of behaviour concerning choice under uncertainty cannot be used to construct an index of psychological value.

THE PARIS COLLOQUIUM, 1952

2. In May 1952, with the help of Professor Darmois, I organised an international colloquium on risk, under the sponsorship of the *Centre National de la Recherche Scientifique*. The participants were K. J. Arrow, Marcel Boiteux, Van Dantzig, Bruno de Finetti, Maurice Fréchet, Milton Friedman, Ragnar Frisch, Robert Gibrat, Georges Th.

Guilbaud, René Hutter, William Jaffé, Henri Lavaill, Jacob Marshak, Edmond Malinvaud, Pierre Massé, Georges Morlat, René Roy, Paul A. Samuelson, L. J. Savage, L. J. Shackle, Jean Ville, Herman Wold, and myself.

I presented two memoirs at this colloquium: 'Généralisation des Théories de l'Equilibre Economique Général et du Rendement Social au Cas du Risque' (Generalisation of the Theories of General Economic Equilibrium and Economic Efficiency to the Case of Risk) (Memoir I) and 'Fondements d'une Théorie Positive des Choix comportant un Risque' (Foundations of a Positive Theory of Choice involving Risk) (Memoir II).[6] These two memoirs were published by the *Centre National de la Recherche Scientifique* in the collective volume *Econométrie*, in its collection *Colloques Internationaux* (International Colloquia).[7] A summary of the first was published in 1953 under the same title in *Econometrica* (Memoir I bis).[8]

During the colloquium, the neo-Bernoullian formulation was defended in various forms by de Finetti, Friedman, Marshak, Samuelson, and Savage,[9] and my conflicting views led to heated discussion.[10]

After the colloquium, I wrote a third memoir: 'Fondements d'une Théorie des Choix Comportant un Risque et Critique des Postulats et Axiomes de l'Ecole Américaine' (The Foundations of a Positive Theory of Choice Involving Risk, and a Critical Analysis of the Postulates and Axioms of the American School) (Memoir III) in which I developed in more detail the arguments I had put forward at the colloquium. This memoir was annexed to the volume of the colloquium[11] and published later as a book in 1955 under the same title.[12] In the meantime, a summary had been published under the same title in *Econometrica* (Memoir III bis).[13] Unfortunately, this, like Memoir III was in French, which meant that most English-speaking economists had no direct access to it; at best, they only got the indirect and therefore imperfect review which could be deduced from various comments that were made on it.[14,15]

THE 1952 EXPERIMENT

3. After the International Symposium on Random Choice, in 1952, I organised an experiment to analyse the behaviour of 'rational' men confronted with choice associated with risk. It was limited to people generally considered as rational, and who had a good knowledge of

probability theory. The Questionnaire used for the inquiry was later published in 1953 in the *Journal de la Société de Statistique de Paris* under the title 'La Psychologie de l'Homme Rationnel devant le Risque. La Théorie et l'Expérience' (The Psychology of Rational Behaviour in the Presence of Risk – Theory and Experience).[16]

The experiment took a double form. A limited investigation covering 49 subjects was carried out during a seminar[17] based on that part of the Questionnaire for which immediate answers could be given.[18] In parallel, an inquiry based on the whole Questionnaire was carried out. There were 101 respondents to this in all, so that the short questionnaire was returned by 150 people and the full questionnaire by 101. A first statistical analysis was carried out in 1952–1953.

Of the 101 complete responses, 55 were returned by students of the *Ecole Nationale Supérieure des Mines*; only 15 of these 55 files were selected in 1952, to avoid giving too much weight to this group. The respondents retained were those who stated that they had worked on their questionnaire with care. In addition, 9 forms had arrived late, so that in all 101 files (150–40–9), were processed in the statistical analysis done in 1952–53, of which 52 were complete questionnaires (101–40–9) and 49 short questionnaires.

The thorough analysis of these 150 files, of which 101 related to the complete questionnaire, meant a considerable burden of work, and I underestimated the size of the job[19] which was only very partly started in 1952 and 1953. As my time was completely absorbed by a set of other researches and publications,[20] I was unable to carry out a full analysis scientifically worthy of publication, and in the upshot, kept putting off the work from year to year. Only in June 1974, when writing an overview of my work[21] did the occasion arise to resume this analysis.

Summing up, I have suffered delay and am still behind in publishing the results of the 1952 experiment.[22] Essentially, the reason is the amount of work involved in undertaking a satisfactory analysis of the answers I received to the Questionnaire and the many constraints resulting from my professional duties and my other research and publishing activities.

In the light of the scientific importance of the results,[22] I am quite embarrassed by this lag, especially vis-à-vis all those who put so much time and effort into answering the Questionnaire. Fundamentally, however, the survey fully confirmed the arguments I put forward in 1952. *Indeed, my contentions were decisively confirmed, much better than I could have hoped.*

If, as I believe, the value and merit of a theory is to be judged by the results it yields, the analysis I presented in 1952 is strongly supported by the results of the survey of that year.

EXTENSION OF THE THEORIES OF GENERAL ECONOMIC EQUILIBRIUM AND MAXIMUM EFFICIENCY TO THE CASE OF CHOICE WITH UNCERTAINTY

4. *My research into random psychology was only a part of a much greater whole: the generalisation of the theory of economic equilibrium and maximum efficiency to the case of choice with uncertainty.*

The purpose of my 1952 memoir: 'L'extension des théories de l'équilibre économique général et du rendement social au cas du risque' (The Extension of the Theories of General Economic Equilibrium and Maximum Efficiency to the Case of Choice with Uncertainty) (Memoir I)[23] was twofold: to extend both the theory of general economic equilibrium and the theory of maximum efficiency to the case of choice with uncertainty.

The approach taken was to consider a specific model, sufficiently detailed for all important aspects to appear, and for the different effects of interest to be discussed.[24] This approach can easily be generalised.

The model used and the fields of choice considered make it possible to take into account the degree of *propensity for risk or security* explicitly, simply and in a way that lends itself well to theoretical analysis. The model is based also on the consideration of *production functions* representing the composition of risks according to the principles of the probability calculus.

It is a two-good model: a certainly available good and an uncertain good. The fields of choice considered are such that each index of preference is a function of the mathematical expectation and the standard deviation of the uncertain outcomes considered.[25,26] In fact, the shape of the indifference curves corresponding to the trade-off between certain and uncertain goods is entirely different from the shape of these curves when they refer to arbitrage between certainly available goods.[27]

The generalisation of the theory of economic equilibrium is based on the determination of the prices of the certain and uncertain goods considered, subject to the dual condition that each operator maximizes his preference index subject to the budgetary constraint, and that aggregate supply and demand must be equalised by price.[28]

The model is based on the assumption that there are no insurance facilities and no lotteries,[29] but in view of the results obtained in this particular case, the analysis is extended to the general case in which insurance and lotteries are present.[30] The discussion is based on the distinction between risks which cannot be eliminated in aggregate and the risks which cancel out in aggregate.[31]

As regards the generalisation of the theory of maximum efficiency to the case of risk, the particular model studied shows how it is possible to generalise the theorems of equivalence of states of equilibrium and situations of maximum efficiency. The discussion is then extended to the case in which lotteries, insurance companies and friendly societies are present.[32]

In the light of the literature on risk, this study, although relatively short, presents an entirely new approach whose generalisation could be very fruitful.[33]

APPLIED WORK

5. During the years 1953–1954, I undertook concrete application of the theses I had propounded at the 1952 meeting. The opportunity arose in connection with an operational research project for the *Bureau de Recherches Minières de l'Algérie* (Algerian Office of Mining Research). It led to the publication of a memoir in 1957: 'Evaluation des perspectives de la recherche minière sur de grands espaces – Application au cas Algérien' (Method of Appraising Economic Prospects of Mining Exploration over Large Territories – Algerian Sahara Case Study).[34]

This paper summarised the operational research which had been commissioned by the Algerian Office of Mining Research. Its purpose was to make reasonable forecasts, before any effective search was begun, of the economic prospects for mining exploration in *the non-sedimentary Sahara*, and to determine an optimum economic strategy.[35] *A priori, this was a problem without a solution.* However, further research proved that it could be solved.

The analysis presented is based on the development of a probabilistic model and the application of this model to the case studied using available empirical data.

The model treats research as if it were a lottery with tickets costing several hundred million, and prizes of several hundred billion francs of the time.[36] It is based on the fact that mining statistical distributions conform remarkably to well determined laws: values of deposits are lognormally distributed, the probability of discovery follows a Poisson distribution, while dimension-free parameters such as the standard deviation of a lognormal distribution are normally distributed.[37]

Unbelievable as it may seem, *the data are what one would expect if* the probability laws concerning mining deposits were the same for each million km^2 tract, whatever the *non-sedimentary* geological nature of the terrain. This result is observed in the data for countries already explored, so that the laws of distribution for unexplored countries can be deduced.[38] The first step was to determine the laws of the statistical distribution of the values of mining deposits.[39] I used the lognormal distribution systematically,[40] with excellent results.[41]

The second step was to develop a three-stage statistical model based on the consideration of research for mineral traces, prospection of these traces, and exploration of mineable areas. The corresponding probabilities of success are denoted p_1, p_2 and p_3; the probability for the project as a whole p.[42]

The analysis made it possible to determine the distribution of the global value of deposits which might be discovered in the non-sedimentary Sahara,[43] and to work out the probable economic return to exploration, and its variability as a function of the area of the tract explored.[44] Overall, the study led to accurate and consistent estimates of what had seemed beforehand to defy analysis.

This study was inspired throughout by my theoretical and empirical research on risk, which I was continuing at the same time.[45] *The guiding principle was to offer the Mining Research Office of Algeria a reasonable compromise between the mathematical expectation of the gains that might be expected and the probability of ruin.*

ANALYSIS OF THE ANSWERS TO THE 1952 QUESTIONNAIRE
(1974–1975)

6. During 1974 and 1975, preparing for the publication of the present volume, I proceeded to make a thorough analysis of the answers to the 1952 Questionnaire. This was carried out over three periods during which the methodological approach was progressively perfected.

First Period (February–April 1974)

(a) *In the first period* a general analysis was performed of the work done in 1952 and 1953 and methods of graphical analysis of the answers developed, greatly superior to those used in 1952–53.[46] The conclusions from the analysis of the 101 files containing fully completed questionnaires[47] were essentially the following:[48]

(1) An index of psychological value (cardinal utility) exists and can be determined from the questions related to the intensity of preference,[49] which are *absolutely independent of any consideration of random choices whatsoever. This index is approximately loglinear.*

(2) For each series of questions, the corresponding neo-Bernoullian index can be built up.[50] *These indexes differ significantly from each other.* All the answers are extraordinarily consistent, and it is possible to draw the curves representing the neo-Bernoullian indices of each subject with surprising precision.

(3) No subject acts according to the neo-Bernoullian principle in respect of all the series of questions.

Second Period (June 1974–August 1975)

(b) *In the second period*, sixteen complete questionnaires were analysed in full detail. Methods were developed for calculating the averages of the replies for a given group. The behaviour of different groups was analysed and compared. A method was also established for representing the field of random choice of a subject corresponding to his full set of answers.

During these first two periods, I concluded, *as a first approximation but covering a wide range of variation*, that the cardinal utility of different subjects can be represented by a *single loglinear formulation.* But this approximation does not seem acceptable *for very small or very great variations* of the envisaged gains in relation to the capital actually held. However, up to October 1975, all my attempts to represent the cardinal utility of all the subjects *using a single nonloglinear expression* had failed.

Third Period (October–December 1975)

(c) *During the third and last period,* I succeeded in defining a relatively complex but very suggestive method of analysing the non-loglinear case. Considering the Group *P* of 9 subjects (of the preceding sample of 16 respondents studied) for whom no phenomenon of satiety was present, this method led to the conclusion that *it is possible to represent the cardinal utility of different subjects with the same non-loglinear formulation over the full range of the argument.* The corresponding curve, is, for sufficiently large values of the argument, of logistic shape, and is asymptotically horizontal for very large sums.[51]

Given the extraordinary coherence of the results obtained, I undertook a further survey in November 1974 of six conscientious students attending my seminar in monetary analysis at the Paris-X University. For this group *R*, I found the same results. I then considered all those among the 45 unused files of the 1952 survey, which presented no phenomenon of satiety,[52] and compared the 9 corresponding subjects (Group *Q*) with the nine subjects (Group *P*), belonging to the group of the 16 subjects considered above, that satisfied this condition. *The results for all three groups P, Q and R are remarkably and indeed surprisingly consistent*; they can be represented by the same non-loglinear curve for each group of subjects on average; and this consistency may vouch for the validity of their interpretation.

In April 1974, at the end of the first period, I had intended to limit this paper essentially to an overview of the controversial issues and the presentation of the results of the 1952 experiment. Thus this volume could have been published early in 1975. But the amount of work involved in exploiting the answers of the 1952 experiment, and the importance of the new results obtained delayed the drafting of this paper. *I felt I had to finish the whole analysis to be able to present with absolute certainty the conclusions flowing from it.*[53]

In the end, I felt it would be necessary to publish, *as a separate volume*, the analysis of the answers to the 1952 Questionnaire, the presentation of the methods employed and of the numerical data used, and the detailed justification of the conclusions I reached.

I had hoped to present a general view of all this work in this memoir, but even for such a condensed presentation there was not enough room, and I had to give up the idea. Thus I will limit myself, in Appendix C to the present study, to some brief comments on fifteen charts among the several hundred which will be presented in the book devoted to the detailed analysis of the 1952 experiment and of its results.

I accept full responsibility for the delay in the publication of this volume, to which Ole Hagen has devoted himself so untiringly, but the reader will doubtless agree with me on the necessity of basing the conclusions presented on a complete and unchallengeable analysis of the replies to the 1952 Questionnaire.

EXTENSION OF THE THEORETICAL ANALYSIS OF FIELDS OF CHOICE INVOLVING RISK

7. During the three years 1974–1976, partly in connection with the preparation of this paper, I have been led to study four domains of risk theory thoroughly: the gamblers' ruin, the St. Petersburg Paradox, the foundations of the concept of probability, and the concept of psychological value.

Concerning the theory of the gamblers' ruin, I have extended the field of application of de Finetti's theorem,[54] and linked his theory to the Cramér's collective risk theory.[55]

My work on the St. Petersburg Paradox resulted in a new explanation of the paradox based on the theory of the gamblers' ruin and the trade-off between mathematical expectation and the probability of ruin.[56]

The analysis of the foundations of the concept of objective and subjective probability led me to an axiomatic presentation of the foundations of the probability calculus which is, I believe, free of any logical contradiction.

Finally, I have been led to consider two new axioms: the axiom of homogeneity for cardinal utility, and the axiom of cardinal isovariation. These axioms can yield a partial specification of the index of cardinal utility and of the index of preference representing a field of random choice. The consequences of the first postulate appear to be fully borne out by the analysis of the 1952 experiment.

These different researches have enabled me to ground my 1952 theory on a triple set of axioms dealing with, respectively, the concept of the psychological value of a certain gain, the concepts of objective and subjective probability, and the concept of the psychological value of a random prospect.

I intend to publish all these results as soon as time and opportunity allow, but they could not be included in the present paper.[57] Nevertheless, they are taken into account, at least for the main points.

THE FRAMEWORK OF THE PRESENT MEMOIR

8. In the following sections, I will present successively: a general commentary on the main points of my 1952 paper, which appear essential in view of the subsequent discussion (Chapter II); a brief critical analysis of the basic concepts of the American School after 1952 (Chapter III); my rejoinder to critics of my 1952 memoir (Chapter IV); and, finally, Conclusions, Theory and Experience (Chapter V).[58]

I will present also in four appendices: Comments on the Von Neumann–Morgenstern theory of random choice concerning the axioms of the *Theory of Games* (Extracts of my 1951 memoir 'Notes théoriques sur l'incertitude de l'avenir et le risque', Theoretical notes on the uncertainty of the future and risk) (Appendix A); Complements to my 1952 demonstration of the identity of the cardinal utility and the neo-Bernoullian index when it exists, and also the proof of a mathematical theorem useful for the analysis of the psychological value of a random prospect (Appendix B); an overall review of some results and conclusions of the analysis of the responses to the 1952 Questionnaire (Appendix C); and finally some views on the concept of probability (Appendix D).

Throughout the discussion, I will limit myself to essential features, referring the reader to my 1952 paper whenever possible. For clarity, I have used the same notation.[59,60] The main symbols used are set forth in Paragraph 11.2 below.

To simplify the presentation, I have relegated to the Notes some points which, *although in my view very important*, are not indispensable in the body of the main text.

To facilitate its use, the Bibliography of this memoir has been divided in ten Sections, in which the reader will easily find the references of the works cited.

Finally I have thought it useful to reproduce and discuss some comments I received from certain correspondents. These are of marked interest *since they express a number of widely held objections*. I have not named these correspondents, since *it is ideas, and only ideas, that should be discussed, independently of who express them*.[61,61*]

CHAPTER II

THE ALLAIS 1952 THEORY OF CHOICE
WITH UNCERTAINTY

> It would be definitely unrealistic ... to confine ourselves to the mathematical expectation only, which is the usual but not justifiable practice of the traditional calculus of 'moral probabilities'.
>
> JACOB MARSCHAK, 1938[62]

MY POSITION REMAINS FUNDAMENTALLY THE SAME

9. The main elements arguing for a positive restatement of the theory of random choice were presented, together with a critical analysis of the theories of the Bernoulli school, in the memoir I wrote in 1952. Two decades of reflection, conferences and lectures lead me to maintain *entirely* all the analyses of this memoir. However, I am now in a position further to buttress the arguments I set forth at the time, and to specify the elements on which more stress should be laid.

The purpose of this section is to state the essential reasons for this,[63] examining successively the fundamentals of my positive theory of 1952, my 1952 criticism of the American School, and my position today; and to facilitate the discussion of the objections raised to the conclusions of my 1952 paper.[64]

A. FUNDAMENTALS OF MY POSITIVE THEORY OF 1952 – AXIOMATIC FOUNDATIONS

CONSIDERATION OF MONEY VALUES

10. Although the 1952 study was not formally presented as a sequence of axioms, *its axiomatic foundation is evident*, and essentially consists of the four following:

456

Axiom (I): Existence of a System of Probabilities

10.1. For any operator, a random prospect can be represented by a set of positive or negative gains g_i, each with probabilities p_i satisfying the basic principles of probability theory, and in particular the condition[65]

(1) $p_1 + p_2 + \cdots + p_n = 1.$

The probabilities considered are defined from the observed frequencies of events which repeat themselves, and *independently* of the consideration of the value attributed to any random prospect whatsoever.[66]

Axiom (II): Existence of an Ordered Field of Choice

10.2. It is assumed that for each operator the choices involving risk are made from the consideration of an ordinal index

(2) $S = S[C + g_1, C + g_2, \ldots, C + g_n, p_1, p_2, \ldots, p_n],$

which is a function of the gains g_i and the corresponding probabilities p_i such that any random prospect (P_1) will be preferred to (P_2) if its index S_1 is higher than the index S_2 of (P_2). It is assumed that the conditions $S_1 \geqslant S_2$, $S_2 \geqslant S_3$ entail $S_1 \geqslant S_3$.[67]

The symbol C denotes the subject's own valuation of his stock of assets. It is the present value of his stream of future income, as estimated subjectively by himself.

Axiom (III): Axiom of Absolute Preference

10.3. We have

(3) $S[C + g_1', C + g_2', \ldots, C + g_n', p_1, p_2, \ldots, p_n]$
       $\leqslant S[C + g_1'', C + g_2'', \ldots, C + g_n'', p_1, p_2, \ldots, p_n],$

if[68]

(4) $g_1' \leqslant g_1'', g_2' \leqslant g_2'', \ldots, g_n' \leqslant g_n''.$

Axiom (IV): Axiom of Composition

10.4. Axiom (IV) may be formulated as follows:

Any set of random prospects considered at a given time may be reduced to a single random prospect by application of the two fundamental principles of the probability theory of addition and multiplication. Likewise any set of choices between random prospects may be reduced to a single choice by application of the same principles.

This axiom corresponds to the same general principle of composition of random prospects which I applied in various sections of my 1952 memoir, for instance §§4, 48 and 64, and it involves numerous applications. Here are its main applications:

Application (IVa) – Composite random prospect

Let us consider the two random prospects:

(P') $g'_1, g'_2, \ldots, g'_n, p'_1, p'_2, \ldots, p'_n,$

(P'') $g''_1, g''_2, \ldots, g''_n, p''_1, p''_2, \ldots, p''_n.$

It results from Axiom (IV) that the composite random prospect (P) corresponding to the probability α of obtaining the random prospect (P') and the probability $(1 - \alpha)$ of obtaining the random prospect (P''), and which may be represented symbolically by

$$(P) = \alpha(P') + \beta(P''), \qquad \alpha + \beta = 1,$$

is constituted by gains

$$g'_1, g'_2, \ldots, g'_n, g''_1, g''_2, \ldots, g''_n,$$

with probabilities

$$\alpha p'_1, \alpha p'_2, \ldots, \alpha p'_n, \beta p''_1, \beta p''_2, \ldots, \beta p''_n.$$

That is the application I considered in my discussion of the Samuelson's axiom (§64 of my 1952 memoir).

Application (IVb) – Composition of composite random prospects

Let us consider the random prospect constituted by the probability α of obtaining the composite random prospect $\beta(P_1) + (1 - \beta)(P_2)$ and the probability $(1 - \alpha)$ of obtaining the random prospect (P_2). By application of Axiom (IV) we have

$$(5) \qquad \alpha[\beta(P_1) + (1 - \beta)(P_2)] + (1 - \alpha)(P_2) = \alpha\beta(P_1) + (1 - \alpha\beta)(P_2).$$

That is precisely the Axiom 3Cb of von Neumann–Morgenstern.[69]

Application (IVc) – Composition of a series of elementary games

Let us consider a series of N successive rounds of an elementary game corresponding to the random prospect (P):

$$g_1, g_2, \ldots, g_n, p_1, p_2, \ldots, p_n.$$

According to Axiom (IV) the random prospect resulting from N successive drawings may be deduced by considering the multinomial probability distribution corresponding to the expansion of the expression $(p_1 + p_2 + \cdots + p_n)^N$. That is this application of Axiom (IV) I have considered in the discussion of the justification of the neo-Bernoullian formulation by the law of large numbers (§48 of my 1952 memoir).

Application (IVd) – Composition at a given time of a series of successive random choices considered at that time

Let us suppose that at a given time a subject considers different successive random choices between random prospects: (P_0) and (P_0'), (P_1) and (P_1'), ..., (P_n) and (P_n'), etc.

According to Axiom (IV) of composition these successive random choices may be reduced to a single random choice considered at that time.

Taking again the example I gave in my 1952 memoir (§4), let us consider the four independent random prospects

$$(P_0) \begin{cases} \alpha_0 : g_0 \\ 1 - \alpha_0 : 0 \end{cases} \qquad (P_0') \begin{cases} 1 : g_0' \end{cases} \qquad (P_1) \begin{cases} \alpha_1 : g_1 \\ 1 - \alpha_1 : 0 \end{cases} \qquad (P_1') \begin{cases} 1 : g_1'. \end{cases}$$

According to Axiom (IV) the two successive choices (P_0) or (P_0'), (P_1) or (P_1'), may be reduced to a single choice between the four random prospects (P_0P_1), (P_0P_1'), $(P_0'P_1)$, $(P_0'P_1')$ resulting from the application of the probability multiplication rule. Thus the random prospect (P_0P_1) is constituted by gains $g_0 + g_1, g_0, g_1, 0$ with probabilities $\alpha_0\alpha_1$, $\alpha_0(1 - \alpha_1)$, $(1 - \alpha_0)\alpha_1$, $(1 - \alpha_0)(1 - \alpha_1)$, respectively.

In my 1952 memoir I constantly but implicitly admitted the Axiom (IV) of composition, and I made different applications of it, those corresponding to cases (a), (c) and (d) above. However I made no application (IVb) corresponding to the Axiom 3Cb of von Neumann–Morgenstern, but this axiom represents only an immediate application of my Axiom (IV).

Implications of the Axioms

10.5. It is entirely incorrect to argue that this theory is not really a theory because it is very general. If this were so, the theory of choice with certainty would also warrant the same statement. Nobody has made this statement yet.[70]

The theory in no way implies considering cardinal utility. It only implies the existence of a field of ordered choice which satisfies the axiom of absolute preference.[71]

As the index of ordinal preference can be taken as any increasing function of S, we may use as an index the certain value V deemed equivalent to the random prospect (P) [72,73]

$$(6) \qquad g_1, g_2, \ldots, g_n, p_1, p_2, \ldots, p_n,$$

V being defined by a relation of the form

$$(7) \qquad V = F(g_1, g_2, \ldots, g_n, p_1, p_2, \ldots, p_n).$$

In continuous notation, the index S is a functional

$$(8) \qquad S = S[\varphi(g)]$$

of the probability density function $\varphi(g)$.[74] The index S thus depends *on the whole probability distribution of monetary gains.*[75]

Instead of S, it is possible to consider the functional

$$(9) \qquad V = V[\varphi(g)]$$

of the probability density function $\varphi(g)$. Naturally S is an increasing function of V.

CONSIDERATION OF PSYCHOLOGICAL VALUES (CARDINAL UTILITY)

11. The consideration of psychological values (cardinal utility) is useful *only* for a thorough analysis of the psychology of random choice. A fifth axiom is then required.

Axiom (V): Existence of an Index of Psychological Value

11.1. The *intensity* of *ordinal* preferences can be represented by a *cardinal* index[76]

$$(1) \qquad \bar{s} = \bar{s}(C + V),$$

which is defined, up to a linear transformation, from the answers to questions *independent of any random prospect*. Its properties and determination are studied in Appendix C, Sections II and VI, below.

It follows from relation (2) of §10 that this axiom makes it possible to represent random choice by a cardinal index

(2) $\quad \bar{S} = \bar{S}(C + g_1, C + g_2, \ldots, C + g_n, p_1, p_2, \ldots, p_n),$

with

(2*) $\quad \bar{s}(C + V) = \bar{S}(C + g_1, C + g_2, \ldots, C + g_n, p_1, p_2, \ldots, p_n).$

In continuous notation, we have

(3) $\quad \bar{S} = h[\psi(\gamma)],$

with[77]

(4) $\quad \gamma = \bar{s}(C + g),$

where $\psi(\gamma)$ represents the probability density of psychological value γ.

The cardinal index $\bar{S}$ therefore depends *on the whole probability distribution of psychological values.*[78] It is a functional of the probability density function $\psi(\gamma)$.

The index of psychological value is determined directly from the answers to appropriate questions, *without reference of any kind to a system of random choice.*[79]

In the discrete case, relation (8) of §10 may be written

(4*) $\quad \bar{s}(V) = h[\bar{s}(g_1), \bar{s}(g_2), \ldots, \bar{s}(g_n), p_1, p_2, \ldots, p_n].$

NOTATION

11.2. As in my 1952 memoir[80] the symbols S and $\bar{S}$ denote respectively the ordinal and cardinal indexes of preference for the random prospects $g_1, g_2, \ldots, g_n, p_1, p_2, \ldots, p_n$. The lower case symbols s and $\bar{s}$ denote the ordinal and cardinal indexes relating to certainly available gains. Thus we have

(5) $\quad \bar{s}(g) = \bar{S}(g, g, \ldots, g, p_1, p_2, \ldots, p_n).$

It may assist the reader if I list the meaning of the various symbols employed in my 1952 and the present study[81]

(6) S = ordinal preference index (ordinal utility),

(7) $\bar{S}$ = cardinal preference index (cardinal utility),

(8) $S = S(C + g_1, \ldots, C + g_n, p_1, \ldots, p_n)$,

(9) $\bar{S} = \bar{S}(C + g_1, \ldots, C + g_n, p_1, \ldots, p_n)$,

(10) $\gamma(X) = \bar{s}(X)$,

(11) $\gamma = \gamma(C + g) = \bar{s}(C + g)$,

(12) $\bar{s}(C + u) = \bar{S}(C + u, \ldots, C + u, p_1, \ldots, p_n)$,

(13) $\varphi(g)$ = density of the probability distribution
           of the monetary gain g,

(14) $\psi(\gamma)$ = density of the probability distribution
           of the psychological values γ,

(15) C = the own worth estimate of a given person,

with

(15*)
$$\varphi(g)\, dg = \psi(\gamma)\, d\gamma = \psi[\gamma(C + g)]\frac{d\gamma(C + g)}{dg}\, dg.$$

Naturally the notation $\bar{S}$ and $\bar{s}$ does not represent at all the mathematical expectation of S and s.

Simplified Notation

11.3. *To simplify the presentation,* $S(C + g_1, \ldots, C + g_n, p_1, \ldots, p_n)$ *may be replaced by* $S(g_1, \ldots, g_n, p_1, \ldots, p_n)$, *and similarly for the* $\bar{S}$ *and* γ *functions. This is for simplification only. It should be remembered throughout that* S, $\bar{S}$ *and* γ *are as defined by relations (8), (9) and (11). For some developments, this reminder is essential.*

THE CONCEPT OF RATIONALITY

12. It is my view that the necessary and sufficient conditions for rationality are
(a) the pursuit of consistent ends,
(b) the use of means appropriate to these ends.

For random choices, these conditions imply, but only imply, the three following conditions:
- an ordered field of choice,
- obedience to the axiom of absolute preference,
- consideration of objective probabilities.

In fact, experience shows that people who are generally considered as rational (*on criteria* that are free of all reference to any consideration of random choice) respect these conditions in making their random choices.[82,83]

THE AXIOMATIC FOUNDATIONS OF MY 1952 THEORY

13. The five axioms presented above[84] constitute the basis of the formulation I put forward in 1952. They could easily have been supplemented by a few further axioms to develop a complete and systematic axiomatization. It seemed to me at the time that this *was a question of minor interest in comparison with the aims pursued, namely, understanding the behaviour of reputedly rational persons, and how they ought to behave to meet criteria of perfect rationality.* As Sandretto correctly writes: "It is better to have a non-formalised but good explanation than an axiomatised but complex and superficial theory" (1970, p.90).

The point to be stressed is that the probabilities and the psychological values are defined *independently* of the consideration of any random choice (Axioms (I) and (V)).[85]

B. MY 1952 CRITICISM OF THE AMERICAN SCHOOL

THE NEO-BERNOULLIAN FORMULATION, CORE OF
THE AMERICAN SCHOOL'S THEORIES

14. In my 1952 study, which was a synthesis, I presented both a positive theory of random choice and a critical analysis of the theories of the American School. That analysis cannot be summarised here.[86] The issue is too complex. I will limit myself to stressing a few essential points.

During the 1952 Symposium, two very different concepts were discussed, respectively the index of cardinal preference $\gamma = \bar{s}(g)$[87]

which is a function of a certainly available gain g, and a neo-Bernoullian index $B(g)$ which is also a function of a certainly available gain g. Both were defined subject only to a possible linear transformation.

The existence of the index $B(g)$ is demonstrated by the American School from various systems of axioms which differ from one to the other (von Neumann–Morgenstern, Marschak, Savage, Samuelson, etc.). This index is such that a sure sum of money V is considered as equivalent to a random prospect yielding gains g_i with probabilities p_i if and only if

(I) $$B(C + V) = \sum_i p_i B(C + g_i),$$

which, to simplify, may be written (see §11.3 above)

(I*) $$B(V) = \sum_i p_i B(g_i).$$

This nucleus is common to all the theories of the American School.

The adherents of this school deduce from it that *rational behaviour* involves classifying the random prospects $(g_1, g_2, \ldots, g_n, p_1, p_2, \ldots, p_n)$ in relation to their value V as defined by relation (I).

The neo-Bernoullian authors consider only relation (I*). They never write it as relation (I), which is really the only significant form. Thus they never take into account the influence of capital C, a *very important* element for all empirical research. This is all the more curious as Daniel Bernoulli (1738) explicitly brought the subject's capital into his formulation.[87*]

THE SUCCESSIVE POSITIONS OF THE AMERICAN SCHOOL

15. Two very different theses have been successively supported by the American School.[88]

The first thesis identifies the two concepts $\bar{s}$ and B, i.e. it is contended that

(II) $$B(g) \equiv \bar{s}(g).$$

This is the position taken by von Neumann–Morgenstern in the *Theory of Games* (1944).

The second thesis limits consideration to the index $B(g)$, and claims either that the cardinal index of preference $\bar{s}(g)$ does not exist (first variant),[89] or that the index $B(g)$ can in no case be identified as the cardinal index of preference, whose existence is, however, admitted (second variant).[90]

The criticisms I presented at the 1952 symposium led the supporters of the first position to abandon it completely. I pointed out that it would imply that an economic agent would be considered as acting irrationally in taking account of the probability distribution of cardinal indexes of preference about their mean, and that such a judgment would evidently be inadmissible. This argument could not be refuted, and my adversaries took refuge in relation (I), arguing that the index $B(g)$ could not be identified with cardinal utility $\bar{s}(g)$.[91]

MY OWN POSITION

16. My own position was, and remains, as follows:[92]

(a) A cardinal index of preference $\bar{s}(g)$, representing the psychological value of a gain g, does exist;

(b) We have

(III) $\bar{s}(V) = h[\bar{s}(g_1), \bar{s}(g_2), \ldots, \bar{s}(g_n), p_1, p_2, \ldots, p_n]$,

in which the psychological value $\bar{s}(V)$ of a random prospect is a well-determined function h of the psychological values $\bar{s}(g_i)$ of the gains g_i, and of their probabilities p_i.

In general, this signifies that V, *depends both on the mathematical expectation*

(IV) $\mathscr{E} = \sum p_i \bar{s}(g_i)$

of the cardinal indices $\bar{s}(g_i)$, *and on their probability distribution about their mean.*

(c) An operator whose behaviour responds to the general formulation (III) above cannot be considered as irrational, merely because his preference index *does not reduce* to a function of the mathematical expectation (IV) above.

(d) A rational operator may behave as indicated by the neo-Bernoullian principle (I), but in this case his index $B(g)$ is necessarily identical with his cardinal utility index $\bar{s}(g)$, in other words, in this case relation (I) implies relation (II).[93]

(e) It is just as impossible to determine the cardinal index of preference $\bar{s} = \bar{s}(g)$ from observed random choices as it is to determine it from observed choices of certainly available goods in relation to their prices. Only a direct determination of cardinal utility is possible.[94]

MY REFUTATION OF THE NEO-BERNOULLIAN FORMULATION

17. *Once my opponents denied that a cardinal index $\bar{s}(g)$ could exist, or that if it did, that it could be identified in any way with the Bernoullian indicator $B(g)$, I was forced to place myself on their own ground. I did so by presenting a number of counterexamples which required no assumptions whatsoever as to the existence of a cardinal index of preference.* These fall into two groups:

(a) A first group[95] based on an *abstract definition of rationality*.[96]

(b) A second group based on the *observed behaviour of operators who may be considered as rational* (persons of high scientific achievement, and very well versed in probability theory) (*experimental definition of rationality*).[97]

As these examples were decisive,[98] my adversaries acknowledged that a reputedly 'rational' man might not necessarily act in accordance with their axioms, and instead claimed that in this case, the reputedly rational man was unaware of his irrationality, whether because of false information, insufficient reflection, or errors of judgment.

Clearly, scientific discussion is out of the question if rationality is defined by ascertaining whether behaviour is or is not in conformity with the postulates of the American School.

THE NEO-BERNOULLIAN FORMULATION AND THE
PRINCIPLE OF INDEPENDENCE

18. In fact, it is easy to discern the origin of the errors committed by the American School. The neo-Bernoullian principle (relation (I) above) presupposes that the various terms on the right hand side of relation (I) are *independent*.[99] In reality, there is indisputably *a complementarity effect*, and it cannot be neglected. As an example, consider a lottery consisting of one million tickets at one dollar each, with a single prize of one million dollars. For many highly rational operators the psychological value of a ticket will be entirely different according to whether or not they already own all the other tickets, except one. Ownership of all the tickets but one may raise the psychological value of the last ticket, which secures the certainty of collecting the prize, well above the psychological value of this ticket where the same operator possesses none earlier.[100]

The complementarity effect is the more marked the closer one is to certainty, and all my examples were designed to bring this effect to light.[101]

THE DEFINITION OF RATIONALITY

19. It is clear, and very important to stress, that rationality can never be defined in terms of the correspondence of behaviour to one of the systems of axioms or postulates used by the American School to reach the neo-Bernoullian formulation. If it were, scientific discussion would no longer be possible.

The neo-Bernoullian formulation is in fact a rigorous consequence of any one of these systems. It is obviously futile to debate the proposition that rational people behave according to the neo-Bernoullian formula when rationality is defined as meaning conformity with one of the systems of axioms from which the formula is deduced. This is sheer tautology, and devoid of scientific interest.

It can only make sense to discuss the proposition "rational behaviour is neo-Bernoullian behaviour" *if rationality is defined in a way that makes no direct or indirect reference to the neo-Bernoullian criterion.* This makes it necessary to define what one means by *'rationality'*. Two definitions are conceivable, depending on whether the approach taken is abstract, based on reasoning, or pragmatic, based on experience. It is possible to define rationality, *either abstractly* by referring to the criterion of non-self-contradiction generally used in the social sciences (implying the consistency of ends and the use of appropriate means to achieve them), *or experimentally*, by observing the acts of people *of whom there exist independent grounds, i.e. without recourse to any consideration of random choices, for believing that they behave rationally.*[102] *At all events, the second definition flows from the first because only those whose behaviour is in line with the first are generally considered as rational.*

The proponents of the neo-Bernoullian formulation were never able to give a clear reply to three questions I put to them, to wit: "(1) Do you, directly or not, define rationality as conformity with your axioms? (2) If not, do you admit a theoretical definition of rationality, and which? (3) Apart from such a definition, other than the one corresponding to the obedience to your own axioms, would you be prepared to agree that rationality may be defined in relation to the behaviour of people who are generally considered as rational *in terms of criteria which do not rely on consideration of random choices?*".[103]

In my 1952 study, I gave many examples[104] showing that people *who are commonly accepted as rational (according to criteria totally independent of their behaviour in relation to their random choices)* act in general in a way that is incompatible with the neo-Bernoullian formulation.

Those surveyed in the context of the 1952 experiment were highly conversant with the theory of probabilities, having generally extensive mathematical knowledge and being persons *likely to be commonly considered as 'rational' from the standpoint of all the available criteria, apart from any criteria relating to random choice.*

The findings of the analysis of replies to the 1952 Questionnaire clearly demonstrate the pseudo-evident character of the axioms of the American School. *That so many people so readily accept the formulation is due to the fact that they do not perceive all its implications, some of which, far from being rational, may be very irrational in certain psychological situations.* It is also, and mainly, the result of the conditioning produced by the incessant repetition of its affirmations by the neo-Bernoullian 'establishment'.

Faced with these examples, the supporters of the neo-Bernoullian formulation do not say anything, but: "Such behaviour is against our axioms, so it is irrational". This position is scientifically untenable.

C. MY POSITION TODAY

FUNDAMENTALLY IDENTICAL POSITION, BUT DIFFERENTLY WEIGHTED ARGUMENTS

20. Basically, my position today is the same as in 1952, but I attach somewhat different weight to the various arguments. Some of them now seem to me utterly central. These are the following: consideration of objective probabilities and psychological values determined independently of any random choice; non-existence of a neo-Bernoullian index; conditions of asymptotic validity of the neo-Bernoullian formulation; arbitrage between mathematical expectation and probability of ruin; explanation of the St. Petersburg Paradox.[104*]

CONSIDERATION OF OBJECTIVE PROBABILITIES DETERMINED INDEPENDENTLY OF ANY RANDOM CHOICE

21. *Objective probabilities alone have operational value.* Objective probabilities correspond to repeatable events, in similar conditions. *They are physical quantities which represent a physical reality.*

The founders of the calculus of probabilities: Fermat, Pascal, the Bernoullis (James, Nicholas and Daniel), Laplace, Poisson, Joseph Bertrand, to name only these, defined the probability of an event as the ratio of the number of favourable cases to the total number of possible cases. One condition is stressed: *all cases are 'equally possible'.* Without this restriction the definition would be meaningless. Before counting the chances, their 'equal possibility' must be established.

It may be objected that this definition is built on a vicious circle. How is one to tell if all the cases are 'equally possible'? *The circularity, however, is only apparent.*

First the equal possibility of possible cases may result from conditions of symmetry. In fact, devices can be fabricated to secure almost perfect conditions of symmetry. Such would be the case of drawings carried out by blind persons from a *reference urn* containing identically machined balls, differing only in colour. In this case, the *a priori* probability for each ball to be drawn may be considered as exactly equal to $1/q$ if there are q balls.

On the contrary, if conditions of symmetry cannot be *a priori* ascertained, the objective probability of an event which may be repeated in comparable conditions, *must be understood as a magnitude whose experimental value is the observed frequency of that event.*[105] In the absence of any other information, the observed frequency can be considered as an estimate of the probability, which is the better the longer the series observed. Here the probability cannot be estimated *a priori*. It can only be estimated *a posteriori* from the consideration of a probabilistic model.

As for any other science, the probability theory is based on the consideration of models. *But the confrontation of these models with physical reality can never lead to certainty, contrarily to the other sciences.* For the probability theory can never allow the conclusion that such an event is impossible. It can only enable its probability to be calculated in the framework of a model founded on a system of assumptions.

In the case of dice for example, the most natural assumption *a priori* is that each die is symmetrical, and is cast in such a manner that the 'drawing' takes place in conditions which also guarantee symmetry. From these assumptions we deduce consequences. If the consequences seem to agree with observed data, i.e. in the case considered, if the calculated probability of a difference between frequency and probability, considered in absolute value, greater than the observed difference, is not too small, the model may be deemed valid. If they are not, the model must be rejected. *One has therefore, inevitably, to make a subjective appraisal of the objective validity of the model.* The same is true of any science; indeed, we can even affirm that it is the basis of the scientific approach.[106]

In fact, experience shows that for a given die the observed frequency f_N of a one-spot for example, corresponding to N successive drawings, generally differs significantly from 1/6, and that, admitting the probability $p = 1/6$, the probability of the observed difference $|f_N - p|$ is generally small if N is large. The reason for such a difference is that a die is rarely symmetrical. Thus we are led to attribute to the probability of drawing the one-spot a value p different from 1/6, and in the absence of any other information, we take the observed frequency as an estimate of this probability because it is precisely this hypothesis which gives the realisation of the frequency f_N the greatest probability. In fact taking the frequency f_N as an estimate of the probability p, the model cannot be claimed to be a strict portrayal of reality, but it can depict reality with a degree of approximation the probability of which can be estimated.

There is certainly a very great difference between dice experiments and drawings from a reference urn. If I cast a one-spot ten times in succession using a die about which I have no information at all, I will assert without hesitation that it is loaded. But if ten blind people each draw the same ball in ten successive extractions from an urn containing six identical balls whose manufacture I have been able to monitor (the ball being replaced each time), I would not hesitate to continue to affirm that the probability of drawing that ball is 1/6, and that if the same ball came out ten times running, it is because that particular sequence of drawings was no more, and no less, probable than any other sequence. In fact when indisputable conditions of symmetry do obtain, the *a priori* estimate of the probability deduced from the consideration of these symmetry conditions, *may be viewed as con-*

siderably better than the estimate which could be deduced from the observed frequency in a long series of drawings, whatever the length of the series observed.

Some will say that probability has a subjective character in this case. It has effectively this character in the sense that it represents *a subjective estimate of an objective probability*, which may be considered as deduced from a long earlier experience for all classes of events characterized by symmetry conditions. That is only a direct and immediate application of the fundamental theorem of Bayes: if the probability *a priori* is perfectly determined, the probability *a posteriori* remains equal to it, whatever the result of the drawings carried out.

If on the contrary, as in the case of the dice example considered, I have no information whatsoever on the dice used, the application of the same Bayes theorem will lead me to the conclusion that the probability of casting a one-spot is certainly not equal to 1/6.

It follows that the best definition of an objective probability is the one corresponding to drawings from a reference urn, i.e. an urn meeting conditions of symmetry such that all possible cases may be considered as equally possible. The corresponding probabilities may be called reference probabilities. They permit to gauge the probabilities and they give the measuring scale for probabilities against which all probabilities can be measured. The corresponding probability model may be called the reference urn model. Consideration of a reference urn enables the concept of probability to be grasped in its pure state.

It is effectively possible to consider subjective probabilities corresponding to events which will occur one-time only, for example the probability that it will rain tomorrow, *but they can only be measured in relation to reference probabilities by formulating questions* such as "Do you consider the probability that it will rain tomorrow greater or smaller than the probability of drawing a white ball from a reference urn containing four white balls and one red ball?".[107]

Thus, *subjective* probabilities may be considered. But they can only be defined and measured by reference to objective probabilities. The concept of subjective probability could never have been developed, had the concept of objective probability, suggested by simple observation of coin-tossing and dice games, not preceded it. In fact, *the concept of objective probability is the only operational concept. It is a datum of observation like length, temperature or pressure.* The frequency with which a phenomenon recurs provides a measure of its probability.

To use the same word 'probability' to designate two concepts which differ so fundamentally as objective probability and subjective probability can only lead to dangerous confusion. The word *probability* should be reserved for the consideration of objective probability. Some other wording such as *likelihood coefficient* should be used to refer to what is habitually denoted as subjective probability.[108]

The concept of subjective probability can be used to assess the validity of a probability model. Let us assume for example that for a die, previous information yields an *a priori* probability p^* of throwing a one-spot, p being the real probability. Let us assume that the frequency observed in a series of N throws is f_N and let

$$(1) \qquad P = \text{Probability } \{|f_N - p^*| \leqslant |\varphi_N - p^*|\}$$

be the calculated probability that in a series of N throws, the difference $|\varphi_N - p^*|$ between a given value φ_N of frequency and the probability p^* will be greater than or equal to $|f_N - p^*|$. *We may agree* to consider that the subjective probability

$$(2) \qquad P_s = \text{Subjective probability } \{|p - f_N| \geqslant |p^* - f_N|\}$$

will be equal to the calculated probability P.

If, for instance, one observes that there is only one chance in a thousand for a difference $|\varphi_N - p^*|$ to be greater than or equal to the observed difference $|f_N - p^*|$, it may be agreed to consider that there is only one chance in a thousand for the difference $|p - f_N|$ between the real probability p and the observed frequency f_N to be greater than or equal to the difference $|p^* - f_N|$. *But in any event, this will only be a convention.*

In any event, when we consider events which repeat themselves, *rational behaviour in the presence of choice between random prospects necessarily implies consideration of objective probabilities.* How could we consider as rational a person who would ascribe a probability of 9/10 to heads in a coin-tossing game, if the coin has just come from the Mint?[109]

The *fundamental nature* of the concept of objective probability cannot be defined by a series of axioms any more than time can usefully be defined by a series of axioms. *The concept of objective probability is based on the concept of equal possibility which cannot be reduced to any other.*

However, if probability theory is to be developed, this requires a set of axioms. In this context I now consider it necessary to replace Axiom (I) above (Existence of a system of probabilities)[110] by the two following axioms:

Axiom (IA): Definition of Objective Probabilities

The probability of an event which can repeat itself in similar conditions is a physical magnitude, characterising this event.

When conditions of symmetry exist, the probability of an event is equal to the ratio of the number of favorable cases to the number of equally possible cases.

Drawing from urns under effective conditions of symmetry enables objective reference probabilities to be determined.

In the absence of any other information an approximate measure of the probability of an event is given by the observed frequency of occurrence of this event, and the longer the series of observations, the better the estimation may be considered.[111]

In addition, subjective probabilities could be determined by the following Axiom (IB):

Axiom (IB): Definition of Subjective Probabilities

For a given subject, events can be classified according to their greater or lesser subjective probability by comparison with objective reference probabilities.

The subjective probability $\bar{p}$ of an event whose objective probability p is a reference probability, is equal to this objective probability.

The three basic principles of the theory of objective probabilities (total, compound and inverse probability) apply to subjective probabilities.[112]

THE NON-EXISTENCE OF A NEO-BERNOULLIAN INDEX

22. From any of the various individual systems of axioms of the American School it is possible to prove that there exists an index $B(g)$ such that the monetary value V of the random prospect $(g_1, g_2, \ldots, g_n, p_1, p_2, \ldots, p_n)$ is given by the relation[113]

(1) $B(V) = \sum p_i B(g_i),$

which represents the neo-Bernoullian formulation.

It is a theorem of existence. If the axioms are verified, there necessarily exists one and only one $B(g)$ function which satisfies relation (1), up to a linear transformation.

For a given subject, the question whether his choices correspond effectively to the neo-Bernoullian axioms reduces to ascertaining whether a function $B(g)$ *can be determined from his observed choices* such that relation (1) is always satisfied.

This determination is necessary, for if it is impossible, the theories of the American School are void of operational substance: there is no point invoking *rationality* as a reason for applying the formula (1) above, if the function $B(g)$ remains unknown.[114]

In fact, experience shows that it is generally possible to establish a well-determined $B(g)$ function, *at least approximately, for a given series of questions depending on a single parameter,* which portrays a given subject's replies to these questions in the framework of the neo-Bernoullian formulation (1). However, this function depends on the series of questions considered, and varies from one series of questions to the next.

This was the fundamental conclusion yielded by the analysis of the replies to the 1952 Questionnaire.[115] There was no respondent[116] whose $B(g)$ indicators deduced from their answers to two different series of questions were identical. The first set of questions considered random choices with the probability 1/2 and the second set of questions considered random choices with probabilities in the neighbourhood of unity.

This test of conformity with the neo-Bernoullian formulation is much more efficient than tests of conformity such as the test corresponding to the 'Allais Paradox'.[117] For the Allais Paradox, the percentage of neo-Bernoullian behaviour observed in the data of the 1952 survey ranged from 36% to 52% according to the group considered, with an average value of 47% for 101 respondents. The percentage of cases of neo-Bernoullian behaviour, defined as identity of the $B(g)$ indexes for two different series of questions, was *zero.*[118]

EXISTENCE OF AN INDEX OF PSYCHOLOGICAL VALUE
(CARDINAL UTILITY) DETERMINED INDEPENDENTLY OF ANY
RANDOM CHOICE

23. Analysis of the 1952 Questionnaires establishes *beyond doubt* that there exists for any subject a cardinal index of preference[119]

(1) $\gamma = \bar{s}(g)$.

It is easy to examine the implications of the existence of the cardinal index $\gamma(g)$ from the standpoint of the neo-Bernoullian formulation.

Implications of the Existence of an Index of Psychological Values (Cardinal Utility) for the Neo-Bernoullian Formulation

23.1. Let us consider a subject who *simultaneously* takes account of the mathematical expectation of cardinal utility and its probability distribution about its average. Nobody could argue that he is necessarily acting irrationally.

Let V be the monetary value of the random prospect considered and ω its psychological value. Then (§11 above)

(2) $\omega = \bar{s}(V) = \gamma(V)$.

If it is then assumed that the subject takes into account the whole distribution of psychological values, we have (§11.1, relation (3), above)

(3) $\omega = h[\psi(\gamma)], \qquad \gamma = \bar{s}(g)$,

where $\psi(\gamma)$ represents the probability density of the distribution of psychological values.

Nevertheless were this subject to conform to the neo-Bernoullian formulation, there would exist an index $B(g)$ such that (§22, relation (1), above)

(4) $B(V) = \int_{-\infty}^{+\infty} B(g)\varphi(g)\,dg,$

where $\varphi(g)$ represents the probability density of the distribution of monetary gains g.

For a given value of the parameter X

(5) $\gamma = \gamma(X)$, $B = B(X)$.

Whence it follows that B is a well-determined function

(6) $B = \beta(\gamma)$

of psychological value γ.

Thus from (2), (4) and (6) we should have

(7) $\beta(\omega) = \int_{-\infty}^{+\infty} \beta(\gamma)\psi(\gamma)\,d\gamma,$

where ω is defined by relation (3). It may be seen that in general no function $\beta(\gamma)$ can exist such that relations (3) and (7) are satisfied simultaneously.

The case of discrete distributions

23.1.1. To simplify the discussion, consider the discrete random prospect

(8) $g_1, g_2, \ldots, g_n, p_1, p_2, \ldots, p_n.$

Relations (3) and (4) may be written

(9) $\omega = \gamma(V) = h(\gamma_1, \gamma_2, \ldots, \gamma_n, p_1, p_2, \ldots, p_n),$

(10) $B(V) = \sum p_i B(g_i).$

Using (6), relation (7) may then be written

(11) $\beta(\omega) = \sum p_i \beta(\gamma_i),$

that whence, from (9)

(12) $\beta[h(\gamma_1, \gamma_2, \ldots, \gamma_n, p_1, p_2, \ldots, p_n)] = \sum_i p_i \beta(\gamma_i).$

Let $\beta^{-1}(\beta)$ be the inverse function of

(13) $\beta = \beta(\gamma),$

such that

(14) $\beta^{-1}[\beta(\gamma)] \equiv \gamma.$

Then relation (12) may be written

(15) $h(\gamma_1, \gamma_2, \ldots, \gamma_n, p_1, p_2, \ldots, p_n) = \beta^{-1}\left[\sum p_i \beta(\gamma_i)\right].$

It may thus be seen that for a given field of choice (8) it will generally prove impossible to find a function $\beta = \beta(\gamma)$ such that relation (15) is verified for all γ_i and p_i subject only to the condition

(16) $\sum p_i = 1.$

From this it may be deduced that, in general, there cannot exist a neo-Bernoullian index which simultaneously takes into account both the curvature of cardinal utility and the statistical distribution of cardinal utility about its mean *whatever the random prospect considered.*

On the other hand, if one considers random prospects which depend on a single parameter this impossibility could well not appear. Thus, in the case in which the random outcome considered involves only a single gain of whose probability is p then, from (10) and putting $B(0) = 0$ (which is always possible without loss of generality) we would have

(17) $B(V) = pB(g).$

It can be seen that for a given value of p and for different values of g it will always be possible to determine an index $B(V)$ whatever the monetary value V of the random prospect (g, p) corresponding to relation (9). This means that in this case it is always possible to find an index $\beta(\gamma)$ satisfying relation (15). But there is no reason to find the same index $B(V)$ if one takes a given value of g and different values of p.

In this case it will be impossible, in general, to find a function satisfying relation (15) for the two sets of questions. This fact led me to draw up Questions (IX) ($p = 1/2$) and (VII) ($g = 200$ million 1952 francs) of the 1952 Questionnaire (see Sections III and IV of Appendix C below).

Expansions as Taylor series

23.1.2. Consider changes δg_i, δp_i in the gains g_i and probabilities p_i and the corresponding changes δV, $\delta \omega$ and $\delta \beta = \delta B$, and assume that functions $\beta(\gamma)$ and $h(\gamma_1, \gamma_2, \ldots, \gamma_n, p_i, p_2, \ldots, p_n)$ may be expanded as a Taylor series. Taking only first-order terms and using (9), one may write for changes δg_i in the gains g_i which are sufficiently small relative to the subject's capital

(18)
$$\delta\omega \sim \sum_i c_i\delta\gamma_i + \sum_i d_i\delta p_i,$$

$$\delta\beta = \frac{d\beta(\omega)}{d\omega} \delta\omega,$$

where

(19) $$c_i = \frac{\partial h}{\partial \gamma_i}, \qquad d_i = \frac{\partial h}{\partial p_i}.$$

Further, from (11) we have to within second-order accuracy

(20) $$\delta\beta \sim \sum_i p_i \frac{d\beta(\gamma_i)}{d\gamma_i} \delta\gamma_i + \sum_i \beta(\gamma_i)\delta p_i,$$

Since

(21) $$\sum_i \delta p_i = 0,$$

we may deduce from (18), (20) and (21)

(22)
$$\delta\beta = \frac{d\beta}{d\omega} \delta\omega \sim \frac{d\beta}{d\omega} \left[\sum_i c_i\delta\gamma_i + \sum_{i\neq j} (d_i - d_j)\delta p_i \right]$$

$$\sim \sum_i p_i \frac{d\beta}{d\gamma_i} \delta\gamma_i + \sum_{i\neq j} [\beta(\gamma_i) - \beta(\gamma_i)]\delta p_i$$

to the nearest second-order term, and p_j representing any one probability among the p_i. From (22), we deduce

(23) $$\frac{d\beta}{d\omega} \frac{\partial h}{\partial \gamma_i}(\gamma_1, \gamma_2, \ldots, \gamma_n, p_1, p_2, \ldots, p_n) = \frac{d\beta}{d\gamma_i} p_i,$$

(24) $$\frac{d\beta}{d\omega} \left[\frac{\partial h}{\partial p_i}(\gamma_1, \gamma_2, \ldots, \gamma_n, p_1, p_2, \ldots, p_n) \right.$$

$$\left. - \frac{\partial h}{\partial p_j}(\gamma_1, \gamma_2, \ldots, \gamma_n, p_1, p_2, \ldots, p_n) \right] = \beta(\gamma_i) - \beta(\gamma_j),$$

for all $\gamma_1, \gamma_2, \ldots, \gamma_n$ and $p_1, p_2, \ldots, p_n$.

If the random prospect (8) is interpreted as corresponding to an n tickets lottery, condition (23) implies that the marginal desirability of ticket i corresponding to the probability p_i of winning g_i is independent of the marginal desirabilities of the other tickets $j(g_j, p_j)$. As the function

γ is approximately linear over a broad range of variation in the neighbourhood of any value X (See Section II of Appendix C below), it may be affirmed that for almost all subjects, condition (23) is certainly not verified.

Condition (24) *is even stranger*, for it implies that the difference in any two partial derivatives of ω with respect to probabilities only depends, up to a factor, on the difference $\beta(\gamma_i) - \beta(\gamma_j)$, whereas the function β would be independent of the probabilities p_i.

In point of fact condition (24) would appear psychologically acceptable only if

(25) $\beta(\gamma) \equiv \gamma$,

up to a linear transformation, *which implies identity of the neo-Bernoullian index and the index of cardinal utility. In fact this corresponds to the von Neumann–Morgenstern standpoint (see Appendix A, §A10).*

Case in which the neo-Bernoullian index B should be identified with the index of cardinal utility γ

23.1.3. In this case relation (11) would be written

(26) $\omega = \sum_i p_i \gamma_i$,

which is in fact quite simply relation (10).

It may thus be seen that *analysis of the implications of the neo-Bernoullian formulation leads to the conclusion that the formulation holds for a given subject only if the neo-Bernoullian index is identified with the index of cardinal utility. But if this is so, it can be seen that the subject in question does not allow for the distribution of the cardinal utility about the mean, whereas clearly rationality would not necessarily imply this requirement.*

In particular, for a lottery comprising N tickets with a single prize G, and an operator holding n tickets, we would have

(27) $\omega_n = \gamma(V) = \dfrac{n}{N} \gamma(G)$.

It follows that the increment in utility

(28) $\omega_n - \omega_{n-1} = \dfrac{1}{N} \gamma(G)$

would be totally independent of the number of tickets already held.

Hence for an operator already holding $N - 1$ tickets, the psychological value of the last ticket *which would give him the certainty* of securing the gain G would be the same as that corresponding to the average psychological value of the first $N - 1$ tickets. In fact for virtually all operators, *and even for small values of the ratio of the gain G to the subject's capital C* and values of N of a few units, this is not the case: the preference for security in the neighbourhood of certainty imparts to the last ticket a psychological value (greater than) that of the average psychological value of the $N - 1$ first tickets, as was brought out in the 1952 survey (See Appendix C, Note 28, below).

Some neo-Bernoullians explain the preference for security in the neighbourhood of certainty in terms of a distortion of objective probabilities and their replacement by subjective probabilities. However, in the case of a reference urn for which conditions of symmetry are obtained, the subjective probability for a subject who is rational in the sense of this memoir (§12 above) is equal to the ratio of the number of favourable cases to the number of equally possible cases, and subjective probability may be identified with objective probability (see §21 above and Appendix D below). Quite remarkably, this is precisely Savage's own position (see Savage, 1954, §§4.5 and 4.6 and especially pp.66–67).

Two New Axioms

23.2. The analysis of the answers to the 1952 Questionnaire together with some further reflection led me in 1974 to formulate two new axioms (VI) and (VII).

Axiom (VI): Axiom of invariance and homogeneity of the index of psychological value

23.2.1. The psychology of any subject may be represented by a single index of psychological value (cardinal utility)

$$(29) \qquad \bar{s}(C + g) = \gamma[u = \log(1 + g/C)].$$

This axiom means that *for every subject the index of psychological value is an invariant function of the ratio g/C, C being the subject's capital as estimated by him*. In other words, the cardinal preference function γ is assumed to be the same for each subject.[120]

This property has been used for fitting the data of the 1952 experiment (see Appendix C below) and it gave excellent results.

Two cases were analysed successively: the loglinear approximation (Appendix C II below) and the non-loglinear formulation (Appendix C VI below). In both cases, the results are what one would expect if the axioms of invariance and homogeneity were both verified, at least approximately given the errors inevitably spawned by psychological introspection (see Appendix C, Note 21, below).

Axiom (VII): Axiom of cardinal isovariation

23.2.2. Let

$$(30) \qquad \omega = h[\gamma_1, \gamma_2, \ldots, \gamma_n, p_1, p_2, \ldots, p_n]$$

be the *psychological value* of the random prospect $\gamma_1, \gamma_2, \ldots, \gamma_n$, $p_1, p_2, \ldots, p_n$, in function of the *psychological values* γ_i of the gains g_i (§11 above).

Let us suppose that all the g_i increase in such a manner that all the γ_i increase by the same amount $\Delta\gamma_i = e$ which implies that, for any i, $\gamma_i + \Delta\gamma_i \leqslant \gamma_M$, where γ_M represents the maximum value of γ corresponding to satiety. In such a case, whatever the realised event, the psychological value of the capital of the considered subject increases by e. Thus, it is natural to suppose that the psychological value of the random prospect considered increases by $\Delta\omega = e$. This leads to an axiom which may be called 'axiom of cardinal isovariation', and which may be enunciated as follows.

"The axiom of cardinal isovariation is that

$$(31) \qquad \omega + e = h[\gamma_1 + e, \gamma_2 + e, \ldots, \gamma_n + e, p_1, p_2, \ldots, p_n]$$

for any value of e, subject only to the condition that

$$(32) \qquad \gamma_i + e \leqslant \gamma_M,$$

where γ_M represents the maximum value of γ corresponding to satiety".[121]

It is easy to show that the necessary and sufficient condition for eqn. (31) to hold is that only the differences $\omega - \gamma_1$ and $\gamma_j - \gamma_i$ enter into relation (30). This condition is satisfied if, for instance,

$$(33) \qquad \omega - \gamma_1 = \phi[\gamma_2 - \gamma_1, \ldots, \gamma_n - \gamma_1, p_1, \ldots, p_n]$$

in which ϕ is for a given subject a well-determined function (see Appendix B2 below).

In the continuous case, the axiom of isovariation is equivalent to the condition

$$(34) \qquad \omega = \bar{\gamma} + F[\psi(\gamma - \bar{\gamma})],$$

where F is a functional of the probability density function ψ of the differences $\gamma - \bar{\gamma}$, and $\bar{\gamma} = \mathcal{M}_1$ represents the average value of γ (see Appendix B2 below).

Writing

$$(35) \qquad \mu_n = \frac{1}{n!} \frac{\mathcal{M}_n}{\bar{\gamma}^n},$$

$$(36) \qquad \mathcal{M}_n = \int_{-\infty}^{+\infty} (\gamma - \bar{\gamma})^n \psi(\gamma - \bar{\gamma}) \, d(\gamma - \bar{\gamma}),$$

we may write under very general conditions[122]

$$(37) \qquad \omega = \bar{\gamma} + f[\mu_2, \ldots, \mu_n, \ldots].$$

When all the psychological values γ are equal to their average $\bar{\gamma}$, we have $\mu_2 = \cdots = \mu_n = \cdots = 0$ and $\omega = \bar{\gamma}$. Therefore

$$(38) \qquad f[0, 0, \ldots, 0, \ldots] = 0.$$

The μ_n represent the coefficients of the expansion of the generating function[122]

$$(39) \qquad \varphi(t/\bar{\gamma}) = \sum_0^\infty \mu_n t^n.$$

Thus *when the coefficients μ_n are sufficiently small* we have

$$(40) \qquad \omega \sim \bar{\gamma},$$

which is precisely the neo-Bernoullian formulation.

When this is not the case, *the function $f(\mu_2, \ldots, \mu_n, \ldots)$ represents the greater or lesser propensity for risk-taking relative to the Bernoulli formulation. The higher the value of f the greater the propensity for risk, in other words the function f represents the specific utility of risk.*

The case of an enterprise with a great number of shareholders

23.2.3. For lack of space I cannot develop here all the implications of the axiom of cardinal isovariation. However I think it is necessary to stress that in general *for an enterprise the psychological value reduces to the monetary value*, so that in this case we have

(41) $\gamma = g,$

and here therefore the axiom of cardinal isovariation is written in the discontinuous case by the condition

(42) $V + e = V[g_1 + e, g_2 + e, \ldots, g_n + e, p_1, p_2, \ldots, p_n]$

for any value of e; V representing the monetary value of the random prospect considered (P).

The axiom of cardinal isovariation and the neo-Bernoullian formulation

23.2.4. If the axiom of isovariation is assumed to hold and the neo-Bernoullian formulation taken to be satisfied, it necessarily follows that the neo-Bernoullian index identifies with the index of cardinal utility.

It can in fact be shown that the two equalities (11) and (31)

(43) $\beta(\omega) = \sum p_i \beta(\gamma_i),$

(44) $\omega + e = h(\gamma_1 + e, \gamma_2 + e, \ldots, \gamma_n + e, p_1, p_2, \ldots, p_n),$

necessarily entail

(45) $\beta(\gamma) = \gamma$

up to a linear transformation (Appendix B1 below).

THE ASYMPTOTIC VALIDITY OF THE NEO-BERNOULLIAN FORMULATION WHEN GAINS AND LOSSES ARE RELATIVELY SMALL COMPARED TO THE SUBJECT'S ASSETS

24. There is no difficulty determining the conditions under which the neo-Bernoullian formulation effectively holds. These conditions are independent of the Axioms (VI) and (VII) (§23 above). I will consider in turn the case of monetary and psychological values.

(1) *Monetary Values*

24.1. The operator's field of choice may be defined by the function

(1) $V = V[\varphi(g)],$

in which V is the certainly available sum he judges equivalent to the probability distribution of the gains g corresponding to the probability density $\varphi(g)$.

The conditions for the equivalence of the monetary value V of a random outcome and the mathematical expectation of the monetary gains associated with that outcome

24.1.1. Write

(2) $M_1 = \bar{g} = \displaystyle\int_{-\infty}^{+\infty} g\varphi(g)\,dg,$

(3) $M_n = \displaystyle\int_{-\infty}^{+\infty} (g - \bar{g})^n \varphi(g)\,dg, \quad (n \geq 2),$

(4) $\lambda_n = \dfrac{1}{n!}\dfrac{M_n}{\bar{g}^n},$

where M_1 designates the mathematical expectation of gains g_i and M_n the nth-order moment around the mean $\bar{g}$ of the random prospect considered. Then, since under very general conditions (which will be supposed to be fulfilled) any probability distribution can be described in terms of its various moments,[122] it is always possible to write

(5) $V = H[M_1, \lambda_2, \ldots, \lambda_n, \ldots],$

in which H is a well determined function of the M_n. We have necessarily

(6) $V = M_1$ for $g = \bar{g} = M_1$ whatever g,

which implies

(7) $H[M_1, 0, 0, \ldots, 0, \ldots] = M_1,$

and therefore

(8) $V \sim M_1$ for $\lambda_n \ll 1$ whatever n.

The case of the repetition of N successive unit games of a game J' with global settlement at the end of the games

24.1.2. Now consider an elementary game J' in which the density of the probability distribution of the gains g' is $\varphi'(g')$ and let m and σ^2

denote the corresponding mathematical expectation and variance. Consider a game J consisting of N successive rounds of the game J', *with settlement of gains and losses to be made in a single net amount after the Nth round (thus precluding the possibility of ruin during the N rounds)*. Let V_N be the certainly available sum judged equivalent to the game J.

It is known that the probability distribution of net overall winnings

$$(9) \qquad g_N = g'_1 + g'_2 + \cdots + g'_N$$

will tend in probability, subject to very general conditions which I will assume are satisfied, to a normal distribution for very large values of N (Central limit theorem);[123] in other words, in the case considered

$$(10) \qquad \varphi(g_N) \sim \frac{1}{\sqrt{2\pi}\Sigma_N} \exp\left[-(g_N - \bar{g}_N)^2/2\Sigma_N^2\right] \quad \text{for } N \gg 1,$$

where $\bar{g}_N$ and Σ_N represent the average and the standard deviation of g_N.

Thus, for the N game probability distribution which is approximately normal, the moments are

$$M_{N,1} = \bar{g}_N = Nm = N \int_{-\infty}^{+\infty} g'\varphi(g')\,dg',$$

$$M_{N,2} = \Sigma_N^2 = N\sigma^2,$$

$$(11) \qquad \ldots,$$

$$M_{N,2k} \sim 1 \cdot 3 \ldots (2k-1)(N\sigma^2)^k = \frac{(2k)!}{2^k k!}(N\sigma^2)^k,$$

$$M_{N,2k+1} \sim 0,$$

$$\ldots,$$

using $M_{N,1}, \ldots, M_{N,2k}$ and $M_{N,2k+1}$ to denote the mathematical expectation and the $2k$ and $(2k+1)$th moments of the overall probability distribution of the N rounds considered.[124] From this we deduce

$$(12) \qquad \frac{M_{N,2k}}{M_{N,1}^{2k}} \sim \frac{1 \cdot 3 \ldots (2k-1)(N\sigma^2)^k}{[Nm]^{2k}} = \frac{1 \cdot 3 \ldots (2k-1)\sigma^{2k}}{m^{2k}} \frac{1}{N^k}.$$

Whence from (4), (11) and (12)

$$(13) \qquad \lambda_{N,n} = \frac{1}{n!}\frac{M_{N,n}}{\bar{g}_N^n} \sim 0 \qquad \text{for } N \gg 1,$$

so that from (8)

$$(14) \qquad V_N \sim M_{N,1} = \bar{g}_N = \int_{-\infty}^{+\infty} g_N \varphi(g_N)\, dg_N$$

$$= N \int_{-\infty}^{+\infty} g' \varphi'(g')\, dg' \qquad \text{for } N \geqslant 1,$$

and

$$(15) \qquad \frac{V_N}{\int_{-\infty}^{+\infty} g_N \varphi(g_N)\, dg_N} \to 1 \qquad \text{for } N \to \infty.$$

In discrete notation this last result is written

$$(16) \qquad \frac{V_N}{\Sigma\, p_{N,i} g_{N,i}} \to 1 \qquad \text{for } N \to \infty,$$

where the $p_{N,i}$ represent the probabilities of the values $g_{N,i}$ of g_N.

Thus it can be seen *that under the assumptions stated, in particular excluding the possibility of ruin occurring before the last of the N rounds*, the neo-Bernoullian formulation for monetary values results *asymptotically* from the law of large numbers.[125]

The assumption that settlement does not occur during the N games

24.1.3. *The preceding result can be deduced only on the assumption that net gains and losses are settled in a single transaction after the Nth round.*

However, in the case of a settlement after each game this result holds also approximately *if the probability of ruin before the last Nth round is very low*, which condition may be satisfied if the losses in any individual game (corresponding to negative values of g) are very small in relation to the player's capital.[126]

This analysis sheds considerable light on the meaning of the neo-Bernoullian principle in relation to the law of large numbers when the player is effectively able to take part in a great number of single games. *The neo-Bernoullian principle applied to monetary values is effectively valid if two conditions are met: there must be a large number of successive games, and the probability of ruin in N games must be very small. If these two conditions are not both satisfied, the rule of mathematical expectation of monetary values can lead an operator having a fairly high propensity for security to take altogether irrational decisions.*[127]

(2) *Psychological Values*

24.2. Now consider the expression[128]

(17) $\bar{s}(C + V_N) = h[\psi(\gamma_N)],$

with

(18) $\gamma_N = \bar{s}(C + g_N),$

g_N being defined by (9) and h being a functional of the probability density function $\psi(\gamma_N)$ of psychological value γ_N.[129] Write

(19) $g_N = Nm + u_N.$

When N increases indefinitely, g_N and $var\, u_N$ increase like N.

(a) *The case in which $\gamma = \bar{s}(U)$ tends to a maximum γ_M when U increases indefinitely, with settlement of balances only after completion of N games*

24.2.1. In the case in which the cardinal index

(20) $\gamma = \gamma(U = C + g)$

tends to a limit γ_M when U increases indefinitely – which corresponds to observed data (see Appendix C, Section VI below) – it is easily shown that if settlement is effected as a lump sum after the end of N games J', the neo-Bernoullian formulation

(21) $B(C + V) = \sum p_i B(C + g_i),$

in which V represents the monetary value of a random outcome $(g_1, g_2, \ldots, g_i, \ldots, p_1, p_2, \ldots, p_i, \ldots)$ is verified asymptotically.

Taking the same notation as before, let $p_{N,i}$ denote the probability of the value $g_{N,i}$ of g_N defined by relation (9) with

(22) $\sum p_{N,i} = 1.$

Since the distribution of g_N tends to the normal distribution (10) and since by hypothesis $\gamma(U)$ tends to the limit γ_M when U increases indefinitely, we have according to (22)

(23) $\sum p_{N,i}\gamma(C + g_{N,i}) \to \gamma_M$ for $N \gg 1$.

It follows further from relations (10) and (19) that the monetary value V_N of the random prospect, corresponding to the N successive games J', necessarily increases indefinitely, so that

(24) $\gamma(C + V_N) \to \gamma_M$ for $N \gg 1$.

From (23) and (24), we deduce

(25) $\gamma(C + V_N) \sim \sum p_{N,i}\gamma(C + g_{N,i})$ for $N \gg 1$.

Thus from (23), (24) and (25), it results that the neo-Bernoullian formulation (21) is valid asymptotically, providing that we take

(26) $B(C + X) \equiv \gamma(C + X)$,

up to a linear transformation, i.e. if the neo-Bernoullian index is identified with the index of cardinal utility.

(b) *The case in which $\gamma = \bar{s}(U)$ increases indefinitely with U, with settlement of balances only after completion of N games*

24.2.2. As best as can be judged, the only realistic case corresponds to satiety for very great values of U. This is the case just examined.

It is however of interest to see that *even if this circumstance does not prevail, the neo-Bernoullian formulation would remain asymptotically valid for a large number of classes of function $\gamma = \bar{s}(U)$*, providing the assumption is maintained that settlement takes place at the end of the N games considered.

In this case, the same reasoning as for nominal values may be repeated considering here the mathematical expectation $\mathcal{M}_{N,1} = \bar{\gamma}_N$ of cardinal utility and the moments $\mathcal{M}_{N,n}$ of the distribution whose probability density is $\psi(\gamma_N)$

(27) $\mathcal{M}_{N,1} = \bar{\gamma}_N = \displaystyle\int_{-\infty}^{+\infty} \gamma_N \psi(\gamma_N) \, d\gamma_N,$

(28) $\mathcal{M}_{N,n} = \displaystyle\int_{-\infty}^{+\infty} (\gamma_N - \bar{\gamma}_N)^n \psi(\gamma_N) \, d\gamma_N.$

We may write

(29) $\bar{s}(C + V_N) = F[\mathcal{M}_{N,1}, \mu_{N,2}, \ldots, \mu_{N,n}, \ldots],$

with

$$(30) \qquad \mu_{N,n} = \frac{1}{n!} \frac{\mathcal{M}_{N,n}}{\bar{\gamma}_N^n}.$$

We have necessarily

$$(31) \qquad \bar{s}(C + V_N) = \mathcal{M}_{N,1} = \bar{\gamma}_N \qquad \text{for } \gamma_N = \bar{\gamma}_N \text{ whatever } \gamma,$$

which implies

$$(32) \qquad F[\mathcal{M}_{N,1}, 0, \ldots, 0, \ldots] = \mathcal{M}_{N,1},$$

and therefore

$$(33) \qquad \bar{s}(C + V_N) \sim \mathcal{M}_{N,1} \qquad \text{for } \mu_{N,n} \ll 1 \text{ whatever } n.$$

Condition (33) is satisfied for all classes of the function $\gamma = \bar{s}(C + g)$ such that the condition (13)

$$(34) \qquad \lambda_{N,n} \sim 0 \qquad \text{for } N \gg 1$$

entails

$$(35) \qquad \mu_{N,n} \sim 0 \qquad \text{for } N \gg 1.$$

Since the function $\gamma = \bar{s}(C + X)$ is defined up to a linear transformation and, further, varies relatively slowly in the neighbourhood of any given value of X for $X \gg 1$, and therefore in the neighbourhood of the average $M_{N,1} = \bar{g}_N = Nm$ of the g_N, and since in addition the effect of the law of large numbers is to reduce the relative dispersion about the average $\bar{g}_N$, for the whole set of N unit games, of the net gains $g_{N,i}$ whose probabilities are $p_{N,i}$, it can be considered that, at least for a large number of classes of function $\gamma = \bar{s}(U)$ condition (34) does indeed entail condition (35).[130]

It can thus be seen that condition (34), deduced from the law of large numbers, has the condition

$$(36) \qquad \gamma(C + V_N) \sim \mathcal{M}_{N,1} = \bar{\gamma}_N$$

as a consequence, implying the approximate validity of the neo-Bernoullian formulation for very large values of N if the neo-Bernoullian index is defined by the condition

$$(37) \qquad B(C + X) \equiv \gamma(C + X)$$

up to a linear transformation, i.e. if this index is identified with the cardinal preference index $\gamma = \bar{s}(C + g)$ (cardinal utility).[131]

In discrete notation, the latter result (36) is written

(38) $\bar{s}(C + V_N) \sim \sum p_{N,i}\bar{s}(C + g_{N,i})$.

Conditions for the Asymptotic Validity of the Neo-Bernoullian Formulation

24.3. This discussion shows *that once the assumption is made that settlement is to be in a lump sum after the Nth game, thus precluding the possibility of ruin during the series,* the law of large numbers entails the neo-Bernoullian formulation.

This will, however, also be true, at least approximately, if gains and losses are settled after each game, if for each unit game the ratios g'_i/C of the gains g'_i, associated with an elementary game, to capital C are relatively small, *so that the probability of ruin during the N games remains relatively low.*[132]

It has been suggested that there is no justification for any proposed relationship between the law of large numbers and the neo-Bernoullian formula.[133] In the light of the discussion just completed, this point of view is rather singular. In any event, at the root of the thinking of the proponents of the neo-Bernoullian formulation, is the law of large numbers, at least as far as its historical origin is concerned. Admittedly the neo-Bernoullian formulation flows from conditions of linearity, but this is a purely formal viewpoint, for linearity is actually the consequence, as I stressed in my 1952 study, of the neglect by the American School to take the probability distribution of psychological values about the mean into account. Now the law of large numbers shows precisely that for a large number of games *the relative dispersion* (i.e. the coefficients $\mu_{N,n}$) becomes negligible. The two viewpoints are absolutely identical.

At all events, the *asymptotic validity of the neo-Bernoullian formulation when the probability of ruin remains fairly low* cannot in general warrant its validity in the case of a single game. *There is a yawning gulf between the conduct that is rational in relation to a random choice related to a non-repeatable event, and the conduct that is rational when the event will recur very often and in similar circumstances.*

IMPLICATIONS OF THE NEO-BERNOULLIAN FORMULATION FOR
THE ARBITRAGE BETWEEN MATHEMATICAL EXPECTATION
AND THE PROBABILITY OF RUIN

25. Among all the arguments I put forward in 1952 against the neo-Bernoullian formulation, independently of any recourse to the concept of cardinal utility, one of them appears to me today decisive, and I think I placed too little stress on it in my 1952 memoir.

The Trade-off Between Mathematical Expectation of Monetary Gains and the Probability of Ruin

25.1. Consider a subject whose *ordinal* index of preference is a function

$$(1) \qquad S = f(M, P)$$

of the mathematical expectation M of a random prospect and the associated probability of ruin P.[134]

If $\varphi(g)$ is the probability density of monetary gains g corresponding to the random prospect considered, we have (using continuous notation)

$$(2) \qquad M = \int_{-\infty}^{+\infty} g\varphi(g)\,dg,$$

$$(3) \qquad P = \int_{-\infty}^{-X} \varphi(g)\,dg,$$

where X denotes the subject's capital.[135]

A priori, there is no reason to consider as irrational such a behaviour which consists in the trade-off between the mathematical expectation and the probability of ruin.

The Implications of the Neo-Bernoullian Formulation for the Trade-Off Considered $S = f(M, P)$

25.2. *If the subject acts on the neo-Bernoullian principle*, i.e. if he is rational in the sense understood by the American School, I showed in my 1952 study that condition (1) implies necessarily[136]

$$(4) \qquad S = f(M - aP), \qquad a > 0.$$

Naturally the ordinal index of preference S is an increasing function of the mathematical expectation M of the monetary gains and a decreasing function of the probability of ruin P.

In this case, the indifference curves on the (M, P) space are necessarily parallel straight lines, the equation of which is

(5) $M = K + aP,$ $a > 0,$

where K is a constant, as in Figure 1.

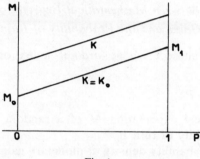

Fig. 1.

Non-Validity of the Formulation $S = f(M - aP)$ for $P = 1$

25.3. In fact the proof given in my 1952 memoir of relation (4) assumes *implicitly* that the probability of ruin P is different from unity. This can easily be verified directly.

Consider the straight line

(6) $K = K_0,$ $K_0 > 0.$

From (5) we have

(7) $M = M_0 = K_0,$ for $P = 0,$

so that from (5), (6) and (7)

(8) $M_1 = a + M_0 > 0$ for $P = 1.$

But to have $P = 1$, we must have

(9) $\varphi(g) = 0$ for $g > -X,$

and in this case, we would have necessarily,

(10) $M_1 < 0$ for $P = 1$,

which is in contradiction with (8).

Thus under the conditions assumed (arbitrage between M and P and validity of the neo-Bernoullian formulation), we have

(11) $S = f(M - aP)$,   only for $P \neq 1$,

but this condition is fully satisfied for all the other values of P, however close they may be to unity.

The Index $S = f(M - aP)$ Cannot be Assumed to Apply for Values of the Probability of Ruin Close to Unity

25.4. Now if we consider a value of the probability of ruin very close to unity

(12) $P = 1 - \varepsilon$, $\varepsilon \ll 1$,

the behaviour described by relation (4) would be, to say the least, very criticizable from the standpoint of rationality.

As a matter of fact, in this particular case and for instance, the neo-Bernoullian formulation would imply that the subject would consider as equivalent an assured gain of $1 million and a random prospect with a higher mathematical expectation, but with a probability of ruin so close to unity as to be practically equivalent to certainty. Thus whatever the value of a could be and *however high the value*

(13) $M = M_1$ for $P = 1 - \varepsilon = 1 - 10^{-10}$,

no subject in possession of his faculties would make this equivalence.

Assume for example, that

(14) $\begin{cases} M_0 = \$1{,}000{,}000 \text{ (one million)} & (a = (M_1 - M_0)/P) \\ M_1 = \$1{,}000{,}000{,}000 \text{ (one billion)} & \text{for } P = 1 - 10^{-10}. \end{cases}$

If the neo-Bernoullian formulation is taken, it reduces to either
  – denying that an operator who bases his decisions on arbitrage between mathematical expectation and probability of ruin could be rational, or
  – accepting that a certain gain of $1 million can rationally be deemed equivalent to a game with a mathematical expectation of $1 billion *but for which ruin would be practically certain.*
In fact both alternatives seem equally indefensible.[137]

The Neo-Bernoullian Index in the Case of a Trade-off
Between Mathematical Expectation of Monetary Gains and
the Probability of Ruin

25.5. If the neo-Bernoullian formulation is valid, the certain value V of a random prospect is given by the relation

(15) $$B(V) = \int_{-\infty}^{+\infty} B(g)\varphi(g)\,dg,$$

in which $B(X)$ represents the neo-Bernoullian index.

If the subject considered carries on an arbitrage between the mathematical expectation M and the probability of ruin P while obeying to the neo-Bernoullian formulation, we should have on the basis of the preceding discussion:

(16) $$V = M - aP,$$

or, from (2) and (3),

(17) $$V = \int_{-\infty}^{-X} (g - a)\varphi(g)\,dg + \int_{-X}^{+\infty} g\varphi(g)\,dg.$$

It is possible to show that the conditions (15) and (17) can both be valid simultaneously only if, up to a linear transformation,[138]

(18)
$$B(g) = g \qquad \text{for } g > -X,$$
$$B(g) = g - a \qquad \text{for } g \leqslant -X.$$

These necessary conditions are also sufficient, for, if they are satisfied, we have from (2), (3), (15) and (18)

(19) $$B(V) = \int_{-\infty}^{-X} (g - a)\varphi(g)\,dg + \int_{-X}^{+\infty} g\varphi(g)\,dg$$
$$= \int_{-\infty}^{+\infty} g\varphi(g)\,dg - a\int_{-\infty}^{-X} \varphi(g)\,dg$$
$$= M - aP,$$

thus verifying that the ordinal index $S = S(V)$, which is a function $S = h(B)$ since $B = B(g)$, is indeed of the form $S = S(M - aP)$.

Relations (18) show clearly that the neo-Bernoullian formulation is *unduly restrictive*.[139] At all events we see that the neo-Bernoullian indicator B can be a continuous function of g for all value of g only when $a = 0$, which reduces the psychology of the subject considered to a simple function of mathematical expectation M.[140]

Incompatibility of the Discontinuity of the Neo-Bernoullian Index $B(g)$ with the Implications of the Neo-Bernoullian Theories

25.6. It results from the proof of the existence of a neo-Bernoullian index that to any assured gain g corresponds an index $B(g)$ with a well defined value (see for example von Neumann–Morgenstern, 1947, §3.5.1., p.27). However it is easily seen that the relations (18) preclude such univocal correspondence.

Following these relations, the index $B(g)$ is depicted as in Figure 2. Now consider the random outcome

$$(20) \qquad \begin{matrix} g_1, p_1, & g_1 > -X, \\ g_2, p_2, & g_2 < -X, \end{matrix}$$

and let V be its value to the subject considered. We should have

$$(21) \qquad \begin{matrix} B(V) = p_1 B(g_1) + p_2 B(g_2), \\ p_1 + p_2 = 1. \end{matrix}$$

From (21) it results that

$$(22) \qquad Om = p_1 Om_1 + p_2 Om_2.$$

On the segment $m_1 m_2$, the point m is the barycenter of points m_1 and m_2 with weights p_1 and p_2.

Using (18), relation (21) is written

$$(23) \qquad B(V) = p_1 g_1 + p_2(g_2 - a).$$

For given values of g_1 and g_2 it is always possible to choose p_1 and p_2 such that the line $M_1 M_2$ cuts the horizontal of ordinate Om at the point M whose abscissa is exactly $-X$. Thus we should have

$$(24) \qquad -X - a < B(V) < -X, \qquad \text{for } V = -X.$$

As the position of M between N_1 and N_2 can be anywhere between the two points M_1 and M_2 considered, it can be seen that for $V = -X$ the index $B(V)$ is *indeterminate*. Thus there is no two-way one to one

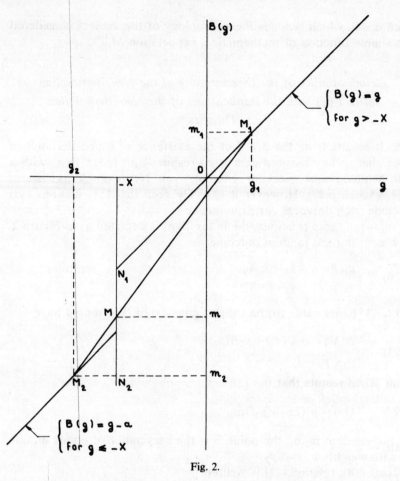

Fig. 2.

correspondence between g and the corresponding index $B(g)$ for any value of g.

The Trade-off Between Mathematical Expectation of the Monetary Gains and the Probability of Ruin, the Neo-Bernoullian Formulation, and the St. Petersburg Paradox

25.7. The discussion above shows that if the neo-Bernoullian formulation holds for a certain subject, the index of preference represented in relation (1) implies relations (18), which must hold whatever the random outcome considered.

It follows, that for the random prospect corresponding to the St. Petersburg Paradox

(25)
$$\text{gains } 2, 2^2, \ldots, 2^n, \ldots,$$
$$\text{probability } \frac{1}{2}, \frac{1}{2^2}, \ldots, \frac{1}{2^n}, \ldots,$$

we should have according to relations (18)

(26) $$V = B(V) = \sum_{n=1}^{n=\infty} \frac{2^n}{2^n} = \infty.$$

However, as we will see in the following §26, no subject will accept to pay a very high price for the right to a single drawing in the game thus defined.

Here again, it is clear that the neo-Bernoullian formulation altogether excludes the rationality of a trade-off between mathematical expectation and the probability of ruin.

The Trade-off Between the Mathematical Expectation of Cardinal Utility and the Probability of Ruin

25.8. Now assume that the subject's psychology can be portrayed by an ordinal index of the form

(27) $$S = f(\mathcal{M}, P),$$

with

(28) $$\mathcal{M} = \sum_i p_i \gamma_i,$$

(29) $$\gamma_i = \bar{s}(g_i),$$

where γ_i denotes the cardinal utility of the gain g_i and $\mathcal{M}$ the mathematical expectation of the γ_i.

The reader can easily verify that if the neo-Bernoullian formulation applies, all the reasoning carried out for monetary values can be transposed for cardinal utilities, and that we should have in this case

(30) $$S = f(\mathcal{M} - aP),$$

with

(31)
$$B(g) = \gamma(g) \qquad \text{for } g > -X,$$
$$B(g) = \gamma(g) - a \qquad \text{for } g \leq -X,$$

where a is a constant.

Here again the discontinuity of the index $B(g)$ for $g = -X$ would show itself to be incompatible with the neo-Bernoullian formulation. The procedure of the proof would be wholly analogous to that considered in §25.6 relating to monetary values.

THE ARBITRAGE BETWEEN MATHEMATICAL EXPECTATION AND THE PROBABILITY OF RUIN, AND THE ST. PETERSBURG PARADOX

26. The *St. Petersburg Paradox*, whose paternity is due to Nicholas Bernoulli[141] is a glaring example of the absurd consequences of blind application of the theory of probable gain.

A banker offers the following game to a player, for a fixed price b: tossing a coin as many times as is necessary for it to fall heads. If this happens on the nth toss, the player wins 2^n units. How much should the player reasonably pay to enter the game?

We calculate the probable gain: one chance in 2 of winning 2, one in 4 of winning 4, one in 8 of winning 8, and so on. The probable gain is then

(1)
$$\frac{2}{2} + \frac{4}{4} + \frac{8}{8} + \cdots = 1 + 1 + 1 + \cdots,$$

which is infinite.

On the theory of probable gain, the conclusion is that the game is to the player's advantage, however much his admittance fee b. This conclusion appears at least questionable.

To explain why nobody would be prepared to pay a very high price for the random outcome corresponding to the St. Petersburg Paradox, several explanations have been put forward: the theory of moral value, the irrationality of considering very small probabilities, the limits on the banker's capital, and the time needed for drawings.

The Theory of Moral Value

26.1. The best known explanation, developed independently by Gabriel Cramer (1704–1752) and Daniel Bernoulli (1700–1782), and subsequently taken up by Laplace (1749–1827), is based on psychological value.[142] If the player's capital is X, the psychological value of a gain g is $\bar{s}(X + g)$, so that by application of the mathematical expectation rule to psychological value instead of monetary value, the monetary value of the random outcome considered is

$$(2) \qquad \bar{s}(X + V) = \frac{1}{2}\, \bar{s}(X + 2) + \cdots + \frac{1}{2^n}\, \bar{s}(X + 2^n) + \cdots,$$

where $\bar{s}(U)$ represents the moral value of the capital U.

Following Daniel Bernoulli by taking psychological value as the logarithmic expression[143]

$$(3) \qquad \bar{s}(X + V) = \lambda \log (X + V) + \mu, \qquad \lambda > 0,$$

where λ and $|\mu|$ may have any values, and considering relation (2), we deduce the following Table:

Value V of the St. Petersburg game for a player of fortune X						
X	0	10	10^2	10^3	10^6	10^9	10^{12}
V	4	5.5	7.9	11.0	20.9	30.8	40.8

This application of the rule of mathematical expectation to the psychological values puts the value V of the stake at \$30.8 for a dollar billionaire, and \$4 for a person with no capital at all. In fact the value V increases with the player's capital X, but it increases approximately only as the logarithm of X.[144]

The Irrationality of Considering Very Small Probabilities

26.2. For Buffon, "*a probability should be regarded as zero if it is very small, i.e. under* 1/10,000", or even, he states later, under 1/1000 (*Essai d'Arithmétique Morale*, Sections XVI and XX).[145] As $2^{10} = 1024$, the value of the game above should amount only to the sum of the first ten terms, i.e. \$10.

Limits on the Banker's Capital

26.3. In Section XVII of his *Essay*, Buffon notes also that the banker would be unable to meet payments of the order of 2^{31} or some 2.15 billion écus, the currency of his time. Today Buffon's statement would be equivalent to saying that the banker would be unable to pay sums of the order of 2^{40} or one thousand billion dollars, a figure of the order of the GNP of the United States.[146]

Even admitting that the banker could pay such a sum but no more, the player's mathematical expectation would be

$$(4) \qquad \frac{2}{2} + \frac{2^2}{2^2} + \cdots + \frac{2^{40}}{2^{40}} \left[1 + \frac{1}{2} + \cdots \right] = 41.$$

Thus the mathematical expectation of the monetary gains cannot be infinite.

Even if the banker's fortune were the same size as one of the world's greatest fortunes, say \$10 billion – roughly 2^{33} – the indicated bet on the basis of the monetary mathematical expectation, taking Buffon's argument into account, would be some \$34.

Time Needed for Drawings

26.4. Buffon also remarks (Section XVIII) that to toss a coin 2^{20}, or some million times, would take more than thirteen years for a six-hour gaming day. For 2^{24} tosses, 52 years would be required, and so on. Thus it would be unrealistic to take account of possibilities which could not be realised in practice.

Partial or Total Inadequacy of the Proposed Explanations

26.5. To explain the St. Petersburg Paradox, the theory of psychological value certainly holds, at least in part,[147] *for the individual*, but it is wholly irrelevant for a capitalistic firm operating according to the rules of the market. *Here linearity becomes the rule.* To see this, it is only necessary to assume that the firm's capital is held by a very large number of shareholders: all effects of curvature of cardinal utility disappear.

The argument, in any case very contestable, that very small probabilities should be ignored by a rational man, is valid only if one game only is to be played, for an event whose probability of occurrence p in a single drawing is small, for instance equal to 1/10,000, becomes practically certain to occur if a very large number N of games is played: its probability to occur at least once in N games is

$$(5) \qquad q = 1 - (1 - p)^N,$$

or $q \sim 9,999/10,000$ for $N = 92,099$.

As regards the limit on the banker's holdings, the argument put forward is that the player cannot consider his mathematical expectation as unlimited; but the fact remains that there are players, or syndicates of players, who would be well prepared to pay a very high price, in any case much more than 41 dollars, for the possibility of a gain of the order of one year's American gross national product, if their propensity to risk is strong.

With respect to the objection regarding the time needed physically to toss the coin a very large number of times, it can be easily eliminated by envisaging agreement on another procedure to generate the same random outcome, such as computer simulation.[148]

The Analysis of the St. Petersburg Paradox

26.6. A valid analysis of the St. Petersburg Paradox implies *a careful distinction between various cases.*

The first concerns the number of games. One game being defined as the sequence of tosses made until heads appears, it is necessary to be precise whether the banker's offer is good for one game only, or is held open for N games, however large N may be.

The second distinction is also of capital importance: is settlement to be made after each game, or in a lump sum corresponding to the net balance after N games? In the first case, the player may be ruined before he reaches the Nth game. In the second case, he can only be ruined if at the end of the Nth game his aggregate winnings are too low to enable him to finance his stakes, which amount to N times the unit bet. It is assumed that a machine can be used to produce a random outcome equivalent to N games in a limited time, however great the value of N.

The set of the different interesting eventualities is schematised below:

The St. Petersburg Game

Possible Variants		Number of Games N		
		1	$N \gg 1$	∞
Settlement	After each game	A	B	C
	After last of N games $(N > 1)$		D	E

Cases B and D correspond to situations in which the law of large numbers applies. Cases C and E correspond to an infinite number of games. As limit cases, they are easier to study.

Variant A: N = 1

Everything clearly depends on the size of the player's and the banker's capital. If the latter is \$10 billion $(\sim 2^{33})$, a player or a syndicate of players with a high propensity for risk may pay quite a high price to participate in a single game. *Caeteris paribus*, the price will be the higher the greater the number of players, since the more players, the more attenuated the effect of the decline in marginal psychological value.

If *enough players are associated, the curvature of the index of cardinal utility has no effect, since the syndicates utility index is necessarily linear, at least over a very wide domain.*

Now it is certain that, according to the greater or lesser propensity for risk of the syndicate's members, the price b which the syndicate will be ready to pay for a game, may exceed or fall below the mathematical expectation of \$33, corresponding to the case where the banker's fortune is \$10 billion.

To explain this brings us back to the central thesis of this paper, namely that the rule of mathematical expectation cannot be a rational principle for decision taking in the case of a single game.

In this case, to define the value V of a single game, one is led to a function of the form

(6) $V = F[g_1, g_2, \ldots, g_n, p_1, p_2, \ldots, p_n]$,

with

(7) $g_i = 2^i, \qquad p_i = 1/2^i$,

n being defined by the condition

(8) $2^n < C < 2^{n+1}$,

where C represents the banker's fortune.

As it follows from the foregoing, the function V could not in general reduce to the mathematical expectation, which in this instance is equal to n.

Variant E: $N = \infty$, no settlement after each game

Whatever his capital, the banker's ruin is absolutely certain. The player will win the whole fortune of the banker, *however large his bet on a unit game.*

There is no upper limit to the bet since the player is certain to recover the aggregate amount bet, and with it the fortune of the banker, whose ruin is *certain*.

The consideration of variant E shows that Bertrand's objections to the thesis that it is absurd to apply the principle of mathematical expectation,[149] are fully borne out *if settlement is on an aggregate basis after N games, and if a practically infinite number of games can be realised by mechanical means in a very short time. Here none of the explanations of the St. Petersburg Paradox advanced so far are valid any longer because there is no longer any paradox.*

Variant D: $N \gg 1$, no settlement after each game

If N is extremely large, e.g. 10^{40}, the situation is similar to that described for variant E. The St. Petersburg game is highly favourable to the player even if his stake for each game is very high.

Variant C: $N = \infty$, settlement after each game

In the case of an infinite number of games and of a settlement after each game, we are brought to the classical problem of the player's ruin in an infinite number of games.

For a given price b of the game *the greater N, the more the law of large numbers seems to operate in the player's favour and against the banker, but the greater in reality the player's probability of ruin.*

If we suppose to simplify that the banker's fortune is infinite, at least on paper, and if we design by X the player's fortune, by b the price paid for each game, and by P the probability of the player's ruin for an infinite number of games, we can calculate, from the general theory of the gambler's ruin, the function $P = P(X, b)$, and so determine the price b paid for each game as a function $b = b(X, P)$ of the player's fortune X and his probability of ruin P.[150] A few results are presented in the following table.

	Price b paid for each game				
X \ P	10^{-9}	10^{-4}	$\frac{1}{2}$	$1 - 10^{-4}$	$1 - 10^{-9}$
10^4	9.2	10.2	13.9	26.7	43.3
10^5	12.3	13.5	17.2	30.0	46.6
10^6	15.7	16.8	20.6	33.3	49.9
10^9	25.6	26.8	30.5	43.3	59.9

X = player's fortune.
P = probability of the player's ruin, the banker's fortune being supposed to be infinite.

Thus, assuming that the banker's fortune is infinite, at least on paper, let us consider a player whose fortune is one billion dollars. Despite the player's fortune and his infinite mathematical expectation for each game, we see that his probability of ruin is 9,999/10,000 if the price of each game is \$43, and $1 - 10^{-9}$ if the price is \$60. By contrast, if our billionaire stakes only \$25 per game, he reduces his probability of ruin to an insignificant value 10^{-9}.

Consider the case of a finite number N of games, for each of which the mathematical expectation is m. If we do not take the probability of ruin into account, the mathematical expectation M_N for N games is

$$(9) \qquad M_N = N(m - b),$$

where b is the price to pay for one game.

But if we take into account the probability of ruin, the mathematical expectation M_N for N games becomes

$$(10) \qquad M_N^* = (1 - P_N)E_N - P_N X, \qquad (E_N > M_N)$$

where X is the player's capital, P_N the probability of the player being ruined in N games, and E_N the conditional mathematical expectation in the absence of ruin.

Thus considering eqn. (10) in the two cases considered (b = \$60 and b = \$25 with $X = 10^9$), the mathematical monetary expectation M_N is infinite, whatever the price b, since m and N are infinite. Yet in the first case, ruin is all but certain, whereas in the second, it is extremely improbable.

Clearly in this case the unit bet *b* must be set very low, even for a most wealthy player, if the probability of ruin is to be reduced sufficiently. The same is true for a syndicate of a very great number of players, for which no phenomenon of satiety can occur, and for which the linearity of the cardinal utility index is the rule.

For this it results that in this case the real explanation of the St. Petersburg Paradox can be founded only on the arbitrage between mathematical expectation and the probability of ruin. It also follows that the neo-Bernoullian principle is validly applied only where the chance of ruin is negligible.

Variant B: $N \gg 1$, settlement after each game

This case is much more difficult to discuss and at least for the time being, eludes precise evaluation. However, it can be shown that for sufficiently high values of N, the position is similar to variant C.

Comparison of Cases B' and D' for a Very Rich Banker and a Syndicate with a Large Number of Members

26.7. If the case of a syndicate having a large number of players, of a very rich banker, and of a machine producing very rapidly the result of a very large number of games N, comparison of cases B' and D', corresponding to cases B and D when the banker's fortune is limited, is highly instructive.

In the case D', settlement follows the nth game. Even if a very high price *b* is paid per unit game, the mathematical expectation that is roughly equal to the banker's fortune F, is large, and the probability of ruin extremely low.

In the case B', settlement follows each game, and the situation differs totally. For the same value of N, and even if the stake per unit game *b* is very low, the probability of ruin can rise close to unity. If the probability of ruin is left out of account, the mathematical expectation remains practically equal to the banker's fortune. It may be reduced substantially if allowance is made for the probability of ruin, i.e., taking relation

(10*) $M_N^* = (1 - P_N)E_N - P_N X, \qquad E < F < N(m - b)$ for $N \gg 1$.

where E is the conditional mathematical expectation. *Thus we see that in this case, the probability of ruin plays a decisive role.*

The Arbitrage Between Mathematical Expectation and the Probability of Ruin

26.8. In the cases B and C the explanation of the St. Petersburg Paradox which I have given offers a perfect illustration of the trade-off a subject may be led to between mathematical expectation and the probability of ruin.

In fact the psychology of the entrepreneur is typified by this arbitrage: he attempts to maximise an index of the type

(11) $S = f(M, P),$

where M is the mathematical expectation and P the probability of ruin.

But, in general, such behaviour is in *total conflict* with the neo-Bernoullian principle.[151]

In the concrete case of the mining exploration study I worked on in the 1950's, it would have been wrong to advise the exploring company to prospect in the Sahara, or anywhere else, on the sole grounds of positive mathematical expectation, since this expectation was associated with a very low probability of success.[152] *For a random outcome of this kind, mathematical expectation is much less important than the very high probability of failure and ruin.* There is little point entering a game with a positive mathematical expectation if there is from the outset a high chance of being forced out of it by ruin.

The entrepreneur who is not averse to risk is, and should be, concerned to be able to continue taking risks, i.e. to play. For this, he must avoid launching activities for which the dispersion of gains and losses is so great that the probability of ruin becomes very high, even though the mathematical expectation is positive and very great.

In the case of mining exploration, a sufficiently low probability of ruin is obtainable only if the prospecting company can investigate a sufficiently large area. If it operates over too small a prospection zone, its ruin is inevitable.

CHAPTER III

A CRITICAL ANALYSIS OF THE BASIC
CONCEPTS OF THE POST-1952 THEORIES OF
THE AMERICAN SCHOOL

> We must demand that the set of operations
> equivalent to any concept be a unique set, for
> otherwise there are possibilities of ambiguity
> in practical applications which we cannot
> admit ....
> If we have more than one set of operations
> we have more than one concept, and strictly
> there should be a separate name to correspond
> to each different set of operations.
>
> PERCY W. BRIDGMAN[153]

THE APPROACHES OF THE AMERICAN SCHOOL SINCE 1952:
THEORETICAL MODELS AND EMPIRICAL RESEARCH

27. Since 1952, the analysis of behaviour with respect to random choice has given rise to an immense volume of literature in two directions: the development of *theoretical models* to represent rational behaviour, and *empirical research* into actual behaviour.

The *theoretical work* has had the twofold aim of seeking to develop new, more attractive postulates to justify the neo-Bernoullian formulation; analysing the implications of the neo-Bernoullian formulation and casting the theories into forms better adapted to empirical research.[154] All this work has called forth a considerable effort, but has not yielded any genuinely new result.

Very many attempts have been made to test the neo-Bernoullian formulation *experimentally*,[155] mostly conducted in the hope of having it confirmed, *but whatever the method, every investigation has turned out against it*. As a conclusion of their thorough analysis of empirical research, in 1975, MacCrimmon and Larsson rightly conclude:

507

Suppose individuals violate the axioms in the choices they make, and especially when these choices have been the result of careful thought. If they would like to rely on the assistance of a theory of decision making, they have three main options:

(1) they can maintain the choices they have made and conclude that the axioms are not relevant for them in this situation (or perhaps in any situation),

(2) they can change their choices to bring them in line with the axioms, or

(3) they can change the theory to make it consistent with their choices.

Since many careful, intelligent decision makers do seem to violate some axioms of expected utility theory, even upon reflection of their choices, it does seem worthwhile exploring this third option of considering modifications to the standard theory. It would seem that, sooner or later, any convincing changes will have to be made at the level of the axioms.

In the light of the analysis presented in my 1952 paper, the results of the analysis of the answers to the 1952 Questionnaire, and the preceding discussion, it is easy to see why. *There is no neo-Bernoullian index such that actual random choices can be represented by the neo-Bernoullian formulation.*[156]

Practically all the work done has been in the neo-Bernoullian frame. However, in the course of years, with the successive failures met by the experiments devised to justify the neo-Bernoullian formulation, and as this formulation has led its proponents into untenable positions, a growing number of dissident voices has brought it under criticism and held that it be scrapped.[157] *Basically the critics have put forward arguments very similar, or even identical to these I presented in my 1952 work.*

Space is lacking here to give even a summary account of this vast literature[158] and I shall limit my discussion to a critical analysis of the basic concepts of the American School since 1952.

The literature displays utter confusion as regards four basic concepts: cardinal utility and the neo-Bernoullian index; probability and a 'coefficient of likelihood' or of 'plausibility'; successive drawings over time and reduction to a simple random choice of future drawings; and finally rationality of behaviour.[158*]

CONFUSION BETWEEN THE NEO-BERNOULLIAN INDEX AND THE INDEX OF CARDINAL UTILITY

28. The word 'utility' is used throughout practically all the literature as a label for two different concepts: cardinal utility in the sense defined by Jevons[159] and as used in the present study,[160] and a neo-Bernoullian index satisfying the formulation[161]

$$B(V) = \sum p_i B(g_i).$$

Taking Savage's theory as an example,[162] *there is no justification for using the term 'index of utility' to refer to the index whose existence he demonstrates subject to certain conditions.* It is impossible to show that this index represents cardinal utility in the usual sense of the term. In the 1952 Symposium, moreover, Savage's fallback position was to claim that the index whose existence he had demonstrated had nothing to do with cardinal utility. *One can therefore only speak of the neo-Bernoullian index in Savage's sense, and no more.*

To treat this index on the same footing as cardinal utility is *deliberately to delude* the unwarned reader into believing that the theory on which it is based provides a measure of cardinal utility. This is an *anti-scientific attitude, for it consists of using the same word to encompass two entirely different concepts.* As a matter of fact, the neo-Bernoullian index whose existence Savage claims to have proved *only exists on paper.* It does not exist for the real man. This was a fundamental result of the 1952 experiment, for the neo-Bernoullian indexes which can be deduced from the answers to different series of questions *differ radically from one series to the next.*[163]

Notwithstanding allegations to the contrary by certain authors, the distinction between cardinal utility and the neo-Bernoullian index does not rest on 'futile questions of semantics', but constitutes an issue of fundamental importance.

Karl Borch (1975b) writes:

... (the decision maker) can also follow Bernoulli and *assume* that the ordering exists, and *set out to determine the underlying utility function.*[164]

This assertion may be doubly questioned. In the first place, the neo-Bernoullian formulation can determine a neo-Bernoullian index, but not the cardinal utility. Secondly, if the neo-Bernoullian formulation is hypothesised, the $B(g)$ indexes derived are *altogether different* for the various series of questions considered, as was shown by the analysis of the answers to the 1952 Questionnaire. *In fact for none of the cases studied does a unique $B(g)$ index exist.*[165]

The confusion between the neo-Bernoullian index and cardinal utility is all the more serious in that some authors dispute the existence of cardinal utility. Many commentators have invoked the authority of Pareto here, showing that they have altogether misunderstood his point of view. This was twofold. Pareto showed that there was no need whatever to call on the concept of cardinal utility to develop the theories of general economic equilibrium and economic efficiency. But in *parallel*, and at the height of his thought, i.e. in the *Treatise on Sociology*, Pareto used the concept of cardinal utility in constructing the general theory of society he presented, and there assumed that cardinal utilities could be compared by the use of suitable weighting coefficients.[166,167]

THE CONFUSION BETWEEN OBJECTIVE PROBABILITY, SUBJECTIVE PROBABILITY, AND THE COEFFICIENTS REFERRED TO AS PROBABILITIES BY THE NEO-BERNOULLIANS

29. Similar confusion arises from the use in the literature of the word '*probability*' to relate to three entirely different concepts: objective probability defined by reference to the frequency of occurrence of repeatable events,[168] the subjective probability of an event which will occur once only,[168] and the coefficients referred to in the neo-Bernoullian literature as '*probabilities*'.

Subjective probability has made its appearance in the development of science with D'Alembert in the middle of the 18th century, in his *Réflexions sur le Calcul des Probabilités* (1761) and, over the past fifty years, has played an ever-growing role to the detriment of objective probability. However, considerable confusion has been generated in the process. In fact from an historical point of view the concept of the subjective probability of a non-recurrent event, was derived directly from the concept of objective probability. Thus Borel proposed to determine subjective probabilities by referring to objective probabilities, through the so-called 'bet method'.[169]

In fact, the only way to confer concrete meaning on the concept of subjective probability is to ask a subject whether he considers that a certain non-recurrent event is more or less likely than the extraction of a given ball from a reference urn.[170] In this particular case, moreover, it would probably be better to speak of a coefficient of likelihood or plausibility rather than of subjective probability. To speak of the probability that the sun will not rise tomorrow has no concrete meaning. It may be convenient to speak of an *index of likelihood or plausibility*, but this cannot be identified with the concept of objective probability suggested by the observation of events which can repeat themselves.[171]

The definition of subjective probability by referring to objective probability is simple and natural. If it were abandoned, another approach altogether would be required. The definition proposed by de Finetti, a supporter of *subjective probability*, is the following:

Roughly speaking, the value *p*, given by a person for the probability $P(E)$ of an event *E*, means the price he is just willing to pay for a unit amount of money conditional on *E*'s being true. That is, the preferences on the basis of which he is willing to behave (side effects being eliminated) are determined, with respect to gains or losses depending on *E*, by assuming that an amount *S* conditional on *E* is evaluated at *pS*. That must be asserted only for sufficiently small amounts, the general approach should deal in the same way with utility, a concept that, for want of space, is not discussed here.[172]

This definition must be strongly criticised. The answers to the 1952 Questionnaire[173] show that the ratio

(1) $k = X'/pX$

of the certain value X' judged equivalent to the *objective* probability $p = 0.9$ of a gain X of about one dollar was unity for only 23% of respondents, as will be seen from the following distribution for 102 subjects:

$$0.39 < k \leqslant 0.83 \qquad \text{34 subjects}$$
$$0.83 < k \leqslant 0.99 \qquad \text{34 subjects}$$
$$k = 1 \qquad \text{23 subjects}$$
$$1.01 \leqslant k \leqslant 1.11 \qquad \text{11 subjects.}$$

This indicates that on de Finetti's definition, subjective probability would differ from objective probability in about 75% of the cases, and by over 20% about one-third of the cases. This, obviously, would be an unacceptable conclusion. All the subjects considered had advanced training in mathematics and statistics, and *it is out of the question* for one-third of them to have put the chance of drawing a given ball from an urn containing ten identical balls at a figure perceptibly different from 1/10. In fact, what de Finetti is considering, is neither objective probability nor a coefficient of likelihood or plausibility, but a coefficient which for clarity should be labelled a 'de Finetti coefficient', covering a concept which differs altogether from the concept of probability.

The same observation may be presented against the concept Savage designates as probability. Nothing proves, and everything invalidates the proposition that the coefficients implied by Savage's theory can be treated as if they were the *probabilities*, such as it was possible to define them after centuries of analysis of card and dice games and urn drawings.

In fact, there is no justification at all for Savage to refer to the coefficients his theory considers as probabilities.

This is another case in which a discussion of semantics is not futile, but *fundamental*. To repeat, *an essential principle of the scientific method is the use of a given word to mean one thing and one thing only.*

For very small sums, a probability of 1/6 is defined by de Finetti (and Savage) as the ratio of the equivalent certain value to the possible gain which has that probability.[174] For a person greatly averse to risk, this would mean putting the subjective probability of drawing a given ball among the six identical balls in an urn at well below 1/6 – for example 1/12. *This is completely unreasonable*, but the explanation is simple. De Finetti and Savage call the coefficient 1/12 a probability, *whereas it should in no way be identified with a probability.*

In reality, *even for a person whose Savage coefficient is* 1/12, *the subjective probability of extracting a given ball is rigorously equal to* 1/6, *if he is scientifically aware,*[175] *and in this specific case subjective probability will be identified with objective probability. The example considered above shows that probability as defined by de Finetti and Savage is neither objective nor subjective probability.* It is a coefficient that might be referred to as de Finetti or Savage's coefficient, and no more. It follows that *when the same word probability is used to designate three entirely different concepts*, namely, objective probability, subjective probability defined with respect to objective probability, and a coefficient labelled as *probability* by de Finetti and Savage, which cannot be identified with the two preceding concepts, *a scientific discussion becomes very difficult.*

Savage's theory is claimed *to enable probability and utility to be determined simultaneously.*[176] What it actually does is to assign the names *utility* and *probability*, respectively, to a neo-Bernoullian index $B(g)$ and a weighting coefficient designated arbitrarily as p. However, both are *mythical* concepts, and a method has yet to be found for the actual determination of the $B(g)$ indexes and the p weighting coefficients (which, to repeat, Savage has, with no justification at all, identified as utility and probability).

For any given person, this determination can only be made by analysing his answers to questions on determinate random choices. But there is no way to guarantee that the subject will attribute to the term 'probability' the meaning it is given in Savage's theory. If the convention were introduced that the two concepts Savage labels 'utility' and 'probability' should be referred to as B_s and P_s (the subscript s in honour of Savage's paternity), without recourse to any other concept or to any other words, it would very rapidly be seen that their determination is impossible.[177,178]

The above discussion shows clearly that the concept defined by de Finetti and Savage and which they call probability is really a coefficient which would take account *simultaneously* of subjective probability defined with respect to objective probability, and the degree of preference for security. It is not a probability, but a coefficient which should more aptly be named after de Finetti or Savage, depending on the case considered. *Neither author, however, devised a procedure for accurate and consistent measurement of the two coefficients they called 'utility' and 'probability'.*

In reality, cardinal utility as a means of expressing the intensity of preference should be derived directly, without reference to random choice. This effectively can be done, as the analysis of the 1952 experiment proves once and for all.[179] *Similarly, probability should only be defined in respect of events which can repeat themselves, and when the estimate can be subjected to empirical verification.*[180]

This is not to say that we cannot consider the random outcome of a given, or an infinite number of games,[181] but the basic probabilities must be objective probabilities in this case.

When cardinal utility is defined and measured directly with reference to the intensity of preference as disclosed from the answers to appropriate questions,[182] and probability with reference to frequency, as deduced *a priori* from the Laplace definition considering the ratio of the number of favourable to the number of equally possible cases under satisfactory conditions of symmetry (e.g. an *urn of reference*), or estimated *a posteriori* from actual data using a probability model, it becomes possible to discuss and observe the properties of fields of random choices.

Bernoulli actually based his formulation *on the weighting of psy-*

chological values (cardinal utilities) by objective probabilities. This was the right way. Outside this approach there is only confusion, and the use of refined mathematics is only a veil which *conceals and adulterates* both the real content of the *concrete* phenomena to be analysed, and the meaning and scope of the axiomatic theories proposed.

THE CONFUSION BETWEEN A SET OF SUCCESSIVE DRAWINGS OVER TIME AND THE REDUCTION TO A SINGLE RANDOM OUTCOME OF SUCCESSIVE DRAWINGS CONSIDERED AT A GIVEN TIME

30. Various kinds of confusion stem from the failure to reduce a sequence of successive random choices considered at a given time to a single random outcome. Samuelson committed this error early on.[183] This confusion is present in one form or another throughout the whole literature (Savage, Markowitz, Luce, Raïffa, Borch, etc.).[184]

If, for example, we consider N successive games whose gains and the corresponding probabilities are

$$g'_1, g'_2, \ldots, g'_n, p'_1, p'_2, \ldots, p'_n,$$

the decision at a given time to play N games depends on the consideration of the gains and the probabilities

$$g_1, g_2, \ldots, g_n, p_1, p_2, \ldots, p_n$$

corresponding to N unit games from the application of the two basic principles of total and compound probability, with allowance for the possibility of ruin during the course of the N games. *This is the only distribution which it is correct to consider in analysing the choice between alternative random outcomes.*[185,186,187]

THE CONFUSION BETWEEN THE CONCEPT OF RATIONALITY AND THE PRINCIPLE OF CONFORMITY WITH THE NEO-BERNOULLIAN PRINCIPLE

31. As far as I know, no supporter of the neo-Bernoullian formulation has given a definition of *rationality* which is independent of the axioms of the American School. Such a definition is necessary, however, in view of their justification of the neo-Bernoullian formulation in terms of its *rational* character.[188,189]

When we consider the whole literature on the subject, we can only be struck by the manner according to which rationality is defined. Thus in his 1952 paper, *Cardinal Utility*, Strotz writes:

The rationality of these axioms seemed self-evident, but we ought now explain just what the meaning of rational is. A test for the propriety of using the word rational here is the following. Consider any person not deemed insane who holds contradictory preferences such as those illustrated here. Imagine that we explain to this person the nature of the contradiction pointing out clearly how his preference violate our axioms. Will he in consequence of understanding the nature of the contradiction decide that his preferences are ill-founded and proceed to change them, or will he persist in his original preferences even though it is entirely clear to him exactly what precepts his preferences violate. If for nearly every person holding contradictory preferences an understanding of the character of the contradiction induces him to straighten out his preferences, then the von Neumann–Morgenstern axioms may properly be regarded as precepts of rational choice. My own feeling is that it would be a strange man indeed who would persist in violating these precepts once he understood clearly in what way he was violating them (p.393).

In fact, such a commentary results in defining rationality by the obedience to the axioms of the neo-Bernoullian theory.

In the same way Luce and Raïffa (*Games and Decisions*, 1957) write:[190]

A natural procedure, then, is ... to agree upon some consistency rules .... In this way a consistent pattern is imposed ... (p.24).

However, they nowhere state what the conditions for consistency are. In fact it all turns out to be circular reasoning. *Consistency* is defined with reference to the axioms, and the axioms are justified by the condition of *consistency*. They write further:

We then postulate that *of two alternatives ... a player ... will attempt to maximise expected utility* (Postulate IX). The logical quality of this postulate bears some consideration. We shall take it to be *entirely tautological in character* in the sense that the postulate does not describe behavior but it describes the word 'preference'. With this interpretation the problem is not to attempt to verify the postulate but rather to devise suitable empirical techniques to determine individual preferences .... To make applications it will be necessary to devise ways to determine these preferences *which satisfy* (IX) ... (p.50).

However, one seeks in vain for some discussion as to whether the postulate is effectively tautological. For that matter, what is a tautological postulate? If the words are taken in their ordinary meaning, a tautological postulate is one that means nothing. Then why bother stating it? In fact, it would still be necessary to show that the subject's field of choice can be consistently determined from his answers to different sets of questions.

Actually, there is nothing tautological about Postulate IX, and since it is equivalent to the neo-Bernoullian formulation, it can be tested against observed data. The results of the 1952 experiment refute it, for it is impossible to determine from the various series of questions a unique neo-Bernoullian index, whose mathematical expectation the operators would seek to measure.[191]

Again, Luce and Raïffa write:

Postulate IX is often described as a postulate of rational behavior. *This is all right provided only that one does not impute to rationality more than is contained in Postulate IX* (p.50).

This is tantamount to defining rationality as Postulate IX, and to be perfectly clear they should have added Postulate X: '*Rationality is behaviour consistent with Postulate IX*'. Actually, this definition of rationality in terms of obeying Postulate IX shows the highly restricted and relative sense in which the Luce and Raïffa concept of rationality must be interpreted. It is quite difficult to see any real content in the propositions put forward.

In his *Economics of Uncertainty* (1968) Karl Borch reverts constantly to the concept of rationality.[192] Thus he writes:

The idea that *intelligent* (*or rational*) people ought to make their decisions so that the mathematical expectation of the gain is maximized goes back to the beginning of probability theory (p.14); ... it is *natural* to assume that a *rational* person is indifferent as to whether his prospect is modified in this way or not (p.26); ... we then formulated three simple conditions which the rule ought to satisfy if it was to be acceptable to *intelligent logical people*... (p.27); This means that, since the mathematics is beyond doubt, the validity of the theorems must depend on the validity of the axioms, i.e., on whether *rational* decision-makers actually observe these axioms .... Axiom 3 assumes *some sophistication* on the part of the decision maker, *or at least that he understands the rudiments of probability theory*... (p.30); It is easy to see that this class of functions is not rich enough to represent all the preference orderings which we will admit as '*rational*'... (p.32); The decision rule (of the business man considered) is different from the rule derived from the Bernoulli Principle, and this should lead us to suspect trouble ...; this means that the decision rule, in spite of its intuitive appeal, *must contain some contradiction in the sense that it violates some of our three axioms* (p.39).

One of my correspondents (1975) expresses the same view

A necessary condition to qualify as rational is one has a mapping having the properties specified in the Ramsey–Savage Theory.

All these statements which repeatedly flow from the pens of the American School, are *pure assertions*, put up *without proof* and completely void of meaning *unless 'rationality'* is defined by reference to the axioms of the American School. However, there can be no doubt that the propositions:

(1) *Postulate*: the only rational behaviour is behaviour conforming to the axioms of the American School

(2) *Theorem*: anyone who does not conform to these axioms is irrational.

are empty of any real scientific content.[193]

Again, one of my correspondents writes to me:

I consider the definition of *'rationality'* as a rather uninteresting purely semantic question, and I think most mathematicians feel this way.... The questions are of course without interest to a mathematician, who feels free to define his concepts as he finds convenient.

I cannot agree with such a statement. This is more than mere semantics. The *only* justification advanced for the American School axioms is their alleged character of rationality. *If the concept of rationality has no real meaning, it should be dropped. If it has, that meaning should be made clear.*[194]

CHAPTER IV

CRITICISM OF THE ALLAIS 1952 ANALYSIS:
REJOINDERS

> The attitude of prejudice leads one to reject all
> that lies outside the frame of familiar assump-
> tions.
>
> ANDRÉ-MARIE AMPERE, 1823[195]

MY REFUTATION OF THE NEO-BERNOULLIAN FORMULATION
VIEWED BY THE PARTISANS OF THE AMERICAN SCHOOL

32. *A careful scrutiny of the criticisms addressed to my 1952 memoir
is of incontestable scientific interest, because it can throw much light
on certain especially difficult points in the general theory of random
choice. This is not a question of finding out who is right or wrong,
although that is not without scientific interest. It has to do with clear
perception of the crucial questions on which attention should focus.*

All the criticisms that I have seen, either adulterate the arguments I
set down in 1952, or involve paralogical reasoning. Nowhere is the
general theory I put forward in 1952 properly discussed, and in
general, the discussion of the 'Allais Paradox' has been limited to an
examination of only one of the illustrations I have given of my
general theory,[196] without referring in any way to the theory itself.[197]

On the whole, I think that most of the criticisms levied against my
theory have been concentrated on points of detail, and have failed to
address the core arguments of the 1952 presentation. In all cases, my
arguments have been truncated, and most of the time, my thinking
misinterpreted, as though better to be able to refute it.

These remarks apply in particular to the critical analysis of
Edwards (1954), Savage (1954), Luce and Raïffa (1957), Morlat (1957),
Fels (1959), Markowitz (1959), Suppes (1959), Morrisson (1967),
Borch (1968), and Raïffa (1968).[198]

The only general criticisms put forward have been those of Mor-

518

genstern and Amihud, presented in this volume. I believe my replies will help elucidate the debate. My own view is that the criticisms levied against my theory cannot be maintained. I am none the less very grateful for them, since they addressed essential questions, and that they provide an excellent summary statement of some widely-held opinions.

Although the voluminous correspondence I received in the 1950's contained a substantial number of suggestions and remarks, and although quite some circulation has been given to some examples I produced to illustrate my objections to the neo-Bernoullian formulation, my work has been subjected to very little critical analysis or follow-up in the literature, and that little often without precise reference. The fact that the 1952 memoir was not available in English may have had something to do with this, and doubtless also, my inability to publish the results of the 1952 experiment for many long years, by reason of the volume of work involved, as I have noted earlier.[199]

The dogmatism and the intolerance of *some* adherents of the American School, which has continued to dominate the academic world, may also account in part for the blanket of silence muffling a dissident view. It was Chamfort who said[200] *"Those who are right twenty four hours before the others are considered during twenty four hours as short on common sense"*. Change hours to years, and his remark still holds good.

I have often been told that I would end up as the lone voice defending an *untenable* position. However, I have always been able to count on some faithful supporters.[201] It is also significant that during twenty five years of teaching and with a very few exceptions, all my students, having reviewed all the facets of the question, took their stand against the conclusions of the American School. This shows that if the issues are presented without bias, the positions taken are very different from those in the literature.

Maybe I should stress that the *distinguishing feature of error is the belief that one is right*. It is therefore difficult to identify, at a given moment, what is '*truth*'. This remark applies to everything I have written on risk, but the reader will also agree that it applies to those who do not share my opinions, and in particular, the defenders of the neo-Bernoullian formulation. This general observation on the nature of error cannot but foster some caution.

Yet there are two criteria of truth: a criterion of apparent truth and a criterion of real truth. On the first, *apparent truth at a given time in a given place is the view held by public opinion, or, if the question is specialised, the experts' view.* Thus at the epoch of Galileo and Kepler, the apparent truth was that the earth stood still, and that the sun rotated about it. *The criterion of real truth is conformity with facts.* On this criterion it matters not that the majority believes in a certain apparent truth: the only effective test is the extent to which the theory put forward agrees with the facts. *This is the only criterion that can be used, no other, by he who would act scientifically.*[202]

Some, as it seems, have interpreted the non-publication of the results of the 1952 experiment as meaning that I had realised that my investigations in 1952 were based on an erroneous approach.[203] This is *as gratuitous* an assumption as the assumption of independence on which the theories of the American School are grounded. In my teaching proper as well as in my guest lectures, I have continued to maintain the same point of view since 1947. Be this as it may, had I changed my mind, I would have considered it my *absolute duty* to say so, and to state where I had found the error to lie.

CRITICISM OF MY PRESENTATION OF THE THEORIES OF THE AMERICAN SCHOOL

33. My presentation of the theories of the American School in 1952 gave rise to a number of different criticisms.

The American School or the Neo-Bernoullian School

33.1. I have often been told that the criticisms formulated in my 1952 study should have been addressed to the neo-Bernoullian school, not the American School. Thus one of my correspondents (1975) wrote to me:

I do not like the term 'Ecole américaine'. The 'Expected Utility Theorem' was proved by Frank Ramsey about 1925 and published in 1931, after his death. He saw the result as a direct continuation of Keynes' 'Treatise on Probability'. I find Ramsey's statement of the theorem, and his proof more attractive than that given by von Neumann in 1947. Ramsey's result is a special case of a more general theorem proved in 1954 by Savage, who gives most of the credit to Bruno de Finetti. In the book you are preparing for the *Theory and Decision Library*, I hope you will not give the Americans all the credit (or blame) for a theorem which is more European in its origin than most central results in mathematical economics.

In the light of these arguments, my first reaction was to adopt this point of view, and to replace the expression *'American School'* by *'Bernoullian School'*. However, on further reflection, the term Bernoullian School seemed less proper, for what Bernoulli said is far removed from the peremptory and dogmatic views of the American School.

May I recall here that for Daniel Bernoulli[204] *psychological value, i.e. cardinal utility, exists independently of the consideration of random outcomes; that he considered objective probabilities, and that his purpose was only to present a model which could explain the St. Petersburg Paradox; that he was perfectly aware that this model was not a general one; and that he did not attach any normative value to his formulation.* His application of his formulation to the St. Petersburg Paradox was fully reasonable, and he never claimed that this application could be considered as rational in all cases.[205]

Certainly, I might have chosen to refer to the *'neo-Bernoullian School'* (including Ramsey and de Finetti among others), but taking into account the *geographical centre of all the studies* over the past thirty years, I thought it more suitable to keep the reference to the *'American School'*. But I must say that I hesitated for some time before deciding to leave the title of the 1952 study stand.

The Axioms of the Theory of Games

33.2. Amihud (1974) reproaches me with having failed explicitly to criticise the axioms of the *Theory of Games*:

It follows that the subject of criticism should not be the expected utility proposition ... which is a well proven theorem ... but its underlying axioms. Yet it is hard to find out which one of those suggested by von Neumann and Morgenstern is considered incorrect by Allais. The much criticized axioms of independence and substitution are not necessary to establish the existence of a measurable utility (in the von Neumann–Morgenstern sense). Even when the substitution axiom is introduced by Herstein and Milnor (1953) – which enables them to drop the much criticized continuity axiom – it is introduced in a very weak form: If $u \sim v$ then for any $w, \frac{1}{2}u + \frac{1}{2}w \sim \frac{1}{2}v + \frac{1}{2}w$. This axiom is not subject to the criticism mounted against the independence axiom, nor is it sensitive to the threshold criticism.

It is true that the criticisms in my 1952 study were mainly addressed to the axioms in Savage's and Samuelson's theories,[206] but I could equally easily have made similar criticisms about von Neumann–Morgenstern's or Marschak's axioms, and did so in a paper which I read in 1951 at the Louvain Econometric Congress, which I have had no opportunity to publish.[207]

As I observed in that paper, the central axioms are von Neumann–Morgenstern's Axioms 3Ba and 3Bb[208] and Marschak's fourth, of which Samuelson's axiom is a variant; and as regards the *Theory of Games* the two axioms 3Ba and 3Bb are those which I consider as fundamentally incorrect. The Herstein/Milnor axiom cited by Amihud is *basically* of the same nature as Samuelson's axiom, and it carries the same implications of linearity and independence.

All these axioms exclude from the analysis what is really the fundamental component of the theory of random choice: the shape of the probability distribution of the psychological values associated with monetary gains. All these axioms are equivalent in the sense that they all lead to the same formulation

(1) $B(V) = \sum p_i B(g_i)$.

In fact this formulation which constitutes the core common to all the American theories, is valid only if the number of unit games is very large, and if the corresponding probability of ruin can be taken as negligible[209] and I fully share the view of Morgenstern (1974):

Now the von Neumann-Morgenstern utility theory, as any theory, is also only an approximation to an undoubtedly much richer and far more complicated reality than what the theory describes in a simple manner.

This statement by Morgenstern is of capital interest.[210] It implies that for Morgenstern himself the neo-Bernoullian formulation does not represent reality on essential points. *This theory, then, cannot be retained. The whole question is to determine what theory should be substituted for it.* My critics believe that it cannot be the one I put forward in my 1952 memoir. I hold the opposite belief. *That is what the debate is about.*

Morgenstern (1974) also writes:

Instead of merely postulating the existence of a number for the purposes of game theory, which we easily could have done, we decided that we could obtain one by looking at the basic fact of uncertainty and it took very little time to formulate our axioms and give the necessary motivation. The proof, that the axioms yield a number of the desired properties with some additional comment, was published only in the second edition of our work in 1947, although we naturally had the proof already in 1944 and even earlier. This theory is not a fundamental building stone for game theory, but it is, of course, most welcome.

Neither von Neumann nor I thought in the least that what we said would be the last word on preferences and utility. We did think, however, that it was nice to offer one of the first rigorous axiomatizations of a fundamental concept of economics. It is one of the great pleasures of my life that those few passages on utility theory we wrote have provided so much stimulus for others to concern themselves deeply and in a fresh manner with the notion of utility which is forever basic for any economic theory.

There can be no denying that the *Theory of Games* was extremely stimulating, and like many others – although probably for different reasons – I am grateful to Von Neumann and Morgenstern. But in my opinion it is not possible to claim that the axiomatic formulation of the *Theory of Games* of 1947 includes "the *basic* fact of uncertainty". The fundamental element of the theory of random choice is preference for security or for risk, and basically this has no place *whatever* in the neo-Bernoullian formulation.

This criticism is not intended to play down the importance of the *Theory of Games* in any way. Although I consider that its fundamental axioms are ungrounded, it provided precious stimulus for thought. From it streamed a steady flow of reflection, new theorising and empirical research, and despite the inhibiting effects of the brand of intolerant and antiscientific dogmatism to which it often gave rise, it was, on balance, a very useful contribution.

Alleged Bias in My Portrayal of the American School's Theories

33.3. Some writers have reproached me for an inadequate presentation of the theses of the American School.[211] May I simply point out that in my study, I set forth the American School's axioms in perfectly clear terms, and further, added examples to illustrate them. (See for instance my presentation of Samuelson's axiom in §§64 and 71 of my 1952 memoir.)

May I also return immediately to my critics the reproach they address to me. One seeks in vain in the analyses which have been made of my 1952 memoir for an accurate statement of the criticisms I presented there, and there is no way for the reader to obtain a valid and objective idea of my own theses from the accounts which have been made of them. Yet my 1952 memoir was preceded by a very clear summary of the twelve essential points. But my critics have given only a pale, distorted shadow of it when it has been taken up at all.[212]

In any case at the very time when the 'Allais Paradox' formed the subject of very numerous discussions, it is somewhat surprising that in over two decades no partisan of the American School envisaged to having the 1952 memoir translated into English, so placing at the disposal of the English-speaking reader the arguments on which rests the first and, to my knowledge, the most complete refutation of the theories of the American School. Is it not the condition of any progress in science to facilitate dialogue and to circulate dissident views?[213]

CRITICISMS BASED ON AN ERRONEOUS PRESENTATION OF MY ANALYSIS

34. Some writers have attributed a position to me which I do not hold. Amihud (1974), for example, writes:

The poor construction of Allais' theory is particularly apparent in that its scope is not defined at all. I shall relate to what he calls "l'élément spécifique de la psychologie du risque", namely the variance of the subjectively distorted probability distribution of the psychologically distorted monetary outcomes of a lottery. It is not clear what this proposition is based on. It does not have any theoretical ground, and its empirical support is very weak at best. Researchers in psychology have not been able yet to determine this one way or the other.

In fact I have never suggested that consideration of the variance of psychological values should be adopted as a normative rule. I simply stated[214] that the specific element of risk theory is the need to allow for the *shape* of the probability distribution of psychological values represented by the probability density $\bar{\psi}(\gamma)$ of these values, i.e., that the moments of all orders, and *in particular* but not exclusively the second moment, cannot be left out of account.

The examples which I have given pertaining to the variance of distributions are only illustrations of the general theory, *and I never said that they have general descriptive value, or that they could represent a normative rule*. In §58 of my memoir, for example, I investigated a psychological structure of the type $S = S(M, \Sigma)$ *only for Gaussian probability distributions*, case for which the principle of absolute preference is satisfied, and I have demonstrated that *in general* a trade-off $S = S(M, \Sigma)$ is not acceptable because it does not satisfy the axiom of absolute preference (Notes 83 and 84 of my 1952 memoir to which corresponds Appendix V of the English translation of the 1952 memoir). But the only object of doing so was to show that *the neo-Bernoullian formulation is much more restrictive than rationality need imply.*[215]

Amihud (1974) also writes:

In a review article, Edwards (1961) states that "variance preferences are necessarily confounded with utility, and skewness preferences with probability, for two alternative bets. So all research on variance preferences so far is ambiguous". Luce (1962) expresses that same opinion, and a more recent survey (Lee, 1971) confirms that "at the present time it is difficult to foresee whether the concepts 'variance and skewness preferences' have a useful future within decision theory", since the research results in this field may be adequately explained by using the expected utility (or subjective expected utility) theory (Lee, p.114).

Therefore it may be suspected that what Allais suggested will result in double-counting the effect of the variance of the monetary outcomes of a lottery: once through the distortion of the monetary values, and once through accounting directly for their variance.

Next to be asked is why Allais focuses only on the second moment of the subjectively distorted probability distribution of the psychologically distorted monetary outcomes of a lottery?

This assertion will seem rather astonishing to the reader who takes the trouble to refer to §21 (and the Notes 32, 33 and 34 to that section) of my 1952 study,[216] in which I emphasised the symmetry of the effects of elements I, III and IV of the psychology of risk, and stressed that the symmetry of the effects of the curvature of the index of psychological value and of its dispersion confused all the discussion.[217]

Amihud (1974) goes on:

It is also possible to show that some of the decision rules suggested by Allais are leading to conflicting choices. In one case, Allais suggests to choose between lotteries by the mean and variance of their outcomes, where preference is positively related to the first moment and negatively related to the second. In another case he suggests to choose by the mean and the probability of loss (the loss being greater than the gain), with positive and negative preference, respectively. Let us assume, then, two preference functions $S_1 = f(M - a\Sigma)$ $S_2 = g(M - bQ)$ where S is the "satisfaction" index, M is the mean, Σ^2 is the variance, Q is the probability of loss.

Again I can only repeat that I never proposed the formulations $S = f(M, \Sigma)$ or $S = g(M, P)$, where P represents the probability of ruin, as decision rules: they were intended only as examples to illustrate the general theory.[218] Thus, again the trade-off $S = f(M, \Sigma)$ was considered only for Gaussian probability distributions and to show that in this particular case the neo-Bernoullian formulation is much more restrictive than rationality need imply. As regards the compromise between mathematical expectation and the probability of ruin, all I said was that although *this compromise is in general incompatible with the Bernoulli formulation, it seems nevertheless impossible to view as irrational a person whose field of choice is based on it.* One of my correspondents (1975) has also written to me:

Luce and Raïffa dismiss your discussion of the dispersion as "a Common Fallacy" in 11 lines. You never answered such criticism, or developed your ideas.

In reality, the eleven-line refutation of "Fallacy 2" by Luce and Raïffa (1957, p.32), which my correspondent refers to has nothing to do with me, for *I have never claimed* that the index for a rational man must be of the form $S(M, \Sigma)$. I only asserted, and still assert, that a person whose index is represented by a function of this form cannot be considered as irrational, providing of course that his index satisfies the axiom of absolute preference (§58 of my 1952 memoir).[219]

But apart from this, Luce and Raïffa's *argument rests only on a paralogism* (like all the pseudo-demonstrations of the proponents of the American theories). They write:

This is a completely wrong interpretation of the utility notion . . . . It misses the point of utility theory. The principal result of utility theory for risk is that a linear index can be defined which reflects completely a person's preferences among the risky alternatives. If the fallacy actually made sense, then it would be a beautiful example to show that a utility theory is impossible (1957, p.32).

Actually, Luce and Raïffa forget a small detail. But it is an essential one. *The utility theory they mention is not universally accepted.*[220] It is a *highly specific* theory whose validity is tied to that of the axiom of independence on which it is based.[221] *If that axiom cannot be maintained, which it cannot, their reasoning collapses. And in any event, it would still remain to be shown that the index which Luce and Raïffa refer to as measuring utility actually represents utility.*[222]

NON-THEORY OR THEORY?

35. Many authors refuse to see my 1952 study as anything more than a series of counterexamples intended to refute the American School's theories, and some go so far as to deny that my analysis has the character of a positive theory of random choice. Best is, undoubtedly, to examine their arguments.

Morgenstern's Argument

35.1. Morgenstern (1974) writes:

Has [a] more refined system been developed since [the Theory of Games] and is it implied and used by Allais . . . ? In my view the answer is negative.

What has been done instead by Allais . . . can be characterized as an attempt to show *counterexamples which would conclusively demonstrate that individuals have a 'utility of gambling'* such that these examples would destroy the universal claim of the theory.

Regarding counterexamples: it is easy to falsify the statement 'all swans are white' by showing one black swan. But it is not as easy to contradict an axiomatic theory which fulfils all the requirements of such a theory, as ours does. Instead of generalities *one would expect that a new axiom be established* to be fitted into the existing system, however modified. Then a proof should be given for the type and kind of utility that the modified system defines . . . . Nothing of this seems to have been done.

It is necessary to realize that a modification and extension of a theory can only be made in the proper *domain* of the theory.

I want to make it absolutely clear that I believe – as von Neumann did – that *there may be a pleasure of gambling, of taking chances, a love of assuming risks, etc.* . . . . But what we did say and what I do feel I have to repeat even today after so many efforts have been made by so many learned men, is that the matter is still very elusive. I know of no axiomatic system worth its name that specifically incorporates a specific pleasure of utility of gambling together with a general theory of utility. Perhaps it will be offered tomorrow. I am not saying that it is impossible to achieve it in a scientifically rigorous manner. I am only saying (as we did in 1944) that this is a very deep matter. I would be delighted if one could go beyond *the instinctive feeling . . . which I share . . . that there is such an inclination towards, or aversion against, gambling and establish a rigorous theory.*

I consider that these assertions are not justified, and that they do not correspond to the theory I have presented in my 1952 memoir. Although that my theory was not formally presented as a sequence of axioms, *its axiomatic basis is evident.* It is based essentially on the five following axioms: existence of a system of probabilities, existence of an ordered field of choice, axiom of absolute preference, axiom of composition, existence of an index of psychological value,[223] and it allows for what I consider to be the fundamental element of risk, namely the distribution of psychological valuès around their mean.

Morgenstern (1974) further writes:

If our preferences are only partially ordered ... which means, grossly speaking, that they are in considerable disarray ... then there is no presently known guiding principle for optimal allocation. Yet we do hope to have one in our personal affairs and we struggle to come to one in social situations. This is achieved by decisions which *impose* a greater order and it is that system we are looking at when as economists we discuss preferences, orderings, etc....

We are thus at least several steps removed from the underlying reality. These facts seem to me to be more important that the question whether a possible utility of gambling has to be axiomatized, welcome though that would be.

This passage is at least very questionable. Our preferences vis-à-vis risk may be perfectly ordered, and representable by an index of preference

(1) $S = S(g_1, g_2, \ldots, g_n, p_1, p_2, \ldots, p_n),$

without having to impose greater order on them through postulates which would apply to all operators.

If, for example, I consider the index of preference

(2) $S = S(A, B, \ldots, C),$

for the certainly available consumer goods $A, B, \ldots, C$, the corresponding field of choice may be perfectly ordered without adding any further restriction which would be imposed on all subjects. John may prefer to drink Burgundy with his pepper steak, where Jack would prefer Bordeaux.[224] Similarly, an operator may violate the neo-Bernoullian formulation if he has a strong taste for either safety or risk; this does not necessarily lead him to be branded as irrational. In fact *there is no need to order the random choices of all subjects imposing determinate preferences on them according to a universally applicable axiomatic conception.*[225] *It would even be antiscientific to do so,* for the variety of psychological patterns cannot be eliminated.

Amihud's Argument

35.2. Amihud (1974) writes:

Now it may be that the set of axioms proposed by von Neumann and Morgenstern is not as general as Allais would like it to be. Yet, a more general formulation of the axioms *takes its toll in a poorer predictive power*, as is the case with Allais' theory. The determination of the trade-off between the generality of the theory and its precision is made so that it adequately explains those phenomena and problems which are of the greatest importance to the behavioral science practitioners.

I do not think that Allais' paradox can be considered to offer such a problem. It deals with a most unrealistic situation which has a very little relevance to the economics of uncertainty, for which the von Neumann–Morgenstern theory provides so well [See comments by Edwards (1954) and Borch (1968)].

These new arguments may also be questioned. It is true that the Allais theory of 1952 is less restrictive than that of von Neumann–Morgenstern, but the conclusion that its predictive power is weaker is false. The 1952 experiment yielded the results one would expect if it were true that *not a single respondent's decisions* were in line with the neo-Bernoullian formulation.[226] *Thus if I were to make a forecast for any one respondent picked at random, it would be that his showing for the 1952 Questionnaire as a whole would* be non-neo-Bernoullian; and my prediction would be better than Morgenstern's.

But this is not the real issue. The nub of the matter is that *the same person sampled twice over an interval of a few months will give the same answers to the same questions,*[227] and therefore that his behaviour can be predicted in the light of the Allais theory.

The same point applies here as for the theory of choice in general. If a person's index of preference is

$$(3) \qquad S = S(A, B, \ldots, C),$$

where $A, B, \ldots, C$ are certainly available goods, the only rationality constraint is that $(A_2, B_2, \ldots, C_2)$ will not be preferred to $(A_1, B_1, \ldots, C_1)$ if $A_2 < A_1, B_2 < B_1, \ldots, C_2 < C_1$. This is the axiom of absolute preference. *A priori*, the predictive power of the theory of choice will be very weak, but if a person's behaviour is kept under observation, it is generally possible to make consistent forecasts of his future behaviour. Some prefer their meat rare, others well done. There is no universal index of preference which can represent these different tastes, but if a subject has hitherto always ordered his steak underdone, he can be predicted to continue doing so. Amihud's error lies here.

As regards the alleged unrealistic nature of the examples I have presented, I can only repeat that there is no way to bring out the pseudo-evident nature of the axioms underlying the neo-Bernoullian formulation other than through extreme examples, i.e. cases in which the effects of complementarity become so important that few of those whose behaviour is investigated could deliberately ignore them.[228]

Amihud (1974) adds:

When we consider Allais' Foundation on its own merits, one thing emerges: While Allais' theory may describe *ex post* why choices between risky lotteries are made in a certain way, it fails to suggest a method to predict these choices *ex ante*; while it can explain any choice as 'rational', based on some psychological (or any other) consideration, it is exempted from the acid test of proving its predictive power as correct, and thus it is sheltered from any paradox.

Again these are very questionable assertions. As I noted above in my response to Morgenstern's arguments, it is true that *a priori* the Allais theory of 1952 cannot predict how a given person will react when confronted with a particular random choice; but no economist or psychologist on earth could forecast *a priori* whether a subject taken at random will prefer frankfurters or hot dogs. By contrast, and this experiment was carried out, when surveyed at intervals of six months, the respondents' answers to the same questions relative to given random choices were perfectly consistent.

At all events on the basis of the Allais theory it is possible to predict that in almost every case it is impossible to find an index capable of representing in conformity with the neo-Bernoullian formulation the random choices made by subjects selected at random for different sets of questions. My analysis of replies to the 1952 Questionnaire enables me to advance this proposition in all certitude [see below Appendix C, Sections III, IV and V].

A General View

35.3. These various arguments are taken up very clearly by one of my correspondents (1975) as follows:

You write that your paper from 1952 "*permet* de fonder une théorie complète . . .". This may be correct, but it is a statement which requires a proof. I cannot see that you have proved this statement anywhere in your published work.

The two assumptions or axioms, (i) there exists a function $V = V(g_1, \ldots, g_n, p_1, \ldots, p_n)$, and (ii) Préférence absolue, do *not constitute a theory*. You must *assume something more*; at least about the shape of the function. I cannot see that you ever have been precise on this point.

I do not think your "*Fondements d'une théorie positive...*" gives a complete theory, although as you say it "No theory without theorems" and an experimental scientist will call a theory void, unless it contains some conclusions which can be refuted by experiments or observations. Your 'theory' contains neither theorems nor refutable statements.

On the other hand, you have designed some experiments to refute the Bernoulli Principle, and this has led to a valuable discussion of the 'Allais Paradox'. This is a negative result and not a positive theory . . . .

My frank opinion can at present be summarized as follows:

(i) Your criticism of the Bernoulli Principle has been extremely successful. It has led to widespread and seminal discussion, and it may be the direct cause of many reformulations and generalizations in decision theory. I hope the book which you edit for the *Theory and Decision Library* will contain a broad survey of this movement, which you started single-handed.

(ii) *Your attempts to create a new positive theory have so far come to nothing.* I hope your new book will give us this complete theory formulated with full logical rigor, or alternatively a clear statement that no theory can be built on your "Fondements".

This argument has the advantage of permitting a discussion of essential points:

(a) First, a theory would be void if it contains no conclusions which experience or observation may refute. Milton Friedman had already made this point in my 1950 seminar, and I discussed it in §44 of my 1952 memoir.[229] *I cannot but maintain now the analysis I presented then.* Friedman's objection cannot be sustained at all.

In fact the question is not as simple as it appears at the outset. To convince us, let us consider N successive drawings (with replacement) made by different blind persons from a reference urn containing an equal number of white and black balls. The probability of drawing a white ball is 1/2. Nevertheless, *whatever the frequency f_N of drawing a white ball in the course of the N drawings, it will be compatible with the theory.* In the case considered, the proposition that the probability is one half cannot hence be contradicted. Yet who would deduce that the theory of probabilities has no scientific value?

Let us also examine two theories, one that the earth is a sphere, the other that it is a spheroid. The first can be contradicted by facts and it is false. The second which is much more general cannot be contradicted by facts and it is true. Can it be contended that the first theory alone is scientific?

The example of the traditional theory of choice given in my 1952 memoir is in fact entirely decisive. This theory considers functions of indifference $S = S(A, B, \ldots, C)$ which are not otherwise specified. *This theory cannot be misproven by observation since it is effectively capable of representing all the psychologies.* No-one can, however, conceive of discarding it merely for the one reason that being very general it is compatible with every psychology. The same holds true for my random choice theory which is based on a very general index of preference $S = S(g_1, g_2, \ldots, g_n, p_1, p_2, \ldots, p_n)$.

(b) Secondly, it is inaccurate to claim that I have nowhere specified the properties of the function $V = V(g_1, g_2, \ldots, g_n, p_1, p_2, \ldots, p_n)$. They have indeed been discussed.[230] If it has only been possible to specify these properties in very general form, this is because fields of random choice are complex, an aspect of reality that cannot be eliminated.[231] Further, my study proves some important theorems bearing on the implications for the neo-Bernoullian theory of the general theory which I presented.[232]

(c) Thirdly, as I have already indicated, the analysis presented in 1952 led to the development of a Questionnaire which led to some extremely important results and *permitted the formulation of predictions of the behaviour of subjects faced with uncertainty which were fully borne out by the answers to the survey.*[233] Thus, it is difficult to maintain that this is an empty theory.

(d) Finally, my correspondent suggests that my theory is not restrictive enough. But this is a somewhat strange criticism. *If, precisely, the neo-Bernoullian School's theories are open to criticism, it is for the very reason that they are unduly restrictive, and utterly distort reality in a manner that cannot be justified.* The neo-Bernoullian theories are too simple, not to say too simplistic, for the complexity of the reality they purport to represent. I cannot agree more that in general the simpler the theory, the better it is: I have argued this many times.[234] *But simplicity is only one of the conditions a theory must satisfy to be acceptable. The prime condition for its validity is its agreement with the facts.* From this standpoint, a good theory should offer a good description of nature. It is somewhat strange for a scientist to brand a theory as inadequately deductive and overly descriptive if, with a minimum of assumptions, it is capable of offering a good portrayal of observed facts.

The formulation of the psychology of risk which I set forth in 1952 is in precise terms. It is logical and consistent mathematically. But its postulates are much less restrictive than those underlying the theories of the American School. Some critics do not admit this; however, any restrictions imposed on it, such as the conformity to the neo-Bernoullian principle, would involve a serious distortion of reality, and it would lose its scientific validity. This is precisely the difficulty with the neo-Bernoullian theories. *They may be fascinating from a mathematical point of view, but they offer no scientific interest in terms of a better understanding of reality.*

I am not a professional mathematician. Mathematics interests me and I use it as far, and only as far, as it constitutes *a tool to further our understanding of natural phenomena.*

INTERPRETATION OF THE SO-CALLED 'ALLAIS PARADOX'

36. The counterexample relating to Savage's theory which I gave in my 1952 memoir[235] generated endless discussion in the United States, and has become known as the 'Allais Paradox'.[236] For many subjects, it turned out to be decisive.[237] The proponents of the neo-Bernoullian formulation have tried to explain it away in terms of *'errors'* committed by the subjects, *'inadequate reflection'*, or *'insufficient information'*. The best course is to set forth their arguments.[238]

Savage's Argument

36.1 During the 1952 Paris Colloquium, I had Savage respond over lunch to a list of some 20 questions. His answer to each was incompatible with the basic axioms of his own theory. He was immediately troubled, and asked for time to think. A week later he told me that his reactions during our lunch conversation had indeed run counter to his own axioms, but that after further reflection, he had concluded that his responses, contrary to his axioms, were explained by the fact that he had behaved irrationally. Thus, he defined rationality by his axioms, and he judged his answers irrational because they infringed the axioms!

The explanation he presented two years later, in his *Foundations of Statistics* (1954), in the section devoted to discussion of the counterexample to his theory which I had published in §63 of my 1952 memoir,[239] is as follows:

Savage considers the Table I (p.103, Savage 1954), corresponding to my counterexample, in which the 1952 french francs have been converted to dollars on the basis of one dollar for 200 francs.

TABLE I

Prizes in Units of $100,000 in a lottery realizing Gambling 1–4
(Situations A, B, C and D)

		Ticket Number		
		1	2–11	12–100
Situation 1 (First Choice)	Gamble I (Situation A)	5	5	5
	Gamble 2 (Situation B)	0	25	5
Situation 2 (Second Choice)	Gamble 3 (Situation C)	5	5	0
	Gamble 4 (Situation D)	0	25	0

Savage starts by admitting that his immediate reaction was to prefer situation A to B, while preferring situation D to C, which contradicts his own principle. He contends, however, that it would be an error to maintain these preferences. To correct it, he presents the following line of reasoning (pp.102–103):

To illustrate, let me record my own reactions to the example with which this heading was introduced. When the two situations were first presented, I immediately expressed preference for gamble 1 (Allais' situation A) as opposed to gamble 2 (Allais' situation B) and for gamble 4 (Allais' situation D) as opposed to gamble 3 (Allais' situation C), and I still feel an intuitive attraction to these preferences. But I have since accepted the following way of looking at the two situations, which amounts to repeated use of the sure thing principle.

One way in which situations A, B, C, D (Gambles 1–4) could be realised is by a lottery with a hundred numbered tickets and with prizes according to the schedule shown in Table I.

Now, if one of the tickets numbered from 12 through 100 is drawn, it will not matter, in either situation, which gamble I choose. I therefore focus on the possibility that one of the tickets numbered from 1 through 11 will be drawn, in which case situations 1 and 2 are exactly parallel. The subsidiary decision depends in both situations on whether I would sell an outright gift of $500,000 for a 10 to 1 chance to win $2,500,000. A conclusion that I think has a claim to universality, or objectivity. Finally, consulting my purely personal taste, I find that I would prefer the gift of $500,000 and, accordingly, that I prefer Gamble 1 to Gamble 2 and (contrary to my initial reaction) Gamble 3 to Gamble 4.

It seems to me that in reversing my preference between Gambles 3 and 4 *I have corrected an error. There is, of course, an important sense in which preferences, being entirely subjective, cannot be in error: but in a different, more subtle sense they can be.*[240]

The reasoning Savage deploys to correct his "error" is *fundamentally the same* used by Samuelson in 1952 when he put forward the very appealing postulate (at least at first sight) which I subjected to critical analysis in §64 of my 1952 memoir. As I showed there, *Samuelson's reasoning reduces to the destruction of the complementarity effect which, for a great many persons, may exist in the neighbourhood of certainty.*

Be this as it may, Savage presents my counterexample without saying a word about the general theory on which it is based, and likewise is silent as to my critical analysis in 1952 of Samuelson's reasoning (§64), although his own new argument is fundamentally the same as that put forward by Samuelson in 1952. Thus Amihud (1974) is wrong in writing:

The same holds for the reformulation of Allais' experiment by Savage, who ultimately corrected his choice, *having recognized his mistake.* It is regrettable that Allais does not discuss these reformulations of his famous experiment, nor that he confronts their arguments with his,

for the refutation of Savage's argument was already presented in my 1952 study (§64, *Choices in the neighbourhood of certainty undermining Samuelson's Substitutability Principle*) since, as indicated above, Savage's reasoning is fundamentally the same used by Samuelson.[241]

In fact, Savage's *reformulation* of my counterexample has no value at all, as it changes the nature of the problem completely, eliminating – as did Samuelson – the complementarity effect operating in the neighbourhood of certainty.[242] It is no surprise that MacCrimmon (1968) did not find consistent answers to my counterexample, in its original version and as *reformulated* by Savage. MacCrimmon and Larsson's paper (1975) in this book is also very suggestive.

To say, as Amihud (1974) does, that:

The reason for answers to be in disagreement with the von Neumann–Morgenstern axioms is *laziness or difficulties in computing which result in mistakes* is a purely gratuitous affirmation. I could just as validly suggest that when there is agreement with these axioms, the reason is *laziness or difficulties in computing, which result in mistakes.*[243]

The same observations apply integrally, and with practically *no change*, to the reasoning of Markowitz (1959) (pp.218–224)[244] and Raïffa, 1970 (Chapter IV, Section 9).[245,246,247]

Morgenstern's Argument

36.2. Morgenstern (1974) writes:

This also takes care of the matter whether those questioned would *"correct"* their behavior if it were pointed out to them that they "act" in violation of the expected utility hypothesis. That theory, as formulated by the von Neumann–Morgenstern axioms, is normative in the sense that the theory is *"absolutely convincing"* which implies that men will act accordingly. *If they deviate from the theory, an explanation of the theory and of their deviation will cause them to re-adjust their behavior.* This is similar to the man who tries to build a *perpetuum mobile* and then is shown that this will never be possible. Hence, on understanding the underlying physical theory, he will give up the vain effort. *Naturally, it is assumed that the individuals are accessible intellectually whether it be physics or utility that is being explained to them.* In that sense there is a limitation since there are certainly persons for whom this is impossible. *Whether they then should be called "irrational" is a matter of taste.*

In a Colloquium regularly held at New York University, students who however were well versed in the von Neumann–Morgenstern theory, were exposed to several of the same experiments made by Allais . . . . The result was that they conformed immediately and exactly to the expected utility hypothesis, quite differently from the school teachers. Was this due to their familiarity with the theory? Or did they not enjoy the uncertainty? . . . Were the persons used in the experiments made by Allais . . . equally capable of calculating properly and also aware that the millions of francs and crowns were not forthcoming? Did they *know* what problem the experiments wanted to settle?

I need simply state that those questioned in the 1952 survey were perfectly aware of the meaning of the questions which were put during my seminar (June 11th, 1952) of the *National Center of Scientific Research*, at which Savage himself was present and had the opportunity to make his views known.[248]

By contrast, I must again stress that *my argument, whenever presented by a proponent of the neo-Bernoullian formulation, has invariably been truncated and voided of its real substance.* For instance, consider the illustration I gave to invalidate Samuelson's axiom, so appealing at first sight,[249] according to which the condition

$$(P_1) < (P_2)$$

entails

$$(P'_1) \equiv \alpha(P_1) + (1 - \alpha)(P_3) < (P'_2) \equiv \alpha(P_2) + (1 - \alpha)(P_3),$$

whatever the values of α and (P_3). I stressed that this axiom is equivalent to the assumption that "the order of preference as between (P_1) and (P_2) is unaffected by being compounded with any outcome (P_3) whatever", which "clearly implies that there is no complementarity effect which could reverse this order of preference".[250] I noted that "given this observation, it is easy to find examples of men who, although considered as rational, exhibit behaviour violating this axiom", and that "*it is enough to find cases* in which (P_3) taken in conjunction with (P_1) and (P_2) has different effects of complementarity (or non-complementarity) which can change the order of preference".[251] I then illustrated this by an example which many commentators have cited;[252] *but the utterly fundamental argument, given in full in my 1952 memoir (that there is a complementarity effect in the neighbourhood of certainty) and of which the example given was a mere illustration, has to the best of my knowledge never been reproduced by these same commentators.* Thus the term "*complementarity effect*" does not figure in any of the critical analyses of Savage (1954), Fels (1959), Markowitz (1959), Suppes (1959), Borch (1968), Raïffa (1968). Yet this is one of the fundamental points of my criticism of the neo-Bernoullian theories.[253]

Their approach is indeed somewhat astonishing. They present only the numerical example, and merely show that it is incompatible with Samuelson's axiom, which is so appealing at first sight; but they do not show why it calls for criticism, i.e. they pass over my basic argument in silence, *while the example, which is only a specific illustration of a general theory, is pinpointed as a wayward curiosity concealing an "error" which is easily brought to light.* This way of doing things is not compatible *with the requirements of scientific method.* In any case, by omitting reference to the general theory of which the example is but an illustration, the proponents of the American School rendered the example difficult to understand, and therefore "*paradoxical*".

The same observations could be presented concerning the comments of my critics on the illustration I gave in my 1952 memoir (§63) to refute Savage's axiom (Allais' Paradox). One searches in vain in

Savage's book for the least allusion to my argument founded on the consideration of the complementarity effect.

As regards *"rationality"* or *"irrationality"* being *"a matter of taste"*, this is a pure assertion. That some prefer carrots to cabbage is a matter of taste, but the assertion that weight does not exist is beyond the bounds of taste. *In the field of the psychology of uncertainty, he who makes a claim which can be proved to overlook an important characteristic of risk phenomena, is in the same position as he who affirms that weight does not exist.*

Morgenstern (1974) adds:

The frequent remarks about this or that decision as being "rational" or not are also open to doubt. For example, in game theory one does not start out with an idea of "rationality"; rather, that is a concept to be *derived* and given meaning to from the theory. One merely assumes that the players prefer a greater payoff to a lesser one. But the behavior necessary to achieve this is deduced from the theory. Similarly here: there is no *a priori* notion of "rational" that could be used in describing the action of an individual of whom one does not know in advance whether he is risk-averse or not. If he is, one kind of action is indicated; if he is not, another one. Only then could one say – if one has a theory! – whether the individual was acting rationally. *After all even a risk-averter can make mistakes!"*

But the whole point is that if *one observes* that in the examples considered in my 1952 memoir,[254] a subject exhibits a behavior contrary to the neo-Bernoullian formulation, it is perfectly impossible to say that *"he makes mistakes"*, since, precisely according to Morgenstern, error can only be established in relation to rationality defined in terms of conformity with neo-Bernoullian theory.[255]

On the consideration of large sums and small probabilities, Morgenstern (1974) writes:

Besides this difficulty of exposing individuals to almost unrecognizably small probabilities there is added another one. And it is difficult to say which is more formidable: that is the matter of the objects which are being offered: Millions, even tens of millions of Norwegian crowns, French francs or even dollars. The chances are offered to school teachers,... or to otherwise not specified persons, but presumably ordinary (economically speaking) individuals who do not normally, if ever, contemplate to come into possession of millions! This then corresponds to letting bodies move with speeds approaching that of light, thereby going far beyond the limits of classical mechanics, as mentioned above.

At first sight, this argument may appear as irresistible. However, since according to me the neo-Bernoullian formulation yields a very valuable approximation when the sums involved are small in relation to a person's capital, and when the number of games is large (but not for a single game),[256] *the only way* to demonstrate that neo-Bernoullian behaviour would be irrational in a large number of cases is to identify extreme cases relating to large sums, with probabilities close to either zero or unity. *These are precisely the cases in which the complementarity effect may become very important.* If this irrationality of the neo-Bernoullian formulation, at least for some subjects, may become absolutely evident in some extreme cases, this means that there are many instances, *which are not necessarily extreme cases,* in which the neo-Bernoullian formulation is inapplicable. This approach is equivalent to the *reductio ad absurdum* proof which plays such a large role in mathematics.

At all events, the 1952 experiment[257] shows that *answers were consistent* when the sums involved were less than a hundred times the respondent's capital, with an error of only a few percentage points; and the answers given on follow-up questioning a few months later were practically the same.[258] During the 1952 Colloquium in Paris, Savage himself was able to answer questions involving very large sums and small probabilities (see §36.1 above).

However, *behavioral inconsistency with the neo-Bernoullian formulation is not limited to large sums and small probabilities.* As the 1952 experiment showed, a person who is not generally considered as irrational, faced with a single, non-renewable choice, may well take ten dollars in cash rather than gamble on an even chance of winning $22 or nothing (See also §29 above).

Amihud's Argument

36.3. Amihud (1974) writes:

[The von Neumann–Morgenstern axiom 3Cb] may look rather like an algebraic identity, but as a behavioral axiom it implies the exclusion of the "utility of gambling", i.e., it is irrelevant whether a lottery is presented in two stages or in one, provided the (compounded) probabilities of the final outcomes remain the same. A violation may occur when the individual draws a certain pleasure from the particular structure of the lottery....

But, if no preference for any particular form is admitted ... as is the case in Allais's experiment – what accounts for the violation? *The reason may be a mistake arising from difficulty in calculations or laziness.* If it was not so, the individuals who chose in an inconsistent manner would not have reversed their initial choices after being presented with a detailed breakdown of the lottery, as happened in Markowitz's, Savage's and MacCrimmon's cases.

Amihud here takes up the point of view of von Neumann and Morgenstern which is broadly admitted in the literature following the *Theory of Games*. However as a matter of fact *the crucial axiom is not 3Cb, but 3Ba and 3Bb*.[259]

But more fundamentally, as I explained abundantly in 1952, and have repeated above, there is in fact no computing error, and still less laziness at all. There is, quite simply, *a complementarity effect* which may entirely disappear if the random process is realized at two successive stages, and if for the second drawing, the subject knows the result of the first.[260]

If in the case of Savage, Markowitz and MacCrimmon, the subjects reversed their initial choices, the reason why was simply that *they realised that these choices violated the axioms of the neo-Bernoullian formulation, whereas they had postulated that these axioms defined rationality.* No more, no less. To say it yet again, *this postulate remains to be justified, and its pseudo-obvious character is unmasked immediately a subject has been enlightened as to the effects of complementarity.*

About my apologue of the traveller from Marseille,[261] Amihud (1974) writes:

It may be wrong to infer from the individual's choice in one situation to his choice in another, if he himself does not consider the situations as equivalent and if he does not claim to employ the same set of rules in each of them . . . .

Formally, this has been known in the American school as the 'state preference approach'. This theory states that the individual may not possess a unique von Neumann–Morgenstern utility function for money, but his utility is contingent upon the different "states of the world". Moreover, in each state of the world, the von Neumann–Morgenstern utility function (being homogeneous up to a linear transformation) can be expressed such that $U_k(L_k) = 0$, $U_k(M_k) = 1$, where L_k is the maximum loss in state k, and M_k is the maximum gain in that state.

This approach then, 'exempts' the individual from consistency of preferences between states, but requires such a consistency within each state. This may explain the *inconsistencies* cited by Allais, and it may also account for his famous paradox.

This passage is ambiguous, and could cause confusion. It may mean that the neo-Bernoullian index deduced from the American theories is not necessarily identical for the same subject considered at different times and in different circumstances. Alternatively, it may mean that there may be a series of different indexes for the same individual at a given moment.

If the first interpretation is right, the existence of different indexes at different times offers no explanation of the so-called '*inconsistencies*' demonstrated by Allais in 1952. If the second interpretation is intended, it is *unsustainable*. Whatever their specific approaches, all the theories of the American School *demonstrate the existence of a unique neo-Bernoullian index at a given moment of time*, with a corresponding determinate field of random choice. In fact, the solution proposed by Morrisson (1967), based on the subject's "asset position",[262] which Amihud considers as "in agreement with the von Neumann–Morgenstern theory", *could only provide an explanation if the second interpretation is adopted, and this would be altogether unacceptable.*

Certainly, Morrisson's final position is not as radical as Amihud suggests somewhat too hastily it seems. As a matter of fact Morrisson ends his article with the following comment:

This paper is not meant as a solution to Allais's paradox; in fact it is not at all obvious that one *correct* decision rule even exists for this problem. Instead, a new way of looking at the Allais lotteries has been presented, indicating that a subject's asset position should be explicitly included in any set of axioms that purport to define *normative or rational behavior*. Finally, it must be concluded that Allais' paradox offers an interesting 'proving ground' for theories of optimal decision making, especially when the possible outcomes may completely change a person's way of life.

DOUBTS REGARDING THE VALIDITY OF THE 1952 EXPERIMENT AND THE ANALYSIS OF THE REPLIES

37. Some writers have cast doubts on the validity of my 1952 Questionnaire. Morgenstern (1974) writes:[263]

The point that for testing individuals – for anything! – in regard to a possible preference for gambling, one has to consider situations within their normal experience and not outlandish situations, was already made by W. Edwards. *This eminent psychologist spoke from the basis of an experience with experiments which it is indispensable to have but which, as far as I know, may not be possessed by ... Allais ....* It is, of course, much to be welcomed that one even wishes to experiment in economics, where this is a much neglected field. It is interesting, however, that there are even supporters of the von Neumann–Morgenstern theory who discuss such hypothetical situations (in order to reject Allais' structures). One of them is Markowitz in his valuable book on portfolio selection.

From Morgenstern this argument is somewhat unexpected, for it is a straight appeal to established authority. I will limit my comment to Pareto's observation that, to a large extent, the history of science reduces to the history of the mistakes of 'competent' men.[264] It is astonishing, to say the least, that a mind as open as Morgenstern's should make such a peremptory judgment of a Questionnaire of which all the details had been published in January 1953 in the *Journal de la Société Statistique de Paris*, but whose underlying theory and findings had not yet been published at the time he was writing.

Amihud (1974) makes a like point:

The problem of ill-constructed and poorly controlled psychological experiments which claim to test for one effect but actually test for another is well known. It may be suspected that Allais' experiment which led to the paradox is just of that kind: What does it test for, finess of perception, or consistency (in the von Neumann and Morgenstern sense)? Or, it may be claimed that its first part presents the individual with entirely different situations than the second one, or at least make him perceive so. Then, the individual uses different preferences in each part, and inconsistencies arise.* [*It is to be assumed that the individual's preference are in accordance with the von Neumann–Morgenstern axioms].

The assertion that my 1952 Questionnaire was ill-constructed remains to be proved. As of now, *very remarkable* results have been yielded by the analysis carried out so far.[265]

As far as the 'inconsistencies' are concerned, they can appear only if it is assumed that the respondents' preferences are in accordance with the von Neumann–Morgenstern axioms; but there are no more inconsistencies if this assumption is not retained, and experience proves that in general it cannot be retained.
Morgenstern (1974) adds.

One should now point out that the domain of our axioms on utility theory is also restricted. Perhaps we should have pointed that out, instead of assuming that this would be understood *ab ovo*. For example the probabilities used must be within certain plausible ranges and not go to 0.01 or even less to 0.001, then to be compared to other equally tiny numbers such as 0.02, etc. Rather one imagines that a normal individual would have some intuition of what 50 : 50 or 25 : 75 means etc. Naturally, one may *postulate* that he might be able to calculate correctly. But then this need and ability must be introduced explicitly into the experiments, yet this has not been done by the critics.

The least that can be said about this last comment on the part of Morgenstern is that it is surprising. The von Neumann–Morgenstern theory *is presented as a general theory.* It carries no restrictions as to its range of applicability. In fact there would be no point in putting forward a highly refined theory implying in particular the principle of compound probabilities were one to suppose that the subjects were not capable of having a precise idea of a probability of one hundredth. What can statistical tests based on *significance levels* mean, if we must understand that those who use them could have no accurate idea of what a probability of 1/100 implies? At all events the replies to the 1952 Questionnaire displayed a high degree of consistency (see Sections II, III, IV and V of Appendix C below).

CRITICISMS OF MY CONCEPTION OF RATIONALITY

38. My conception of rationality has been criticised by Amihud (1974). He writes:[266]

Much of the criticism of Allais against the von Neumann–Morgenstern expected utility theory is based on examples of choices which may be generally considered as rational but (according to Allais) will be labeled as irrational by the expected utility theory which, he believes, proposes that "un homme rationnel doit se conformer à la formulation de Bernoulli". This is an erroneous interpretation. The theory merely claims that *if* in a certain situation, given a choice between certain lotteries, *an individual agrees that his behavior is in accordance with the von Neumann–Morgenstern axioms – then an inconsistency in choices may be pointed out as irrational.* Or, as Morgenstern put it: "Consider an individual who *professes to possess* a utility function *as described by the von Neumann–Morgenstern axioms of expected utility.* If it is shown to him that in his actual behavior he deviates from that function, *the theory, being absolutely convincing,* will tell him how he should modify his behavior in order to conform to his own chosen preference system".

Clearly, any observation of any pattern of choice whatsoever is insufficient by itself to determine rationality (or irrationality). Irrationality is rather a *result* of an action taken by an individual *who has agreed to accept this particular definition of rationality.*

This passage can mean only one thing: that rationality is defined as conformity with the axioms of the *Theory of Games.* But if rationality is indeed defined as subservience to the neo-Bernoullian axioms, there is no longer anything to discuss.

Yet, it seems, Morgenstern does not appear to have fallen into this trap, at least if one refers to the text of the Morgenstern (1972) article from which Amihud cites an altogether insufficient extract. This is what Morgenstern actually says about the use of a theory:[267]

If the individual, for example, expresses the desire to behave 'optimally' in a specific situation or environment, the theory will tell him how he *ought* to behave. *The individual will then follow this advice if the theory is 'absolutely convincing'. This 'convincing' means the intellectual (and practical) acceptance of the theory for its predictive worth.* The individual, or agent (e.g. the government) has to understand the theory in order to develop this degree of confidence. Only then will he allow his behavior to be guided, and possibly be changed by the theory. It is assumed, of course that the theory in question is sufficiently specific to be able to guide behavior. Few theories in the social sciences have reached this state . . . .

He goes on to say what '*absolutely convincing*' means when applied to the neo-Bernoullian formulation:

The 'convincing' is equivalent to the conviction of a mathematical calculation in which mistakes can be pointed out. The person having calculated wrongly will acknowledge and correct the mistakes because the computing procedures are completely convincing.

  This is the manner in which *any* descriptive theory can be interpreted as being 'normative'. This normative property is based on the acceptance of the theory. There is thus no conflict with the above statements about the relations of 'ought' and 'is' propositions, i.e., that neither type follows from the other.[268]

It could not have been better said. *To act as a normative guide, a theory must be accepted as valid.*

If I am given the opportunity to play 10,000 games each involving a sum that is negligible in relation to my capital, the best rule I can apply is the mathematical expectation of monetary values.[269] For the operation of the law of large numbers, *the theoretical consequence* of probability theory, which has been verified in every experiment carried out to this day, will lead me certainly, as this word must be understood in probability theory, to achieve a preferable situation.

However, if the choices before me correspond to my refutation of Samuelson's substitutability axiom,[270] I can be rational by acting in violation of the neo-Bernoullian formulation, because Allais' 1952 theory has enlightened me as to the mistake I would really make, if I am prudent, by neglecting the complementarity effect in the neighbourhood of certainty, and also because most people who are both prudent and generally considered as rational would likewise act in violation of this principle.

It is *entirely legitimate,* as indicated by Morgenstern, to define rationality by the consistency of the principles which are admitted and the decisions taken. *This is moreover the abstract definition of rationality which I gave in my* 1952 *memoir* (§52) and which in my view implies: (A) the pursuit of self-coherent means, and (B) the use of means appropriate to the ends pursued. From the standpoint of my theory, conditions (A) and (B) themselves imply: (a) that the range of choices be ordered; (b) that the axiom of absolute preference be respected; and (c) that objective probabilities be considered. In my opinion they imply nothing more.

But precisely the whole question is to know which theory – the neo-Bernoullian formulation or the 1952 Allais theory – *should be adopted.* Since, according to Morgenstern, rationality should be defined, and here I am in total agreement with him, by the consistency between the axioms admitted and the random choices made, it follows that the axioms themselves cannot be justified in the name of rationality unless they may be logically deduced from other axioms, themselves possessing the character of evidence. Such is precisely the case for propositions (a), (b) and (c) of my theory which may be deduced from propositions (A) and (B) above. However, such is not the case for Principles 3Ba and 3Bb of the *Theory of Games* which do not in themselves present any character of evidence (see §A6 below) and which cannot be deducted from other general propositions such as propositions (A) and (B) above.

Amihud (1974) also writes:

On the other hand, Allais defines rationality as either the criterion of 'internal consistency', implying the coherence of desired ends and the use of appropriate means for attaining them; *or,* the observed behavior of 'people who can be regarded as acting in a rational way'. This definition is subjective and may be wrong. Is rationality synonymous with 'normality'? Is it defined statistically? In an experiment cited below, a group of business executives presented with Allais' paradox was split almost evenly in their answers; who, then, is rational and who is not? Moreover, it can be shown that there are rational types of behavior (in Allais' sense) which do not obey his basic axiom of absolute preference. Consider a man who gambles against his good friend and wants to let him win. He is perfectly rational by Allais' definition, yet he intentionally does not choose the lottery which yields the greatest gain for all possible outcomes, thus violating the axiom of absolute preference. Is he rational or is he not?[271]

This argument proves absolutely nothing. First, I have never suggested that in the situations described by my examples, a rational man's answer, to be rational, must infringe the neo-Bernoullian formulation. I simply said, and have constantly repeated, that a person cannot be branded as irrational *on the sole grounds* that his behaviour violates the axioms of the neo-Bernoullian formulation. For some of the examples I presented, some of the answers agree with the neo-Bernoullian formulation and others do not. This in no way constitutes proof that those answers which agree with this formulation are irrational, but it proves that there are people who are considered as rational and who take decisions that are incompatible with this formulation. *That is enough for me.*

As far as the example of a player who wants to let his friend win is concerned, it is utterly 'irrelevant'.

First, it should be observed at the outset that Amihud's example also invalidates von Neumann's and Morgenstern's theory. Should the latter in fact be valid, then so is the axiom of absolute preference.

Second, at all events, the example put forward by Amihud is of an entirely different nature to that generally admitted by all the random choice theoreticians. In fact, the field of choice which is considered here by Amihud is *not* defined by an index

$$S = S(g_1, g_2, \ldots, g_n, p_1, p_2, \ldots, p_n),$$

but by an index

$$S = S(g_1, g_2, \ldots, g_n, p_1, p_2, \ldots, p_n, S'),$$

where S' is the index of preference of the player's friend:

$$S' = S'(-g_1, -g_2, \ldots, -g_n, p_1, p_2, \ldots, p_n).$$

It is quite clear that if the index S of the player is an increasing function of the index S' of the other player, whereas S' is an increasing function of the $-g_i$, the classification of random prospects $(g_1, g_2, \ldots, g_n, p_1, p_2, \ldots, p_n)$ may be entirely different from those that would be noted if S were independent of S'.

Thus it goes without saying that the decisions considered here by Amihud are of an altogether different character from those of the current theories of random choice, and in any event, *the same objection* could be raised against all the neo-Bernoullian theories *since the considered neo-Bernoullian index $B(g)$ is implicitly supposed to be independent of the neo-Bernoullian indices of the other people.* Thus in the present debate, Amihud's argument *cannot be maintained.*

CHAPTER V

CONCLUSIONS: THEORY AND EXPERIENCE

The assertion that whatever is thought by the majority must therefore be in accord with reality is one that wholly ignores the facts of experience; such an assertion can be believed only for motives to which experience is irrelevant...

'Experience shows that the opinion of 'competent' men are often wholly incompatible with reality, and the history of science is the history of the mistakes of the 'competent'. Such an opinion can only be used as an indication of the concordance of a given theory with reality, as providing it with a greater or lesser degree of likelihood, according to the state of knowledge and the competence of he who expresses the opinion; never can it be taken as an experimental proof of the theory, for such proof can only be had by direct or indirect experience...

'The role of judge in the logical–experimental sciences can only be taken by experience; but it is understandable that in certain cases it may be delegated to 'competent' men provided that they have not been chosen in the light of the orientation of the answer it is hoped to obtain; that the question is put to them with sufficient clarity; that they act in the name of experience, and not so as to impose a certain belief; and lastly, that their verdict can always be taken before the final court of appeal of experience.[272]

VILFREDO PARETO, 1916[272]

547

THE EFFECTIVE STRUCTURE OF THE ALLAIS THEORY

39. It seems probable to me, although I am not altogether sure, that the criticisms addressed to my 1952 memoir spring from a basic misunderstanding of the conditions which should be satisfied by a general theory of random choice.

My critics, it seems, expect this theory to lead to an axiomatic definition of probability and utility. *My approach is entirely different.* My starting point is, on the one hand, the hypothesis of the existence of objective probability defined with reference to observed frequency,[273] *independently of all considerations of random choice*; and, on the other hand, the hypothesis of the existence of psychological value (or cardinal utility), defined directly with reference to the intensity of preference for certainly available sums, *again independently of all considerations of random choice.*[274]

The general theory of random choices I present takes probability and psychological value *as given*, and so reduces to the analysis of the properties of fields of choice for uncertain outcomes which are defined by a set of psychological values with given probabilities.

Thus, as far as my theory is concerned, there is no point asking for an axiomatic definition of probability and psychological value, since *these concepts are assumed to exist over and above any consideration of choice between uncertain outcomes.*

If the debate is placed on this terrain, as I think it should be, *there are two entirely distinct series of questions to be discussed: whether the fundamental concepts of objective probability and psychological value indeed exist, and the formulation of a theory of random choice based on these concepts.*

There is an immense literature on the existence of objective probabilities. It has been argued that they exist; and that they do not. Personally, I am convinced they exist (See §21 and Appendix D below).

The issue of the existence of psychological values representing the intensity of ordinal preferences was *settled once and for all* by the analysis of the answers to the 1952 Questionnaire.[275] *There can be no doubt that the concept of psychological value corresponds to a phenomenon of reality, and that psychological value is a magnitude which can be measured using appropriate direct methods.*[275*]

If it is agreed that objective probability and psychological value exist, the general theory of random choice boils down to the theory of fields of choice, i.e. to the theory of determination of certain monetary sums which are deemed to be the worth of uncertain outcomes composed of sets of psychological values with determinate objective probabilities.

The study of these fields of choice can then be subjected to an axiomatic analysis analogous to that currently used for fields of choice as between certainly available goods.

As I have already indicated, the formulation presented in my 1952 memoir was based essentially on five axioms, namely Axioms I to V above,[276] and as further indicated, I have since been led to complete Axiom I by two Axioms IA and IB[277] and to give consideration to two further axioms: Axioms VI and VII above.[278]

In all, the present formulation of my theory may essentially be based on the following eight axioms:

Axioms on the Fundamental Concepts.

  Axioms of existence of probabilities.
    Axiom IA: *objective probabilities* (§21 above).
    Axiom IB: *subjective probabilities* (§21 above).
  Axioms of psychological values.
    Axiom of existence: Axiom V (§11 above).
    Axiom of invariance and homogeneity: Axiom VI (§23 above).

Axioms on Fields of Random Choice.

  Axiom on the existence of an ordered field of choice: Axiom II (§10 above).
  Axiom of absolute preference: Axiom III (§10 above).
  Axiom of composition: Axiom IV (§10 above).
  Axiom of isovariation: Axiom VII (§23 above).

This set of axioms is naturally *far less strong* than the set of axioms of the neo-Bernoullian theories but this is inevitable and results from the nature of things. *The essential difference between my theory and the neo-Bernoullian theories results from the substitution of the principle of absolute preference in place of the principle of independence, which constitutes the central element of all the neo-Bernoullian theories.*

A theorem of particular importance which can be deduced from this set of axioms deals with the asymptotic validity of the neo-Bernoullian formulation when a large number of games can be played and when the sums at stake for each game are small in relation to the player's capital, i.e. when the probability of ruin is negligible.[279]

ALLAIS' AND VON NEUMANN–MORGENSTERN'S AXIOMS

40. The correspondence between these eight axioms and von Neumann–Morgenstern's axioms (See Appendix A below, §§A2, A6 and A8) can easily be established (see the Table on p.551).

Of Allais' Axioms IA (*Objective Probability*) and IB (*Subjective Probability*), only IA has been admitted by von Neumann–Morgenstern, but it is not given explicitly (*Theory of Games*, 1947, §3.3.3, p.19).

Allais' Axiom V of *existence of psychological* value (cardinal utility) has no equivalent in the *Theory of Games*. Von Neumann–Morgenstern's theory demonstrates that an index *B*, which satisfies to the neo-Bernoullian formulation and which they label '*utility*', exists. Allais' Axiom VI of *invariance and homogeneity* has no equivalent either.

Allais' Axiom II of *existence of an ordered field of choice* corresponds to Axiom 3A of the *Theory of Games* (1947, pp.26–27).

Allais' *composition* Axiom IV corresponds to Axiom 3Cb of the *Theory of Games* (see Appendix A, §A8 below).

On the whole, the fundamental difference lies between Allais' Axiom III of absolute preference and Axioms 3Ba and 3Bb of the Theory of Games that it replaces (see Appendix A, §A6 below).

Allais' Axiom III of absolute preference can be seen to be evident once a little thought is given to it, but this is by no means the case for the von Neumann–Morgenstern Axioms 3Ba and 3Bb which are much stronger, but not obvious at all.[280] May I recall here what von Neumann–Morgenstern write in the *Theory of Games*:

Each axiom should have an immediate intuitive meaning by which its appropriateness may be judged directly (1947, §3.5.2, p.25).

May I also quote Paul Levy:

The works in which the authors satisfy themselves with stating axioms, which most often are no more obvious than the theorem they want to demonstrate, and deducing from it the demonstration of this theorem, are of no interest (1925, p.12; Bibliography, Section III, below).

Utility of Random Prospects: Correspondence and Consequences of Axioms

ALLAIS	VON NEUMANN–MORGENSTERN
Fundamental Concepts	
Probability existence axioms	
IA – Objective probability	Admitted but not stated explicitly
IB – Subjective probability	Not admitted
Psychological value axioms	
V – Axiom of existence	Not admitted but demonstrated
VI – Axiom of invariance and homogeneity	Not admitted
Fields of Random Choice	
II – Existence of an ordered field of choice	Axioms 3Aa and 3Ab (completeness and transitivity)
III – Axiom of absolute preference	Substituted for Axioms 3Ba and 3Bb
IV – Axiom of composition	Axiom 3Cb is a particular case of Allais' Axiom IV
VII – Axiom of isovariation	Not admitted but demonstrable

Consequences of axioms

$$\omega = \bar{\gamma} + F[\psi(\gamma - \bar{\gamma})]$$

$$\bar{\gamma} = \int_{-\infty}^{+\infty} \gamma\psi(\gamma)\,d\gamma$$

$$F = f(\mu_2, \ldots, \mu_n, \ldots)$$

$$\omega = \gamma(C + V)$$

$$\gamma = \gamma(C + g)$$

$$B(V) = \int_{-\infty}^{+\infty} B(g)\varphi(g)\,dg$$

The Allais Axiom VII of *isovariation* has no equivalent in von Neumann–Morgenstern, but, from the neo-Bernoullian formulation, we get the identity

$$B(V) + e = \sum p_i[B(g_i) + e],$$

whatever e. Thus the neo-Bernoullian formulation satisfies Allais' Axiom VII.

As to Axioms 3Bc and 3Bd of the Theory of Games (1947, pp.26–27) they are but the expression of a continuity property and seem of rather minor importance to me.

For both von Neumann–Morgenstern and for Allais: (a) the probabilities considered are objective probabilities as defined in the present memoir (see §21 above and Appendix D below) and may be defined *independently* of any consideration of random choice. (b) The cardinal utilities representing the intensity of preference correspond to a reality, *independently* of any consideration of random choice.

The two basic differences are the following: (a) for Allais the index of cardinal utility may be determined directly *independently* of any consideration of random choice (see Appendix C, Section II below). For von Neumann–Morgenstern, on the other hand, the index of cardinal utility may be determined only by considering random choices. (b) By postulating Axioms 3Ba and 3Bb, von Neumann–Morgenstern are led to the neo-Bernoullian formulation (implying the axiom of *absolute preference*) whereas Allais admits only the axiom of *absolute preference*, which is much less restrictive than Axioms 3Ba and 3Bb.

On the whole, the correspondence between the Allais and von Neumann–Morgenstern axioms may be presented in the preceding Table (p.551).

The meaning of the Allais formulation has been already commented above (Foreword and §23). If we adopt the interpretation of von Neumann–Morgenstern, i.e. $B(g) \equiv \gamma(g)$, we see that the two formulations differ only by the consideration of the term F, functional of the probability density $\psi(\gamma)$ of the psychological values γ about their mean $\bar{\gamma}$, which is a function of the moments $\mu_2, \ldots, \mu_n, \ldots$ of the probability distribution of the psychological values (see Table, p.551, above). The functional F (or the function f) represents the psychological value of the probability distribution of psychological values about their mean, corresponding to the specific element of psychology towards risk.[280*]

THE NATURE OF A SCIENTIFIC THEORY

41. Morgenstern very pertinently cites the examples of Newton's Theory of Gravity, Maxwell's Theory of Electromagnetism and Planck's Quantum Theory, and concludes: *"This shows that there is no absolute theory; all theories are only approximations"*. But his examples are a perfect illustration of my point of view. Thus, whereas the theory of gravity is verified to within a second of an arc, i.e. with an accuracy to the nearest millionth, the neo-Bernoullian formulation of the *Theory of Games* only applies in the very particular case of a sequence of a large number of unit games, for each of which the possible losses are negligible in relation to the player's assets, so that the probability of ruin is very low.[281]

All these considerations lead one to reflect on the nature of theories, and the proper criteria for maintaining some and rejecting others.

A theory must attempt to represent the essential features of reality, and to depict them by a model. The model must be based on a system of axioms or postulates. These must be deduced from experience. From these axioms and postulates it is necessary to deduce all the consequences they imply, and no others. The initial assumptions and their deduced consequences must be confronted with observed data. *If this shows that the theory is incompatible with reality, it must be rejected.* If the theory is compatible, it may be accepted, at least for the time being, but if two alternative theories meet this condition, the simpler of the two must be preferred. Any theory which is maintained must be capable of bringing to light the weaknesses of the other theories. Lastly, *the value of a theory, whether in physics or economics, must not be appraised in terms of its mathematical interest, but of its explanatory power in relation to observed reality.* Mathematics must be used only to the extent that this is strictly necessary.[282]

Every model, then, has three stages: the development of the assumptions formulated as axioms or postulates, the deduction of all the consequences of the assumptions and no others, and the confrontation of the assumptions with observed data. The second phase, if correct, is purely logical and mathematical, i.e. tautological by its very nature, and considered in itself its mathematical interest is its only interest. For the interpretation and explanation of phenomena, the value of a theory depends only on the value of the first and third phases.

The theory set forth in my 1952 memoir fully satisfies all these conditions. That is not the case of the theories of the American School, *essentially because they are contradicted by the facts.*[283]

The non-validity of the neo-Bernoullian formulation is proved by the simple fact that it is generally impossible to determine a neo-Bernoullian index able to represent simultaneously random choices in the neighbourhood of certainty and for values of 1/2 of the probability. *My theory enables this impossibility to be predicted for almost all the subjects* in virtue of the preference for security in the neighbourhood of certainty displayed when large sums are involved; *this holds true even for subjects for whom analysis of their choices reveals a strong propensity to risk far from certainty.*[284]

All the American theories of the neo-Bernoullian formulation share two features: the accuracy with which the deductive process is carried out, and the presence of a common element in their conclusions, namely, the rule of maximisation of the mathematical expectation of a certain index. In fact this rule, taken as a principle, implies the existence of conditions of independence and linearity which cannot be justified either by more thorough theoretical analysis or by observation of facts.

In themselves, the deductions of any scientific theory are, and can only be, tautological. If they are not, there is a defect somewhere in the reasoning. *The difficulty lies elsewhere. It is in the confrontation of the theory's postulates* and axioms, and their consequences, with reality. What establishes geometry as a science is the basic conformity of its postulates with nature, at least with a certain degree of approximation. *Without this conformity, no mathematical model, even if built up by the world's greatest mathematician using the most refined mathematical tools, can be any more than a simple flight of fancy.*

To be scientific, any model must be based on axioms and postulates which are in profound agreement with experience. This is the difference between the theories of risk of the neo-Bernoullian school and the theory of geometry. The American theories are based on intellectually interesting models which develop all the necessary consequences of a certain system of axioms, and it is of considerable value to be aware of these consequences. *But the fact remains that the power and aesthetic beauty of the proofs does not constitute any justification whatsoever of the axioms.*[285]

NOTES

[1] Aldous Huxley, 1932, *Brave New World*, Penguin Modern Classics, 1975, pp.42 and 183.
[2] Irving John Good, 1968, 'Statistical Fallacies', *International Encyclopaedia of the Social Sciences*, MacMillan, Vol. 5, p.292.
[3] Claude Bernard, 1865, *Introduction à l'étude de la médecine expérimentale*, Garnier-Flammarion, 1966, pp.75, 76, 84 and 85. (Translation by M. Allais.)

NOTES TO CHAPTER I: INTRODUCTION (Notes 4–61)

[4] W. S. Jevons, 1871, *The Theory of Political Economy*, Penguin Books, 1970, p.260.

§§1–2. 1936 *Researches and the* 1952 *Paris Colloquium* (Notes 5–15)

[5] In fact, no opportunity occurred to apply the result of these thoughts, because, meanwhile, statistical analysis covering a longer period led me to the conclusion that the mathematical expectation associated with the method examined was, if not negative, at best too close to zero for the method to be reasonably applied in practice. However, my reflection on the question had been very suggestive for me.
[6] Before these papers were written, I had presented at the Econometric Congress of Louvain, 1951, a memoir *'Notes théoriques sur l'incertitude de l'avenir et le risque'* (Theoretical notes on the uncertainty of the future and risk) (39pp.) with three annexes: 'Définition et Propriétés de la Satisfaction Absolue' (Definition and Properties of Cardinal Utility) (7pp.); 'Examen de l'hypothèse logarithmique' (Analysis of the log-linear hypothesis (6pp.); 'Confrontation de la théorie exposée avec les théories de von Neumann–Morgenstern et de Marschak' (Confrontation of the theory presented with the theories of von Neumann–Morgenstern and Marschak) (20pp.) (Bibliography below, Section I).

The main passages of the body of this memoir were reproduced in memoirs I and II of 1952 (Bibliography below, Section I, Note 1, and Section X, Note 6). Unfortunately, I had not the opportunity, as I had intended, to publish the three annexes. In Appendix A below, I give the main points made in Annex III of my 1951 memoir concerning the von Neumann–Morgenstern theory.
[7] *International Colloquium on the Foundations and Applications of Risk Theory*, 1952, pp.81–120 and 127–140 (Bibliography, Section I, below).
[8] *Econometrica*, 1953, pp.269–290 (Bibliography, Section X, below).
[9] To my great regret, it was not possible to invite Morgenstern to the Paris Colloquium of May 1952.

The *Centre National de la Recherche Scientifique* was prepared to finance the cost of bringing at most three participants from the U.S.A. As Morgenstern had given a series of lectures in France a few months earlier during a stay of several months in Europe (Sept. 1951–Feb. 1952) (at the end of 1951), the Statistical Institute of the University of Paris, the director of which was Professor Darmois, accorded priority to Milton Friedman, Jacob Marschak and Paul Samuelson. There was no problem as regards Arrow and Savage, both of whom were in Europe at the time. I tried to obtain an additional appropriation to finance a fourth place at the Colloquium for Morgenstern, but did not succeed. This was all the greater a pity in that Morgenstern identified the neo-Bernoullian indicator with cardinal utility, and that he recognised that the neo-Bernoullian formulation does not take into account the greater or lesser propensity for risk.

What for instance is one to think of the policy of the C.N.R.S. at the time, who refused to change three first-class tickets for four tourist-class tickets, an excellent example of 'irrationality of choice'.

[10] See especially pp.34–35, 37–39, 40, 47–48, 151–163, 194–197, and 245–247 of the Colloquium volume (Note 7 above).

Unfortunately, this book, published in French was given limited distribution and the discussions to which the Colloquium gave rise remained inaccessible, not only to English speaking readers, but also to the majority of French readers.

This can only be deplored, for the views exchanged after the presentation of each paper are very suggestive.

[11] Paris International Colloquium on Risk Theory, 1952, pp.257–332 (Bibliography below, Section I, Note 2).

The English version of this memoir, *The Foundations of a Positive Theory of Choice involving Risk and a Criticism of the Postulates and Axioms of the American School*, is reproduced without any modification in the present book and is indicated below by the reference M.

In the English version, the Appendices I to V correspond to the Notes 33, 57, 84, 85, 88, 89 and 110 of the 1952 French text.

[12] *Imprimerie Nationale*, 1955. The text of this book is identical to the memoir III of 1952. It differs only in presentation by the addition of a citation from Blaise Pascal's *Pensées*, and of a few lines in Note 4.

[13] *Econometrica*, 1953, pp.503–546. Econometrica agreed to publish this study only after interminable discussions, so greatly was its argument out of line with the ideas then currently held. An echo of it is to be found in the note by Ragnar Frisch preceding the article (p.503).

Ole Hagen refers to it in his 1969 paper: *Separation of Cardinal Utility and Specific Utility of Risk* (pp.90–91):

> In 1953 *Econometrica* brought an article by M. Allais in which he attacks 'l'école américaine', in particular the hypothesis that choices under un-certainty aim at maximizing the expectation of ex post utility. He in-dicates that expectation is only one aspect of the prospect, here as elsewhere, and that dispersion must also be taken into account.
>
> It is interesting to note the prehistory of its acceptance for publication as it is told in an editorial note. First some heated verbal exchanges, then the manuscript was sent back and forth between author and referees and

finally printed as is "on the author's responsibility" and with the apologetic expression of hope that it will prevent inbreeding in this field.

One would then expect a barrage of adverse comments to follow its publication, but the immediate reaction was complete silence, at least for two years, of *Econometrica*. And the inbreeding has continued and is jealously preserved.

(see also Note 197 below).

[14] So it was with *the memoirs I and I bis* (see §4 below, and Bibliography, Section X, Notes 6 and 7). This I regret all the more in that my approach in the two papers, for the reasons I gave during the symposium (see pp.47–48 of the Colloquium volume), although apparently less general, actually goes closer to the heart of things than Arrow's approach. One of my correspondents (1975) wrote:

> It is a really pioneering paper, and I am both sorry and surprised that it has not had the same impact as the paper presented by Arrow at the Colloquium in 1952.

[15] Finally, for the Congress of French Speaking Economists, 24–25 May, 1954, I presented a paper on the Theory of Games, *Observations présentées à la suite de l'exposé de G. Th. Guilbaud sur la Théorie des Jeux* (Bibliography below, Section V), in which I added further remarks to those I had presented in the earlier papers in 1951 and 1952.

§3. *The* 1952 *Experiment* (Notes 16–22)

[16] Bibliography below, Section VI. Comments on questions VI, VII and IX of this Questionnaire will be found in Appendix C below (pp.614–627).

[17] *Groupe de Recherches Economiques et Sociales*, Seminar of June 11, 1952.

[18] I.e. except for questions VI, VII, VIII and IX dealing with the construction of the neo-Bernoullian index (See §6 below).

[19] There were about 400 questions in the Questionnaire form.

[20] In particular on the application of risk theory to mining research (see §5 and Note 35 below), on money (Allais, 'Explication des Cycles Economiques par un Modèle non Linéaire à Régulation Retardée', *Metroeconomica*, April, 1956, pp.4–83), and on gravitation (1953–1959, see esp. Allais, 1959, 'Should the Laws of Gravitation be Reconsidered', *Aero Space Engineering*, Vol. 18, No. 9, pp.46–52, No. 10, pp.51–55, and No. 11, p.55; see also Note 35 below).

[21] M. Allais, 1974, *Contributions originales à la Science Economique*, 1943–1974, Centre d'Analyse Economique, 1974, 170pp.

[22] See §6 above and Appendix C below. One of my correspondents (1977) reproaches me for the delay in publishing the results of the 1952 survey. He writes:

> You kept these results secret for twenty five years!... Your readers will be disappointed that you, when you return to this subject after more than twenty years, again publish an incomplete and provisional account. Your

promises of a separate volume and publication as soon as time allows are certainly sincere, but carry little credibility. Could you not take a few months more and give a proper presentation of your 'triple set of axioms'? It should also be possible to give a better and more self-contained report of the experiment without using more space than Appendix C.

I am very sensible of this reproach. I tried to state the reasons for the delay in §§3 and 6 of this memoir. The fact is that one cannot do everything, and over the past twenty five years, I have considered that other areas of investigation were of more interest and had a higher priority than my work on risk.

Perhaps I was wrong. But then the same reproach of not having published important results for so many years could be made equally validly in other areas of my researches. In these areas, the results which I have obtained and which I have not yet published for lack of sufficient time are as important as these corresponding to the 1952 experiment.

Be this as it may, it was altogether impossible to render an account of the analysis of the 1952 experiment other than that given in Appendix C. The publisher could not have included a longer text, given that my 1952 paper is also included in this volume. And any further delay was *unthinkable*, and would not have been acceptable either to the publisher or the other contributors.

It pained me to have to adopt the course I did, considering the remarkable results obtained, especially in regard to the analysis of the non-loglinear case of cardinal utility (see §6 and Appendix C, Section VI) (pp.451–454 and 632–634).

§4. *Extension of the Theories of General Economic Equilibrium and Maximum Efficiency to the Case of Choice with Uncertainty* (Notes 23–33)

[23] Memoirs I and I bis of 1952 (see §2 above).
[24] A totally different approach is presented by Arrow in his paper 'Role des valeurs boursières pour la répartition la meilleure des risques' presented during the same Colloquium (Volume of the Colloquium, pp.41–47). Arrow's approach seems both too general (it does not specify either the psychology of the operators or how one risk can be transformed into another) and too restricted (he assumes convexity). See my observations (*Proceedings*, pp.47–48), and Note 7 above.

Similar remarks apply to Debreu's subsequent formulation (*Theory of Value*, 1959, Chapter 7, pp.88–102).

For a critical analysis of the convexity hypothesis, see Allais, 1971, 'Les théories de l'équilibre économique général et de l'efficacité maximale', *Revue d'Economie Politique*, May–June 1971, pp.331–409 (published subsequently in English; see p.681 below).
[25] Allais, *Econometrica*, 1953, pp.271–275.
[26] Such preference indexes do not satisfy the neo-Bernoullian principle, which does not take into account the dispersion of psychological values (see Allais, *Econometrica*, 1953, p.275, Note 13, and §§13 and 34 below). *In any case, they are used for illustrative purposes only.*

[27] As regards the discussion of the model considered, the text published in *Econometrica* was less extensive than the text published in the Colloquium volume (pp.81–109). See especially pp.88–98 of this volume (first reference in Section X of the bibliography below).

[28] Allais, *Econometrica*, 1953, §§7–8, pp.276–277.

[29] Ibid., §§7–12, pp.276–279.

[30] Ibid., §§13–20, pp.279–283.

[31] Ibid., §1, p.270 and §24, pp.285–286.

[32] Ibid., §§24–30, pp.285–289.

[33] The model presented has permitted a thorough discussion of some essential features of an economy in which uncertain goods exist (see Note 14 above).

§5. *Applied Work* (Notes 34–45)

[34] At Professor J. Marschak's request, this paper was translated into English and published in 1957 in the American Review *Management Science*. The following year, it was awarded the Lanchester prize of the John Hopkins University and the Operations Research Society of America.

[35] M. Allais, 1957, *Method of Appraising Economic Prospects of Mining Exploration over Large Territories*. See the Summary, pp.285–289, the Introduction, §1, pp.289–291, and the Conclusions, pp.317–319.

The work owed much to the cooperation of Mr Blondel, Director of the 'Bureau d'Etudes Géologiques et Minières Coloniales', for collecting empirical data (Note 7, p.291), and of Mr de Beauregard, Director of the 'Bureau de Recherches Minières de l'Algérie', as regards financial data on mining exploration (Introduction, §1, p.298). The study was carried out in 1953 and 1954 and yielded numerous papers (See the 22 notes indicated in the bibliography, Annex VIII, p.344).

A general study was to be published later on. Unfortunately, I fell seriously ill in the first half of 1955, and, pushed for time, quickly drafted a very condensed paper (the one analysed hereunder) for the Petropolis Congress of the International Statistical Institute (June, 1955).

Later on, from 1953 to 1960, I carried out experimental research into gravity, a considerable and time consuming project (see Note 20 above). Events in Algeria and Mr Blondel's death in 1959 were further obstacles to the pursuit of this work.

As a result, the 1955 paper was never supplemented by the general study I had planned to write, and it contains few enough of the results obtained, although they are of substantial scientific interest.

[36] The French monetary reform of December, 1958, defined the 'new franc', the value of which was a hundred 'old francs'.

[37] Ibid., §4, pp.292–293.

[38] Ibid., Introduction, p.286, §17, p.298; §§19–20, pp.299–302, and §35, p.316.

[39] This work was done using the empirical data determined by Mr Blondel.

[40] Ibid., Annex VII, pp.340–343.

[41] Ibid., §§8–18, pp.295–299, and Annex II, pp.322–331.

[42] Ibid., §§2–7, pp.291–295. See particularly §4, pp.292–293, where the principal parameters of the model are defined.

[43] Ibid., §§26–34, pp.308–316.
[44] Ibid., §§34–35, pp.315–316.
[45] See Sections 2 to 4 above.

§6. *Analysis of the 1952 Experiment* (Notes 46–53)

[46] In April 1974, this work led to a summarising note: 'La Psychologie de l'Homme Rationnel devant le Risque – La Théorie et l'Expérience – Résultats du Sondage de 1952' (*Centre d'Analyse Economique*, Note 3064, May 6th, 1974, 9pp.).
[47] See §3 above (pp.447–449).
[48] With five exceptions: Arrow, Baumol, Friedman, Marschak and Savage. The three last respondents based themselves on an index of 'cardinal utility', which they chose *a priori*, and as a function of which they determined their answers using the neo-Bernoullian formulation (see Note 116 below).

Morgenstern and Samuelson did not answer the Questionnaire.
[49] Questions VI of the Questionnaire; see Appendix C, Section II below.
[50] Questions VII, VIII and IX. For an analysis of questions VII and IX, see Appendix C, Sections III and IV below (pp.620–627).
[51] To determine cardinal utility in the non-loglinear case, I considered an auxiliary function that I have called the generating function (see Appendix C, Section VI below) (p.632).
[52] Those respondents are those who gave finite answers to questions 651 to 654 on the determination of cardinal utility.

If satiety is present, the questions VI of the Questionnaire are too few in number to yield reliable results. However, the non-loglinear cardinal preference function determined for the group of respondents who gave no evidence of satiety, offers an excellent portrayal of the replies by those subjects for whom satiety was present.

In any case, for every subject and for sums exceeding a certain multiple of his fortune, satiety appears, which leads to an horizontal asymptote for the cardinal utility represented as a function of a certainly available gain. On all these points see Appendix C, Section VI below (pp.632–634).
[53] See Appendix C below, Section VII (p.634).

§7. *Theoretical Analysis* (Notes 54–57)

[54] On de Finetti's theorem, see Note 126 below and Dubourdieu 1952, Chapter V, pp.163–173; on the problem of the gambler's ruin, see also the various references listed in Section VII of the bibliography (pp.678–679).
[55] See §26 below. On de Finetti's theory of the gambler's ruin and on collective risk theory, see Dubourdieu, 1952, Chapters V and VI, esp. pp.258–260; Cramér, 1955; and Beard, Pentikäinen and Pesonen, 1969 (Bibliography, Section VIII below, p.679).

On the Saint Petersburg Paradox, see the various references in Section IX of the Bibliography below (p.680).
[56] See §§25 and 26 below (pp.491–506).
[57] These different results will be described in forthcoming publications.

§8. *The Framework of the Present Memoir* (Notes 58–64)

[58] Naturally, when necessary, this memoir will refer to the volume describing the whole processing and the detailed analysis of the 1952 experiment, which I hope to be able to publish soon.

The reader will find in Appendix C below a brief analysis of some of the results obtained (pp.611–654).

[59] Although I now feel that some of it could have been improved. Today, for example, I would choose to denote the index of ordinal preference as *I* rather than *S*, as I have done in my publications since 1967. But I have preferred to leave my 1952 memoir completely unchanged.

[60] For brevity, and as I have already indicated (Note 11 above) the 1952 paper is referred to below as M.

[61] Reading some of the observations made by some of my critics or my correspondents, to whom I am grateful for the points they make, I had the feeling that they sometimes were somewhat passionned to the detriment of objectivity.

Certain critics of my 1952 memoir did not hesitate to speak of my 'polemic temerity' (Fels, 1959, p.136) or 'Allais' polemic against the American School' (Suppes, 1959, p.499). This is no basis for scientific debate.

If I respect the opinions of my opponents, I would only ask them to respect mine. But, wherever I have found them to be excessive, I shall refrain from any comments on their judgments.

As I wrote to one of my correspondents in 1977:

> For you, as far as I can see from your comments, any contradiction by my opponents is scientific criticism, but if I contradict them, it is simply personal attacks. Here we leave the domain of science to enter that of emotion and prejudice.

[61*] Initially, the draft of this memoir was to follow this pattern:
I. Introduction.
II. The Allais' 1952 theory of random choice.
III. A critical analysis of the theories of the American School after 1952.
   (A) Basic concepts
   (B) Theoretical approaches
   (C) Empirical research
   (D) Dissident viewpoints.
IV. Answers to critics of the Allais' 1952 analysis.
V. Fundamental concepts
   (A) The concept of probability
   (B) The concept of the psychological value of a given sum (cardinal utility)
   (C) The concept of the psychological value of a random prospect.
VI. Axiomatic presentation of the Allais' theory.
VII. Observed data.
VIII. Conclusions.
Appendix A: Von Neumann and Morgenstern's theory of random choice.
Appendix B: Mathematical appendix.

By reason of the lack of both space and time, I had to give up this ambitious plan at the beginning of 1977 and to decide the suppression of Sections IIIB, IIIC and IIID of Chapter III, and Chapters V, VI and VII.

The present Appendix C is a shortened version of the intended Chapter VII. Similarly, the existing Appendix D is a shortened version of Section A of the intended Chapter V.

NOTES TO CHAPTER II: THE ALLAIS 1952 THEORY OF CHOICE WITH UNCERTAINTY (Notes 62–152)

[62] Jacob Marschak, *Money and the Theory of Assets*, Econometrica, October 1938, p.320. This was in fact Marschak's initial view.

[63] Especially in the light of the results obtained in processing the 1952 experiment, and their analysis (see §6 above, and Appendix C below).

[64] See Part IV below, §32–40 (pp.518–546).

§10. *Consideration of Money Values* (Notes 65–75)

[65] M, §2 (pp.38–39).

[66] M, §5, and §21 below. This axiom is not explicitly formulated by von Neumann–Morgenstern (pp.42 and 469–473).

[67] M, §2. This axiom corresponds to von Neumann–Morgenstern's Axioms 3A (see Appendix A below, §A2) (pp.38–39 and 592–594).

[68] M, §3. This axiom replaces von Neumann–Morgenstern Axioms 3Ba and 3Bb. Its implications are naturally far weaker. See Appendix A, §A6 below.

[69] On the von Neumann–Morgenstern Axiom 3Cb, see Appendix A below, §§A2 and A8 (pp.592–594, 599).

[70] M, §44, and §39 below (pp.65–66 and 548–550).

[71] On the properties of the function $S(g_1, g_2, \ldots, g_n, p_1, p_2, \ldots, p_n)$ see M, §2, and M, §41, Note 42 (pp.38–39 and 134).

[72] M, §§2 and 10 (pp.38–39,45).

[73] M, §2, relation 5 (p.39).

[74] To simplify, I consider only the probability density $\varphi(g)$ instead of the more general concept of the probability function

$$F(g) = \text{Probability } \{u \leqslant g\}.$$

Fundamentally, the discussion which follows is in no way affected by this simplification.

[75] *And not simply on the variance of the monetary gains*, a view which has been ascribed to me, but wrongly (see §34 below, pp.524–526).

§11. *Consideration of Psychological Values* (Notes 76–81)

[76] On the determination of this cardinal index, see below Annex C, Section II, and the Bibliography, Section II. See also M, §§8 and 9, and Allais, 1943, *A la Recherche d'une Discipline Economique, L'Economie Pure*, §§68–70, pp.156–177.

[77] M, §10, relations 4–5, and §23 (pp.45 and 55).

[78] *And not simply on the variance of psychological values*, a view which has been also ascribed to me, but wrongly (see Note 72 above and §34 below, pp.562 and 524–526).

[79] See §23 and Appendix C, Section II, below.

The concept of psychological value (or cardinal utility) was introduced by Daniel Bernoulli, in 1738, to explain the *St. Petersburg Paradox* (§26 below) and was used again by Laplace, 1812 and 1814, in his theory of moral expectations. Both adopted a logarithmic formulation. A thorough economic analysis of this concept was presented by Jevons, 1871.

Many attempts have been made in the past to compute cardinal utility from an analysis of demand laws. They generally cannot succeed. The reason is because the equations of general economic equilibrium and economic efficiency only involve the ordinal preference index (ordinal utility) (see Allais, 1943, *A la Recherche d'une Discipline Economique*, §70, pp.176–177).

Fisher, 1927 developed a method of computing the marginal utility as a function of the income, under the assumption that the goods consumed may be classified into independent groups. It boils down to admit the hypothesis

$$\bar{S} = \psi_A(A) + \psi_B(B) + \cdots + \psi_C(C)$$

(see Appendix A below, Note 5, p.602). But he did not publish any empirical application.

Frisch, 1926 and 1932, assumes that the cardinal utility $\bar{S} = \bar{S}(A, B, \ldots, C)$ is a function $\bar{S} = \bar{S}(R, P)$ where R stands for nominal income and P for the price level. René Roy, 1943, worked on a similar hypothesis, but his results are only valid under the condition

$$A \frac{\partial \bar{S}}{\partial A} + B \frac{\partial \bar{S}}{\partial B} + \cdots + C \frac{\partial \bar{S}}{\partial C} = K$$

where K is a constant (see Allais, 1965, *La loi héréditaire, relativiste et logistique de la demande de monnaie et la structure des surfaces d'indifférence*, Centre d'Analyse Economique, 56pp.; to be published soon).

However, although consideration of cardinal utility is not necessary in order to develop the theories of economic equilibrium and maximum efficiency, it is *essential* for any general theory of society, because the distribution of income within a given family, and all political decisions regarding the distribution of incomes, imply inter-personal comparisons (see especially Vilfredo Pareto, 1916, *Treatise on Sociology*, §2131, Note 1 in particular; Allais, 1959, *Les Conditions d'une Société Libre*, §II.1, La définition d'une société libre par référence à une situation de minimum de contrainte, pp.38–39; Allais, 1961, *L'influence des Besoins sur la Production des Biens de Consommation*, pp.139–140, 149–150 and pp.178–180, 1967, *Les Conditions de l'Efficacité dans l'Economie*, §§13–14 and 86, pp.13–16 and 80–82; and Allais, 1968, *Pareto*, International Encyclopaedia of the Social Sciences, Volume 11, pp.402–403 and 405).

The reader will find interesting historical data about cardinal utility in Stigler, 1950, and Georgescu Roegen, 1968. See also the other references given in Section II of the Bibliography (pp.665–667).

[80] See Note 59 above (p.561).

[81] M, §§2, 8 and 10 (pp.38–39, 44 and 45).

§§12–13. *The Concept of Rationality and the Axiomatic Foundations of My* 1952 *Theory* (Notes 82–85)

[82] See M, §§47, 51, 52 and 53; see also §§19, 31 and 38 and Note 193 below.

[83] This is demonstrated by the analysis of the results of the 1952 experiment (see §6 above, and Appendix C below, pp.451–454 and 611–654).

[84] §§10 and 11 above. On the axiomatic formulation of my theory at the present time see §§39 and 40 below (pp.456–462 and 547–552).

[85] §§10 and 11 above, knd §§21 and 23 below (pp.451–454, 469–473, and 475–483).

§§14–15. *The Neo-Bernoullian Formulation* (Notes 86–91)

[86] The reader will find an abstract of the twelve main points in the *Summary* which opens my 1952 memoir. See also the somewhat more developed abstract in my 1953 memoir, 'La psychologie de l'homme rationnel devant le risque – La théorie et l'expérience' (The Psychological of Rational Behavior in the Presence of Risk – Theory and Experience) pp.47–53 (see the Bibliography below, Section VI).

[87] Which I referred to at the time as "satisfaction absolue" (absolute satisfaction) (M, §§8) (p.44).

[87*] See hereunder Note 155; Appendix A, Note 4; and Appendix C, §C19 and Notes 24* and 30* (pp.576, 602, 628–631 and 637–639).

[88] M, §§49–52 (pp.74–79).

[89] Such was Samuelson's position during the 1952 Paris Colloquium.

[90] Such was de Finetti's position during the 1952 Paris Colloquium.

During the Colloquium, de Finetti maintained that the neo-Bernoullian index $B(g)$ *simultaneously* takes account of the curvature of the cardinal index of preference and the dispersion of monetary gains. On this point, see my reply: Proceedings of the Colloquium, 1952, pp.159–162 and 196–197 (Bibliography, Section I). See also M, §21, especially Notes 32, 33 and 34.

Today, de Finetti's position remains unchanged: see this volume: de Finetti, 'A Short Confirmation of My Standpoint' (pp.161–162).

I can only reiterate my reply to him in 1952 (Proceedings of the Symposium, pp.161–162):

> According to de Finetti my argumentation (M, §20) based on the distinction between the probability distributions I and II of psychological values (cardinal utility) with the same average $\bar{y}$, would be admissible only if the neo-Bernoullian index $B(x)$ was identical (up to a linear transformation) to the index of psychological value $\bar{s}(x)$. Then according to him the function $B(x)$ would be a non-linear function
>
> $$B(x) = F[\bar{s}(x)],$$
>
> which precisely would take into account the subject's psychology with respect to the probability distribution of $\bar{s}(x)$.
>
> It is true that in this case my argument against the neo-Bernoullian formulation would not hold.

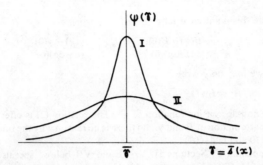

In reality however, this circumstance appears hardly admissible, for, if in some particular cases, one can conceive the existence of a non linear transformation $F[\bar{s}(x)]$ of $\bar{s}(x)$ such that the consideration of mathematical expectation $\Sigma\, p_iB(x_i)$ could lead to a correct choice, *I consider it impossible to conceive that the same transformation could remain valid if very different probability distributions are considered*, like the two represented below with the same average $\bar{\gamma}$.

My thesis is:

(1) If a neo-Bernoullian index existed, it would necessarily be identical to the index of psychological value up to a linear transformation.

(2) The neo-Bernoullian formulation based on consideration of the mathematical expectation $\Sigma\, p_i\bar{s}(x)$ neglects an essential element, the probability distribution of $\bar{s}(x)$ about its average.

(3) In these conditions, it is impossible in general that an index $B(x)$ can exist such that consideration of the mathematical expectation $\Sigma\, p_iB(x_i)$ can lead to rational choices.

In actual fact, the analysis of the 1952 survey showed that for every subject (and for de Finetti in particular) there is no way to determine a $B(x)$ indicator taking account simultaneously of the curvature of the index of cardinal preference (cardinal utility) and the greater or lesser degree of preference for security, *for different sets of questions.* Thus the two indicators $B_{1/2}$ and B_{200} determined in Annex C below (Sections III and IV) cannot be deduced from one another by choosing appropriate values of the parameters representing the subject's wealth, and making a suitable linear transformation (see also §C19 below, and §§22, 28 and 29, as well as Note 154, pp.628–631, 473–474, 508–514 and 574–576).

[91] M, §50 (pp.75–77).

§§16–19. *Criticism of the Neo-Bernoullian Formulation*
(Notes 92–104)

[92] M, §§2–48, especially §§3, 10, 20, and 46–48 (pp.38–73).

[93] The identification of the two indices $\gamma(g)$ and $B(g)$ needs to be proved (see M, Note 110, which corresponds to Appendix V of the English translation; see also Appendix B below). But it cannot be deduced from the fact that the two indexes $B = B(g)$ and $\gamma = \bar{s}(g)$, being assumed to exist, are both defined up to a linear transformation.

To make this point clear let

(1) $B^*(g) = \dfrac{B(g) - B(0)}{(dB/dg)(0)}$, $\gamma^*(g) = \dfrac{\gamma(g) - \gamma(0)}{(d\gamma/dg)(0)}$.

A priori we may only write

(2) $B^* = f(\gamma^*)$,

f being a non-decreasing function of γ^*. The relation (2) is effectively invariant in any linear transformation of B and γ, and there is no reason why the function f should be linear (pp.128–130 and 604–607).

[94] See Appendix C, Sections II, V, VI and VII below; see also §§11, 23, 28 and 29 below (pp.614–620, 627–634, 460–462, 475–483 and 508–514).

[95] M, §§55–59 (pp.80–86).

[96] M, §52 and §12 above (pp.78–79 and 462–463).

[97] M, §§53 and 60–65, and §12 above. See especially M, §64.

[98] *My adversaries' behaviour in respect of these counterexamples turned out to be anti-Bernoullian* (See below, §36, and Allais, 1957, 'Sur la théorie des choix aléatoires, Réponse à la critique de Georges Morlat', p.386) (pp.533–541).

[99] See §14 above, and M, §§63, 68 and 70. On the implicit independence principle of von Neumann–Morgenstern see Appendix A, §A4 (pp.463–464, 88–90, 96–99 and 594–596).

[100] See Allais, 1952, *La Psychologie de l'Homme Rationnel devant le Risque*, Questions 43 and 44, p.61 (§3 above). See also the Appendix A, §A4, below (pp.447–449 and 594–596).

[101] See Appendix C, §C2 and Note 8 (pp.612–613 and 635).

[102] §12 above, and §§31 and 38 below (pp.462–463, 514–517 and 543–546).

[103] M, §53, and §38 below (pp.79–80 and 543–546).

[104] M, §§63 and 64 especially(pp.88–92).

§21. *Objective Probabilities* (Notes 104*–112)

[104*] See Foreword, pp.4–7 above.

[105] M, §5. See also §29 and Appendix D, §1 below (pp.42, 510–514 and 655–657).

[106] Allais, 1968, *Economics as a Science*, Cahiers Vilfredo Pareto, pp.5–24.

[107] This seems much better than Borel's method (M, §6), because the last one may be biased by complementary effects. See also §29 and Note 169 below, and Allais, 1976, *Les fondements de la théorie des probabilités* (pp.42–43, 510–514 and 577).

[108] I have kept the term in this memoir only because it has by now been consecrated by repeated use.

[109] M, §52 (pp.78–79).

[110] §10 above, and Appendix D below. See also Allais, 1976, *Les fondements de la théorie des probabilités* (pp.456–460 and 655–663).

[111] One of my correspondents writes: "For von Mises: limit of frequency = probability. Is this what Allais wants to say?".

In fact it seems to me that von Mises' theory of collectives, according to which the frequence would tend to probability in the sense of mathematical analysis, is inconsistent and cannot be defended. (See Appendix D3 below).

[112] On all these points see Appendix D below (pp.655–663).

§§22–23. The Non-Existence of a Neo-Bernoullian Index and Cardinal Utility (Notes 113–121)

[113] §14 above (pp.463–464).

[114] M, §64, Note 95 (pp.90–92 and 138–139).

[115] §6 above, and Appendix C, §C19 below (pp.451–454 and 628–631).

[116] Apart from Friedman, Marschak and Savage, who according to their own statements had set their $B(g)$ indicator beforehand (see Note 48 above).

The analysis of their replies, which is in any event of very great interest, will be presented in the general volume to be devoted to the processing and analysis of the 1952 survey: *The Psychological Structure of Choice Involving Risk.*

[117] See §36 below, and M, §63. See also Appendix C, Note 15 below (pp.533, 88, 636).

[118] §6 above, and Appendix C, §C19 below (pp.451–454 and 628–631).

[119] §6 above, and Appendix C, §C18 (pp.451–454 and 627–628).

[120] The variable $u = \log[1 + g/C]$ is considered because, as a first approximation and in a large domain, the cardinal utility γ is a linear function of u (See Appendix C, Sections II and VI below, pp.614–620 and 632–634).

[121] This axiom is related to the minimum perceptible threshold property discussed in my 1952 memoir above. See M, §69, Note 110, and Appendix V, relations (4) and (5); see also Appendix B below, §B1; (pp.97–98, 128–130, 604–607).

However, in 1952, I considered that Axiom VII assumed complete absence of complementarity (M, Note 109). I now think this to be extremely likely in all cases.

It is noteworthy that Leinfellner and Hagen have independently reached the same axiom (Hagen, 1976, Axiom A11 and Note 31). This axiom is not however essential to the theory discussed in the present memoir.

§24. Asymptotic Validity of the Neo-Bernoullian Formulation (Notes 122–133)

[122] Cramér, 1945, *Mathematical Methods of Statistics*, pp.176–177.

[123] Cramér, ibid., pp.316–317. The central limit theorem is only a generalisation of the theorem of James Bernoulli (1654–1705) on the distribution of the sum of variables obeying the same binomial law, when their number increases indefinitely.

[124] For a normal distribution with variance Σ^2 we have rigorously

$$\mu_{2k} = 1.3\ldots(2k-1)\Sigma^{2k}, \qquad \mu_{2k+1} = 0.$$

(Cramér, ibid., p.212, relation 17.2.3.)

[125] It is worth noting that this demonstration has been made considering the probability distribution resulting from N successive games, i.e. reducing the whole process to a single random choice (See §10.4 above and §30 below, and M, §§4 and 48.4).

[126] For the probability of ruin P_N in N games the player's mathematical expectation is

$$(1) \qquad M_N = (1 - P_N)E_N - P_N X, \qquad (E_N > Nm)$$

where X is his capital and E_N his conditional mathematical expectation in the absence of ruin.

If the number of games N is relatively large, the order of magnitude of P_N can be estimated by considering the probability of ruin P in an infinite number of games, using the following theorem, which is due to de Finetti:

Consider a unit game for which the probability of a gain (positive or negative) between g and $g + dg$ is $\varphi(g)\,dg$, and for which

$$(2) \qquad m = \int_{-\infty}^{+\infty} g\varphi(g)\,dg > 0,$$

where m denotes the mathematical expectation of the game considered.

Let τ be the root of the equation

$$(3) \qquad \int_{-\infty}^{+\infty} \exp(-\tau g)\varphi(g)\,dg = 1, \qquad \tau \geq 0.$$

The probability of ruin of a player whose fortune is X in an infinite sequence of games is

$$(4) \qquad P_\infty(X) = \frac{\exp(-\tau X)}{\mathscr{E}[\exp(\tau\Delta)]},$$

in which Δ represents the amount the player cannot settle in the game in which his ruin is accomplished, and $\mathscr{E}[\exp(\tau\Delta)]$ is the mathematical expectation of $\exp(\tau\Delta)$ (see especially Dubourdieu, 1952, p.168).

As $\tau > 0$ and $\Delta > 0$, we have necessarily

$$(5) \qquad P_\infty(X) \leq \exp(-\tau X).$$

Whence the probability of ruin is the lower the smaller the losses ($g < 0$) relatively to the player's fortune X and the lower their probability. Of course

$$(6) \qquad P_N < P_\infty,$$

since the probability of ruin in N games is naturally lower than the probability of ruin in an infinite number of gains. Moreover, if A is the maximum loss in absolute value, it follows from (4) that

$$(7) \qquad \exp[-\tau(X + A)] < P_\infty(X) \leq \exp[-\tau X],$$

with the equalities arising when $\Delta = 0$: this will happen when the game involves a unique loss a and when the players fortune X and the gains are integral multiples of a, i.e. when the random outcome is written $-a, n_1 a, n_2 a, \ldots, p_0, p_1, p_2, \ldots$, with no restrictions on the probabilities associated with the loss a or the gains $n_1 a, n_2 a, \ldots$ other than the condition $p_0 + p_1 + p_2 + \cdots = 1$.

I recall that

$$(8) \qquad P_\infty = 1 \qquad \text{for } m \leq 0.$$

[127] See M, §48 (pp.70–73).

[128] See §11 above (pp.460–462).

[129] Under very general conditions the probability distribution of γ_N will tend to normal (See Cramér, ibid., pp.218–219, §17.5.2).

[130] The general proof of this proposition cannot be given in this paper; I shall limit myself to indicating the principle on which it is based.

As u_N defined by relation (19)

$$(1) \qquad g_N = Nm + u_N$$

increases like $\sqrt{N}$, we have for $N \gg 1$

(2) $\qquad \gamma(C + Nm + u_N) \sim \gamma(C + Nm) + u_N \dfrac{d\gamma}{dC}(C + Nm).$

(3) $\qquad \bar{\gamma}(C + Nm + u_N) \sim \gamma(C + Nm).$

From these conditions we deduce

(4) $\qquad \mathcal{M}_{N,n} = \displaystyle\int_{-\infty}^{+\infty} (\gamma_N - \bar{\gamma}_N)^n \psi(\gamma_N)\, d\gamma_N$

$\qquad\qquad \sim \displaystyle\int_{-\infty}^{+\infty} \left[\dfrac{d\gamma}{dC}(C + Nm) \right]^n u_N^n \varphi(u_N)\, du_N,$

and since

(5) $\qquad M_{N,n} = \displaystyle\int_{-\infty}^{+\infty} u_N^n \varphi(u_N)\, du_N,$

we have

(6) $\qquad \mathcal{M}_{N,n} \sim \left[\dfrac{d\gamma}{dC}(C + Nm) \right]^n M_{N,n} \qquad$ for $N \gg 1$,

whence, from (13) and (30) (main text)

(7) $\qquad \mu_{N,n} \sim \bar{g}_N^n \left[\dfrac{(d\gamma/dC)(C + Nm)}{\gamma(C + Nm)} \right]^n \lambda_{N,n} \qquad$ for $N \gg 1$.

It can be deduced from this that $\mu_{N,n}$ will tend to zero with $\lambda_{N,n}$ if the coefficient of $\lambda_{N,n}$ on the right-hand side of (7) has an upper boundary.

In the particular case in which the cardinal utility index would be loglinear, i.e.

(8) $\qquad \gamma(X) = \bar{s}(C + X) = \log[C + X],$

(see Appendix C, Section II), it is possible to write

(9) $\qquad \gamma(C + Nm + u_N) \sim \log(C + Nm) + u_N/(C + Nm),$

(10) $\qquad \bar{\gamma}(C + Nm + u_N) \sim \log(C + Nm),$

and hence according to (7)

(11) $\qquad \mu_{N,n} \sim \dfrac{(Nm)^n}{(C + Nm)^n [\log(C + Nm)]^n} \lambda_{N,n} \qquad$ for $N \gg 1$,

and finally

(12) $\qquad \mu_{N,n} \sim \dfrac{1}{[\log(C + Nm)]^n} \lambda_{N,n} \qquad$ for $N \gg 1$.

Thus we see that in this particular case the $\mu_{N,n}$ tend towards zero more rapidly than the $\lambda_{N,n}$.

[131] At the 1952 Symposium, I indicated the possibility of this demonstration:
《Let S be the index of preference

$$S = F[\bar{s}(g_1), \bar{s}(g_2), \ldots, \bar{s}(g_n), p_1, p_2, \ldots, p_n].$$

If we consider the different moments of the probability distribution of $\bar{s}(g)$

$$\mathcal{M}_1 = \sum p_i \bar{s}(g_i),$$

. . . .

$$\mathcal{M}_\nu = \sum p_i [\bar{s}(g_i) - \mathcal{M}_1]^\nu,$$

we would have

$$S = G[\mathcal{M}_1, \mathcal{M}_2, \ldots, \mathcal{M}_\nu, \ldots],$$

a relation which *as a first approximation* would reduce to the neo-Bernoullian formulation

$$S = g(\mathcal{M}_1),$$

when, psychologically, the subject considered would not, in practice, take into account the moments of order greater or equal to 2, or in the case in which these moments are sufficiently small.

Naturally this last eventuality would arise when the number of successive drawings is sufficiently large, so that the relative dispersion of the $\bar{s}(g)$ about their mean becomes negligible》.
(*Colloquium Proceedings*, p.195; see Bibliography, Section I below; see also M, §48.)

The law of large numbers was also applied by Camacho, 1973, 'Maximising expected utility and the rule of long run success'. But apparently Camacho does not take into account the possibility of being ruined during a long sequence of drawings, which implies implicitly assuming comparatively small values for any of the g_i/C.

On the identification of $\bar{s}(g)$ and $B(g)$, see §16d above, and M, §69.

[132] As the probability P_N of ruin in N games is lower than the probability of ruin P_∞ in an infinite number of games, the condition for P_N to be relatively small is that P_∞ be relatively small. But P_∞ can be easily calculated (see Note 126 above) (p.567).

[133] Morlat, 1957 (Bibliography, Section VII below).

In fact, many authors see the law of large numbers as the basic justification of the neo-Bernoullian formulation. For example, Tintner (1954, p.666) writes:

> The von Neumann–Morgenstern theory of choice explains a large class of phenomena by the introduction of the Bernoullian hypothesis, that people try to achieve the maximum possible gain on average in the long run.

and he refers to Marschak's 1952 article: 'Why should Statisticians and Businessmen Maximise Moral Expectation'.

§25. *Mathematical Expectation and Probability of Ruin*
(Notes 134–140)

[134] Equally interesting is the case in which

$$S = f(M_y, P),$$

where M_y represents the mathematical expectation of psychological values and P the probability of ruin (See M, Note 89 to which corresponds the §88 of the Appendix IV of the English translation; see Note 11 above) (pp.127–128 and 556).

[135] For a sequence of N successive games, each with a mathematical expectation of m, and if the probability of ruin in N games is P_N, the principle of compound probabilities yields

$$M_N = (1 - P_N)E_N - P_N X, \qquad (E_N > Nm)$$

where M_N is the mathematical expectation corresponding to N games, X the operator's capital, and E_N the mathematical expectation in the absence of ruin.

In general X is different of the subjective estimate C of his worth by the subject which may take into account the discounted value of his future incomes. The estimate C is considered in §10 above.

On the theory of the gambler's ruin, see especially Bertrand, 1907; Bachelier, 1912; Dubourdieu, 1952, Chapters V and VI; Feller, 1966. See also the other references given in Section VIII of the Bibliography below (pp.679–680).

[136] M, §59 and Appendix IV, §86 (pp.84–86 and 124–125).

[137] On this question see also M, §65 (pp.92–95).

[138] M, Appendix IV, relation 23 of the English translation (Appendix IV of the English translation corresponds to Notes 88–89 of the 1952 French text; see Note 11 above) (pp.124–128 and 556).

[139] In particular a linear expression of $B(g)$ would be completely incompatible with the Bernoulli indexes derived from the responses to the 1952 experiment: *these are not linear* (See §6 above, and Appendix C, Section III and IV below, pp.451–454 and 620–627).

[140] The arbitrage $S = f(M, P)$ just considered differs fundamentally from the case studied by Borch (1968, pp.41–42), in which the underlying principle is the maximisation of mathematical expectation subject to the condition that the probability of ruin is below a given value. I examined this case in my 1952 study (Note 100). It is a highly unrealistic one (p.139 above).

§26. *The St. Petersburg Paradox* (Notes 141–152)

[141] For bibliography on the immense literature dealing with this celebrated Paradox, see mainly: Bernoulli, 1738; Buffon, 1777; Laplace, 1812 and 1814; Bertrand, 1907; Levy, 1925; Borel, 1939; Stigler, 1950; Menger, 1967. See also the other references given in *Section IX* of the Bibliography below (pp.680–681).

The works of the Bernoullis have played an essential role in the development of risk theory: James Bernoulli (1654–1705) for the central limit theorem, Nicholas Bernoulli (1662–1716) for the Saint Petersburg Paradox, and Daniel Bernoulli (1700–1782) for the psychological value and the neo-Bernoullian formulation.

[142] See Daniel Bernoulli, 1738; Laplace, 1812, pp.481–485, and 1814, pp.20–23; see also the other references given in *Section IX* of the Bibliography below.

[143] Daniel Bernoulli's assumption seems completely justified as a first approximation (see below Appendix C, Sections II and V, pp.614–620 and 627–628).
[144] Under the assumption considered the value V is defined as a function of X by the relation

(1) $$\log (X + V) = \frac{1}{2} \log (X + 2) + \frac{1}{2^2} \log (X + 2^2) + \cdots + \frac{1}{2^n} \log (X + 2^n) + \cdots.$$

It may be shown that the quantity

(2) $$V - \frac{\log X}{\log 2} - \alpha,$$

where α is a constant, tends to zero when X increases indefinitely. We have approximately

(3) $$\alpha = 0.942.$$

See Allais, 1976, *Le Paradoxe de Saint Pétersbourg et Théorie de la Ruine des Joueurs* (The St. Petersburg Paradox and the Theory of the Gambler's Ruin).
[145] On the neglecting of small probabilities, see Appendix D, §2, below (pp.657–660).
[146] At the time of Buffon the écu was worth 6 livres Tournois, equivalent to the purchasing power of some 60 French francs or 12 dollars in 1977 (see Allais, 1973, *Classes Sociales et Civilisations*, Economies et Sociétés, No. 17, p.332). The amount considered by Buffon thus represented some 25 billion current dollars.

Buffon's argument was also taken up by Shapley, 1972, although without reference to Buffon.

The speed at which exponentials grow is not generally realised. Let us assume that the unit of value is 1 gram of gold and that this gram of gold was invested at compound interest of 2.65 per cent at the beginning of the fourth millennium. In 1961 this would have amounted to a weight of gold of $6.74 \times 10^{66} \sim 2^{220}$ grams of gold, i.e. a mass of gold slightly exceeding that of as many constellations, each comprising one thousand billion suns, as there have been billionths of seconds since the beginning of the fourth millennium (Allais, 1962, *Le Tiers Monde au Carrefour*, Editions des Cahiers Africains, Brussels, Volume II, Annex V, p.117).
[147] But only in part. Bertrand notes that although the psychological value of very great sums may rise much less rapidly than their nominal value, this has no effect except only insofar as the player refrains from using any gains he makes for altruistic purposes. In this last case, satiety cannot occur (Bertrand, 1907, p.64).
[148] See e.g. Wold, 1965, p.7, Kendall and Stuart, 1969, Volume I, §9.8, p.218, and the references cited by these authors (see Bibliography, Section III).
[149] In his preface to his *Calcul des Probabilités*, 1907, Bertrand writes (pp.XI–XII) [author's translation]

> As regards the St. Petersburg Paradox we must approve simply and absolutely the reply castigated as absurd. Let us suppose Peter owns one million gold sovereigns which he gives to Paul in exchange for the agreed promises. It might be said that he is mad. The investment may appear as reckless; nevertheless it is excellent; the infinite advantage can be

attained. If he plays with obstinacy, he will lose one game, 1000, 1000 million or even a million billion; he should not abandon, but repeat the game so often that the pen will be worn out writing the figure; let him but postpone the settlement of accounts, and his victory is certain, Paul's ruin inevitable. What day? Which century? No one knows: before the end of time, there is no doubt that Peter's gain will be enormous.*

Bertrand's conclusion *cannot be gainsaid.* If settlement is not performed game by game, the banker's ruin is absolutely certain, however great the player's stake per game.

* French text:

Quant au problème de Saint Pétersbourg, il faut approuver absolument et simplement la réponse réputée absurde. Pierre possède, je suppose, un million d'écus et les donne à Paul en échange des promesses convenues. Il est fou! dira-t-on. Le placement est aventureux, mais excellent; l'avantage infini est réalisable. Qu'il joue obstinément, il perdra 1 partie, 1000, 1000 millions, 1 million de milliards peut-être; qu'il ne se rebute pas, qu'il recommence un nombre de fois que la plume s'userait à écrire, qu'il diffère surtout le règlement des comptes, la victoire, pour lui, est certaine, la ruine de Paul inévitable. Quel jour? quel siècle? On l'ignore; avant la fin des temps certainement, le gain de Pierre sera colossal.

[150] However surprising, if not paradoxical, these results may appear, they are no less exact. This is because of the great sensitivity of the probability of ruin to the price of a ticket corresponding to a game.

I cannot here give the detailed justification of these results, which involves some relatively complex calculations. I shall content myself with indicating the principles of these calculations, which stem from the application of the general theory of the gambler's ruin to the case of the St. Petersburg paradox.

Noting that the maximum of the possible loss is equal to $b - 2$, we have according to Note 126 above (pp.567–568).

(1) $\exp[-\tau(X + b - 2)] < P < \exp[-\tau X],$

with

(2) $\frac{1}{2}\exp[-\tau(2 - b)] + \frac{1}{2^2}\exp[-\tau(2^2 - b)] + \cdots + \frac{1}{2^n}\exp[-\tau(2^n - b)] + \cdots = 1.$

Putting

(3) $\tau = 1/2^q$

it is possible to demonstrate that the quantity

(4) $q - b + \beta,$

where β is a constant, tends to zero when X increases indefinitely. We have approximately

(5) $\beta = 0.11$.

For $b \geqslant 10$ the asymptotic value $q_a = b - \beta$ is practically reached, with an error smaller than $1/100$.

In the case of the Table given in the main text we have

(6) $0.998 < k = \exp[-\tau(b-2)] < 1$,

for all values of b, but the two values of b of the first line 9.1 and 10.2 for which we have $k \sim 0.99$.

Very analogous results could be obtained in the case where the banker's fortune F is limited. In this case the probability of ruin P_F of a player whose fortune is X and paying a price b for each game is smaller than the probability of ruin P when the banker's fortune is infinite, but, naturally, the player's mathematical expectation becomes here for an infinite number of games

(7) $M_F = (1 - P_F)F - P_F X$.

It is not infinite but it may be very great if P_F is small and F very great.

The justification of these results will be set forth in a forthcoming study, *The St. Petersburg Paradox, and the Theory of the Gambler's Ruin.*

[151] §25 above (pp.491–498).
[152] §5 above (pp.450–451).

NOTES TO CHAPTER III: A CRITICAL ANALYSIS OF THE BASIC CONCEPTS OF THE POST-1952 THEORIES OF THE AMERICAN SCHOOL (Notes 153–194)

[153] Quoted by D. Ellsberg, 1954, (See Bibliography, Section V, below).

§27. *Theoretical Models and Empirical Research* (Notes 154–158)

[154] Including references subsequent to the *Theory of Games* and previous to 1952, see especially (Bibliography, Section IV):

(a) *On the search for new, more appealing postulates, justifying the neo-Bernoullian formulation*:

Marschak, 1950; Friedman and Savage, 1952; Samuelson, 1952; Herstein and Milnor, 1953; Savage, 1954; Suppes, 1955 and 1961; Davidson and Suppes, 1956; Chipman, 1960, Aumann, 1962; Pratt, Raïffa and Schlaifer, 1964; Luce and Suppes, 1965; Hersanyi, 1966.

Among these works, special attention is drawn to Savage's book, which presents a simultaneous axiomatisation of 'utility' and 'probability'. See also Davidson and Suppes, 1956 (see below, §§28 and 29, pp.508–514).

(b) *On the determination of the implications of the neo-Bernoullian formulation*:

Tobin, 1958; Pratt, 1964; Borch, 1968, 1969, 1974 and 1975; Hadar and Russel, 1969; Levy, 1969 and 1974; Whitmore, 1970; Samuelson, 1970; Tsiang, 1972 and 1974; Bierwag, 1974; Bawa, 1975.

All these works assume the neo-Bernoullian formulation as a starting point and derive its implications as regards the moments of the probability distribution of the monetary gains g from the consideration of the Taylor expansion of the neo-Bernoullian index $B(U_0 + g)$ with respect to g, *these implications being independent of the particular shape of the $B(g)$ index taken into account*. The principle of these studies had already been brought forward by de Finetti, during the 1952 Paris Colloquium (Colloquium Proceedings, p.196).

In fact, all these works implicitly make a wrong assumption, i.e. that the Bernoullian index $B(U_0 + g)$ is able *simultaneously* to represent the psychological value of g and the propensity for risk (or security). As far as the first aspect is considered it is clear that the psychological values $\bar{s}(U_0 + g)$ must be considered instead of the monetary gains g.

Thus to analyse the implications of the neo-Bernoullian formulation, the only correct approach would to consider the function

(1) $$B(C + g) = \beta[\bar{s}(C + g)] = \beta(\gamma),$$

and to expand the function $\beta(\gamma)$ using Taylor's expansion, with respect to the powers of $\gamma - \bar{\gamma}$, $\bar{\gamma}$ being the average value of γ.

Only this could permit to distinguish between the respective effects of the curvature of the cardinal preference index (cardinal utility) and the greater or lesser propensity to risk-taking. (On this point see the Annex to the Appendix III, §85.6 of the English translation of my 1952 memoir, pp.116–124).

All these authors designate the principle of absolute preference (Axiom III of §10 above) by the denomination 'first degree stochastic dominance'. No reference is given to the principle of absolute preference, which was introduced in 1952, i.e., many years earlier, in the French literature (pp.39–41 and 457).

If the neo-Bernoullian index $B(g)$ reduces to a quadratic function

(2) $$B(g) = a + bg + cg^2,$$

it follows from the neo-Bernoullian formulation that the ordinal index of preference may be written

(3) $$S = S[a + bM + cM^2 + c\Sigma^2],$$

where M and Σ represent the mean and the standard deviation of g.

In his papers of 1968, 1969 and 1974, Borch has shown that in general such a field of choice is incompatible with the axiom of absolute preference, so that expression (2) is impossible for the index $B(g)$.

This impossibility had already been demonstrated by Allais, 1952, Notes 83 and 84. In fact Allais, 1952, has shown:

(a) that for a trade-off $S = f(M, \Sigma)$ the principle of absolute preference is satisfied for any Gaussian distribution (Note 83) (pp.137 and 112).

(b) that, whereas for a normal distribution the preference index $S = f(M, \Sigma)$ satisfies

the principle of absolute preference, this property does not hold for the most general
random prospects (Note 84) (pp.137 and 112–114).

(Appendix III of the English translation of the Allais 1952 memoir was Notes 83, 84
and 85 of French text of 1952) (pp.112–114).

Whereas Borch makes reference the Allais proposition (a) he makes no reference at
all to Allais proposition (b).

I have also demonstrated that a trade-off $S = f(M, \Sigma)$ for Gaussian probability
distribution is, in general, incompatible with the neo-Bernoullian formulation (Note 85
of the 1952 memoir which is §84 of the Appendix III of the English translation).

[155] On the empirical research to test the neo-Bernoullian formulation, see especially:
Mosteller and Nogee, 1951; Edwards, 1953, 1954a and b, 1956; Davidson, Siegel and
Suppes, 1955; Royden, Suppes and Walsh, 1957; Davidson and Marschak, 1958;
Lindman, 1965; Dolbear and Lave, 1967; Hagen, 1973 and 1976 (Bibliography, Section
VI). The reader will find a good general survey in Edwards, 1954, 1961 and 1968
(Bibliography, Section I) and especially in the very remarkable paper of MacCrimmon and
Larsson, 1975 reproduced in this volume (Bibliography, Section V).

MacCrimmon and Larsson rightly classify the empirical research relating to the
present paper into two categories which they label 'Common Ratio of Probabilities'
(Decision Problem I, §4) and 'Common Consequence' (Decision Problem II, §5). See
Appendix C below, §C2 and Note 8 (pp.612–613 and 635–636).

To my knowledge, no empirical research work has taken the subject's capital C into
account. This is a pity (see §14 above, and Appendix A, Note 4, and Appendix C, §C19 and
Notes 24* and 30*) (pp.463–464, 602, 628–631, 637–638).

[156] See §§6 and 22 above, and Appendix C below, Section V (pp.451, 473 and 628).

[157] On the criticism of the neo-Bernoullian formulation see especially: Ellsberg, 1954
and 1961; Shackle, 1956; Archibald, 1959; Hagen, 1969, 1972 and 1976; Watkins, 1970
and 1975; MacCrimmon and Larsson, 1975. See also the other references in the
Bibliography, Section V. A trend of thought opposed to the neo-Bernoullian formulation can be seen to be growing with time.

Krelle (1968), Bernard (1974) and Handa (1977) have suggested new but not very
convincing formulations of the utility index of a random prospect. Lesourne (1975)
proposed a particular presentation of the general formulation with an interesting
interpretation.

[158] My original intention was to give in this memoir an overall and thorough presentation of the theoretical work, empirical investigations and critical analysis to which the
neo-Bernoullian formulation has given rise, but space was lacking in the present
volume to do all this. A whole book would be necessary. I had therefore to limit myself
to some very brief comments.

[158*] See Foreword, pp.7–10 above.

§28. Confusion Between the Neo-Bernoullian Index and the Index of Cardinal Utility (Notes 159–167)

[159] Jevons, 1879, Chapter III, and Chapter IV, pp.237–239 of the French translation.

[160] §11 above, and Appendix C, Section II, below (pp.460–462 and 614–620).

[161] See §14 above (pp.463–464).

[162] Savage, 1954, and Friedman and Savage, 1952.

[163] See §6 above, and Appendix C below, Section V, §C19 (pp.451–454 and 628–631).

[164] Karl Borch, 1975, §13.

[165] See §§6 and 22 above; and Appendix C, Sections III, IV and V below (pp.620–632).

[166] See Pareto, 1919, *Traité de Sociologie*, Note 2131 (text following relation 7 to the end). *In the light of this passage, it is impossible to argue that Pareto was anti-cardinalist.* See also Allais, 1968, *Pareto*, Encyclopaedia of the Social Sciences, Vol. 11, pp.402–403 and 405 (See also Note 79 above) (p.563).

[167] The 'anticardinalists' have often been excessively critical; Karl Borch, for example, may have been rather too unjust on Ole Hagen in his 1970 paper 'De siste kardinalister' (The Last Cardinalist).

May I say that Ole Hagen will not be "standing as the last cardinalist, after Frisch and many others, who has got a paper printed".

In fact, in the light of the results of the 1952 experiment (See §6 above and Appendix C, Section II, below), I am tempted to reverse somewhat the Borch formula, and to foresee a time when we will refer to 'the last anti-cardinalist'. But I would regret it, for conflict between points of view is *indispensable* for the progress of science.

§29. *Objective Probability and Neo-Bernoullian 'Probability'*
(Notes 168–182)

[168] See §21 above, and Appendix D below (pp.469–473 and 655–663).

[169] M, §6. However, since the alternatives of the bet can present a complementarity effect together with the events whose probabilities are being considered, I now think that subjective probabilities can only be defined by a direct comparison, without any stake, with objective probabilities (See §21 and Note 107 above) (pp.469–473, 566).

[170] On this definition and the concept of the reference urn, see §21 above.

[171] It is difficult to understand why as clearsighted a thinker as Laplace should have sought to calculate the probability of tomorrow's sunrise by applying the Bayes principle of the probability of causes (Laplace, 1812–1847, Livre II, Chapter VI, pp.433–434, and 1814–1921, Vol. I, p.18), and Bertrand was easily able to present a criticism of Laplace's analysis (Bertrand, 1889–1907, §137, pp.168–169).

[172] De Finetti, 1968, pp.499–500. The last restriction was not present in de Finetti's 1937 study, *La Prévision*, in which he wrote (p.6) "Assume that a person is obliged to estimate the price p for which he would be prepared to exchange *any* positive or negative sum S for the sum pS, if a given event E occurs. We will say that by definition p is the probability he ascribes to E, or more simply, that p is the probability of E (for the person considered: this may be taken as understood whenever no ambiguity is possible)". (The word *any* is italicized by the present author.)

In fact, the general conception of de Finetti today is identical to that of Savage *as regards the simultaneous determination of 'utility' and 'probability'* (See de Finetti, 1968).

[173] Questions II of the Questionnaire. See §6 above, and Appendix C, §C3, below.

[174] See Note 172 above.

[175] That was the case of all the respondents to the 1952 experiment. (See Notes 47 and 48 above, p.560).

[176] Savage's approach, like de Finetti's, is similar to that suggested by Ramsey in 1926 (*Truth and Probability*) and well summarised by Davidson and Suppes (1956):

First find a chance event with subjective probability of one-half, then use this event to determine the utility of outcomes, and finally use the constructed utility function to measure subjective probabilites (pp.264–265).

[177] Proposition that Savage proved himself in compiling my 1952 Questionnaire. He actually followed Ramsey's approach (Note 161 above), and determined his neo-Bernoullian 'utility' index by considering an objective probability of 1/2 *defined directly with respect to drawings from an urn*. In this case, subjective and objective probability were identical.

Having thus defined his neo-Bernoullian 'utility' index using Ramsey's approach, he answered all the questions in the 1952 Questionnaire by applying the neo-Bernoullian formulation, using an objective definition throughout for all the probabilities in the list of questions (See Allais, 1976, *The Psychological Structure of Choice Involving Risk*). In doing so, Savage was discarding an essential part of his theory, and repudiating the conceptions of de Finetti, although he claimed his approach to follow de Finetti's.

[178] See Appendix C, §§C19 and C23 (pp.628–631 and 634).

[179] See §6 above, and Appendix C, Section II, below (pp.451–454 and 614–620).

[180] See §21 above (pp.469–473).

[181] By reducing a sequence of drawings to a single random prospect (M, §4, and §10 above, Axiom IV; see also §30 below) (pp.41–42, 457–459 and 514).

[182] Questions VI of the 1952 Questionnaire (see Appendix C, Section II, below) (p.614).

§30. *Sets of Successive Drawings* (Notes 183–187)

[183] M, §71, Note 122 (p.142).

[184] Thus Borch's counterexample in his work of 1968 (*The Economics of Uncertainty*, §4.8, pp.39–40) *is not valid in relation to the heart of the question*, for it assumes: (a) small sums, (b) continuous repetition of the game. In this case, the law of large numbers applies. *In fact, in order to discuss such an example, all sequences of random choice should be reduced beforehand to a single random choice.* Had Borch done this, there would no longer have been any grounds for the paradoxical conclusion he reached. That is also what he should have done in applying the von Neumann–Morgenstern Axiom 3Cb (See Note 69 above, and Appendix A, §§A2 and A8, p.562).

[185] See M, §2, and §10, Axiom II, above (pp.38–39 and 457).

[186] In fact that is what I did to establish the asymptotic validity of the neo-Bernoullian formulation (§24 above, pp.483–490).

[187] The principle of compounding elementary probabilities corresponds to von Neumann–Morgenstern's Axiom 3Cb (Axiom IV of §10, and Note 67 above; see also Appendix A, §§A2 and A8; pp.457–459, 542, 592–594 and 599).

§31. *The Neo-Bernoullian Concept of Rationality* (Notes 188–194)

[188] None of the neo-Bernoullians replied to the *altogether essential* questions in §53 of my 1952 memoir. These questions were reproduced in my *Econometrica* paper (Oct. 1953, p.521, Note 26, pp.79–80 above).

[189] As for me, I set forth *very explicitly* the two definitions of rationality I conceive as applicable (one abstract, one experimental) in my 1952 paper (See M, §§47, 52 and 53). These definitions are also presented very clearly in my *Econometrica* paper, Oct. 1953, §§16–18, pp.518–521. See also §§12 and 19 above, and §38 below (pp.462, 467, 543).

[190] In the following quotations all italics are mine.

[191] The 1952 Questionnaire actually contained three different sets of questions. (Questions VII, VIII and IX; see Appendix C, §C.3 below.) For each, it was possible to calculate the corresponding neo-Bernoullian indexes for every subject. These three indexes were completely different for any one subject (On indexes $B_{1/2}$ and B_{200}, see Appendix C below, Sections III, IV and V, pp.620–632).

[192] Although the word '*rationality*' is missing from the index of contents of Borch's 1968 book.

[193] One of my correspondents (1975) writes to me:

> I cannot see that you have given any satisfactory definition of rationality. The definition on page 304 of the Colloquium Report is obviously circular. The one on page 304 has no meaning as long as you do not define "coherence" (consistency). You have hardly any right to ask the questions in footnote 72 before you have given your own axiomatic definition of 'rationality'.

The response to these objections is easy and immediate. The definition on page 304 cited by my correspondent is the experimental definition of rationality (M, §53, and §19 above). The claimed circularity does not exist at all. The following is the French text of §53 of my 1952 memoir (p.79 above):

> Si on ne veut pas, ou si on ne peut pas, recourir à une définition abstraite de la rationalité, on ne peut que recourir à l'expérience et observer ce que font effectivement les hommes dont on a par ailleurs des raisons de penser qu'ils se comportent rationnellement.

My correspondent thus totally ignores two words "*par ailleurs*" in my text implying "*independently of any random choice consideration*".

Thus at issue is the observation of how people behave who are generally considered as 'rational' *on criteria that are free of all reference to considerations of random choice*. This is a question *of fact*.

The definition on page 302 cited by my correspondent is the abstract definition of rationality (M, §52, and §19 above). The French word '*cohérent*' simply means '*not contradictory*', i.e. consistent (pp.78–79 and 467–468).

Note 72 corresponds to the three questions recalled above (§19, pp.79–80).

I think my definitions have been given clearly enough to entitle me to ask the members of the American School to say clearly what theirs are.

[194] The same ambiguities and paralogisms *can be found everywhere in the neo-Bernoullian literature*, a fact the reader will easily check by a careful examination of the meaning of every sentence containing the words '*rational*', or '*rationality*'.

To illustrate this, see for instance: von Neumann–Morgenstern, 1947, pp.8, 9, 31, 33; Marschak, 1950, pp.111, 112, 113, 119, 138; Friedman and Savage, 1952, p.463; Strotz, 1953, p.39 (see also his definition of a 'normal' or 'not pathological' man, pp.390–391); Savage, 1954, pp.2, 7 (see also his use of the word 'reasonable', pp.3, 7, 67); Barankin,

1954, pp.25, 26; Suppes, 1955, pp.61, 72 and 1961, p.186; Markowitz, 1959, pp.205–207, 209, 213, 218, 219 and 224; Aumann, 1962, p.446; Pratt, Raïffa and Schlaifer, 1964, p.354 (see also their use of the word '*consistency*', p.357); Harsanyi, 1966, pp.613, 615, 620, 633; Edwards, 1968, p.41.

Nowhere can a definition of '*rationality*' be found which consists of anything but obedience to the axioms underlying the neo-Bernoullian formulation.

NOTES TO CHAPTER IV: CRITICISMS OF THE ALLAIS 1952
ANALYSIS: REJOINDERS (Notes 195–271)

[195] André-Marie Ampère, 1823, *Mémoire sur la Théorie Mathématique des Phénomènes Electro-Dynamiques*, Collection de Mémoires relatifs à la Physique, Tome III, Gauthier-Villars, 1887, p.104 (translation by the author).

§32. *My Refutation of the Neo-Bernoullian Formulation*
(Notes 196–203)

[196] M., §63, and below §36. For illustration see for instance: Savage, 1957, pp.101–103; Luce and Raïffa, 1957, p.25; Borch, 1968, pp.63–66; Raïffa, 1968, Chapter IV, §9.

[197] On this, may I refer to John Watkins' judgment? (1975, *Towards a Unified Decision Theory: A non-Bayesian Approach*, Note 15):

> When in the course of preparing this paper I eventually read Allais (1953) I was at once chagrined to discover how many of my (1970) criticisms of the expected utility approach has already been made, and made better, by him, and heartened by this powerful endorsement of them. This time I will try to make proper acknowledgements to him.
>
> In the meanwhile, partly by way of an excuse for my previous neglect, I will make a complaint about the way Allais has been treated by the 'Bayesian' camp. It was perhaps unfortunate that, among his various powerful criticisms of what he called 'the American School', he gave prominence to an ingenious numerical counterexample (1953, pp.525–8) to Savage's sure-thing principle. In his (1954) work, Savage concentrated exclusively on this. (He admitted that he had at first found it intuitively convincing, but claimed that a careful analysis of it shows that his initial intuition had been mistaken). This seems to have created a widespread impression that Allais's whole criticism hinges on this particular counterexample which, moreover, can be rebutted. For instance, the sole reference to Allais in Luce and Raïffa (1957, p.25) refers to Savage's handling of it; and Raïffa (1968, pp.80f) again concentrates exclusively on it.
>
> It is perhaps also unfortunate that Allais's example concerned gambles involving prizes of hundreds of millions of francs, giving it an air of unreality. This allowed Edwards, in the course of his generally excellent, and influential, review of the development of decision theory, to conclude a brief report on Allais with the remark: "However, from a simple-minded

psychological point of view these (sophisticated examples of Allais) are irrelevant. It is enough if the theory of choice can predict choices involving familiar amounts of money..." (1954; reprinted in 1967, p.42*). Allais's example would not, of course, have lost its force if the prizes had consisted of "familiar amounts of money".

*Edwards, 1954, *The Theory of Decision Making* (see Bibliography below, Section I), reprinted in Edwards and Tversky, 1967, *Decision Making*, Penguin Books (see also Note 13 above, p.556).

[198] The reader will find in Section VII of the Bibliography the references in which some comments are made on my 1952 memoir (an English translation of this memoir is given in Part II of the present volume). For more than twenty years, apart from a few exceptions, a systematic blanket of silence has fallen on this work (see Note 13 above).

It is only recently that it seems to have caught the attention of research workers. I have been very sensible of some supports, such as J. W. N. Watkins' (1975) (See Note 197 above).

As far back as the fifties I was somewhat encouraged by a few comments on my 1952 memoir, republished in 1955. I should like to quote three of these, by Gerhard Tintner, Wilhelm Krelle and Roger Dehem respectively.

The subject of choice under uncertainty has engaged many outstanding economists before. The main problem, the validity of the von Neumann–Morgenstern axioms, remains disputed. Many new and important ideas relating to this subject are contained in this book. I would like to point out especially the contributions of Allais, which are in the best tradition of the great French mathematical economists Cournot and Walras. (Tintner, 1954, p.666)

With rigour, clarity and in a manner accessible to all, M. Allais propounds his argument...

That this (certain developments of the risk theory heretofore admitted) is false is demonstrated by Allais with convincing logic backed up by numerous striking examples...

Allais demonstrates the accuracy of his thesis after carefully and irrefutably defining the concept of rationality. His book is thus a very fine work, which is both clear and intelligible in a subtle and somewhat neglected area of the national economy which will I believe soon come once again to the fore thanks to a more effective investment and prices policy. (Krelle, 1958, pp.18*–19*)

Outstanding theoreticians such as Samuelson, Marschak, Savage and Friedman, have attempted to explain the behaviour of the real individual confronted with a range of random choices and a definition of the rational choices among the uncertain possibilities. The authors base their very rigorous systems on sets of axioms defining rationality. However, M. Allais criticizes these axioms very vigorously and denies their evidence.

> The author once again displays his great powers of penetration and the subtlety of his exceptional intellect. His book is extraordinarily limpid and easy to read despite the dryness of the subject. It should also be said that his arguments are convincing and should confound his critics. (Dehem, 1956, p.159)

[199] See §§3 and 6 above; see also Appendix C below (pp.447–449, 451–454, 611–654).

[200] Chamfort, *Maximes et Pensées*, 1795.

[201] I am particularly grateful to Werner Leinfellner and Ole Hagen for having made it possible to publish this book.

I repeat that the responsibility for the delay in its publication is mine alone (see §6 above).

[202] See Allais, 1966, *Economics as a Science* (Note 106 above).

May I also refer to the three citations placed at the beginning of this study. They probably express the principles on which to base the scientific discussion of the neo-Bernoullian theory much better than I could do.

[203] Thus one of my correspondents wrote to me in February 1975:

> I think, frankly, that most people believe that you agreed that your work from 1952 was based on a fallacy, and that you wanted it to be forgotten. Nobody expected you to publish a 'mea culpa'.

§33. *My Presentation of the Theories of the American School*
(Notes 204–213)

[204] Daniel Bernoulli, 1738 (See Bibliography below, Section II).

[205] One of my correspondents (1977) writes to me: "This is not correct! Quote from Bernoulli in original Latin the statement on which you have your interpretation".

I do not see the point of consulting Bernoulli's original writings in Latin (1738) although of course I could do so. The fact is that *Econometrica* published an authoritative English translation in 1954.

Three points appear beyond dispute in this translation.

(1) From §6 (pp.25–26) the index discussed is the index of cardinal preference (cardinal utility) considered in this memoir (Appendix C, Section II below). Bernoulli's reasoning for justifying the loglinear formulation is independent of any consideration of random outcomes.

(2) His analyses (§§15–17, pp.29–35) indubitably relate to objective probabilities, corresponding to recurrent events (shipwrecks, dice games, . . .). Further, at the time (1738), only objective probabilities were considered. Only with D'Alembert (1761) was the concept of subjective probability explicitly introduced (See Appendix D, §D2 below).

(3) Taking Bernoulli's text as a whole, it is difficult to see that he did anything other than to give illustrations of the application of the principle of the mathematical expectation of cardinal utility.

[206] Mainly because Oskar Morgenstern could not be invited to the Symposium (see Note 9 above, pp.555–556).

[207] Taking into account Amihud's criticism, it seems useful to present in Appendix A,

the English translation of the most relevant parts of the Annex III, 'Confrontation de la théorie exposée avec les théories de von Neumann–Morgenstern et de Marschak' (Confrontation of the theory presented with the theories of von Neumann–Morgenstern and Marschak) of my 1951 memoir *Notes théoriques sur l'incertitude de l'avenir et le risque* (Theoretical notes on the uncertainty of the future and risk) (pp.591–603).

I stressed in this study that von Neumann–Morgenstern had clearly perceived that their formulation discarded what I have always regarded as the fundamental element of the risk (See Appendix A below, §A7, pp.598–599).

[208] And not Axiom 3Cb as von Neumann–Morgenstern suggest (*Theory of Games*, 1947, §3.7.1, p.28). On this point see Appendix A, §§A6 and A8, below (pp.596–599).

Although in my 1951 Louvain study, I presented Axioms 3Ba and 3Bb as the key axioms, the reference to the Axioms 3Ba and 3Bb was unfortunately replaced by inadvertence by a reference to Axiom 3Cb in Note 115 of my 1952 study.

[209] §24 above (pp.483–490).

[210] See Appendix A below, §A7 (pp.598–599).

[211] See for instance Morlat, 1957, p.380.

[212] See Note 197 above (pp.580–581).

[213] One of my correspondents (1977) writes that the reason for this is very simple: "de Finetti, Morgenstern and Savage could all read French, and the 'Allais Theory' seemed only to be a common fallacy".

This is the nub of the question. Who can claim the privilege of being the sole possessor of the truth? In fact the specific feature of error is to believe that one is right.

And if those named indeed knew French, what can be said about all those in the English-speaking countries who have been interested in the theory of risk? (see Note 13 above, pp.556–557).

In any case it is somewhat surprising that in the course of all the debate on the 'Allais Paradox' no-one has reflected that there might after all be some advantage in having Allais himself participate.

§34. *Erroneous Presentation of My Analysis* (Notes 214–222)

[214] M, §§10, 20, 23 and 47 (pp.45, 51–53, 55 and 69–70). The erroneous interpretation of Amihud, 1974, has also been given by Edwards, 1954, p.401, and 1960, p.39; Luce and Suppes, 1965, p.328; Borch, 1969, p.2.

[215] The same observation may be presented on the preference functions considered in my other memoir published in 1952. *L'extension des théories de l'équilibre économique général et du rendement social au cas du risque* (Extension of the Theories of General Economic Equilibrium and Economic Efficiency to the Case of Risk).

[216] *I.e., nine years before Edwards.*

[217] This point is also made, but in more condensed form, in §8 of the extract of my 1952 memoir, which was published in *Econometrica* in 1953 (Memoir III bis, see Bibliography below, Section I).

[218] See §§58 and 59 of my 1952 memoir (pp.84–86).

In view of Amihud's note concerning Tobin's work (1958), I consider it useful to draw attention to the fact that I set forth in my 1952 paper (§58, and Appendix III, §§82–83), i.e. well before Tobin, the conditions under which a preference index of the

type $S = f(M, \Sigma)$ can be compatible with the neo-Bernoullian formulation, and noted that in general it is not. In addition, and contrary to what Amihud suggests, a neo-Bernoullian index of the type $B(g) = a + bg + cg^2$ is, in general, inadmissible, for it does not satisfy the principle of absolute preference (see Note 154 above).
[219] One of my correspondents writes:

> Some people misunderstood you because you did not express your views with sufficient clarity! You never put forward a general theory!...
>
> [Today] your views are in general stated clearly and precisely, and I am only sorry that you did not present your ideas from 1952 with the same clarity 20 years ago – at the time when Savage, and Luce and Raïffa published their books. If you had done it then, your place in the history of decision theory would have been assured, and the theory may have developed along different lines.

Actually, my new memoir basically takes up the main points of my 1952 study. Twenty years ago, I thought – wrongly, it turns out – that the 1952 paper was clear enough to stand on its own, and that exegesis would be pointless. I also completely underestimated the extent to which the majority of the English-speaking academics were ignorant of French.

At all events, if my commentators have misunderstood my point of view, this is probably because too often they have read my 1952 memoir *only superficially*, considering only a few passages from it.

I leave it to the reader to refer to the English translation of my 1952 paper, which is reproduced in full in this book *without modification*, to judge whether it was clear enough or not.

In any case if I may have indeed succeeded in clarifying my standpoints, or stating them more accurately, this is thanks to the reflexion suggested by the criticisms of Morgenstern, Amihud and my other correspondents; in this context, Chapter IV of my memoir is absolutely essential.

Finally, even assuming that my present discussion is much clearer than was the 1952 text, I doubt that, had it been published in 1953, it could have modified decision theory as it stood then. Prejudice was too powerful at the time for a publication to have led to a change in the dominant opinion. Years had to pass before illusions began to be dissolved (see §27 and Note 13 above, pp.507–508 and 556–557).
[220] See §27 above (pp.507–508).
[221] On the axiom of independence, see M, 1952, §§63 and 70; see also Appendix A, §A4 below (pp.88–90, 98–99 and 594–596).
[222] See above §28 (pp.508–510).

§35. *Non-Theory or Theory* (Notes 223–234)

[223] See §§10 and 11 above (pp.456–462).
[224] M, §44(d) (p.67).
[225] Be this as it may, Morgenstern's use of the term *'utility of gambling'* which has a somewhat pejorative sense seems inappropriate to me to represent the fundamental

issue of the theory of random choice, namely, the shape of the probability distribution of the psychological value of monetary gains. I should prefer a more neutral expression, for instance 'the utility of risk taking'.

One of my correspondents (1977) writes that '*utility of gambling*' is the translation of Pascal's term '*Plaisir du Jeu*'. Actually Pascal's expression encompasses both '*the pleasure of gambling*' and '*the pleasure of the game*', corresponding to elements A(IV) and B(2) of my 1952 paper (M, §§20, 27 and 36, pp.51–53, 57–58 and 60).

[226] See §6 above, and Appendix C below, Sections III, IV and V (pp.451–454 and 620–632).

[227] As two experiments made in 1974 and 1975 have shown. The respondents were Ph.D. students at the University of Paris-X, (see §6 above and Appendix C, §§C9, C21 and Chart VI, pp.453, 619–620, 632 and 645).

[228] The consideration of the Charts representing $B_{1/2}$ and B_{200}, (Appendix C, below, Charts VII to XII) shows that the effects whose importance I am underlining, are only marked for relatively large sums and probabilities close to one (pp.646–651).

As regards the works of Edwards (1954) and Borch (1968) referred to by Amihud without specifying the passages he alludes to, their comments on the 'Allais Paradox' betray the same paralogical and inconsistent reasoning as the passages examined above.

[229] M, §44. May I ask the reader to refer to the different arguments I have presented in this §44: they reply in advance to the observations made by my correspondent, like those of Morgenstern and Amihud (pp.65–67).

[230] See M, §21, Note 42*, and §57 (pp.53, 134 and 83). See also my analysis of indifference surfaces in a particular case; Allais, 1953, *L'extension des théories de l'équilibre économique général et du rendement social au cas du risque* (pp.271–275) (see Note 215 above).

[231] However the theoretical research done in connection with the analysis of the 1952 experiment led me to two new axioms VI and VII which I called the *Invariance and Homogeneity* and *Cardinal Isovariation* axioms, which make it possible to specify somewhat the form of fields of choice. In fact the two postulates seem to be borne out by observed data (see §23.2 above, pp.480–483).

[232] See for instance Appendices I to V of the English version of my 1952 memoir (in the 1952 French original these Appendixes were included as text notes; see Note 11 above).

[233] §6 above, and Appendix C below, Sections III, IV and V (pp.451–454 and 620–632).

[234] Allais, 1966, *Economics as a Science* (Note 106 above).

§36. Interpretation of the So-called 'Allais Paradox' (Notes 235–262)

[235] M, §63 (pp.88–90).

[236] Although some authors discussed it without giving the precise reference.

[237] Although it is far from being the most efficient test (See §22 above, and Appendix C below, Note 15 and §C19, pp.473–474, 636 and 628–631).

[238] The italics in the following quotations have been added by the present author.

[239] Savage, 1954, pp.101–103. Savage restates my example in dollars, at a conversion rate of 200 frs = \$1. *To facilitate comparison with my 1952 memoir* (§63), *I have added my original notation in brackets after Savage's* (pp.88–90).

In the paper Savage read at the Paris Colloquium in 1952, *his fundamental axiom was his fifth*. In the December 1952 paper of Friedman and Savage, '*The Expected Utility*

Hypothesis and the Measurability of Utility', this axiom became Postulate 3. *In his* 1954 *book, this became Postulate II 'The Sure Thing Principle'*, §2.7, pp.21–26) (see Bibliography below, Section IV). This correspondence should be kept in mind when comparing the critical analysis of these different texts.

[240] Savage's fundamental axiom is illustrated in Figures 1 and 2 of §63 of my 1952 memoir. These Figures are not reproduced by Savage in his presentation of my counterexample. They are however essential for a correct understanding of my point of view. *It is at the very least amazing* that *none* of the authors who have discussed the 'Allais' Paradox' showed these Figures, nor reproduced the *very short* comment that came with them. How can one possibly criticize an author without first presenting his argument? (pp.88–90).

[241] Two of my correspondents suggest that I never replied to the reasoning of Savage (1954), Luce and Raïffa (1957) and Raïffa (1958) (See Bibliography, Section VIII).

This is not so: these three authors merely reproduced *much less clearly*, the justification presented by Samuelson in 1952, at the Paris Colloquium, of the axiom of substitutability whose specious nature I showed in my 1952 memoir (See M, §71, p.99).

As a matter of fact, one of these two correspondents who was particularly responsive to Raïffa's line of argument (1968) has recognised later, November 1977, that the reasoning presented by Savage, Luce and Raïffa, and Raïffa indeed boils down fundamentally to that of Samuelson.

[242] It is easily seen that, eliminating any possible complementarity effect, Savage's 1952 fifth axiom (related to his 1954 Postulate II; see Note 239 above) leads to the neo-Bernoullian formulation. Here is the argument I set forth during the 1952 Paris Colloquium (Colloquium Proceedings, p.245):

⟨⟨It is easy to see that Savage's fifth axiom implies the Bernoullian formulation by itself; let us consider an urn with three identical balls, but of different colours, to which correspond gains X, Y, Z respectively. Let $S = S(X, Y, Z)$ be the corresponding preference index.

Savage's fifth axiom means that if

$$S(X_0, Y_0, Z_0) = S(X_1, Y_1, Z_0),$$

then

$$S(X_0, Y_0, Z) = S(X_1, Y_1, Z)$$

must be true whatever Z.

This means that in the (X, Y, Z) space, the indifference curves are the same in any plane on a Z ordinate, and that we have:

$$S = F[\varphi(X, Y) + \varphi(Z)],$$

and hence, for symmetry reasons:

$$S = F[\psi(X) + \psi(Y) + \psi(Z)].$$

Since the three balls have an identical probability of being drawn, this formula is equivalent to Bernoulli's:

$$B(V) = [B(X) + B(Y) + B(Z)]/3,$$

where V is the monetary value of the random prospect considered⟩⟩.

[243] See the citation from Good included among the three with which this study opens.

[244] In presenting Markowitz's criticism, Amihud (1974) does not seem to see that his reasoning is none other than Savage's (1954), and that it is basically subject to the same criticisms as those I presented in my 1952 memoir (§64) against Samuelson's axiom.

[245] Raiffa (1970) does not even give the reference to my 1953 paper in *Econometrica* 'Le Comportement de l'Homme Rationnel devant le Risque: Critique des Postulats et Axiomes de l'Ecole Américaine' (The Behavior of Rational Man in the Presence of Risk: Criticism of the Postulates and Axioms of the American School).

[246] Luce and Raïffa (1957) (p.25) merely repeat the criticism by Savage, which they describe as "penetrating".

As regards their own it is improperly attached to their Assumption 1 (p.25), whereas it should relate to their Assumption 4 (p.27). This is somewhat surprising.

[247] See also Morrisson's criticism of Savage (1967, pp.377–378).

[248] Some of the seminar participants had attended the 1952 Paris Colloquium (May 12–17) and so were fully informed of the questions there debated.

Those who responded to the Questionnaire published in the *Journal de la Société Statistique de Paris* (1953) without having participated in these debates, had nevertheless no trouble briefing themselves, since the questionnaire proper was preceded by eleven pages of appropriate comments. See *La Psychologie de l'homme rationnel devant le risque – La théorie et l'expérience* (The Psychology of Rational Behavior in the Presence of Risk–Theory and Experience), pp.47–57. (See §3 above and Appendix C, §C2 below, pp.447–448 and 612–613).

In all of the 101 complete files I hold (§6 above and Appendix C below, §C4), over 80 have been given to me by people who were present at my Seminar of June 11, 1952 in the 'Groupe de Recherches Economiques et Sociales'. During this seminar, after I presented a general introduction, Savage explained his point of view for about twenty minutes.

[249] M, §§64 and 71 (pp.90–92 and 99–103).

[250] M, §64, alinea 2 (p.90).

[251] M, §64, alinea 3 (p.90).

[252] M, §64 (pp.90–92).

[253] See Notes 216 and 197 above. See also and for instance Luce and Raïffa, 1957, p.25; Markowitz, 1959, pp.219–224; Borch, 1968, pp.62–66; Raïffa, 1968, Chapter IV, §9 (Bibliography below, Section I).

See also Fels, 1959; Suppes, 1959; Borch, 1968 (Bibliography below, Section VII).

Drèze alone (1954) makes reference to my *complementarity effect*, though he nonetheless adds:

> This argument is somewhat surprising since the invoked 'complementarity' is inconsistent with the continuity of the preference relation advocated by Allais in other contexts (see Allais, 1952a, Fondements d'une théorie positive des choix comportant un risque). This point will be discussed later.

In fact I do not understand the exact meaning of this argument.

[254] M, §§63 and 64 (pp.88–92).

[255] See §§19 and 31 above (pp.467–468 and 514–517).

[256] See §24 above (pp.483–490).

[257] See §6 above, and Appendix C below, Sections II, III, IV and V (pp.451–454 and 614–632).

[258] Such competent and experienced men as de Finetti and Shackle were able to respond consistently to questions bearing on large sums associated with probabilities that were either very small or very close to unity. However for both the neo-Bernoullian indexes $B_{1/2}$ and B_{200} are incompatible (For de Finetti, see Charts I, VII, X, and XIII below, pp.640, 646, 649 and 652).

As far as Milton Friedman and Jacob Marschak were concerned, they determined their utility index from introspection (see Note 116 above).

In any case Savage himself, using the Ramsey method, could without any difficulty determine his 'utility index' in an interval of the possible gains from ten to one million dollars (Notes 161 and 162 above).

[259] §33 and Note 208 above. See also Appendix A below, §§A6 and A8 (pp.520–524, 583, 596–600).

[260] See M, §§64 and 71, and Notes 122 and 123 (pp.90–92, 99–103 and 42).

The validity of Axiom 3Cb is not equivalent to a two stage choice such as Samuelson suggests, for he places himself '*ex post*', not '*ex ante*' (see M, §71, p.101).

In reality, Axiom 3Cb is equivalent to the combinational rules stated in §4 of my 1952 paper (see §10, Axiom IV of Composition above, and Appendix A, §A8 below, pp.457 and 599).

In fact the Axiom 3Cb is only a particular case of my Axiom IV (see §10.4 above, and Appendix A, §A8 below, pp.457–459 and 599).

[261] See M, §21, Note 32 (pp.53–54).

[262] Morrisson (1967) sets aside, correctly in my view, the would-be explanations of the 'Allais Paradox' based on the distinction between 'risk' and 'uncertainty' (p.377), Savage's reasoning (pp.377–378), and the shape of the utility function (p.382). Morrisson's point of view seems to be reasonably well summarised on pp.378–381 and 383. However, some passages in his exposition are not the most limpid.

The argument in (I) to (III) of p.378 (§1a of p.383) seems fundamentally different from that in pp.379–380 (§IIA, p.383) which, as Borch (1968, the Allais Paradox) correctly pointed out, merely restates Savage's argument (1954), which Morrisson precisely rejects (pp.377–378). In any case, the assumption labelled (1) (pp.378–379) does not strike me as particularly appealing.

§37. *The Validity of the* 1952 *Experiment* (Notes 263–265)

[263] Morgenstern 1974, 'Some Reflections on Utility' (Contribution to the present book).

[264] May I refer to the quotation from Pareto at the end of §40 below, and to those introducing the study as a whole. In any case, Edward's works on random choice (Bibliography, Sections I and VI, below) were done well after my 1952 questionnaire.

[265] See §6 above, and Appendix C below (pp.451–454 and 611–654).

§38. *The Concept of Rationality* (Notes 266–271)

[266] Amihud, 1974, 'Critical Examination of the New Foundation of Utility' (Contribution to this volume).

[267] Morgenstern, 1972, p.711. Italicization is that of Morgenstern.
[268] Ibid., p.712.
[269] See §24 above (pp.483–491).
[270] M, §63. See §36 above (pp.88–90 and 533–541).
[271] Amihud, 1974, ibid.

NOTES TO CHAPTER V: CONCLUSIONS: THEORY AND
EXPERIENCE (Notes 272–283)

[272] *Traité de Sociologie Générale*, 1916, Vol. I, pp.319–320.

§39–40. The Axiomatic Structure of Allais' Theory (Notes 273–280)

[273] Which may either be deduced *a priori* from conditions of symmetry, if they obtain (the fundamental urn probability model) or from *a posteriori* analysis of observed data (see §21 above, pp.469–473).
[274] See §23 above (pp.475–483).
[275] See §6 above, and Appendix C below, Sections II and V (pp.451, 614 and 627).
[275*] Jacques Lesourne writes to me "Is it not necessary to underline that, in considering *in all the cases* the concept of cardinal utility, the Allais theory ensures the total coherence of utility theory in the absence of risk *and* the presence of risk?

How, on the contrary, could one consider the neo-Bernoullian *cardinal* utility concept in the case of risk and to admit *only* the concept of *ordinal* utility in the absence of risk?"
[276] See §§10 and 11 above (pp.456–462).
[277] See §21 above (pp.469–473).
[278] See §25 above (pp.491–498).
[279] See §24 above (pp.483–490).
[280] See §31 and Note 208 above, and Appendix A below (pp.514–517, 583 and 591–603).
[280*] See Foreword pp.4–7; §23, pp.481–483; see also §24, pp.484–490.

§41. The Nature of a Scientific Theory (Notes 281–285)

[281] §24 above (pp.483–490).
[282] See Allais, 1968, *Economics as a Science* (see Note 106 above).
[283] Amihud's study (1974) begins with a citation from Kuhn:

> The act of judgement that leads scientists to reject a previously accepted theory is always based upon more than a comparison of that theory with the world. The decision to reject one paradigm is always simultaneously the decision to accept another, and the judgement leading to that decision involves the comparison of both paradigms with nature *and* with each other.

and Amihud writes:

I shall try to show that Allais' criticism is not sufficiently convincing to reject the expected utility theory, and that the alternative theory suggested by Allais is far from being able to replace that of von Neumann and Morgenstern.

However attractive the Kuhn citation may be, it is not convincing. *If a theory is invalidated by observed data, it is not scientific to maintain in merely because another has not yet been developed.* But even if Kuhn's thesis is accepted, it does not apply here, for *the theory I presented in 1952 is an alternative theory that is compatible with observed data, which the von Neumann–Morgenstern theory is not.* (On this question see also §35.3(a), pp.531–532).

[284] See Appendix C, Sections III, IV and V below (pp.620–632).

[285] Considering its obvious weaknesses, one cannot but wonder why the neo-Bernoullian formulation has kept such a hold for thirty years, and why the American School has displayed such passionate tenaciousness in defending a wholly untenable position at all costs.

The reason can perhaps be easily found out. During a talk in 1975 with an Israelian psychologist, Kahnehan, it appeared to us that a very simple psychological explanation could be given by considering the considerable amount of intellectual investments put into the theories of the American School. Just as a firm (or a State) has great difficulty in renouncing a technique (or a policy) which shows itself basically disadvantageous but in which enormous investments have been made, the neo-Bernoullian of the American School could never give up theories which have cost them so much effort.

This situation brings to mind the statement of the mathematician Frege at the end of the second volume of his master work on arithmetic:

> Nothing is more annoying for a scientist than to see the foundations crumble just as the work is done. A letter from Mr Bertrand Russell put me in this position as I was preparing to bring my manuscript to the printer.

(Eric Temple Bell, *La mathématique, reine et servante des Sciences*, French translation, Payot, 1939, Chapter XX, 4, p.349).

APPENDICES

APPENDIX A: THE VON NEUMANN–MORGENSTERN THEORY OF RANDOM CHOICE

> Do not our postulates introduce, in some oblique way, the hypotheses which bring in the mathematical expectation?... May there not exist in an individual a (positive or negative) utility of the mere act of 'taking a chance', of gambling which the use of the mathematical expectation obliterates?...
>
> It constitutes a much deeper problem to formulate a system, in which gambling has under all conditions a definite utility or disutility.
>
> J. VON NEUMANN AND O. MORGENSTERN,
> *Theory of Games and Economic Behavior*,
> 1947, pp.28 and 629

Considering Morgenstern and Amihud's criticisms in their 1974 contributions, it is useful to annex to the present study extracts of a critical analysis written, twenty eight years ago, in 1951,[1] completing them on a few points. The given references correspond to the 1947 second edition of the *Theory of Games* (pp.8–31 and 617–632).

THE AIMS OF THE VON NEUMANN–MORGENSTERN THEORY

A.1. *As far as can be seen, von Neumann–Morgenstern aim to determine psychological value as defined in the present study.* This seems to result from the following passages:

591

It has been pointed out repeatedly that a numerical utility is dependent upon the possibility of comparing differences in utilities. This may seem – and indeed is – a more far-reaching assumption than that of a mere ability to state preferences . . . .

If [an individual] now prefers A to the 50–50 combination of B and C, *this provides a plausible base* for the numerical estimate that his preference of A over B is in excess of his preference of C over A.

If this standpoint is accepted, then there is a criterion with which to compare the preference of C over A with the preference of A over B. It is well known that thereby utilities – or rather differences of utilities – become numerically measurable . . . (pp.17–18).

To give a simple example: Assume that an individual prefers the consumption of a glass of tea to that of a cup of coffee, and the cup of coffee to a glass of milk. If we now want to know whether the last preference – i.e., difference in utilities – exceeds the former *it suffices* to place him in a situation where he must decide this: Does he prefer a cup of coffee to a glass the content of which will be determined by a 50%–50% chance device as tea or milk (p.18, Note 1).

For all these passages (my italics) it results that von Neumann–Morgenstern indeed aim to determine differences in satisfaction (or utility), that according to them such differences cannot be determined by direct experiment, and that therefore it is necessary to consider indirect experiments considering random choice.

We see also that von Neumann and Morgenstern admit without any real justification propositions which they present as '*plausible*' and which are in reality *very questionable*.

The probabilities von Neumann–Morgenstern consider are objective probabilities, as the following passage shows:

Probability has often been visualized as a subjective concept more or less in the nature of an estimation. Since we propose to use it in constructing an individual, numerical estimation of utility, the above view of probability would not serve our purpose. The simplest procedure is, therefore, to insist upon the alternative perfectly well-founded interpretation of probability *as frequency in long runs*. This gives directly the necessary numerical foothold (p.19).

THE MAIN AXIOMS OF VON NEUMANN AND MORGENSTERN

A.2. Using our notation, i.e. that is using the symbol (P) to represent the random prospect[2]

$$(1) \qquad g_1, g_2, \ldots, g_n, p_1, p_2, \ldots, p_n,$$

the notation $(P) > (P')$ to denote the preference for (P) over (P'), and the notation

$$(P_3) = \alpha(P_1) + (1 - \alpha)(P_2)$$

to represent the random prospect constituted by the probability (α) to obtain (P_1) and the probability $(1 - \alpha)$ to obtain (P_2), von Neumann–Morgenstern's *main axioms* (pp.26–27) may be presented as follows.[3]

(1) *Axiom 3Ab*

The preferences $(P_1) < (P_2)$, $(P_2) < (P_3)$ entail the preference $(P_1) < (P_3)$.

Von Neumann–Morgenstern write: "Axiom 3Ab is the 'transitivity' of preference, a plausible and generally accepted property".

(2) *Axioms 3Ba and 3Bb*

Preference $(P_1) < (P_2)$ implies $(P_1) < \alpha(P_1) + (1 - \alpha)(P_2)$. Likewise $(P_1) > (P_2)$ implies $(P_1) > \alpha(P_1) + (1 - \alpha)(P_2)$.

Von Neumann–Morgenstern write: "This is legitimate since any kind of complementarity (or the opposite) has been excluded" (p.27).

(3) *Axioms 3Bc and 3Bd*

Preferences $(P_1) < (P_3) < (P_2)$ imply the existence of at least one probability α such that $\alpha(P_1) + (1 - \alpha)(P_2) < (P_3)$. Likewise preferences $(P_1) > (P_3) > (P_2)$ imply the existence of at least one probability α such that $\alpha(P_1) + (1 - \alpha)(P_2) > (P_3)$.

Von Neumann–Morgenstern write: "This is plausible 'continuity' assumption" (p.27). "These axioms express ... the Archimedean property" (p.630).

(4) *Axiom 3Cb*

We have

$$\alpha[\beta(P_1) + (1 - \beta)(P_2)] + (1 - \alpha)(P_2) = \gamma(P_1) + (1 - \gamma)(P_2)$$

with $\gamma = \alpha\beta$.

Von Neumann–Morgenstern write: "This is the statement that it is irrelevant whether a combination of two constituents is obtained in two successive steps, – first the probabilities α, $1 - \alpha$, then the probabilities β, $1 - \beta$; or in one operation, – the probabilities γ, $1 - \gamma$ where $\gamma = \alpha\beta$" (p.27).

THE NEO-BERNOULLIAN FORMULATION OF VON NEUMANN–MORGENSTERN

A.3. From these axioms von Neumann–Morgenstern demonstrate the existence of an index $B(X)$ such that

$$(2) \qquad B(C + V) = \sum_i p_i B(C + g_i) \qquad \left[\sum p_i = 1 \right],$$

where C denotes the subject's capital and V the monetary value of the random prospect (P).[4] The function $B(X)$ is interpreted by von Neumann–Morgenstern as representing the cardinal utility of the sum X.

THE IMPLICIT INDEPENDENCE HYPOTHESIS

A.4. If a function $B(X)$ existed, such that *in the most general case, relation* (2) *was satisfied*, the indifference surface would be represented by the condition

$$(3) \qquad \sum p_i B(C + g_i) = \text{constant},$$

and the most general index of preference S (or ordinal utility) would be given by the relation

$$(4) \qquad S = F\left[\sum p_i B(X + g_i) \right],$$

where $F(Z)$ denotes an increasing function of Z.

This can only occur if the goods (g_1, p_1), (g_2, p_2), . . . , (g_n, p_n) corresponding to gains $g_1, g_2, . . . , g_n$ having probabilities $p_1, p_2, . . . , p_n$ could be considered as psychologically independent, but there is no reason in general for this to be so.[5]

The very fact that the occurrence having probability p_i excludes all the others, cannot on its own entail this circumstance, because the desirability of gain g_i with probability p_i obviously depends on the amounts g_k of the other gains associated with probabilities p_k. Thus let us consider a lottery with 1000 tickets among which one ticket only gives a gain, this gain being one million dollars. Without any doubt the psychological value of a ticket for a person would be in general entirely different if he had already inherited 999 tickets, or if had no one, since in the first case the thousandth ticket would give him the certainty of winning one million dollars.

For any operator for whom this is the case, the neo-Bernoullian theory will be contradicted. If, G being the monetary value of the single prize, V_n is the monetary value attributed to the possession of n tickets, then, if we take $B(0) = 0$ which is always possible without any loss of generality, we should have

$$(5) \qquad B(V_n) = \frac{n}{N} B(G),$$

implying

$$(6) \qquad B(V_1) = \frac{1}{N} B(G),$$

$$(7) \qquad B(V_{N-1}) = \frac{N-1}{N} B(G),$$

$$(8) \qquad B(V_N) = \frac{N}{N} B(G).$$

If V_{N-1}^* is thus the value of the last ticket for a player who already has $N - 1$, then

$$(9) \qquad B(V_{N-1}^*) = B(V_N) - B(V_{N-1}) = \frac{1}{N} B(g) = B(V_1),$$

i.e.

$$(10) \qquad V_{N-1}^* = V_1.$$

It is this analysis which led me to formulate questions IV bis (43 and 44) of the 1952 questionnaire (J.S.S.P., 1953, p.61).

Von Neumann and Morgenstern do not seem to have clearly perceived this, at least judging from the following passages whose meaning remains, it is true, *somewhat obscure, because they do not give a precise definition of complementarity.*

By a combination of two events we mean this: let the two events be denoted by B and C and use, for the sake of simplicity, the probability 50%–50%. Then the 'combination' is the prospect of seeing B occur with a probability of 50% and (if B does not occur) with the (remaining) probability of 50%. We stress that the two alternatives are mutually exclusive, *so that no possibility of complementarity and the like exists* (pp.17–18).

Simply additive formulae would seem to indicate that we are assuming absence of any form of complementarity between the things the utilities of which we are combining. It is important to realize, that we are doing this solely in a situation where there can indeed be no complementarity. As pointed out ... the utilities ... *refer to alternatively conceived events*, of which only one can and will become real. *I.e. since the* [*different events of probabilities p_i*] *are in no case conceived as taking place together, they can never complement each other in the ordinary sense* (p.628).[6]

This reasoning rests on a pure paralogism, for the very fact that the realization of event of probability p_i excludes all the others could not in any way imply that the different lottery tickets (g_i, p_i) constitute independent goods, as the preceding example regarding the possession of 999 lottery tickets out of 1,000 shows it very clearly.

THE INTERPRETATION OF THE NEO-BERNOULLIAN INDEX

A.5. Von Neumann–Morgenstern's analysis embodies (we think involuntarily) a constant confusion between two different concepts: a certain function $B(X)$ satisfying the neo-Bernoullian formulation (2) and a certain function $\bar{s}(X)$ representing the psychological value (or cardinal utility) as given directly by our introspection. The result of this confusion is to mask absolutely essential difficulties, for the von Neumann–Morgenstern statements, quoted above in §A1 are not at all evident.

THE VON NEUMANN–MORGENSTERN AXIOMS 3Ba AND 3Bb EXCLUDE THE SPECIFIC ELEMENT OF RISK

A.6. *It is easy to verify that the von Neumann–Morgenstern Axioms 3Ba and 3Bb exclude the specific element of risk*, that is the probability distribution of psychological values about their mean.[7]

Implications of the Axioms 3Ba and 3Bb

A.6.1. In fact the preference

$$(11) \qquad (P_1) < (P_2),$$

may result from a strong propensity to security, for instance if (P_2)

represents a certainly available gain. But the security advantage corresponding to (P_2) may be destroyed if we consider the random prospect $\alpha(P_1) + (1 - \alpha)(P_2)$ so that we may have at the same time the preference (11) and the preference

(12) $(P_1) > (P_3) = \alpha(P_1) + (1 - \alpha)(P_2)$.

Thus we can verify that the propensity to risk or to security is incompatible with von Neumann–Morgenstern's Axioms 3Ba and 3Bb.

Axioms 3Ba and 3Bb and Samuelson's Axiom[8]

A.6.2. Von Neumann–Morgenstern's Axioms 3Ba and 3Bb are only particular cases of Samuelson's substitutability axiom (M §64). So we may verify that Axioms 3Ba and 3Bb are effectively the crucial axioms. For we have:

Axiom 3Ba

(13) $(P_1) < (P_2)$ implies $(P_1) < \alpha(P_1) + (1 - \alpha)(P_2)$.

Samuelson's Axiom (p.90 above)

(14) $(P_1) < (P_2)$ implies $(1 - \alpha)(P_1) + \alpha(P_3) < (1 - \alpha)(P_2) + \alpha(P_3)$

if we take $(P_3) \equiv (P_1)$ Samuelson's axiom becomes identical to Axiom 3Ba. Thus Axiom 3Ba is only a particular case of Samuelson's axiom. Therefore it may be contradicted by analogous examples.

Illustration example[8]

A.6.3. As an illustration, the following example may contradict the Axiom 3Ba:

$$(P_1)\begin{cases} \dfrac{90}{100}\text{:} & 20 \text{ million dollars} \\ \dfrac{10}{100}\text{:} & 0 \end{cases} \qquad (P_2)\begin{cases} \text{certainty} \\ \text{of 1 million} \\ \text{dollars} \end{cases}$$

$$\begin{array}{l} P_3 = \alpha(P_1) + (1 - \alpha)(P_2) \\[2mm] \alpha = \dfrac{9}{10} \end{array} \qquad \begin{cases} \dfrac{81}{100}\text{:} & 20 \text{ million dollars} \\ \dfrac{10}{100}\text{:} & 1 \text{ million dollars} \\ \dfrac{9}{100}\text{:} & 0 \end{cases}$$

It seems really difficult to consider as irrational a prudent man for whom we have at the same time (contrary to Axiom 3Ba)

(a) $(P_1) < (P_2)$,

(b) $(P_1) > (P_3) = \alpha(P_1) + (1 - \alpha)(P_2)$.

Preference (a) results from a strong preference for security, but when certainty disappears, 90 chances in 100 to win 20 million dollars may be much more attractive than 81 chances on 100 to win the same sum though the probability of winning nothing is 10/100 instead of 9/100.

THE PROPENSITY TO RISK OR SECURITY ACCORDING TO VON NEUMANN AND MORGENSTERN

A.7. *The index $B(X)$ being interpreted as representing cardinal utility, it is obvious that formulation (2) of von Neumann–Morgenstern cannot take into account the probability distribution of cardinal utilities since it considers only their mathematical expectation, and so it eliminates the specific element of the theory of random choice.*

It seems unquestionable that von Neumann and Morgenstern did clearly perceive this difficulty, as shown by the following significant quotations (my italics):

Do not our postulates introduce, in some oblique way, the hypotheses which bring in the mathematical expectation.

More specifically: *May there not exist in an individual a (positive or negative) utility of the mere act of taking a chance of gambling which the use of the mathematical expectation obliterates?*

How did our Axioms (3:A)–(3:C) get around this possibility?

As far as we can see, our postulates (3:A)–(3:C) do not attempt to avoid it. *Even that one which gets closest to excluding as a 'utility of gambling'* (3:C:b) (Cf. its discussion in 3.6.2.), seems to be plausible and legitimate – unless a much more refined system of psychology is used than the one now available for the purpose of economics. The fact that a numerical utility – with a formula amounting to the use of mathematical expectations – can be built upon (3:A)–(3:C), seems to indicate this: *We have practically defined numerical utility as being that thing for which the calculus of mathematical expectations is legitimate.* Since (3:A)–(3:C) secure that the necessary construction can be carried out, *concepts like a 'Specific utility of gambling' cannot be formulated free of contradiction on this level.*

This may seem to be a paradoxical assertion. But anybody who has seriously tried to axiomatise that elusive concept will probably concur with it (p.28).

Daniel Bernoulli's well known suggestion to 'solve' the 'St. Petersburg Paradox' by the use of so-called 'moral expectation' (instead of the mathematical expectation) means defining the utility numerically as the logarithm of one's monetary possessions (p.28).

Bernoulli's utility satisfies our axiom and obeys our results.... Thus a suitable definition of utility (which in such a situation is essentially uniquely determined by our axioms) eliminates in this case the specific utility or disutility of gambling, *which prima facie appeared to exist....*

It constitutes a much deeper problem to formulate a system, in which gambling has under all conditions a definite utility or disutility, where numerical utilities fulfilling the calculus of mathematical expectations cannot be defined by any process, direct or indirect. *In such a system some of our axioms must be necessarily invalid.* It is difficult to foresee at this time which axiom or group of axioms is most likely to undergo such a modification (p.629).[6]

It seems probable, that the really critical group of axioms is (3:C) – *or, more specifically, the axiom 3Cb.* This axiom expresses the combination rule for multiple chance alternatives, and it is plausible, that a specific utility or disutility of gambling can only exist if this simple combination rule is abandoned.

Some change of the system (3:A)–(3:C), at any rate involving the abandonment or at least a radical modification of (3:C:b), may perhaps lead to a mathematically complete and satisfactory calculus of utilities, which allows for the possibility of a specific utility or disutility of gambling. *It is hoped that a way will be found to achieve this,* but the mathematical difficulties seem to be considerable. Of course, this makes the fulfillment of the hope of a successful approach by purely verbal means appear even more remote (p.632).[6]

These different passages deserve particularly close attention by authors who state that the neo-Bernoullian formulation (2) *does take account of the more or less strong propensity to risk.* The object of the theory we have submitted in 1952 is to meet precisely the concerns evinced by von Neumann–Morgenstern.[7]

THE REAL IMPLICATIONS OF VON NEUMANN–MORGENSTERN'S AXIOM 3Cb[8]

A.8. *Contrary to von Neumann–Morgenstern's suggestions attributing to Axiom 3Cb the elimination of the risk specific element, and very often taken again in the literature,[9] Axioms 3Ba and 3Bb are those which entail this elimination* as I have indicated above (§A6).[10]

Axiom 3Cb simply corresponds to the reduction of a series of random prospects considered at a given time to a single random prospect as I have indicated in my 1952 memoir (§4). This equivalence appears today in the axiomatic formulation of my theory as a particular case of the 'composition axiom' (Axiom IVb of §10.4 above).

THE DETERMINATION OF PSYCHOLOGICAL VALUES

A.9. It must be recalled that no economic experiment based on certainly available goods can provide a measure of psychological value (or cardinal utility). In fact, economic observation can only yield ratios between desirabilities (marginal utilities) and cannot furnish any information whatsoever on the function of psychological value as such.

Only when the different goods are independent of each other, can this determination be made.[11] However, *this condition of independence is generally not verified.*[12]

As regards random choice, and for the reasons indicated above, *attempts to determine the function of psychological value from the observation of economic decisions involving risk are also necessarily vain.*

Thus only a direct approach of the Fechner–Weber type may result in the determination of psychological value.[13]

THE REAL SCOPE OF THE VON NEUMANN–MORGENSTERN THEORY OF CHOICE INVOLVING RISK

A.10. *From the preceding, it results that von Neumann–Morgenstern theory can be considered as valid only in the limited setting of very restrictive hypotheses* excluding the fundamental element of random choice, that is the more or less marked propensity to risk or security, such as it is characterised by the probability distribution of psychological values about their mean.[14]

In any case it should be stressed that for von Neumann–Morgenstern:

(a) The probabilities considered are *objective probabilities* as defined in the present memoir (see §A1 above and Appendix D below).

(b) They identify the neo-Bernoullian index, whose existence they demonstrate on the basis of their axioms, with the index of cardinal utility. Cardinal utility is assumed to exist independently of any consideration of random choice, but it is considered that it can be determined only on the basis of random choices (§A1 above).

(c) The crucial axioms whose consideration entails the neo-Bernoullian formulation are Axioms 3Ba and 3Bb (§A6 and A8 above).

(d) Since the neo-Bernoullian index is identified with cardinal utility, clearly the neo-Bernoullian formulation cannot take into account
the probability distribution of cardinal utility around its mean, in
other words the specific element of risk (§A7) above).

NOTES TO APPENDIX A

[1] Annex III, *Confrontation de la théorie exposée avec les théories de von Neumann–
Morgenstern et de Marschak* (*Confrontation of the presented theory with the theories of
von Neumann–Morgenstern and Marschak*) or my 1951 memoir submitted to the
European Econometric Congress of Louvain, *Notes théoriques sur l'incertitude de
l'avenir et le risque* (*Theoretical Notes on the Uncertainty of the Future and Risk*)
Bibliography, Section I).

To simplify, I use the notation of the present memoir, and I replace the references to
the main text of my 1951 memoir, which is not reproduced here, by references to my
1952 memoir and to the text of the present memoir.

A few additions have been made (see Notes 3 and 6 below).

[2] Naturally if $p_2 = \cdots = p_n = 0$ the random prospect (P) comes down to the certain gain
g_1.

[3] *As regards the neo-Bernoullian formulation* (2) *below, the entities* $u, v, w, \ldots$ *considered by von Neumann and Morgenstern* (p.26) *must be considered as representing
random prospects* (P_u), (P_v), $(P_w)\ldots$ and the operation $\alpha u + (1 - \alpha)v = w$ represents
the probability α of obtaining the random prospect (P_u) and the probability $1 - \alpha$ of
obtaining the random prospect (P_v). The entity w then represents, with my notation, the
random prospect

$$(P_w) = \alpha(P_u) + (1 - \alpha)(P_v).$$

The correspondence $V = V(u)$, the existence of which von Neumann–Morgenstern
demonstrate (pp.24 and 627), means that an index B corresponds to every entity u, that
is to every random prospect (P), such B satisfies to the neo-Bernoullian formulation.
With my notation the correspondence $V = V(u)$ may be written as $B = B[(P)]$. If the
random prospect (P) reduces itself to a certainly available sum V (Note 2 above), the
index $B(V)$ represents, according to the von Neumann–Morgenstern interpretation, the
cardinal utility (or psychological value) of V.

The interpretation given by von Neumann–Morgenstern in Note 1, p.26, to the
entities $u, v, w, \ldots$: "This is, of course, meant to be the system of (abstract) utilities, to
be characterised by our axioms" *cannot but give rise to confusion, for it is wrong.* In
fact the mathematical demonstrations given in the Appendix (pp.617–632) are *entirely
independent of this interpretation*, the only properties of the considered entities being
these corresponding to axioms and expressing the supposed properties of the preferences (and not of the '*utilities*') concerning the random prospects. This is the very
principle of the axiomatic method, and von Neumann–Morgenstern justly write (p.74):

We have even avoided giving names to the mathematical concepts introduced ... in
order to establish no correlation with any meaning which the verbal associations may
suggest.

The same observation may be presented as regards the interpretation of the entities $u, v, w, \ldots$ given (p.24)

All these observations are absolutely essential.

(This note has been added in 1977 to my 1951 text).

[4] *In fact a more general property is demonstrated by von Neumann–Morgenstern* (p.627): If

$$(1) \qquad (P) = \sum \alpha_i(P_i),$$

we have

$$(2) \qquad B[(P)] = \sum \alpha_i B[(P_i)].$$

From this theorem, we deduce immediately the neo-Bernoullian formulation of §A3. For if the random prospects (P_i) represent sure gains g_i and if V represents the monetary value of the random prospect (P) we have

$$(3) \qquad B(V) = B[(P)],$$

so that (2) may be written

$$(4) \qquad B(V) = \sum \alpha_i B(g_i).$$

In writing the neo-Bernoullian formulation in this form, von Neumann and Morgenstern do not consider the subject's capital C. It would be preferable to write:

$$(5) \qquad B(C + V) = \sum \alpha_i B(C + g_i).$$

However, this omission is only of real significance as regards the psychological interpretation of empirical work.

See §14 and Note 155 above, and Appendix C, §C19 and Notes 24* and 30* below (pp.463–464, 576, 628–631 and 637–639).

[5] See Allais, 1943, *A la Recherche d'une Discipline Economique*, pp.143–144 (Note 17 especially).

May I recall that for a subject whose psychology is represented by the indifference surfaces

$$(1) \qquad S = S(A, B, \ldots, C),$$

the goods $(A), (B), \ldots, (C)$ are called "*independent*" if there exists a transformation $\bar{s} = \psi(S)$ such as

$$(2) \qquad \frac{\partial^2 \bar{s}}{\partial A \, \partial B} = 0,$$

for any pair (A) (B). In this case we have

$$\bar{s}(A, B, \ldots, C) = \psi_A(A) + \psi_B(B) + \cdots + \psi_C(C),$$

where $\psi_A(A), \psi_B(B), \ldots, \psi_C(C)$ represent the independent cardinal utilities corresponding to the goods $(A), (B), \ldots, (C)$ (see p.138, Note 95; p.141, Note 113; and p.563, Note 79).

[6] Added in the second 1947 edition.

[7] Element (AIV), M§20 (pp.51–53).

[8] *The three sections A6.2; A6.3; and A8 have been added in 1977. All the other developments were presented in my 1951 memoir.*

[9] See for instance Massé, 1953, p.22.

[10] The explanation given by Malinvaud (1952) considering that the operation $\alpha u + (1 - \alpha)v = w$ entails the independence property is not any more justified (see Note 3 above).

[11] See Allais, 1943, *A la Recherche d'une Discipline Economique*, Note 5, p.158.

[12] That is the somewhat contestable hypothesis admitted by some economists such as Irving Fisher (1927) in their attempts to determine changes in the desirability of income as a function of income by observation of markets.

[13] See Appendix C, Section II (pp.614–620).

[14] The theory presented by Marschak in his 1950 paper, 'Rational Behavior, Uncertain Prospects and Measurable Utility', which leads to the same formulation than the theory of von Neumann–Morgenstern, does raise analogous observations.

The Marschak postulates have practically the same meaning as von Neumann and Morgenstern's axioms. First Marschak postulate is equivalent to the Axiom 3Ab of von Neumann–Morgenstern. The second axiom of Marschak is a continuity axiom whose meaning is the same as that of Axioms 3Bc and 3Bd of von Neumann–Morgenstern. The fourth axiom of Marschak has implications very similar to those of Axioms 3Ba and 3Bb of von Neumann–Morgenstern. *It is the crucial axiom.*

In fact, the theory of Marschak calls for the same reserves as von Neumann–Morgenstern's theory.

APPENDIX B: MATHEMATICAL APPENDIX

I. IDENTITY OF THE NEO-BERNOULLIAN INDEX $B(g)$ AND PSYCHOLOGICAL VALUE $\gamma(g)$ WHEN THE NEO-BERNOULLIAN FORMULATION IS VALID

Complements to the Demonstration of Appendix V of the 1952 Study

B.1. The demonstration I gave in 1952 of the identity of the neo-Bernoullian index $B(g)$ and of psychological value (or cardinal utility) $\gamma(g)$ when the neo-Bernoullian formulation is valid, was not entirely satisfactory and it must be completed as follows:

In the case of a discrete probability distribution, the psychological value ω of a random prospect is defined by the relation

(1)[1] $$\omega = h[\gamma_1, \gamma_2, \ldots, \gamma_n, p_1, p_2, \ldots, p_n],$$

with

(2) $$\gamma_i = \bar{s}(C + g_i) \qquad i = 1, 2, \ldots, n,$$

(3)[2] $$\omega = \bar{s}(C + V),$$

in which V is the subject's monetary value of the random prospect $g_1, g_2, \ldots, g_n, p_1, p_2, \ldots, p_n$ with $\Sigma p_i = 1$.

The analysis of the properties of the minimum perceptible variations of psychological value leads to the conclusion that we must have

(4) $$\omega + e = h(\gamma_1 + e, \gamma_2 + e, \ldots, \gamma_n + e, p_1, p_2, \ldots, p_n),$$

for any e.[3]

Further, if the neo-Bernoullian formulation is valid, we must have

(5) $$B(C + V) = \sum_i p_i B(C + g_i).$$

From relations (2) and (3) we deduce

(6) $$B(C + g) = \beta(\gamma),$$

604

(7) $B(C + V) = \beta(\omega)$,

in which $\beta(\gamma)$ is a never-decreasing function of γ. According to (6) and (7) relation(5) is then written

(8) $\beta(\omega) = \sum_i p_i \beta(\gamma_i)$.

Hence, according to (4) we must have

(9) $\beta(\omega + e) = \sum_i p_i \beta(\gamma_i + e)$,

for any e.

It is easy to demonstrate that this condition implies that the function $\beta(\gamma)$ must be a linear function of γ, and consequently that the neo-Bernoullian index $B(C + g)$ and the cardinal utility $\bar{s}(C + g)$ are identical up to a linear transformation. This theorem can be enumerated as follows.

THEOREM

If an index $B(C + x)$ exists such that relation (5) is valid and if an index $\gamma(C + x)$ of cardinal utility exists the necessary and sufficient condition for condition (4) to be true for any e is that for any x

(10) $B(C + x) \equiv \bar{s}(C + x)$,

up to a linear transformation.

Proof

B.2. *Relation (9) must remain true whatever the random prospect considered.* Then consider the random prospect

(11) $g_1, 0, p, 1 - p$

and let V_1 and ω_1 denote its monetary and psychological values for the subject considered. Relation (9) is then written

(12) $\beta(\omega_1 + e) = p\beta(\gamma_1 + e) + (1 - p)\beta(e)$,

with

(13) $\gamma_1 = \gamma(C + g_1)$ $\gamma(C) = 0$.

We always may choose p in such a way that

(14) $\omega_1 = \gamma_1/2$

and we may write

(15) $e = na$ $a = \omega_1,$

where n is any integer, which is always possible since e may take any value.

Then eqn. (12) is written

(16) $p\beta[(n+2)a] - \beta[(n+1)a] + (1-p)\beta(na) = 0$

and it must remain valid for any n.

Equation (16) is a linear homogeneous finite difference equation whose solution is known.[4] Let us search a particular solution such as

(17) $\beta(\gamma) = \mu^{\gamma/a}.$

From eqn. (16) we deduce

(18) $p\mu^{n+2} - \mu^{n+1} + (1-p)\mu^n = 0$

or

(19) $p\mu^2 - \mu + 1 - p = 0.$

This equation has two roots

(20) $\mu = 1,$ $\mu = (1-p)/p.$

Only two cases are possible:

(a) $p \neq 1/2$. In this case, the *general* solution of (16) is

(21) $\beta(\gamma) = K\mu^{\gamma/a} + K_1 = K[(1-p)/p]^{\gamma/\omega_1} + K_1.$

(b) $p = 1/2$. In this case, $\mu = 1$ is a double root, and the *general* solution of (16) is

(22) $\beta(\gamma) = K\gamma + K_1.$

The first case is impossible because the function $\beta(\gamma)$ cannot depend on a quantity $[(1-p)/p]^{1/\omega_1}$ which corresponds to a particular random prospect whereas the function $\beta(\gamma)$ must remain the same whatever the prospect considered.

Only the second case is possible. It remains to be verified that we have effectively $p = 1/2$. Substituting the expression of $\beta(\gamma)$ given by (22) into (12), we find

(23) $K(\omega_1 + e) + K_1 = p[K(\gamma_1 + e) + K_1] + (1-p)(Ke + K_1)$

which reduces to

(24) $\omega_1 = p\gamma_1$,

whence from (14)

(25) $p = 1/2$.

Then from (6) and (22) we have

(26) $B(C + g) = K\bar{s}(C + g) + K_1$,

so that when the Bernoullian formulation is valid, the neo-Bernoullian index is identical to the index of psychological value (cardinal utility) up to a linear transformation.[5]

Condition (26) is necessary, but it is also sufficient in the most general case, since from (5)

(27) $B(C + V) + e = \sum_i p_i[B(C + g_i) + e]$,

whatever the value of e. It follows that, given relations (2), (3) and (26), we have

(28) $\omega + e = \sum_i p_i(\gamma_i + e)$.

Thus relation (4) is verified.

II. THE CONDITION THAT FOR ANY GIVEN a WE HAVE
$$X + a = f(x_1 + a, x_2 + a, \ldots, x_n + a)\,^6$$

THEOREM

B.3. *Consider the differentiable function*

(1) $X = f(x_1, x_2, \ldots, x_n)$

and assume that

(2) $X + a = f(x_1 + a, x_2 + a, \ldots, x_n + a)$,

for any value a. The necessary and sufficient condition for (2) *is to have*

(3) $G[\phi_1, \phi_2, \ldots, \phi_n] = 0$,

in which G is an arbitrary function and

(4) $\phi_1 = C_1, \phi_2 = C_2, \ldots, \phi_n = C_n,$

denote n linearly independent integrals of the system

(5) $dX = dx_1 = dx_2 = \cdots = dx_n,$

in which $C_1, C_2, \ldots, C_n$ are constants of integration
Proof
B.4. Differentiating expression (2) with respect to a and taking $a = 0$, we have

(6) $1 = \dfrac{\partial X}{\partial x_1} + \dfrac{\partial X}{\partial x_2} + \cdots + \dfrac{\partial X}{\partial x_n}.$

We know[7] that the general solution of this equation is given by relation (3). We can take for the ϕ_i functions

(7) $\phi_i = x_i - X,$

such that the most general solution of (2) may be written

(8) $G[x_1 - X, x_2 - X, \ldots, x_n - X] = 0,$

which means that the relation between $X, x_1, \ldots, x_n$ only depends on their differences.

ALTERNATIVE FORMULATION

B.5. For some applications (implications of the axiom of cardinal isovariation, §23.22 above), it may be preferable to use other expressions for the n functions ϕ_i. Thus consider the functions

(9)
$$\psi_0 = X - \sum_{i=1}^{n} b_i x_i,$$
$$\psi_1 = x_1 - \sum_{i=1}^{n} b_i x_i,$$
$$\cdots$$
$$\psi_n = x_n - \sum_{i=1}^{n} b_i x_i,$$

in which the b_i are any constants, subject only to the condition

(10) $\sum b_i = 1.$

Under this condition, the functions ψ_i are linear forms of the differences $X - x_i$ and $x_i - x_j$.

We have according to (10)

$$(11) \qquad \sum_{j=1}^{n} b_j \psi_j = \sum_{j=1}^{n} b_j x_j - \sum_{j=1}^{n} b_j \sum_{i=1}^{n} b_i x_i = \sum_{i=1}^{n} b_i x_i \left[1 - \sum_{j=1}^{n} b_j \right] = 0.$$

Taking for the n functions $\phi_1, \phi_2, \ldots, \phi_n$, the functions

$$(12) \qquad \phi_1 = \psi_0, \phi_2 = \psi_1, \ldots, \phi_n = \psi_{n-1}$$

and for the arbitrary function G, the following arbitrary function H of $\psi_0, \psi_1, \ldots, \psi_{n-1}$:

$$(13) \qquad H = H \left[\psi_0, \psi_1, \ldots, \psi_{n-1}, -\frac{1}{b_n} \sum_{i=1}^{i=n-1} b_i \psi_i \right].$$

Taking (11) into account, H is written

$$(14) \qquad H = H[\psi_0, \psi_1, \ldots, \psi_{n-1}, \psi_n].$$

The most general solution of (6) can then be written

$$(15) \qquad \psi_0 = F[\psi_1, \psi_2, \ldots, \psi_n],$$

in which F is an arbitrary function.

We see that the most general solution of equation (2) may be written

$$(16) \qquad X = \bar{x} + F[x_1 - \bar{x}, x_2 - \bar{x}, \ldots, x_n - \bar{x}],$$

with

$$(17) \qquad \bar{x} = \sum_{i=1}^{n} b_i x_i, \qquad \sum_{i=1}^{n} b_i = 1.$$

It is immediately verified that relation (2) is identically satisfied if the function X is defined by relations (16) and (17).

Finally, we see that *the necessary and sufficient condition for condition (2) to be satisfied is that the function X must be defined by the relations (16) and (17).*

NOTES TO APPENDIX B

[1] Relation 4* of §11 and III of §16 above (pp.461 and 465).
[2] §23 (p.475).
[3] M, §§69 and 89. In my 1952 memoir (M, §69, Note 109), I considered that relation

(4) was only valid if the (g_i, p_i) were independent goods. Today I consider that this restriction is not necessary (see Note 121 above) (pp.98, 129, 140 and 567).

In fact relation (4) of §B1 is a consequence of the axiom of *cardinal isovariation* (§23.22 above) (p.481).

[4] Guelfond, *Calcul des Différences Finies*, Dunod, Paris, 1963, pp.308–316.

[5] One of my correspondents (1977) writes: "The given proof is valid only in the particular case corresponding to the random prospect (11)".

This point of view is not justified. Relation (9), which follows from relations (4) and (5), should hold for any random outcome. If, then, for a particular random prospect, these conditions imply relation (26), this latter is in fact a necessary condition for the general validity of condition (4).

It then follows from (26) that in the most general case, condition (4) is indeed satisfied.

[6] This theorem is used in §23.22 above (pp.481–482).

[7] Paul Levy, *Cours d'Analyse, II*, Gauthier-Villars, Paris, 1931, pp.234–235.

APPENDIX C: SELECTED FINDINGS OF THE 1952 EXPERIMENT

The hypothesis that individuals choose among alternatives involving risk as if they were seeking to maximize the expected value of some quantity, which has been called utility, is intended to be a scientific hypothesis enabling correct predictions to be made about individual behavior. It should be accepted – tentatively, of course, as all scientific hypotheses are – if it leads to 'correct' predictions usually, or more frequently that any equally useful alternative; it should be rejected if its predictions are generally contradicted by observation.

MILTON FRIEDMAN AND L. J. SAVAGE
The Expected-Utility Hypothesis and the Measurability of Utility, 1952, p.473.

My closing admission reverses the story of the farmer who regarded everyone in the world as crazy but himself and his wife, and who sometimes wasn't sure about her. I sometimes feel that Savage and I are the only ones in the world who give a consistent Bernoulli answer to questionnaires of the type that Professor Allais has been circulating – but I am often not too sure about my own consistency.

PAUL A. SAMUELSON
Probability, Utility and the Independence Axiom, 1952, p.678.

I. THE 1952 QUESTIONNAIRE

THE 1952 EXPERIMENT

C.1. As has been noted[1] the results obtained in processing the responses to the 1952 Questionnaire were in many regards remarkable

611

and suggestive. However, the very great deal of work involved made it impossible to present all the data in this volume, to review the methods used, some of which were somewhat complex,[2] or to discuss and interpret the results. They will be discussed in a separate volume *The Psychological Structure of Choice Involving Risk: the Theory and Empirical Evidence.*

Nevertheless, it would be a pity not to take the opportunity briefly to describe some of the results here, inasmuch as they can shed light on the general discussion of the theory of random choice, the subject of the present memoir.

THE GUIDING PRINCIPLES OF THE 1952 QUESTIONNAIRE

C.2. The 1952 survey was based on a Questionnaire that was published in 1953 in the Journal of the *Société de Statistique de Paris*[3] under the title: 'La psychologie de l'homme rationnel devant le risque – La théorie et l'expérience' ('The Psychology of Rational Behaviour in the Presence of Risk – Theory and Experience'). Underlying the Questionnaire were two guiding principles: firstly, that by judiciously selected questions it was possible to make a direct determination of the index of psychological values of a subject (cardinal utility):[4] secondly, that the neo-Bernoullian indexes of a subject, determined on the basis of different series of questions, could not be identical.

This is how, at the end of the 1952 Colloquium, I outlined a working method to demonstrate this impossibility as follows (*Proceedings of the Symposium*, p.247):

《The neo-Bernoullian index of an individual can be determined through two separate methods, one of which involves the psychological weight linked with uncertainty near the certainty while the other will not be related to it.

Let V be the certain amount that is thought to be equivalent to a probability p of getting an amount X.

In a first set of questions, a given constant value X_0 can be assumed as X. Taking then $B(0) = 0$, which is always possible, we get[5]

$$(1) \qquad B(V) = pB(X_0).$$

When p is close to 1, we will see the influence of the preference for certainty.[6]

In a second set of questions, we can assume a fixed value p_0, not too close to unity as p, and we get:

(2) $B(V) = p_0 B(X)$.

Here, the preference for security near the certainty will not intervene.[7]

The two methods give a way of building the $B(X)$ index. *If the neo-Bernoullian theory is valid at all*, it should produce in the two cases the same function $B(X)$ for a given rational individual. In fact, I think it not to be so, at least in general, and I intend to put it to an experiment that seems crucial to me.⟩⟩

These two sets of questions led to the consideration of the indices B_{200} and $B_{1/2}$ examined in Sections IV and III below.[8] As will be seen, the two indices differ significantly from one another.[9]

THE QUESTIONS ASKED

C.3. The Questionnaire comprised ten sets of questions:[8]

Questions I and X: To determine the general characteristics of the psychology of respondents to risk.

Questions VI: To determine the cardinal index of preference $\bar{s}$.[10]

Questions II to V: To appraise the consistency of decisions with the neo-Bernoullian principle (Conformity Tests).[11]

Questions VII, VIII and IX: To determine the neo-Bernoullian index $B(g)$ corresponding to different sets of questions.[12]

THE ANALYSIS OF THE EXPERIMENT

C.4. As has been stated (§3 above), the experiment yielded 101 fully compiled returns, of which 55 were handed in by students at the *Ecole des Mines*. Not to give too much weight to this group, only fifteen of these replies were processed. Of the total of 61 files processed a group of 16 was chosen on a purely accidental basis and such that, at least as a first approximation, they can be viewed as a random selection. These returns were from 9 participants in the *Groupe de Recherches Economiques et Sociales*: Anonymous A_1,[13] Charreton, Desrousseaux, Jacquelin, Jouven, Malinvaud, Rabussier, Roman,[14] Saint Guilhem; four foreign personalities: de Finetti,

Galvenius, Richardson and Zonderland; and three students at the
Ecole des Mines: Brun, Delsol and Leborgne.

The responses to all 400 questions in the Questionnaire were
processed, but *for simplicity*, and however interesting some results
could be,[15] *I will deal here only with the results concerning the
determination of the index of psychological value (cardinal utility)
derived from the Questions VI, those concerning the neo-Bernoullian
index $B_{1/2}$ (Questions IX), and those concerning the neo-Bernoullian
index B_{200} (Questions VII).* For the same reason, only fifteen of the
several hundred or so charts to be reproduced in the general volume are
shown in this volume (pp.640–654), with a minimum of comment.

II. DETERMINATION OF THE CARDINAL INDEX
OF PREFERENCE

DETERMINATION OF THE CURVE REPRESENTING THE
CARDINAL PREFERENCE INDEX $\bar{s}(U)$

C.5. If U denotes the subject's evaluation of his capital stock, real or
potential, his index of cardinal preference $\bar{s}(U)$ yields an estimate of
the intensity of his preferences relatively to different possible values
of U.[16] In other words, if U_4 is preferred to U_3 with the same intensity
as U_2 is preferred to U_1, we have

$$(1) \qquad \bar{s}(U_4) - \bar{s}(U_3) = \bar{s}(U_2) - \bar{s}(U_1),$$

whence the index $\bar{s}$ is determined up to a linear transformation.
Condition (1) is illustrated by Figure A1.

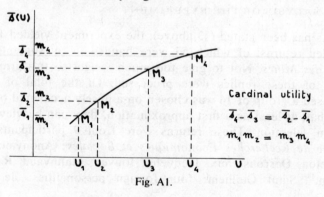

Fig. A1.

If any two arbitrary chosen values of $\bar{s}$, such as $\bar{s}_1$ and $\bar{s}_2$, are assigned for any two values U_1 and U_2 ($U_1 < U_2$), determination of the value U for which

(2) $\bar{s}(U) - \bar{s}_1 = \bar{s}_2 - \bar{s}(U)$,

determines the abscissa U of the point the ordinate of which is $(\bar{s}_1 + \bar{s}_2)/2$. Likewise the value U for which

(3) $\bar{s}(U) - \bar{s}_2 = \bar{s}_2 - \bar{s}_1$,

yields the abscissa U corresponding to the ordinate $2\bar{s}_2 - \bar{s}_1$. Finally, the value of U for

(4) $\bar{s}_1 - \bar{s}(U) = \bar{s}_2 - \bar{s}_1$

determines the abscissa U corresponding to the ordinate $2\bar{s}_1 - \bar{s}_2$.

Consequently, *if a subject can respond to questions from which may be determined the value U_4 for which the interval (U_3, U_4) is considered as psychologically equivalent to the interval (U_1, U_2),* where U_1, U_2 and U_3 have given values, the curve depicting his cardinal preference index can be built up step by step,[17] affording the conclusion that *the concept of a cardinal preference index is an operational one.*

In the discussion below, we will write[18]

(5) $U = U_0 + X$, $x = (U_0 + X)/U_0$,

where U_0 is the subject's subjective estimate of his capital worth, and X a possible gain. To the two psychologically equivalent intervals (U_3, U_4) and (U_1, U_2) there then correspond two psychologically equivalent variations $X_4 - X_3$ and $X_2 - X_1$ of X.

The function $\bar{s}(U)$ is plotted on semi-log paper, using a log-scale for U and a linear scale for $\bar{s}$. We will write

(6) $u = \log U$.

THE RESPONSES X TO QUESTIONS VI

C.6. The purpose of the Questions VI is to determine intervals of psychologically equal value. As an illustration, we may take Question 651 and de Finetti's response:[19]

Question 651	Answer	Degree of Conviction with which given[21]
Is your preference, for an inheritance of 10 millions rather than no inheritance stronger than your preference for an inheritance of		
– 150 millions rather than 10 millions	no	AH
– 100 millions rather than 10 millions	no	PAH
– 60 millions rather than 10 millions	no	H
– 40 millions rather than 10 millions	yes	BH
– 30 millions rather than 10 millions	yes	H
– 25 millions rather than 10 millions	yes	PAH

What is the approximate level X at which your preference changes?	45 millions

All the figures were presented in millions of 1952 francs.[20] The meaning of the indications of the last column is as follows:[21]
- BH, much hesitation
- H, hesitation
- PAH, almost with hesitation
- AH, without hesitation

de Finetti's answer to this question yields the conclusion that using U_0^* to denote his estimated capital worth, the intervals $(U_0^*, U_0^* + 10)$ and $(U_0^* + 10, U_0^* + 45)$ are psychologically equivalent.

Questions 651 *to* 654 deal with the psychological equivalence of the intervals

$$(U_0^*, U_0^* + A) \qquad \text{and} \qquad (U_0^* + A, U_0^* + X),$$

where X is the subject's answer. The value of A for the four questions was:

$$\text{Q. 651:} \quad A = 10, \qquad \text{Q. 653:} \quad A = 50,$$
$$\text{Q. 652:} \quad A = 25, \qquad \text{Q. 654:} \quad A = 100.$$

Questions 631 *and* 632 deal with the psychological equivalence of the intervals

$$(U_0^* + B, U_0^* + X) \qquad \text{and} \qquad (U_0^* + C, U_0^* + D)$$

with

$$Q.\ 631:\quad B = 250,\quad C = 500,\quad D = 1000,$$
$$Q.\ 632:\quad B = 100,\quad C = 200,\quad D = 400\ .$$

Questions 633 *and* 634 deal with the psychological equivalence of the intervals

$$(U_0^* + X,\ U_0^* + E)\qquad\text{and}\qquad(U_0^* + F,\ U_0^* + G)$$

with

$$Q.\ 633:\quad E = 100,\quad F = 800,\quad G = 1000,$$
$$Q.\ 634:\quad E = \ 10,\quad F = \ 80,\quad G = \ 100,$$

where X is the subject's answer.

It follows from the above that the responses X to Questions VI can be used to determine the shape of the function representing the cardinal preference index.

Two hypotheses were examined in succession: loglinearity and non-loglinearity of the index. For simplicity, only the results for the loglinear hypothesis are given here.[22]

DETERMINATION OF THE CARDINAL PREFERENCE INDEX: LOGLINEAR HYPOTHESIS

C.7. As the cardinal preference index $\bar{s}$ is defined subject to a linear transformation, we can write in the loglinear case[23]

$$(7)\qquad \bar{s} = m[\log(U_0^* + X) - \log(U_0^*)].$$

For a given value of m, this is equivalent to setting the two constraints

$$(8)\qquad \bar{s}(X = 0) = 0,$$

$$(9)\qquad d\bar{s}/d\log(U_0^* + X) = m.$$

Using five moduli semi-log paper, it is convenient to take a unit change in $\bar{s}$ as corresponding to a change in $U_0^* + X$ covering two moduli. With this scaling, the curve depicting the cardinal preference index $\bar{s}$ as a function of

$$(10)\qquad u = \log U = \log(U_0^* + X)$$

is a straight line passing through the point $(U = U_0^*, \bar{s} = 0)$ with a slope of

(11) $m = 1/(2 \log_e 10) = 0.2171,$

as it is indicated on Figure A2.

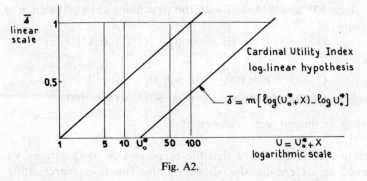

Fig. A2.

Under the loglinear hypothesis, therefore, the determination of the cardinal index of preference is equivalent to the determination of an estimate U_0^* of U_0 for which the responses X correspond to a set of points that are as close as possible to the straight line of slope m which passes through the point U_0^*.

For a determinate value of U_0, we can use our knowledge of the equivalent intervals $(U_0 + X_3, U_0 + X)$ and $(U_0 + X_1, U_0 + X_2)$ to determine the ordinate at $U_0 + X$, since we have

(12) $\bar{s}(U_0 + X) - \bar{s}(U_0 + X_3) = \bar{s}(U_0 + X_2) - \bar{s}(U_0 + X_1),$

where $\bar{s}$ is given by relation (7).

By convention, we will take as our estimate of U_0^* the value of U_0 which minimises the sum of the squares $(u - u^*)^2$ of deviations taken parallel to the $u = \log U$ axis.

In *Chart I,** the eight points corresponding to de Finetti's answers X to Questions VI are plotted for the estimate $U_0^* = 17$ of U_0. These answers are indicated on the Table shown on Chart I. For the value $U_0^* = 17$, the standard deviation of the residuals is 0.15. Under the loglinear assumption, this corresponds to a standard error of 15% in the assessment of the $U_0^* + X$. Chart I shows that, in de Finetti's case, the loglinear assumption gives a good fit of the answers X.

---

* Charts I–XV appear on pp.640–654.

For illustrative purposes, the loglinear fits obtained for four other subjects are presented in *Chart II*. $\log(1 + X/U_0^*)$ is plotted on the abscissa instead of $\log(U_0^* + X)$. It may be observed that the loglinear adjustments are approximately valid for

$$20 \leqslant x = 1 + X/U_0^* \leqslant 3{,}000.$$

PORTRAYING THE SET OF FITTINGS FOR A GIVEN GROUP

C.8. If $\log(1 + X/U_0^*)$ is plotted on the abscissa, the straight line depicting the cardinal index is the same for each subject, so that the set of answers for a certain group of respondents can be portrayed on the same graph.

A detailed analysis of the results shows that the answers to Questions 651 to 654 are much more significant and yield a better determination of the values of U_0^* than those to Questions 631 to 634. For this reason, *Chart III* is presented, showing for group g the distribution of the points corresponding to the answers to Questions 631 to 634 and 651 to 654. The better grouping of the points for Questions 631 to 634 stems from the very nature of these questions.

Chart IV shows the points corresponding to Questions 651 to 654 for the two groups g_1 and g_2.

PORTRAYING A GROUP AVERAGE

C.9. For a given group and a given question, the average for the group may be taken as the barycentre of the points depicting the individual subjects. In other words, the abscissa of the average point for n subjects and a given question is the *geometric* mean of $\log(1 + X/U_0^*)$ for the n subjects, and its ordinate is the *arithmetic* mean of the corresponding $\bar{s}$ values.

Chart V shows the points corresponding to the 'average' subject in groups g, g_1 and g_2. The corresponding estimates $\overline{U_0^*}$ of U_0 are equal to the geometric means of the U_0^* of the group's members. It can be seen that if 'average' subjects are considered, the loglinear hypothesis yields very good fits for $u < 1000$.

As I noted earlier,[23*] I ran a further experiment in 1974, covering a few Ph.D. students at the University of Paris X. They were asked similar questions to those in the 1952 survey, but the intervals were bigger. For illustration *Chart VI* represents the obtained results for a group of four students who, according to their declarations, determined their answers with great care.[24] The results, again, are very remarkable.

At least as a first approximation, the results obtained confirm the loglinear hypothesis of Daniel Bernoulli.

III. DETERMINATION OF THE NEO-BERNOULLIAN INDEX $B_{1/2}$

THE NEO-BERNOULLIAN INDEX $B_{1/2}$

C.10. Questions IX can be drawn on to find the certain value X' attributable to a gain of X whose probability is

(13) $p = 1/2$.

Let $B(U)$ be the neo-Bernoullian index corresponding to the sum U. According to the neo-Bernoullian formulation we should have

(14) $B(U_0 + X') = pB(U_0 + X) + (1 - p)B(U_0)$,

where U_0 denotes the capital worth of the subject as appraised by himself.[24*]

As $B(U)$ is defined up to a linear transformation, *it is always possible to take the two conditions*

(15) $B(U_0) = B_0 = 0$,

(16) $B(U_1) = B(U_0 + X_1) = B_1$,

where B_1 represents the value attributed to $B(U_1)$ for a given value U_1 of U. The two conditions express the fact that the curve of the neo-Bernoullian index must pass through the two points

(17) M_0 $U = U_0$ $B(U_0) = 0$,

(18) M_1 $U = U_1$ $B(U_1) = B_1$.

Given (13) and (15), condition (14) is written

(19) $B(U_0 + X') = \frac{1}{2} B(U_0 + X)$.

This relation defines the neo-Bernoullian index $B_{1/2}$ for the subject considered. U_0 is an unknown parameter to be estimated.

THE RESPONSES X' TO QUESTIONS IX

C.11. As an illustration, here is *de Finetti's* reply to Question 96:

Question 96	Answer	Degree of Conviction with which given[25]
Would you prefer		
– an even chance of winning 100 millions or nothing		
– or the immediate cash sum of:		
5 millions	no	PAH
10 millions	no	H
20 millions	no	BH
25 millions	no	BH
30 millions	yes	BH
35 millions	yes	BH
40 millions	yes	H
50 millions	yes	AH
70 millions	yes	AH

At what approximate level X' does   28 millions
your preference change?

All figures were presented in millions of 1952 francs (as regards the indications of the last column, see §C.10 above).

DETERMINING THE CURVE OF THE NEO-BERNOULLIAN INDEX $B_{1/2}$

C.12. For the 16 subjects considered, there exists an index of cardinal preference which can be portrayed as a first approximation by a straight line, and the replies to the Questions VI can be used to make an estimate U_0^* of U_0.

So as to compare the index $B_{1/2}$ easily with the index of cardinal preference $\bar{s}$, the greatest value of X being 1 billion "old" francs, it is convenient to take for $B(U_0 + 1000)$ the value of $\bar{s}$ for $U = U_0 + 1000$. Thus, we have

(20) $B_1 = B(U_0^* + 1000) = m[\log(U_0^* + 1000) - \log U_0^*],$

(21) $m = 0.5/\log_e 10 = 0.2171,$

where U_0^* is the estimate of U_0 obtained from analysis of the responses of the subject to the Questions VI.

In de Finetti's case, $U_0^* = 17$, and the coordinates of M_0 and M_1 are[26]

M_0: $U_0 = U_0^* = 17,$ $B_0 = B(17) = 0,$

M_1: $U_1 = U_0^* + 1000 = 17 + 1000 = 1017,$

       $B_1 = B(1017)$ $= 0.888.$

The set of his answers to Questions IX is indicated on the Table shown on *Chart VII*.

The point M_1 being given, relation (5) immediately yields the point M_2 corresponding to Question 98. Its coordinates are

M_2: $U_2 = U_0^* + X' = 17 + 200 = 217,$ $B_2 = B_1/2 = 0.444.$

The curve we are looking for should pass through the points M_0, M_1 and M_2, and a first approximation to it may be deduced by drawing a smooth arc C_1 through them.

Now there is a well-determined value of $B(U_0^* + 200)$ corresponding to this arc. Question 97 then yields the coordinates of a third point M_3 of coordinates.

M_3: $U_3 = U_0^* + X' = 17 + 50 = 67,$

       $B_3 = \frac{1}{2}B(U_0^* + 200) = \frac{1}{2}B(217).$

This third point does not fall exactly on the arc C_1 drawn earlier because the answers X' to Questions 98 and 97 may be considered as in some error. This leads to an adjustment of the first drawing of the smooth curve, such that the points M_2 and M_3 are as close as possible to the curve C_2 (see Figure A3). The same process of successive approximation is carried on for the following questions.

Experience shows that by successive approximations a curve is rather rapidly reached such that, although the points $M_2, M_3 \ldots$ obtained do not be exactly on it, they are not very far away. *Chart VII* shows the results of this process for the case of de Finetti. It can be seen that the curve satisfies condition (17) with a very close degree of accuracy for each of the Questions 90 to 98.

Experience further shows that the curve obtained in this way is determined with considerable precision. The goodness of fit deteriorates markedly once the path traced departs from the optimum.

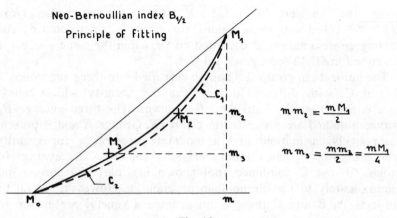

Fig. A3.

If it is taken that a neutral attitude to risk is implicit in the neo-Bernoullian formulation, it can be seen that in the present case depicted by the line M_0M_1, de Finetti's $B_{1/2}$ curve, all of which lies to the right of M_0M_1, indicates a propensity for risk taking in the random choices considered incompatible with the neo-Bernoullian formulation.

Chart VIII is presented to illustrate three typical forms of fitting corresponding to the index $B_{1/2}$. $\mathrm{Log}\,(1 + X/U_0^*)$ is plotted on the abscissa instead of $\mathrm{Log}\,(U_0^* + X)$. *Malinvaud's* case is similar to de Finetti's. By contrast, *Saint-Guilhem* shows a marked propensity for security, and *Jacquelin*'s propensity for security is extremely high.

The case in which no estimate U_0 deduced by considering the index of cardinal utility is available is examined in §C.19.2 below.

DEPICTING A GROUP AVERAGE

C.13. The average neo-Bernoullian index $B_{1/2}$ for a given group is obtained by considering the geometric means $\overline{U_0^*}$, $\overline{U_0^* + X}$, $\overline{U_0^* + X'}$ of the U_0^*, $U_0^* + X$ and $U_0^* + X'$ of the members of the group for each question. These means may be considered as corresponding to the 'average subject' in the group.

The fit for the 'average subject' is carried out in the same way as described in the preceding section, but using the preceding geometric means. In other words, the 'average subject' is considered to have

given the answer $(X') = \overline{U_0^* + X'} - \overline{U_0^*}$ for the value $(X) =$
$\overline{U_0^* + X} - \overline{U_0^*}$. Using these values, the graph is constructed by successive approximation of the fitted curve, using the same process as
described in §C.12 for a given subject.

The subjects in group G [27] can be classified into three subgroups A,
B and C, with different propensities for security which can be
ascertained from the individual $B_{1/2}$ curves. The three average $B_{1/2}$
curves obtained are presented in *Chart IX*. Groups A and B present,
respectively, a marked and a moderate preference for security,
whereas group C has a mild preference for risk. The average for
groups B and C combined (not shown in Chart IX) corresponds
approximately to neo-Bernoullian psychology. However, for all the
subjects A, B and C there is on average a general preference for
security.

In all cases, the neo-Bernoullian indices $B_{1/2}$ corresponding to the
fitted curves differ significantly from the cardinal preference indices
depicted by the straight lines M_0M_1.

IV. DETERMINATION OF THE NEO-BERNOULLIAN INDEX B_{200}

THE NEO-BERNOULLIAN INDEX B_{200}

C.14. Questions VII can be used to ascertain the certain value X'
attributable to a gain, with probability p, of

(22) $X = 200$ millions of 1952 francs.

Let $B(U)$ be the neo-Bernoullian index corresponding to the sum U.
The neo-Bernoullian formulation implies that we should have

(23) $B(U_0 + X') = pB(U_0 + X) + (1 - p)B(U_0),$

where U_0 is the subject's capital worth as assessed by himself.

Using the same approach as for the index $B_{1/2}$, we choose for the
two points M_0 and M_1 which may be arbitrary selected

(24) $B(U = U_0^*) = B_0 = 0,$

(25) $B(U = U_1 = U_0^* + 200) = B_1 = m[\log(U_0^* + 200) - \log U_0^*],$

where U_0^* is the estimate of U_0 obtained for the subject considered
by analysing his answers to Question VI, and 200 corresponds to the
gain of 200 millions francs considered in the Questions VII.

From (22), (23) and (24) we deduce

(26) $B(U_0 + X') = pB(U_0 + 200)$.

This relation defines the neo-Bernoullian index B_{200} for the considered subject. U_0 is an unknown parameter to be estimated.[28]

THE REPLIES X' TO QUESTIONS VII

C.15. As an illustration, here is de Finetti's reply to Question 74:

Question 74	Answer	Degree of conviction with which given[29]
Would you prefer – 98 per cent chance of winning 200 millions associated with a 2 per cent chance of nothing to the immediate cash sum of:		
5 millions	no	PAH
10 millions	no	PAH
20 millions	no	PAH
30 millions	no	PAH
40 millions	no	PAH
50 millions	no	H
70 millions	no	H
100 millions	no	H
150 millions	no	BH
What is the approximate level X' at which your preference changes?	160 millions	

All figures were presented in millions of *1952 francs*[20] (as regards the indications of the last column, see §C.10 above).

DETERMINING THE CURVE OF THE NEO-BERNOULLIAN
INDEX B_{200}

C.16. We consider de Finetti's case, for which $U_0^* = 17$. The coordinates of M_0 and M_1 are[30]

M_0: $U_0 = U_0^* = 17$, $B_0 = B(17) = 0$,

M_1: $U_1 = U_0^* + 200 = 217$, $B_1 = B(217) = 0.553$.

As M_1 is given, the point M corresponding to one of the Questions VII is deduced immediately using relation (26). Thus for Question 74, the coordinates of the point M_4 are

$$M_4: \quad U_4 = U_0^* + X' = 17 + 160 = 177,$$

$$B_4 = 0.98B_1 = 0.542.$$

Chart X, plotted for de Finetti's answers, shows that a continuous and regular curve can easily be run through the eight points corresponding to Questions VII. The tangent at M_1 can be seen to be almost horizontal. The fit shows a high preference for security in the neighbourhood of certainty and a mild preference for risk in the neighbourhood of M_0.

Chart XI is presented to show three typical fits of the neo-Bernoullian index B_{200}. $\log(1 + X/U_0^*)$ is plotted on the abscissa instead of $\log(U_0^* + X)$.

Without exception, the tangent at M_1 is almost horizontal, i.e. all the subjects have a high preference for security in the neighbourhood of certainty.

In the neighbourhood of the point M_0, Jacquelin shows a very strong preference for security while Malinvaud presents a strong preference for risk.

The radical difference in the nature of the fittings B_{200} and the fittings $B_{1/2}$ should be stressed. For the B_{200} fittings, the observed points, marked by a cross, are *completely* independent of the fitted curve which interpolate them. To the contrary, it results from the fitting process that for the fittings $B_{1/2}$, the points marked with a cross *depend on* the shape of the admitted fitting curve. There is therefore *interdependence* between the points corresponding to observed data and the curve which fits these data best in conformity with the neo-Bernoullian formulation.

PORTRAYING A GROUP AVERAGE

C.17. The average neo-Bernoullian index B_{200} for a given group is obtained by considering the geometric means $\overline{U_0^*}$, $\overline{U_0^* + X}$, $\overline{U_0^* + X'}$ of the U_0^*, $U_0^* + X$, $U_0^* + X'$, of each member of the group, for each question. These means may be considered as corresponding to the 'average subject' in the group.

Using these means, fitting proceeds as just described above for the individual subject. In other words, the 'average subject' is considered to have given the answer $(X') = \overline{U_0^* + X' - U_0^*}$ for the value $(X) = \overline{U_0^* + X - U_0^*}$. Using these values, the fitted curve is developed as just described in the preceding §C.16.

The members of group G can be classified into three subgroups (a), (b) and (c), according to the degree of preference for security they exhibit in the individual B_{200} fittings. The three average B_{200} indices are plotted in *Chart XII*.

Each of the three groups has a very marked preference for security in the neighbourhood of certainty. This is most intense for the members of group (a).

In the neighbourhood of the point M_0, i.e. for low values of the probability, the group (a) displayed a strong preference for security, whereas group (c) displayed a strong preference for risk.

For the three groups (a), (b) and (c) as a whole, one observes on average a strong preference for security in the neighbourhood of probabilities close to unity and a moderate preference for risk for low probabilities.

In all cases, the B_{200} neo-Bernoullian indices of the fitted curves *differ significantly* from the indices of cardinal preference depicted by the straight lines M_0M_1 and also *differ significantly* from the neo-Bernoullian indices $B_{1/2}$.

V. INTERPRETATION OF THE RESULTS

The results set forth above yield three main conclusions.

1. EXISTENCE OF AN INDEX OF CARDINAL UTILITY

C.18. The respondents were able to reply consistently to questions designed to allow their index of cardinal utility to be constructed.

As a first approximation and for each subject the index appears to be loglinear over a wide range of variation which covers some three moduli and a half of a base 10 scale, i.e. over values of the ratio $x = (U_0 + X)/U_0$ up to 3000.

Beyond this, the replies received indicate that satiety appears and the index of cardinal utility is no longer loglinear. In fact for values of

x greater than 10^4, those questioned seemed no longer capable of giving a precise reply to the questions put. Naturally U_0 is an unknown whose value has to be determined for each person surveyed.

For small values of x, systematic deviations from the loglinear fitting are observed such that on the whole the loglinear approximation is truly satisfactory only within the interval

(27) $20 \leqslant x = 1 + x/U_0 \leqslant 3,000$.

2. NON-EXISTENCE OF A NEO-BERNOULLIAN INDEX TO DEPICT THE RANDOM CHOICES CORRESPONDING TO DIFFERENT SETS OF QUESTIONS

C.19. Two cases must be considered, depending on whether there is an estimate of the parameter U_0 available from the replies to the Questions VI on the cardinal preference index (Section II), or whether no such estimate can be made, or if made, is not to be taken into account.

(a) *Case in Which an Estimate of U_0 Corresponding to the Cardinal Preference Index Is Available*

C.19.1. For those subjects for whom an estimate of the parameter U_0 is available, the neo-Bernoullian indexes $B_{1/2}$ and B_{200} can be determined as shown in §C.12 and C.16 above.

From the results obtained we may deduce that the index of cardinal utility $\bar{s}$, and the two neo-Bernoullian indices $B_{1/2}$ and B_{200}, all differ significantly from one another.

The conclusion from this is that *the risk psychology of all the subjects tested is basically different from the neo-Bernoullian formulation.*

It is *well worth noting* that for many respondents the $B_{1/2}$ neo-Bernoullian index, corresponding to a probability of 1/2 is not very different from the index of cardinal preference. In other words, the neo-Bernoullian principle seems to hold approximately for some subjects in the absence of either practical certainty or gross uncertainty. But this identity cannot be observed *for the same respondents'* neo-Bernoullian index B_{200}.

Even more remarkably, there is a *surprising structural similarity* in the $B_{1/2}$ and B_{200} indexes of individual respondents, indicating the existence of fundamental invariances in their psychological reactions to random choices.

It further follows that the *experiment* itself proved groundless all the *a priori* objections put forward in 1952 as to the possibility of obtaining valuable and coherent replies to the whole questionnaire.

(b) *Case in Which an Estimate of U_0 Corresponding to the Cardinal Preference Index Is Not Used, Whether Because It is Not Available or Set Aside*

C.19.2. If the estimate of U_0 deduced from the answers to Questions VI relating to cardinal utility, is left out of account, or, if it could not be determined, the analysis of the consistency of the replies to Questions IX and VII relating to the indexes $B_{1/2}$ and B_{200} may be made very easily.

Indeed, the possibility of being able to identify both indexes $B_{1/2}$ and B_{200} does not depend on the value of U_0^* considered, for to choose one value of U_0^* rather than another boils down to making the same transformation in the scale of the co-ordinates for both indexes. For the purpose here considered, one can *without loss of generality* construct both indexes $B_{1/2}$ and B_{200} by taking $U_0^* = 0$.

Since both series of Questions IX and VII include the same question on the assured gain judged equivalent to a probability of 0.5 of winning 200 million of 1952 francs and a probability of 0.5 of winning nothing (Questions 97 and 77), since the attention of the subjects had been drawn on this identity, and since the neo-Bernoullian index is defined up to a linear transformation, one may in order to determine the indexes $B_{1/2}$ and B_{200} corresponding to the Questions IX and VII, take the same two conditions

$$(28) \quad \begin{aligned} B_0 &= B(0) = 0, \\ B_1 &= B(200) = 1. \end{aligned}$$

The determination of the two indexes $B_{1/2}$ and B_{200} can then be done for the interval $(0 < X < 200)$ using the methods which were described in §C.12 and C.16 above. For the fittings of the index $B_{1/2}$, the ordinate of the point corresponding to $X = 1000$ was taken as equal to twice the ordinate of the curve fitted for the value of X' judged equivalent to a probability of 0.5 of winning 1000 million. Here, one should proceed in this way, as the process of determining the index $B_{1/2}$ is founded on the consideration of pairs of values X and X', such that both these values are in the interval (0/200).

It is then seen that for each subject the fitted curves corresponding to the indexes $B_{1/2}$ and B_{200} are significantly different.

To illustrate, the *Charts XIII, XIV, and XV* show the fittings for de Finetti, Jacquelin and Malinvaud, the position of each of whom was markedly different either for their personal worth (characterised by the U_0^* yielded by the analysis of psychological values, Section II above) or their psychology vis-à-vis risk.

It will be observed that for the index B'_{200} the tangent at the point M_1 is almost horizontal, whereas it is far from horizontal for the index $B_{1/2}$. *This reflects a strong preference for security in the neighbourhood of certainty for all the subjects.*

The point of intersection of the curves $B_{1/2}$ and B_{200} has *no particular meaning* because it corresponds to the same question for both sets of Questions IX and VII (the two Questions 97 and 77 are identical).

It will also be observed that the fits obtained are *very similar* to those which one could deduce from the fits portrayed in Charts VII, VIII, X and XI by proportional transformations in the scales of co-ordinates and by replacing $U_0^* + X$ by X for the U abscissae. It is important to underline that in these transformations of co-ordinates, *the neo-Bernoullian formulation remains invariant.*

We verify that in the three cases considered, the two indexes $B_{1/2}$ and B_{200} *differ very significantly.* The same statement can be made for all other subjects.

It is very highly probable, not to say absolutely certain, that similar results would have been obtained for other series of questions. In particular, it is practically certain that, whatever the position of the point M_1 on the curve depicting the index $B_{1/2}$, the tangent as M_1 would remain close to horizontal. One would then have for instance the following for Jacquelin (Figure A4).

One can then consider that it is indeed impossible to find the same neo-Bernoullian index to represent all the random choices made.

It can thus be concluded that even setting aside consideration of the cardinal utility index, we are led to the same conclusion as in the

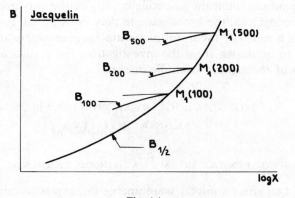

Fig. A4.

preceding case (a), i.e. that the psychology vis-à-vis risk of the subjects considered differs significantly from the psychology implied by the neo-Bernoullian formulation.

I feel it necessary to stress once again that not taking the subject's capital C into account can be justified as regards the demonstration that a neo-Bernoullian index does not exist for any subject, that can depict his psychology vis-à-vis risk for different series of questions. However this representation is much less meaningful than that used for the Charts VII to XII, and in fact, the lesser or greater preference for risk or security can only be assessed through comparison of the neo-Bernoullian indexes corresponding to various series of questions with the index of cardinal utility.

3. CONSISTENCY OF THE REPLIES

C.20. All the answers to the various questions proved to be remarkably consistent. The deviations from the fitting curves of the indexes correspond to relative errors of a comparable order of magnitude. These are errors of measurement very analogous to the errors committed in the measurement of the physical magnitudes.

In general, from one subject to another, one notices a marked variety in their reactions vis-à-vis risk. It can be compared to the variety observed in relation to consumption goods. It is in striking contrast with the observation of the first approximation validity of the same loglinear formulation of cardinal utility for all the subjects.

Taking into account the scientific quality of the very great majority of those consulted, the broad sample they constituted, the great care with which most of them did elaborate their answers, and the conclusions to be drawn from the investigation, the results obtained are certainly of *the highest* scientific interest.

VI. THE NON-LOGLINEAR FORMULATION OF CARDINAL UTILITY

THE NON-LOGLINEAR FORMULATION OF CARDINAL UTILITY

C.21. In fact some subjects were unable to answer certain questions, the X values for these questions being practically infinite. This is because, for values exceeding 10^4 of the parameter

$$x = (U_0 + X)/U_0,$$

there is hardly any further increase in cardinal utility, and the corresponding curve becomes horizontally asymptotic.[31] Then we may understand why some subjects with a relatively low value of U_0 could reply only to Question 651, since for them, Questions 652, 653 and 654 did correspond to a situation of satiety.

Thus it can be stated that although the loglinear formulation performs well over a wide range of variation, it does not apply beyond a certain threshold.

Analysis of the non-loglinear case is rendered very difficult by the small number of questions in heading VI of the 1952 Questionnaire.

In this analysis, I have been guided throughout by the conviction that it should be possible as a first approximation to find *a single non-loglinear formulation which gives a first approximation portrayal of the psychology of all subjects.*

To determine it, I considered three groups of subjects:

Group P: The 9 of the sample of 16 respondents studied about (§C.4 above) who answered all the Questions 651 to 654.

Group Q: All the other respondents remaining sample of 45 (= 61 − 16) of the 1952 experiment (§C.4 above) who answered all the Questions 651 to 654, constituting a second group of nine subjects.

Group R: Six students attending the Clement Juglar seminar at Paris-X University, who also answered all these questions in 1974.

Although for these 24 subjects the estimates of the values of capital U_0 in francs (1952) varied widely, the highest value of U_0 being 400 times greater than the lowest, it was in fact possible to determine a single function

(29) $\bar{s} = f[\log x]$,

which satisfactorily portrayed the average psychology of each of the three groups over a wide range of variation

(30) $1 < x < 10^4$.

The methods used[32] to reach this formulation are quite complex and cannot be described here, even summarily. They lead to a single formulation f of cardinal utility which is the same whichever group of subjects is considered.

In this formulation, cardinal utility $\bar{s}$ tends to a maximum as X increases indefinitely. In practice, this maximum is reached for

(31) $x > 10{,}000$.

The formulation f, I found, permits a remarkably close fit for all the observed values of X/U_0. In particular, it provides an explanation for the deviations observed in the loglinear adjustments for small[33] and large values of X/U_0 and explains why the loglinear adjustments are good only for values of X/U_0, such that approximately[34] (relation 27 above)

(32) $20 < x = 1 + X/U_0 < 3{,}000$.

The analysis that was performed leads to a remarkable interpretation of the results corresponding to low values of x.[35]

This formulation explains also why some subjects whose value of U_0 is very low were unable to answer certain questions. This occurs when the value of X is such as to bring the function f close to its maximum, corresponding to a state close to satiety.

On the whole, the derived formulation proves to be markedly superior to the loglinear formulation throughout the observed values of X/U_0.

Thus we see that it is perfectly feasible to depict the indexes of cardinal preference of *all* the respondents *by a single function*. The index of cardinal preference may therefore be considered to be an *invariant* function of the ratio $x = (U_0 + X)/U_0$.

NON-EXISTENCE OF A NEO-BERNOULLIAN INDEX TO PORTRAY THE RANDOM CHOICES CORRESPONDING TO DIFFERENT GROUPS OF QUESTIONS

C.22. Consideration of the non-loglinear formulation for cardinal utility naturally *leaves unaffected* the conclusions above concerning the impossibility, of finding for each subject a single neo-Bernoullian index which could be identified simultaneously with $B_{1/2}$ and B_{200}.

VII. GENERAL OVERVIEW

C.23. The results obtained from the 1952 experiment described above enable four essential propositions to be demonstrated:

(a) *A cardinal preference index exists and can be determined.*

(b) It is approximately *logarithmic* in shape, except for extremely high sums.

(c) *For all the persons surveyed* (who, it is recalled, were familiar with probability theory, could be *a priori* considered as rational,[36] and were perfectly aware of the doctrinal implications of the Questionnaire) replies corresponding to the indices $B_{1/2}$ and B_{200} show that their behaviour cannot be explained by the neo-Bernoullian formulation, since for each subject it is impossible to represent his answers to Questions IX and VII by a unique neo-Bernoullian index.[37]

(d) From one subject to another, there is a degree of variety in psychology vis-à-vis risk very similar to the differences in psychology vis-à-vis consumption goods. *However, for all the subjects, there is to be seen a very strong preference for security in the neighbourhood of certainty once the sums involved become substantial.*

(e) *The proof of the existence of an index of cardinal preference (representing psychological value) sweeps away all support for the neo-Bernoullian formulation, as regards rational subjects, if the neo-Bernoullian index is identified with cardinal utility, as it should be,*[38] for it is not possible to consider that it would be irrational to take account, not only of the mathematical expectation, but also of the probability distribution of psychological values about their mean.

These results *totally* invalidate the neo-Bernoullian doctrine which is currently accepted by so many economists and statisticians.

NOTES TO APPENDIX C

[1] §6 above (pp.451–454).

[2] That is especially the case of the method for fitting a non-loglinear index of psychological value (cardinal utility) to the data (see Section VI below).

[3] §3 and §6 above (pp.447–449 and 451–454).

[4] See §11 above and Section II below (pp.460–462 and 614–620).

[5] This relation is deduced from the neo-Bernoullian condition

$$B(C + V) = pB(C + X_0) + (1 - p)B(C)$$

with

$$B(C) = 0,$$

where C represents the subject's capital (see §11.3 and 14 above).

[6] Questions VII of the Questionnaire correspond to $X_0 = 200$ millions (see Section IV, §C.14 below, pp.624–625).

[7] Questions IX of the Questionnaire correspond to $p = 1/2$ (see Section III, §C.10 below, p.620).

[8] MacCrimmon and Larsson have made an extensive study of the test which I used in my 1952 Questionnaire (Questions 39 and 39 bis, J.S.S.P., 1953, p.60) and which they have called the *Common Ratio Test*. In fact the *complementarity effect* in the neighbourhood of certainty can also be brought in evidence by questions such as:

(1) Do you prefer C_1 or D_1?

C_1: 1 million with probability 1.00,

D_1: 5 million with probability 0.80.

(2) Do you prefer C_2 or D_2?

C_2: 1 million with probability 0.05,

D_2: 5 million with probability 0.04.

The neo-Bernoullian formulation implies that the preference $C_1 > D_1$ should entail the preference $C_2 > D_2$, and vice versa. In general, the prudent prefer C_1 to D_1, but nevertheless prefer D_2 to C_2.

The theory underlying these questions is immediate. Let V_1, V_1', V_2 and V_2' be the certain values attaching to the outcomes C_1, D_1, C_2 and D_2. Let $B(X)$ be the neo-Bernoullian index. As $B(0)$ can always be taken as zero, we should have, according to the neo-Bernoullian formulation

$$
\begin{aligned}
B(V_1) &= p_1 B(X_1),\\
B(V_1') &= p_1' B(X_2),\\
B(V_2) &= p_2 B(X_1),\\
B(V_2') &= p_2' B(X_2),
\end{aligned}
$$
(1)

with, in this instance

(2) $X_1 = 1$ million, $X_2 = 5$ million,

    $p_1 = 1,$ $p_1' = 0.8,$ $p_2 = 0.05,$ $p_2' = 0.04,$

(3) $p_1'/p_1 = p_2'/p_2.$

Therefore we should have

(4) $B(V_1)/B(V_1') = B(V_2)/B(V_2'),$

whatever the values of X_1, X_2, p_1, p_1', p_2 and p_2', subject only to condition (3). Thus if $V_1 > V_1'$, we should have $V_2 > V_2'$ whatever the function $B(X)$.

On this very interesting test, see MacCrimmon and Larsson, 1975, Section 4, *Common Ratio of Probabilities* (pp.350–359 above).

[9] See §C19 below (pp.628–631).

[10] See Section II below (pp.614–620).

[11] Questions II were designed to test the propensity to safety or risk for small sums (M, §62). Questions III were designed to test Savage's fifth axiom of his 1952 paper (Contribution to the 1952 Paris Colloquium), i.e. Postulate II, *the sure thing principle*, of his 1954 book (see Note 215 above). This test corresponds to the 'Allais Paradox' (see M, §63, and §36 above). Questions IV and V, very different in principle from Questions III, were also designed to test the validity of the neo-Bernoullian formulation (see Note 15 below).

[12] The replies to Questions IX and VII are examined in Sections III and IV below. For Questions VIII see Note 28 below (pp.620–627 and 628).

[13] Respondents could remain anonymous if they wished; others authorised publication of their names.

[14] The file of Roman's answers to Questions VII and IX was wrongly classified in 1952, and was recovered in 1975 only *after* the averages for these questions had been calculated. This mistake explains why Roman's answers to Questions VII and IX are omitted from the computation of the average for the $B_{1/2}$ and B_{200} indexes. In reality, the inclusion of his answers would not have influenced the conclusions, for his psychology is in radical opposition to the neo-Bernoullian formulation.

[15] Thus and for instance, *due to lack of space*, I am unable to discuss here the results obtained for the four *conformity tests* corresponding to Questions II, III, IV and V for which the replies of 101 subjects were analysed in July 1952. These results may be summarised as follows:

Percentage of replies in violation of the neo-Bernoullian formulation

Questions II	77%	
Questions III	46%	(Allais' Paradox)
Questions IV	82%	
Questions V	35%	

With respect to the 'Allais Paradox', the percentage of 46% for the rate of violation of the neo-Bernoullian formulation is effectively of the same order of magnitude as the percentage of 40% found by MacCrimmon (1968) and recalled by Amihud (1974) (see §36 above, pp.533–541).

See especially the very interesting detailed analysis given by MacCrimmon and Larsson (1975, Section V) of the results obtained by different authors who have found rates of violation of the same order of magnitude, from 27% to 59%. See also the experiments analysed by MacCrimmon (1975, Section IV) which relates to the comparison of random choices near and far from certainty, for which the rate of violation is of the order of 65% (pp.350–369 above).

The above Table shows that *the test of the 'Allais Paradox' is far from being the strongest* against the neo-Bernoullian formulation. The most effective test proved to be that corresponding to Questions IV, with 82% of the subjects submitting replies not in accord with the neo-Bernoullian formulation (see Allais, May 1974, *Résultats du sondage de* 1952; and October 1975, *Les tests de compatibilité des choix avec le principe bernoullien*).

The essential result is that none of the tests is as effective in invalidating the neo-Bernoullian formulation as that corresponding to the non-compatibility of the neo-Bernoullian indices $B_{1/2}$ and B_{200} corresponding to Questions IX and VII (see §C19 below, pp.628–631). In this case the rate of violation is 100%.

[16] $\bar{s}(U)$ represents the cardinal preference index, $s(u)$ the ordinal preference index (see §11.2 above, pp.461–462).

[17] See Allais, *A la Recherche d'une Discipline Economique*, 1943, pp.156–177; see also the *Introduction to the second edition*, 1953, No. 12.

[18] In fact with the notation of §11.2 we have (pp.461–462)

$$U_0 = C$$

and

$$U = U_0 + X = C + X.$$

The symbol U_0 is used in this appendix for reasons of convenience.

[19] Of all the answers I received, de Finetti's was without doubt *the most remarkable in terms of the scientific conscientiousness and great intellectual honesty* with which he responded to the various questions.

[20] To form an idea of the current purchasing power equivalent, the sums mentioned should be multiplied by 3/100 to yield an approximation of the corresponding figures in new francs, as of 1976. In October 1952, exchange rates were 350 'old francs' for one dollar and 980 'old francs' for a pound sterling.

[21] Taking these indications into account, it was possible to establish for each subject an index of '*psychological indetermination*', which represents the degree of precision of the subject's answers.

[22] The techniques required for analysis of the non log-linear case are relatively complex (see §6 above, and Section VI below, pp.453–454 and 632–634).

[23] Napierian logarithms throughout.

[23*] §6 above (pp.451–454).

[24] For reason of convenience the loglinear fitting of Chart VI has been made considering the arithmetic averages of the X for the group of four subjects considered.

[24*] It may be recalled that for a satisfactory analysis of the psychology of random choices, the neo-Bernoullian formulation should be written in the form

$$(1) \qquad B(C + V) = \sum p_i(C + g_i),$$

in which C represents the subject's capital (see §14; Note 155; Appendix A, Note 4 above; and Note 30* hereunder; pp.463–464, 576, 602 and 638).

I also recall that in this Appendix, the subject's capital C is written U_0 (see Note 18 above).

[25] See §C.6 and Note 21 above (p.616).

[26] According to relations (20) and (21) above (p.621), we have for $U_0^* = 17$:

$$B_1 = m[\log 1017 - \log 1000].$$

[27] This group does not include Roman (see Note 14 above).

[28] For the Questions VIII of the 1952 Questionnaire we have

$$B(U_0 + X') = pB(U_0 + 0.01),$$

the value unit being one million of *1952 francs*. Their principle is identical to that of Questions VII. But the sums involved are relatively small.

For lack of space it is impossible to present here the very interesting results of the analysis of the answers to these questions. For the vast majority of subjects a preference is observed for security in the neighbourhood of certitude. This invalidates the neo-Bernoullian formulation.

[29] See §C.6 and Note 21 above (p.616).

[30] Relation (25) above (p.624).

[30*] It is again recalled, that if for any value of U_0^* (in particular for a value of zero) the two indexes $B_{1/2}$ and B_{200} corresponding to the same conditions (28) of §C.19.2 differ markedly, this will necessarily be true for any other value of U_0^*.

In other words, in this case, one would seek in vain a value of U_0^* for which both indexes $B_{1/2}$ and B_{200}, defined respectively by the relations

(1) $B(U_0^* + X') = \dfrac{1}{2} B(U_0^* + X),$

(2) $B(U_0^* + X') = pB(U_0^* + 200),$

with

(3) $B(U_0^*) = 0,$

(4) $B(U_0^* + 200) = 1,$

did not differ significantly from each other.

If this possibility existed, one would be able to determine the subject's capital U_0 from the consideration of his random choices only. In fact this is impossible.

Actually, it is easy to see the link between the presentation used in the Charts VII to XII and the presentation used in the Charts XIII to XV. To illustrate, let us consider the curves $B_{1/2}$ of the Charts VII and XIII for De Finetti. Let a_1 and b_1 be the co-ordinates of point M_1 of the Chart VII, and a_2 and b_2 those of the point M_2 of the Chart XIII, corresponding to $B_{1/2}$. Then:

(5) $a_1 = \log (U_0^* + X),$

(6) $a_2 = \log X,$

and

(7) $b_2 = \dfrac{b_2(a_2 = 200)}{b_1^*(a_1 = 217)} \, b_1 = \dfrac{1}{0.444} \, b_1.$

The value $b_1^* = 0.444$ is equal to the ordinate of the point whose abscissa is $a_1 = U_0^* + 200 = 217$ of the curve fitted in Chart VII.

The neo-Bernoullian formulation

(8) $B(U_0^* + X') = \dfrac{1}{2} B(U_0^* + X)$

is invariant under such a transformation, since the index B is defined up to a linear transformation and condition (8) holds whatever the scale used for the abscissa.

Similar remarks can be made for the other Charts.

[31] The case of satiety, was examined for the first time in the literature by Cramer, 1728, cited by Daniel Bernoulli, 1738, at the end of his study (*Econometrica*, 1954, pp.33–34). See also Buffon, 1777, Sections XV and XVI.

[32] They are essentially based on consideration of an auxiliary function which I have named the '*generating function*'.

[33] Corresponding to the Question 651 (see §C.6 above, pp.615–617).

[34] In fact with a margin of error of less than 2%, the function f may be reduced to a linear function of $\log x$ for

$$6 < x = 1 + X/U_0 < 1700.$$

This explains why loglinear adjustments give good results only for values of U_0/X which are neither too small nor too great (see conditions (30), p.633).

[35] For lack of space this very complex analysis, unfortunately, cannot be given in the present paper.

[36] In the sense precised in §19 and Note 193 above (pp.467–468 and 579).

[37] See §C.19 above; see also §22 above; (pp.628–631 and 473–474).

[38] See §§16d, 23.1 and Appendix BI above (pp.465, 475–480 and 604–607).

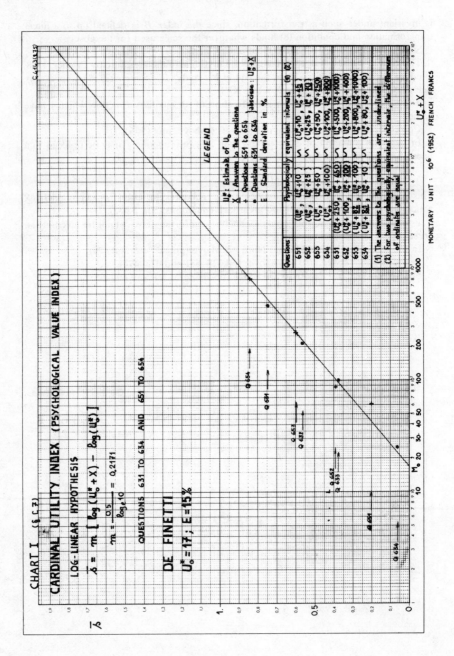

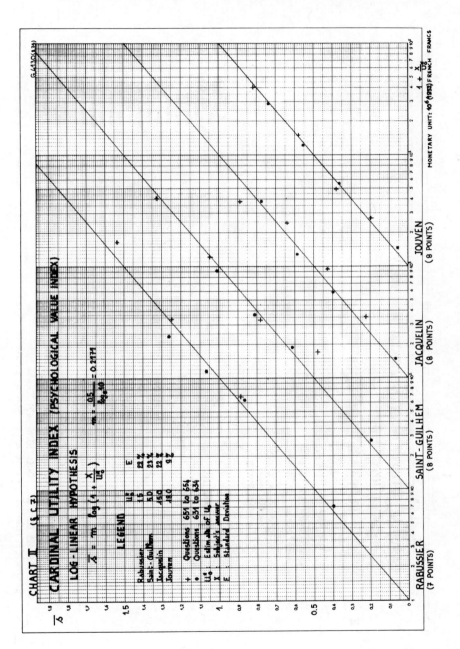

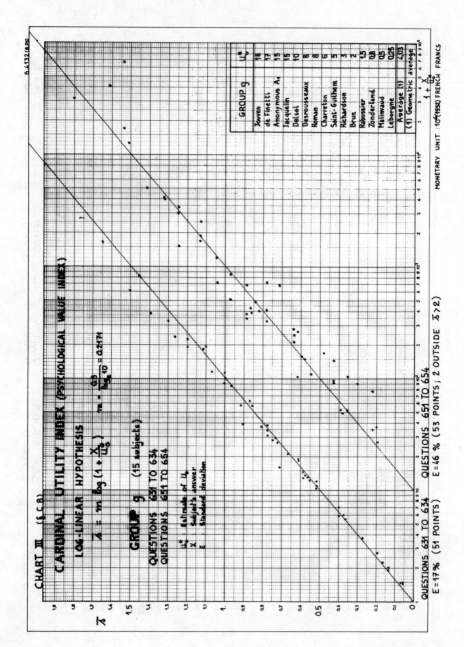

CHART II (S.C.B)

CARDINAL UTILITY INDEX (PSYCHOLOGICAL VALUE INDEX)

LOG-LINEAR HYPOTHESIS

$$\gamma = m \log \left(1 + \frac{X}{U_0}\right) \qquad m = \frac{0.5}{\log_{10} 10} = 0.2174$$

GROUP g   (15 subjects)

QUESTIONS 631 TO 634
QUESTIONS 651 TO 654

U_0^* : Estimation of U_0
X   : Subject's answer
E   : Standard deviation

QUESTIONS 631 TO 634)   QUESTIONS 651 TO 654
E = 17% (51 POINTS)   E = 46 % (53 POINTS ; 2 OUTSIDE $\bar{\gamma} > 2$)

GROUP g	U_0^*
Xouven	18
de Finetti	17
Anonymous A₁	15
Jacquelin	15
Delsol	10
Desrousseaux	8
Roman	8
Charreton	6
Saint-Guilhem	5
Richardson	3
Brun	2
Rabossier	1.5
Zonderland	0.8
Malinvaud	0.5
Lebergue	0.25
Average (1)	4.03
(1) Geometric average	$1 + \frac{X}{U_0}$

MONETARY UNIT : 10⁶(1952) FRENCH FRANCS

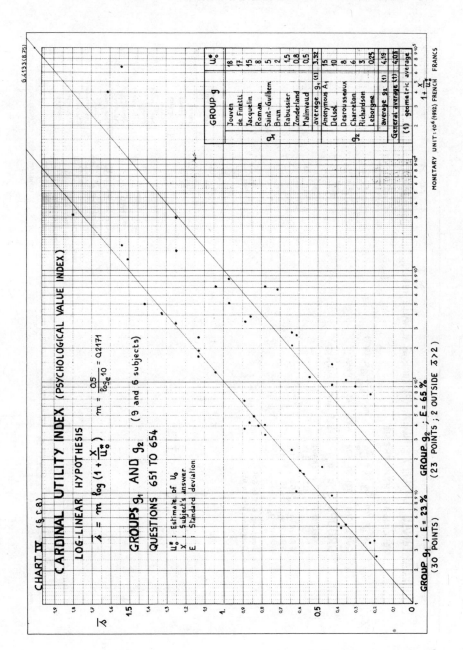

CHART IV   (§ C 8)

CARDINAL UTILITY INDEX (PSYCHOLOGICAL VALUE INDEX)

LOG-LINEAR HYPOTHESIS

$$\bar{\mathfrak{z}} = m \log \left(1 + \frac{X}{U_o^*}\right) \qquad m = \frac{0.5}{\log_e 10} = 0.2171$$

GROUPS g_1 AND g_2 (9 and 6 subjects)

QUESTIONS 651 TO 654

U_o^* : Estimate of U_o
X : Subject's answer
E : Standard deviation

GROUP g		U_o^*
g_1	Jouven	18
	de Finetti	17
	Jacquelin	15
	Roman	8
	Saint-Guilhem	5
	Brun	2
	Rabussier	1.5
	Zonderland	0.8
	Malinvaud	0.5
	average g_1 (1)	3.52
g_2	Anonymous A_1	15
	Delsol	10
	Desrousseaux	8
	Charretton	6
	Richardson	3
	Leborgne	0.25
	average g_2 (1)	4.19
	General average (†)	4.05

(1) geometric average

$$1 + \frac{X}{U_o^*}$$

MONETARY UNIT : 10^6 (1952) FRENCH FRANCS

GROUP g_1 ; E = 23 %   GROUP g_2 ; E = 65 %
(30 POINTS)   (23 POINTS ; 2 OUTSIDE $\bar{\mathfrak{z}} > 2$)

G.4133 (8.75)

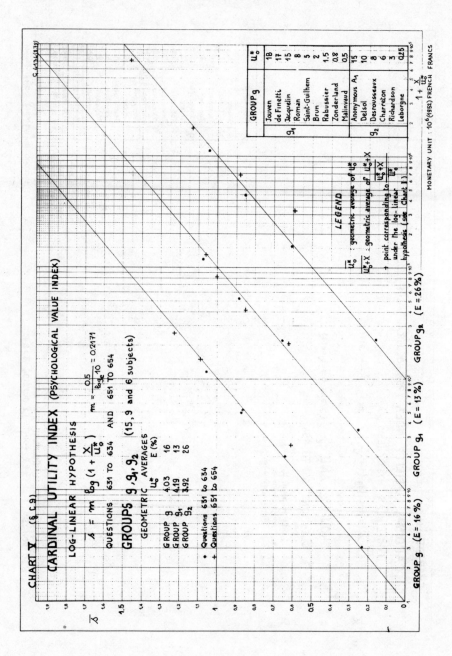

CHART V (§ C 9)

CARDINAL UTILITY INDEX (PSYCHOLOGICAL VALUE INDEX)

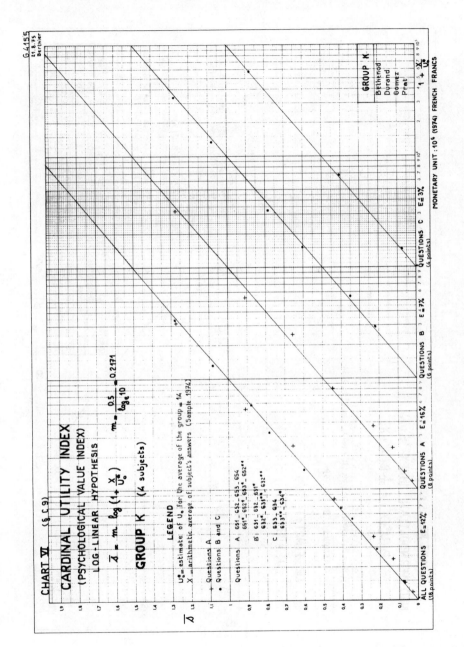

CHART VI (§ C 9)

CARDINAL UTILITY INDEX
(PSYCHOLOGICAL VALUE INDEX)

LOG - LINEAR HYPOTHESIS

$$\bar{A} = m \, \log\left(1 + \frac{X}{U_o^*}\right) \qquad m = \frac{0.5}{\log_e 10} = 0.2171$$

GROUP K (4 subjects)

LEGEND

U_o^* = estimate of U_o for the average of the group = ¼
X = arithmetic average of subject's answers (Sample 1974)

+ Questions A
● Questions B and C

Questions A: 651 – 652, 653, 654
               651*, 652, 653*, 652**
           B: 631 – 632, 631**
               632*, 631**, 632**
           C: 633, 634
               633**, 634*

GROUP K

Bethenod
Durand
Gomez
Pret

MONETARY UNIT : 10⁶ (1974) FRENCH FRANCS

ALL QUESTIONS   QUESTIONS A   QUESTIONS B   QUESTIONS C
(18 points)   E=12% (8 points) E=16% (6 points) E=7% (4 points) E=3%

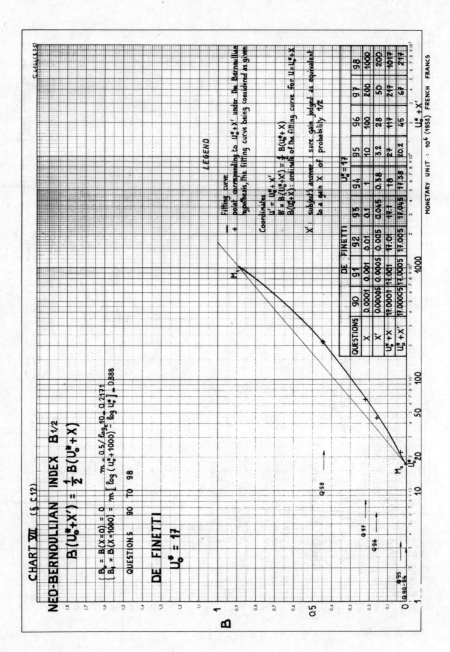

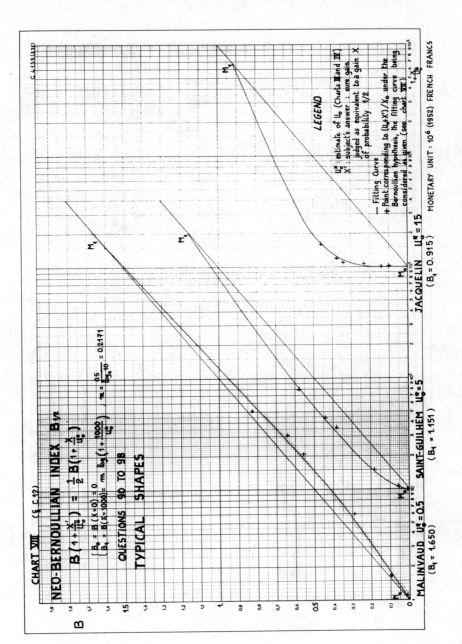

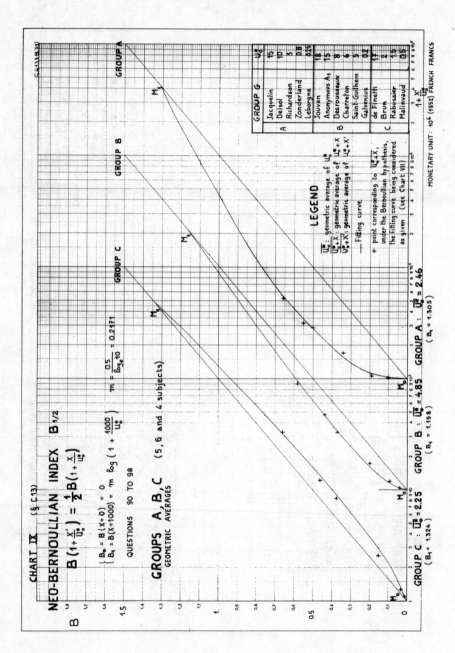

CHART IX   (§ C 13)

NEO-BERNOULLIAN INDEX $B_{1/2}$

$$B\left(1+\frac{X'}{U_0^*}\right) = \frac{1}{2}B\left(1+\frac{X}{U_0^*}\right)$$

$\begin{cases} B_0 = B(X=0) = 0 \\ B_1 = B(X=1000) = m \log\left(1+\frac{1000}{U_0^*}\right) \end{cases}$ $m = \frac{0.5}{\log_e 10} = 0.2171$

QUESTIONS 90 TO 98

GROUPS A, B, C
GEOMETRIC AVERAGES   (5, 6 and 4 subjects)

GROUP G

GROUP G		U_0^*
A	Jacquelin	15
	Deïsol	10
	Richardson	3
	Zonderland	0.8
	Leborgne	0.15
B	Jouven	18
	Anonymous A_1	15
	Desrousseaux	8
	Charreton	6
	Saint-Guilhem	5
	Galvenius	0.2
C	de Finetti	1.7
	Brun	2
	Rabuissier	1.5
	Malinvaud	0.5

LEGEND

$\overline{U_0^*}$: geometric average of U_0^*
$\overline{U_0^* + X}$: geometric average of $U_0^* + X$
$\overline{U_0^* + X'}$: geometric average of $U_0^* + X'$

—— Fitting curve

+ point corresponding to $\overline{U_0^* + X}$,
under the Bernoullian hypothesis,
the fitting curve being considered
as given (see Chart VII)

MONETARY UNIT: 10^6 (1952) FRENCH FRANCS

$1+\frac{X}{U_0^*}$

GROUP A : $\overline{U_0^*} = 1.305$ GROUP A : $\overline{U_0^*} = 2.46$
($B_1 = 1.305$)

GROUP B : $\overline{U_0^*} = 4.85$
($B_1 = 1.158$)

GROUP C : $\overline{U_0^*} = 2.25$
($B_1 = 1.324$)

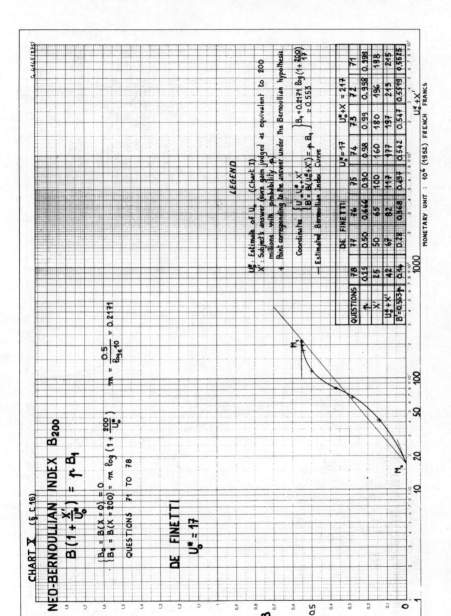

CHART X (§ C.16)

NEO-BERNOULLIAN INDEX B₂₀₀

$$B\left(1 + \frac{X'}{U_0^*}\right) = \gamma \cdot B_1$$

$$\begin{cases} B_0 = B(X=0) = 0 \\ B_1 = B(X=200) \end{cases}$$

$$B(X=200) = m \log\left(1 + \frac{200}{U_0^*}\right) \qquad m = \frac{0.5}{\log_e 10} = 0.2171$$

QUESTIONS 71 TO 78

DE FINETTI

$$U_0^* = 17$$

LEGEND

U_0^*: Estimate of U_0 ((Chart I)
X': Subject's answer (sure gain judged as equivalent to 200
millions with probability γ)
$+$ Point corresponding to the answer under the Bernoullian hypothesis

Coordinates $\begin{cases} U_0^* = {}^*U_0 + X' \\ B = B(U_0^* + X') = \gamma \cdot B_1 \end{cases}$ $\begin{cases} B_1 = 0.2171 \log\left(1 + \frac{200}{17}\right) \\ = 0.555 \end{cases}$

— Estimated Bernoullian Index Curve

QUESTIONS		78	77	76	75	74	73	72	71
			DE FINETTI			$U_0^* = 17$		$U_0^* + X = 217$	
γ		0.15	0.50	0.664	0.90	0.98	0.99	0.998	0.998
X'		25	50	65	100	160	180	196	198
$U_0^* + X'$		42	67	82	117	177	197	215	215
$B = 0.553\gamma$		0.14	0.28	0.368	0.493	0.542	0.547	0.547	0.5515

MONETARY UNIT : 10⁶ (1952) FRENCH FRANCS

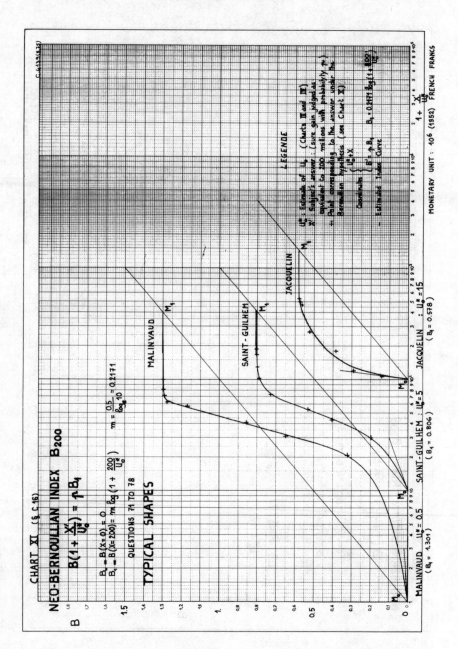

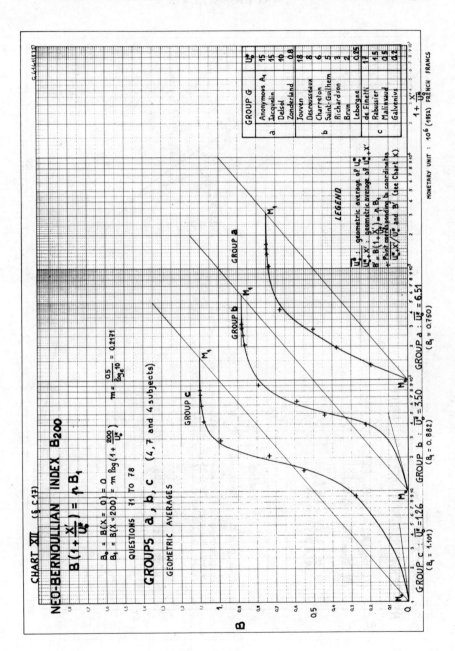

CHART XII (§ C.13)

NEO-BERNOULLIAN INDEX B200

$$B\left(1 + \frac{X'}{U_\xi^*}\right) = r \, B_4$$

$B_o = B(X = 0) = 0$
$B_4 = B(X = 200) = m \log\left(1 + \frac{200}{U_\xi^*}\right)$

$m = \dfrac{0.5}{\log_e 10} = 0.2171$

QUESTIONS 71 TO 78

GROUPS a, b, c   (4, 7 and 4 subjects)

GEOMETRIC AVERAGES

GROUP c

GROUP b

GROUP a

M₁

LEGEND

U_ξ^* : geometric average of U_ξ^*
U_ξ^*, X' : geometric average of U_ξ^*, X'
$B' = B\left(1 + \frac{X'}{U_\xi^*}\right) = r \, B_4$
+ Point corresponding to coordinates
$U_\xi^*, X'/U_\xi^*$ and B' (see Chart X).

GROUP c : $\overline{U_\xi^*} = 1.26$ GROUP b : $\overline{U_\xi^*} = 3.50$ $\overline{U_\xi^*} = 6.51$ GROUP a : $\overline{U_\xi^*} = 0.750$
($B_4 = 1.101$)   ($B_4 = 0.882$)   ($B_4 = 0.750$)

$1 + \frac{X'}{U_\xi^*}$

MONETARY UNIT : 10⁶ (1952) FRENCH FRANCS

	GROUP G	U_ξ^*
a	Anonymous A₄	15
	Jacquelin	15
	Delsol	10
	Zanderland	0.8
	Jouven	18
	Desrousseaux	8
b	Charreton	6
	Saint-Guilhem	5
	Richardson	3
	Brun	2
	Leborgne	0.25
	de Finetti	17
c	Rabusier	1.5
	Malinvaud	0.5
	Galvenius	0.2

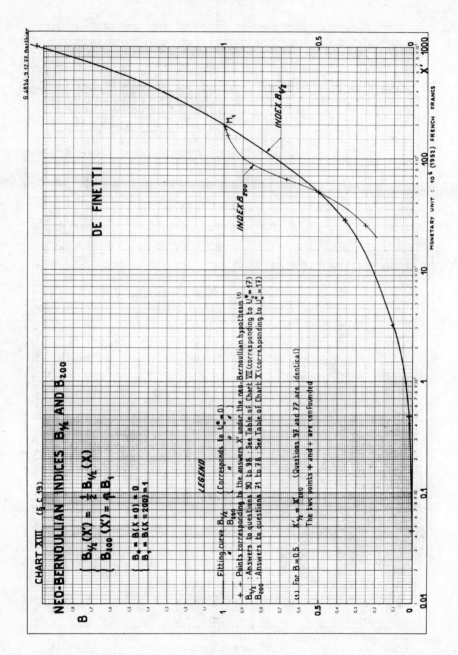

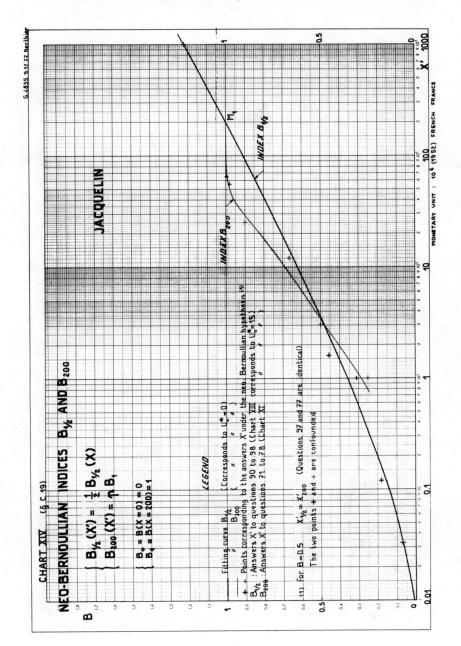

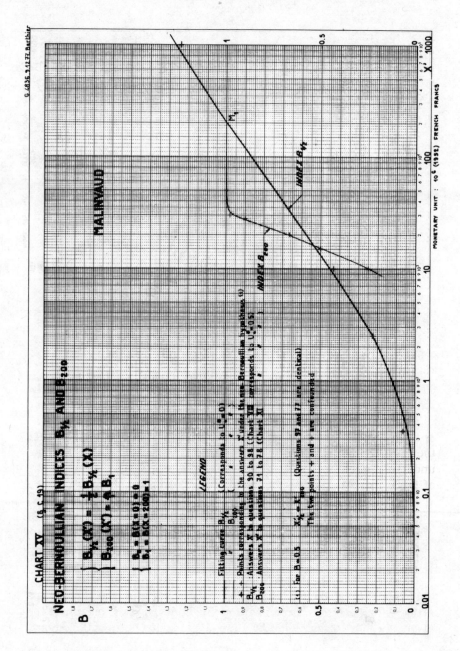

CHART XV (5, C, 19)

NEO-BERNOULLIAN INDICES B_{y_2} AND B_{200}

APPENDIX D: ON THE CONCEPT OF PROBABILITY

> If one's attention is focused on the mathematical difficulties of complicated problems, it is easily possible to pass over the difficulties of the fundamentals.
>
> RICHARD VON MISES,
> *Probability, Statistics and Truth*, 1946, p.82

> A probability, however tiny, is separated from an impossibility by an impassable abyss that cannot be crossed.
>
> MAX PLANCK,
> *A Survey of Physics,*
> *A Collection of Lectures and Essays,*
> 1925, Chapter III.

The following comments are simply intended to supplement the indications given in Sections 10, 21, 29 and 39 above, to reply to some observations made by readers of the first draft of this study.

They are by no means intended to be exhaustive, and in any case they are far from perfect; but it is hoped that they will facilitate understanding of a standpoint which cannot be identified with any one of the theories that have been put forward to date.

In fact, *no theory of random choice whatsoever can be satisfactorily elaborated without a previous thorough study of the concept of probability.*

THE THEORIES OF PROBABILITIES

D.1. The general theory of random events that developed from the 17th century on has been marked by controversies regarding the axioms which should underlie it to avoid any contradiction. Some

655

schools contend that probability only has meaning in terms of the frequencies observed in physical processes, others that probability is basically a subjective notion. Still others think that the general theory of random events should remain a purely mathematical construct, while others consider it essentially as a theory depicting concrete reality in the same manner as the physical theories.

Whether or not they are developed in axiomatic form, probability theories may be classified into three main groups: *classical theory and related theories* defining probabilities on the basis of the concept of equal possibility, itself depending on the consideration of symmetry conditions; *theories founded on the definition of probabilities on the basis of frequencies, and theories relying on a subjective conception of probability.* Classical theory may be regarded as both objective and subjective.

All probability theories take as their starting point the three principles of addition, multiplication and inversion of probabilities, some as theorems, others as axioms or definitions. From this starting point all deduce the same corpus of propositions. *They differ on only two points: the definition and interpretation of the concept of probability, and the appropriate way to apply the theory to real life. Here and here alone lie the fundamental difficulties.*

All probability theories are confronted with the same proposition: *it is impossible fully to verify a probability judgment; whatever happens, the event which occurs may always be considered as compatible with the probability judgment.* This is because the theory of probability can only lead to the determination of probabilities, and consequently, it cannot yield any forecast with absolute certainty. However small the probability, the corresponding event can always arise. *Thus, no event can confirm or refute an inference based on probability theory.* This theory cannot therefore be 'verified' in the sense in which 'verification' is understood for a physical theory.

A theory may effectively be considered as a probability theory only inasmuch as it provides a link between mathematical probability and the frequency observed, and between mathematical theory and physical reality. *This link implies a response to three questions:* how to predict the frequency effectively observed on the basis of an *a priori* assessment of probability? How to assess probability on the basis of observed frequencies? How to explain that nature obeys probabilistic models?

Answers to the two first questions are given already in Laplace's analytical theory of probabilities (1812). Only Henry Poincaré really tackled the third one (1903, 1908, and 1912). *This third question is by far the most difficult.* Relevant answers to the first two questions indeed depend on the analysis of the third. *Unfortunately no fully satisfactory answer to this third question is available at present.*

At all events, the purely axiomatic mathematical theories yield no real answer to these three fundamental questions. In this sense, they are not theories of probability. *In itself, and for instance, Bernoulli's law of large numbers yields no information on observed reality, for it merely represents the enumeration of the possible eventualities, based on the axiom of equal possibility. It is merely a theorem in mathematical combinatorial analysis and nothing more.*

(For a discussion of these various points and on a possible synthesis of the classical, frequentist and subjective theories, see Allais, 1976, *Les fondements de la théorie des probabilités*).

On the history of probability theory, see Laplace, 1814, pp.94–106; Todhunter, 1865. On classical theory, see Laplace, 1812 and 1814; Poincaré, 1903, 1908 and 1912. For frequentist theories, see mainly: Mises, 1920 and 1932; Cantelli, 1935; Frechet, 1955. For subjective theories, see mainly: Keynes, 1921; Levy, 1925; Ramsey, 1926; De Finetti, 1937 and 1938; Borel, 1939; Jeffrey, 1947; Savage, 1952 and 1954. On purely axiomatic probability theory, see mainly: Kolmogorov, 1933; Cramér, 1945; Gnedenko, 1963; Dugué, 1968. For an overview, see Kendall, 1949; Good, 1950; and Wright, 1975. See also the other references in Section III of the Bibliography below.

As a matter of fact, *the most penetrating insights into the nature and scope of probability theory may generally be found in the works of the probability theory's founders and their disciples – much more so than in the more recent axiomatic theories which by-pass the fundamental issues.*

D'ALEMBERT'S PRINCIPLE OF THE 'PRACTICAL
IMPOSSIBILITY' OF EVENTS WITH A SMALL PROBABILITY

D.2. In order to overcome the basic difficulty resulting from the impossibility of verifying a probabilistic model with full certainty, and to allow a link to be established between theory and reality, most authors have been led to introduce a new more or less explicit postulate: *Any event whose probability is below a certain threshold can be viewed as 'practically' impossible.* In fact such a postulate is *really unacceptable.*

If however, such a postulate is abandoned, as it should, it must be recognised that in the field of random events it is impossible to make any forecast with certainty. In other words, any absolute verification of probability theory is altogether impossible. *But this impossibility derives from the very nature of things, and it cannot be eliminated.*

To treat events having a very low probability as being impossible can only lead to insurmountable difficulties. By its very nature, probability theory can only lead to judgments of probabilities. The fact that an event occurs, can never be viewed as either confirming or invalidating a given probability model. If for instance in a series of 10 successive drawings (with replacement), a white ball is extracted eight times from a reference urn containing 5 white and 5 black balls, it is only possible to calculate the probability of this event to occur, or if we prefer the probability of drawing a white ball at least 8 times out of 10. Nothing more than this can be said.

In fact, the decision of taking, or not taking, into account the small probabilities raises a question of the greatest importance, not only for the probability theory as a whole, but also *and more especially for the theory of random choice.*

Fréchet, 1955 (pp.208–213), names *principle of Buffon–Cournot* the principle of not taking into account low probabilities, while admitting that its paternity can be traced back to D'Alembert, but without giving any precise reference.

It is, in fact, D'Alembert who stated this principle first. In his *Reflexions sur le Calcul des Probabilités*, 1761 (Sections XI, XII and XIII), he writes:

A distinction must be made between that which is possible metaphysically and that which is possible physically . . . it is *metaphysically possible* to throw a pair of six-spots on two dice a hundred times in succession, but it is *physically impossible*, because it has never happened and never will.

D'Alembert's principle that small probabilities should be ignored, was taken up by Buffon, 1777, in his *Arithmétique Morale* (Sections XVI and XX), and then by Cournot, 1843, in his *Théorie des Chances et des Probabilités* (pp.77–82). Buffon writes (Section XVI and XX):

The value of a probability should be regarded as zero as soon as it is very small, i.e. less than 1/10,000, or even less 1/1000.

Cournot sets *'physical impossibility'* or *'impossibility in practice'* in contrast to *'metaphysical impossibility'* or *'absolute impossibility'*. For Cournot:

A physically impossible event is one whose mathematical probability is infinitely small; this single remark confers on the theory of mathematical probability consistency, and objective and phenomenological value.

In fact, D'Alembert's comments (pp.8–12) are more opposite and detailed than Cournot's or Buffon's. He particularly puts down some quite fundamental questions:

What is the span beyond which it becomes possible to regard a probability as zero? . . . Supposing we posit it, for example, at the point at which the probability is 1/1000, how should we estimate the probabilities which differ only slightly from it, although they are greater . . . or which represent relatively large fractions, such as 1/4 or 1/8?

From the standpoint of scientific deontology, it is to be regretted that Buffon failed to refer to D'Alembert, whose ideas on small probabilities he built on, and that Cournot failed to mention either Buffon or D'Alembert, on whose work he patently based his own conception on small probabilities. Too often great minds seem deliberately to wish to mask their debt to their predecessors. Examples of this are only too abundant, nowadays as much as formerly.

The principle of neglecting small probabilities, which should therefore be called D'Alembert's principle, is *implicitly or explicitly* admitted by most of the contemporary theories, but *fundamentally it is utterly inadmissible,* for it leads to logical inconsistencies; and nobody has ever been able to determine the threshold beyond which small probabilities should be neglected, or the rules by which the objective probabilities should be modified once this path could be taken.

At all events, for the theory of choice in the face of risk, the threshold value below which a probability could be considered to correspond to a *'practically impossible'* event would clearly depend on the size of the sums at issue. Most certainly for many people a probability of 1/1000 of losing $10 can be neglected, whereas at the same time the same probability of being totally ruined cannot. Be this as it may, if this circumstance is to be analysed, it is useless to have recourse to the really unacceptable principle of neglecting small probabilities, treating a small probability as if it were one of zero. It is sufficient, and much more appropriate, to consider, as indicated in this memoir an ordinal preference index such as $S = S(g, p)$ where p is the probability of a monetary gain g.

The distinction between '*actual (or practical) impossibility*' and '*absolute impossibility*' is scientifically inadmissible. Any event with a very low probability *can practically happen* for the simple reason that however big an N, the drawing of N white balls out of N drawings with replacement, in a reference urn containing as many black balls as white balls, is *just as possible as any other sequence of drawings that will be observed*.

As to the events with probability zero, they correspond to an infinite value of N. *Since infinite sequences cannot be achieved, such events evade any experimental control.*

Actually, the concept of probability is derived from the concept of '*equal possibility*', and *this concept cannot be reduced to any other*. The consideration of a very low probability can never lead to certainty. Besides, nobody can give a rigorous definition of what a '*small probability*' is.

It follows that the estimation of a probability can never lead to any conclusion whatsoever that can be stated outside the field of the theory of probability.

MY GENERAL CONCEPTION OF THE PROBABILITY THEORY

D.3. My general conception of the theory of probability can be summarized as follows:

(1) The probability of an event likely to occur repeatedly under the same conditions is a *physical quantity corresponding to a physical reality*.

(2) The consideration of the device of an *urn of reference* in which symmetry conditions do obtain, makes it possible to define the probability as the ratio of the number of favourable cases to the total number of equally possible cases.

The process of drawing from an urn of reference *makes it possible to grasp the concept of probability in its pure state. It cannot be reduced to any other.*

It is in fact the *only* process really capable of defining the concept of objective probability. It gives the measuring scale for probabilities against which all probabilities can be measured.

(3) *The whole of the theory of probability can be deduced down from the axiom of equal possibility corresponding to symmetry conditions* for the model of the urn of reference. This axiom corresponds to an *abstract model*, which is an *idealisation of physical experience. In fact, this axiom is more or less implicitly admitted by every theory. It constitutes the real basis of probability theory.*

(4) It can be admitted as an axiom that actual symmetry conditions actually obtain in the experimental set up of an urn of reference, as defined in §21 above.

This axiom has a fundamentally subjective character. It corresponds to a *subjective judgment* over a physical process. The resulting probability estimate is *a subjective estimate of an objective probability.*

(5) *In the absence of any other information*, the observed frequency provides an estimate of probability, which may be considered as the better the longer the series observed.

However, if actual symmetry conditions do exist (*which is the case in an urn of reference*) the subjective estimate of the objective probability, based on the consideration of the ratio of the number of favourable cases to the total number of equally possible cases, must be preferred to the one based on the observed frequency, *whatever the length of the series of observations taken into account.*

(6) The assimilation of an event with a very small probability to a 'practically impossible' event is *always to be rejected, however small the value of the probability considered.*

(7) There is *no real contradiction* between the axiom of equal possibility and the fact that in an infinite set of drawings (with replacement) from an urn containing an equal number of black and white balls, it is effectively possible to extract the same ball each time, indefinitely.

The axiom of equal possibility relates to each unit drawing. In no way does it imply the asymptotic convergence of the frequency towards the probability in the sense of mathematical analysis when the number of drawings effected increases indefinitely.

(8) The confrontation of theory and observed reality in the field of probability *raises problems that differ altogether* from those generally met in the physical sciences: *here any certain verification is totally impossible.*

All that can be said is that out of two probability models likely to represent an event that really happened, one should prefer, in the absence of any other information, the one for which the probability of occurrence of that event is the largest.

At all events, appraisal of the validity of a probability model in the light of observed data is a matter of subjective appreciation.

(9) The agreement generally found between the propositions deduced by probability theory from the axiom of equal possibility and observed data should be interpreted as a proof of the validity of this axiom, from which *all* these propositions flow.

Nevertheless, the axiom of equal possibility, which is fundamentally based on an assumption of symmetry, can be considered only as an idealisation of experience, since in a given drawing, the ball extracted will be either black or white. This shows that symmetry is not total, and that the departure of reality from perfect symmetry, although small indeed, is nevertheless enough to cause a white ball to be extracted rather than a black one (or *vice versa*), in the case of a reference urn containing an equal number of black and white balls.

As Henry Poincaré clearly perceived, it is *in the association with general conditions of symmetry of the effects of small causes* that one should seek the reasons for the agreement that is generally found between observed data and deductions from probability theory.

(10) *Subjective probability is a derived concept which can only be defined from the concept of a reference probability* (i.e. from the consideration of an objective reference probability).

It follows that for *the urn reference model, subjective probability is necessarily equal to the corresponding objective probability.*

(11) *The concept of the subjective probability attaching to a non-repeatable event is altogether different in nature from the concept of objective probability, which corresponds to a physical reality.*

For non-repeatable events, another terminology should be introduced *to avoid confusion*, replacing the expression 'subjective probability' by the expression '*coefficient of plausibility, or likelihood*'.

(12) The link between probability theory and reality implies the answer to *three fundamental questions*: how to predict frequency

from probability; how to estimate probability from observed frequency; how to explain that nature can be generally represented by probabilistic models.

(13) In any case, the interpretation of the differences observed between the *a priori* probability and the *observed* frequency in relation to the validity of a probability model *relies on a subjective judgment involving subjective probabilities.*

(14) In the last analysis, the theory of probability is essentially based on three entirely different classes of deductions:

(a) more or less complex *calculations of combinatory analysis*, which form the mathematical theory of probability and are all based implicitly or explicitly on the *axiom of equal possibility* (axiomatic theory of probability).

(b) *subjective judgments* to interpret empirical relations between observed frequencies and calculated probabilities (statistical analysis).

(c) *explanatory attempts* as regards the observed possibility of representing physical reality using probability models (physical theory).

(15) As the reader will easily see, the general conception of the probability theory which rests on the above considerations differs from that of the classical theories, the frequentists theories, the subjectivist theories and the axiomatic theories (see §D.1 above), although it has numerous affinities with each of these.

At all events, and in contrast with some developments found in all of these theories, *this conception is free of any logical contradiction as regards the link to be established between probability theory and observed reality.*

BIBLIOGRAPHY

I. OVERVIEWS OF THE THEORY OF CHOICE UNDER UNCERTAINTY

Allais, Maurice: (1951) 'Notes Théoriques sur l'Incertitude de l'Avenir et le Risque' ('Theoretical Notes on the Uncertainty of the Future and Risk'), Paper submitted to the European Econometric Congress, Louvain, Centre d'Analyse Economique, 72pp.

Allais, Maurice: (1952a) 'Fondements d'une Théorie des Choix Comportant un Risque' ('Foundations of a Theory of Random Choice'), Colloque International de Paris sur les 'Fondements et Applications de la Théorie du Risque en Econométrie', Paris, 12–17 Mai, 1952. *Econométrie*, Colloques Internationaux du Centre National de la Recherche Scientifique, Vol. XL, Paris, 1953, pp.127–140.[1]

Allais, Maurice: (1952b) *Fondements d'une Théorie Positive des Choix comportant un Risque et Critique des Postulats et Axiomes de l'Ecole Américaine* (*Foundations of a Positive Theory of Choice involving Risk, and a Criticism of the Postulates and Axioms of the American School*), *Econométrie*, Colloques Internationaux du Centre National de la Recherche Scientifique, Vol. XL, Paris, 1953, pp.257–332.[2] (See also pp.34–35, 37–39, 40, 47–48, 151–163, 194–197 and 245–247.)

This memoir was republished in Vol. 144 of the *Annales des Mines*, special issue, 1955, and again as a separate volume, under the same title by the Imprimerie Nationale, 1955.

The English version of this memoir appears without any modification in the present book (pp.27–145).

Allais, Maurice: (1952c) A summarised version was published under the title 'Le Comportement de l'Homme Rationnel devant le Risque: Critique des Postulats et Axiomes de l'Ecole Américaine' ('The Behavior of Rational Man facing Risk: Criticism of the Postulates and Axioms of the American School') in *Econometrica*, Vol. 21, No. 4, Oct. 1953, pp.503–546.[3]

Allais, Maurice: (1976) 'Fondements axiomatiques de la théorie positive des choix', ('Axiomatic Foundations of the Positive Theory of Choice'), Centre d'Analyse Economique, 25 pp.

Arrow, K. J.: (1958) 'Utilities, Attitudes, Choices: A Review Note', *Econometrica* 26, 1–23 (a); republished in L. R. Amey (Ed.), *Readings in Management Decision*, Longman, 1973, pp.46–86 (b).

Arrow, K. J.: (1963) 'Utility and Expectation in Economic Behavior'. In Sigmund Koch (Ed.), *Psychology: A Study of a Science. Volume 6: Investigations of Man as Socius: Their Place in Psychology and the Social Sciences*, McGraw-Hill, New York, pp.724–752.

Baumol, William J.: (1961) *Economic Theory and Operations Analysis*, Chapters 17–19, Prentice Hall.

Borch, Karl: (1968) *The Economics of Uncertainty*, Princeton University Press.

Chernoff, Herman: (1968) 'Decision Theory', *International Encyclopedia of the Social Sciences*, Vol. 4, Macmillan and Free Press, pp.62–66.

Colloque sur les Fondements et Applications de la Theorie du Risque, (Colloquium on the Foundations and Applications of Risk Theory), Paris, (1952). Actes du Colloque. Contributions of G. Th. Guilbaud, L. J. Savage, K. Arrow, B. de Finetti, M. Friedman,

H. Wold, P. A. Samuelson, P. Massé and G. Morlat, J. Marschak, M. Boiteux, J. Ville, R. Frisch and M. Allais, 12–17 Mai, 1952, Colloques Internationaux, Vol. XL, *Econometrie*, Centre National de la Recherche Scientifique, Paris, 1953.

Edwards, Ward: (1954) 'The Theory of Decision Making', *Psychological Bulletin* 51, 380–417.

Edwards, Ward: (1960) *Psychophysical Decision Theories*, The University of Michigan, Engineering Psychology Group, Willow Run Laboratories, Mimeo, doc., 62 pp.

Edwards, Ward: (1961) 'Behavioral Decision Theory', *Annual Review of Psychology* 12, 473–498.

Edwards, Ward: (1968) 'Decision Making: Psychological Aspects', *International Encyclopedia of the Social Sciences* 4, 34–42.

Gerard-Varet, Louis-André: (1973) 'Utilité de Bernoulli, Probabilité subjective et Décision en Incertitude', Thèse pour le Doctorat d'Etat ès-Sciences Economiques, 12 Novembre 1973, Université de Dijon, 303 pp.

Khamei, Anvar: (1969) 'Contribution à l'Etude de l'Utilité Espérée et sa Maximisation', Thèse présentée à la Faculté de Droit et des Sciences Economiques et Sociales de l'Université de Fribourg, Switzerland.

Luce, R. Duncan, and Raiffa, Howard: (1957) *Games and Decisions: Introduction and Critical Survey*, A study of the Behavioral Models Project, Bureau of Applied Social Research, Columbia University, New York: Wiley. First issued in 1954 as *A Survey of the Theory of Games*, Columbia University, Bureau of Applied Social Research, Technical Report No. 5.

Luce, R. Duncan, and Suppes, Patrick: (1965) 'Preference, Utility and Subjective Probability'. In R. Duncan Luce, Robert R. Bush, and Eugene Galanter (Eds.), *Handbook of Mathematical Psychology*, Volume 3, Wiley, New York, pp.249–410.

Markowitz, H. M.: (1959) *Portfolio Selection*, Yale University Press.

Marschak, Jacob: (1968) 'Decision Making: Economic Aspects', *International Encyclopedia of the Social Sciences* 4, 42–55.

Menges, Günter: (1973) *Economic Decision Making – Basic Concepts and Models*, Longman, London.

Raiffa, Howard: (1968) *Decision Analysis*, Addison Wesley, Reading, Mass.

Sandretto, René: (1970) 'L'Analyse Axiomatique et la Science Economique – Application à la Théorie de la Décision face à l'Incertitude', Mémoire pour le Diplôme d'Etudes Supérieures de Sciences Economiques, Université de Lyon.

Tribus, Myron: (1969) *Rational, Descriptions, Decisions and Designs*, Pergamon Press.

II. ON THE CONCEPT OF PSYCHOLOGICAL VALUE
(OR CARDINAL UTILITY)

Allais, M.: (1943) *A la Recherche d'une Discipline Economique*, Première Partie: L'Economie Pure. (*In Quest of an Economic Discipline*, Part I, Pure Economics), Chapter II, Satisfactions Absolues, pp.156–177, Ateliers Industria, 852 pp. and Annexes, 68 pp. Second edition under the title: *Traité d'Economie Pure* (*Treatise on Pure Economics*), Imprimerie Nationale, 1952, 5 Vol., 1000 pages (the second edition is identical to the first, apart from the addition of a new introduction, 63 pp.).

Allais, M.: (1959) 'Les conditions d'une Société Libre', §II.1, *Revue des Travaux de l'Académie des Sciences Morales et Politiques*, Vol. 112, January 1959, pp.307–322.

Allais, M.: (1961) 'L'Influence, des Besoins sur la Production des Biens de Consommation', pp.139–140, 149–150, and 178–180; in *L'Evolution et le Rôle des Besoins de Biens de Consommation dans les Divers Régimes Economiques*, Centre National de la Recherche Scientifique, Paris, 1963, pp.133–194.

Allais, M.: (1967) 'Les Conditions de l'Efficacité dans l'Economie', §§13, 14 and 86, Ecole Nationale Supérieure des Mines de Paris.
Italian translation: 'Le Condizioni Dell' Efficienza Nell' Economia', in *Programmazione E Progresso Economico*, Centro Studi e Ricerche su Problemi Economico-Sociali, Franco Angeli Editore, Milano, 1969, pp.13–153, 169–181, 207–208 and 221–242.

Allais, M.: (1968) Pareto, *International Encyclopaedia of Social Sciences*, Vol. II, pp.402–403.

Allais, M.: (1976) 'Fondements Axiomatiques du Concept de Valeur Psychologique' ('Axiomatic Foundations of the Concept of Psychological Value'), Centre d'Analyse Economique, 15 pp.

Armstrong, W. E.: (1939) 'The Determinateness of the Utility Function', *The Economic Journal* XLIX, 453–468.

Bernoulli, Daniel: (1738) 'Exposition of a New Theory on the Measurement of Risk', *Econometrica*, 22, 1954, pp.23–36. First published as 'Specimen theoriae novae de mensura sortis'. Contains notes by Louise Sommer and footnotes by Carl Menger.

Colin Clark, Grant: (1973) *The Marginal Utility of Income*, Oxford Economic Papers, July 1973, and Monash University, Clayton, Victoria, Australia.

Fisher, Irving: (1927) 'A Statistical Method for Measuring "Marginal Utility" and Testing the Justice of a Progressive Income Tax'. In Jacob H. Hollander (Ed.), *Economic Essays: Contributed in Honor of John Bates Clark*, Macmillan, New York, pp.157–193.

Frisch, Ragnar: (1926) 'Sur un problème d'économie pure', *Norsk Mathematisk forenings skrifer*, Series 1, No. 16, 1–40.

Frisch, Ragnar: (1932) *New Methods of Measuring Marginal Utility*, Tübingen, Germany.

Georgescu-Roegen, Nicholas: (1968) 'Utility', *International Encyclopedia of the Social Sciences* 16, 236–267.

Gerlach, Muriel Wood: (1957) 'Interval Measurement of Subjective Magnitudes with Subliminal Differences', Technical Report No. 7, Applied Mathematics and Statistics Laboratory, Stanford Univ.

Jevons, W. Stanley: (1871) *The Theory of Political Economy*, 5th edition, Kelley, 1957. French translation: *La Théorie de l'Economie Politique*, Giard, 1909.

Jordan, Ch.: (1949) 'Sur l'Impôt Equitable et sur l'Utilité Marginale de la Monnaie', *Economia Internazionale* 11, 206–220.

Kennedy, Ch.: (1954) 'Concerning Utility' *Economica*, New Series, XXI, pp.7–21.

Lange, Oscar: (1934) 'The Determinateness of the Utility Function', *Review of Economic Studies*, June, pp.218–225.

Laplace, Pierre-Simon: (1812) *Théorie Analytique des Probabilités*, Livre II, Chapitre X, De l'Espérance morale. Oeuvres de Laplace, Tome VII, Imprimerie Royale, Paris, 1847, pp.474–488.

Laplace, Pierre-Simon: (1814) *Essai Philosophique sur les Probabilités*. 2 Vols., Paris, Gauthier-Villars, 1921, Vol. 1, pp.20–23.
English translation: *A Philosophical Study on Probabilities*, 1951, Dover, New York.

Morgan, James N.: (1945) 'Can we Measure the Marginal Utility of Money?', *Econometrica* 13, 129–153.

Pareto, Vilfredo: (1916) *Trattato di Sociologia Generale* (*Treatise of General Sociology*) Barbera, Firenze, 2 Vols. Published in French as: *Traité de Sociologie*, Payot, Paris, 1919, 2 Vols., 1763 pp. (Droz, Geneva, 1818 pp.). Published in English as: *The Mind and Society*, Dover, New York, 1935, 2 Vols., 2033 pp.

Philips, Louis: (1972) 'A Dynamic Version of the Linear Expenditure Model', *The Review of Economic and Statistics*, Vol. LIV, No. 4, November 1972, Harvard University Press, pp.450–458.

Roy, René: (1942) *De l'Utilité – Contribution à la Théorie des Choix*. Hermann, Paris, 47 pp.

Roy, René: (1943) *Eléments d'Econométrie*, Fascicule I, Centre de Documentation Universitaire, Paris, 118 pp.

Shapley, Lloyd S.: (1975) 'Cardinal Utility from Intensity Comparisons', A Report prepared for United States Air Force Project Rand, R–1683–PR, Santa-Monica, Ca, 16 pp.

Stigler, George J.: (1950) 'The Development of Utility Theory'. In Joseph J. Spengler and William R. Allen (Eds.), *Essays in Economic Thought: Aristotle to Marshall*. Chicago: Rand McNally, 1969, pp.606–655. First published in Volume 58 of the *Journal of Political Economy*, August–October 1950, pp.307–327 and 373–396.

Suppes, P., and Noiret, H.: (1954) 'Axiomatisation and Representation of Difference Structures', Report 2, Department of Philosophy, Standford Univ., mimeo.

Taylor, Lester D., and Weiserbs, Daniel: (1972) 'On the Estimation of Dynamic Demand Functions', *The Review of Economics, and Statistics*, Vol. LIV, November 1972, No. 4, Harvard University Press, pp.459–465.

III. ON THE CONCEPT OF PROBABILITY

Allais, Maurice: (1976) 'Les fondements de la théorie des probabilités' ('The Foundations of Probability Theory'), Centre d'Analyse Economique, 64 pp.

Allais, M.: (1976) 'Réalisation d'un processus aléatoire correspondant à une probabilité donnée', ('Realisation of a Random Process corresponding to a given probability'), Centre d'Analyse Economique, 6 pp.

Bayes, Thomas: (1763) 'A Letter from the Late Reverend Mr. Thomas Bayes to John Canton. An Essay towards Solving a Problem in the Doctrine of Chances', *Philosophical Transactions*, Vol. LIII, 1763, London, pp.269–271 and 370–418.

Borel, Emile: (1939) *Valeur pratique et philosophie des probabilités*, Paris, Gauthier-Villars.

Borel, Emile: (1949) 'Probabilité et Certitude'. *Dialectica*, Vol. 3, No. 9–10, pp.24–27.

Cantelli, F. P.: (1935) 'Considérations sur la convergence dans le calcul des probabilités', *Annales de l'Institut Henri Poincaré*, Vol. V, Presses Universitaires de France, pp.1–50.

Cournot, M. A. A.: (1843) *Exposition de la Théorie des Chances*, Hachette, Paris, 448 pp.

Ceresole, Pierre: (1915) 'L'irréductibilité de l'intuition des probabilités et l'existence de propositions mathématiques indémontrables', *Archives de Psychologie*, Tome XV, Genève, pp.255–305.

Cramér, Harald: (1945) *Mathematical Methods of Statistics*, Princeton University Press, 1946.

Cramér, Harald: (1959) *The Elements of Probability Theory and some of its Applications*, Wiley, New York.

D'Alembert, Jean Le Rond: (1761) 'Réflexions sur le Calcul des Probabilités', *Opuscules Mathématiques*, Tome II, Paris, 1961, pp.1–25.

Dreze, Jacques H.: (1959) 'Les Probabilités "Subjectives" ont-elles une Signification Objective?', *Economie Appliquée*, pp.55–70.

Dugue, Daniel: (1968) 'Calcul des Probabilités', *Encyclopaedia Universalis*. Vol. 13, pp.575–585.

Du Pasquier, Gustave: (1926) *Le calcul des probabilités. Son évolution mathématique et philosophique*, Hermann, Paris, 304 pp.

De Finetti, Bruno: (1937) 'La Prévision: ses Lois Logiques, ses Sources Subjectives', *Annales de l'Institut Henri Poincaré* **VII**, I, Paris.
English translation: 'Foresight: Its Logical Laws, Its Subjective Sources'. In Henry E. Kyburg and Howard E. Smokler (Eds.), *Studies in Subjective Probabilities*, Wiley, New York, 1964, pp.93–158.

De Finetti, Bruno: (1939) Compte Rendu critique du Colloque de Genève sur la Théorie des Probabilités. Vol. VIII, Hermann, 1939, Paris.

De Finetti, Bruno: (1949) Le Vrai et la Probable. *Dialectica*, 1949, Vol. III, n° 9–10, pp.78–92.

De Finetti, Bruno: (1951) Expérience et théorie dans l'élaboration et dans l'application d'une doctrine scientifique. Revue de Métaphysique et de Morale. Paris: Armand Colin.

De Finetti, Bruno: (1968) Probability: Interpretations. *International Encyclopedia of the Social Sciences*, 12, pp.496–505.

See also de Finetti, Bruno, in Section IV.

Frechet, Maurice: (1938) 'Les Principaux Courants dans l'Evolution Récente des Recherches sur le Calcul des Probabilités', *Colloque consacré à la Théorie des Probabilités*, Vol. I, pp.19–23, Hermann, Paris.

Frechet, Maurice: (1938) 'Exposé et Discussion de Quelques Recherches Récentes sur les Fondements du Calcul des Probabilités', *Colloque consacré à la Théorie des Probabilités*, Vol. II, pp. 23–55, Hermann, Paris.

Frechet, Maurice: (1954) 'Un Problème Psychologique sur les Probabilités Subjectives Irrationnelles', *Journal de Psychologie Normale et Pathologique*, pp.431–438, Paris, Presses Universitaires de France.

Frechet, Maurice: (1955) *Les Mathématiques et le Concret*, Philosophie de la Matière, Paris, Presses Universitaires de France.

Frechet, Maurice: (1955) 'Sur l'Importance en Econométrie de la Distinction entre les Probabilités Rationnelles et Irrationnelles', *Econometrica* **23**, pp.303–307.

Gini, Corrado: (1949) 'Concept et mesure de la probabilité', *Dialectica*, 1949, Vol. III, Nos. 9–10, pp.36–54.

Gnedenko, Boris V.: (1963) *The Theory of Probability*, New York, Chelsea, First published as *Kurs theorii veroiatnostei*.

Good, I. J.: (1950) *Probability and the Weighting of Evidence*, London, Griffin.

Jeffreys, Harold: (1947) *Theory of Probability*. Clarendon Press, Oxford.

Jevons, W. Stanley: (1958) '*The principles of Science. A Treatise on Logic and Scientific Method*', Chapter X: The Theory of Probability, pp.197–217, Dover Publications, Inc., New York, 786 pp.

Kendall, M. G.: (1949) 'On the Reconciliation of Theories of Probability', *Biometrika*, Vol. XXXVI, pp.101–116.

Kendall, M. G., and Stuart, A.: (1969) *The Advanced Theory of Statistics*, Vol. I, *Distribution Theory*, 439 pp.

Kendall, M. G., and Stuart, A.: (1973) *The Advanced Theory of Statistics*, Vol. 2, *Inference and Relationship*, 723 pp.

Keynes, John Maynard: (1931) *A Treatise on Probability*, Macmillan, London.

Kolmogorov, A. N.: (1933) *Foundations of the Theory of Probability*, Chelsea Publishing Company, New York, 1956, 84 pp.

Koopman, B. O.: (1946) Reviews of Nine Papers on Probabilities of Williams, Nagel, E., Riechenbach, H., Carnap, R., Margenau, H., Bergmann, G., V. Mises, L., Kaufman, F., Williams, D., *Mathematical Reviews*, pp.186–193.

Kruskal, William H., and Kendall, M. G.: (1968) 'Statistics', *International Encyclopedia of the Social Sciences*, Vol. 15, pp.206–232.

Laplace, Pierre-Simon, (1812) *Théorie Analytique des Probabilités*, Livre II, Chapitre I, Principes généraux, pp.195–197.

Laplace, Pierre-Simon, (1814) *Essai Philosophique sur les Probabilités*, Vol. I, pp.2–11. See also Laplace, Section II and III above.

Levy, Paul: (1925) *Calcul des Probabilités*, Gauthier-Villars, Paris.

Levy, Paul: (1937) *Théorie de l'addition des variables aléatoires*, Chapitre I: 'Les fondements de la notion de probabilité', pp.1–10, Gauthier-Villars, Paris.

Levy, Paul: (1949) 'Les Fondements du Calcul des Probabilités', *Dialectica*, Vol. 3, No. 9–10, pp.55–64.

Von Mises, Richard: (1920) *Probability, Statistics and Truth*, Second English edition, 1956, Allen, London and Macmillan, New York, 244 pp.

Von Mises, Richard: (1932) 'Théorie des Probabilités. Fondements et Applications', *Annales de l'Institut Henri Poincaré*, Fasc. II, Vol. III, pp.137–190, Paris.

Poincare, H.: (1903) *La Science et l'Hypothèse*, Chapitre XI, 'Le Calcul des Probabilités', Bibliothèque de Philosophie Scientifique, Flammarion, Paris, 1927.

Poincare, H.: (1908) *Science et Méthode*, Chapitre IV, Le Hasard. Bibliothèque de Philosophie Scientifique, Flammarion, Paris, 1927.

Poincare, H.: (1912) *Calcul des Probabilités*, 2ème Ed., Gauthier-Villars, Paris, 1923.

Ramsey, Frank P.: (1926–1928) *The Foundations of Mathematics and Other Logical Essays*, Chapter 7, 'Truth and Probability', and Chapter 8, 'Further Considerations', Littlefied and Adams, New York, 1965.

Ramsey, Frank P.: (1926) 'Truth and Probability', In Henry E. Kyburg, Jr. and Howard E. Smokler (Eds.), *Studies in Subjective Probabilities*, New York, Wiley, pp.61–92.

Reichenbach, H.: (1937) 'Les fondements logiques du calcul des probabilités', *Annales de l'Institut Henri Poincaré*, Vol. VII, Fasc. V, pp.268–348, Paris.

Roberts, Harry V.: (1968) 'Bayesian Inference', *International Encyclopedia of the Social Sciences*, Vol. 2, pp.28–33.

Schrödinger, Erwin: (1947) 'The Foundation of the Theory of Probability', *Proceedings of the Royal Irish Academy*, Vol. LI, pp.51–56 and 141–146.
Steffenson, J. F.: (1938) 'Fréquence et probabilité, Colloque consacré à la Théorie des Probabilités', *Les Fondements du Calcul des Probabilités*, pp.67–78, Hermann, Paris.
Todhunter, I.: (1865) *History of the Mathematical Theory of Probability from the Time of Pascal to that of Laplace*, Chelsea Publishing Company, Bronx, New York, 1965, 624 pp.
Ville, Jean: (1939) *Etude Critique de la Notion de Collectif*, Paris, Gauthier-Villars.
Von Wright, Georg Henrik: (1975) 'Historical Development of Probabilitie Areas of Mathematics', *Encyclopaedia Britannica*, Vol. II, pp.666–669.
Wold, Herman: (1965) 'A Graphic Introduction to Stochastic Process', in *Bibliography on Times Series and Stochastic Processes*, Oliver and Boyd, London, pp.7–76.

IV. THE NEO-BERNOULLIAN THEORIES OF THE AMERICAN SCHOOL

Arrow, Kenneth J.: (1951) 'Alternative Approaches to the Theory of Choice in Risk-Taking Situations', *Econometrica* 19, 404–437.
Arrow, Kenneth J.: (1965) *Aspects of the Theory of Risk-bearing*, Helsinki, Academic Bookstore.
Aumann, Robert J.: (1962) Utility Theory Without the Completeness Axiom. *Econometrica*, 30, 445–462. Corrections in Volume 32 of *Econometrica*.
Barankin, Edward W.: (1954) 'Toward an Objectivistic Theory of Probability', *Proceedings of the Third Berkeley Symposium on Mathematical Statistics and Probability*, University of California, Dec. 1954, Jun. Jul. 1955, pp.21–52.
Bawa, Vijay S.: (1975) 'Optimal Rules for Ordering Uncertain Prospects', *Journal of Financial Economics* 2, 95–121.
Bierwag, G. O.: (1974) 'The Rationale of the Mean-Standard Deviation Analysis: Comment', *The American Economic Review*, June 1974, Vol. LXIV, No. 3, pp.431–433.
Block, H. D., and Marschak, Jacob: (1960) 'Random Orderings and Stochastic Theories of Responses', Cowles Foundation for Research in Economics. Paper No. 147. Also In Olkin, Ghurye, Hoeffding, Madow and Mann (Eds.), *Contributions to Probability and Statistics*, Stanford Univ. Press, pp.97–132.
Borch, Karl: (1968) 'Indifference Curves and Uncertainty', *Swed. J. of Economics*, pp.20–24.
Borch, Karl: (1969) 'A Note on Uncertainty and Indifference Curves', *The Review of Economic Studies*, XXXVI, pp.1–4.
Borch, Karl: (1970) 'De Siste Kardinalister', *Stasökonimisk Tidsskrift* 4, 156–161.
Borch, Karl: (1973) 'Expected Utility Expressed in Terms of Moments', *Omega* (1973) pp.331–343.
Borch, Karl: (1974) 'The Rationale of the Mean-Standard Deviation Analysis: A Comment', *The American Economic Review* LXIV, 428–430.
Borch, Karl: (1975a) 'The Place of Uncertainty in the Theories of the Austrian School'. In J. R. Hicks and W. Weber (Eds.), *Carl Menger and the Austrian School of Economics*, pp.61–74.
Borch, Karl: (1975b) 'Utility and Stochastic Dominance', (Contribution to this volume.)

Chipman, John S.: (1960) 'The Foundations of Utility', *Econometrica* **28**, 193–225.

Davidson, Donal, and Suppes, Patrick: (1956) 'A Finitistic Axiomatization of Subjective Probability and Utility', *Econometrica* **24**, 264–275.

Debreu, Gérard: (1958) 'Stochastic Choice and Cardinal Utility', *Econometrica* **26**, 440–445; and Cowles Foundation Paper No. 125.

Debreu, Gérard: (1959) 'Topological Methods in Cardinal Utility Theory'. In Arrow, Karlin and Suppes (Eds.), *Mathematical Methods in the Social Sciences*, Proceedings of the First Stanford Symposium, Stanford Mathematical Studies in the Social Sciences, IV, pp.16–27.

Debreu, Gérard: (1975) 'Least Concave Utility Functions', Institute of Business and Economic Research, Center for Research in Management Science, Berkeley, Working Paper, IP–231.

Dreze, J.: (1954) 'Savage on Subjective Probability and Utility', Carnegie Institute of Technology, mimeo. doc., 31 pp.

Dreze, J.: (1957) 'On the Identifiability of Subjective Probabilities and Measurable Utilities', Carnegie Institute of Technology, mimeo. doc., 69 pp.

Dreze, J.: (1960) 'Fondements Logiques de la Probabilité Subjective et de l'Utilité', Centre National de la Recherche Scientifique, Colloques Internationaux, *La Décision*, C.N.R.S., 1961, pp.73–89.

De Finetti, B.: (1952) 'Rôle de la Théorie des Jeux dans l'Economie et Rôle des Probabilités Personnelles dans la Théorie des Jeux', Colloque International sur les Fondements et Applications de la Théorie du Risque, Colloques internationaux, Vol. XL, *Econométrie*, Centre National de la Recherche Scientifique, Paris, pp.49–63.

De Finetti, B.: (1960) 'Dans quel Sens la Théorie de la Décision est-elle et doit-elle être "Normative"', Centre National de la Recherche Scientifique, Colloques Internationaux, *La Décision*, C.N.R.S., 1961, pp.159–171.

De Finetti, B.: (1976) 'A Short Confirmation of my Standpoint', (Contribution to this volume).

See also de Finetti, B., in Section III.

Friedman, Milton, and Savage, L. J.: (1948) 'The Utility Analysis of Choices Involving Risk', *Journal of Political Economy* **56**, 279–304.

Friedman, Milton, and Savage, L. J.: (1952) 'The Expected-Utility Hypothesis and the Measurability of Utility', *The Journal of Political Economy* LX, 463–475. Republished in *Readings in Price Theory*, pp. 57–96, American Economic Association, Homewood, Ill: Irwin.

Friedman, Milton, and Savage, L. J.: (1953) 'Choice, Chance, and the Personal Distribution of Income', *The Journal of Political Economy*, Vol. LXI, August 1953, No. 4, pp.277–290.

Georgescu-Roegen, Nicholas: (1954) 'Choice, Expectations, and Measurability'. In Nicholas Georgescu-Roegen (Ed.), *Analytical Economics: Issues and Problems*. Cambridge, Mass. pp.184–215: Harvard Univ. Press, 1966. First published in Volume 68 of the *Quarterly Journal of Economics*.

Grandmont, Jean-Marie: (1970) 'Continuity Properties of a von Neumann–Morgenstern Utility', *Journal of Economic Theory* **4**, 45–57.

Hadar, J., and Russell, W.: 'Rules for Ordering Uncertain Prospects', *The American Economic Review*, Vol. LIX, No. I, pp.25–34.

Hakansson, Nils H.: (1970) 'Friedman-Savage Utility Functions Consistent with Risk Aversion', *The Quarterly Journal of Economics* **LXXXIV**, 472–487.

Harsanyi, John C.: (1953) 'Cardinal Utility in Welfare Economics and in the Theory of Risk-Taking', *The Journal of Political Economy*, pp.434–435.

Harsanyi, John C.: (1955) 'Cardinal Welfare, Individualistic Ethics, and Interpersonal Comparisons of Utility', *The Journal of Political Economy*, Vol. LXIII, No. 4, pp.309–322.

Harsanyi, John C.: (1966) 'A General Theory of Rational Behavior in Game Situations', *Econometrica* **34**, 613–635.

Herstein, I. N., and Milnor, John: (1953) 'An Axiomatic Approach to Measurable Utility', *Econometrica* **21**, 291–297.

Levy, Haim: (1969) 'A Utility Function Depending on the First Three Moments', *The Journal of Finance*, Sept., 1969, pp.715–719.

Levy, Haim: (1974) 'The Rationale of the Mean-Standard Deviation Analysis: Comment', *The American Economic Review*, June 1974, Vol. LXIV, No. 3, pp.434–441.

Majumdar, Tapas: (1958) 'Behaviourist Cardinalism in Utility Theory', *Economica*, New Series, XXV, 26–34.

Malinvaud, E.: (1952) 'Note on von Neumann-Morgenstern's Strong Independence Axiom', *Econometrica*, Vol. 20, No. 4, October 1952, p.679.

Marschak, Jacob: (1950) 'Rational Behavior, Uncertain Prospects and Measurable Utility. Cowles Commission Papers', New Series, No. 43. Reprinted from *Econometrica*, Vol. 18, No. 2, April 1950.

Marschak, Jacob: (1952) 'Why "Should" Statisticians and Businessmen Maximize Moral Expectation?', Cowles Commission Papers, New Series, No. 53, pp.493–506. Reprinted from *Proceedings of the Second Berkeley Symposium on Mathematical Statistics and Probability*, University of California Press, 1951.

Marschak, Jacob: (1954–1964) 'Scaling of Utility and Probability'. In Martin Shubik (Ed.) *Game Theory and Related Approaches to Social Behavior: Selections*, Wiley, New York, pp.95–109.

Marschak, Jacob: (1958) *Stochastic Theories of Choice*, The Institute of Management Sciences, Yale Univ. Mimeo. doc.

Marschak, Jacob: (1959) 'Binary-Choice Constraints and Random Utility Indicators'. In Arrow, Karlin and Suppes (Eds.), *Mathematical Methods in the Social Sciences*, Proceedings of the First Stanford Symposium, Stanford Mathematical Studies in the Social Sciences, IV, 1960, pp.312–330; and Cowles Foundation Paper No. 155.

Morgenstern, Oskar: (1954) 'Experiment and Large Scale Computation in Economics'. In Oskar Morgenstern (Ed.), *Economic Activity Analysis*, Wiley, New York, pp.483–554.

Morgenstern, Oskar: (1972) 'Descriptive, Predictive and Normative Theory', *Kyklos* **4**, 699–714.

Morlat, Georges: (1956) 'De l'Usage du Calcul des Probabilités en Matière Economique', *Revue d'Economie Politique*, pp.889–906.

Morlat, Georges: (1960a): 'Un article de M. J. L. Milnor: les Jeux contre Nature', *Economie Appliquée* **13**, 27–36.

Morlat, Georges: (1960b) 'L'Incertitude et les Probabilités', *Economie Appliquée* **17**, 37–53.

Von Neumann, John, and Morgenstern, Oskar: (1944) *Theory of Games and Economic Behavior*, Princeton University Press, Second edition, 1947.

Pratt, John: (1964) 'Risk Aversion in the Small and in the Large', *Econometrica* 32 122–135.

Pratt, John W., Raiffa, Howard, and Schlaifer, Robert: (1964) 'The Foundations of Decision under Uncertainty: An Elementary Exposition', *Journal of the American Statistical Association*, 353–375.

Radner, Roy, and Marschak, Jacob: (1954) 'Note on Some Proposed Decision Criteria', *Cowles Commission Papers*, New Series, **96**, pp.61–68.

Raiffa, Howard: (1968) *Decision Analysis*, (see Section I).

Samuelson, Paul A.: (1952) 'Probability, Utility and the Independence Axiom', *Econometrica* **20**, 670–678.

Samuelson, Paul A.: (1952) 'Utility, Preference, and Probability', Colloque International d'Econometrie 'Les Fondements et Applications de la Théorie du Risque en Econométrie', Centre National de la Recherche Scientifique, Paris. Also in J. E. Stiglitz (Ed.), *Collected Scientific Papers of Paul A. Samuelson*, (1966) 1970, M.I.T. Press, pp.127–137.

Samuelson, Paul A.: (1963) 'Risk and Uncertainty: A Fallacy of Large Numbers', *Scientia*, April–May. Also in J. E. Stiglitz (Ed.), *Collected Scientific Papers of Paul A. Samuelson* (1966) 1970, M.I.T. Press, pp.153–159.

Samuelson, Paul A.: (1970) 'The Fundamental Approximation Theorem of Portfolio Analysis in Terms of Means, Variances and Higher Moments', *The Review of Economic Studies*, Vol. XXXVII, No. 112, pp.537–542.

Savage, Leonard: (1952) 'Une Axiomatisation de Comportement raisonnable face à l'Incertitude', Colloque International d'Econométrie 'Fondements et Applications de la Théorie du Risque en Econométrie', 12–17 May 1952, *Econométrie*, 1953, Collection des Colloques internationaux, **XL**, pp.29–40, Paris, Centre National de la Recherche Scientifique.

Savage, Leonard: (1954) *The Foundations of Statistics*, Wiley, New York.

Simon, Herbert A.: (1957) 'A Behavioral Model of Rational Choice'. In Herbert A. Simon (Ed.), *Models of Man*, Wiley, New York, pp.241–260.

Simon, Herbert A.: (1959) 'Theories of Decision-making in Economics and Behavioral Science'. *American Economic Review* **49**, 253–283.

Strotz, Robert H.: (1952) 'Cardinal Utility'. *The American Economic Review*, XLIII, May 1953, 384–397; and Cowles Commission Paper, New Series, No. 75.

Suppes, Patrick: (1955) 'The Role of Subjective Probability and Utility in Decision Making', *Proceedings of the Third Berkeley Symposium on Mathematical Statistics and Probability*, Dec. 1954 and June–July 1955, pp.61–73, Univ. of California.

Suppes, Patrick: (1960) 'Behavioristic Foundations of Subjective Probability and Utility', Centre National de la Recherche Scientifique, Colloques Internationaux, *La Décision*, C.N.R.S., 1961, pp.89–105.

Suppes, Patrick: (1961) 'Behavioristic Foundations of Utility', *Econometrica* **29**, 186–203.

Tobin, J.: (1958) 'Liquidity Preference as a Behavior Towards Risk', *Review of Economic Studies*, pp.65–86.

Tsiang, S. C.: (1972) 'The Rationale of the Mean-Standard Deviation Analysis, Skewness Preference, and the Demand for Money', *The American Economic Review*, Vol. LXII, No. 3, pp.354–371.

Tsiang, S. C.: (1974) 'The Rationale of the Mean-Standard Deviation Analysis: Reply and Errata for Original Article', *The American Economic Review*, June 1974, Vol. LXIV, No. 3, pp.442–450.

Whitmore, G. A.: (1970) 'Third-Degree Stochastic Dominance', *The American Economic Review*, Vol. LX, No. 3, pp.457–459.

V. CRITICAL ANALYSIS OF THE NEO-BERNOULLIAN FORMULATION OF THE THEORIES OF THE AMERICAN SCHOOL

Allais, M.: (1952) *Fondements d'une Théorie Positive des Choix comportant un Risque et Critique des Postulats et Axiomes de l'Ecole Américaine* (See Section I above).

Allais, M.: (1954) 'Observations présentées à la suite de l'exposé sur "La Théorie des Jeux" de M. Guilbaud', ('Observations on M. Guilbaud's Exposition of the Theory of Games'), *Congrès des Economistes de Langue Française*, Paris, pp.143–163.

Allais, M.: (1957) 'Sur la Théorie des Choix Aléatoires' ('On the Theory of Random Choice'), *Revue d'Economie Politique*, 1953, No. 3, pp.381–390.

Alchian, A. A.: (1953) 'The Meaning of Utility Measurement', *The American Economic Review* XLIII, 26–51.

Archibald, G.C.: (1959) 'Utility, Risk and Linearity', *The Journal of Political Economy* LXVII, 437–451.

Armstrong, W. E.: (1948) 'Uncertainty and the Utility Function', *The Economic Journal* LVIII, 1–11.

Baumol, William J.: (1951) 'The Neumann-Morgenstern Utility Index – An Ordinalist View', *The Journal of Political Economy* LIX, 1–14.

Bernard, Georges: (1962) 'Incertitude et Expertise – Exemple d'un Problème d'Investissement', *Revue française de recherche opérationnelle*, pp.181–192.

Bernard, Georges: (1963) 'Valeur, Temps et Incertitude dans l'Idée de l'Utilité', C.N.R.S., Séminaire d'Econométrie de René Roy, Paris, 72 pp.

Bernard, Georges: (1974) 'On Utility Functions', *Theory and Decision* 5, 205–242.

Camacho, A.: (1973) 'Maximizing Expected Utility and the Rule of Long Run Success', (Contribution to this volume).

Coombs, C. H.: (1961) 'A Study of Decision Making under Risk'. In *La Décision*, Colloques Internationaux, Centre National de la Recherche Scientifique, Paris, 1961, pp.63–72.

Ellsberg, D.: (1954) 'Classic and Current Notions of "Measurable Utility"', *The Economic Journal* LXIV, No. 255, pp.528–557.

Ellsberg, D.: (1961) 'Risk, Ambiguity and the Savage Axioms', *Quarterly Journal of Economics* 75, 643–669.

Fellner, William: (1961) 'Distortion of Subjective Probabilities as a Reaction to Uncertainty, *The Quarterly Journal of Economics*, Vol. LXXV, Nov. 1961, pp.670–689.

Fishburn, Peter C.: (1975) 'On the Nature of Expected Utility' (Contribution to this volume.)

Frisch, Ragnar: (1953) 'Allocution de clôture du Colloque International sur le Risque de 1952' (Closing Speech, International Symposium on Risk, May 1952), XL, Symposia, *Centre National de la Recherche Scientifique*, Paris, pp.252–255.

Hagen, Ole: (1966) 'Risk Aversion and Incentive Contracting', *The Journal of the Economic Society of Australia and New Zealand*, pp.416–429.

Hagen, Ole: (1967) 'Elements of Value', *Statsøkonomisk Tidsskrift*, No. 1, pp.39–51.

Hagen, Ole: (1969) 'Separation of Cardinal Utility and Specific Utility of Risk in Theory of Choices under Uncertainty', *Statsøkonomisk Tidsskrift*, No. 3, pp.81–107.

Hagen, Ole: (1972) 'A New Axiomatization of Utility under Risk', *Teorie A Methoda*, IV/2, pp.55–80.

Hagen, Ole: (1976) 'Towards a Positive Theory of Preferences under Risk' (Contribution to this volume.)

Hagen, Ole: (1977) 'Utility and Morality'. In R. Henn and O. Moeschlin (Eds.), *Mathematical Economics and Game Theory*, Essays in Honor of Oskar Morgenstern, Springer-Verlag.

Handa, Jagdish: (1977) 'Risk, Probabilities, and a New Theory of Cardinal Utility', *Journal of Political Economy* **85**, 97–122.

Krelle, W.: (1968) *Präferenz und Entscheidungstheorie*, Mohr, Tübingen.

Lesourne, Jacques: (1975) 'A Multiperiod Interpretation of Individual Behavior in a Probabilistic Environment', *SEMA*, 25pp.

MacCrimmon, Kenneth, and Larsson, Stig: (1975) 'Utility Theory: Axioms versus "Paradoxes"' (Contribution to this volume.)

Marschak, Jacob: (1938) 'Money and the Theory of Assets', *Econometrica*, October 1938, pp.311–325.

Masse, Pierre: (1951) 'Le Mécanisme des Prix et de l'Intérêt dans une Economie Concurrentielle Aléatoire', *Revue d'Economie Politique*, January–February 1951, pp.74–99.

Masse, Pierre: (1953) 'Réflexions sur les Comportements Rationnels en Economie Aléatoire', *Cahiers du Séminaire d'Econométrie*, C.N.R.S., Paris, pp.11–58.

Masse, M. P., and Morlat, M. G.: (1952) 'Sur le Classement Economique des Perspectives Aléatoires', Colloque international sur les Fondements et Applications de la théorie du risque, *Econométrie*, Colloques Internationaux, Vol. XL, Centre National de la Recherche Scientifique, Paris, pp.165–199.

Menges, Günter: (1975) 'Comparison of Decision Models and some Suggestions' (Contribution to this volume.)

Raiffa, Howard: (1961) 'Risk, Ambiguity, and the Savage Axioms (Ellsberg's and Fellner's paper): Comment', *The Quarterly Journal of Economics* LXXV, 4, 690–694.

Samuelson, Paul A.: (1950) 'Probability and the Attempts to Measure Utility', *The Economic Review*, Tokyo, Keizai Kenkyu, Hitotsubashi University. Also in J. E. Stiglitz (Ed.), *Collected Scientific Papers of Paul A. Samuelson*, 1966, Vol. I, pp.117–123, M.I.T. Press.

   This paper is followed by a Postscript (ibid., pp.124–126) explaining why Samuelson changed his mind soon after the publication of this paper.

Shackle, G. L. S.: (1956) 'Expectation and Cardinality', *The Economic Journal*, 262, LXVI, pp.211–220.

Watkins, John: (1970) *Imperfect Rationality. Explanation in the Behavioural Sciences.* Edited by R. Borger and F. Cioffi, C.U.P., pp.167–230.

Watkins, John: (1975) 'Towards a Unified Decision Theory: a Non-Bayesian Approach.'
   Mimeo. Doc., 47 pp. The London School of Economics and Political Science.
Wold, H.: (1952) 'Ordinal Preferences or Cardinal Utility?' *Econometrica* **20**, No. 4,
   pp.661–665.

VI. EMPIRICAL RESEARCH INTO THE PSYCHOLOGY OF
RANDOM CHOICE

Allais, M.: (1952) 'La psychologie de l'homme rationnel devant le risque – La théorie et
   l'expérience', *Journal de la Société de Statistique de Paris*, January–March 1953,
   pp.47–73.
   English translation: 'The Psychology of Rational Behaviour in the Presence of
   Risk – Theory and Experience', *Centre d'Analyse Economique*, Mimeo. doc. 3289,
   Dec. 75, 44 pp.
Allais, M.: (1954) 'Evaluation des perspectives economiques de la recherche minière
   sur de grands espaces – Application au Sahara Algérien', *Bulletin de l'Institut International de Statistique*, Tome XXXV, 4, Rio de Janeiro, 1957, pp.89–140; *Revue de
   l'Industrie Minérale*, Paris, January 1956, pp.329–383.
   English translation: 'Method of Appraising Economic Prospects of Mining Explora-
   tion over Large Territories – Algerian Sahara Case Study', *Management Science*, Vol.
   3, No. 4, July 1957, pp.285–347.
      A more complete version was published as a separate volume under the same title:
   'Evaluation des Perspectives Economiques de la Recherche Minière sur de Grands
   Espaces', Bureau de Recherche Minière de l'Algérie, Alger, 1957, 101 pp.
Allais, M.: (1974) 'Résultats du sondage de 1952' ('Results of the 1952 Experiment'),
   Centre d'Analyse Economique, Doc. No. 3063, 6 May 1974, 9 pp.
Allais, M.: (1976) *The Psychological Structure of Choice Involving Risk – The Theory
   and Empirical Evidence'*. In preparation (about 400pp. and 300 Charts).
Block, H. D., and Marschak, Jacob: (1960) 'Random Orderings and Stochastic Theories
   of Responses', Cowles Foundation for Research in Economics. Paper No. 147. Also
   in Oklin, Ghurye, Hoeffding, Madow and Mann, (Eds.) *Contributions to Probability
   and Statistics*, Stanford Univ. Press, pp.97–132.
Cureton, Edward E.: (1968) 'Psychometrics', *International Encyclopedia of the Social
   Sciences*, Vol. 13, pp.95–112.
Davidson, Donald, and Marschak, Jacob: (1958) 'Experimental Tests of Stochastic
   Theory', Technical Report No. 17, Applied Mathematics and Statistics Laboratory,
   Stanford Univ.
Davidson, Donald, Siegel, Sidney, and Suppes, Patrick: (1955) 'Some Experiments and
   Related Theory on the Measurement of Utility and Subjective Probability', Report
   No. 4, Stanford Value Theory Project and Dept. of Philosophy, Stanford Univ.
Davidson, Donald, and Suppes, Patrick: (1957) *Decison Making: An Experimental
   Approach.* In collaboration with Sidney Siegel, Stanford Univ. Press.
Dolbear, F. Trenery, and Lave, Lester B.: (1967) 'Inconsistent Behavior in Lottery
   Choice Experiments', *Behavior Science* **12**, pp. 14–23.
Edwards, Ward: (1953) 'Probability-Preferences in Gambling', *American Journal of
   Psychology* **66**, 349–364.

Edwards, Ward: (1954a) 'Probability-Preferences among Bets with Differing Expected Values', *American Journal of Psychology* **67**, 56–67.

Edwards, Ward: (1954b) 'The Reliability of Probability-Preferences', *American Journal of Psychology* **67**, 68–95.

Edwards, Ward: (1956) 'Reward Probability, Amount, and Information as Determiners of Sequential two-alternative Decisions', *Journal of Experimental Psychology* **52**, 177–188.

Edwards, Ward: (1962) 'Dynamic Decison Theory and Probabilistic Information Processing', *Human Factors* **4**, 59–73.

Edwards, Ward: (1965) 'Optimal Strategies for Seeking Information: Models for Statistics, Choice Reaction Times, and Human Information Processing', *Journal of Mathematical Psychology* **2**, 312–329.

Edwards, Ward, Lindman, Harold, and Phillips, Lawrence D.: (1963) 'Emerging Technologies for Making Decisions', *New Directions in Psychology* II, Holt, New York, pp.261–325.

Edwards, Ward, Lindman, Harold, and Savage, Leonard Y.: (1963) 'Bayesian Statistical Inference for Psychological Research', *Psychological Review* **70**, 193–242.

Hagen, Ole: (1973) 'Testing av nytteforventningshypotesen', ('Testing the Expected Utility Hypothesis', Norwegian), *Sosialøkonomen*, No. 5.

Hagen, Ole: (1973) 'New Foundations of Utility: Allais versus Morgenstern', working paper presented at a seminar in Heidelberg, Die Norwegische Handelshochschule, Bergen, 15 pp.

Hagen, Ole: (1976) 'Towards a Positive Theory of Preferences under Risk' (Contribution to this volume.)

L'Hardy, Ph., Hericourt, F., Marchand, O., Turc, A.: (1971) 'Théorie de l'Aversion pour le Risque: Un Essai de Confrontation à des Résultats Empiriques', *Annales de l'INSEE* **8**, 25–81.

Lindman, Harold R.: (1965) 'The Simultaneous Measurement of Utilities and Subjective Probabilities', Ph.D. Dissertation, Univ. of Michigan.

Luce, R. Duncan, and Suppes, Patrick: (1965) 'Preference, Utility and Subjective Probability' (see Section I above).

MacCrimmon, K. R.: (1965) 'An Experimental Study of the Decision-Making Behavior of Business Executives', Ph.D. Dissertation, Univ. of California at Los Angeles.

MacCrimmon, K. R.: (1968) 'Descriptive and Normative Implication of the Decision-Theory Postulates'. In K. Borch and J. Mossin (Eds.), *Risk and Uncertainty*, St. Martin's Press, New York, pp.3–32.

MacCrimmon, Kenneth R., and Larsson, Stig: (1975) 'Utility Theory: Axioms versus "Paradoxes"' (see Section V).

Mosteller, Frederick, and Nogee, Philip: (1951) 'An Experimental Measurement of Utility', *Journal of Political Economy* **59**, 371–404.

Peterson, Cameron R., Schneider, Robert J., and Miller, Alan J.: (1965) 'Sample Size and the Revision of Subjective Probabilities', *Journal of Experimental Psychology* **69**, 522–527.

Peterson, Cameron R., et al.: (1965) 'Internal Consistency of Subjective Probabilities', *Journal of Experimental Psychology* **70**, 526–533.

Phillips, Lawrence D., Hays, William L., and Edwards, Ward: (1966) 'Conservatism in Complex Probabilistic Inference', *IEEE Transactions on Human Factors in Electronics*, **HFE-7**, 7–18.

Royden, Halsey L., Suppes, Patrick, and Walsh, Karol: (1957) 'A Model for the Experimental Measurement of the Utility of Gambling', Technical Report No. 14, Applied Mathematics and Statistics Laboratory, Stanford Univ.

Suppes, Patrick, and Walsh, Karol: (1957) 'A Nonlinear Model for the Experimental Measurement of Utility', Technical Report No. 11, Applied Mathematics and Statistics Laboratory, Stanford Univ.

VII. CRITICAL ANALYSIS OF ALLAIS' 1952 POSITIVE THEORY OF CHOICE

Amihud, Yakov: (1974) 'Critical Examination of the New Foundation of Utility', (Contribution to this volume.)

Borch, Karl: (1968) 'The Allais Paradox: A Comment', *Behavioral Science* **13**, No. 6, pp.488–490.

Dehem, Roger: (1956) 'Appréciations sur les "Fondements d'une Théorie Positive des Choix Comportant un Risque et Critique des Postulats et Axiomes de l'Ecole Américaine" by Maurice Allais', *L'Actualité Economique* (Canada), April–June, 1956, No. 1, p.159.

Fels, Eberhard: (1959) 'Fondements d'une Théorie Positive des Choix comportant un Risque et Critique des Postulats et Axiomes de l'Ecole Américaine, by Maurice Allais', *Econometrica*, Book Reviews, **27**, 135–137.

Krelle, Wilhelm: (1958) 'Fondements d'une Théorie Positive des Choix Comportant un Risque et Critique des Postulats et Axiomes de l'Ecole Américaine, Maurice Allais', *Weltwirtschaftliches Archiv*, Band 80, 1958, Heft I, pp.17–18.

Marschak, Jacob: (1975) 'Utilities, Psychological Values, and the Training of Decision Makers' (Contribution to this volume.)

Morgenstern, Oskar: (1974) 'Some Reflections on Utility' (Contribution to this volume.)

Morlat, G.: (1957) 'Sur la Théorie des Choix Aléatoires – Critique des idées de Maurice Allais', *Revue d'Economie Politique* **3**, 378–380.

Morrison, D. G.: (1967) 'On the Consistency of Preferences in Allais' Paradox', *Behavioral Science*, 373–383.

Suppes, Patrick: (1959) 'Fondements d'une Théorie Positive des Choix comportant un Risque et Critique des Postulats et Axiomes de l'Ecole Américaine, by Maurice Allais', *Econometrica*, Book Reviews, **27**, 498–500.

Tintner, Gerhard: (1954) 'Observations on the "Fondements d'une Théorie Positive des Choix comportant un Risque et Critique des Postulats et Axiomes de l'Ecole Américaine" by Maurice Allais', *The American Economic Review*, Sept. 1954, Vol. XLIV, No. 4, p.666.

Complementary references on Allais' 1952 Theory (other Sections of this Bibliography)

Section I. Overviews of the Theory of Choice Under Uncertainty

Arrow (1958b) p.51; (1963) pp.739–749: Baumol (1961) p.339: Borch (1968) pp.44, 46, 62–65, 76, 196: Edward (1954) pp.394, 401 and 411; (1960) pp.39 and 43: Gerard-Varet (1973) pp.43–45, 50–53, 62, 181: Khamei (1969) pp.20–21, 55, 67, 116–117, 179, 182,

188–190, 193–194, 199–203: Luce and Suppes (1965) p.338: Luce and Raïffa (1957) pp.25 and 485: Markowitz (1959) pp.209, 218–224, 228, 307: Marschak (1968) pp.48 and 53: Menges (1973) pp.24, 40, 44, 219: Raïffa (1968) Chapter IV, §9 and Chapter X, §3: Sandretto (1970) pp.8, 22, 26, 35, 54–56, 59–60, 66–78, 89.

Section IV. The neo-Bernoullian Theories of the American School

Block and Marschak (1960) p.123: Borch (1968) p.20; (1969) p. 2; (1975): Dreze (1954) pp.5–7: Grandmont (1970): Morlat (1956) p.903; (1960): Savage (1954) pp.29, 97, 101–103, 271.

Section V. Critical Analysis of the neo-Bernoullian Formulation of the Theories of the American School

Bernard (1962) p.189; (1963) pp.38, 40, 44, 51; (1974): Camacho (1973): Coombs (1961) p.64: Ellsberg (1954) pp.529, 545: Fishburn (1975): Hagen (1969) pp.84, 90–92, 101–103, 107; (1972) pp.57–59, 64, 69, 75, 79; (1976); (1977): Lesourne (1975): MacCrimmon and Larsson (1975): Masse (1953) pp.28–30: Menges (1975): Watkins (1975) pp.34, 35, 38, 50 and 51 (see especially Note 15, p.50): Handa (1977) pp.97–98, 105 and 115–117.

Section VIII. On the Theory of the Gamblers Ruin

Borch (1960a) p.35; (1960b) p.188; (1961) p.181.

Section X. General Theories of Economic Equilibrium and Maximum Efficiency in the Case of Risk

Borch (1962) pp.438–439; (1968) p.339: Malinvaud (1966) pp.210, 224: Guesnerie and Montbrial (1972) §§1 and 6.1.

VIII. ON THE THEORY OF THE GAMBLERS RUIN

Allais, M.: (1975) 'La Théorie Générale de la Ruine des Joueurs' ('The General Theory of the Gamblers Ruin'), Centre d'Analyse Economique.
Bachelier, Louis: (1912) *Calcul des Probabilités*, Tome I. Gauthier-Villars, Paris, 516 pp.
Beard, R. E., Pentikäinen, T., and Pesonen, E.: (1969) *Risk Theory*, Methuen, London.
Bertrand, J.: (1889) *Calcul des Probabilités*; Chap. VI, 'La Ruine des Joueurs', Gauthier-Villars, Paris, 2nd edn., 1907.
Borch, Karl: (1960a) 'Reciprocal Reinsurance Treaties seen as a Two-Person Co-operative Game', *Skandinavisk Aktuariediskrift*, pp.29–58.
Borch, Karl: (1960b) 'Reciprocal Reinsurance Treaties', *The Astin Bulletin*, Vol. I, Part IV, pp.170–191.
Borch, Karl: (1961) 'The Safety Loading of Reinsurance Premiums', *The Skandinavisk Aktuarietidskrift*, Uppsala 1961, pp.163–184.
Borch, Karl: (1967) 'The Theory of Risk', *Journal of the Royal Statistical Society*, Serie B, Vol. 29, No. 3, pp.432–467.

Borch, Karl: (1968) 'Decision Rules Depending on the Probability of Ruin', *Oxford Economic Papers* **20**, 1–10.

Cramer, Harald: (1955) *Collective Risk Theory*, Reprinted from the Jubilee Volume of Föräkringsaktiebolaget Skandia, Skandia Insurance Company.

Dubourdieu, J.: (1952) *Théorie Mathématique du Risque dans les Assurances de Répartition*, Monographies des Probabilités, Fasc. VIII, I, Paris, Gauthier-Villars.

Feller, William: (1950–1966) *An Introduction to Probability Theory and its Applications*, Vol. I, Chap. XIV, and II, Chap. VI, X, XI and XII, Second edition, 1957, Wiley.

Laplace, Pierre-Simon: (1812) *Théorie Analytique des Probabilités*, Livre II, Chapter II, pp.205–300 (See Section II above).

IX. ON THE SAINT PETERSBURG PARADOX

Allais, M.: (1976) 'Le Paradoxe de Saint-Pétersbourg et la Théorie de la Ruine des Joueurs', ('The Saint Petersburg Paradox and the Theory of the Gamblers Ruin'), Centre d'Analyse Economique; 50 pp.

D'Alembert, Le Rond: (1761) *Réflexions sur le Calcul des Probabilités*, (see Section III above).

Bernoulli, Daniel: (1738) Exposition of a New Theory on the Measurement of Risk, (see Section II above).

Bertrand, J.: (1889) *Calcul des Probabilités*, Préface, pp.IX–XII, and Chap. III, 'Espérance mathématique', pp.59–64. (see Section VIII above).

Borel, Emile: (1939) *Valeur Pratique et Philosophie des Probabilités*, pp.63–66, (see Section III above).

Buffon, G. L.: (1777) 'Essai d'Arithmétique Morale', *Supplément à l'Histoire naturelle*, Vol. IV. Reproduced in *Un autre Buffon*, Hermann, 1977, pp.47–59.

Gorovitz, Samuel: (1973) 'The St. Petersburg Puzzle', (Contribution to this volume.)

Laplace, Pierre-Simon: (1812) *Théorie Analytique des Probabilités*. Livre II, Chapter X. 'De l'Espérance morale', pp.474–487. (see Section II above).

Laplace, Pierre-Simon: (1814) *Essai Philosophique sur les Probabilités*, pp.20–23. (see Section II above).

Levy, Paul: (1925) *Calcul des Probabilités*, Chap. VI, 'Critique de la Théorie du Gain Probable', pp.113–133. (see Section III above).

Menger, Karl: (1967) 'The Role of Uncertainty in Economics', Chapter 16 in *Essays in Mathematical Economics in Honor of Oskar Morgenstern*, Princeton.

Poincare, H.: (1912) *Calcul des Probabilités*, pp.66–68 (see Section III above).

Samuelson, Paul A.: (1959) 'The St. Petersburg Paradox as a Divergent Double Limit', *International Economic Review*, January. Also in J. E. Stiglitz (Ed.), *Collected Scientific Papers of Paul A. Samuelson*, (1966) 1970, M.I.T. Press, pp.146–153.

Samuelson, Paul A.: (1977) 'St. Petersburg Paradoxes: Defanged, Dissected, and Historically Described', *Journal of Economic Literature*, March 1977, Vol. XV, No. I, pp.24–55.

Shapley, L. S.: (1972) 'The Petersburg Paradox – A Con Game?' The Rand Corporation, Mimeo. Doc. Santa Monica, California.

Stigler, George J.: (1950) 'The Development of Utility Theory', pp.373–377 (see Section II above).

X. GENERAL THEORIES OF ECONOMIC EQUILIBRIUM AND MAXIMUM EFFICIENCY IN THE CASE OF RISK

Allais, M.: (1952) 'L'extension des théories de l'équilibre économique général et du rendement social au cas du risque' ('Extension of the Theories of General Economic Equilibrium and Economic Efficiency to the Case of Risk')[5]. Colloque de Paris sur les Fondements et Applications de la Théorie du Risque (Section I above), pp.81–120. A summarised version was published under the same title in *Econometrica*, Vol. 21, 1953, No. 2, pp.269–290[6].

Allais, M.: (1971) 'Les théories de l'équilibre économique général et de l'éfficacité maximale. Impasses récentes et nouvelles perspectives', *Revue d'Economie Politique*, May–June 1971, No. 3, pp.331–409. English translation: 'Theories of General Equilibrium and Maximum Efficiency. Recent Blind Alleys and New Perspectives', in *Equilibrium and Disequilibrium in Economic Theory*, Reidel, Dordrecht, 1977, pp.129–201.

Arrow, K. J.: (1952) 'Le rôle des valeurs boursières pour la répartition la meilleure des risques', Colloques Internationaux, XL, *Econometrie*, pp.41–48.
English translation: 'The Role of Securities in the Optimal Allocation of Risk Bearing', *Review of Economic Studies*, 1964, Vol. XXXI.

Borch, Karl: (1962) 'Equilibrium in a Reinsurance Market', *Econometrica*, Vol. 30, No. 3, July, 1962, pp.424–445.

Borch, Karl: (1968) 'Economic Equilibrium under Uncertainty', *International Economic Review*, Vol. 9, No. 3, pp.339–347.

Debreu, G.: (1959) *Theory of Value*, Wiley, New York.

Malinvaud, Edmond: (1966) 'La Prise en charge des risques dans l'allocation des ressources', Colloques Internationaux du Centre National de la Recherche Scientifique, Biarritz, 2–9 Sept. 1966, *Editions du Centre National de la Recherche Scientifique*, Paris, 1968, pp.205–231 and 587–599.

Guesnerie, Roger, and De Montbrial, Thierry: (1972) 'Allocation under Uncertainty: A Survey'. In J. Dreze (Ed.), *Allocation under Uncertainty, Equilibrium and Optimality*.

NOTES ON BIBLIOGRAPHY

[1] Memoir II of 1952, see §2 above.
[2] Memoir III, see §2 above. This memoir which I wrote after the Colloquium in the light of the discussion, was annexed to the C.N.R.S. volume (pp.257–332).
[3] Memoir III bis, see §2, above.
[4] Detailed Analysis of the 1952 Experiments and of its results (see Appendix C above).
[5] Memoir I of 1952 (See §2 above).
[6] Memoir I bis of 1953 (See §2 above).

INDEXES

NOTE TO SUBJECT INDEXES

Theoretical controversy often involves controversy in the use of words in relation to concepts. Further, placing a word in context may involve an interpretation of which the author may not approve. The parts of this volume written by Professor Allais have been indexed under his own responsibility. Thus the subject index beginning on p. 685 corresponds to Allais' Foreword (pp. 3–11), his 1952 Memoir (presented as Part II of this book, pp. 27–143) and his 1977 Memoir (presented as Part V, pp. 453–681). Allais' notation is summarised at the end of this index.

The other parts of this book, written by different authors with different views and from different academic disciplines, differ from him and between themselves in this respect. If an author uses the expression 'utility index' he may mean a measure of a concept that another claims does not exist, and this may be mutual. 'Inconsistency' may mean what anybody will see as a logical error, or an observation not compatible with a theoretical model.

To avoid making the index controversial, the index for these parts is essentially based on words, not ideas or concepts, and no attempts are made to subdivide according to context. Cross references do not imply that words are synonyms, only that the reader interested in one word may find relevant information under another. This subject index, corresponding to the Introductory Survey (Part I) (pp. 13–24) and Parts III and IV of the book (pp. 149–434), begins on p. 701.

The reader searching for treatment of an idea, may find some help in reading Part I: Editorial Introduction, and using the Table of Contents to distinguish the authors in the page numbers.

On the other hand, there is only one Name Index for the whole book.

O. H.

SUBJECT INDEX
TO PARTS I (FOREWORD), II AND V

References to notes are preceded by the letter n. Thus 137n80 means p. 137, note 80.

685

ALLAIS' NOTATION

Allais' notation: 461–462 (Allais 1977 notation is identical to Allais' 1952 notation)
psychological value index (or cardinal utility index)

$\gamma(x) = \bar{s}(X)$: 462 and 44 §8; corresponds to the cardinal utility concept in the Jevon's sense of the anglo-saxon literature: 43–44; 460–461; 563n79; the letter $\bar{s}$ corresponds to the Allais' 1952 denomination 'satisfaction absolue', i.e. psychological value 133n15′

objective probability p: 38; 457; subjective —— $\bar{p}$ 48

gains (positive or negative) of a random prospect g: 38; 457

probability density $\varphi(C + g)$ of monetary values g of a random prospect; simplified notation $\varphi(g)$: 45; 462; —— $\psi(\gamma)$ of psychological values $\gamma = \bar{s}(C + g)$, or simplified notation $\gamma = \bar{s}(g)$: 45; 462

standard deviation Σ of monetary values g: 84; —— σ of psychological values $\gamma = \bar{s}(C + g)$, or simplified notation $\gamma = \bar{s}(g)$: 119

probability of ruin P: 92; 491

capital
– psychological estimate of subject's monetary capital, C: 38; 457
– monetary value of subject's capital, X: 492
– estimate of C deduced by analysis of the 1952 experiment, U_0: 615

ordinal index of preference of random prospects, $S = S(C + g_1, \ldots, C + g_n, p_1, \ldots, p_n)$: 462
– simplified notation $S = S(g_1, \ldots, g_n, p_1, \ldots, p_n)$: 44 and 462; or $S = S[\varphi(g)]$: 460
– the letter S corresponds to Allais 1952 denomination 'satisfaction': 561n59

psychological value (or cardinal index of preference, or cardinal utility index) of a random prospect:
– as a function of the probability distribution of monetary gains g, $\bar{S} = \bar{S}(C + g_1, \ldots, C + g_n, p_1, \ldots, p_n)$ or $\bar{S} = \bar{S}[\varphi(C + g)]$; simplified notation, $\bar{S} = \bar{S}(g_1, \ldots, g_n, p_1, \ldots, p_n)$, or $\bar{S} = \bar{S}[\varphi(g)]$: 462
– as a function of the probability distribution of psychological values $\gamma = \bar{s}(C + g)$; simplified notation $\gamma = \bar{s}(g)$: $\bar{S} = (\gamma_1, \ldots, \gamma_n, p_1, \ldots, p_n)$ or $\bar{S} = \bar{S}[\psi(\gamma)]$: 462

monetary value of a random prospect, V:
– consideration of the monetary values of gains g: $\bar{s}(C + V) = \bar{S}(C + g_1, \ldots, C + g_n, p_1, \ldots, p_n)$: simplified notation, $\bar{s}(V) = \bar{S}(g_1, \ldots, g_n, p_1, \ldots, p_n)$: 45 and 461, or $\bar{s}(V) = \bar{S}[\varphi(g)]$: 45, 460
– consideration of psychological values γ: $\omega = \bar{s}(C + V)$ or simplified notation: $\omega = \bar{s}(V) = h[\bar{s}(g_1), \ldots, \bar{s}(g_n), p_1, \ldots, p_n]$, or $\bar{s}(V) = h[\psi(\gamma)]$: 6; 45; 461; 475

cardinal utility of risk taking, $f: f = \omega - \Sigma_i p_i \gamma_i = f(\mu_2, \ldots, \mu_n, \ldots)$; $\mu_2, \ldots, \mu_n, \ldots,$ moments of the probability distribution of psychological values γ $(n \geqslant 2)$: 6, 482, 551

simplified notation: 462 §11.3

SUBJECT INDEX
TO PARTS I (INTRODUCTORY SURVEY), III AND IV

Action space 335
Actual choices 350
Actual function 226
Adaptive criterion 428
Additivity 15, 272, 286
Allais
  hypothesis 166, 168
  paradox 17, 150f, 223, 250, 277, 289,
    297, 312, 323, 327, 361, 369; *see also*
    Common consequence, Common
    ratio
  School 330
  situations 323
  theory 19, 151, 154, 158, 272
  model 150
  -type violations, choices 368, 388
American hypothesis 168, 175
American School 17, 150, 152, 163, 168
Applicability 350
Applications 254, 307
Archimedean axioms, properties, etc.
  182, 244, 254, 256
Arrow's axioms 340f
Axiom
  argument 366
  confirmity —— 150
  of cardinal isovariation 272, 481
  of continuity 334
  of monotone sequence 343
  of monotony 343, 424
  of partition of event 344
  rate of substitution —— 208, 217f, 220
  relationality —— 248
  repetition —— 209, 221
  set of ——s 307, 312, 334
  specific additional unique ——s 313
  system 175f, 312f, 319, 335, 346, 394,
    399f, 402
  totally ordering —— 206

utility —— 333, 335, 363, 382f, 388
Axiomatic
  foundation 414, 417
  model 271ff
  system 414, 420
  theory 177
Axiomatization 130, 175, 255, 306, 319,
  321f, 324, 326f
  self-theoretical —— 306
Axiom-based
  choices 366
  rules 374, 376, 384

Bayes'
  principle 414
  theorem 413, 415
Bayesian
  analysis 20, 259, 261f, 267, 268, 426
  probabilities 415
  process 223
Behavior
  actual 350
  adaptive 428
  future 303, 307, 310
Behavioristic structure 326
Behavioristic value theory, etc. 21, 303,
  304, 309–314, 316, 322ff;
  common structure of 321f
  foundation, empirical 307
Bergen paradox 278, 285, 290
Bernoulli
  model 415
  principle 193, 194, 197, 199, 413, 427;
    empirical 413
Boolean properties 326
Brouwerian
  structure 316, 321
  value-structure 318

701